Scotland

Orkney &
Shetland
p397

Northern Highlands
& Islands
p347

Northeast
Scotland
p211

Inverness & the
Central Highlands
p293

Southern   Central
Highlands &   Scotland
Islands   p177
p237   Edinburgh
                            p53
Glasgow
p107   Southern
             Scotland
             p139

Isabel Albiston, Andy Symington, Neil Wilson, Barbara Woolsey

Contents

ROYAL PALACE P57

MSP BUILDING,
SCOTTISH PARLIAMENT P61

ANTON_IVANOV/SHUTTERSTOCK ©

MIROSLAV_1/GETTY IMAGES ©

ARCHITECT:ENRIC MIRALLES, CORNFIELD/SHUTTERSTOCK ©

Contents

JACOBITE STEAM
TRAIN P335

ON THE ROAD

BLAIR CASTLE P327

Contents

GLEN NEVIS P337

COVID-19

We have re-checked every business in this book before publication to ensure that it is still open after the COVID-19 outbreak. However, the economic and social impacts of COVID-19 will continue to be felt long after the outbreak has been contained, and many businesses, services and events referenced in this guide may experience ongoing restrictions. Some businesses may be temporarily closed, have changed their opening hours and services, or require bookings; some unfortunately could have closed permanently. We suggest you check with venues before visiting for the latest information.

Right:
The Highlands

Welcome to Scotland

It's the weather. Seriously. We get four proper seasons here (sometimes in one day) and that means you get to enjoy the same landscapes in a range of different garbs – August hills clad in purple heather, native woodlands gilded with autumn colours, snow-patched winter mountains, and Hebridean machair sprinkled with spring wildflowers. The weather's unpredictability means even the wettest day can be suddenly transformed by parting clouds and slanting shafts of golden light. Sheer magic.

By Neil Wilson, Writer
🐦 @neil3965

For more about our writers, see p480

MIKADUN/SHUTTERSTOCK ©

Scotland

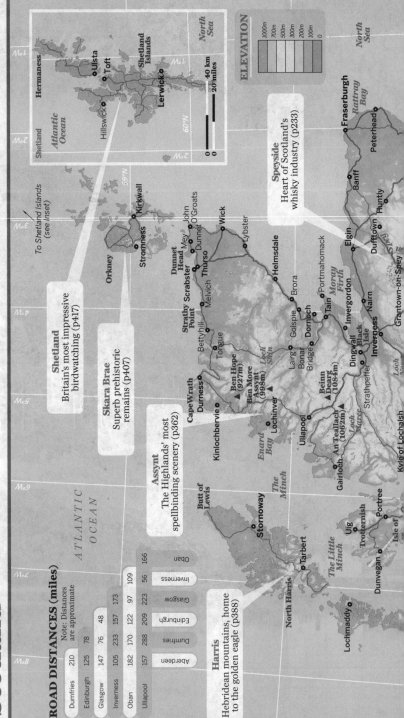

ROAD DISTANCES (miles)
Note: Distances are approximate

	Aberdeen	Dumfries	Edinburgh	Glasgow	Inverness	Oban
Dumfries	210					
Edinburgh	125	78				
Glasgow	147	76	48			
Inverness	105	233	157	173		
Oban	182	170	122	97	109	
Ullapool	157	288	209	223	56	166

Harris
Hebridean mountains, home to the golden eagle (p388)

Assynt
The Highlands' most spellbinding scenery (p362)

Skara Brae
Superb prehistoric remains (p407)

Shetland
Britain's most impressive birdwatching (p417)

Speyside
Heart of Scotland's whisky industry (p233)

To Shetland Islands (see inset)

ELEVATION

1000m
700m
500m
300m
200m
100m
0

Top Experiences

1 EXPERIENCE EDINBURGH

Scotland's capital is famous for its festivals, but there's much more to the city than that. Edinburgh is a place of many moods: visit in March to see the castle silhouetted between a blue spring sky and a yellow haze of daffodils, or on a chill December morning with the fog snagging the spires of the Royal Mile, rain on the cobblestones and a warm glow beckoning from the window of a pub.

Above: Princes Street Gardens (p69)

Edinburgh Castle

Edinburgh's castle watches over the city centre like a benevolent monarch. It's the calm centre of the capital's history, hosting 12th-century St Margaret's Chapel, Edinburgh's oldest building – but also a buzzing events venue and a superb viewpoint. p56

Right: Edinburgh Military Tattoo (p79)

Calton Hill

The most atmospheric of the Scottish capital's seven hills is nicknamed 'Edinburgh's Acropolis'. Calton's summit is crowned with pillared neoclassical monuments and an astronomical observatory turned art gallery. Hike up here to enjoy one of the finest sunsets in the city. p71

Edinburgh Festival & Fringe

Every year since 1947 – with a break in 2020 – Edinburgh has welcomed the world with an extravaganza of festivals. Its venerable cobbled streets, medieval courtyards and Georgian terraces ring with music and mayhem, drama and dance, comedy and culture. p78

Above: Babolin Theatre cast (p79)

2 HIT THE TRAILS

The best way to get inside Scotland's landscapes is to hike them. Despite the vagaries of wind and weather, midges and mud, walking here is always a pleasure as well as a challenge, with countless trails – long and short, easy and hard – begging to be tramped. For experienced hikers the hilltops beckon, with no fewer than 282 Munros (summits of 3000ft and over) waiting to be bagged.

West Highland Way

Top of the wish list for many hikers is the 96-mile West Highland Way from Milngavie (near Glasgow) to Fort William, a challenging week-long walk through some of the country's finest scenery, finishing in the shadow of its highest peak, Ben Nevis. p37

Below: West Highland Way

BRIAN BLADES/SHUTTERSTOCK ©

Ben Nevis

The allure of Scotland's highest peak is strong – around 100,000 people a year set off up the summit trail, though not all make it to the top. The reward is a truly magnificent view. p338

Above: Ben Nevis

Loch Leven Heritage Trail

It's not just the Highlands that have great hiking – this all-abilities trail around the biggest lake in the Scottish lowlands offers fine scenery and fascinating wildlife. p206

Right: Loch Leven

3 ICONIC WILDLIFE

LEONIEK VAN DER VLIET/SHUTTERSTOCK ©

Sparsely populated, and with large areas of wild land, Scotland is an important sanctuary for all sorts of wildlife. Amazing birdwatching is on offer throughout the country, but the golden eagle and the seabird cities of Shetland take first prize for spectacle. Scotland is also great for marine wildlife. In July and August many west-coast cruise operators can almost guarantee sightings of minke whales, dolphins and porpoises.

Golden Eagles

Golden eagles have come to symbolise Scotland's wild mountain landscapes. The Eagle Observatory in Harris provides one of the country's best opportunities for viewing this iconic species. p389

Seabird Cities

The vast colonies of gannets, guillemots, puffins and kittiwakes at Hermaness, Noss and Sumburgh Head in Shetland provide one of British birdwatching's most impressive experiences. p427

Above: Puffins on the Treshnish Isles (p289)

Whales & Dolphins

Gairloch Marine Wildlife Centre is one of dozens of operators running wildlife-watching boat trips to see harbour porpoises, common dolphins, minke whales and – if you're lucky – orcas. p368

4 MAJESTIC MOUNTAINS

From hiking and mountain-biking through the Cairngorms' ancient pine forests to skiing and mountaineering amid snowy summits, Scotland's mountains provide a year-round playground for outdoor enthusiasts. For photographers there are jaw-dropping landscapes at every turn – mountain and sea are intimately entwined in a gloriously scenic embrace, from the vertiginous sea cliffs of remote Cape Wrath to the distinctive pillared peaks of Assynt and the haunting, desolate beauty of Glencoe.

MATT ELLIOTT/SHUTTERSTOCK ©

LUKAS BISCHOFF PHOTOGRAPH/SHUTTERSTOCK ©

Cairngorms

In the boulder-strewn, 4000ft-high plateau of the Cairngorms, Scotland harbours an oupost of subarctic tundra, the haunt of ptarmigan and snow bunting, red deer and reindeer. p309

Above top: Red deer stag in Cairngorms National Park

Assynt

The Highlands abound in breathtaking views, but in the far northwest things become truly awe-inspiring. The isolated peaks of Assynt provide some of Scotland's most spellbinding scenery. p362

Above left: Highlands susnet

Glen Coe

Scotland's most famous glen combines dramatic scenery with deep history. Some of the glen's finest walks – to the Lost Valley, for example – follow routes used by clanspeople trying to flee attackers. p331 Above: Glen Coe

5 HARVEST OF THE SEA

One of the great pleasures of a visit to Scotland is the opportunity to indulge in the sea's rich harvest. The cold, clear waters provide some of the most sought-after seafood in Europe, with much of it being whisked straight from the quayside to waiting restaurant tables from London to Lisbon. Fortunately there are plenty of places to sample this bounty right here.

Haar

This restaurant makes the most of seafood landed in the fishing harbours of Fife. The signature dish delivers local lobster with a trademark Asian twist, swimming in mirin-scented butter. p194

Loch Bay

Nestled on the coast of the Waternish peninsula in northwest Skye, this modest farmhouse kitchen has blossomed into a Michelin-starred restaurant that works some classic French magic on the local shellfish. p383

Captain's Galley

Sustainability, traceability and seasonality are the keywords at this north-coast restaurant where the owner can tell you the name of the boat that caught the fish you're eating. p358

6 ISLAND HOPPING

Much of the unique character of western and northern Scotland is down to the expansive vistas of sea and islands – there are more than 900 islands off Scotland's coast, of which almost 100 are inhabited. A network of ferry services links these islands to the mainland and each other, and it's possible to hop all the way from Arran to the Outer Hebrides, touching the mainland only at Kintyre and Oban.

Orkney

In Orkney you'll discover a near-treeless landscape of lochs, low hills and red sandstone sea cliffs, and a culture more Scandinavian than Scottish. p400

Below: Old Man of Hoy seat stack (p411), Orkney

Outer Hebrides

The name Hebrides comes from the Norse *havbredey* – 'isles at the edge of the ocean' – alluding to the broad vistas of sky and sea that characterise the islands' landscape. p384

Above: Isle of Lewis (p385)

Coll & Tiree

A scenic ferry trip from Oban leads to this pair of contrasting islands. Tiree is flat and green and ringed by gorgeous strands of white shell sand, while Coll is rugged, rocky and peaceful. p287

Right: Tiree homes

7 WHISKY TASTING

Islay

Islay is a gentle blend of rich farmland, picturesque villages, broad sandy beaches and – most famously – whisky distilleries. No fewer than nine turn out the island's distinctive peaty, smoky malts. p262

Macallan

This Speyside brand is famous for its intense, fruity single malts finished in oloroso sherry casks, and for its architecturally stunning visitor centre, a veritable cathedral of a distillery. p234

Left: Macallan distillery

Glenmorangie

One of the world's best known single malt whiskies, Glenmorangie (accent on the second syllable) is made near the Highland town of Tain, using the tallest whisky stills in Scotland. p351

Scotland's national drink – from the Gaelic *uisge bagh,* meaning 'water of life' – has been distilled here for more than 500 years. More than 100 distilleries are still in operation across the country, producing hundreds of varieties of single malt, with new ones opening every year. Learning to distinguish the smoky, peaty whiskies of Islay from, say, the flowery, sherried malts of Speyside has become a hugely popular pastime.

Top: Lagavulin distillery (p264)

8 EXPLORING PREHISTORY

Few sights conjure up the mystery and romance of Scotland like the prehistoric monuments that punctuate the landscape from Orkney to Kintyre. When visiting ancient sites it can be difficult to bridge the gulf of years to sense a connection with the people that built them, but Scotland's superb prehistoric remains have an immediate impact. To explore these places at dawn, before the crowds arrive, is to step back in time and sense something truly ancient.

Skara Brae

Few places offer a better glimpse of everyday Stone Age life than Skara Brae in Orkney, with its carefully constructed fireplaces, beds, cupboards and cisterns. p407

Left: Skara Brae

Kilmartin Glen

This peaceful Argyllshire glen is home to a prehistoric landscape peopled with stone circles, burial cairns, hill forts and rocks carved with mysterious 'cup-and-ring' patterns. p258

Above left: Kilmartin Glen

Callanish Standing Stones

These 5000-year-old stones are the archetypal stone circle, with weathered slabs of banded gneiss arranged in worship around a central monolith. p387

Above right: Callanish Standing Stones

9 CASTLES GALORE

Whether you're looking for desolate stone fortresses looming out of the mist, majestic strongholds towering over historic towns, or luxurious palaces built by lairds more concerned with show and status than with military might – Scotland has the lot. Most Scottish castles have a story or 10 to tell of plots, intrigues, imprisonments and treachery, and many have a phantom rumoured to stalk their halls or parapets.

Stirling Castle

Rivalling (some would say exceeding) Edinburgh Castle in architectural magnificence, Stirling's fortress crouches atop its crag like a dragon guarding the gateway to the north. p178

Above top: Stirling Castle

Kisimul Castle

Perched on an island off Castlebay in Barra – it takes a boat trip to get there – this picturesque Hebridean castle has been the seat of Clan MacNeil for 600 years. p394

Above left: Kisimul Castle

Urquhart Castle

Although in ruins for almost 300 years, the photogenic towers and turrets of Urquhart Castle still provide visitors with a lookout where they can scan the waters of Loch Ness for signs of monsters. p306

Above: Urquhart Castle

10 BIRTHPLACE OF GOLF

STEPHEN BRIDGER/SHUTTERSTOCK ©

St Andrews

The hallowed turf of the Old Course – first played on in the 15th century, and overlooked by the Royal and Ancient Golf Club (founded 1754) – is a place of pilgrimage for golfers from all over the world. p194

Left top: St Andrews

Royal Dornoch

This classic links course topped the list of the World's Top 100 Golf Courses in 2020. p353

Gleneagles

Scotland's best inland golf resort combines scenic beauty with technical challenge in three superb championship courses that have hosted several major world tournaments. p206

Left bottom: Gleneagles

MATT HOOPER/SHUTTERSTOCK ©

Scotland invented the game of golf and is still revered as its spiritual home by amateurs and champions alike. Links courses are the classic experience here – bumpy coastal affairs where the rough is machair and the main enemy is the wind, which can make a disaster of a promising round in an instant. St Andrews, the historic Fife university town, is golf's headquarters, and an irresistible destination for anyone who loves the sport.

Need to Know

For more information, see Survival Guide (p455)

Currency
Pound sterling (£)

Language
English, Gaelic and Lallans

Visas
Generally not needed for stays of up to six months. The UK is no longer a member of the European Union.

Money
ATMs widely available; credit cards widely accepted, though not in all restaurants or B&Bs.

Mobile Phones
The UK uses the GSM 900/1800 network. Local SIM cards can be used in unlocked phones.

Time
Greenwich Mean Time

Driving
In Scotland, drive on the left.

When to Go

Cool to mild summers, cold winters

Lerwick
GO mid-May–mid-July

Stornoway
GO May–Sep

Inverness
GO May–Sep

Fort William
GO May–Sep

Edinburgh
GO year-round

High Season (Jul & Aug)

→ Accommodation prices 10% to 20% higher (book ahead if possible).

→ Warmest time of year, but often wet.

→ Midges at their worst in Highlands and islands.

Shoulder (May, Jun & Sep)

→ Wildflowers and rhododendrons bloom in May and June.

→ Statistically, the best chance of dry weather, minus midges.

→ June evenings have daylight till 11pm.

Low Season (Oct–Apr)

→ Rural attractions and accommodation often closed.

→ Snow on the hills November to March.

→ Gets dark at 4pm in December.

→ Can be very cold and wet from November to March.

Useful Websites

Lonely Planet (lonelyplanet. com/scotland) Destination information, hotel bookings, traveller forum and more.

VisitScotland (www.visitscot land.com) Official tourism site; booking services.

Internet Guide to Scotland (www.scotland-info.co.uk) Best online tourist guide to Scotland.

Traveline (www.traveline.info) Up-to-date public-transport timetables.

ScotlandsPeople (www.scot landspeople.gov.uk) Official genealogical website that lets you search the indexes to old parish and statutory registers, as well as census returns.

Important Numbers

Country code	🎧 44
International access code	🎧 00
Emergencies	🎧 112 or 999
Police (non-emergencies)	🎧 101

Exchange Rates

Australia	A$1	£0.55
Canada	C$1	£0.58
Euro zone	€1	£0.90
Japan	¥100	£0.71
New Zealand	NZ$1	£0.52
USA	US$1	£0.74

For current exchange rates, see www.xe.com.

Daily Costs

Budget: Less than £40

➡ Dorm bed: £13–25

➡ Wild camping: free

➡ Takeaway fish and chips: £4–8

Midrange: £40–130

➡ Double room at midrange B&B: £60–100

➡ Bar lunch: £12

➡ Dinner at midrange restaurant: £30

➡ Car hire per day: £35–40

➡ Petrol costs per mile: around 15p

Top End: More than £130

➡ Double room at high-end hotel: £130–250

➡ Dinner at high-end restaurant: £40–60

➡ One-way flight to islands: £65–130

Opening Hours

Hours may vary throughout the year; in rural areas many places have shorter hours from around October to April. In the Highlands and islands, Sunday opening is restricted.

Banks 9.30am–4pm Monday to Friday, some to 1pm Saturday.

Nightclubs 9pm–1am Thursday to Saturday.

Post offices 9am–6pm Monday to Friday, to 12.30pm Saturday.

Pubs 11am–11pm Monday to Thursday, to 1am Friday and Saturday, 12.30–11pm Sunday; lunch noon–2.30pm, dinner 6–9pm daily.

Restaurants Lunch noon–2.30pm, dinner 6–9pm.

Shops 9am–5.30pm Monday to Saturday, often 11am–5pm Sunday.

Arriving in Scotland

Edinburgh Airport Airlink 100 bus runs from the airport to South St David St, at the east end of Princes St (one way/return £4.50/7.50, 30 minutes), near the main train station, via Haymarket and the West End every 12 minutes from 4am to 1am and every 30 minutes through the night. Trams run from the airport to the city centre (one way/return £6.50/9, 33 minutes, every six to eight minutes from 6.15am to 10.45pm). An airport taxi to the city centre costs around £20 and takes 20 to 30 minutes.

Glasgow Airport Bus 500 runs every 10 or 15 minutes (half-hourly or hourly late at night, 24 hours a day) from Glasgow Airport to Buchanan bus station via Central and Queen Street train stations (one way/return £8.50/14, 25 minutes). A taxi costs around £25.

Getting Around

Transport in Scotland can be expensive compared to the rest of Europe, and bus and rail services are sparse in more remote parts of the country. For up-to-date timetables, visit Traveline (www.traveline.info).

Car Useful for travelling at your own pace, or for visiting regions with minimal public transport. Cars can be hired in cities and major towns. Drive on the left.

Train Relatively expensive, with extensive coverage and frequent departures in central Scotland, but only a few lines in the northern Highlands and southern Scotland.

Bus Cheaper and slower than trains, but useful for more remote regions that aren't serviced by rail.

Boat A network of car ferries links the mainland to the islands of western and northern Scotland.

For much more on **getting around**, see p462

First Time Scotland

For more information, see Survival Guide (p455)

Checklist

➡ Make sure your passport is valid for at least six months past your arrival date.

➡ Make all necessary bookings (for accommodation, events and travel).

➡ Check airline baggage restrictions.

➡ Inform your debit-/credit-card company of your travels.

➡ Arrange appropriate travel insurance.

➡ Check if you can use your mobile (cell) phone in Scotland.

What to Pack

➡ Passport

➡ Driving licence

➡ Good walking shoes or boots

➡ Waterproof jacket

➡ Camera

➡ UK electrical adapter

➡ Insect repellent

➡ Binoculars

➡ Hangover cure (all that whisky, you know)

Top Tips for Your Trip

➡ Quality rather than quantity should be your goal: instead of a hair-raising race to see everything, pick a handful of destinations and give yourself time to linger. The most memorable experiences in Scotland are often the ones where you're doing very little.

➡ If you're driving, get off main roads when you can. Some of the country's most stunning scenery is best enjoyed on secondary or tertiary roads that wind their narrow way through standout photo ops.

➡ Make the effort to greet the locals. The best experiences of Scotland are to be had courtesy of the Scots themselves, whose helpfulness, friendliness and fun has not been exaggerated.

➡ Be prepared for midges – tiny biting flies that can make life a misery in summer in the Highlands. Bring insect repellent, antihistamine cream and long-sleeved shirts and trousers.

What to Wear

Scotland is a fairly casual destination and you can wear pretty much whatever you like all the time. For fancy dinners, smart casual is all that's required.

Summer days can be warm but rarely hot, so you'll always want something around your legs and shoulders when the inevitable cool sets in.

The factor that will determine your outfits the most is the weather, which also means that a light, waterproof jacket should always be close at hand.

Sleeping

Book in advance, especially in summer, at weekends, and on islands. If you're going to be in Edinburgh in August (festival month) or at Hogmanay (New Year), book as far ahead as possible – a year is recommended.

B&Bs Small, family-run houses that are generally good value. More luxurious versions resemble boutique hotels.

Hotels Range from half a dozen rooms above a pub to restored country houses and castles, with a commensurate variety of rates.

Hostels A good choice of hostels, many housed in historic buildings.

Money

➡ The British currency is the pound sterling (£), with 100 pence to a pound. 'Quid' is the slang term for pound.

➡ Three Scottish banks issue their own banknotes, meaning there's quite a variety of different notes in circulation. They are legal currency in England, too, but you'll sometimes run into problems changing them. They are also harder to exchange once you get outside the UK.

➡ Euros are accepted in Scotland only at some major tourist attractions and a few upmarket hotels – it's always better to use sterling.

Bargaining

A bit of mild haggling is acceptable at flea markets and antique shops, but everywhere else you're expected to pay the advertised price.

Tipping

Hotels £1 per bag is standard; gratuities for cleaning staff are completely at your discretion.

Pubs Not expected unless table service is provided, then £1 for a round of drinks.

Restaurants For decent service, 10%; up to 15% at more expensive places. Check to see if service has been added to the bill already (most likely for large groups).

Taxis Fares are generally rounded up to the nearest pound.

Grassmarket (p68), Edinburgh

Etiquette

Although largely informal in their everyday dealings, the Scots do observe some rules of etiquette.

Greetings Shake hands with men, women and children when meeting for the first time. Scots expect a firm handshake with eye contact.

Conversation Generally friendly but often reserved, the Scots avoid conversations that might embarrass.

Table service In general, cafes have table service, but pubs do not. In some pubs, you should order food at the bar, others will have staff take your order.

Buying your round at the pub Scots generally take it in turns to buy a round of drinks for the whole group. In pubs, you're expected to pay for drinks when you order them.

Eating

It's wise to book ahead for midrange restaurants, especially at weekends. Top-end restaurants should be booked at least a couple of weeks in advance.

Cafes Open during daytime, cafes are good for a casual breakfast or lunch, or simply a cup of coffee.

Pubs Most of Scotland's pubs serve reasonably priced meals, and many can compete with restaurants on quality.

Restaurants Scotland's restaurants range from cheap and cheerful to Michelin starred, and they cover every cuisine you can imagine.

What's New

Just as Scotland begins to look forward to the easing of Covid-19 pandemic restrictions, it has to confront the effects of Brexit on its fragile economy. The final departure from the European Union on 1 January 2021 has put the issue of Scottish independence firmly back on the agenda.

Campervan Crush

Scotland has always been a popular tourist destination, but the Covid-19 pandemic saw the numbers of UK citizens taking a holiday on their home territory go through the roof. The motorhome sector in particular took off – the Caravan & Motorhome Club signed up 1000 more members per week than usual, and at Indie Campers, the UK's largest campervan rental company, July bookings were up 350% compared with 2019.

Combined with the popularity of the North Coast 500 driving route, which celebrated its fifth anniversary in 2020, and the fact that many campsites had closed because of the pandemic, the result was mayhem. Not only were motorhomes causing traffic jams on the narrow and twisting single-track roads that characterise much of Scotland's northern Highlands and islands, but the overcrowding of campsites meant many vehicles were overnighting wherever they could; some were even disposing of sewage from their waste tanks at roadside parking spots.

Many Highland businesses are heavily reliant on tourism income and don't want to deter visitors, but worry about the effect of overcrowding. You can help by making sure you book campsite space well in advance, and avoid driving large vehicles on unsuitable roads, notably the Bealach na Ba to Applecross, the 'Wee Mad Road' between Lochinver and Coigach, and the road from Craignure to Iona on Mull.

Edinburgh Accommodation

Two openings at either end of the budget range sum up the wide appeal of the capital's accommodation options. The Court (p82) is a new hostel that has been built in a former Victorian jail in the heart of the

---

LOCAL KNOWLEDGE

WHAT'S HAPPENING IN SCOTLAND

Neil Wilson, Lonely Planet writer

Like the rest of the world, Scotland's experience of 2020 was dominated by the Covid-19 pandemic. Apart from the devastating loss of life and the effects on public health and the economy, the crisis showed up a marked difference in approach and communication between the Scottish parliament in Edinburgh and the UK parliament in London. In particular, the Scottish First Minister Nicola Sturgeon won acclaim for her clear and consistent messaging, to the extent that polls showed her as more popular than UK Prime Minister Boris Johnson, even in England.

At the same time, popular support for Scottish independence rose to its highest levels ever, with polls showing 58% in favour (excluding 'don't knows') as opposed to the 45% who voted in favour in the 2014 referendum.

Meanwhile, Glasgow is set to host the United Nations Climate Change Conference (COP26) in November 2021, which could be hooked onto the city's ambitious sustainability goals – it aims to become Britain's first carbon-neutral city by 2030.

Old Town, with dorms based around banks of Japanese-style sleeping pods and sleekly minimalist lounge and kitchen areas. At the other end of the spectrum – in all ways – is the House of Gods (p82), an over-the-top designer extravaganza of a hotel occupying a former gap site on the Cowgate.

Braemar's Highland Games Centre

The Duke of Rothesay Highland Games Pavilion in Braemar is home to this new centre (p319) devoted to the history of Highland Games in general, and the Braemar Gathering (held annually since 1832) in particular, as well as the Royal Family's links with Braemar.

Kirk Gallery

The former parish church of St Andrew in Tankerness in Orkney has undergone a stunning conversion into a gallery (p405) for local jewellery designer Sheila Fleet. The old church is flooded with light streaming through stained-glass windows, a fitting backdrop for the displays of hand-crafted designer jewellery.

Loch Ness 360º

Loch Ness 360º (p305) is a new hiking trail that loops for 80 miles around Loch Ness, starting and finishing in Inverness. The trail is divided into six day-long sections, with stops in Drumnadrochit, Invermoriston, Fort Augustus, Foyers and Dores.

Saorsa 1875

Housed in a Scottish Baronial mansion in the pretty Highland Perthshire town of Pitlochry, Saorsa 1875 (p326) is the UK's first 100% vegan hotel – furnishings, toiletries and cleaning products are all vegan, as well as the food and drink.

Moat Brae

Moat Brae (p162), an elegant Georgian villa built in 1823, captured the imagination of a schoolboy who attended nearby Dumfries Academy in the 1870s. That boy was JM Barrie, who was inspired by Moat Brae and its 'enchanted gardens' to create the story of Peter Pan. The house, restored to its former glory, opened to the public in 2019.

LISTEN, WATCH & FOLLOW

For inspiration and up-to-date news, visit www.lonelyplanet.com/scotland/articles.

The Chaotic Scot (www.thechaoticscot.com) Travel stories and experiences from all over Scotland.

Glasgow Live (www.glasgowlive.co.uk) News, what's-on listings, and food and drink recs from Scotland's biggest city.

Insta: Tom Duffin (@tomduffinphotographer) Superbly atmospheric images of Edinburgh's (and Scotland's) landscapes and cityscapes.

Twitter: Walkhighlands (@walkhighlands) Gorgeous photos and a fount of ideas for scenic walks.

Good Morning Scotland Weekend Edition (www.bbc.co.uk/podcasts/radioscotland) Weekly news and current affairs round-up from BBC Radio Scotland.

FAST FACTS

Food trend Veganism

Number of islands More than 900

Annual whisky exports 1.3 billion bottles (2019)

Population 5.45 million

SCOTLAND   USA   ENGLAND

👤 ≈ 80 people per sq km

Macallan Distillery

The new Macallan distillery (p234) and visitor centre is a stunning piece of contemporary architecture that took six years to build. Made from vast spans of engineered timber cut into the hillside, its wavy turf roof echoes the lines of the local Moray hills.

Outlook

This new glass-walled restaurant (p88) perched atop Edinburgh's Calton Hill enjoys some of the finest views in the city accompanied by some of the finest food.

Accommodation

Find more accommodation reviews throughout the On the Road chapters (from p51)

Find more accommodation reviews throughout the On the Road chapters (from p51)

PRICE RANGES

The following price ranges refer to a double room with bathroom.

£ less than £65

££ £65–130

£££ more than £130

Accommodation Types

B&Bs Small, family-run houses that are usually good value. The more luxurious offerings are similar to boutique hotels.

Hotels Range from a handful of rooms above a pub to restored country houses and castles. Prices vary accordingly.

Hostels A good choice of institutional and independent hostels, many housed in historic buildings.

Bothies Simple shelters, often in remote places; many are maintained by the Mountain Bothies Association (www.mountainbothies.org.uk).

Bunkhouses Have stoves for heating and cooking and may supply utensils. They may have mattresses, but you'll still need a sleeping bag. There will be toilets but probably no showers.

Camping Most commercial campsites offer a variety of pitches – hardstanding and grass, with or without electricity – and accept tents, campervans and caravans; some are caravan only.

Rental Accommodation Self-catering accommodation is very popular in Scotland, and staying in an apartment in a city, or a cottage in the country, gives you the opportunity to get a feel for a place and its community. The minimum stay is usually one week in the summer peak season, and three days or less at other times.

Best Places to Stay

Best on a Budget

Budget accommodation usually means hostels, so you'll find the widest choice in places that traditionally attract backpackers – cities such as Edinburgh and Inverness have a wide range of attractive and competitively priced spots. You'll also find a good choice in places that attract hikers, surfers and other outdoors enthusiasts – Fort William, Aviemore, the islands and the far northwest, for example.

➡ Code – The Court (p82), Edinburgh

➡ Murray Library Hostel (p199), Anstruther

➡ Flower House (p123), Glasgow

➡ Iona Hostel (p287), Iona

➡ Callander Hostel (p247), Callander

➡ Craignure Bunkhouse (p281), Mull

Best for Families

The best family-oriented places tend to be holiday resorts, country hotels (though they can be expensive) and farmhouse B&Bs within weekend getaway distance of cities such as Edinburgh and Glasgow, so consider looking at southern Scotland, Argyll, Fife and Perthshire.

➡ Crieff Hydro (p208), Crieff

➡ Grasshoppers (p122), Glasgow

➡ Lickisto Blackhouse Camping (p390), Harris

➡ Loch Ness Inn (p307), Drumnadrochit

➡ Baile-na-Cille (p388), Lewis

Best for Solo Travellers

Many guest houses and hotels in Scotland charge much the same for a single traveller as for a couple sharing a double room; in fact, single rooms can be downright hard to find. If you want to meet other travellers, your best bet is backpacker hostels with buzzing common rooms, and convivial B&Bs where guests enjoy breakfast conversations around a communal kitchen table.

➡ Citizen M (p122), Glasgow
➡ Lazy Crofter Bunkhouse (p360), Durness
➡ Backpackers Plus (p276), Oban
➡ Jessie Mac's (p324), Dunkeld
➡ West Manse (p414), Westray

Best Historic Hotels

Scotland has a rich legacy of country houses, castles and stately homes that have been converted into hotels. Places like these offer the chance to indulge in four-poster beds, Victorian baths, antique furniture and candlelit dining rooms, and to stroll through landscaped gardens that would once have been the preserve of the rich and powerful.

➡ Prestonfield (p82), Edinburgh
➡ Fonab Castle Hotel (p326), Pitlochry
➡ Knockinaam Lodge (p175), Portpatrick
➡ Links House Hotel (p353), Dornoch
➡ Glengorm Castle (p284), Mull

Booking

Book in advance, especially in summer, at weekends, and on islands (where options are often limited). Book at least two months ahead for July and August. If you're going to be in Edinburgh in August (festival month) or at Hogmanay (New Year), book as far ahead as possible – a year is recommended.

Lonely Planet (www.lonelyplanet.com/scot land/hotels) Find independent reviews, as well as recommendations on the best places to stay – and then book them online.

Glengorm Castle (p283), Mull

Cool Camping (www.coolcamping.com) Booking service for offbeat, remote and interesting campsites, including 'glamping' options.

Cottages & Castles (www.cottages-and-castles. co.uk) Listings of self-catering accommodation in cottages and historic buildings throughout Scotland, including dog-friendly and last-minute options.

Hostelling Scotland (www.hostellingscotland. org.uk) Has a network of reasonably priced hostels and produces a free hostelling guide and listing that's available from tourist offices.

Scottish Independent Hostels (www.hostel-scotland.co.uk) Listings of independent hostels not covered by the Hostelling Scotland network.

VisitScotland (www.visitscotland.com/accom modation) Accommodation approved by the official tourist board. VisitScotland tourist offices offer an accommodation-booking service.

Month by Month

January

The nation shakes off its Hogmanay hangover and gets back to work, but only until Burns Night comes along. It's cold and dark, but the skiing can be good.

✗ Burns Night

Suppers all over the country (and the world for that matter) are held on 25 January to celebrate the anniversary of national poet Robert Burns, with much eating of haggis, drinking of whisky and reciting of poetry.

🎊 Celtic Connections

Glasgow hosts the world's largest winter music festival, a celebration of Celtic music, dance and culture, with participants arriving from all over the globe. Held mid- to late January. (p120)

🎊 Up Helly Aa

Half of Shetland dresses up with horned helmets and battleaxes in this spectacular re-enactment of a Viking fire festival, with a torchlit procession leading the burning of a full-size Viking longship. Held in Lerwick on the last Tuesday in January. (p421)

February

The coldest month of the year is usually the best for winter mountaineering, ice climbing and skiing. The days are getting longer, and snowdrops begin to bloom.

☆ Six Nations Rugby Tournament

Scotland, England, Wales, Ireland, France and Italy battle it out in this prestigious tournament (www. sixnationsrugby.com), held February to March. Home games are played at Murrayfield, Edinburgh.

🎿 Fort William Mountain Festival

The UK's Outdoor Capital celebrates the peak of the winter season with ski and snowboard workshops, talks by famous climbers, kids' events and a festival of mountaineering films (www.mountainfestival. co.uk).

April

The bluebell woods on the shores of Loch Lomond come into flower and ospreys arrive at their Loch Garten nests. Weather is improving, though heavy showers are still common.

☆ Rugby Sevens

A series of weekend, seven-a-side rugby tournaments held in various towns throughout the Borders region in April and May, kicking off with Melrose in early April. Fast and furious rugby (sevens was invented here), crowded pubs and great craic. (p144)

🎊 Shetland Folk Festival

The end of April sees this engagingly eccentric music festival, with performances of traditional music from around the world staged everywhere from Lerwick pubs to remote island village halls. (p420)

May

Wildflowers on the Hebridean machair, hawthorn hedges in bloom and cherry blossom in city parks – Scottish weather is often at its best in May.

✯ Burns an' a' That

Ayrshire towns are the venues for performances of poetry and music, children's events, art exhibitions and more in celebration of the Scottish bard. (p160)

🍷 Spirit of Speyside Whisky Festival

Based in the Moray town of Dufftown, this festival of whisky, food and music involves five days of distillery tours, knocking back the 'water of life', cooking, art and outdoor activities. Held late April to early May in Moray and Speyside. (p234)

✯ Fèis Ìle

Islay sees a week-long celebration of traditional Scottish music and whisky. Events include *ceilidhs* (evenings of traditional Scottish entertainment), pipe-band performances, barbecues and lots of whisky-related fun. (p262)

June

Argyllshire is ablaze with pink rhododendron blooms as the long summer evenings stretch on till 11pm. Border towns are strung with bunting to mark gala days and Common Ridings.

✯ Common Ridings

Following the age-old tradition that commemorates the ancient conflict with England, horsemen and -women ride the old boundaries of common lands, along with parades, marching bands and street parties. Held in various Border towns; the Jedburgh event (www.jethartcallantsfestival.com) is one of the biggest and best.

July

School holidays begin, as does the busiest time of year for resort towns. It's high season for Shetland birdwatchers.

✯ Hebridean Celtic Festival

The gardens of Lews Castle in Stornoway provide the scenic setting for this four-day extravaganza of folk, rock and Celtic music. (p386)

August

It's festival time in Edinburgh (www.edinburghfestivalcity.com) and the city is crammed with visitors. On the west coast, this is the peak month for sighting minke whales and basking sharks.

☆ Edinburgh Festival Fringe

The world's biggest festival of the performing arts. Takes place over 3½ weeks in August, the last two weeks overlapping with the first two of the Edinburgh International Festival. (p79)

☆ Edinburgh International Festival

The world's top musicians and performers congregate in Edinburgh for three weeks of diverse and inspirational music, opera, theatre and dance. Ends on the first Saturday in September. The program is usually available from April. (p79)

October

Autumn brings a blaze of colour to the forests of Highland Perthshire and the Trossachs, as the tourist season winds down and thoughts turn to log fires and malt whiskies in country-house hotels.

☆ Enchanted Forest

Crowds gather in Faskally Wood at Pitlochry to experience this spectacular sound-and-light show. Three weeks of events occasionally spill into November. (p325)

December

Darkness falls mid-afternoon as the shortest day of the year approaches. The often cold and wet weather is relieved by Christmas and New Year festivities.

✯ Hogmanay

Christmas celebrations in Edinburgh (www.edinburghschristmas.com) culminate in a huge street party on Hogmanay on 31 December. The fishing town of Stonehaven echoes an ancient, pre-Christian tradition with its procession of fireball-swinging locals who parade to the harbour and fling their blazing orbs into the sea (www.stonehaven fireballs.co.uk; p82)

Itineraries

Inverness
Kyle of Lochalsh
Skye
Plockton
Culloden Battlefield
Glen Shiel
Loch Ness
Invergarry
Fort William
Glen Coe
Ben Nevis (1344m)
Pitlochry
The Trossachs
Callander
Stirling
EDINBURGH

1 WEEK — A Highland Fling

This tour takes in Scotland's scenic and historical highlights.

No trip to Scotland would be complete without a visit to **Edinburgh**, and even if your Scottish trip lasts only a week, the capital is worth two days of your time. On day three, head northwest to **Stirling** to see Scotland's other great castle, then on to the **Trossachs** for your first taste of Highland scenery (overnight in Callander).

Day four starts with a scenic drive north via **Glen Coe** and **Fort William**, then along the Great Glen to **Loch Ness** in time for an afternoon visiting Urquhart Castle and the Loch Ness Centre & Exhibition. An evening cruise on Loch Ness rounds out the day; spend the night in **Inverness**.

On day five visit **Culloden Battlefield**, then drive west via Achnasheen and **Plockton** to **Kyle of Lochalsh** and cross the bridge to the **Isle of Skye**. Devote day six to Dunvegan Castle and the Trotternish peninsula.

Spend your last day taking the long drive back south – the scenic route goes via **Glen Shiel**, **Invergarry**, Spean Bridge (pause at the Commando Monument), Laggan and then south on the A9 to Edinburgh, with a stop in **Pitlochry**.

Best of Scotland

Castles, whisky, mountain scenery and the legendary Isle of Skye – this route covers the best that Scotland has to offer.

From **Edinburgh** head north to Fife and turn east along the coastal road through the fishing villages of the **East Neuk** (pause for a seafood lunch at Anstruther or St Monans) to the home of golf, **St Andrews**. Stay a night or two – heck, play a round of golf – before continuing north to **Dundee** and **Glamis Castle**, with its royal associations. A scenic drive north through the mountains leads to **Braemar**, a good place to spend the night.

A feast of castles lies ahead as you make your way east along Royal Deeside – take your time and visit (at the very least) the royal residence of **Balmoral Castle** and the fairy-tale **Crathes Castle** on your way to the granite city of **Aberdeen**. Overnight here.

Now strike west again along the A944, visiting **Castle Fraser** and **Craigievar Castle** before heading north to **Dufftown** and Aberlour in the heart of Speyside. Base yourself here for at least a day while you explore the local whisky distilleries – there are some good places to eat, plus the Quaich whisky bar at the nearby Craigellachie Hotel.

Head northwest to **Elgin** and its magnificent ruined cathedral, then west on the A96, visiting **Fort George** and **Culloden** on the way to Inverness. **Inverness** itself is worth a night or two – there are some excellent hotels and restaurants, and the opportunity for a side trip to **Loch Ness** (Drumnadrochit for monster spotters; Dores Inn for foodies).

Now for a glorious drive from Inverness to **Torridon** via Kinlochewe through some incredible mountain scenery; try to spend a night at the Torridon hotel. Then head south via **Applecross** and the pretty village of **Plockton** to Kyle of Lochalsh and the bridge to **Skye**.

Spend two days exploring Scotland's most famous island before taking the ferry from Armadale to Mallaig, and follow the Road to the Isles in reverse, stopping to visit **Glenfinnan**, where Bonnie Prince Charlie raised his Highland army in 1745. Overnight at **Fort William**, and drive back to Edinburgh via the scenic road through **Glen Coe** and along the bonnie banks of **Loch Lomond**.

Island Hopscotch
1 WEEK

This scenic, island-hopping route is usually done by car, but also makes a brilliant cycling tour (270 miles, including the 60 miles from Ullapool to Inverness, making both start and finish accessible by rail).

From **Oban** it's a five-hour ferry crossing to **Barra**; plan to spend the night here (book ahead). On day two, after a visit to Kisimul Castle and a tour around the island, take the ferry to **South Uist**. Walk the west coast's wild beaches, sample local seafood and perhaps go fishing on the island's trout lochs. Continue through Benbecula and **North Uist**, prime birdwatching country.

Overnight at Lochmaddy on North Uist (or if you're camping, Balranald Campsite is a must) before taking the ferry to **Harris**, whose west coast has some of Scotland's most spectacular beaches. The road continues north from **Tarbert**, where you'll find good hotels, through rugged hills to **Lewis**.

Don't go directly to Stornoway, but loop west via the **Callanish Standing Stones** and **Arnol Blackhouse**. Spend your final night in **Stornoway** (eat at Digby Chick), then take the ferry to **Ullapool** for a scenic drive to **Inverness**.

Border Raid
5 DAYS

Southern Scotland is often overlooked by visitors, but fans of Robert Burns and Sir Walter Scott will find much to enjoy here.

From **Edinburgh** pay a visit to Sir Walter Scott's former home at **Abbotsford**, followed by the beautiful Border abbeys of **Melrose** and nearby Dryburgh; Melrose is a charming place to stay the night, with a choice of good hotels.

Next morning head west on the A708 to Moffat, passing through glorious scenery around St Mary's Loch. Stop the night at **Dumfries**, visiting the first of several sights related to Scotland's national poet Robert Burns, making a short side trip to spectacular **Caerlaverock Castle**.

Take the A76 northwest towards Ayr, and spend the rest of day three in **Alloway** visiting Burns' birthplace (and other Burns-related sites); nearby **Ayr** has plenty of accommodation options.

North now to **Wemyss Bay** and the ferry to **Rothesay** on the Isle of Bute, where you can visit stunning Mount Stuart, one of Scotland's most impressive stately homes. Spend the night on the island, then return to the mainland and head east to **Glasgow**.

Plan Your Trip
The Great Outdoors

Scotland is a brilliant place for outdoor recreation, and has something to offer everyone, from those who enjoy a short stroll to full-on adrenaline junkies. Although hiking, golf, fishing and cycling are the most popular activities, there is an astonishing variety of other things to do.

Walking

Scotland's wild, dramatic scenery and varied landscape have made walking a hugely popular pastime for locals and tourists alike. There really is something for everyone, from after-breakfast strolls to the popular pastime of Munro bagging (p38).

Planning

For gentle walks along clearly defined tracks, the most planning you'll need to do is to take a look at the weather forecast and decide how many layers to wear. Highland hikers should be properly equipped and cautious, as the weather can become vicious at any time of year. After rain, peaty soil can become boggy, so always wear stout shoes or boots and carry extra food and drink – many unsuspecting walkers have had to survive an unplanned night in the open. Don't depend on mobile (cell) phones (though carrying one with you is a good idea, and can be a lifesaver if you can get a signal). Leave a note with your route and expected time of return with your accommodation, or text/email details to someone you can rely on to contact the emergency services if you don't get back to them when expected.

The best time of year for hill walking is usually May to September, though snow

Best Outdoor Experiences

⇒ Hiking the West Highland Way
⇒ Climbing Ben Nevis
⇒ Cycle touring the Outer Hebrides
⇒ Mountain biking the 7Stanes trails
⇒ Sea kayaking in Shetland

Essential Hill Walking Gear

⇒ Good waterproofs
⇒ Spare warm clothing
⇒ Map and compass (know how to use them!)
⇒ Mobile (cell) phone (but don't rely on it)
⇒ First-aid kit
⇒ Head torch (and spare batteries)
⇒ Whistle (for emergencies)
⇒ Spare food and drink
⇒ Bivvy bag

Safety Checklist

⇒ Check the weather forecast before you go
⇒ Let someone know your plans
⇒ Set your pace and objective to suit the slowest member of your party
⇒ Don't be afraid to turn back if the going becomes too difficult

BEATING THE MIDGES

Forget Nessie. The Highlands have a real monster in their midst: a voracious, blood-sucking female fully 2mm long, known as *Culicoides impunctatus* – the Highland midge. (The male midge is an innocent vegetarian.) The bane of campers and as much a symbol of Scotland as the kilt or the thistle, they can drive sane folk to distraction as they descend in swarms of biting misery. Though mostly vegetarian, the female midge needs a dose of blood in order to lay her eggs. And like it or not, if you're in the Highlands in summer, you've just volunteered as a donor.

The midge season lasts from late May to early September, with June and August being the worst months. Climate change has seen warmer, damper springs and summers that seem to suit the midges just fine – in recent years they've increased both in numbers and in range. They're at their worst in the morning and evening, especially in calm, overcast weather; strong winds and strong sunshine help keep them away.

You can get an idea of how bad they are going to be in your area by checking the **midge forecast** (www.smidgeup.com/midge-forecast; only operates during midge season).

Be Prepared!

Cover up by wearing long trousers and long-sleeved shirts, and (if the midges are really bad) a head net (available in most outdoor shops) worn over a brimmed hat. Also be sure to use a repellent.

Many kinds of repellents have been formulated over the decades, some based on natural ingredients such as citronella and bog myrtle, but until recently there was only one that worked reliably – DEET, which is a nasty, industrial chemical that smells bad, stings your eyes and seems to be capable of melting plastic. A repellent called Saltidin (marketed under the brand name Smidge) is both effective and pleasant to use.

There's another substance that has shot to prominence since 2005, despite not being marketed as an insect repellent. Avon's 'Skin So Soft' moisturiser spray is regularly used as a midge repellent by the Royal Marines, forestry workers and water engineers, as well as thousands of outdoor enthusiasts. You can find it in most outdoor stores in the west of Scotland. Not only does it keep the midges at bay, it claims to leave your skin feeling 'velvety soft'.

---

can fall on the highest summits even in midsummer. Winter walking on the higher hills of Scotland requires the use of an ice axe and crampons and is for experienced mountaineers only.

Access & Rights of Way

There is a tradition of relatively free access to open country in Scotland, a custom that was enshrined in law in the 2003 Land Reform (Scotland) Bill, popularly known as 'the right to roam'. The Scottish Outdoor Access Code (www.outdooraccess-scotland.scot) states that everyone has the right to be on most land and inland waters, providing they act responsibly.

You should avoid areas where you might disrupt or disturb wildlife, lambing (generally mid-April to the end of May), grouse shooting (from 12 August to the third week in October) or deer stalking (1 July to 15 February, but the peak period is August to October). You can get up-to-date information on deer stalking in various areas through the Heading for the Scottish Hills (www.outdooraccess-scotland.scot/hftsh) service.

Local authorities aren't required to list and map rights of way, so they're not shown on Ordnance Survey (OS) maps of Scotland, as they are in England and Wales. However, the Scottish Rights of Way & Access Society (www.scotways.com) keeps records of these routes, provides and maintains signposting, and publicises routes in its guidebook, *Scottish Hill Tracks*.

You are free to pitch a tent almost anywhere that doesn't cause inconvenience to

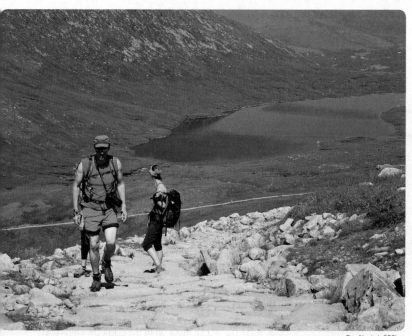

Ben Nevis (p338)

others or damage to property, as long as you stay no longer than two or three nights in any one spot, take all litter away with you, and keep well away from houses and roads. (Note that this right does not extend to the use of motorised vehicles to reach camping spots.)

Long-Distance Footpaths

Scotland has no fewer than 29 official long-distance footpaths (ie waymarked trails), which are all described on the website www.scotlandsgreattrails.org.uk. Each trail also has its own dedicated website, and at least one print guidebook, such as those published by Cicerone (www.cicerone.co.uk) and Rucksack Readers (www.rucsacs.com).

West Highland Way

This classic hike – the country's most popular long-distance trail – stretches for 96 miles through some of Scotland's most spectacular scenery, from Milngavie (mull-*guy*), on the northwestern fringes of Glasgow, to Fort William.

The route begins in the Lowlands, but the greater part of the trail is among the mountains, lochs and fast-flowing rivers of the western Highlands. After following the eastern shore of Loch Lomond and passing Crianlarich and Tyndrum, the route crosses the vast wilderness of Rannoch Moor and reaches Fort William via Glen Nevis, in the shadow of Britain's highest peak, Ben Nevis.

The path is easy to follow, making use of old drove roads (along which Highland cattle were once driven to Lowland markets), an old military road (built by troops to help subdue the Highlands in the 18th century) and disused railway lines.

Best done from south to north, the walk takes about six or seven days. Many people round it off with an ascent of Ben Nevis. You need to be properly equipped, with good boots, waterproofs, maps, a compass, and food and drink, for the northern part of the walk. Midge repellent is also essential.

It's possible to do just a day's hike along part of the trail. For example, the Loch Lomond Water Bus allows you to walk the section from Rowardennan to Inversnaid, returning to your starting point by boat.

The West Highland Way Official Guide, by Bob Aitken and Roger Smith, is the most comprehensive guidebook, while the Harvey map *West Highland Way* covers the entire route in a single waterproof sheet.

Accommodation shouldn't be too difficult to find, though between Bridge of Orchy and Kinlochleven it's limited. At peak times (May, July and August), book accommodation in advance. There are some youth hostels and bunkhouses on or near the path, and it's possible to camp in some parts. A list of accommodation is available from tourist offices.

For more information, see www.west-highlandway.org.

Speyside Way

This long-distance footpath follows the course of the River Spey, one of Scotland's most famous salmon-fishing rivers. It starts at Buckie and first follows the coast to Spey Bay, east of Elgin, then runs inland along the river to Aviemore in the Cairngorms (with branches to Tomintoul and Dufftown). There are plans to extend the trail to Newtonmore, but as of 2020 it had only reached Kincraig.

The 66-mile route has been dubbed the 'Whisky Trail' as it passes near a number of distilleries, including Glenlivet and Glenfiddich (p234), which are open to the public. If you stop at them all, the walk may take considerably longer than the usual three or four days! The first 11 miles from Buckie to Fochabers makes a good day hike (allow four to five hours).

The Speyside Way, a guidebook by Jacquetta Megarry and Jim Strachan, describes the trail in detail. Check out the route at www.speysideway.org.

Munro Bagging

At the end of the 19th century an eager hill walker, Sir Hugh Munro, published a list of Scottish mountains measuring over 3000ft (914m) in height – he couldn't have realised that in time his name would be used to describe all Scottish mountains over 3000ft, and that keen hill walkers would set themselves the target of reaching the summit of (or bagging) all of Scotland's 282 Munros.

To the uninitiated it may seem odd that Munro baggers see venturing into mist, cloud and driving rain as time well spent. However, for those who can add one or more ticks to their list, the vagaries of the weather are part of the enjoyment, at least in retrospect. Munro bagging is, of course, more than merely ticking off a list – it takes you to some of the wildest and most beautiful corners of Scotland.

Once you've bagged all the Munros you can move on to the Corbetts – hills over 2500ft (700m), with a drop of at least 500ft (150m) on all sides – and the Donalds – lowland hills over 2000ft (610m). And for connoisseurs of the diminutive, there are the McPhies: 'eminences in excess of 300ft (90m)' on the island of Colonsay.

Further Information

Every tourist office has leaflets (free or for a nominal charge) of suggested walks

TOP 10 SHORT WALKS

➡ Quiraing (p383) (Isle of Skye) One to two hours; bizarre rock pinnacles.

➡ Steall Meadows (p337) (Glen Nevis) One to two hours; waterfall beneath Ben Nevis.

➡ Lost Valley (p332) (Glen Coe) Three hours; impressive mountain scenery.

➡ Ben A'an (p246) (The Trossachs) Three hours; views over Loch Katrine.

➡ Loch an Eilein (p312) (Aviemore) One hour; lovely lochan (small loch) amid Scots pines.

➡ Morrone (p319) (Braemar) Three hours; steep climb to hilltop viewpoint.

➡ Plodda Falls (p303) (Cannich) One hour; dizzying viewpoint above waterfall.

➡ Duncansby Head (p356) (John O'Groats) One hour; spectacular sea stacks.

➡ Stac Pollaidh (p364) (Coigach) Two to four hours; ascent of miniature mountain.

➡ Old Man of Hoy (p411) (Orkney) Three hours; Britain's tallest sea stack.

SIX OF THE BEST GOLF COURSES

St Andrews (p194) The public Old Course is the game's spiritual home, and you can't help but be awed by the history and atmosphere here. The 17th – the Road Hole – is famous for its blind drive, nasty bunker and seriously sloping green. Several other courses for all abilities make this Scotland's premium golfing destination.

Turnberry (☎01655-334060; www.turnberry.co.uk; Maidens Rd, KA26 9LT) Now owned by Donald Trump, Turnberry's Ailsa is one of Scotland's most prestigious links courses, with spectacular views of Ailsa Craig offshore.

Royal Dornoch (p353) Up north, the sumptuous championship course rewards the journey with picture-perfect links scenery and a quieter pace to things.

Machrihanish Dunes (p262) On the Kintyre peninsula, this Old Tom Morris–designed course is one of Scotland's most scenic. There's no easing into your round here; strike long and clean on the first or you'll be on the beach – literally.

Gleneagles (p206) Three brilliant courses and a five-star hotel with truly excellent service make this legendary Perthshire destination a great choice for golfing breaks.

Muirfield (☎01620-842123; www.muirfield.org.uk; Duncur Rd, Muirfield, Gullane EH31 2EG) Handy to Edinburgh, this private course on land reclaimed from the sea allocates some public tee times. It's one of Scotland's more traditional – and many would say outrageously sexist – institutions, and hit the headlines in 2017 when it finally allowed women to join its ranks.

that take in local points of interest. Lonely Planet's *Best Day Walks Great Britain* is a comprehensive resource, covering short walks and longer all-day hikes, including a good selection in Scotland. For general advice, VisitScotland's **Walking in Scotland** (http://walking.visitscotland.com) website describes numerous routes in various parts of the country, and also offers safety tips and other useful information. **WalkHighlands** (www.walkhighlands. co.uk) is an online database of more than 2000 walks, complete with maps and detailed descriptions.

Golf

A round in the home of golf isn't about nostalgia: the sport is part of Scotland's fabric. Playing here is a unique experience; you're almost guaranteed heart-stopping scenery and a friendly atmosphere whatever the weather. Scotland's tradition of public courses means that outstanding golf is usually accompanied by sociable moments and warm hospitality.

History

The first known mention of golf is from 1457, when James II banned it to prevent archery, crucial for military reasons, from being ignored as an activity.

The oldest club is the Honourable Company of Edinburgh Golfers (1744), based at Muirfield. In 1754 the Royal and Ancient Golf Club of St Andrews, which became the game's governing body, was born.

Modern golf really evolved in the late 19th and early 20th centuries. Legendary figures such as James Braid and Old Tom Morris designed courses across Britain; the latter was a founding figure of the Open Championship and won it four times.

Scotland is also very much at the forefront of international professional golf, with high-profile events such as the 2018 Open at Carnoustie, the 2019 Solheim Cup at Gleneagles and the 2022 Open at St Andrews.

Where to Play

With more golf courses per capita than any other country, Scotland offers a bewildering choice. A selection of world golf's most iconic courses offers some of the sport's most famous holes, with deep, challenging bunkers where you might only get out backwards, if at all. But there's also great pleasure to be had on simpler, local fairways eked out by small Highland or island communities, where

TOP FIVE CYCLING ROUTES

Hebridean Way (www.visitouterhebrides.co.uk/hebrideanway) 185 miles, six days; from Vatersay to Butt of Lewis in the Outer Hebrides.

Whisky & Burns Cycling Tour (www.gallowaycycling.com/whisky-and-burns) 84 miles, three days; guided tour of Robert Burns and Scotch whisky heritage sites in Galloway.

Loch Leven Heritage Trail (www.pkct.org/loch-leven-heritage-trail) 14 miles, half-day; an all-abilities circuit around Central Scotland's largest loch.

Assynt-Achiltibuie Circular (https://ridewithgps.com/routes/6581845) 76 miles, one or two days; an engaging tour through the stupendous scenery of the northwest Highlands.

Applecross Peninsula Loop (https://welovemountains.net/applecross) 42 miles, one (long) day; the most challenging, as well as one of the most beautiful, cycle routes in Scotland.

you'll have to improvise shots over the sheep or deer nibbling at the green.

Links Courses

Links – the seaside courses where modern golf was born – present unique challenges with their undulating fairways, unforgiving rough, vertical bunkers and enormous greens that can resemble the Scottish Highlands in miniature. They're usually wholly treeless, with gorse, heather and machair making up the vegetation. But that's not to say they're easy. Far from it.

Largely unplanned, on sandy uncultivable ground between the fields and the sea, they follow the contours of the landscape. Exposed and unprotected, they are at the mercy of wind and weather: on a sunny day you can post flattering scores, but a healthy sea breeze means that approaches into scarily angled greens need meticulous execution. It pays to listen to locals.

Further Information

When to Play

Summer is most enjoyable – long daylight hours mean you can tee off at 6am or 7pm. Courses are busy in these months, though; a good compromise is to play in May or September.

Resources

VisitScotland (www.visitscotland.com/golf) Useful information, including on discount golf

passes. Publishes *Golf in Scotland,* a free annual brochure listing courses, costs and accommodation information.

Scotland Golf (www.scottishgolfcourses.com) Good for investigating courses to play.

Costs

A round at an unfashionable rural course may cost as little as £10. Showpiece courses charge green fees of £160 to £250 and up in high season. It's more economical in winter, is often cheaper midweek, and 'twilight' rates (teeing off after 4pm or so) can save you up to 50% at some clubs.

Cycling

Cycling is an excellent way to explore Scotland. There are hundreds of miles of forest trails and quiet minor roads, and dedicated cycle routes along canal towpaths and disused railway tracks. Depending on your energy and enthusiasm, you can take a leisurely trip through idyllic glens, stopping at pubs along the way, or head off on a long and arduous road tour.

The network of signposted cycle routes maintained by Sustrans (www.sustrans. org.uk) makes a good introduction. Much of the network is on minor roads or cycle lanes, but there are long stretches of surfaced, traffic-free trails between Callander and Killin, between Oban and Ballachulish, on Royal Deeside, and along the Union and Forth & Clyde canals between Glasgow and Edinburgh.

But it's the minor roads of the northwest Highlands, the Outer Hebrides, Orkney and Shetland that are the real attraction for cycle tourers, offering hundreds of miles of peaceful pedalling through breathtaking landscapes. The classic Scottish cycle tour is a trip around the islands of the west coast, from Islay and Jura north via Mull, Coll and Tiree to Skye and the Outer Hebrides (bikes travel for free on Calmac car ferries).

Further Information

Many regional tourist offices have information on local cycling routes and places to hire bikes. They also stock cycling guides and books. Other resources:

VisitScotland (www.visitscotland.com/see-do/active) Publishes a useful free brochure, *Active Scotland,* and has a website with more information.

Sustrans (www.sustrans.org.uk) For up-to-date, detailed information on Scotland's cycle-route network.

Cycling UK (www.cyclinguk.org) A membership organisation offering comprehensive information about cycling in Britain.

Mountain Biking

A combination of challenging, rugged terrain, a network of old drove roads, military roads and stalkers' paths, and legislation that enshrines free access to the countryside has earned Scotland a reputation as one of the world's top mountain-biking destinations. Fort William has hosted the UCI Mountain Bike World Championships every year since 2007.

Scotland offers everything from custom-built forest trails with berms, jumps and skinnies to world-class downhill courses such as those at Laggan Wolftrax and Nevis Range. But perhaps the country's greatest appeal is its almost unlimited potential for adventurous, off-road riding. Areas such as the Galloway hills, the Angus Glens, the Cairngorms, Lochaber, Skye and most of the northwest Highlands have large roadless regions where you can explore to your heart's content.

Top trails include Glen Feshie, Glenlivet and Rothiemurchus Forest in the Cairngorms, Spean Bridge to Kinlochleven via the Lairig Leacach and Loch Eilde Mor, and the stretch of the West Highland Way between Bridge of Orchy and Kinlochleven. The 37-mile loop from Sligachan on Skye (south through Glen Sligachan to Camasunary, over to Kilmarie, and back north via Strath Mor) was voted by *Mountain Bike Rider* magazine as the best off-road trail in Britain. Check out the Where to Ride link on www.dmbins.com.

The ultimate off-road experience is a coast-to-coast ride. There's no set route and no waymarking, so it's as much a planning and navigational challenge as a physical one. A coast-to-coast trip can be as short as the 36 miles from Ullapool to Bonar Bridge via Glen Achall and Glen Einig, or as long as the 250 miles from Aberdeen to Ardnamurchan (90% off road). The most popular coast-to-coast route is from Fort William to Montrose (starting and finishing at a railway station) via Fort Augustus, Aviemore, Tomintoul, Ballater and Edzell, taking in the Corrieyairack Pass, the Ryvoan Pass, Glen Builg, Glen Tanar and Glen Esk (195 miles). You can camp wild along the way, book accommodation at B&Bs and hostels, or join a guided expedition with an organisation such as Wilderness Scotland (p43).

SALMON FISHING ON THE TAY

The Tay is Europe's most famous salmon river, attracting anglers from all over the world (the season runs from 15 January to 15 October). The British record rod-caught salmon, weighing in at a whopping 64lb (29kg) was hooked in the Tay near Dunkeld in 1922 by local woman Georgina Ballantine.

Salmon fishing has an air of exclusivity and can be expensive, but anyone – even complete beginners – can have a go. There's lots of information on the FishTay website (www.fishtay.co.uk), but novices would be best to hire a guide – check out Fishinguide Scotland (p263).

ALTERNATIVE ACTIVITIES

Horse Riding

VisitScotland publishes the *Riding in Scotland* (http://riding.visitscotland.com) brochure, which lists riding centres around Scotland. The Trekking & Riding Society of Scotland (www.ridinginscotland.com) can provide information on horse-riding courses and approved riding centres.

Yachting

The west coast of Scotland, with its myriad islands, superb scenery and challenging winds and tides, is widely acknowledged to be one of the finest yachting areas in the world. Beginners can take a Royal Yachting Association (www.rya.org.uk) training course in yachting or dinghy sailing at many schools around the coast.

Surfing

Even with a wetsuit you definitely have to be hardy to enjoy surfing in Scottish waters. That said, the country does have some of the best surfing breaks in Europe; the north and west coasts, particularly around Thurso and in the Outer Hebrides, have outstanding, world-class surf. For more information, contact Hebridean Surf (www.hebrideansurf.co.uk).

Scuba-Diving

It may lack coral reefs and warm waters, but Scotland offers some of the most spectacular scuba diving in Europe. There are dizzying drop-offs, challenging drift dives and fascinating wildlife, ranging from colourful jewel anemones and soft corals to giant conger eels, monkfish and inquisitive seals. There are also hundreds of fascinating shipwrecks. For more information, contact the Scottish Sub Aqua Club (www.scotsac.com).

Rock Climbing

Scotland has a long history of rock climbing and mountaineering, with many of the classic routes on Ben Nevis and Glen Coe having been pioneered in the 19th century.

Scottish Rock volumes 1 and 2, by Gary Latter, and the Scottish Mountaineering Club's *Scottish Rock Climbs* are excellent guidebooks that cover the whole country.

Mountaineering Council of Scotland (www.mountaineering.scot) General background and information.

Scottish Mountaineering Club (www.smc.org.uk) Publisher of climbing guidebooks.

UK Climbing (www.ukclimbing.com) Discussion forums and databases of crags and routes.

Top Five MTB Trail Centres

7stanes (www.7stanesmountainbiking.com) Series of seven forest-trail centres strung across the Southern Uplands, with fantastic trails for all skill levels from beginner to expert.

Nevis Range (www.nevisrange.co.uk/bike) Ski resort offering summer sport in the form of a world-championship downhill course, and a 3.7-mile red-grade cross-country trail from the top station of the gondola.

Witch's Trails (www.nevisrange.co.uk/bike) Has 22 miles of forest road and single track in the shadow of Ben Nevis. Hosts the annual cross-country world championships and the annual 10 Under the Ben endurance event.

Laggan Wolftrax (http://scotland.forestry.gov.uk/visit/laggan-wolftrax) Forest centre near Newtonmore with everything from novice trails and a bike park to hard cross-country and a challenging black route with drop-offs, boulder fields and rock slabs.

Highland Wildcat (www.highlandwildcat.com) The hills above Golspie harbour have the biggest single-track descent in the country (390m drop over 4 miles, from the top of Ben Bhraggie almost to sea level). Plenty for beginners and families, too.

Fishing

Fishing – coarse, sea and game – is enormously popular in Scotland; its lochs and rivers are filled with salmon, sea trout, brown trout and Arctic char. Fly fishing in particular is a joy – it's a tricky but rewarding form of angling, closer to an art form than a sport.

Fishing rights to most inland waters are privately owned and you must obtain a permit to fish in them – these are usually readily available from the local fishing-tackle shop or hotel, which are also great sources of advice and local knowledge. Permits cost from around £5 to £20 per day, but salmon fishing on some rivers – notably the Tweed, Dee, Tay and Spey – can be much more expensive (up to £150 a day).

For wild brown trout the close season is 7 October to 14 March inclusive. The close season for salmon and sea trout varies between districts; it's generally from mid-October to mid-January.

FishPal (www.fishpal.com/scotland) provides a good introduction, with links for booking fishing on various rivers and lochs.

Canoeing & Kayaking

Scotland's islands, sea lochs and indented coastline provide some of the finest sea kayaking in the world. There are sheltered lochs and inlets ideal for beginners, long and exciting coastal and island tours, and gnarly tidal passages that will challenge even the most expert paddler, all amid spectacular scenery and wildlife – encounters with seals, dolphins and even whales are relatively common.

The inland lochs and rivers offer excellent Canadian and white-water canoeing. Lochs Lomond, Awe and Maree all have uninhabited islands where canoeists can set up camp, while a study of the map will suggest plenty of cross-country expeditions involving only minor portages. Classic routes include Fort William to Inverness along the Great Glen; Glen Affric; Loch Shiel; and Loch Veyatie–Fionn Loch–Loch Sionascaig in Assynt.

There are dozens of companies offering sea-kayaking and canoeing courses and guided holidays, including the following:

Killin Outdoor Centre (p249)

Summer Isles Sea Kayaking (p362)

Sea Kayak Oban (p275)

Sea Kayak Shetland (p425)

Whitewave Outdoor Centre (p374)

Wilderness Scotland (☑01479-420020; www.wildernessscotland.com)

Further Information

Scottish Canoe Association (www.canoescotland.org) Publishes coastal navigation sheets and organises tours, including ones for beginners.

The Northern Isles (by Tom Smith and Chris Jex) A detailed guide to sea kayaking the waters around Orkney and Shetland.

The Outer Hebrides (by Mike Sullivan, Robert Emmott and Tim Pickering) A detailed guide to sea kayaking around the Western Isles.

Scottish Sea Kayak Trail (www.scottishseakayak-trail.com; by Simon Willis) Covers the Scottish west coast from the Isle of Gigha to the Summer Isles.

Snow Sports

There are five ski centres in Scotland, offering downhill skiing and snowboarding:

Cairngorm Mountain (p314) (1097m) Has around 23 miles of runs spread over an extensive area.

Glencoe Mountain Resort (p332) (1108m) Has six tows and two chairlifts.

Glenshee Ski Resort (p43) (920m) Situated on the A93 between Perth and Braemar; offers Scotland's largest network of lifts and widest range of runs.

Lecht 2090 (p43) (793m) The smallest and most remote centre, on the A939 between Ballater and Grantown-on-Spey.

Nevis Range (p339) (1221m) Near Fort William; offers the highest ski runs, the grandest setting and some of the best off-piste potential in Scotland.

The high season is from January to April, but it's sometimes possible to ski from as early as November to as late as May. Conversely, the fickleness of Scottish weather means it's also possible for resorts to close temporarily in season due to high winds or lack of snow.

VisitScotland's *Ski Scotland* brochure is useful and includes a list of accommodation options. General information, and weather and snow reports, can be obtained from Ski Scotland (www.ski-scotland.com) and Winterhighland (www.winterhighland.info).

Whale Watching

Scotland has cashed in on the abundance of minke whales off its coast by embracing whale watching. There are now dozens of operators around the coast offering whale-watching boat trips lasting from a couple of hours to all day; some have whale-sighting success rates of 95% in summer.

The best places to base yourself for whale watching include Oban, the Isle of Mull, Skye and the Outer Hebrides. Orkney and Shetland offer the best chance of spotting orcas (killer whales), while the Moray Firth has a resident population of bottlenose dolphins. Seals, porpoises and dolphins can be seen year-round, but minke whales are most commonly spotted from June to August, with August the peak month for sightings.

The Hebridean Whale & Dolphin Trust (https://hwdt.org) has lots of information on the species found in Scottish waters, and how to identify them. A booklet entitled *Is It a Whale?* is available from tourist offices and bookshops, and provides tips on identifying the various marine mammals that you're likely to see.

The Scottish Marine Wildlife Watching Code (www.snh.scot/marinecode) provides guidance on best practice and legal considerations.

Outfits operating whale-watching cruises include the following:

➡ Sea Life Surveys (p282)
➡ Seafari Adventures (p278)
➡ Aquaxplore (p378)
➡ Gairloch Marine Cruises (p368)
➡ Hebridean Whale Cruises (p368)
➡ Arisaig Marine (p341)
➡ Hebridean Adventures (p386)

Birdwatching

Scotland is the best place in the British Isles (and in some cases, the only place) to spot bird species such as the golden eagle, white-tailed eagle, osprey, corncrake, capercaillie, crested tit, Scottish crossbill and ptarmigan. The country's coast and islands also provide some of Europe's most important seabird nesting grounds.

There are more than 100 ornithologically important nature reserves managed by Scottish Natural Heritage (www.nnr.scot), the Royal Society for the Protection of Birds (www.rspb.org.uk) and the Scottish Wildlife Trust (www.swt.org.uk).

Further information can be obtained from the Scottish Ornithologists Club (www.the-soc.org.uk).

Plan Your Trip
Family Travel

Scotland is one giant adventure playground for kids, with endless miles of sandy beaches, world-class mountain-biking trails, ruined (and not-so-ruined) castles to explore, and seas filled with whales, seals and dolphins. And it's the birthplace of favourite characters such as Harry Potter, Peter Pan and Katie Morag.

Children Will Love...

Outdoor Fun

Edinburgh Zoo, Edinburgh (p75) Giant pandas, interactive chimpanzee enclosure, penguins on parade...

Cairngorm Reindeer Centre, Aviemore (p313) Hike into the hills to hand-feed Scotland's only herd of reindeer.

Falkirk Wheel, Falkirk (p186) Take a boat trip along the Union Canal and pass through a huge rotating boat lift.

Mabie Farm Park, New Abbey (p165) Animals and activities, including soft play area, donkey rides, petting and feeding sessions.

Landmark Forest Adventure Park, Carrbridge (p314) Forest park with nature trail, wildlife hides and a treetop high-wire adventure course.

Luskentyre, Harris (p390) Go beachcombing, kite-flying, dog walking, bird spotting or just plain wandering on one of Scotland's best beaches.

Hands-On Action

National Museum of Scotland, Edinburgh (p67) Lots of interactive exhibits, and trail leaflets for kids to follow and fill in.

Scottish Lighthouse Museum, Fraserburgh (p230) Learn about lighthouses and find out how to move a 4.5-ton lamp assembly with one finger!

Mull Aquarium, Tobermory (p281) Has touch pools where kids can get familiar with starfish, crabs, sea urchins and anemones.

Keeping Costs Down

Sleeping

Children under a certain age (usually 12) can often stay free with their parents in hotels, but check first, and be prepared for upmarket B&Bs that won't accept children at all. Mid-range B&Bs often have excellent-value family rooms, or you could rent a whole dorm in a youth hostel, which often have private ensuites and four or six beds.

Eating Out

Look for places that offer a children's menu, serving smaller portions at reduced prices. In general, eating out at lunchtime or early evening (pre-6.30pm) is cheaper than choosing a mainstream evening slot.

Sightseeing

Almost all tourist attractions have reduced admission fees for children, though the age cut-off varies; under-fives are often free. Many also offer family tickets, admitting one or two adults and up to two children at a reduced rate.

Transport

Typically, children under five travel for free on public transport when accompanied by a fare-paying adult, and children aged five to 15 pay half the adult fare. Scotrails's Family & Friends Railcard (£30 per year) offers big discounts for up to four adults and four children travelling together.

Scottish Crannog Centre, Kenmore (p330) Watch demonstrations of Iron Age technology and try to start a fire by rubbing two bits of wood together.

Museum of Lead Mining, Wanlockhead (p169) Visit Scotland's highest village, take a tour of a real lead mine, and have a go at panning for gold.

Moat Brae, Dumfries (p162) The house and garden that inspired the creator of Peter Pan is set up so kids can explore its secrets interactively.

Rainy-Day Distractions

Real Mary King's Close, Edinburgh (p57) Older children will enjoy the ghost stories and creepy atmosphere.

Scotland's Secret Bunker, Fife (p199) Head underground to explore this Cold War–era nuclear shelter and its James Bond atmosphere.

Loch Ness Centre & Exhibition, Drumnadrochit (p307) View film footage of monster sightings and learn about hoaxes and optical illusions.

Cruachan Power Station, Loch Awe (p290) Ride an electric bus into the heart of a mountain to admire a subterranean power station.

Jacobite Steam Train, Fort William (p335) All aboard the Hogwarts Express across the iconic viaduct that stars in the Harry Potter films.

Stealth Learning

Our Dynamic Earth, Edinburgh (p67) Loads of great stuff about geology, ecology and climate, from earthquake simulators to real icebergs.

New Lanark Visitor Centre, Lanark (p154) Follow the hologram 'spirit' of 10-year-old Annie Macleod, learning about child workers in the 19th-century textile industry.

Highland Folk Museum, Kingussie (p316) Guides in 18th-century costume demonstrate woodcarving, wool-spinning and baking oatcakes on a peat fire.

Dunrobin Castle, Golspie (p353) The impressive falconry display here teaches unexpected lessons not just about birds, but also history and language.

Region by Region

Edinburgh

Edinburgh has plentiful attractions for kids. During the Edinburgh and Fringe Festivals (p79) there's lots of street theatre, especially on High St and at the foot of the Mound, and in December there's a Ferris wheel and fairground rides in Princes Street Gardens (p69) and an ice rink in St Andrew Sq.

Glasgow

Glasgow boasts excellent family attractions, including Glasgow Science Centre (p118) and the People's Palace (p114), and there are several family-friendly apartment-hotels.

Southern Scotland

The Scottish Borders are good for hiking and mountain biking. Some great abbeys and castles, like Culzean (p161) and Hermitage (p148), make an effort to keep kids engaged. Good beaches around Troon, Irvine and Largs.

Central Scotland

Scottish history is everywhere here. Scotland's kings were crowned at Scone Palace (p202), and Stirling Castle (p178) is a fortress straight out of *Braveheart*.

Northeast Scotland

The northeast (p211), with its abundance of castles, stately homes and whisky distilleries, is more adult-oriented. But there's family fun to be had at Discovery Point (p214), Aberdeen Beach (p223) and the Grampian Transport Museum (p231).

Southern Highlands & Islands

This part of the country is made for water sports and boat trips, plus there are castles to explore and child-friendly attractions such as Cruachan Power Station (p290).

Inverness & the Central Highlands

Excellent for outdoor family activities, especially cycling and skiing. Loch Ness has plenty of family attractions, including cruises and the Loch Ness Centre & Exhibition (p307). Arisaig and Morar have sandy beaches and child-friendly campsites.

Northern Highlands & Islands

Distances are greater here, so bring distractions for long drives and ferry crossings. But the scope for outdoor adventures

is unlimited, from beachcombing to whale-watching trips to climbing hills.

Orkney & Shetland

Prehistoric sites are the big draw in Orkney – crawling into the Maeshowe (p407) burial chamber and exploring ancient homes at Skara Brae (p407). Don't miss the Shetland Museum (p418) and climbing the lighthouse at Sumburgh Head (p424).

Good to Know

Look for the 🏵 icon for family-friendly suggestions throughout this guide.

Baby-changing facilities Most modern public toilets, especially those in train and bus stations and other tourist attractions, have baby-changing rooms.

Stuff for babies Supermarkets and pharmacies sell baby formula, nappies (diapers), ready-made baby food and sterilising solutions.

Prams & strollers Cobbled streets, staircases and narrow pavements make the Old Town areas of Edinburgh and Stirling hard to get around; best bring a backpack-style carrier.

Eating out in pubs A lot of pubs are family-friendly and some have great beer gardens where kids can run around. While many Scottish pubs are forbidden by law to admit children under 14, those with a Children's Certificate admit accompanied under-14s between 11am and 8pm; ask the bartender.

Breastfeeding Breastfeeding in public is widely accepted and actively encouraged by government campaigns.

Car travel It's a legal requirement for children under 12 years of age, or under 135cm in height regardless of age, to use a safety seat. Most car-hire companies can provide these, but it's worth booking in advance.

Useful Resources

Lonely Planet Kids (www.lonelyplanetkids.com) Loads of activities and great family-travel blog content.

Edinburgh for Under Fives (www.efuf.co.uk) Has a useful website and guidebook (published 2016).

MumsNet (www.mumsnet.com) No-nonsense advice from a vast network of UK mums.

Kids' Corner

Say What?

Yes	Aye
Pretty	Bonnie
Good	Braw
Grey, miserable (weather)	Dreich

Did You Know? ℹ️

- The Perthshire town of Dull is paired with the town of Boring in Oregon, USA.

- JK Rowling wrote the first Harry Potter in Edinburgh.

Have You Tried?

Haggis A sheep's stomach bag stuffed with heart, liver and lungs.

STOCKCREATIONS/SHUTTERSTOCK ©

PLAN YOUR TRIP FAMILY TRAVEL

Regions at a Glance

Which regions of Scotland you choose to visit will naturally depend on how much time you have, and whether you've been here before. First-time visitors will want to squeeze in as many highlights as possible, so they could try following the well-trodden route through Edinburgh, the Trossachs, Pitlochry, Inverness, Loch Ness and the Isle of Skye.

It takes considerably more time to explore the further-flung corners of the country, but the ruined abbeys and castles of the Borders, the jaw-dropping scenery of the northwest Highlands and the gorgeous white-sand beaches of the Outer Hebrides are less crowded and ultimately more rewarding. The long journey to Orkney or Shetland means that you'll want to devote more than just a day or two to these regions.

Edinburgh

Culture
History
Food

Festival City

The Scottish capital is a city of high culture where, each summer, the world's biggest arts festival rises, phoenix like, from the ashes of its rave reviews and box-office records to evoke yet another string of superlatives.

Edinburgh Castle

Edinburgh Castle has played a pivotal role in Scottish history. The growth of the city from its medieval origins and the parallel development of Scottish nationhood is documented in its excellent museums.

Dining Out

Edinburgh has more restaurants per head of population than any other UK city. The eateries range from stylish but inexpensive bistros and cafes to gourmet restaurants with Michelin stars.

p53

Glasgow

Culture
Music
Style

Kelvingrove Art Gallery & Museum

Glasgow's mercantile, industrial and academic history has left the city with a legacy of museums and art galleries, dominated by this grand Victorian cathedral of culture.

King Tut's Wah Wah Hut

Glasgow is the star of Scotland's live-music scene, with venues like King Tut's Wah Wah Hut staging gigs from local start-ups to top international acts.

Charles Rennie Mackintosh

From Charles Rennie Mackintosh's iconic buildings and interiors and the centre's grand Victorian architecture, to the fashion boutiques of the Italian Centre and design exhibitions at the Lighthouse, Glasgow stakes its claim as Scotland's most stylish city.

p107

Southern Scotland

Historic Buildings
Architecture
Activities

Great Abbeys

Ruined abbeys dot Scotland's southern border. The Gothic ruins of Melrose, Jedburgh, Dryburgh and Sweetheart and the martial towers of Hermitage Castle, Caerlaverock Castle and Smailholm are eloquent testimony to a turbulent past.

Dumfries House

This region is rich in Robert Adam–designed mansions such as Culzean Castle, Paxton House, Floors Castle and Mellerstain House, but the preserved Chippendale time capsule that is Dumfries House takes top place.

Mountain Biking

The rounded, heather-clad hills of the Southern Uplands can't compete with the Highlands for scenery, but the 7stanes trails offer some of the UK's most challenging mountain biking.

p139

Central Scotland

Activities
Coastal Scenery
Historic Buildings

The Home of Golf

Scotland is the home of golf, and the Old Course at St Andrews – the world's oldest – is on every golfer's wish list. The game has been played here for more than 600 years.

East Neuk of Fife

The scenic coastline of the East Neuk of Fife is dotted with picturesque harbours and quaint fishing villages, their history recounted in the excellent Scottish Fisheries Museum in Anstruther.

Stirling Castle

Some say that Stirling has the country's finest castle, but the region has plenty of others worth visiting, including Castle Campbell, Kellie Castle, Doune Castle and St Andrews Castle.

p177

Northeast Scotland

Culture
Historic Buildings
History

Speyside Distilleries

The Speyside region, around Dufftown in Moray, is the whisky distillery's epicentre. Around 50 distilleries open their doors during the twice-yearly Spirit of Speyside festival; many open year-round.

Scottish Baronial Style

Aberdeenshire and Moray have the country's greatest concentration of Scottish Baronial castles, from the turreted splendour of Craigievar and Fyvie to the restrained elegance of Crathes and Balmoral.

Pictish Stones

The northeast is the ancient heartland of the Picts, whose mysterious carved stones (dating from the 7th and 8th centuries) can be seen in places such as Aberlemno and St Vigeans Museum.

p211

Southern Highlands & Islands

Nature
Geography
Food

Whales & Eagles

This region is home to spectacular wildlife, from magnificent white-tailed sea eagles in Mull to minke whales and basking sharks cruising the west coast.

Island-Hopping

Island-hopping is a great way to explore the western seaboard, and the islands here – Islay with its whisky distilleries, mountainous Jura, scenic Mull, the little jewel of Iona, and Colonsay, Coll and Tiree – provide a brilliant introduction.

Harvest of the Sea

Whether you dine at a top restaurant in Oban or Tobermory, or eat with your fingers on the harbourside, the rich harvest of the sea is one of the region's biggest drawcards.

p237

Inverness & the Central Highlands

Activities
Royalty
Legends

Hiking & Skiing

Aviemore and Fort William offer outdoor adventure galore. Try climbing Ben Nevis, walking the West Highland Way, biking the trails around Loch Morlich or skiing the slopes of Cairngorm.

Royal Deeside

The valley of the River Dee between Ballater and Braemar has been associated with the royal family since Queen Victoria acquired her holiday home, Balmoral Castle.

The Loch Ness Monster

Scotland's most iconic legend, the Loch Ness monster, hails from here. You might not spot Nessie, but the scenery of the Great Glen makes a visit worthwhile, as does Culloden battlefield, the undoing of another Scottish legend, Bonnie Prince Charlie.

p293

Northern Highlands & Islands

Scenery
Activities
History

Mountains & Beaches

From the peaks of Assynt and Torridon and the jagged pinnacles of the Cuillin Hills to the dazzling beaches of the Outer Hebrides, this region's big skies and lonely landscapes are the very essence of Scotland.

Adventure Sports

The northwest is one huge adventure playground for hikers, mountain bikers, climbers and kayakers, and provide the chance to see some spectacular wildlife.

The Clearances

The abandoned rural communities of the north teach much about the Clearances, especially Arnol Blackhouse and Skye Museum of Island Life. The region is also rich in prehistoric remains, including the famous standing stones of Callanish.

p347

Orkney & Shetland

History
Wildlife
Music

Skara Brae

These islands have a fascinating Viking heritage and prehistoric villages, tombs and stone circles. Skara Brae is northern Europe's best-preserved prehistoric village; Maeshowe is one of Britain's finest Neolithic tombs.

Birdwatching

Shetland's cliffs teem in summer with gannets, fulmars, kittiwakes, razorbills, puffins and Arctic terns. Nature reserves include Hermaness on Unst, Scotland's northernmost inhabited island.

Folk Festivals

The pubs of Kirkwall, Stromness and Lerwick are ideal for exploring the traditional-music scene, with impromptu fiddle and guitar sessions. Both Orkney and Shetland host annual folk-music festivals.

p397

On the
Road

AT A GLANCE

POPULATION
513,210

OLDEST UNIVERSITY
University of Edinburgh, founded in 1582

BEST TABLE WITH A VIEW
Outlook (p88)

BEST BOUTIQUE HOTEL
House of Gods (p82)

BEST TRAD PUB
Café Royal Circle Bar (p91)

WHEN TO GO
May Good weather (usually), flowers and cherry blossom everywhere and (gasp!) no crowds.

Aug Festival time! Crowded and mad but irresistible.

Dec Christmas decorations, cosy pubs with open fires, ice skating in Princes Street Gardens.

Royal Mile (p56)
MATTHI/SHUTTERSTOCK ©

Edinburgh

E dinburgh is a city that begs to be explored. From the vaults and wynds (narrow lanes) that riddle the Old Town to the urban villages of Stockbridge and Cramond, it's filled with quirky, come-hither nooks that tempt you to walk just a little bit further.

But there's more to Edinburgh than sightseeing – there are top shops, world-class restaurants and a bacchanalia of bars to enjoy. This is a city of pub crawls and impromptu music sessions, late-night drinking, all-night parties and wandering home through cobbled streets at dawn.

All these superlatives come together at festival time in August, when it seems as if half the world descends on Edinburgh for one enormous party. If you can possibly manage it, join them.

N 0 ___ 1 km
0 ___ 0.5 miles

Firth of Forth

Western Harbour
Leith Docks

Royal Yacht Britannia 2

Victoria Dock
Albert Dock

Lindsay Rd

Kitchin 5
Commercial St
Salamander St

GRANTON
Granton Rd
Lower Granton Rd
W Granton Rd
WARDIE
Boswall Parkway
PILTON
TRINITY
Victoria Park Rd
Ferry Rd

Crewe Rd N
Ainslie Park
Ferry Rd

Telford Rd
Crewe Rd S

WARRISTON

Leith Links

LEITH
Duke St
Easter Rd
Lochend Rd

Inverleith Row
CANONMILLS

Broughton Rd
McDonald Rd
Pilrig St
Leith Walk

Lochend Loch

INVERLEITH

COMELY BANK
Inverleith Park

Craigleith Rd
Comely Bank Rd

STOCKBRIDGE
See New Town Map (p72)
London Rd

Queensferry Rd

London Rd

DEAN VILLAGE
Queen St
NEW TOWN
Waverley Station

St Margaret's Loch

WEST END
Princes St

Whinny Hill

Holyrood Park

Roseburn Tce
Edinburgh Castle 1
OLD TOWN
Real Mary King's Close 6

Haymarket Station
Sandy Bell's 4

W Approach Rd
DALRY
Dundee St
TOLLCROSS
See Old Town Map (p64)

Clerk St
Minto St

Arthur's Seat 3

Queen's Dr

Gilmore Pl
BRUNTSFIELD
The Meadows
Melville Dr

GORGIE
Union Canal

MERCHISTON
MARCHMONT

NEWINGTON

Slateford Rd

Grange Rd

Priestfield Rd

See Edinburgh Map (p58)

SHANDON
GREENHILL
Newbattle Tce

Ashley Tce
Colinton Rd

Grange Loan
W Savile Tce

Dalkeith Rd

The Inch Park

MORNINGSIDE

Colinton Rd
Cluny Gdns
Morningside Dr
Blackford Pond
Rosslyn Chapel 7
(5mi)

Craiglockhart Pond

Edinburgh Highlights

1 **Edinburgh Castle** (p56)
Taking in the views from the battlements.

2 **Royal Yacht Britannia** (p74) Nosing around the Queen's private quarters.

3 **Arthur's Seat** (p65)
Climbing to the summit of the city's miniature mountain.

4 **Sandy Bell's** (p93)
Listening to live Scottish folk music.

5 **Kitchin** (p90) Enjoying the finest of Scottish cuisine.

6 **Real Mary King's Close** (p57) Exploring Edinburgh's subterranean history in these haunted vaults.

7 **Rosslyn Chapel** (p101)
Trying to decipher the Da Vinci Code at this mysterious chapel.

History

Edinburgh owes its existence to the Castle Rock, the glacier-worn stump of a long-extinct volcano that provided a near-perfect defensive position guarding the coastal route from northeast England into central Scotland.

In the 7th century the Castle Rock was called Dun Eiden (meaning 'Fort on the Hill Slope'). When it was captured by invaders from the kingdom of Northumbria in northeast England in 638, they took the existing Gaelic name 'Eiden' and tacked it onto their own Old English word for fort, 'burh', to create the name Edinburgh.

Originally a purely defensive site, Edinburgh began to expand in the 12th century when King David I held court at the castle and founded the abbey at Holyrood. The royal court came to prefer Edinburgh to Dunfermline and, as parliament followed the king, Edinburgh became Scotland's capital. The city's first effective town wall was constructed around 1450, enclosing the Old Town as far east as Netherbow and south to the Grassmarket. This overcrowded area – by then the most populous town in Scotland – became a medieval Manhattan, forcing its densely packed inhabitants to build upwards instead of outwards, creating tenements five and six storeys high.

The capital played an important role in the Reformation (1560–1690), led by the Calvinist firebrand John Knox. Mary, Queen of Scots held court in the Palace of Holyroodhouse for six brief years, but when her son James VI acceded to the English throne in 1603 he moved his court to London. The Act of Union in 1707 further reduced Edinburgh's importance, but its cultural and intellectual life flourished.

In the second half of the 18th century a planned new town was created across the valley to the north of the Old Town. During the Scottish Enlightenment (c 1740–1830), Edinburgh became known as 'a hotbed of genius', inhabited by leading scientists and philosophers such as David Hume and Adam Smith.

In the 19th century the population quadrupled to 400,000, not much less than today's population, and the Old Town's tenements were taken over by refugees from the Highland Clearances and the Irish famines. A new ring of crescents and circuses was built to the north of the New Town, and grey Victorian terraces spread south of the Old Town.

In the 1920s the city's borders expanded again to encompass Leith in the north, Cramond in the west and the Pentland Hills in the south. Following WWII the city's cultural life blossomed, stimulated by the Edinburgh International Festival and its fellow traveller, the Fringe, both held for the first time in 1947 and now recognised as world-class arts festivals.

Edinburgh entered a new era following the 1997 referendum vote in favour of a devolved Scottish parliament, which first convened in 1999 in a controversial modern building at the foot of the Royal Mile. The 2014 independence referendum saw Scots vote to remain part of the United Kingdom, but Brexit – with the UK finally splitting from the EU at the end of 2020 – has reignited interest in Scotland seeking its own path.

⊙ Sights

Edinburgh's main attractions are concentrated in the city centre – on and around the Old Town's Royal Mile between the castle and Holyrood, and in the New Town. A major exception is the Royal Yacht *Britannia,* which is in the redeveloped docklands district of Leith, 2 miles northeast of the centre.

If you tire of sightseeing, good areas for aimless wandering include the posh suburbs of Stockbridge and Morningside, the pretty riverside village of Cramond and the winding footpaths of Calton Hill and Arthur's Seat.

⊙ Old Town

Edinburgh's Old Town stretches along a ridge between the castle and Holyrood, and tumbles southward down Victoria St and West Bow to the broad expanse of the Grassmarket and the mossy stones of Greyfriars Kirkyard. It's cleft along its spine by the cobbled ravine of the Royal Mile.

Half the fun is just exploring this medieval maze, but the Old Town is also home to the city's most important historical sights – Edinburgh Castle, St Giles Cathedral, the Real Mary King's Close and Greyfriars Kirkyard, along with the Museum of Edinburgh and the National Museum of Scotland.

Until the founding of the New Town in the 18th century, old Edinburgh was an overcrowded, unsanitary hive of humanity squeezed between the boggy ground of the Nor' Loch (North Loch, now drained and occupied by Princes Street Gardens) to the north and the city walls to the south and east. The only way for the town to expand was upwards, and the five- and six-storey tenements that were raised along the Royal Mile in the 16th and 17th centuries were the skyscrapers of their day, remarked upon with wonder by visiting writers such as Daniel Defoe. All classes of society, from beggars to magistrates, lived cheek by jowl in these urban ant nests, the wealthy occupying the middle floors – high enough to be above the noise and stink of the streets, but not so high that climbing the stairs would be too tiring – while the poor squeezed into attics, basements, cellars and vaults amid rats, rubbish and raw sewage.

The renovated Old Town tenements still support a dwindling city-centre community – many flats have been converted to short-term holiday lets – and today the street level is crammed with cafes, restaurants, bars, backpacker hostels and tacky souvenir shops.

◉ Royal Mile

★**Edinburgh Castle**   CASTLE
(Map p64; ☎0131-225 9846; www.edinburgh castle.scot; Castle Esplanade, EH1 2NG; adult/child £17.50/10.50, audio guide £3.50/1.50; ⊘9.30am-6pm Apr-Sep, to 5pm Oct-Mar, last entry 1hr before closing; 🚌23, 27, 41, 42) Edinburgh Castle has played a pivotal role in Scottish history, both as a royal residence – King Malcolm Canmore (r 1058–93) and Queen Margaret first made their home here in the 11th century – and as a military stronghold. The castle last saw military action in 1745; from then until the 1920s it served as the British army's main base in Scotland. Today it is one of Scotland's most atmospheric and popular tourist attractions.

The brooding, black crags of Castle Rock, rising above the western end of Princes St, are the very reason for Edinburgh's existence. This rocky hill was the most easily defended hilltop on the invasion route between England and central Scotland, a route followed by countless armies from the Roman legions of the 1st and 2nd centuries CE to the Jacobite troops of Bonnie Prince Charlie in 1745.

The **Entrance Gateway**, flanked by statues of Robert the Bruce and William Wallace, opens to a cobbled lane that leads up beneath the 16th-century **Portcullis Gate** to the cannons ranged along the Argyle and Mills Mount Batteries. The battlements here have great views over the New Town to the Firth of Forth.

At the far end of Mills Mount Battery is the famous **One O'Clock Gun**, where crowds gather to watch a gleaming WWII 25-pounder fire an ear-splitting time signal

---

EDINBURGH IN...

Two Days

A two-day trip to Edinburgh should start at Edinburgh Castle, followed by a stroll down the Royal Mile to the Scottish Parliament Building (p61) and the Palace of Holyroodhouse (p65). You can work up an appetite by climbing Arthur's Seat (p65), then satisfy your hunger with dinner at Ondine (p86) or Cannonball Restaurant (p85). On day two spend the morning in the National Museum of Scotland (p67), then catch the bus to Leith for a visit to the Royal Yacht Britannia (p74). In the evening, have dinner at one of Leith's many excellent restaurants, or scare yourself silly on a guided ghost tour (p77).

Four Days

Two more days will give you time for a morning stroll around the Royal Botanic Garden (p75), followed by a trip to the enigmatic and beautiful Rosslyn Chapel (p101), or a relaxing afternoon visit to the seaside village of Cramond (p75) – bring binoculars (for birdwatching and yacht-spotting) and a book (to read in the sun). Dinner at Aizle (p87) or Gardener's Cottage (p87) could be before or after your sunset walk to the summit of Calton Hill (p71). On day four head out to the pretty harbour village of Queensferry, nestled beneath the Forth Bridges, and take a cruise to Inchcolm Island (p104).

at exactly 1pm (every day except Sundays, Christmas Day and Good Friday).

South of Mills Mount, the road curls up leftwards through **Foog's Gate** to the highest part of Castle Rock, crowned by the tiny, Romanesque **St Margaret's Chapel**, the oldest surviving building in Edinburgh. It was probably built by David I or Alexander I in memory of their mother, Queen Margaret, sometime around 1130 (she was canonised in 1250). Beside the chapel stands **Mons Meg**, a giant 15th-century siege gun built at Mons (in what is now Belgium) in 1449.

The main group of buildings on the summit of Castle Rock is ranged around Crown Sq, dominated by the shrine of the **Scottish National War Memorial**. Opposite is the Great Hall, built for James IV (r 1488–1513) as a ceremonial hall and used as a meeting place for the Scottish parliament until 1639. Its most remarkable feature is the original, 16th-century hammer-beam roof.

The **Castle Vaults** beneath the Great Hall (entered via the **Prisons of War Exhibition**) were used variously as storerooms, bakeries and a prison. The vaults have been renovated to resemble 18th- and early 19th-century prisons, where graffiti carved by French and American prisoners can be seen on the ancient wooden doors.

On the eastern side of the square is the **Royal Palace**, built during the 15th and 16th centuries, where a series of historical tableaux leads to the highlight of the castle: a strongroom housing the **Honours of Scotland** (the Scottish crown jewels), among the oldest surviving crown jewels in Europe. Locked away in a chest following the Act of Union in 1707, the crown (made in 1540 from the gold of Robert the Bruce's 14th-century coronet), sword and sceptre lay forgotten until they were unearthed at the instigation of novelist Sir Walter Scott in 1818. Also on display here is the Stone of Destiny (p71).

Among the neighbouring **Royal Apartments** is the bedchamber where Mary, Queen of Scots, gave birth to her son James VI, who was to unite the crowns of Scotland and England in 1603.

★ **Real Mary King's Close**   HISTORIC BUILDING
(Map p64; ☎ 0131-225 0672; www.realmarykingsclose.com; 2 Warriston's Close, EH1 1PG; adult/child £17.95/11.25; ☺ hours vary, approx 9.30am-9pm Apr-Oct, 10am-5.30pm Nov-Mar;

☒ 23, 27, 41, 42) Edinburgh's 18th-century City Chambers were built over the sealed-off remains of Mary King's Close, the lower levels of this medieval Old Town alley have survived almost unchanged amid the foundations for 250 years. Now open to the public, this spooky, subterranean labyrinth gives a fascinating insight into the everyday life of 17th-century Edinburgh. Costumed characters lead tours through a 16th-century town house and the plague-stricken home of a 17th-century gravedigger. Advance booking is recommended; check hours online.

The scripted tour, complete with ghostly tales and gruesome tableaux, can seem a little naff, milking the scary and scatological aspects of the close's history for all they're worth. But there are also things of genuine interest to see: there's something about the crumbling 17th-century **tenement room** that makes the hair rise on the back of your neck, with tufts of horsehair poking from collapsing lath-and-plaster walls that bear the ghost of a pattern, and the ancient smell of stone and dust thick in your nostrils.

In one of the former bedrooms off the close, a psychic once claimed to have been approached by the ghost of a little girl called Annie. It's hard to tell what's more frightening – the story of the ghostly child, or the bizarre heap of tiny dolls and teddies left by sympathetic visitors.

National War Museum of Scotland   MUSEUM
(Map p64; www.nms.ac.uk; EH1 2NG; incl in Edinburgh Castle entry; ☺ 9.45am-5.45pm Apr-Oct, to 4.45pm Nov-Mar; ☒ 23, 27, 41, 42) At the western end of Edinburgh Castle, to the left of the castle tearooms, a road leads down to the National War Museum of Scotland, which brings Scotland's military history vividly to life. The exhibits have been personalised by telling the stories of the original owners of the objects on display, making it easier to empathise with the experiences of war than any dry display of dusty weaponry ever could.

Scotch Whisky Experience   MUSEUM
(Map p64; www.scotchwhiskyexperience.co.uk; 354 Castlehill, EH1 2NE; adult/child from £17/8; ☺ 10am-6pm Apr-Jul, to 5pm Aug-Mar; ☒ 23, 27, 41, 42) A former school houses this multimedia centre that takes you through the making of whisky, from barley to bottle,

Edinburgh

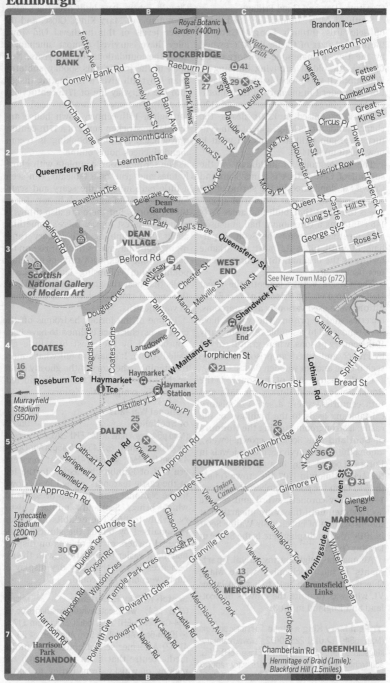

Royal Botanic Garden (400m)

Brandon Tce

Water of Leith

COMELY BANK

STOCKBRIDGE

Henderson Row

Fettes Ave

Comely Bank Rd

Raeburn Pl

41

Clarence St

Fettes Row

Orchard Brae

Comely Bank Ave

Comely Bank St

27

Raeburn St

29

Dean St

Leslie Pl

Cumberland St

Great King St

Dean Park Mews

Danube St

Circus Pl

India St

Howe St

S Learmonth Gdns

Lennox St

Ann St

Heriot Row

Frederick St

Queensferry Rd

Learmonth Tce

Eton Tce

Moray Pl

Queen St

Castle St

Hill St

Doune Tce

Gloucester La

Young St

George St

Rose St

Ravelston Tce

Belgrave Cres

Dean Gardens

Dean Path

Bell's Brae

Belford Rd

8

DEAN VILLAGE

Queensferry St

See New Town Map (p72)

2

Scottish National Gallery of Modern Art

Belford Rd

14

WEST END

Rothesay Tce

Chester St

Alva St

Castle Tce

Douglas Cres

Melville St

Coates Gdns

Manor Pl

Palmerston Pl

Shandwick Pl

Spittal St

Magdala Cres

Lansdowne Cres

West End

Bread St

COATES

W Maitland St

Torphichen St

Lothian Rd

16

Roseburn Tce

Haymarket Tce

Haymarket

21

Haymarket Station

Morrison St

Murrayfield Stadium (950m)

Distillery La

Dalry Pl

25

Dalry Rd

Orwell Pl

26

DALRY

22

W Approach Rd

Fountainbridge

Tollcross

36

Cathcart Pl

FOUNTAINBRIDGE

9

37

Springwell Pl

Dundee St

Gilmore Pl

Leven St

31

Downfield Pl

Viewforth

W Approach Rd

Union Canal

Gibson Tce

Learmington Tce

Glengyle Tce

MARCHMONT

Tynecastle Stadium (200m)

Dundee St

Dundee Tce

Dorset Pl

Granville Tce

Viewforth

Morningside Rd

Whitehouse Loan

30

Bryson Rd

Watson Cres

Temple Park Cres

Polwarth Gdns

Merchiston Park

13

Forbes Rd

Bruntsfield Links

Harrison Rd

W Bryson Rd

Polwarth Gve

Polwarth Tce

W Castle Rd

E Castle Rd

Merchiston Ave

MERCHISTON

Harrison Park

SHANDON

Napier Rd

Chamberlain Rd

GREENHILL

Hermitage of Braid (1mile); Blackford Hill (1.5miles)

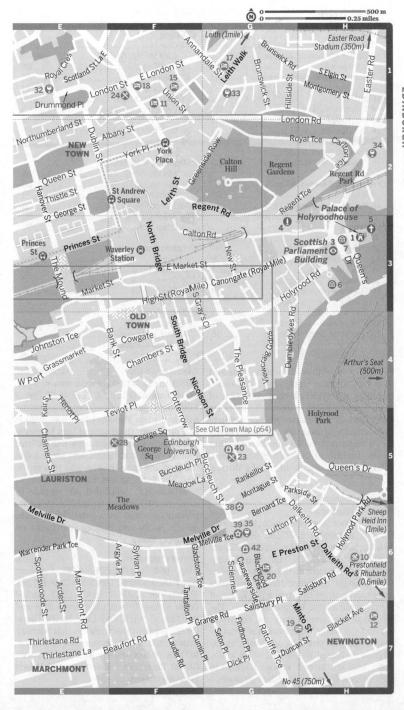

0 — 500 m
0 — 0.25 miles

Easter Road Stadium (350m)

Leith (1mile)

Royal Cres
Scotland St La E.
32
Drummond Pl
London St
E London St
24
18
15
11
Union St
33
Leith Walk
Annandale St
Brunswick Rd
Brunswick St
Hillside Cres
S Elgin St
Montgomery St
Easter Rd

London Rd

Northumberland St
NEW TOWN
Dublin St
Albany St
York Pl
York Place
Greenside Row
Royal Tce
Carlton Tce
Carlton
34

Queen St
Thistle St
George St
St Andrew Square
Leith St
Calton Hill
Regent Gardens
Regent Rd Park
Palace of Holyroodhouse
5
1
7
3

Hanover St
Princes St
Princes St
The Mound
Waverley Station
North Bridge
Calton Rd
New St
Regent Tce
Regent Rd
4
Scottish Parliament Building
Queen's Dr

Market St
E Market St
High St (Royal Mile)
Canongate (Royal Mile)
S Gray's Cl
Holyrood Rd
6
Dumbiedykes Rd

Johnston Tce
OLD TOWN
Bank St
Cowgate
Chambers St
South Bridge
The Pleasance
Viewcraig Gdns
Arthur's Seat (500m)

W Port
Grassmarket
Teviot Pl
Potterrow
Nicolson St
Holyrood Park

Heriot Pl
Lady
Chalmers St
28
George Sq
George Sq
Edinburgh University
See Old Town Map (p64)
40
23
Queen's Dr

LAURISTON
Buccleuch Pl
Meadow La
Buccleuch St
Rankeillor St
Montague St
Parkside St
Holyrood Park Rd

The Meadows
38
Bernard Tce
Dalkeith Rd
Sheep Heid Inn (1mile)

Melville Dr
Melville Dr
Melville Tce
39 35
Lutton Pl
E Preston St
Dalkeith Rd
10
Prestonfield & Rhubarb (0.6miles)

Warrender Park Tce
Sylvan Pl
Gladstone Tce
42
Blackwood Cres
20
Causewayside
Sciennes
Salisbury Rd
Salisbury Pl

Spottiswoode St
Arden St
Marchmont Rd
Argyle Pl
Tantallon Pl
Grange Rd
Seton Pl
Findhorn Pl
Ratcliffe Tce
Minto St
19
Duncan St
Blacket Ave
12
NEWINGTON

Thirlestane Rd
Thirlestane La
MARCHMONT
Beaufort Rd
Lauder Rd
Cumin Pl
Dick Pl
No 45 (750m)

Edinburgh

in a series of exhibits, demonstrations and talks that combine sight, sound and smell, including the world's largest collection of malt whiskies (3384 bottles!). The pricier tours include extensive whisky tastings and samples of Scottish cuisine. There's also a restaurant called Amber (p86) that serves traditional Scottish dishes with, where possible, a dash of whisky thrown in.

Camera Obscura & World of Illusions   MUSEUM
(Map p64; www.camera-obscura.co.uk; Castlehill, EH1 2ND; adult/child £16.50/12.50; ⊙9am-10pm Jul & Aug, 9.30am-8pm Apr-Jun, Sep & Oct, 9.30am-7pm Nov-Mar; 🚌23, 27, 41, 42) Edinburgh's camera obscura is a curious 19th-century device – in constant use since 1853 – that uses lenses and mirrors to throw a live image of the city onto a large horizontal screen. The accompanying commentary is entertaining and the whole experience has a quirky charm, complemented by an intriguing exhibition dedicated to illusions of all kinds. Stairs lead up through various displays to the **Outlook Tower**, which offers great views over the city.

Gladstone's Land   HISTORIC BUILDING
(NTS; Map p64; ☎0131-226 5856; www.nts.org.uk; 477 Lawnmarket, EH1 2NT; 🚌23, 27, 41, 42) One of Edinburgh's most prominent 17th-century merchants was Thomas Gledstanes, who in 1617 purchased the tenement later known as Gladstone's Land. It contains fine painted ceilings, walls and beams, and some splendid furniture from the 17th and 18th centuries. The building has undergone a major refurbishment, scheduled to reopen by summer 2021 with a traditional ice-cream parlour on street level, exhibitions on the middle floors, and holiday apartments on the upper floors.

Writers' Museum   MUSEUM
(Map p64; ☎0131-529 4901; www.edinburghmuseums.org.uk; Lady Stair's Close, EH1 2PA; ⊙10am-5pm; 🚌23, 27, 41, 42) FREE Tucked down a close between the Royal Mile and the Mound you'll find Lady Stair's House (1622), home to this museum that contains manuscripts and memorabilia belonging to three of Scotland's most famous writers: Robert Burns, Sir Walter Scott and Robert Louis Stevenson.

St Giles Cathedral
CHURCH

(Map p64; www.stgilescathedral.org.uk; High St, EH1 1RE; ⊘9am-7pm Mon-Fri, to 5pm Sat, 1-5pm Sun Apr-Oct, 9am-5pm Mon-Sat, 1-5pm Sun Nov-Mar; ⌂23, 27, 41, 42) FREE The great grey bulk of St Giles Cathedral dates largely from the 15th century, but much of it was restored in the 19th century. One of the most interesting corners of the kirk is the Thistle Chapel, built in 1911 for the Knights of the Most Ancient & Most Noble Order of the Thistle. The elaborately carved Gothic-style stalls have canopies topped with the helms and arms of the 16 knights – look out for the bagpipe-playing angel amid the vaulting.

Properly called the High Kirk of Edinburgh (it was only a true cathedral – the seat of a bishop – from 1633 to 1638 and from 1661 to 1689), the church was named after the patron saint of cripples and beggars. The interior lacks grandeur but is rich in history: a Norman-style church was built here in 1126 but was destroyed by English invaders in 1385 (the only substantial remains are the central piers that support the tower). St Giles was at the heart of the Scottish Reformation, and John Knox served as minister here from 1559 to 1572.

There are several ornate monuments in the church, including the tombs of James Graham, Marquis of Montrose, who led Charles I's forces in Scotland and was hanged in 1650 at the Mercat Cross; and his opponent, Covenanter (an adherent of the Scottish Presbyterian Church) Archibald Campbell, Marquis of Argyll, who was decapitated in 1661 after the restoration of Charles II. There's also a bronze memorial to author Robert Louis Stevenson, and a copy of the National Covenant of 1638.

By the side of the street, outside the western door of St Giles, is the Heart of Midlothian, set into the cobblestone paving. This marks the site of the Tolbooth. Built in the 15th century and demolished in the early 19th century, the Tolbooth served variously as a meeting place for parliament, the town council and the General Assembly of the Reformed Kirk, before becoming law courts and, finally, a notorious prison and place of execution. Passers-by traditionally spit on the heart for luck (don't stand downwind!).

At the other end of St Giles is the Mercat Cross, a 19th-century copy of the 1365 original, where merchants and traders met to transact business and royal proclamations were read.

John Knox House
HISTORIC BUILDING

(Map p64; www.scottishstorytellingcentre.com; 43-45 High St, EH1 1SR; adult/child £6/1; ⊘10am-6pm daily Jul & Aug, Mon-Sat Sep-Jun; ⌂35) The Royal Mile narrows at the foot of High St, beside the jutting facade of John Knox House. This is the oldest surviving tenement in Edinburgh, dating from around 1490. John Knox, an influential church reformer and leader of the Protestant Reformation in Scotland, is thought to have lived here from 1561 to 1572. The labyrinthine interior has some beautiful painted-timber ceilings and an interesting display on Knox' life and work.

Museum of Edinburgh
MUSEUM

(Map p64; ☏0131-529 4143; www.edinburghmuseums.org.uk; 142 Canongate, EH8 8DD; ⊘10am-5pm Mon & Thu-Sat, noon-5pm Sun; ⌂300) FREE You can't miss the colourful facade of Huntly House (it featured in Season 3 of the TV series Outlander), opposite the Tolbooth clock on the Royal Mile. Built in 1570, it houses a museum covering Edinburgh from prehistory to the present. Exhibits of national importance include an original copy of the National Covenant of 1638, but the big crowd-pleaser is the dog collar and feeding bowl that once belonged to Greyfriars Bobby (p67), the city's most famous canine citizen.

◉ Holyrood & Arthur's Seat

★ Scottish

Parliament Building
NOTABLE BUILDING

(Map p58; ☏0131-348 5200; www.parliament.scot; Horse Wynd, EH99 1SP; ⊘9am-6.30pm Tue-Thu, 10am-5pm Mon, Fri & Sat in session, 10am-5pm Tue-Thu in recess; ⌂35) FREE The Scottish Parliament Building, designed by Catalan architect Enric Miralles (1955–2000), was opened by the Queen in October 2004. The ground plan of the complex is said to represent a 'flower of democracy rooted in Scottish soil' (best seen looking down from Salisbury Crags). Free, one-hour tours (advance bookings recommended) include visits to the Debating Chamber, a committee room, the Garden Lobby and the office of a member of parliament (MSP).

Miralles believed that a building could be a work of art. However, this weird concrete confection at the foot of Salisbury

Royal Mile

A GRAND DAY OUT

Planning your own procession along the Royal Mile involves some tough decisions – it would be impossible to see everything in a single day, so it's wise to decide in advance what you don't want to miss and shape your visit around that. Remember to leave time for lunch, for exploring some of the Mile's countless side alleys and, during festival time, for enjoying the street theatre that is bound to be happening in High St.

The most pleasant way to reach the Castle Esplanade at the start of the Royal Mile is to hike up the zigzag path from the footbridge behind the Ross Bandstand in Princes St Gardens (in springtime you'll be knee-deep in daffodils). Starting at **① Edinburgh Castle** means that the rest of your walk is downhill. For a superb view up and down the length of the Mile, climb the **② Camera Obscura's Outlook Tower** before visiting **③ Gladstone's Land** and **④ St Giles Cathedral**.

ROYAL VISITS TO THE ROYAL MILE

1561: Mary, Queen of Scots arrives from France and holds an audience with John Knox.
1745: Bonnie Prince Charlie fails to capture Edinburgh Castle, and instead sets up court in Holyroodhouse.
2004: Queen Elizabeth II officially opens the Scottish Parliament building.

CLAUDIO DIVIZIA / SHUTTERSTOCK ©

Edinburgh Castle
If you're pushed for time, visit the Great Hall, the Honours of Scotland and the Prisons of War exhibit. Head for the Half Moon Battery for a photo looking down the length of the Royal Mile.

Camera Obscura's Outlook Tower

MINGKWAN DOILOM/ SHUTTERSTOCK ©

Gladstone's Land
The 1st floor houses a faithful recreation of how a wealthy Edinburgh merchant lived in the 17th century. Check out the beautiful Painted Bedchamber, with its ornately decorated walls and wooden ceilings.

LUNCH BREAK

Eggs Benedict at **Edinburgh Larder**; steak and chips at **Maxie's Bistro**; slap-up seafood at **Ondine**.

Royal Scottish Academy
Scott Monument
Heart of Midlothian
City Chambers
NORTH BRIDGE
Scottish National Gallery
Princes St Gardens
THE MOUND
HIGH ST
CASTLEHILL
GEORGE IV BRIDGE
Scotch Whisky Experience

If history's your thing, you'll want to add **⑤ Real Mary King's Close**, **⑥ John Knox House** and the **⑦ Museum of Edinburgh** to your must-see list.

At the foot of the mile, choose between modern and ancient seats of power – the **⑧ Scottish Parliament** or the **⑨ Palace of Holyroodhouse**. Round off the day with an evening ascent of Arthur's Seat or, slightly less strenuously, Calton Hill. Both make great sunset viewpoints.

TAKING YOUR TIME

Minimum time needed for each attraction:
Edinburgh Castle two hours
Gladstone's Land 45 minutes
St Giles Cathedral 30 minutes
Real Mary King's Close one hour (tour)
Scottish Parliament one hour (tour)
Palace of Holyroodhouse one hour

Real Mary King's Close
The guided tour is heavy on ghost stories, but a highlight is standing in an original 17th-century room with tufts of horsehair poking from the crumbling plaster, and breathing in the ancient scent of stone, dust and history.

Canongate Kirk

CANONGATE

ST MARY'S ST

SOUTH BRIDGE

ron Kirk

Our Dynamic Earth

Scottish Parliament
Don't have time for the guided tour? Pick up a 'Discover the Scottish Parliament Building' leaflet from reception and take a self-guided tour of the exterior, then hike up to Salisbury Crags for a great view of the complex.

Palace of Holyroodhouse
Find the secret staircase joining Mary, Queen of Scots' bedchamber with that of her husband, Lord Darnley, who restrained the queen while his henchmen stabbed to death her secretary (and possible lover), David Rizzio.

St Giles Cathedral
Look out for the Burne-Jones stained-glass window (1873) at the west end, showing the crossing of the River Jordan, and the bronze memorial to Robert Louis Stevenson in the Moray Aisle.

HEARTLAND ARTS / SHUTTERSTOCK ©

DAVID IONUT / SHUTTERSTOCK ©

Old Town

Crags initially left the good people of Edinburgh scratching their heads in confusion. What does it all mean? The strange forms of the exterior are each symbolic in some way, from the oddly shaped windows on the western wall (inspired by the silhouette of *The Reverend Robert Walker Skating on Duddingston Loch,* one of Scotland's most famous paintings) to the asymmetrical panels on the main facade (representing a curtain being drawn aside – a symbol of open government).

The **Main Hall**, inside the public entrance, has a low, triple-arched ceiling of polished concrete, like a cave, or cellar, or castle vault. It is a dimly lit space, the starting point for a metaphorical journey from this relative darkness up to the **Debating Chamber** (sitting directly above the Main Hall), which is, in contrast, a palace of light – the light of democracy. This magnificent chamber is the centrepiece of the parliament, designed not to glorify but to humble the politicians who sit within it. The windows face Calton Hill, allowing parliamentarians to look up to its monuments (reminders of the Scottish Enlightenment), while the massive, pointed oak beams of the roof are suspended by steel threads above the MSPs' heads like so many Damoclean swords.

The public areas of the building – the Main Hall, where there is an exhibition, shop and cafe, and the public gallery in the Debating Chamber – are open to visitors (free tickets are needed for the public gallery – see the website for details). If you want to see the parliament in session, check the website to see when it will be sitting – business days are normally Tuesday to Thursday year-round.

★ **Arthur's Seat**   VIEWPOINT

(Holyrood Park; 🚌35) The rocky peak of Arthur's Seat (251m), carved by ice sheets from the deeply eroded stump of a long-extinct volcano, is a distinctive feature of Edinburgh's skyline. The view from the summit is well worth the walk, extending from the Forth bridges in the west to the distant conical hill of North Berwick Law in the east, with the Ochil Hills and the Highlands on the northwestern horizon. You can hike from Holyrood to the summit in around 45 minutes.

★ **Palace of Holyroodhouse**   PALACE

(Map p58; ☎0303 123 7306; www.rct.uk; Canongate, Royal Mile, EH8 8DX; adult/child incl audio guide £16.50/9.50; ⏰9.30am-6pm, last entry 4.30pm Apr-Oct, to 4.30pm, last entry 3.15pm Nov-Mar; 🚌35) This palace is the royal family's official residence in Scotland but is more famous as the 16th-century home of the ill-fated Mary, Queen of Scots. The highlight of the tour is **Mary's Bedchamber**, home to the unfortunate queen from 1561 to 1567. It was here that her jealous second husband, Lord Darnley, restrained the pregnant queen while his henchmen murdered her secretary – and favourite – David Rizzio. A plaque in the neighbouring room marks the spot where Rizzio bled to death.

The palace developed from a guesthouse attached to Holyrood Abbey that was extended by James IV in 1501. The oldest surviving part of the building, the northwestern tower, was built in 1529 as a royal apartment for James V and his wife, Mary of Guise. Mary, Queen of Scots, spent six turbulent years here, during which time she debated with John Knox, married both her second and third husbands, and witnessed Rizzio's murder.

Old Town

◉ Top Sights

◉ Sights

⊕ Activities, Courses & Tours

⊜ Sleeping

⊗ Eating

⊖ Drinking & Nightlife

⊕ Entertainment

⊝ Shopping

The self-guided audio tour leads you through a series of impressive royal apartments, culminating in the **Great Gallery**. The gallery's 89 portraits of Scottish kings were commissioned by Charles II and supposedly record his unbroken lineage from Scota, the Egyptian pharaoh's daughter who discovered the infant Moses in a reed basket on the banks of the Nile. The tour continues to the oldest part of the palace, which contains Mary's Bedchamber, connected by a secret stairway to her husband's bedroom, and ends with the ruins of Holyrood Abbey.

The palace is closed during royal visits; check the website for dates.

Holyrood Abbey   ABBEY
(Map p58; www.historicenvironment.scot; Canongate, EH8 8DX; free with Palace of Holyroodhouse; ⊙9.30am-6pm, last entry 4.30pm Apr-Oct, to 4.30pm, last entry 3.15pm Nov-Mar; 🚌35) David I founded this abbey in the shadow of Salisbury Crags in 1128. It was probably named after a fragment of the True Cross (*rood* is an old Scots word for cross), said to have been brought to Scotland by David's mother, St Margaret. Most of the ruins date from the 12th and 13th centuries, although a doorway in the far-southeastern corner has survived from the original Norman church. Admission is included in the cost of a Palace of Holyroodhouse (p65) ticket.

Queen's Gallery   GALLERY
(Map p58; www.rct.uk; Horse Wynd, EH8 8DX; adult/child £7.80/3.90, with Holyroodhouse £21.90/12; ⊘9.30am-6pm, last entry 4.30pm Apr-Oct, to 4.30pm, last entry 3.15pm Nov-Mar; 🖳35) This stunning modern gallery, which occupies the shell of a former church and school, is a showcase for exhibitions of art from the Royal Collections. The exhibitions change every six months or so; for current details, check the website.

Our Dynamic Earth   MUSEUM
(Map p58; www.dynamicearth.co.uk; Holyrood Rd, EH8 8AS; adult/child £15.95/9.95; ⊘10am-5.30pm Easter-Oct, to 6pm Jul & Aug, 10am-5.30pm Wed-Sun Nov-Easter; 🖫; 🖳35) Housed in a modernistic white marquee, Our Dynamic Earth is an interactive, multimedia journey of discovery through Earth's history from the Big Bang to the present day. Hugely popular with kids of all ages, it's a slick extravaganza of whiz-bang special effects and 3D movies cleverly designed to fire young minds with curiosity about all things geological and environmental. Its true purpose, of course, is to disgorge you into a gift shop where you can buy toy dinosaurs and souvenir T-shirts.

◉ South of the Royal Mile

★**National Museum of Scotland**   MUSEUM
(Map p64; ☑0300 123 6789; www.nms.ac.uk; Chambers St, EH1 1JF; ⊘10am-5pm; 🖫; 🖳35, 45) FREE Elegant Chambers St is dominated by the long facade of the National Museum of Scotland. Its extensive collections are spread between two buildings: one modern, one Victorian – the golden stone and striking architecture of the new building (1998) make it one of the city's most distinctive landmarks. The museum's five floors trace the history of Scotland from geological beginnings to the present, with many imaginative and stimulating exhibits. Audio guides are available in several languages. Fees apply for special exhibitions.

The modern building connects with the original Victorian museum, dating from 1861, the stolid, grey exterior of which gives way to a beautifully bright and airy, glass-roofed exhibition hall. The old building houses an eclectic collection covering natural history, archaeology, design and fashion, science and technology, and the decorative arts of ancient Egypt, the Islamic world, China, Japan, Korea and the West.

★**Surgeons' Hall Museums**   MUSEUM
(Map p64; ☑0131-527 1711; www.museum.rcsed.ac.uk; Nicolson St, EH8 9DW; adult/child £8/4.50; ⊘10am-5pm; 🖳all South Bridge buses) Housed in a grand Ionic temple designed by William Playfair in 1832, these three fascinating museums were originally established as teaching collections. The **History of Surgery Museum** provides a look at surgery in Scotland from the 15th century to the present day. Highlights include the exhibit on murderers Burke and Hare (p68), which includes Burke's death mask and a pocketbook made from his skin, and a display on Dr Joseph Bell, who was the inspiration for the character of Sherlock Holmes.

The adjacent **Dental Collection**, with its wince-inducing extraction tools, covers the history of dentistry, while the **Pathology Museum** houses a gruesome but compelling 19th-century collection of diseased organs and excised tumours pickled in formaldehyde.

Greyfriars Kirkyard   CEMETERY
(Map p64; www.greyfriarskirk.com; Candlemaker Row, EH1 2QQ; ⊘24hr; 🖳2, 23, 27, 35, 41, 42, 45) Greyfriars Kirkyard is one of Edinburgh's most evocative cemeteries, a peaceful green oasis dotted with elaborate monuments. Many famous Edinburgh names are buried here, including poet Allan Ramsay (1686–1758); architect William Adam (1689–1748); and William Smellie (1740–95), editor of the 1st edition of the *Encyclopaedia Britannica*. If you want to experience the graveyard at its scariest – inside a burial vault, in the dark, at night – go on a City of the Dead (p77) guided tour.

A more recent addition to the graveyard's reputation is the idea that it is the resting place of JK Rowling's famous villain Voldemort. Rowling is said to have been inspired to create the dark lord by the grave of 19th-century gentleman Thomas Riddell, who died in 1806 aged 72.

Greyfriars Bobby Statue   MONUMENT
(Map p64; cnr George IV Bridge & Candlemaker Row, EH1 2QQ; 🖳2, 23, 27, 35, 41, 42, 45) Probably the most popular photo opportunity in Edinburgh, the life-size statue of Greyfriars Bobby, a Skye terrier who captured the hearts of the British public in the late 19th century,

68

stands outside Greyfriars Kirkyard. From 1858 to 1872 the wee dog maintained a vigil over the grave of his master, an Edinburgh police officer. The story was immortalised in a novel by Eleanor Atkinson in 1912, and in 1961 was made into a movie by – who else? – Walt Disney.

The statue is always surrounded by crowds of visitors taking photos of themselves posing beside the little dog. Bobby's own grave, marked by a small, pink-granite stone, is just inside the entrance to Greyfriars Kirkyard, behind the monument, and you can see his original collar and bowl in the Museum of Edinburgh (p61).

Grassmarket STREET
(Map p64; 🖵2) The site of a cattle market from the 15th century until the start of the 20th century, the Grassmarket has always been a focal point of the Old Town. It was once the city's main place of execution, and over 100 martyred Covenanters are commemorated by a monument at the eastern end, where the gallows used to stand. The notorious murderers Burke and Hare operated from a now-vanished close off the western end.

Nowadays the broad, open square, lined by tall tenements and dominated by the looming castle, has many lively pubs and restaurants, including the **White Hart Inn** (Map p64; ☎0131-226 2806; www.white-hart-edinburgh.co.uk; 34 Grassmarket, EH1 2JU; ⊙11am-midnight Sun-Thu, to 1am Fri & Sat; 🖵2), which was once patronised by Robert Burns. Claiming to be the city's oldest pub in continuous use (since 1516), it also hosted William Wordsworth in 1803. **Cowgate** – the long, dark ravine leading eastwards from the Grassmarket – was once the road along which cattle were driven from the

THE RESURRECTION MEN

In 1505 Edinburgh's newly founded Royal College of Surgeons was officially allocated the corpse of one executed criminal per year for the purposes of dissection. But this was not nearly enough to satisfy the curiosity of the city's anatomists, and in the following centuries an illegal trade in dead bodies emerged, which reached its culmination in the early 19th century when the anatomy classes of famous surgeons such as Professor Robert Knox drew audiences of up to 500.

The readiest supply of corpses was to be found in the city's graveyards, especially Greyfriars. Grave robbers – who came to be known as 'resurrection men' – plundered newly buried coffins and sold the cadavers to the anatomists, who turned a blind eye to the source of their research material.

This gruesome trade led to a series of countermeasures, including the mort safe – a metal cage that was placed over a coffin until the corpse had begun to decompose; you can see examples in Greyfriars Kirkyard (p67) and on level five of the National Museum of Scotland (p67). Watchtowers, where a sexton, or relatives of the deceased, would keep watch over new graves, survive in St Cuthbert's and Duddingston kirkyards.

The notorious William Burke and William Hare, who kept a lodging house in Tanner's Close at the western end of the Grassmarket, took the body-snatching business a step further. When an elderly lodger died without paying his rent, Burke and Hare stole his body from the coffin and sold it to the famous Professor Knox. Seeing a lucrative business opportunity, they figured that rather than waiting for someone else to die, they could create their own supply of fresh cadavers by resorting to murder.

Burke and Hare preyed on the poor and weak of Edinburgh's Grassmarket, luring them back to Hare's lodging house, plying them with drink and then suffocating them. Between December 1827 and October 1828, they murdered at least 16 people and sold their bodies to Professor Knox. When the law finally caught up with them, Hare turned king's evidence and testified against Burke.

Burke was hanged outside St Giles Cathedral in January 1829 and, in an ironic twist, his body was given to the anatomy school for public dissection. His death mask, and a pocketbook made from his flayed skin, are still on display in the Surgeons' Hall Museums (p67).

It was as a result of the Burke and Hare case that the *Anatomy Act* 1832 – regulating the supply of cadavers for dissection, and still in force today – was passed.

pastures around Arthur's Seat to the safety of the city walls. Today it is the heart of Edinburgh's nightlife, with around two dozen clubs and bars within five minutes' walk of each other.

◉ New Town

Edinburgh's New Town lies north of the Old, on a ridge running parallel to the Royal Mile and separated from it by the valley of Princes Street Gardens. Its regular grid of elegant Georgian terraces is a complete contrast to the chaotic tangle of tenements and wynds that characterises the Old Town, and is the world's most complete and unspoilt example of Georgian architecture and town planning.

Apart from the streetscape, the main sights are the art galleries and gardens on Princes St, and the Scottish National Portrait Gallery near St Andrew Sq, all within walking distance of each other.

◉ Princes Street

Princes St is one of the world's most spectacular shopping streets. Built up on the north side only, it catches the sun in summer and allows expansive views across Princes Street Gardens to the castle and the crowded skyline of the Old Town.

★**Princes Street Gardens** GARDENS
(Map p64; Princes St; ⊙dawn-dusk; ☐all Princes St buses, ☐Princes St) FREE These beautiful gardens lie in a valley that was once occupied by the Nor' Loch (North Loch), a boggy depression that was drained in the early 19th century. At the gate beside the Mound is the **Floral Clock**, a working clock laid out in flowers; it was first created in 1903 and the design changes every year.

In the middle of the western part of the gardens is the **Ross Bandstand** (www.rossbandstand.org), a venue for open-air concerts in summer and at Hogmanay, and the stage for the famous fireworks concert during the Edinburgh International Festival (there are plans to replace the bandstand with a modern pavilion).

The gardens are split in the middle by **the Mound** – around two million cartloads of earth that were dug out from foundations during the construction of the New Town and dumped here to provide a road link across the valley to the Old Town. The road was completed in 1830.

Scott Monument MONUMENT
(Map p72; www.edinburghmuseums.org.uk; East Princes Street Gardens, EH2 2EJ; tours £6; ⊙10am-4pm; ☐all Princes St buses, ☐Princes St) The eastern half of Princes Street Gardens is dominated by the massive Gothic spire of the Scott Monument, built by public subscription in memory of novelist Sir Walter Scott after his death in 1832. The exterior is decorated with 64 carvings of characters from his novels; inside you can see an exhibition on Scott's life, and join a tour to climb the 287 steps to the top for a superb view of the city.

Scottish National Gallery GALLERY
(Map p72; ☑0131-624 6200; www.nationalgalleries.org; The Mound, EH2 2EL; ⊙10am-5pm Fri-Wed, to 7pm Thu; ☐all Princes St buses, ☐Princes St) FREE Designed by William Playfair, this imposing classical building with its Ionic porticoes dates from 1850. Its octagonal rooms, lit by skylights, have been restored to their original Victorian decor of deep-green carpets and dark-red walls. The gallery houses an important collection of European art from the Renaissance to the post-Impressionism era, with works by Verrocchio (Leonardo da Vinci's teacher), Tintoretto, Titian, Holbein, Rubens, van Dyck, Vermeer, El Greco, Poussin, Rembrandt, Gainsborough, Turner, Constable, Monet, Pissarro, Gauguin and Cézanne.

The upstairs galleries (14 to 18) house portraits by Allan Ramsay and Sir Henry Raeburn, and a clutch of **Impressionist paintings**, including Monet's *Poplars on the River Epto,* Van Gogh's colourful *Orchard in Blossom* and Gauguin's hallucinatory *Vision of the Sermon.* But the painting that really catches your eye is the gorgeous portrait *Lady Agnew of Lochnaw* by John Singer Sargent.

The basement galleries dedicated to **Scottish art** include glowing portraits by Allan Ramsay and Sir Henry Raeburn, rural scenes by Sir David Wilkie and Impressionistic landscapes by William MacTaggart. Look out for Sir George Harvey's hugely entertaining *A Schule Skailin'* (A School Emptying) – a stern *dominie* (teacher) looks on as the boys stampede for the classroom door, one reaching for a confiscated spinning top. Kids will love the fantasy paintings of Sir Joseph Noel Paton in room B5; the incredibly detailed canvases are crammed with hundreds of tiny fairies, goblins and elves.

Recent research has suggested that the iconic 1790s painting of *The Reverend Robert Walker Skating on Duddingston Loch*, historically attributed to Sir Henry Raeburn, may in fact be the work of French artist Henri-Pierre Danloux.

Each January the gallery exhibits its **collection of Turner watercolours**, bequeathed by Henry Vaughan in 1900. Antonio Canova's white marble sculpture, **The Three Graces**, is owned jointly with London's Victoria & Albert Museum; when not in London it can be seen in room 10.

There's a charge for some special exhibitions.

◉ George Street & Charlotte Square

Until the 1990s George St – the major axis of the New Town – was the centre of Edinburgh's financial industry and Scotland's equivalent of Wall St. Today the big financial firms have moved to premises in the modern Exchange office district west of Lothian Rd, and George St's former banks and offices house upmarket shops, pubs and restaurants.

At the western end of George St is **Charlotte Sq**, the architectural jewel of the New Town, designed by Robert Adam shortly before his death in 1791. The northern side of the square is Adam's masterpiece and one of the finest examples of Georgian architecture anywhere. **Bute House**, in the centre at No 6, is the official residence of Scotland's first minister, the equivalent of London's 10 Downing St.

Georgian House   HISTORIC BUILDING
(NTS; Map p72; www.nts.org.uk; 7 Charlotte Sq, EH2 4DR; adult/child £8/6; ⊙10am-5pm Apr-Oct, 11am-4pm Mar & Nov, closed Dec-Feb; 🚍19, 36, 37, 41, 47) The National Trust for Scotland's Georgian House has been beautifully restored and furnished to show how Edinburgh's wealthy elite lived at the end of the 18th century. The walls are decorated with paintings by Allan Ramsay, Sir Henry Raeburn and Sir Joshua Reynolds, and there's a fully equipped 18th-century kitchen complete with china closet and wine cellar.

◉ St Andrew Square & Around

Not as architecturally distinguished as its sister Charlotte Sq at the opposite end of George St, St Andrew Sq is dominated by the fluted column of the **Melville Monument**, commemorating Henry Dundas, 1st Viscount Melville (1742–1811). Dundas was the most powerful Scottish politician of his time, often referred to when alive as 'Harry IX, the Uncrowned King of Scotland'. Following the Black Lives Matter protests of 2020, a plaque was added to the monument explaining Dundas' role in delaying Britain's abolition of the slave trade.

The impressive Palladian mansion of **Dundas House**, constructed between 1772 and 1774 on the eastern side of the square, was built for Sir Laurence Dundas (1712–81; no relation to Viscount Melville). It has been the head office of the Royal Bank of Scotland since 1825 and has a spectacular domed banking hall dating from 1857 (you can nip inside for a look).

The square has seen some major changes since the central garden was opened to the public in 2008, with several upmarket restaurants now ranged along the south side, and the **Edinburgh Grand** luxury apartment complex on the east, housed in a gorgeous 1940s art deco building.

A short distance along George St is the **Church of St Andrew & St George**, built in 1784 with an unusual oval nave. It was the scene of the Disruption of 1843, when 451 dissenting ministers left the Church of Scotland to form the Free Church.

★ Scottish National Portrait Gallery   GALLERY
(Map p72; ☑0131-624 6200; www.nationalgalleries.org; 1 Queen St, EH2 1JD; ⊙10am-5pm; ♿; 🚍all York Pl buses, 🚇St Andrew Sq) **FREE** The Venetian Gothic palace of the Scottish National Portrait Gallery is one of the city's top attractions. Its galleries illustrate Scottish history through paintings, photographs and sculptures, putting faces to famous names from Scotland's past and present, from Robert Burns, Mary, Queen of Scots, and Bonnie Prince Charlie to the late Sir Sean Connery, comedian Billy Connolly and poet Jackie Kay. There's an admission fee for special exhibitions.

The gallery's interior is decorated in Arts and Crafts style, and nowhere more splendidly than in the **Great Hall**. Above the Gothic colonnade a processional frieze painted by William Hole in 1898 serves as a 'visual encyclopedia' of famous Scots, shown in chronological order from Calgacus (the chieftain who led the Caledonian

THE STONE OF DESTINY
....

On St Andrew's Day 1996 a block of sandstone – 26.5 inches by 16.5 inches by 11 inches in size, with rusted iron hoops at either end – was installed with much pomp and circumstance in Edinburgh Castle. For the previous 700 years it had lain in London, beneath the Coronation Chair in Westminster Abbey. Almost all English, and later British, monarchs from Edward II in 1307 to Elizabeth II in 1953 have parked their backsides firmly over this stone during their coronation ceremony.

The legendary Stone of Destiny – said to have originated in the Holy Land, and on which Scottish kings placed their feet (not their bums; the English got that bit wrong) during their coronation – was stolen from Scone Abbey near Perth by Edward I of England in 1296. It was taken to London and there it remained for seven centuries – except for a brief removal to Gloucester during WWII air raids, and a three-month sojourn in Scotland after it was stolen by Scottish Nationalist students at Christmas in 1950 – as an enduring symbol of Scotland's subjugation by England.

The Stone of Destiny returned to the political limelight in 1996, when the then Scottish Secretary and Conservative Party MP Michael Forsyth arranged for the return of the sandstone block to Scotland. A blatant attempt to boost the flagging popularity of the Conservative Party in Scotland prior to a general election, Forsyth's publicity stunt failed miserably. The Scots said thanks very much for the stone and then, in May 1997, voted every Conservative MP in Scotland into oblivion.

Many people, however, believe Edward I was fobbed off with a shoddy imitation in 1296 and that the true Stone of Destiny remains safely hidden somewhere in Scotland. This is not impossible – some descriptions of the original stone state that it was made of black marble and decorated with elaborate carvings. Interested parties should read *Scotland's Stone of Destiny* by Nick Aitchinson, which details the history and cultural significance of Scotland's most famous lump of rock.

tribes into battle against the Romans) to writer and philosopher Thomas Carlyle (1795–1881). The murals on the 1st-floor balcony depict scenes from Scottish history, while the ceiling is painted with the constellations of the night sky.

The gallery's selection of 'trails' leaflets adds a bit of background information while leading you around the various exhibits; the Hidden Histories trail is particularly interesting.

◉ Calton Hill

Calton Hill (Map p72; 📖104, 113, 124), rising dramatically above the eastern end of Princes St, is Edinburgh's acropolis, its 100m summit scattered with grandiose memorials dating mostly from the first half of the 19th century. It is also one of the best viewpoints in the city, with a panorama that takes in the castle, Holyrood, Arthur's Seat, the Firth of Forth, the New Town and the full length of Princes St.

On the southern side of the hill, on Regent Rd, is the modernist facade of **St Andrew's House** (Map p72; Regent Rd, EH1 3DG; 📖15, 18), built between 1936 and 1939 and housing the civil servants of the Westmin-

ster government's Scottish Office until they were moved to the new Scottish Executive building in Leith in 1996.

Just beyond St Andrew's House, and on the opposite side of the road, is the imposing **Royal High School** building, dating from 1829 and modelled on the Temple of Theseus in Athens. Former pupils include Robert Adam, Alexander Graham Bell and Sir Walter Scott. It now stands empty. To its east, on the other side of Regent Rd, is the 1830 **Burns Monument** (Map p58; Regent Rd, EH8 8DR; 📖104, 113, 124), a Greek-style memorial to Robert Burns.

You can reach the summit of Calton Hill via the road beside the Royal High School or by the stairs at the eastern end of Waterloo Pl. The largest structure on the summit is the **National Monument** (Map p72; 📖104, 113, 124), an overambitious attempt to replicate the Parthenon in Athens and intended to honour Scotland's dead in the Napoleonic Wars. Construction – paid for by public subscription – began in 1822, but funds ran dry when only 12 columns had been completed.

Looking a bit like an upturned telescope – the similarity is intentional – and offering

New Town

superb views, the **Nelson Monument** (Map p72; www.edinburghmuseums.org.uk; £6; ⊙10am-7pm Mon-Sat, noon-5pm Sun Apr-Sep, 10am-4pm Mon-Sat Oct-Mar; 🚍104, 113, 124) was built to commemorate Admiral Lord Nelson's victory at Trafalgar in 1805.

The design of the **City Observatory** (Map p72; ☎0131-556 1264; www.collectivegallery.net; ⊙10am-5pm Tue-Sun Apr-Jul & Sep, to 4pm Oct-Mar, to 6pm daily Aug; 🚍104, 113, 124) FREE, built in 1818, was based on the ancient Greek Temple of the Winds in Athens. Its original function was to provide a precise, astronomical timekeeping service for marine navigators, but smoke from Waverley train station forced the astronomers to move to Blackford Hill in the south of Edinburgh in 1895. The observatory has been redeveloped as a stunning space for contemporary visual art, and it is now open to the public for the first time in its history.

⊙ West End & Dean Village

★ Scottish National Gallery of Modern Art   GALLERY
(Map p58; ☎0131-624 6200; www.nationalgalleries.org; 75 Belford Rd, EH4 3DR; ⊙10am-5pm; 🚍13) FREE Edinburgh's gallery of modern art is split between two impressive neoclassical buildings (Modern One and Modern Two surrounded by landscaped grounds some 500m west of Dean Village. As well as showcasing a stunning collection of paintings by the popular, post-Impressionist Scottish Colourists – in *Reflections, Balloch,* Leslie Hunter pulls off the improbable trick of making Scotland look like the south of France – the gallery is the starting point for a walk along the Water of Leith. Fees apply for some exhibitions.

The main collection, known as **Modern One**, concentrates on 20th-century art, with various European movements represented by the likes of Matisse, Picasso,

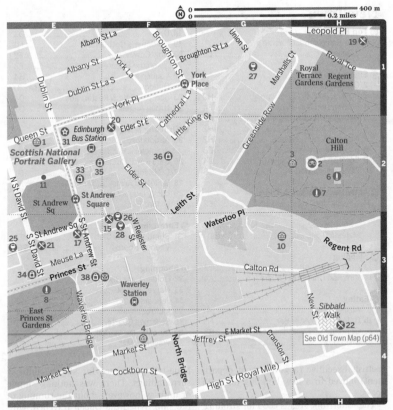

Kirchner, Magritte, Miró, Mondrian and Giacometti. American and English artists are also represented, but most space is given to Scottish painters – from the Scottish Colourists of the early 20th century to contemporary artists such as Peter Howson and Ken Currie.

There's an excellent **cafe** (Map p58; www. heritageportfolio.co.uk; mains £4-10; ⏰10am-4.30pm; 🛜🧒) downstairs, and the surrounding park features sculptures by Henry Moore, Rachel Whiteread and Barbara Hepworth, among others, as well as a 'landform artwork' by Charles Jencks, and the **Pig Rock Bothy**, a rustic timber event and exhibition space created in 2014 as part of the Bothy Project (www.theboth-yproject.org).

A footpath and stairs at the rear of the gallery lead down to the **Water of Leith Walkway**, which you can follow along the river for 4 miles to Leith.

Scottish National Gallery of Modern Art – Modern Two   GALLERY
(Map p58; www.nationalgalleries.org; Belford Rd, EH4 3DR; ⏰10am-5pm; 🚌13) **FREE** Directly across Belford Rd from Modern One, another neoclassical mansion (formerly an orphanage) houses its annexe, Modern Two, which is home to a large collection of sculpture and graphic art created by Edinburgh-born artist Sir Eduardo Paolozzi. One of the 1st-floor rooms houses a recreation of Paolozzi's studio, while the rest of the building stages temporary exhibitions of modern art.

⊙ Leith

Leith's history as Edinburgh's port is evident in its waterfront setting, with old warehouses converted into luxury flats, and a lush crop of trendy bars and restaurants along the river. The area was given an additional boost in the late 1990s when the

New Town

Scottish Executive (a government department) moved to a new building on Leith docks.

The waterfront area is good for strolling, but the main attractions are Ocean Terminal (p96), a shopping and leisure complex, and the former Royal Yacht *Britannia*, which is moored alongside.

★ **Royal Yacht Britannia**   SHIP
(www.royalyachtbritannia.co.uk; Ocean Terminal, EH6 6JJ; adult/child incl audio guide £17/8.75; ⊙9.30am-6pm Apr-Sep, to 5.30pm Oct, 10am-5pm Nov-Mar, last entry 1½hr before closing; P; ⑪11, 22, 34, 36, 200) The former Royal Yacht *Britannia* was the British royal family's floating holiday home from the time of her launch in 1953 until her decommissioning in 1997, and is now permanently moored in front of Ocean Terminal. The tour, which you take at your own pace with an audio guide (available in 30 languages), lifts the curtain on the everyday lives of the royals, and gives an intriguing insight into the Queen's private tastes. It's best to book online in advance.

Britannia is a monument to 1950s decor, and the accommodation reveals Her Majesty's preference for simple, unfussy surroundings. There was nothing simple or unfussy, however, about the running of the ship. When the Queen travelled, with her went 45 members of the royal household, 5 tonnes of luggage and a Rolls-Royce that was carefully squeezed into a specially built garage on the deck. The ship's company consisted of an admiral, 20 officers and a 220-strong crew.

The decks (of Burmese teak) were scrubbed daily, but all work near the royal accommodation was carried out in complete silence and had to be finished by 8am. A thermometer was kept in the Queen's bathroom to make sure the water was the correct temperature, and when the ship was in harbour one crew member was charged with ensuring that the angle of the gangway never exceeded 12 degrees. Note the mahogany windbreak that was added to the balcony deck in front of the bridge: it was put there to stop wayward breezes from blowing up skirts and inadvertently revealing the royal underwear.

Britannia was joined in 2010 by the 1930s racing yacht *Bloodhound*, which was owned by the Queen in the 1960s. *Bloodhound* is moored alongside *Britannia* (except in July and August, when she is away cruising) as part of an exhibition about the royal family's love of all things nautical.

The Majestic Tour (p78) bus runs from Waverley Bridge to *Britannia* during the ship's opening times.

⊙ Greater Edinburgh

★**Royal Botanic Garden**   GARDENS
(☑ 0131-248 2909; www.rbge.org.uk; Arboretum Pl, EH3 5LR; ⊙ 10am-6pm Mar-Sep, to 5pm Feb & Oct, to 4pm Nov-Jan; ☐ 8, 23, 27) **FREE** Edinburgh's Royal Botanic Garden is the second-oldest institution of its kind in Britain (after Oxford's), and one of the most respected in the world. Founded near Holyrood in 1670 and moved to its present location in 1823, its 28 beautifully landscaped hectares include splendid **Victorian glasshouses** (admission £7), colourful swathes of rhododendron and azalea, and a world-famous rock garden. There are entrances to the gardens on Inverleith Row (city buses) and Arboretum Pl (Majestic Tour bus only).

The **John Hope Gateway visitor centre** is housed in a striking, environmentally friendly building overlooking the entrance on Arboretum Pl, and has exhibitions on biodiversity, climate change and sustainable development, as well as displays of rare plants from the institution's collection and a specially created biodiversity garden.

Edinburgh Zoo   ZOO
(☑ 0131-334 9171; www.edinburghzoo.org.uk; 134 Corstorphine Rd, EH12 6TS; adult/child £19.95/11.35; ⊙ 10am-6pm Apr-Sep, to 5pm Oct & Mar, to 4pm Nov-Feb; ⊕; ☐ 12, 18, 26, 31, 100) Opened in 1913, Edinburgh Zoo is one of the world's leading conservation zoos. Its captive breeding programme has helped save many endangered species, including Siberian tigers, pygmy hippos and red pandas. The main attractions are the two **giant pandas**, Tian Tian and Yang Guang, who arrived in December 2011, and the **penguin parade** (the zoo's penguins go for a walk every day at 2.15pm). The zoo is 2.5 miles west of the city centre.

Cramond   AREA
(☐ 41) With its moored yachts, stately swans and whitewashed houses spilling down the hillside at the mouth of the River Almond, Cramond is the most picturesque corner of Edinburgh. It is also rich in history. The Romans built a fort here in the 2nd

EDINBURGH FOR CHILDREN

Edinburgh has plentiful attractions for children, and most things to see and do are child-friendly. During the Edinburgh and Fringe Festivals there's lots of street theatre for kids, and in December there's a Ferris wheel and fairground rides in Princes Street Gardens and an ice rink in St Andrew Sq.

There are good, safe playgrounds in most Edinburgh parks, including Princes Street Gardens West, Inverleith Park (opposite the Royal Botanic Garden), George V Park (New Town), the Meadows and Bruntsfield Links.

Some more ideas for outdoor activities include exploring the Royal Botanic Garden, going to see the animals at Edinburgh Zoo, visiting the statue of Greyfriars Bobby (p67) and feeding the swans and playing on the beach at Cramond.

If it's raining, you can visit the Discovery Centre, a hands-on activity zone on level 3 of the National Museum of Scotland (p67), play on the flumes at the **Royal Commonwealth Pool** (Map p58; ☑ 0131-667 7211; www.edinburghleisure.co.uk; 21 Dalkeith Rd; adult/family £6.40/12; ⊙ 5.30am-9.15pm Mon-Fri, to 7.15pm Sat, to 4.15pm Sun; ⊕; ☐ 2, 14, 30, 33, 37), try out the earthquake simulator at Our Dynamic Earth (p67), or take a tour of the haunted Real Mary King's Close (p57).

Need to Know

Resources Edinburgh for Under Fives (www.efuf.co.uk) has a useful website and guidebook (published 2016). *The List* (www.list.co.uk/kids) events guide has a kids' section.

Public Transport Up to two children under five may travel free when accompanied by a fare-paying adult. Children five to 15 pay half the adult fare.

century CE, but recent archaeological excavations have revealed evidence of a Bronze Age settlement dating from 8500 BCE, the oldest known settlement site in Scotland. It's 5 miles northwest of the city centre.

Originally a mill village, Cramond has a historic 17th-century church and a 15th-century tower house, as well as some rather unimpressive Roman remains, but most people come to enjoy the walks along the river to the ruined mills and to stroll along the seafront. On the riverside, opposite the cottage on the far bank, is the **Maltings** (www.cramondheritage.org.uk; Riverside, Cramond EH4 6NY; ⊙2-5pm Sat & Sun Apr-Sep, daily during Edinburgh Festival; ▣41) **FREE**, which hosts an interesting exhibition on Cramond's history.

🏃 Activities

Edinburgh has plenty of places to perk up your sagging muscles with a spot of healthy exercise. Football and rugby fans can shout themselves hoarse at one of the city's three major stadiums, and golfers can take their pick from around 90 courses in and around the city.

Walking

Edinburgh is lucky to have several good walking areas within the city boundary, including Arthur's Seat (p65), Calton Hill (p71), **Blackford Hill** (Charterhall Rd, EH9 3HR; ▣24, 38, 41), **Hermitage of Braid** (www.facebook.com/friendsofhermitage; ▣5, 11, 15, 16), **Corstorphine Hill** (www.corstorphinehill.org.uk; Clermiston Rd N, EH12 6UR; ℗; ▣26) and the coast and river at Cramond (p75). The

Pentland Hills (www.pentlandhills.org), which rise to over 500m, stretch southwest from the city for over 15 miles, offering excellent high- and low-level walking.

You can follow the **Water of Leith Walkway** (www.waterofleith.org.uk/walkway) from the city centre to Balerno (8 miles), and continue across the Pentlands to Silverburn (6.5 miles) or Carlops (8 miles), and return to Edinburgh by bus. Another good walk is along the **Union Canal towpath**, which begins in Fountainbridge and runs all the way to Falkirk (31 miles). You can return to Edinburgh by bus at Ratho (8.5 miles) or Broxburn (12 miles), or by bus or train from Linlithgow (21 miles).

The **Scottish Rights of Way & Access Society** (☎0131-558 1222; www.scotways.com) provides information and advice on walking trails and rights of way in Scotland.

Cycling

Edinburgh and its surroundings offer many excellent opportunities for cycling (see www.citycyclingedinburgh.info and www.cycling-edinburgh.org.uk). The main off-road routes from the city centre out to the countryside follow the **Union Canal towpath** and then the **Water of Leith Walkway** from Tollcross southwest to Balerno (7.5 miles) on the edge of the Pentland Hills, and the **Innocent Railway Cycle Path** from the southern side of Arthur's Seat eastwards to Musselburgh (5 miles) and on to Ormiston and Pencaitland.

There are several routes through the **Pentland Hills** that are suitable for mountain bikes. For details ask at any bike

---

UNDERGROUND EDINBURGH

As Edinburgh expanded in the late 18th and early 19th centuries, many old tenements were demolished and new bridges were built to link the Old Town to the newly built areas to its north and south. South Bridge (built between 1785 and 1788) and George IV Bridge (built between 1829 and 1834) lead south from the Royal Mile over the deep valley of Cowgate, but so many buildings have been constructed around them that you can hardly tell they're bridges – George IV Bridge has a total of nine arches, but only two are visible; South Bridge has no fewer than 18 hidden arches.

These **subterranean vaults** were originally used as storerooms, workshops and drinking dens. But as Edinburgh's population swelled in the early 19th century with an influx of penniless Highlanders cleared from their lands, and Irish refugees from the potato famine, the dark, dripping chambers were given over to slum accommodation and abandoned to poverty, filth and crime.

The vaults were eventually cleared in the late 19th century, then lay forgotten until 1994, when the **South Bridge vaults** were opened to guided tours. Certain chambers are said to be haunted, and one particular vault was investigated by paranormal researchers in 2001.

shop, or check out www.pentlandhills.org. The Spokes *Edinburgh Cycle Map* (www. spokes.org.uk; available from cycle shops) shows all the city's cycle routes.

Bikes can be hired from:

Biketrax (Map p58; ☑ 0131-228 6633; www. biketrax.co.uk; 11-13 Lochrin Pl, EH3 9QX; hybrid/ e-bike per day from £25/48; ☺ 9.30am-6pm Mon-Fri, to 5.30pm Sat, noon-5pm Sun, longer hours Apr-Sep; ☺ all Tollcross buses) Hybrid bikes, road bikes, mountain bikes, e-bikes and Brompton folding bikes.

Cycle Scotland (Map p64; ☑ 0131-556 5560; www.cyclescotland.co.uk; 29 Blackfriars St, EH1 1NB; tour per person from £35, rental per day from £25; ☺ 10am-6pm Mon-Sat; ☺ 35) Top-quality bikes; rates include helmet, lock and repair kit.

Golf

There are 19 golf courses in Edinburgh itself, and another 70 within 20 miles of the city, including some of the most famous links courses in the world – Muirfield, Gullane and St Andrews. For details of other courses in and around Edinburgh, check out www.scottishgolfcourses.com.

Scenic golf courses in Edinburgh include:

Braid Hills Public Golf Course (☑ 0131-447 6666; www.edinburghleisure.co.uk/venues/ braid-hills-golf-course; Braid Hills Approach, EH10 6JY; green fees weekday/weekend £27.50/28.50) Charming but challenging course to the south of the city centre.

Duddingston Golf Course (☑ 0131-661 7688; www.duddingstongolfclub.co.uk; Duddingston Rd W, EH15 3QD; green fees £40-60) Picturesque setting at the foot of Arthur's Seat.

☞ Tours

Edinburgh has a wealth of walking tours that allow you to explore the city by theme, as well as a number of hop-on, hop-off bus tours that run between the city's top sights.

Walking Tours

There are plenty of organised walks around Edinburgh, many of them related to ghosts, murders and witches.

Edinburgh Literary Pub Tour   WALKING
(Map p64; www.edinburghliterarypubtour.co.uk; Beehive Inn, Grassmarket, EH1 2JU; adult/student £16/14; ☺ 7.30pm daily May-Sep, limited days Oct-Apr) An enlightening two-hour trawl through Edinburgh's literary history – and

its associated howffs (pubs) – in the entertaining company of Messrs Clart and McBrain. One of the city's best walking tours (departing from Beehive Inn).

City of the Dead Tours   WALKING
(Map p64; ☑ 0131-225 9044; www.cityof thedeadtours.com; 26a Candlemaker Row, EH1 2QE; adult/concession £14/10; ☺ 9pm Easter-Oct, 8.30pm Tue & Thu-Sat Nov-Easter) This nightly tour of Greyfriars Kirkyard is probably the scariest of Edinburgh's 'ghost' tours. Many people have reported encounters with the Mackenzie Poltergeist, the ghost of a 17th-century judge who persecuted the Covenanters and who now haunts their former prison in a corner of the kirkyard. Not suitable for children under 12.

Cadies & Witchery Tours   WALKING
(Map p64; ☑ 0131-225 6745; www.witcherytours. com; 84 West Bow, EH1 2HH; adult/child £10/7.50; ☺ 7pm year-round, plus 9pm Apr-Sep; ☺ 2) The becloaked and pasty-faced Adam Lyal (deceased) leads a 'Murder & Mystery' tour of the Old Town's darker corners. These tours are famous for their 'jumper-ooters' – costumed actors who 'jump oot' when you least expect it. There's also a 2pm tour of Greyfriars Kirkyard (adult/child £15/12).

Mercat Tours   WALKING
(Map p64; ☑ 0131-225 5445; www.mercattours. com; Mercat Cross, EH1 1RF; adult/child £16/11; ☺ 10am-9.30pm; ☺ 35) Mercat offers a wide range of fascinating history walks and 'Ghosts & Ghouls' tours, but its most famous is Ghostly Underground, a visit to the hidden, haunted subterranean vaults beneath South Bridge. Tours depart from the Mercat Cross.

Rebus Tours   WALKING
(Map p64; ☑ 0131-553 7473; www.rebustours. com; Royal Oak, Infirmary St, EH1 1LT; per person £20; ☺ noon Sat) A two-hour guided tour of the 'hidden Edinburgh' frequented by novelist Ian Rankin's fictional detective, John Rebus. Not recommended for children under 10.

Trainspotting Tours   WALKING
(www.leithwalks.co.uk; per person £10, minimum charge £20; ☺ by arrangement) A tour of locations from Irvine Welsh's notorious 1993 novel *Trainspotting*, and the 1996 film of the book, delivered with wit and enthusiasm. Not suitable for kids.

Invisible (Edinburgh)

WALKING

(☑ 07500-773709; www.invisible-cities.org; per person from £12) This venture trains homeless people as tour guides to explore a different side of the city. Tour themes include Crime & Punishment (including Burke and Hare, p68) and Powerful Women (from Maggie Dickson to JK Rowling). Must be booked in advance; check the website for times and meeting points.

Boat Tours

3 Bridges Tour

BOATING

(www.edinburghtour.com/3-bridges-tour; adult/child £25/12; ⊙ departs 10am & noon Fri-Sun) This tour begins with a bus trip from St Andrews Sq in Edinburgh to South Queensferry, where you board a boat for a cruise beneath the three bridges that span the Firth of Forth – two road and one rail, dating from 1890 to 2017 – and then go to spot seals at Inchcolm Island (p104), with the option of going ashore to visit the abbey ruins.

Bus Tours

Open-topped buses leave from the north side of St Andrew Sq, near the east end of Princes St, and offer hop-on, hop-off tours of the main sights, taking in the New Town, the Grassmarket and the Royal Mile. They're a good way to get your bearings, although with a bus map and a Day Saver bus ticket you could do much the same thing (but without the commentary).

Bright-red, open-top **City Sightseeing** (Map p72; www.edinburghtour.com; adult/child £16/free; ⊙ daily year-round except 25 Dec) buses depart every 20 minutes from St Andrew Sq.

Majestic Tour (Map p72; www.edinburgh tour.com; adult/child £16/free; ⊙ daily year-round except 25 Dec) has hop-on, hop-off buses departing every 15 to 20 minutes from St Andrew Sq to the Royal Yacht *Britannia* at Ocean Terminal via the New Town, the Royal Botanic Garden and Newhaven, returning via Leith Walk, Holyrood and the Royal Mile.

🎆 Festivals & Events

Edinburgh hosts an amazing number of festivals throughout the year, notably the Edinburgh International Festival, the Edinburgh Festival Fringe and the Military Tattoo. Hogmanay, Scotland's New Year's celebration, is also a peak party time.

April

Edinburgh International Science Festival

FESTIVAL

(☑ 0131-226 0005; www.sciencefestival.co.uk; ⊙ Apr) First held in 1987, the two-week Science Festival hosts a wide range of events, including talks, lectures, exhibitions, demonstrations, guided tours and interactive experiments designed to stimulate, inspire and challenge. From dinosaurs to ghosts to alien life forms, there's something to interest everyone.

Beltane

CULTURAL

(www.beltane.org; tickets £10-15; ⊙ 30 Apr) A pagan fire festival that marks the end of winter and the rebirth of spring, Beltane was resurrected in modern form in 1988 and is now celebrated annually on the summit of Calton Hill. The spectacular rituals involve lots of fire, drumming, body paint and sexual innuendo (well, it's a fertility rite, after all).

Held annually on the night of 30 April into the early hours (around 1am) of 1 May.

May

Imaginate Festival

PERFORMING ARTS

(☑ 0131-225 8050; www.imaginate.org.uk; late May-early Jun) Britain's biggest festival of performing arts for children, Imaginate is a week-long event suitable for kids aged three to 12. Groups from around the world perform classic tales like *Hansel and Gretel* as well as new material written especially for a young audience.

June

Edinburgh International Film Festival

FILM

(www.edfilmfest.org.uk; ⊙ Jun) One of the original Edinburgh Festival trinity, having first been staged in 1947 along with the International Festival and the Fringe, the two-week June film festival is a major international event, serving as a showcase for new British and European films, and staging the European premieres of one or two Hollywood blockbusters.

Royal Highland Show

FAIR

(☑ 0131-335 6200; www.royalhighlandshow. org; Royal Highland Centre, Ingliston EH28 8NB; adult/child £32/free; ⊙ late Jun) Scotland's hugely popular national agricultural show is a four-day feast of all things rural, with everything from showjumping and tractor driving to sheep shearing and falconry. Countless pens are filled with coiffed show cattle and pedicured prize ewes. The

FESTIVAL CITY

August in Edinburgh normally sees a frenzy of festivals, with several world-class events running at the same time. The Covid-19 pandemic saw them all cancelled for the first time in 2020, but hopefully they should return in 2021.

Edinburgh Festival Fringe

When the first Edinburgh Festival was held in 1947, eight theatre companies didn't make it onto the main programme. Undeterred, they grouped together and held their own minifestival – on the fringe – and an Edinburgh institution was born. Today the **Edinburgh Festival Fringe** (☏ 0131-226 0026; www.edfringe.com; ⊘ Aug) is the biggest festival of the performing arts anywhere in the world.

Since 1990 the Fringe has been dominated by stand-up comedy, but the sheer variety of shows on offer is staggering – everything from chainsaw juggling and performance poetry to Tibetan yak-milk gargling. So how do you decide what to see? There are daily reviews in the *Scotsman* newspaper – one good *Scotsman* review and a show sells out in hours – but the best recommendation is word of mouth. If you have the time, go to at least one unknown show – it may be crap, but at least you'll have your obligatory 'worst show I ever saw' story.

The big names play at megavenues organised by big agencies such as Assembly (www.assemblyfestival.com) and Gilded Balloon (www.gildedballoon.co.uk), and charge megaprices (£15 to £20 a ticket and up, with some famous comedians notoriously charging more than £30), but there are plenty of good shows in the £5 to £15 range and lots of free stuff – check out www.freefestival.co.uk and www.freefringe.org.uk.

The Fringe takes place over three-and-a-half weeks, the last two weeks overlapping with the first two of the Edinburgh International Festival.

For bookings and information, head to the **Edinburgh Festival Fringe Office** (Map p64; ☏ 0131-226 0026; www.edfringe.com; 180 High St, EH1 1QS; ⊘ noon-3pm Mon-Sat mid-Jun–mid-Jul, 10am-6pm daily mid-Jul–1 Aug, 9am-9pm daily Aug; ☷ all South Bridge buses).

Edinburgh International Festival

First held in 1947 to mark a return to peace after the ordeal of WWII, the **Edinburgh International Festival** (☏ 0131-473 2000; www.eif.co.uk; ⊘ Aug-Sep) is festooned with superlatives – the oldest, biggest, most famous, best in the world. The original was a modest affair, but today hundreds of the world's top musicians and performers congregate in Edinburgh for three weeks of diverse and inspirational music, opera, theatre and dance.

The festival takes place over the three weeks ending on the first Saturday in September; the programme is usually available from April. Tickets for popular events, especially music and opera, sell out quickly, so book as far in advance as possible. You can buy tickets in person at the **Hub** (Map p64; ☏ 0131-473 2015; www.thehub-edinburgh.com; Castlehill, EH1 2NE; ⊘ ticket centre 10am-5pm Mon-Fri; ☏; ☷ 23, 27, 41, 42), by phone or online.

Edinburgh Military Tattoo

August in Edinburgh kicks off with the **Edinburgh Military Tattoo** (☏ 0131-225 1188; www.edintattoo.co.uk; ⊘ Aug), a spectacular display of military marching bands, massed pipes and drums, acrobats, cheerleaders and motorcycle display teams, all played out in front of the magnificent backdrop of the floodlit castle. Each show traditionally finishes with a lone piper, dramatically lit, playing a lament on the battlements. The Tattoo takes place over the first three weeks of August (from a Friday to a Saturday); there's one show at 9pm Monday to Friday and two (at 7.30pm and 10.30pm) on Saturday, but no performance on Sunday.

Edinburgh International Book Festival

Held in a little village of marquees in the middle of Charlotte Sq, the **Edinburgh International Book Festival** (☏ 0845 373 5888; www.edbookfest.co.uk; Charlotte Sq Gardens, EH2 4DR; ⊘ Aug) is a fun fortnight of talks, readings, debates, lectures, book signings and meet-the-author events, with a cafe-bar and tented bookshop thrown in. The festival usually coincides with the first two weeks of the Edinburgh International Festival.

show is held over a long weekend (Thursday to Sunday).

July

Edinburgh International Jazz & Blues Festival   MUSIC
(www.edinburghjazzfestival.com; ☉Jul) Held annually since 1978, the Jazz & Blues Festival pulls in top talent from all over the world. It runs for nine days, beginning on a Friday, a week before the Fringe and Tattoo begin. The first weekend sees a carnival parade on Princes St and an afternoon of free, open-air music in Princes Street Gardens.

Edinburgh Food Festival   FOOD & DRINK
(www.edfoodfest.com; George Sq Gardens, EH8 9JZ; ☉Jul) This four-day festival, based in George Square Gardens, precedes the opening of the Edinburgh Fringe with a packed programme of talks, cookery demonstrations, tastings, food stalls and entertainment.

August

The Edinburgh International Festival, the Edinburgh Festival Fringe, the Edinburgh International Book Festival and the Military Tattoo are all held around the same time in August (p79).

December

Edinburgh's Hogmanay (p82) is the biggest winter festival in Europe.

Edinburgh's Christmas   CHRISTMAS
(☎0131-510 0395; www.edinburghchristmas.com; ☉late Nov-early Jan) First held in 2000, the Christmas bash includes a big street parade, Christmas markets, a fairground and Ferris wheel, and a circular open-air ice rink in St Andrew Sq.

🛏 Sleeping

Edinburgh offers a wide range of accommodation options, from moderately priced guesthouses set in lovely Victorian villas and Georgian town houses to expensive and stylish boutique hotels. There are also plenty of chain hotels, and a few truly exceptional hotels housed in magnificent historic buildings.

At the budget end of the range, there is no shortage of youth hostels and independent backpacker hostels, which often have inexpensive double and twin rooms.

🏃 City Walk
Old Town Alleys

START CASTLE ESPLANADE
END COCKBURN ST
LENGTH 1 MILE; ONE TO TWO HOURS

This walk explores the alleys and side streets around the Royal Mile, and involves a bit of climbing up and down steep stairs.

Begin on the ❶ **Castle Esplanade**, which provides a grandstand view south over the Grassmarket; the prominent quadrangular building with all the turrets is George Heriot's School. Head towards Castlehill and the start of the Royal Mile.

The 17th-century house on the right is known as ❷ **Cannonball House** because of the iron ball lodged in the wall (look between, and slightly below, the two largest windows on the wall facing the castle). The ball was not fired in anger but marks the gravitation height to which water would flow naturally from the city's first piped water supply.

The low, rectangular building across the street (now a touristy tartan-weaving mill) was originally the reservoir that held the Old Town's water supply. On its western wall is the ❸ **Witches Well**, where a bronze fountain commemorates around 4000 people (mostly women) who were executed between 1479 and 1722 on suspicion of witchcraft.

Go past the reservoir and turn left down Ramsay Lane. Take a look at ❹ **Ramsay Garden** – one of Edinburgh's most desirable addresses – where late-19th-century apartments were built around the octagonal Ramsay Lodge, once home to poet Allan Ramsay. The cobbled street continues around to the right below student residences to the towers of the ❺ **New College**, home to Edinburgh University's Faculty of Divinity. Nip into the courtyard to see the statue of John Knox (a firebrand preacher who led the Protestant Reformation in Scotland, and was instrumental in the creation of the Church of Scotland in 1560).

Just past the New College, turn right and climb the stairs into Milne's Court, a student residence belonging to Edinburgh University. Exit into the Lawnmarket, cross the street (bearing slightly left) and duck into **⑥ Riddell's Court**, a restored Old Town close at No 322–328. You'll find yourself in a small courtyard, but the house in front of you (built in 1590) was originally the edge of the street (the building you just walked under was added in 1726 – look for the date inscribed on the doorway on the right). The arch with the inscription *Vivendo discimus* (We live and learn) leads into the original 16th-century courtyard.

Go back into the street, turn right and right again down Fisher's Close, which leads to the delightful Victoria Tce, strung above the cobbled curve of shop-lined Victoria St. Wander right, enjoying the view – **⑦ Maxie's Bistro** (p86), at the far end of the terrace, is a great place to stop for a drink – then descend the stairs at the foot of Upper Bow and continue downhill to the Grassmarket. At the eastern end, outside Maggie Dickson's pub, is the **⑧ Covenanters Monument**, which marks the site of the gallows where more than 100 Covenanters were martyred in the 17th century.

If you're feeling peckish, the Grassmarket has several good places to eat and a couple of good pubs – poet Robert Burns once stayed at the **⑨ White Hart Inn** (p68). Head east along the gloomy defile of the Cowgate,

passing under the arch of George IV Bridge – the buildings to your right are the law courts, while high up to the left you can see the complex of buildings behind Parliament Sq. Past the courts, on the right, is **⑩ Tailors Hall** (built 1621, extended 1757), now a hotel and bar but formerly the meeting place of the Companie of Tailzeours (Tailors' Guild).

Turn left and climb steeply up Old Fishmarket Close, a typical cobbled Old Town wynd, and emerge once more onto the Royal Mile. Across the street and slightly downhill is **⑪ Anchor Close**, named for a tavern that once stood there. It hosted the Crochallan Fencibles, an 18th-century drinking club that provided its patrons with an agreeable blend of intellectual debate and intoxicating liquor. The club was founded by William Smellie, editor of the 1st edition of the *Encyclopedia Britannica*; Burns was its best-known member.

Go down Anchor Close to finish the walk on **⑫ Cockburn St**, one of the city's coolest shopping strips, lined with gift shops and clothing boutiques. The street was cut through Old Town tenements in the 1850s to provide an easy route between Waverley station and the Royal Mile.

EDINBURGH'S HOGMANAY

Edinburgh's Hogmanay (☑ 0131-510 0395; www.edinburghshogmanay.com; street-party tickets £25; ⊘ 30 Dec-1 Jan) Edinburgh's Hogmanay is the biggest winter festival in Europe, with events including a torchlit procession, a huge street party and the famous 'Loony Dook', a chilly sea-swimming event on New Year's Day. To get into the main party area in the city centre after 8pm on 31 December you'll need a ticket – book well in advance.

Traditionally, the New Year has always been a more important celebration for Scots than Christmas. In towns, cities and villages all over the country, people fill the streets at midnight on 31 December to wish each other a Guid New Year and, yes, to knock back a dram or six to keep the cold at bay.

In 1993 Edinburgh's city council had the excellent idea of spicing up Hogmanay by organising some events, laying on some live music in Princes St and issuing an open invitation to the rest of the world. Most of them turned up, or so it seemed, and had such a good time that they told all their pals and came back again the next year.

🛏 Old Town

★ Code – The Court   HOSTEL £
(Map p64; ☑ 0131-510 9380; www.codehostels.com; 1a Parliament Sq, EH1 1RF; dm/d from £21/68; ☺) It would be hard to get any closer to the action on the Royal Mile than this hostel housed in a converted Victorian jail, tucked behind St Giles Cathedral. The dorms consist of pod-style bunks with privacy screens, spacious storage with combination locks, and bedside phone-charging points. The atmospheric private rooms occupy former prison cells, while the public areas are bright, modern and appealing.

Safestay Edinburgh   HOSTEL £
(Map p64; ☑ 0131-524 1989; www.safestay.com; 50 Blackfriars St, EH1 1NE; dm £27-37, tw from £70; @☺; 🖵35) A big, modern hostel with a convivial cafe where you can buy breakfast, and mod cons such as keycard access and charging stations for mobile phones and laptops. Lockers in every room, a huge bar and a central location just off the Royal Mile make this a favourite among the young, party-mad crowd – don't expect a quiet night!

★ Witchery by the Castle   B&B £££
(Map p64; ☑ 0131-225 5613; www.thewitchery.com; Castlehill, EH1 2NF; ste from £395; P; 🖵23, 27, 41, 42) Set in a 16th-century Old Town house in the shadow of Edinburgh Castle, the Witchery's nine lavish Gothic suites are extravagantly furnished with antiques, oak panelling, tapestries, open fires, four-poster beds and roll-top baths, and supplied with flowers, chocolates and complimentary champagne. It's overwhelmingly popular – you'll have to book several months in advance to be sure of getting a room.

★ House of Gods   BOUTIQUE HOTEL £££
(Map p64; ☑ 0131-230 0445; www.houseofgodshotel.com; 233 Cowgate, EH1 1JQ; r from £159; ☺) Forget minimalist – this new hotel in the heart of the Old Town is what might be called 'maximalist'. The over-the-top decor runs to burgundy velvet wall coverings and curtains, faux tiger-skin cushions, gold-tasselled lampshades and marble-lined bathrooms, and the decadence extends to the hotel's cocktail bars, which cultivate an aura of rock and roll debauchery.

Grassmarket Hotel   HOTEL £££
(Map p64; ☑ 0131-220 2299; www.grassmarkethotel.co.uk; 94-96 Grassmarket, EH1 2JR; s/d/tr from £202/215/266; ☺; 🖵2) An endearingly quirky hotel set in a historic Grassmarket tenement in the heart of the Old Town, this place has bedroom walls plastered with front pages from the *Dandy* (a DC Thomson comic published in Dundee) and coffee stations supplied with iconically Scottish Tunnock's teacakes and Irn-Bru. Some bargain rates are available directly through the website.

🛏 Holyrood & Arthur's Seat

★ Prestonfield   BOUTIQUE HOTEL £££
(☑ 0131-668 3346; www.prestonfield.com; Priestfield Rd, EH16 5UT; r/ste from £355/445; P ☺ ☺) If the blonde wood and brushed steel of modern boutique hotels leave you cold, then this is the place for you. A 17th-century mansion set in 8 hectares of parkland (complete with peacocks and Highland

cattle), Prestonfield is draped in damask and packed with antiques – look out for original tapestries, 17th-century embossed-leather panels and £500-a-roll hand-painted wallpaper.

The sumptuous bedrooms are supplied with all mod cons, including Bose sound systems and internet-enabled plasma-screen TVs. The hotel is southeast of the city centre, east of Dalkeith Rd.

New Town

Code – The Loft
APARTMENT £

(Map p72; 0131-659 9883; www.codecoliv ing.com; 50 Rose St N Lane, EH2 2NP; per week pod/tw/apt £99/200/300; ; Princes St) This bold experiment in 'co-living' offers short- to mid-term rental accommodation in innovative sleeping pods that offer more privacy than bunks (up to three people per room, with shared toilet and shower room), and shared kitchen and living areas. There's also a twin/double room and a luxurious double apartment called the Penthouse, complete with kitchenette and roof terrace.

★14 Hart Street
B&B ££

(Map p58; 07795 203414; www.14hartstreet. co.uk; 14 Hart St, EH1 3RN; r from £95; ; 8) Centrally located and child friendly, 14 Hart Street is steeped in Georgian elegance and old Edinburgh charm. There are three generous bedrooms, all en suite, and a sumptuous dining room where guests can enjoy breakfast at a time of their choosing. Indulgent extras include whisky decanters and shortbread in every room. There is sometimes a two-night-stay minimum.

Broughton Townhouse
GUESTHOUSE ££

(Map p58; 0131-558 9792; www.brought on-hotel.com; 37 Broughton Pl, EH1 3RR; s/d/f from £80/120/150; ; 8) This five-bedroom Georgian guesthouse combines great value with a great location, on a relatively quiet street a few minutes' walk from the restaurants and nightlife of Broughton St and Edinburgh's gay village, and just 10 minutes' walk from Princes St.

Ramsay's B&B
B&B ££

(Map p58; 0131-557 5917; www.ramsaysbed andbreakfastedinburgh.com; 25 East London St, EH7 4BN; r from £100; ; 8) The four bright and fresh bedrooms in this tastefully decorated Georgian town house make a great base for exploring the New Town, with the vibrant bar and restaurant scene of Broughton's gay

village just around the corner. Breakfasts are freshly prepared, with kippers on the menu as well as the usual options.

★Kimpton
Charlotte Square
BOUTIQUE HOTEL £££

(Map p72; 0131-240 5500; www.kimpton charlottesquare.com; 38 Charlotte Sq, EH2 4HQ; r from £340; ; all Princes St buses) Arriving in this modern makeover of a classic Georgian New Town establishment (formerly the Roxburghe Hotel) feels like being welcomed into a country-house party. Service is friendly and attentive without being intrusive, and the atmosphere is informal. In the bedrooms, designer decor meets traditional tweed, and breakfast is served in a lovely glass-roofed garden courtyard.

West End & Dean Village

★Dunstane Houses
BOUTIQUE HOTEL £££

(Map p58; 0131-337 6169; www.theduns tane.com; 4 West Coates, EH12 5JQ; r from £220, ste £445; ; 12, 26, 31, 100) Dunstane House and its companion, Hampton House, are large Victorian villas dating from the 1860s, but totally refurbished in 2017. Gorgeous modern styling complements the many original features, including period fireplaces, stained-glass windows and ornate cornices. The rooms are individually decorated with designer fabrics and wallpapers, while the luxury suites have four-poster beds, chaise longues and roll-top copper baths.

★B+B Edinburgh
HOTEL £££

(Map p58; 0131-225 5084; www.bb-edin burgh.com; 3 Rothesay Tce, EH3 7RY; d/ste from £233/354; ; West End) Built in 1883 as a grand home for the proprietor of the *Scotsman* newspaper, this Victorian extravaganza of carved oak, parquet floors, stained glass and elaborate fireplaces was given a designer makeover to create a striking contemporary hotel. Rooms on the 2nd floor are the most spacious, but the smaller top-floor rooms enjoy the finest views.

South Edinburgh

Sherwood Guest House
B&B ££

(Map p58; 0131-667 1200; www.sherwood-ed inburgh.com; 42 Minto St, EH9 2BR; d/tr from £95/145; ; all Newington buses) One of the most attractive guesthouses on Minto

BOOKING SERVICES

If you arrive in Edinburgh without a place to stay, the Edinburgh tourist office (p98) booking service will try to find a room to suit you (and will charge a £5 fee if successful). If you have the time, pick up the tourist office's accommodation brochure and ring around yourself.

VisitScotland (www.visitscotland.com/accommodation) Wide range of options from the official website.

Lonely Planet (www.lonelyplanet.com/hotels) Recommendations and bookings.

This is Edinburgh (www.edinburgh.org) Promotional website with wide range of accommodation and weekend-break offers.

St's B&B strip, the Sherwood is a refurbished Georgian terrace house decked out with hanging baskets and shrubs. Inside are six en-suite rooms that combine period features with modern fabrics and neutral colours.

No 45   B&B **££**

(☑0131-667 3536; www.edinburghbedbreakfast.com; 45 Gilmour Rd, EH16 5NS; s/d from £80/127; 🛜; 🚌all Newington buses) A peaceful setting, a large garden and friendly owners contribute to the appeal of this Victorian terrace house, which overlooks the local bowling green. The decor is a blend of 19th and 20th century, with bold Victorian reds, pine floors and a period fireplace in the lounge, and a 1930s vibe in the three spacious bedrooms. Occasional two-night-stay minimum.

★**Southside Guest House**   B&B **£££**

(Map p58; ☑0131-466 6573; www.southsideguesthouse.co.uk; 8 Newington Rd, EH9 1QS; s/d from £145/180; 🛜; 🚌all Newington buses) Though set in a typical Victorian terrace, the Southside transcends the traditional guesthouse category and feels more like a modern boutique hotel. Its seven stylish rooms, featuring the clever use of bold colours and modern furniture, ooze interior design. Breakfast is an event, with Buck's Fizz (cava mixed with orange juice) on offer to ease any hangovers.

Albyn Townhouse   B&B **£££**

(Map p58; ☑07973 146210; www.albyntownhouse.co.uk; 16 Hartington Gardens, EH10 4LD; s/d from £101/154; 🅿🛜; 🚌11, 15, 16, 23, 36, 45) Set in a refurbished Victorian town house tucked away at the end of a quiet cul-de-sac in the fashionable Bruntsfield district, this B&B is a real home away from home. Designer-ish decor doesn't detract from the welcoming atmosphere, and the owners (plus their charming dog) are only too pleased to offer advice on where to go and what to see.

94DR   BOUTIQUE HOTEL **£££**

(Map p58; ☑0131-662 9265; www.94dr.com; 94 Dalkeith Rd, EH16 5AF; r from £130; 🅿; 🚌2, 14, 30, 33) This peaceful and elegant guesthouse is a sensitively restored Victorian town house with six individually designed bedrooms with views towards either Salisbury Crags or the Pentland Hills. Extras include complimentary use of bicycles, a well-equipped honesty bar, seriously impressive breakfasts cooked by the chef-owner, and a lovely conservatory and garden.

🛏 Leith

Edinburgh Central Youth Hostel   HOSTEL **£**

(HS; Map p58; ☑0131-524 2090; www.hostellingscotland.org.uk; 9 Haddington Pl, EH7 4AL; tw from £52; @🛜; 🚌all Leith Walk buses) This modern, purpose-built hostel, off Leith Walk about a half-mile north of Waverley train station, is a big, flashy, five-star establishment with its own cafe-bistro as well as a self-catering kitchen, smart and comfortable dorms and private rooms, and mod cons including keycard entry and plasma-screen TVs. Private rooms only during the Covid-19 pandemic.

★**Sheridan Guest House**   B&B **££**

(☑0131-554 4107; www.sheridanedinburgh.com; 1 Bonnington Tce, EH6 4BP; r from £125; 🅿🛜; 🚌11) Flowerpots filled with colourful blooms line the steps of this little haven hidden away north of the New Town. The eight bedrooms (all en suite) blend crisp colours with contemporary furniture, stylish lighting and colourful paintings, which complement the house's clean-cut Georgian lines. The breakfast menu adds omelettes, pancakes with maple syrup, and scrambled eggs with smoked salmon to the usual offerings.

Sandaig Guest House   B&B **££**

(☑0131-554 7357; www.sandaigguesthouse.co.uk; 5 East Hermitage Pl, Leith Links, EH6 8AA;

d/f from £90/130; ☎; ⌨21, 25) From the welcoming glass of sherry to the cheerful goodbye wave, the owner of the Sandaig knows a thing or two about hospitality. Numerous details make staying here a pleasure, from the boldly coloured decor to the crisp cotton sheets, big fluffy towels and refreshing power showers, plus a breakfast menu that includes porridge with cream and maple syrup.

★**Fingal** LUXURY HOTEL **£££**

(☑0131-357 5000; www.fingal.co.uk; Alexandra Dock, EH6 7DX; r from £300; ☎) If a tour of the Royal Yacht *Britannia* has whetted your appetite for a life afloat, you can book yourself into this floating hotel housed in a converted lighthouse maintenance vessel. Under the same management as the *Britannia*, the ship has been fitted out to the highest standard, with 14 luxurious cabins and suites that will make you feel like a pampered royal.

✕ Eating

Eating out in Edinburgh has changed beyond all recognition since the 1990s. Back then, sophisticated dining meant a visit to the Aberdeen Angus Steak House for a prawn cocktail, steak (well done) and chips, and Black Forest gateau. Today, central Edinburgh has more restaurants per head of population than any other UK city, including a handful of places with Michelin stars.

✕ Old Town

★**Mums** CAFE **£**

(Map p64; ☑0131-260 9806; www.monster mashcafe.co.uk; 4a Forrest Rd, EH1 2QN; mains £9-13; ⊙9am-10pm Mon-Sat, 10am-10pm Sun; ☎✦; ⌨2, 23, 27, 35, 41, 42, 45) ∅ This nostalgia-fuelled cafe serves up classic British comfort food that wouldn't look out of place on a 1950s menu – bacon and eggs, bangers and mash, shepherd's pie, fish and chips. But there's a twist – it's all top-quality nosh freshly prepared from local produce. There's also a good selection of bottled craft beers and Scottish-brewed cider.

★**Union Brew Lab** CAFE **£**

(Map p64; ☑0131-662 8963; www.brewlabcof fee.co.uk; 6-8 S College St, EH8 9AA; mains £4-6; ⊙9am-5.30pm; ☎; ⌨all South Bridge buses) ∅ Students with iPads lolling in armchairs, sipping carefully crafted espressos amid art-

fully distressed brick and plaster, recycled school-gym flooring, old workshop benches and lab stools…this is coffee-nerd heaven. There's good food, too, with hearty soups and crusty baguette sandwiches. In summer try the refreshing cold-brew coffee.

Scott's Kitchen SCOTTISH, CAFE **£**

(Map p64; ☑0131-322 6868; www.scottskitch en.co.uk; 4-6 Victoria Tce, EH1 2JL; mains £8-10; ⊙9am-6pm; P☎; ⌨23, 27, 41, 42) Green tile, brown leather and arched Georgian windows lend an elegant feel to this modern cafe, which combines fine Scottish produce with international favourites. Fill up on a breakfast (served till noon) of eggs Benedict or bacon baps, or linger over a lunch of haggis bonbons, crunchy calamari or a smoked ham and Scottish cheddar sandwich.

Edinburgh Larder CAFE **£**

(Map p64; ☑0131-556 2350; www.edinburgh larder.co.uk; 15 Blackfriars St, EH1 1NB; mains £9-15; ⊙8am-5pm Mon, Thu & Fri, 8.30am-5pm Sat & Sun; ✦; ⌨35) This bright and cheerful cafe, handily located just off the Royal Mile, puts the focus on seasonal Scottish produce (a map on the wall highlights its suppliers). Dishes range from brunch favourites such as eggs Benedict, to a Taste of Scotland platter that includes hot and cold smoked salmon, organic cheeses, oatcakes and salad leaves.

★**Cannonball Restaurant** SCOTTISH **££**

(Map p64; ☑0131-225 1550; www.contini.com; 356 Castlehill, EH1 2NE; mains £15-30; ⊙noon-3pm & 5.30-10pm Tue-Sat; ☎✦; ⌨23, 27, 41, 42) The historic Cannonball House next to Edinburgh Castle's esplanade has been transformed into a sophisticated restaurant and whisky bar where the Contini family work their Italian magic on Scottish classics to produce dishes such as haggis balls with marmalade and mustard, and lobster thermidor with macaroni and cheese.

Mother India's Cafe INDIAN **££**

(Map p64; ☑0131-524 9801; www.motherindia. co.uk; 3-5 Infirmary St, EH1 1LT; dishes £5-9; ⊙4-9pm Mon & Tue, noon-9pm Wed, Thu & Sun, noon-10pm Fri & Sat; ☎✦; ⌨all South Bridge buses) A simple concept pioneered in Glasgow has captured hearts and minds – and stomachs – here in Edinburgh: Indian food served in tapas-size portions, so that you can sample a greater variety of deliciously different dishes without busting a gut. It's hugely popular, so book a table to avoid disappointment.

Devil's Advocate
PUB FOOD ££

(Map p64; ☎ 0131-225 4465; www.devilsad vocateedinburgh.co.uk; 9 Advocates Close, EH1 1ND; mains £15-23; ⊗ food served noon-3pm & 5-10pm; ☎; ☐ 23, 27, 41, 42) No trip to Edinburgh is complete without exploring the narrow closes (alleys) that lead off the Royal Mile. Lucky you if your explorations lead to this cosy split-level pub-restaurant set in a converted Victorian pump house, with a menu of top-quality pub grub – the smoked fish and charcuterie platters are irresistible. It gets rammed on weekends, so book ahead.

Maxie's Bistro
BISTRO ££

(Map p64; ☎ 0131-226 7770; www.maxiesbis tro.com; 5b Johnston Tce, EH1 2PW; mains £10-27; ⊗ noon-11pm; ☎☝; ☐ 23, 27, 41, 42, 67) This candlelit bistro, with its cushion-lined nooks set amid stone walls and wooden beams, is a pleasant setting for a cosy dinner, but at summer lunchtimes people queue for the tables on the terrace overlooking Victoria St. The food is dependable, ranging from pasta, steak and stir-fries to seafood platters and daily specials. It's best to book, especially in summer.

Amber
SCOTTISH ££

(Map p64; ☎ 0131-477 8477; www.scotchwhis kyexperience.co.uk; 354 Castlehill, EH1 2NE; mains £15-20; ⊗ 11am-8pm; ☎☝; ☐ 23, 27, 41, 42) You've got to love a place where the waiter greets you with the words, 'I'll be your whisky adviser for this evening'. Located in the Scotch Whisky Experience (p57), this whisky-themed restaurant manages to avoid the tourist clichés and creates genuinely interesting and flavoursome dishes using top Scottish produce, with a suggested whisky pairing for each dish.

★ Grain Store
SCOTTISH £££

(Map p64; ☎ 0131-225 7635; www.grain store-restaurant.co.uk; 30 Victoria St, EH1 2JW; mains £24-32; ⊗ noon-2.30pm & 6-9.45pm Mon-Sat, noon-2.30pm & 6-9.30pm Sun; ☐ 2, 23, 27, 41, 42) An atmospheric upstairs dining room on picturesque Victoria St, the Grain Store has a well-earned reputation for serving the finest Scottish produce, perfectly prepared in dishes such as halibut with fried squid and mussel bisque, and roe deer venison with celeriac, beetroot and kale. The two-course lunch for £14 is good value.

★ Ondine
SEAFOOD £££

(Map p64; ☎ 0131-226 1888; www.ondineres taurant.co.uk; 2 George IV Bridge, EH1 1AD; mains £22-38; ⊗ noon-9pm Wed-Sat, noon-4pm Sun; ☎; ☐ 23, 27, 41, 42) 🌿 Ondine is one of Edinburgh's finest seafood restaurants, with a menu based on sustainably sourced fish. Take a seat at the curved Oyster Bar and tuck into oysters with shallot dressing, shellfish bisque, lobster thermidor, a *fruits de mer* platter or just good old haddock and chips (with minted pea puree, just to keep things posh).

White Horse Oyster & Seafood Bar
SEAFOOD £££

(Map p64; ☎ 0131-629 5300; www.whitehorseoys terbar.co.uk; 266 Canongate, EH8 8AA; seafood platters £48-95; ⊗ 4-10pm Mon-Fri, noon-10pm Sat & Sun; ☐ 35) One of Edinburgh's oldest pubs has been transformed into this intriguing seafood restaurant. The decor is bare stone and wood panelling in shades of slate grey and brown, providing a dark canvas on which white platters of colourful shellfish and crustaceans shine all the more brightly. The menu also includes 'small plates' (£8 to £15), which can be ordered tapas-style.

✗ Holyrood & Arthur's Seat

★ Rhubarb
SCOTTISH £££

(☎ 0131-225 1333; www.prestonfield.com; Prestonfield, Priestfield Rd, EH16 5UT; mains £23-40; ⊗ noon-8pm; ℗ 🌿) Set in the splendid 17th-century Prestonfield Hotel (p82), Rhubarb is a feast for the eyes as well as the taste buds. The over-the-top decor of rich reds set off with black and gold and sensuous surfaces – damask, brocade, marble and gilded leather – are matched by the intense flavours and rich textures of the modern Scottish cuisine. Vegetarian and vegan menus available.

Take your postprandial coffee and brandy upstairs to the sumptuous fireside sofas in the Tapestry and Leather rooms. A two-/three-course lunch menu is available for £27/33.

✗ New Town

Urban Angel
CAFE £

(Map p72; ☎ 0131-225 6215; www.urban-angel.co.uk; 121 Hanover St, EH2 1DJ; mains £6-11; ⊗ 8am-5pm Mon-Fri, 9am-5pm Sat & Sun; 🍴☝; ☐ 23, 27) 🌿 A wholesome deli that puts the emphasis on fair-trade, organic and locally sourced produce, Urban Angel is also a delightfully informal cafe-bistro that serves all-day brunches (porridge with honey, pancakes, eggs Benedict), mix-and-match salads and a wide range of light, snacky meals.

★ **Gardener's Cottage**　　SCOTTISH ££
(Map p72; 📞0131-558 1221; www.thegarden erscottage.co; 1 Royal Tce Gardens, London Rd, EH7 5DX; 2-/3-course lunch £15/19, 6-course dinner £60; ⊙noon-2pm & 5-10pm Mon-Fri, 10am-2pm & 5-10pm Sat & Sun; 🚌all London Rd buses) 🍴 This country cottage in the heart of the city, bedecked with flowers and fairy lights, offers one of Edinburgh's most interesting dining experiences – two tiny rooms with communal tables made of salvaged timber, and a set menu based on fresh local produce (most of the vegetables and fruit are from its own organic garden). Bookings essential; brunch served at weekends.

★ **Aizle**　　SCOTTISH ££
(Map p72; 📞0131-527 4747; www.aizle.co.uk; Kimpton Charlotte Square Hotel, 38 Charlotte Sq, EH2 4HQ; 6-course dinner £70; ⊙5-9pm Wed-Sun; 📞; 🚌all Princes St buses) If you tend to have trouble deciding what to eat, Aizle (the name is an old Scots word for 'spark' or 'ember') will do the job for you. There's no menu here, just a six-course dinner

conjured from a monthly 'harvest' of the finest and freshest local produce (listed on a blackboard), and presented beautifully – art on a plate.

Café Royal Oyster Bar　　SEAFOOD ££
(Map p72; 📞0131-556 1884; www.caferoyaledin burgh.com; 17a W Register St, EH2 2AA; mains £15-23, fillet steak £40; ⊙noon-2.30pm & 5.30-9.30pm Mon-Fri, noon-9.30pm Sat & Sun; 🚇St Andrew Sq) Pass through the revolving doors on the corner of West Register St and you're transported back to Victorian times – a palace of glinting mahogany, polished brass, marble floors, stained glass, Doulton tiles, gilded cornices and starched table linen so thick it creaks when you fold it. The menu is mostly classic seafood, from oysters on ice to Scottish lobster thermidor.

Dishoom　　INDIAN ££
(Map p72; 📞0131-202 6406; www.dishoom.com; 3a St Andrew Sq, EH2 2BD; mains £9-15; ⊙8am-10pm Mon-Fri, 9am-10pm Sat & Sun; 📞📶📱; 🚇St Andrew Sq) This Edinburgh restaurant was the Dishoom minichain's first opening outside London. Inspired by the Irani cafes of Mumbai, it serves exquisite Indian street food in upmarket surroundings; the breakfasts, including the signature bacon nan, are legendary. Hugely popular – book

---

BEST VEGETARIAN RESTAURANTS

David Bann (Map p64; 📞0131-556 5888; www.davidbann.com; 56-58 St Mary's St, EH1 1SX; mains £12-15; ⊙noon-10pm Mon-Fri, 11am-10pm Sat & Sun; 📱; 🚌35) If you want to convince a carnivorous friend that cuisine à la veg can be every bit as tasty and inventive as a meat-muncher's menu, take them to David Bann's stylish restaurant – dishes such as strudel filled with mushroom, rosemary, Isle of Arran cheese and Heather Ale with polenta chips and shallot sauce are guaranteed to win converts.

Holy Cow (Map p72; 34 Elder St, EH1 3DX; mains £6-12; ⊙10am-10pm; 📱) This hard-to-find cafe is hidden in a New Town basement close to the bus station, but well worth seeking out for its vegan burgers (portobello mushroom, Vietnamese tofu or soya and kidney bean, with chunky fries), and fresh and zingy Mexican salads loaded with chilli, coriander and lime juice.

Kalpna (Map p58; 📞0131-667 9890; www.kalpnarestaurant.com; 2-3 St Patrick Sq, EH8 9EZ; mains £8-13; ⊙noon-2pm & 5.30-10.30pm; 📱; 🚌all Newington buses) A long-standing Edinburgh favourite, Kalpna is one of the best Indian restaurants in the country, vegetarian or otherwise. The cuisine is mostly Gujarati, with a smattering of dishes from other parts of India. The all-you-can-eat lunch buffet (£9) is superb value.

Mosque Kitchen (Map p64; www.mosquekitchen.com; 31 Nicolson Sq, EH8 9BX; mains £5-7; ⊙11am-8pm; 📱📶; 🚌all South Bridge buses) Expect shared tables and disposable plates, but this is the place to go for cheap, authentic and delicious homemade curries, kebabs, pakoras and nan bread, all washed down with lassi or mango juice. It caters to Edinburgh's Central Mosque but welcomes all – local students have taken to it big time. No alcohol.

well ahead, or be prepared to queue for a table. A vegan menu is available.

Dome
SCOTTISH ££

(Map p72; ☎0131-624 8624; www.thedomeedinburgh.com; 14 George St, EH2 2PF; mains £16-23, 2-/3-course lunch £20/25; ⊘10am-10pm; ☞☝; ☐St Andrew Sq) Housed in the magnificent neoclassical former headquarters of the Commercial Bank, with a lofty glass-domed ceiling, pillared arches and mosaic-tiled floor, the Grill Room at the Dome is one of the city's most impressive dining rooms. The menu is solidly modern Scottish, with great steaks and seafood, or try afternoon tea in the elegant Georgian Tea Room. Reservations strongly recommended.

Contini
ITALIAN ££

(Map p72; ☎0131-225 1550; www.contini.com; 103 George St, EH2 3ES; mains £18-24; ⊘8am-10pm Mon-Fri, 10am-10.30pm Sat, 11am-8pm Sun; ☜☞☝; ☐all Princes St buses) A palatial Georgian banking hall enlivened by fuchsia-pink banners and lampshades is home to this lively, family-friendly Italian bar and restaurant, where the emphasis is on fresh, authentic ingredients (produce imported weekly from Milan; homemade bread and pasta) and the uncomplicated enjoyment of food.

Ivy on the Square
BRITISH ££

(Map p72; ☎0131-526 4777; www.theivyedinburgh.com; 6 St Andrew Sq, EH2 2BD; mains £15-19; ⊘8am-midnight Mon-Sat, 9am-10.30pm Sun; ☜☞; ☐St Andrew Sq) The first Scottish outpost of London's famous celebrity haunt, the Ivy in Covent Garden, this classy but informal brasserie serves up traditional British dishes, from eggs Benedict for brunch through afternoon tea to the Ivy's classic dishes of steak, egg and chips, or shepherd's pie (made with red wine sauce and topped with cheesey mashed potato). A vegan menu is available.

Scottish Cafe & Restaurant
SCOTTISH ££

(Map p72; ☎0131-225 1550; www.contini.com; The Mound, EH2 2EL; mains £9-15; ⊘9am-5pm Mon-Wed, Fri & Sat, to 7pm Thu, 10am-5pm Sun; ☜☝; ☐Princes St) ⏺ This appealing modern restaurant, part of the Scottish National Gallery (p69) complex, has picture windows providing a view along Princes Street Gardens. Try traditional Scottish dishes such as Cullen skink (smoked-haddock soup) and leek-and-potato soup, or

seasonal, sustainably sourced produce including smoked salmon and trout, free-range chicken and pork.

★Outlook
SCOTTISH £££

(Map p72; ☎0131-322 1246; www.thelookoutedinburgh.co; Calton Hill, EH7 5AA; lunch/dinner from £28/34; ⊘noon-9.30pm Tue-Thu, 10am-9.30pm Fri-Sun; ☞) ⏺ This glass-walled restaurant perched on top of Calton Hill enjoys some of the finest views in the city, and some of the finest food. Run by the same folk as Gardener's Cottage (p87), it has a menu consisting of a tray of seven small dishes (including a vegetarian option) prepared using whatever fresh local produce is in season, plus a choice of sides and wines.

★L'Escargot Bleu
FRENCH £££

(Map p58; ☎0131-557 1600; www.lescargotbleu.co.uk; 56 Broughton St, EH1 3SA; mains £19-25; ⊘noon-2.30pm & 5.30-10pm Mon-Thu, noon-3pm & 5.30-10.30pm Fri & Sat; ☝; ☐8) This cute little bistro is as Gallic as garlic but makes fine use of quality Scottish produce – the French-speaking staff will lead you knowledgeably through a menu that includes authentic Savoyard *tartiflette,* beef bourguignon and Basque-style mussels. Two-course *menu du jour* lunch/dinner costs £13/15.

✖ West End & Dean Village

Cafe Milk
CAFE £

(Map p58; ☎0131-629 6022; www.cafemilk.co.uk; 232 Morrison St, EH3 8EA; mains £6-9; ⊘7.30am-4pm Mon-Fri, 8am-4pm Sat, 8am-3pm Sun; ☜☞; ☐Haymarket) ⏺ This is fast food with a conscience – natural, nutritious, locally sourced and freshly prepared, from organic porridge to courgette, lemon and feta fritters, and North Indian dal with rice or flatbread. Take away, or sit in and soak up the retro vibe amid old Formica tables and battered school benches. There are branches at **Fruitmarket Gallery** (Map p72; www.fruitmarket.co.uk; 45 Market St, EH1 1DF; ⊘11am-6pm; ☝; ☐all North Bridge buses) and **Edinburgh Sculpture Workshop** (☎0131-551 4490; www.edinburghsculpture.org; 21 Hawthornvale, EH6 4JT; ⊘9.30am-5pm Mon-Sat; ☐; ☐7, 11).

★Kanpai Sushi
JAPANESE ££

(Map p64; ☎0131-228 1602; www.kanpaisushi.co.uk; 8-10 Grindlay St, EH3 9AS; mains £9-15, sushi per piece £4-10; ⊘ noon-2.30pm & 5-10.30pm Tue-Sat; ☐ all Lothian Rd buses) What is arguably Edinburgh's best sushi restaurant impresses with its minimalist interior, fresh, top-quality fish and elegantly presented dishes – the squid tempura comes in a delicate woven basket, while the sashimi combo is presented as a flower arrangement in an ice-filled stoneware bowl. Bookings recommended.

★ **Timberyard**   SCOTTISH ££
(Map p64; ☑ 0131-221 1222; www.timberyard.co; 10 Lady Lawson St, EH3 9DS; mains £16-22, 5-course set menu £50; ⊘ noon-2pm & 5.30-9.30pm Tue-Sat; ☎☑☝; ☐ 2, 300) ✪ Ancient, worn floorboards, cast-iron pillars, exposed joists, and tables made from slabs of old mahogany create a rustic, retro atmosphere in this slow-food restaurant where the accent is on locally sourced produce from artisan growers and foragers. Typical dishes include honey-glazed monkfish with saffron, samphire and leek, and pigeon with radicchio, chanterelles and sherry.

✖ Stockbridge

Scran & Scallie   GASTROPUB ££
(Map p58; ☑ 0131-332 6281; www.scranandscallie.com; 1 Comely Bank Rd, EH4 1DR; mains £14-21; ⊘ noon-10pm Mon-Fri, 8.30am-10pm Sat & Sun; ☎☝☺; ☐ 24, 29, 42) ✪ Established by the Michelin-starred team responsible for Kitchin (p90), this laid-back gastropub adds a modern chef's touch to old-time dishes such as chicken-liver parfait, sausage and mash, and fish pie. There are also quality versions of classic pub grub such as burgers, steak pie, and fish and chips, and veggie options that include a spelt-and-lentil burger.

Taisteal   INTERNATIONAL ££
(Map p58; ☑ 0131-332 9977; www.taisteal.co.uk; 1-3 Raeburn Pl, EH4 1HU; 2-/3-course meal £25/30; ⊘ noon-2.30pm & 6-9.30pm Tue-Sat; ☐ 24, 29, 36, 42) ✪ Taisteal is the Gaelic word for 'travel', so it's no surprise that the menu in this convivial bistro is a fusion of Scottish produce with influences and flavours from around the world – pea and jalapeño soup with ham-hock croquette, and venison Wellington with butternut squash and blackberries are typical concoctions. There's also a five-/seven-course tasting menu for £40/50.

✖ South Edinburgh

Söderberg (The Meadows)   CAFE £
(Map p58; ☑ 0131-228 5876; www.soderberg.uk; 27 Simpson Loan, EH3 9GG; sandwiches £5-7, cakes £3; ⊘ 8.30am-5.30pm; ☑☝; ☐ 23, 27, 45, 47, 300) This Swedish-style coffee house produces its own home-baked pastries and breads, which form the basis of lunchtime sandwiches with fillings such as roast beef with beetroot and caper salad, and roast butternut squash with sunblush tomato pesto. Breakfast (served till noon) can be a basket of breads with conserves and cheeses, or yoghurt with granola and fruit.

★ **Locanda de Gusti**   ITALIAN ££
(Map p58; ☑ 0131-346 8800; www.locandadegusti.com; 102 Dalry Rd, EH11 2DW; mains £14-28; ⊘ 5.30-10pm Mon-Wed, 12.30-2pm & 5.30-10pm Thu-Sat; ☝; ☐ 2, 3, 4, 25, 33, 44) This bustling family bistro, loud with the buzz of conversation and the clink of glasses and cutlery, is no ordinary Italian but a little corner of Naples, complete with hearty Neapolitan home cooking by friendly head chef Rosario. The food ranges from light and tasty ravioli tossed with butter, sage and nutmeg to delicious platters of grilled seafood.

★ **First Coast**   SCOTTISH ££
(Map p58; ☑ 0131-313 4404; www.first-coast.co.uk; 97-101 Dalry Rd, EH11 2AB; 2-/3-course dinner £22/26; ⊘ noon-2pm & 5-11pm Mon-Sat; ☎☑☝; ☐ 2, 3, 4, 25, 33, 44) This popular neighbourhood bistro has a striking main dining area with sea-blue wood panelling and stripped stonework, and a short and simple menu offering hearty comfort food such as maple-syrup- and mustard-glazed ham hock with spinach and nutmeg mash, or cod in banana leaf with lemon, basil, aubergine and shrimp paste. Lunchtime and early evening there's an excellent two-/three-course menu for £14.50/16.

★ **Loudon's Café & Bakery**   CAFE ££
(Map p58; www.loudons.co.uk; 94b Fountainbridge, EH3 9QA; mains £9-13; ⊘ 7.30am-5pm Mon-Fri, 8am-5pm Sat & Sun; ☎☑☝; ☐ 1, 34, 35, 300) Organic bread and cakes baked on the premises, ethically sourced coffee, daily and weekend newspapers scattered about, even some outdoor tables – what's not to like? The weekend all-day brunch (8am to 4pm) includes eggs Benedict, granola with yoghurt, and vegan vanilla pancakes. A **second branch** (Map p72; ☑ 0131-556 7734;

2 Sibbald Walk, EH8 8FT; mains £9-13; ⊙8am-3pm Mon-Fri, to 4pm Sat & Sun; 🚇35) opened in 2020 at the New Waverley development just off the Royal Mile.

✕ Leith

Pitt
MARKET **£**

(📞07534 157477; www.thepitt.co.uk; 125 Pitt St, EH6 4DE; entry £2; ⊙noon-8pm Sat, noon-6pm Sun Mar-Dec; 🚇7, 14, 21) A weekly street-food market surrounded by industrial warehouses, the Pitt is a little bit of East London in north Edinburgh. The regularly changing food trucks sell anything from butter-milk-fried chicken burgers to halloumi bao buns to haggis to sweet-potato pierogi (dumplings). Choose a drink from the wine and gin bars, or the Barneys beer truck selling local craft ales.

The vibe is rustic and outdoorsy, with live bands, wooden pallet seating and fire barrels for warming your hands.

★ Fishers Bistro
SEAFOOD **££**

(📞0131-554 5666; www.fishersbistros.co.uk; 1 The Shore, EH6 6QW; mains £12-26; ⊙noon-10.30pm Mon-Sat, 12.30-10.30pm Sun; 🛜🚪👶; 🚇16, 22, 35, 36) This cosy little restaurant, tucked beneath a 17th-century signal tower, is one of the city's best seafood places. The menu ranges widely in price, from cheaper dishes such as classic fish cakes with lemon-and-chive mayonnaise to more expensive delights such as a whole Fife lobster with garlic-and-herb butter and chips (£45).

★ Restaurant Martin Wishart
FRENCH **£££**

(📞0131-553 3557; www.restaurantmartinwishart.co.uk; 54 The Shore, EH6 6RA; 3-course lunch £39, 4-course dinner £75; ⊙noon-1.30pm & 7-9pm Wed-Sat; 🚪; 🚇16, 22, 35, 36) 🌱 In 2001 this restaurant became the first in Edinburgh to win a Michelin star, and it's retained it ever since. The eponymous chef has worked with Albert Roux, Marco Pierre White and Nick Nairn, and brings a modern French approach to the best Scottish produce, from sautéed foie gras and langoustines with braised fennel to a six-course vegetarian tasting menu (£80).

★ Kitchin
SCOTTISH **£££**

(📞0131-555 1755; www.thekitchin.com; 78 Commercial Quay, EH6 6LX; 3-course lunch/dinner £39/90; ⊙noon-2.30pm & 6-10pm Tue-Sat; 🚪; 🚇16, 22, 35, 36) Fresh, seasonal, locally sourced Scottish produce is the philosophy

that's won a Michelin star for this elegant but unpretentious restaurant. The menu moves with the seasons, of course, so expect fresh salads in summer and game in winter, and shellfish dishes such as Orkney scallops baked in the shell with white wine, vermouth and herbs when there's an 'r' in the month.

Chop House Leith
STEAK **£££**

(📞0131-629 1919; www.chophousesteak.co.uk; 102 Constitution St, EH6 6AW; mains £17-30; ⊙noon-3pm & 5-10.30pm Mon-Fri, noon-10.30pm Sat & Sun; 🛜; 🚇16, 22, 35, 36) A modern take on the old-fashioned steakhouse, this 'bar and butchery' combines slick designer decor (the ceramic brick tiles are a nod to traditional butcher shops) with a meaty menu of the best Scottish beef, dry-aged for at least 35 days and chargrilled to perfection (chateaubriand for two goes for £80). Sauces include bone-marrow gravy and Argentine chimichurri. Cool cocktails, too.

🍷 Drinking & Nightlife

Edinburgh has always been a drinkers' city. It has more than 700 pubs – more per square mile than any other UK city – and they are as varied and full of character as the people who drink in them, from Victorian palaces to stylish pre-club bars, and from real-ale howffs (meeting places, often pubs) to cool cocktail lounges.

🍷 Old Town

★ Cabaret Voltaire
CLUB

(Map p64; www.thecabaretvoltaire.com; 36-38 Blair St, EH1 1QR; ⊙5pm-3am Tue-Sat, 8pm-1am Sun; 🛜; 🚇all South Bridge buses) An atmospheric warren of stone-lined vaults houses this self-consciously 'alternative' club, which eschews huge dance floors and egotistical DJ worship in favour of a 'creative crucible' hosting an eclectic mix of DJs, live acts, comedy, theatre, visual arts and the spoken word. Well worth a look.

★ Bow Bar
PUB

(Map p64; www.thebowbar.co.uk; 80 West Bow, EH1 2HH; ⊙noon-midnight; 🍴; 🚇2, 23, 27, 41, 42) One of the city's best traditional-style pubs (it's not as old as it looks), serving a range of excellent real ales, Scottish craft gins and a vast selection of malt whiskies, the Bow Bar is often standing-room only on Friday and Saturday evenings.

Bongo Club   CLUB
(Map p64; www.thebongoclub.co.uk; 66 Cowgate, EH1 1JR; ⊙11pm-3am Tue & Thu, 7pm-3am Fri-Sun; ☎; ⬚2) Owned by a local arts charity, the weird and wonderful Bongo Club has a long history of hosting everything from wild club nights and local bands to performance art and kids comedy shows.

Dragonfly   COCKTAIL BAR
(Map p64; ☎0131-228 4543; www.dragonfly cocktailbar.com; 52 West Port, EH1 2LD; ⊙4pm-1am; ☎; ⬚2) A superstylish lounge bar with a Raffles of Singapore vibe – it's all crystal chandeliers, polished wood and Asian art – Dragonfly has won rave reviews for both its innovative cocktails and its designer decor. Grab a seat on the neat little mezzanine, from where you can look down on the bar as the Singapore Slings are being slung.

Salt Horse Beer Shop & Bar   BAR
(Map p64; ☎0131-558 8304; www.salthorse. beer; 57-61 Blackfriars St, EH1 1NB; ⊙4pm-midnight Mon-Fri, noon-1am Sat, 12.30pm-midnight Sun; ⬚35) Tucked off the Royal Mile, this independent hybrid combines great beer, food, and a shop next door selling around 400 beers to drink in or take away. Work your way through 12 keg lines of local and imported beers and a small but perfectly formed menu of handmade burgers, Scotch eggs, and cheese and charcuterie platters.

Liquid Room   CLUB
(Map p64; www.liquidroom.com; 9c Victoria St, EH1 2HE; ⊙live music from 7pm, club nights 10.30pm-3am; ⬚2, 23, 27, 41, 42) Set in a subterranean vault deep beneath Victoria St, the Liquid Room is a superb club venue with a thundering sound system. There are regular club nights every Friday and Saturday, as well as

TOP FIVE TRADITIONAL PUBS

Bennet's Bar (Map p58; ☎0131-229 5143; www.kilderkingroup.co.uk; 8 Leven St, EH3 9DX; ⊙11am-1am; ⬚all Tollcross buses) Situated beside the King's Theatre (Map p58; www. capitaltheatres.com/kings), Bennet's (established in 1839) has managed to hang on to almost all of its beautiful Victorian fittings, from the stained-glass windows and the ornate mirrors to the wooden gantry and the brass water taps on the bar (for your whisky – there are over 100 from which to choose).

Café Royal Circle Bar (Map p72; ☎0131-556 1884; www.caferoyaledinburgh.com; 17 W Register St, EH2 2AA; ⊙11am-11pm Mon-Wed, to midnight Thu, to 1am Fri & Sat, to 10pm Sun; ☎; ⬚Princes St) The Café Royal is perhaps *the* classic Edinburgh pub; its main claims to fame are its magnificent oval bar and its Doulton tile portraits of famous Victorian inventors. Sit at the bar or claim one of the cosy leather booths beneath the stained-glass windows, and choose from the seven real ales on tap.

Athletic Arms (Diggers; Map p58; ☎0131-337 3822; www.athleticarms.com; 1-3 Angle Park Tce, EH11 2JX; ⊙11am-1am; ☎; ⬚1, 34, 35) Nicknamed for the cemetery across the street – gravediggers used to nip in and slake their thirst here – the Diggers dates from 1897. It's still staunchly traditional – the decor has barely changed in 100 years – and is a beacon for real-ale drinkers, serving locally brewed 80-shilling ale. It's packed to the gills with football and rugby fans on match days.

Abbotsford (Map p72; ☎0131-225 5276; www.theabbotsford.com; 3 Rose St, EH2 2PR; ⊙11am-11pm Mon-Thu, to midnight Fri & Sat, 12.30-11pm Sun; ☎; ⬚all Princes St buses) One of the few pubs in Rose St that has retained its Edwardian splendour, the Abbotsford has long been a hang-out for writers, actors, journalists and media people, and has many loyal regulars. Named after Sir Walter Scott's country house, it dates from 1902; the pub's centrepiece is a splendid mahogany island bar. There's a good selection of real ales.

Sheep Heid Inn (www.thesheepheidedinburgh.co.uk; 43-45 The Causeway, EH15 3QA; ⊙11am-11pm Mon-Thu, to midnight Fri & Sat, noon-11pm Sun; ⬚☎; ⬚42) Possibly the oldest inn in Edinburgh (with a licence dating back to 1360), the Sheep Heid feels more like an upmarket country pub than an Edinburgh bar. Set in the semirural shadow of Arthur's Seat (p65), it's famous for its 19th-century skittles alley and its lovely little beer garden.

DJs and live bands on other nights. Check the website for upcoming events.

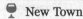

New Town

Lucky Liquor Co
COCKTAIL BAR

(Map p72; ☑ 0131-226 3976; www.luckyliquorco.com; 39a Queen St, EH2 3NH; ⊙ 4pm-1am; ☐ 24, 29, 42) This tiny, black-and-white bar is all about the number 13: 13 bottles of base spirit are used to create a daily menu of 13 cocktails. The result is a playful list with some unusual flavours, such as tonka-bean liqueur, coconut champagne and salted grapefruit soda (though not necessarily all in the same glass!), served by a fun and friendly crew.

Bramble
COCKTAIL BAR

(Map p72; ☑ 0131-226 6343; www.bramblebar.co.uk; 16a Queen St, EH2 1JE; ⊙ 4pm-1am; ☐ 23, 27) One of those places that easily earns the sobriquet 'best-kept secret', Bramble is an unmarked cellar bar (there's only an inconspicuous brass nameplate beneath a dry-cleaner's shop) where a maze of stone and brick hideaways conceals what is arguably the city's best cocktail venue. No beer taps, no fuss, just expertly mixed drinks.

Joseph Pearce's
PUB

(Map p58; ☑ 0131-556 4140; www.bodabar.com; 23 Elm Row, EH7 4AA; ⊙ 11am-midnight Sun-Thu, to 1am Fri & Sat; ☎️; ☐ all Leith Walk buses) This traditional Victorian pub has been remodelled and given a new lease of life by the Swedish owners. It's a real hub of the local community, with good food (very family friendly before 5pm), a relaxed atmosphere, and events like Monday-night Scrabble games and August crayfish parties.

Guildford Arms
PUB

(Map p72; ☑ 0131-556 4312; www.guildfordarms.com; 1 W Register St, EH2 2AA; ⊙ 11am-11pm Mon-Thu, to 11.30pm Fri & Sat, 12.30-11pm Sun; ☎️; ☐ St Andrew Sq) Located in a side alley off the east end of Princes St, the Guildford is a classic Victorian pub full of polished mahogany, gleaming brass and ornate cornices. The range of real ales is excellent – try to get a table in the unusual upstairs gallery, with a view over the sea of drinkers below.

Oxford Bar
PUB

(Map p72; ☑ 0131-539 7119; 8 Young St, EH2 4JB; ⊙ noon-midnight Mon-Thu, 11am-1am Fri & Sat, 12.30-11pm Sun; ☎️; ☐ all Princes St buses) The

---

LGBTIQ+ EDINBURGH

Edinburgh has a small – but perfectly formed – gay and lesbian scene, centred on the area around Broughton St (known affectionately as the 'Pink Triangle') at the eastern end of New Town.

Scene Alba (www.scenealba.co.uk) is a monthly magazine covering queer culture in Scotland, with listings of gay-friendly pubs and clubs in Edinburgh and Glasgow.

Useful contacts:

Edinburgh LGBT Centre (www.lgbthealth.org.uk; 4 Duncan Pl; ⊙ 9am-5pm Mon-Fri; ☐ 21, 25, 34, 35, 49)

Lothian LGBT Helpline (☑ 0300 123 2523; www.lgbthealth.org.uk/helpline; ⊙ noon-9pm Tue & Wed, 1-6pm Thu & Sun)

Pubs & Clubs

CC Blooms (Map p72; ☑ 0131-556 9331; www.ccblooms.co.uk; 23 Greenside Pl, EH1 3AA; ⊙ 11am-3am; ☎️; ☐ all Leith Walk buses) The raddled old queen of Edinburgh's 1990s gay scene has been given a shot in the arm, with two floors of deafening dance and disco every night. It can get pretty crowded after 11pm and the drinks can be overpriced, but it's worth a visit – go early, or sample the wild Church of High Kicks cabaret show on Sunday nights.

Regent (Map p58; ☑ 0131-661 8198; 2 Montrose Tce, EH7 5DL; ⊙ noon-1am Mon-Sat, 12.30pm-1am Sun; ☎️; ☐ 35) This is a pleasant gay local with a relaxed atmosphere (no loud music) that serves coffee and croissants as well as excellent real ales, including Deuchars IPA and Caledonian 80/-. It's the meeting place for various community groups including Bear Scots (second Saturday of the month) and the Ruby Fruits (first Sunday of the month).

Oxford is that rarest of things: a real pub for real people, with no 'theme', no frills and no pretensions. 'The Ox' has been immortalised by Ian Rankin, author of the Inspector Rebus novels, whose fictional detective is a regular here (as is the author himself). There's occasional live folk music.

Cumberland Bar   PUB

(Map p58; ☑ 0131-558 3134; www.cumber landbar.co.uk; 1-3 Cumberland St, EH3 6RT; ⊘ noon-midnight Mon-Wed, to 1am Thu-Sat, 11am-11pm Sun; 🕾; 🚍 23, 27) Immortalised as the stereotypical New Town pub in Alexander McCall Smith's serialised novel *44 Scotland Street*, the Cumberland has an authentic, traditional wood-brass-and-mirrors look (despite being relatively new) and serves well-looked-after, cask-conditioned ales and a wide range of malt whiskies. There's also a pleasant little beer garden.

 Leith

★ **Roseleaf**   BAR

(☑ 0131-476 5268; www.roseleaf.co.uk; 23-24 Sandport Pl, EH6 6EW; ⊘ 10am-1am; 🕾 🐕; 🚍 16, 22, 35, 36) Cute, quaint, and decked out in flowered wallpaper, old furniture and rose-patterned china (cocktails are served in teapots), the Roseleaf could hardly be further from the average Leith bar. The real ales and bottled beers are complemented by a range of speciality teas, coffees and fruit drinks (including rose lemonade), and well-above-average pub grub (served from 10am to 10pm).

Lioness of Leith   BAR

(☑ 0131-629 0580; www.thelionessofleith.co.uk; 21-25 Duke St, EH6 8HH; ⊘ noon-1am Mon-Thu, 11am-1am Fri-Sun; 🕾; 🚍 21, 34, 35) Duke St was always one of the rougher corners of Leith, but the emergence of pubs like the Lioness is a sure sign of gentrification. Distressed timber and battered leather benches are surrounded by vintage objets trouvés, a pinball machine and a pop-art print of Allen Ginsberg. There are good beers and cocktails, and a tempting menu of gourmet burgers.

Teuchters Landing   PUB

(☑ 0131-554 7427; www.teuchtersbar.co.uk; 1c Dock Pl, EH6 6LU; ⊘ 10.30am-1am; 🕾; 🚍 16, 22, 35, 36) A cosy warren of timber-lined nooks and crannies housed in a single-storey red-brick building (once a waiting room for ferries across the Firth of Forth), this real-ale and malt-whisky bar also has tables on a floating terrace in the dock.

Port O'Leith   PUB

(☑ 0131-554 3568; www.facebook.com/theporto leithbar; 58 Constitution St, EH6 6RS; ⊘ 11am-1am Mon-Sat, noon-1am Sun; 🚍 16, 22, 35, 36) This good old-fashioned local boozer has been sympathetically restored – it appeared in the 2013 film *Sunshine on Leith*. Its nautical history is evident in the form of flags and cap bands left behind by visiting sailors (Leith docks are just down the road). Pop in for a pint and you'll probably stay until closing time.

☆ Entertainment

Edinburgh has a number of fine theatres and concert halls, and there are independent art-house cinemas as well as mainstream movie theatres. Many pubs offer entertainment ranging from live Scottish folk music to pop, rock and jazz, as well as karaoke and quiz nights, while a range of stylish modern bars purvey house, dance and hip-hop to the pre-clubbing crowd.

As with cities all around the world, Edinburgh's nightlife was decimated by restrictions introduced to help control the Covid-19 pandemic, but many venues have coped by staging online events.

Live Music

Edinburgh is a great place to hear traditional Scottish (and Irish) folk music, with a mix of regular spots and impromptu sessions. The Gig Guide (www.gigguide.co.uk) is a free email newsletter and listing website covering live music in Scotland.

★ **Sandy Bell's**   TRADITIONAL MUSIC

(Map p64; ☑ 0131-225 2751; 25 Forrest Rd, EH1 2QH; ⊘ noon-1am Mon-Sat, 12.30pm-midnight Sun; 🚍 2, 23, 27, 35, 41, 42, 45) This unassuming pub has been a stalwart of the traditional-music scene since the 1960s (the founder's wife sang with the Corries). There's music every weekday evening at

ⓘ **WHAT'S ON**

ⓘ **WHAT'S ON**

The List (www.list.co.uk) is an excellent, comprehensive free listings website and magazine covering what's on in Edinburgh and Glasgow. Published every two months, it's available from most newsagents.

9pm, and from 2pm Saturday and 4pm Sunday, plus lots of impromptu sessions.

Caves
LIVE MUSIC

(Map p64; www.unusualvenuesedinburgh.com; 8-12 Niddry St S, EH1 1NS; 35) A spectacular subterranean venue set in the ancient stone vaults beneath the South Bridge, the Caves stages a series of one-off club nights and live-music gigs, as well as *ceilidh* (traditional music) nights during the Edinburgh Festival. Check the What's On link on the website for upcoming events.

Henry's Cellar Bar
LIVE MUSIC

(Map p64; 0131-629 2992; www.facebook.com/henryscellarbar; 16 Morrison St, EH3 8BJ; free-£10; 9pm-3am Sun & Tue-Thu, 8pm-3am Mon, 7pm-3am Fri & Sat; all Lothian Rd buses) One of Edinburgh's most eclectic live-music venues, Henry's has something going on most nights of the week, from rock and indie to 'Balkan-inspired folk', and from funk and hip-hop to hardcore, staging both local bands and acts from around the world.

Bannerman's
LIVE MUSIC

(Map p64; www.facebook.com/bannermans bar; 212 Cowgate, EH1 1NQ; noon-1am Mon-Sat, 12.30pm-1am Sun; ; 35) A long-established music venue – it seems like every Edinburgh student for the last four decades spent half their youth here – Bannerman's straggles through a warren of old vaults beneath South Bridge. It pulls in crowds of students, locals and backpackers with live rock, punk and indie bands five or six nights a week.

Jazz Bar
JAZZ, BLUES

(Map p64; www.thejazzbar.co.uk; 1a Chambers St, EH1 1HR; £3-7; 5pm-3am Sun-Fri, 1.30pm-3am Sat; ; 35, 45) This atmospheric cellar bar, with its polished parquet floors, bare stone walls, candlelit tables and stylish steel-framed chairs, is owned and operated by jazz musicians. There's live music every night from 9pm to 3am, and on Saturday from 3pm. As well as jazz, expect bands playing blues, funk, soul and fusion.

Voodoo Rooms
LIVE MUSIC

(Map p72; 0131-556 7060; www.thevoodoo rooms.com; 19a W Register St, EH2 2AA; free-£20; 4pm-1am Mon-Thu, noon-1am Fri-Sun; St Andrew Sq) Decadent decor of black leather, ornate plasterwork and gilt detailing creates a stylish setting for this complex of bars and performance spaces above the Café Royal

(p91), hosting everything from classic soul and Motown to blues nights, jam sessions and live local bands.

Cinemas

Film buffs will find plenty to keep them happy in Edinburgh's art-house cinemas, while popcorn munchers can choose from a range of multiplexes.

Filmhouse
CINEMA

(Map p64; 0131-228 2688; www.filmhousecin ema.com; 88 Lothian Rd, EH3 9BZ; tickets £7-11; ; all Lothian Rd buses) The Filmhouse is the main venue for the annual Edinburgh International Film Festival (p78) and screens a full programme of art-house, classic, foreign and second-run films, with lots of themes, retrospectives and 70mm screenings. It has wheelchair access to all three screens.

Cameo
CINEMA

(Map p58; 0871 902 5723; www.picturehous es.com; 38 Home St, EH3 9LZ; tickets £7.90-12.40; ; all Tollcross buses) The three-screen, independently owned Cameo is a good old-fashioned cinema (first opened in 1914) showing an imaginative mix of mainstream and art-house movies. There's a programme of late-night films and Sunday matinees, and the seats in screen 1 are big enough to get lost in.

Classical Music, Opera & Ballet

Edinburgh is home to the Scottish Chamber Orchestra (SCO; www.sco.org.uk), one of Europe's finest orchestras and well worth hearing. Its performances are usually held at Queen's Hall (Map p58; 0131-668 2019; www.thequeenshall.net; Clerk St, EH8 9JG; box office 10am-5.15pm Mon-Sat, or to 15min after show begins; all Newington buses) or Usher Hall.

Scottish Opera (www.scottishopera. org.uk) and the Royal Scottish National Orchestra (RSNO; www.rsno.org.uk) are based in Glasgow but regularly perform in Edinburgh, at the Edinburgh Festival Theatre and Usher Hall, respectively.

Edinburgh Festival Theatre
THEATRE

(Map p64; 0131-529 6000; www.capitalthe atres.com/festival; 13-29 Nicolson St, EH8 9FT; box office 10am-7.30pm; all South Bridge buses) A beautifully restored art deco theatre with a modern all-glass frontage, the Festival is the city's main venue for opera, dance and ballet, but also stages musicals, concerts, drama and children's shows.

Usher Hall   CLASSICAL MUSIC

(Map p64; ☑ 0131-228 1155; www.usherhall.co.uk; Lothian Rd, EH1 2EA; ⊙ box office 10am-5.30pm, to 8pm show nights; ☐ all Lothian Rd buses) The architecturally impressive Usher Hall hosts concerts by the RSNO and performances of popular music.

St Giles Cathedral   CLASSICAL MUSIC

(Map p64; www.stgilescathedral.org.uk; High St, EH1 1RE; ☐ 23, 27, 41, 42) The big kirk on the Royal Mile plays host to a regular and varied programme of classical music, including popular lunchtime and evening concerts and organ recitals. The cathedral choir sings at the 10am and 11.30am Sunday services.

Theatre, Musicals & Comedy

★ **Summerhall**   THEATRE

(Map p58; ☑ 0131-560 1580; www.summer hall.co.uk; 1 Summerhall, EH9 1PL; ⊙ box office 10am-6pm; ☐ 41, 42) Formerly Edinburgh University's veterinary school, the Summerhall complex is a major cultural centre and entertainment venue, with old halls and lecture theatres (including an original anatomy lecture theatre) now serving as venues for drama, dance, cinema and comedy. It's also one of the main venues for events during the Edinburgh International Festival (p79).

Royal Lyceum Theatre   THEATRE

(Map p64; ☑ 0131-248 4848; www.lyceum.org.uk; 30b Grindlay St, EH3 9AX; ⊙ box office 10am-5pm Mon-Sat, to 7pm show nights; ♿; ☐ all Lothian Rd buses) A grand Victorian theatre located beside Usher Hall, the Lyceum stages drama, concerts, musicals and ballet.

Traverse Theatre   THEATRE

(Map p64; ☑ 0131-228 1404; www.traverse.co.uk; 10 Cambridge St, EH1 2ED; ⊙ box office 10am-6pm Mon-Sat, to 7pm show nights; ☎; ☐ all Lothian Rd buses) The Traverse is the main focus for new Scottish writing; it stages an adventurous programme of contemporary drama and dance. The box office is only open on Sunday (from 4pm) when there's a show on.

Stand Comedy Club   COMEDY

(Map p72; ☑ 0131-558 7272; www.thestand.co.uk; 5 York Pl, EH1 3EB; tickets £3-18; ⊙ from 7.30pm Mon-Sat, from 12.30pm Sun; ☐ St Andrew Sq) The Stand, founded in 1995, is Edinburgh's main independent comedy venue. It's an intimate cabaret bar with performances every night and a free Sunday lunchtime show.

Sport

Edinburgh has two rival football (soccer) teams playing in the Scottish Premier League – **Heart of Midlothian** (aka Hearts, nicknamed the Jam Tarts or Jambos), founded in 1874, and **Hibernian** (aka Hibs, Hibbies or Hi-bees), founded in 1875.

Hearts has their home ground at **Tynecastle Stadium** (www.heartsfc.co.uk; Gorgie Rd, EH11 2NL; ☐ 1, 2, 3, 25, 33), southwest of the city centre in Gorgie. Hibernian's home ground is northeast of the city centre at **Easter Road Stadium** (www.hibernianfc.co.uk; 12 Albion Pl, EH7 5QG; ☐ 1, 13, 35).

The domestic football season lasts from August to May and most matches are played at 3pm on Saturday or 7.30pm on Tuesday or Wednesday.

Each year, from January to March, Scotland's national rugby team takes part in the Six Nations Rugby Union Championship (www.sixnationsrugby.com). The most important fixture is the clash against England for the Calcutta Cup, which takes place in Edinburgh in even-numbered years (and at Twickenham in London in odd-numbered years). At club level, the season runs from September to May.

🔒 Shopping

Princes St is Edinburgh's principal shopping street, lined with all the big high-street stores, with many smaller shops along pedestrianised Rose St, and more expensive designer boutiques on George St and Thistle St.

For more offbeat shopping – including fashion, music, crafts, gifts and jewellery – head for the cobbled lanes of Cockburn, Victoria and St Mary's Sts, all near the Royal Mile in the Old Town; William St in the western part of the New Town; and the Stockbridge district, immediately north of the New Town.

There are two big shopping centres in the New Town – **Waverley Mall** (Map p72; ☑ 0131-557 3759; www.waverleymall.com; Waverley Bridge, EH1 1BQ; ⊙ 9am-7pm Mon-Sat, 10am-6pm Sun; ☐ all Princes St buses), at the eastern end of Princes St, and the massive new development of **St James Quarter** (Map p72; www.stjamesquarter.com; 1 Leith St, EH1 3SS; ☐ St Andrew Sq) at the top of Leith St.

There's also **Multrees Walk** (Map p72; www.multreeswalk.co.uk; St Andrew Sq, EH1 3DQ; ☐ St Andrew Sq), a designer shopping complex with a flagship Harvey Nichols store

DON'T MISS

EDINBURGH FARMERS MARKET

The **Edinburgh Farmers Market** (Map p64; ☑ 0131-220 8580; www.facebook.com/edinburghfarmersmarket; Castle Tce, EH1 2AE; ⊕9am-2pm Sat; ☐ all Lothian Rd buses), a colourful weekly event, attracts stallholders who sell everything from wild boar, venison and home-cured pedigree bacon to organic bread, free-range eggs, honey and handmade soap.

on the eastern side of St Andrew Sq, and **Ocean Terminal** (☑ 0131-555 8888; www.oceanterminal.com; Ocean Dr, EH6 6JJ; ⊕10am-8pm Mon-Fri, to 7pm Sat, 11am-6pm Sun; ☎; ☐11, 22, 34, 36, 200), a huge mall in Leith.

🏛 Old Town

Armstrong's   VINTAGE
(Map p64; ☑ 0131-220 5557; www.armstrongsvintage.co.uk; 83 Grassmarket, EH1 2HJ; ⊕10am-5.30pm Mon-Thu, to 6pm Fri & Sat, noon-6pm Sun; ☐2) Armstrong's is an Edinburgh fashion institution (established in 1840, no less), a quality vintage-clothes emporium offering everything from elegant 1940s dresses to funky 1970s flares. Aside from the retro fashion, it's a great place to hunt for preloved kilts and Harris tweed, or to seek inspiration for that fancy-dress party.

Ragamuffin   FASHION & ACCESSORIES
(Map p64; ☑ 0131-557 6007; www.facebook.com/ragamuffinclothesandknitwear; 278 Canongate, EH8 8AA; ⊕10am-6pm Mon-Sat, noon-5pm Sun; ☐35) Quality Scottish knitwear and fabrics, including cashmere from Johnstons of Elgin, Fair Isle sweaters and Harris tweed.

Geoffrey (Tailor) Inc   FASHION & ACCESSORIES
(Map p64; ☑ 0131-557 0256; www.geoffreykilts.co.uk; 57-59 High St, EH1 1SR; ⊕9.30am-6pm Mon-Sat, 10.30am-5.30pm Sun; ☐35) Geoffrey can fit you out in traditional Highland dress, or run up a kilt in your own clan tartan. The store's offshoot, **21st Century Kilts** (www.21stcenturykilts.com; based at Duntarvie Castle in West Lothian), offers modern fashion kilts in a variety of fabrics.

Bill Baber   FASHION & ACCESSORIES
(Map p64; ☑ 0131-225 3249; www.billbaber.com; 66 Grassmarket, EH1 2JR; ⊕9am-6pm Mon-Sat;

☐2) This family-run designer-knitwear studio has been in the business for more than 40 years, producing stylish and colourful creations using linen, merino wool, silk and cotton.

Royal Mile Whiskies   DRINKS
(Map p64; ☑ 0131-225 3383; www.royalmilewhiskies.com; 379 High St, EH1 1PW; ⊕10am-6pm; ☐23, 27, 41, 42) If it's a drap of the cratur ye're after, this place has a selection of single malts in miniature and full-size bottles. There's also a range of blended whiskies, Irish whisky and bourbon, and you can buy online, too.

🏛 New Town

Jenners   DEPARTMENT STORE
(Map p72; ☑ 0131-225 2442; www.houseoffraser.co.uk; 48 Princes St, EH2 2YJ; ⊕9.30am-6.30pm Mon-Wed, to 8pm Thu, to 7pm Fri, 9am-7pm Sat, 11am-6pm Sun; ☐ Princes St) Founded in 1838, and acquired by House of Fraser in 2005, Jenners is the 'Grand Old Lady' of Scottish department stores. It stocks a wide range of quality goods, both classic and contemporary.

Plans for Jenners to move to new premises in St James Quarter in 2021 have been put on hold because of the Covid-19 pandemic.

Harvey Nichols   DEPARTMENT STORE
(Map p72; ☑ 0131-524 8388; www.harveynichols.com; 30-34 St Andrew Sq, EH2 2AD; ⊕10am-6pm Mon-Wed, to 8pm Thu, to 7pm Fri & Sat, 11am-6pm Sun; ☐ St Andrew Sq) The jewel in the crown of Edinburgh's shopping scene has four floors of designer labels and eye-popping price tags.

🏛 Stockbridge

⭐**Golden Hare Books**   BOOKS
(Map p72; ☑ 0131-629 1396; www.goldenharebooks.com; 68 St Stephen St, EH3 5AQ; ⊕10am-6pm; ☐24, 29, 36, 42) Independent bookshops don't get lovelier than this. The Golden Hare – voted UK Independent Bookshop of the Year in 2019 – boasts a top-notch selection of books, an enchanting children's nook, and a small but perfectly formed events programme. A must if you love books, book design and beautiful shops.

Stockbridge Market
MARKET

(Map p72; www.stockbridgemarket.com; cnr Kerr & Saunders Sts; ⊙10am-5pm Sun; 🚌24, 29, 36, 42) On Sunday the local community's focus is Stockbridge Market, set in a leafy square next to the bridge that gives the district its name. Wares range from fresh Scottish produce to handmade ceramics, jewellery, soaps and cosmetics. Grab an espresso from Steampunk Coffee, which operates out of a 1970s VW campervan.

Galerie Mirages
JEWELLERY

(Map p58; ☑0131-315 2603; www.galeriemirages.com; 46a Raeburn Pl, EH4 1HL; ⊙10am-5.30pm Mon-Sat, noon-4.30pm Sun; 🚌24, 29, 42) An Aladdin's cave packed with jewellery, textiles and handicrafts from all over the world, Mirages is best known for its silver, amber and gemstone jewellery in both culturally traditional and contemporary designs.

🏠 South Edinburgh

Meadows Pottery
CERAMICS

(Map p58; ☑0131-662 4064; www.themeadowspottery.com; 11a Summerhall Pl, EH9 1QE; ⊙10am-5pm Mon-Fri, to 4.30pm Sat; 🚌2, 41, 42) This small shop sells a range of colourful, high-fired oxidised stoneware, both domestic and decorative, all hand thrown on the premises. If you can't find what you want, you can commission custom-made pieces.

Backbeat
MUSIC

(Map p58; ☑0131-668 2666; 31 E Crosscauseway, EH8 9HE; ⊙10am-5.30pm Mon-Sat; 🚌all Newington buses) If you're hunting for secondhand vinyl from way back, this cramped little shop has a stunning and constantly changing collection of jazz, blues, rock and soul, plus lots of '60s and '70s stuff, though you'll have to take some time to hunt through the clutter.

Lighthouse
BOOKS

(Map p64; ☑0131-662 9112; www.lighthousebookshop.com; 43 W Nicolson St, EH8 9DB; ⊙11am-6pm Mon-Sat, 11.30am-5pm Sun; 🚌41, 42) Lighthouse is a radical independent bookshop that supports both small publishers and local writers. It stocks a wide range of political, gay and feminist literature, as well as non-mainstream fiction and nonfiction.

🏠 Leith

Kinloch Anderson
FASHION & ACCESSORIES

(☑0131-555 1390; www.kinlochanderson.com; 4 Dock St, EH6 6EY; ⊙9am-5.30pm Mon-Sat; 🚌16, 22, 35, 36) One of the best tartan shops in Edinburgh, Kinloch Anderson was founded in 1868 and is still family run. It is a supplier of kilts and Highland dress to the royal family.

ℹ️ Information

EMERGENCY

You can report a crime in person at the following 24-hour police stations, or by calling the non-emergency number (for crimes that have already taken place, eg a theft). Use the emergency number (999 or 112) for crimes in progress or where there is a risk of injury or loss of life.

Gayfield Square Police Station (☑non-emergency 101; www.scotland.police.uk; Gayfield Sq, EH1 3NW; ⊙24hr; 🚌all Leith Walk buses)

St Leonards Police Station (☑non-emergency 101; www.scotland.police.uk; 14 St Leonards St, EH3 8DY; ⊙24hr; 🚌14)

INTERNET ACCESS

There are countless cafes, pubs and restaurants all over Edinburgh offering free wi-fi. Internet cafes like **Here** (☑0131-228 9097; 23 Leven St, EH3 9LH; ⊙9am-8pm; 🛜; 🚌all Tollcross buses) are a dying breed, but can be useful if you lose your phone or need access to a printer.

MEDIA

Newspapers The Scotsman (www.scotsman.com) is a quality daily covering Scottish, UK and international news, sport and current affairs; Scotland on Sunday is the weekend newspaper from the same publisher. The Edinburgh Evening News (www.edinburghnews.com) covers news and entertainment in the city and its environs.

Radio The BBC Radio Scotland (www.bbc.co.uk/radioscotland) programme Good Morning Scotland, from 6am weekdays, covers Scottish current affairs.

MEDICAL SERVICES

For urgent medical advice you can call the **NHS 24 Helpline** (☑111; www.nhs24.scot). Chemists (pharmacists) can advise you on minor ailments. At least one local chemist remains open round the clock – its location will be displayed in the windows of other chemists.

For urgent dental treatment, you can visit the walk-in **Chalmers Dental Centre** (☑0131-536 4800; www.nhslothian.scot.nhs.uk; 3 Chalmers St, EH3 9EW; ⊙9am-4.45pm Mon-Thu, to

4.15pm Fri; 🚌 23, 27, 35, 45, 47). In the case of a dental emergency in the evenings or at weekends, call the **Lothian Dental Advice Line** (🖉 0131-536 4800; ⊙ 5-10pm Mon-Fri, 9am-10pm Sat & Sun).

Boots (🖉 0131-225 6757; 48 Shandwick Pl, EH2 4SA; ⊙ 8am-8pm Mon-Fri, 9am-6pm Sat, 10.30am-5pm Sun; 🚌 West End) Chemist open longer hours than most.

Edinburgh Royal Infirmary (🖉 0131-536 1000; www.nhslothian.scot.nhs.uk; 51 Little France Cres, Old Dalkeith Rd, EH16 4SA; ⊙ 24hr; 🚌 7, 8, 24, 33, 38, 49) Edinburgh's main general hospital; has a 24-hour accident and emergency department.

Western General Hospital (🖉 0131-537 1000; www.nhslothian.scot.nhs.uk; Crewe Rd S, EH4 2XU; ⊙ 8am-9pm; 🚌 16, 19, 24, 29, 37, 38, 47) For non-life-threatening injuries and ailments, you can attend the Minor Injuries Clinic here without having to make an appointment.

Royal Hospital for Children and Young People (🖉 0131-536 0000; www.nhslothian. scot; 51 Little France Cres, Old Dalkeith Rd, EH16 4SA; ⊙ 24hr; 🚌 7, 8, 24, 33, 38, 49) Brand new hospital (opened January 2021) with a casualty department for children aged under 13; located next to the Edinburgh Royal Infirmary.

Edinburgh Rape Crisis Centre (🖉 08088 01 03 02; www.rapecrisisscotland.org.uk)

POST

The UK postal system is generally reliable. You can find up-to-date rates at www.royalmail.com.

Edinburgh City Post Office (Map p72; upper level, Waverley Mall, Princes St, EH1 1BQ; ⊙ 10am-5.30pm Mon-Sat; 🚌 all Princes St buses)

Frederick St Post Office (Map p72; 40 Frederick St, EH2 1EY; ⊙ 9am-5.30pm Mon & Wed-Fri, 9.30am-5.30pm Tue, 9.30am-12.30pm Sat; 🚌 24, 29, 42)

St Mary's St Post Office (Map p64; 46 St Mary's St, EH1 1SX; ⊙ 9am-5.30pm Mon-Fri, to 12.30pm Sat; 🚌 35)

TOURIST INFORMATION

Edinburgh Tourist Office (Edinburgh iCentre; Map p64; 🖉 0131-473 3820; www.visitscot land.com/info/services/edinburgh-icen tre-p234441; 249 High St, Royal Mile, EH1 1YJ; ⊙ 10am-4.30pm Mon-Sat, to 4pm Sun Oct-Mar, longer hours Apr-Sep; ⊙; 🚌 23, 27, 41, 42) Accommodation-booking service, free city maps, gift shop and bookshop, and sales of tickets for CalMac ferries and CityLink and National Express buses.

USEFUL WEBSITES

Edinburgh Festival Guide (www.edinburgh festivalcity.com) Everything you need to know about Edinburgh's many festivals.

Lonely Planet (www.lonelyplanet.com/edin burgh) Destination information, hotel bookings, traveller forum and more.

The List (www.list.co.uk) Local listings and reviews for restaurants, bars, clubs and theatres.

VisitScotland Edinburgh (www.visitscotland. com/edinburgh) Official Scottish tourist board site.

🛈 Getting There & Away

AIR

Edinburgh Airport (EDI; 🖉 0844 448 8833; www.edinburghairport.com), 8 miles west of the city, has numerous flights to other parts of Scotland and the UK, Ireland and mainland Europe.

Loganair (LM; 🖉 0344 800 2855; www.loga nair.co.uk) operates flights daily (except Sunday) from Edinburgh to Orkney and Shetland, and weekly to Stornoway.

BUS

Edinburgh Bus Station (Map p72; St Andrew Sq, EH1 3DX; left-luggage lockers per 12hr £8-12; ⊙ 4.30am-midnight Sun-Thu, to 12.30am Fri & Sat; 🚌 St Andrew Sq) is at the northeastern corner of St Andrew Sq, with pedestrian entrances from the square and from Elder St. For timetable information, contact **Traveline** (🖉 0871 200 22 33; www.traveline.info).

Scottish Citylink (🖉 0871 266 3333; www. citylink.co.uk) buses connect Edinburgh with all of Scotland's cities and major towns. The following are sample one-way fares departing from Edinburgh.

Destination	Fare (£)
Aberdeen	35
Dundee	18.60
Fort William	39
Glasgow	8.50
Inverness	34
Portree	57
Stirling	9.30

It's also worth checking with **Megabus** (🖉 0900 1600 900; https://uk.megabus.com) for cheap intercity bus fares (from as little as £5) from Edinburgh to Aberdeen, Dundee, Glasgow, Inverness and Perth.

There are various buses to Edinburgh from London and the rest of the UK.

CAR & MOTORCYCLE

Arriving in or leaving Edinburgh by car during the morning and evening rush hours (7.30am to 9.30am and 4.30pm to 6.30pm Monday to Friday) is an experience you can live without. Try to time your journey to avoid these periods.

Major roads leading into and out of Edinburgh:
➡ M90 north to Perth
➡ M9 northwest to Stirling
➡ M8 west to Glasgow
➡ A7 south to Galashiels
➡ A68 south to Melrose and Jedburgh
➡ A1 southeast to Berwick-upon-Tweed

TRAIN

The main rail terminus in Edinburgh is **Waverley train station**, located in the heart of the city. Trains arriving from, and departing for, the west also stop at **Haymarket station**, which is more convenient for the West End.

You can buy tickets, make reservations and get travel information at the **Edinburgh Rail Travel Centre** (Waverley station, EH1 1BB; ⊙5am-midnight Mon-Sat, 7am-midnight Sun; 🚌all Princes St buses). For fare and timetable information, phone the **National Rail Enquiry Service** (☑03457 48 49 50; www.nationalrail.co.uk) or use the journey planner on the website.

If you're travelling as a pair, consider purchasing a **Two Together Railcard** (www.twotogether-railcard.co.uk; per year £30), which offers you one-third off your combined fares on train rides taken throughout Great Britain (outside peak travel times).

ScotRail (☑0344 811 0141; www.scotrail.co.uk) operates regular train services from Edinburgh to:

Aberdeen (£37, 2½ hours, hourly)
Dundee (£20, 1¼ hours, hourly)
Glasgow (£15.30, 50 minutes, every 15 minutes)
Inverness (£45, 3½ hours)

ℹ Getting Around

TO/FROM THE AIRPORT
Bus

Lothian Buses operates a number of services to the airport (www.lothianbuses.co.uk/airport). Airlink 100 runs from South St David St (between Princes St and St Andrew Sq) to the airport (one way/return £4.50/7.50, 30 minutes, every 12 minutes from 4am to midnight) via the West End and Haymarket. Skylink services 200 and 300 run from the airport to Ocean Terminal via north Edinburgh, and to Surgeons' Hall via west Edinburgh, respectively.

ℹ **BUS INFO ON YOUR PHONE**

Transport for Edinburgh has created free smartphone apps (www.tfeapp.com) that provide route maps, time-tables and live waiting times for city buses and trams. The companion m-tickets app allows you to buy bus and tram tickets on your phone (minimum purchase is £4).

Taxi

An airport taxi to the city centre costs around £20 and takes about 20 to 30 minutes.

Tram

Edinburgh Trams (www.edinburghtrams.com) run from the airport to the city centre (one way/return £6.50/9, 33 minutes, every six to eight minutes from 6.15am to 10.45pm).

BICYCLE

Thanks to the efforts of local cycling campaign group Spokes (www.spokes.org.uk) and a bike-friendly city council, Edinburgh is well equipped with bike lanes and dedicated cycle tracks. You can buy a map of the city's cycle routes from most bike shops.

Biketrax (p77) rents out mountain bikes, hybrid bikes, road bikes, Brompton folding bikes and e-bikes. You'll need a debit- or credit-card deposit and photographic ID.

BUS

Bus timetables, route maps and fare guides are posted at all main bus and tram stops, and you can pick up a copy of the free *Lothian Buses Route Map* from Lothian Buses' **TravelHub** (Map p64; 31 Waverley Bridge, EH1 1BQ; ⊙9am-5pm Mon-Sat; 🚌all Princes St buses).

Adult fares within the city are £1.80; purchase from the bus driver. Children aged under five travel free and those aged five to 15 pay a flat fare of 90p.

On Lothian Buses you must pay the driver the exact fare, but First buses will give change. Lothian bus drivers also sell a day ticket (£4.50) that gives one day of unlimited travel on Lothian buses and trams (within the City Zone, ie not including the airport); a family day ticket (up to two adults and three children) costs £9.50.

Night-service buses, which run hourly between midnight and 5am, charge a flat fare of £3.

You can also buy a Ridacard (from TravelHub; not available from bus drivers) that gives unlimited travel for one week for £20.

Lost-property enquiries should be made online (www.lothianbuses.com/lost-property).

CAR & MOTORCYCLE

Though useful for day trips beyond the city, a car in central Edinburgh is more of a liability than a convenience. There is restricted access on Princes St, George St and Charlotte Sq, many streets are one way, and finding a parking place in the city centre is like striking gold. Queen's Dr around Holyrood Park is closed to motorised traffic on Sunday.

Car Rental

All the big international car-rental agencies have offices in Edinburgh, including **Avis** (0344-544 6059; www.avis.co.uk; 24 E London St, EH7 4BQ; 8am-6pm Mon-Fri, to 3pm Sat, 10am-2pm Sun; 10,11) and **Europcar** (0371-384 3453; www.europcar.co.uk; Platform 2, Waverley Station, EH1 1BB; 7am-5pm; all Princes St buses).

There are many smaller, local agencies that offer better rates. **Arnold Clark** (0131-333 0124; www.arnoldclarkrental.com; 16-18 Bankhead Dr, EH11 4DJ; 8am-6pm Mon-Fri, to 5pm Sat, to 4pm Sun) charges from £37/189 per day/week for a small car, including VAT and insurance. It's close to Edinburgh Park train station and tram stop.

Parking

There's no parking on main roads into the city from 7.30am to 6.30pm Monday to Saturday. Also, parking in the city centre can be a nightmare.

On-street parking is controlled by self-service ticket machines from 8.30am to 6.30pm Monday to Saturday, and costs from £2.40 to £4.90 per hour, with a 30-minute to four-hour maximum.

If you break the rules, you'll get a fine, often within minutes of your ticket expiring – Edinburgh's parking wardens are both numerous and notorious. The fine is £60, reduced to £30 if you pay up within 14 days. Cars parked illegally will be clamped or towed away. There are large, long-stay car parks at the Omni Centre, Blackfriars St, Castle Tce, Holyrood Rd and Fountain Park. Motorcycles can be parked free at designated areas in the city centre.

TAXI

Edinburgh's black taxis can be hailed in the street, ordered by phone (extra 80p charge) or picked up at one of the many central ranks. The minimum charge is £3 (£4 at night) for the first 450m, then 25p for every subsequent 168m – a typical 2-mile trip across the city centre will cost around £6 to £7. Tipping is up to you – because of the high fares, local people rarely tip on short journeys, but they occasionally round up to the nearest 50p on longer ones.

Central Taxis (0131-229 2468; www.taxis-edinburgh.co.uk)

City Cabs (0131-228 1211; www.citycabs.co.uk)

TRAM

Edinburgh's tram system (www.edinburghtrams.com) consists of one line from Edinburgh Airport to York Pl, at the top of Leith Walk, via Haymarket, the West End and Princes St.

Tickets are integrated with the city's Lothian Buses, costing £1.80 for a single journey within the city boundary, or £6.50 to the airport. Trams run every eight to 10 minutes Monday to Saturday and every 12 to 15 minutes on Sunday, from 5.30am to 11pm.

DAY TRIPS ON THE BORDERS RAILWAY

The longest stretch of new railway line to be built in the UK for more than 100 years, the Borders Railway (www.scotrail.co.uk/scotland-by-rail/borders-railway) opened in 2015, linking Edinburgh with Tweedbank near Melrose. With trains running every 30 minutes, it's a great way to take day trips into the countryside south of the capital.

Top of the list of attractions is Abbotsford (p445), Sir Walter Scott's country house, which lies a pleasant 20-minute walk from the terminus at Tweedbank, most of it along the banks of the River Tweed. Other trips are described in the *Borders Railway Guide* (£9.90; www.bordersrailwayguide.co.uk), available from Edinburgh tourist office.

AROUND EDINBURGH

Queensferry

POP 9030

Queensferry, also known as South Queensferry, is at the narrowest part of the Firth of Forth where ferries have crossed to Fife from the earliest times. The village takes its name from Queen Margaret (1046–93), who gave pilgrims free passage across the firth on their way to St Andrews. Ferries continued to operate until 1964, when the graceful **Forth Road Bridge** was opened; this was followed by a second road bridge, the **Queensferry Crossing** (2017).

ROSSLYN CHAPEL

Rosslyn Chapel (Collegiate Church of St Matthew; ☏0131-440 2159; www.rosslynchapel.com; Chapel Loan, Roslin, EH25 9PU; adult/child £9/free; ☉9.30am-6pm Mon-Sat Jun-Aug, to 5pm Sep-May, noon-4.45pm Sun year-round; ᴾ; 🚍37) Many years may have passed since Dan Brown's novel *The Da Vinci Code* came out, but floods of visitors still descend on the beautiful and enigmatic church made famous by the book – Rosslyn Chapel. Built in the mid-15th century for Sir William St Clair, third prince of Orkney, it has an ornately carved interior – at odds with the architectural fashion of its time – that's a monument to the mason's art, rich in symbolic imagery. Hourly talks by qualified guides are included with admission.

As well as flowers, vines, angels and biblical figures, the carved stones include many examples of the pagan Green Man; other figures are associated with Freemasonry and the Knights Templar. Intriguingly, there are also carvings of plants from the Americas that predate Columbus' voyage of discovery. The symbolism of these images has led some researchers to conclude that Rosslyn is some kind of secret Templar repository, and it has been claimed that hidden vaults beneath the chapel could conceal anything from the Holy Grail or the head of John the Baptist to the body of Christ himself. The chapel is owned by the Scottish Episcopal Church and services are still held here on Sunday mornings.

The chapel is on the eastern edge of the village of Roslin, 7 miles south of Edinburgh's centre. Lothian bus 37 to Penicuik Deanburn runs from Edinburgh's West End to Roslin (£1.80, one hour, every 15 minutes). Note that bus 37 to Bush does not go via Roslin, you want bus 37 to Penicuik – check the bus front and if in doubt ask the driver.

Predating the first road bridge by 74 years, the magnificent **Forth Bridge** – only outsiders ever call it the Forth Rail Bridge – was one of the finest engineering achievements of the 19th century. Opened in 1890 as the world's first major steel structure, it has three huge cantilevers spanning 1630m and took 53,000 tonnes of steel, 6.5 million rivets and the lives of 73 men to build.

Hopetoun House HISTORIC BUILDING
(☏0131-331 2451; www.hopetoun.co.uk; EH30 9SL; adult/child house & grounds £11.50/6, grounds only £5.50/3.50; ☉10.30am-5pm Easter-Sep, last entry 4pm; ᴾ) One of Scotland's finest stately homes, Hopetoun House has a superb location in lovely grounds beside the Firth of Forth. The family seat of the earls of Hopetoun, it has two parts: the older, built between 1699 and 1707 and dominated by a splendid stairwell with (modern) trompe l'oeil paintings, and the newer, designed between 1720 and 1750 by three members of the Adam family – William and his sons Robert and John.

The highlights are the red and yellow Adam drawing rooms, lined in silk damask, and the view from the roof terrace. Britain's most elegant equine accommodation – where the earls once housed their pampered racehorses – is now the stylish **Stables Kitchen** (☏0131-331 3661; mains £5-11, afternoon tea per person £22; ☉11am-4.30pm Easter-Sep; 🍴), a delightful spot for lunch or afternoon tea.

The 2428-hectare grounds, where red deer roam in summer, offer sweeping Firth of Forth views. Rangers lead walks on the last Sunday of the month at 3.30pm, as well as activities such as foraging, pond-dipping and bushcraft.

Hopetoun House is 2 miles west of Queensferry along the coast road. Driving from Edinburgh, turn off the A90 onto the A904 just before the Forth Bridge and follow the signs.

★ Forth Boat Tours BOATING
(☏0131-331 3030; www.forthtours.com; Hawes Pier, EH30 9TB; adult/child £16/9, with Inchcolm stopover £21/12.60; ☉Easter-Oct; 👶) Forth Boat Tours runs daily 1½-hour trips along the Firth of Forth, heading beneath its three majestic bridges, storied islands and shoreline landmarks (including the epic Edinburgh skyline) to Inchcolm (p104). Most voyages offer a 1½-hour stopover on the island, a place of blonde beaches, squawking seabirds and abandoned defences that's famed for its medieval abbey – it's well worth it.

Rosslyn Chapel

DECIPHERING ROSSLYN

Rosslyn Chapel is a small building, but the density of decoration inside can be overwhelming. It's well worth buying the official guidebook by the Earl of Rosslyn first; find a bench in the gardens and have a skim through before going into the chapel – the background information will make your visit all the more interesting. The book also offers a useful self-guided tour of the chapel, and explains the legend of the Master Mason and the Apprentice.

Entrance is through the ❶ **north door**. Take a pew and sit for a while to allow your eyes to adjust to the dim interior; then look up at the ceiling vault, decorated with engraved roses, lilies and stars, (Can you spot the sun and the moon?). Walk left along the north aisle to reach the Lady Chapel, separated from the rest of the church by the ❷ **Mason's Pillar** and the ❸ **Apprentice Pillar**. Here you'll find carvings of ❹ **Lucifer**, the Fallen Angel, and the ❺ **Green Man**. Nearby are ❻ **carvings** that appear to resemble Indian corn (maize). Finally, go to the western end and look up at the wall – in the left corner is the head of the ❼ **Apprentice**; to the right is the (rather worn) head of the ❽ **Master Mason**.

ROSSLYN CHAPEL & THE DA VINCI CODE

Dan Brown was referencing Rosslyn Chapel's alleged links to the Knights Templar and the Freemasons – unusual symbols found among the carvings, and the fact that a descendant of its founder, William St Clair, was a Grand Master Mason – when he chose it as the setting for his novel's denouement. Rosslyn is indeed a coded work, written in stone, but its meaning depends on your point of view. See *The Rosslyn Hoax?* by Robert LD Cooper for an alternative interpretation of the chapel's symbolism.

EXPLORE SOME MORE

After visiting the chapel, head downhill to see the spectacularly sited ruins of Roslin Castle, then take a walk along leafy Roslin Glen.

Lucifer, the Fallen Angel
At head height, to the left of the second window from the left, is an upside-down angel bound with rope, a symbol often associated with Freemasonry. The arch above is decorated with the Dance of Death.

The Apprentice
High in the corner, beneath an empty statue niche, is the head of the murdered Apprentice, with a deep wound in his forehead above the right eye. Legend says the Apprentice was murdered in a jealous rage by the Master Mason. The worn head on the side wall to the left of the Apprentice is that of his mother.

The Master Mason
❽

N..Do..

Baptistry

PRACTICAL TIPS

Local guides give hourly talks throughout the day, which are included in the admission price. No photography is allowed inside the chapel.

Green Man
On a boss at the base of the arch between the second and third windows from the left is the finest example of more than a hundred 'green man' carvings in the chapel, pagan symbols of spring, fertility and rebirth.

MISTY RIVER / SHUTTERSTOCK ©

Crypt

④

② ⑤
Mason's Pillar

③

orth Aisle

Altar

Choir

South Aisle

⑥

⑦

The Apprentice Pillar
This is perhaps the chapel's most beautiful carving. Four vines spiral up the pillar, issuing from the mouths of eight dragons at its base. At the top is Isaac, son of Abraham, lying bound upon the altar.

OSCAR ELIAS/ALAMY STOCK PHOTO ©

Indian Corn
The frieze around the second window on the south wall is said to represent Indian corn (maize), but it predates Columbus' discovery of the New World in 1492. Other carvings seem to resemble aloe vera.

❶ Getting There & Away

Queensferry lies on the southern bank of the Firth of Forth, 8 miles west of Edinburgh city centre. Lothian Country (www.lothiancountry.co.uk) bus 43 runs from Edinburgh (Princes St) to the village centre (£2.80, 45 minutes, every 20 minutes). It's a 10-minute walk from the bus stop to Hawes Pier.

Trains go from Edinburgh's Waverley and Haymarket stations to Dalmeny station (£4.90, 15 minutes, two to four hourly). From the station exit, Hawes Pier is five minutes' walk along a footpath (across the road, behind the bus stop) that leads north beside the railway and then downhill under the Forth Bridge. The village centre is 15 minutes away – head left when the footpath forks, via the scenic woodland of Ferry Glen.

Inchcolm

Inchcolm Abbey   ABBEY

(HES; www.historicenvironment.scot; KY3 0UA; adult/child £6/3.60; ⊙ 9.30am-5.30pm Apr-Sep, to 4pm Oct) Known as the 'Iona of the East', the island of Inchcolm (meaning 'St Columba's Island') lies east of the Forth bridges, less than a mile off the Fife coast. Only 800m long, it's home to the ruins of Inchcolm Abbey, one of Scotland's best-preserved medieval abbeys, founded by Augustinian priors in 1123.

Access is by ferry (www.maidoftheforth.co.uk; Hawes Pier, EH30 9TB; adult/child £21/11.60) from Queensferry. The trip also gives you the chance to see the island's grey seals, as well as puffins and other seabirds.

Forth Boat Tours (p101) also run trips to the island, including a cruise beneath the three Forth bridges.

North Berwick & Around

North Berwick is an attractive Victorian seaside resort with long sandy beaches and a small harbour. It's also a popular golfing destination, with three courses in and around the town and a dozen more within easy reach, including the world-famous Open Championship course at Muirfield (www.muirfield.org.uk).

Scottish Seabird Centre   NATURE CENTRE

(☑ 01620-890202; www.seabird.org; The Harbour, EH39 4SS; adult/child £11.95/7.95; ⊙ 10am-6pm Apr-Aug, to 5pm Feb, Mar, Sep & Oct, to 4pm Nov & Dec, 11am-4pm Jan; ℗ ♿) ✐ Top marks to the bright spark who came up with the idea for this centre, an ornithologist's paradise that uses remote-control video cameras sited on Bass Rock and other islands to relay live images of nesting gannets and other seabirds (including puffins if you're lucky). You can control the cameras yourself and zoom in on scenes of cosy gannet domesticity. For real-life close encounters of the bird kind, check out the Seabird Boat Trips offered by the centre.

Tantallon Castle   RUINS

(HES; ☑ 01620-892727; www.historicenvironment.scot; EH39 5PN; adult/child £6/3.60; ⊙ 9.30am-5.30pm Apr-Sep, 10am-4pm Oct-Mar; ℗) Perched on a cliff 3 miles east of North Berwick is the spectacular ruin of Tantallon Castle. Built around 1350, the red-sandstone fortress was the residence of the Douglas earls of Angus (the Red Douglases), defended on one side by a series of ditches and on the other by an almost sheer drop into the sea. Often attacked, it finally succumbed to an English bombardment in the 17th century – but its battlement views remain as mighty as ever.

Dirleton Castle   CASTLE

(HES; ☑ 01620-850330; www.historicenvironment.scot; Dirleton EH39 5ER; adult/child £6/3.60; ⊙ 9.30am-5.30pm Apr-Sep, 10am-4pm Oct-Mar; ℗) ✐ Two miles west of North Berwick is this impressive medieval fortress with massive round towers, a drawbridge and a horrific pit dungeon, surrounded rather incongruously by beautiful, manicured gardens.

Seabird Boat Trips   BOATING

(☑ 01620-890202; www.seabird.org; The Harbour, EH39 4SS; adult/child from £26/10; ⊙ Easter-autumn) The Scottish Seabird Centre runs catamaran and high-speed RIB boat trips exploring the Forth islands' riotous birdlife – including the squawking, spiralling spectacle of the world's largest northern gannet colony on Bass Rock, and a plethora of puffins on the Isle of May (the UK's top breeding site). Choose from short cruises or stopovers with several hours to get acquainted.

❶ Getting There & Away

North Berwick is 24 miles east of Edinburgh. East Coast operates two bus services between Edinburgh and North Berwick: the 124 (£4.90, 1¼ hours, every 30 minutes) and the X5

(£4.90, one hour, hourly Monday to Saturday). Both stop at Dirleton Castle.

Eve Coaches (www.eveinfo.co.uk) bus 120 from North Berwick to Dunbar stops near Tantallon Castle (£1.50, 11 minutes, hourly).

There are frequent trains between North Berwick and Edinburgh (£7, 35 minutes, hourly).

Linlithgow

POP 13,460

This ancient royal burgh is one of Scotland's oldest towns, though much of it 'only' dates from the 15th to 17th centuries. Birthplace of Mary, Queen of Scots, and other Stuart monarchs, it's also traversed by the scenic Union Canal on its journey from Falkirk to Edinburgh.

The town centre radiates around the ornately carved Cross Well, which dates from the 19th century. Despite some ugly modern buildings and occasional traffic congestion, it retains a certain charm, and the town makes a worthwhile day trip from Edinburgh.

There's a self-service tourist information point (☑01506-282720; www.linlithgow burghhalls.com; Burgh Halls, The Cross, EH49 7AH; ☺9am-5pm Mon-Sat, 11am-5pm Sun; 🗣) in the Burgh Halls, near the Linlithgow Palace entrance.

Linlithgow Palace   PALACE

(HES; ☑01506-842896; www.historicenvironment.scot; Kirkgate; adult/child £9/5.40; ☺9.30am-5.30pm Apr-Sep, 10am-4pm Oct-Mar; P) ✔ This magnificent loch-side palace was begun by James I in 1424, and became a favourite royal residence – James V was born here in 1512, as was his daughter Mary (later Queen of Scots) in 1542, and Bonnie Prince Charlie visited in 1745. The elaborately carved King's Fountain, the centrepiece of the palace courtyard, flowed with wine during Charlie's stay – commissioned by James V in 1537, it's Britain's oldest fountain. Atop the northwestern tower are sweeping views from Queen Margaret's Bower.

Visit on a Sunday in July or August and you'll be able to see the courtyard fountain in action. Summer also sees the palace wind the clock back to medieval times with its two-day Spectacular Jousting tournament – check dates online.

❶ Getting There & Away

Linlithgow is 15 miles west of Edinburgh and is served by frequent trains from the capital (£5.80, 20 minutes, four every hour). The train station is 250m east of the town centre.

You can also cycle from Edinburgh to Linlithgow along the Union Canal towpath (21 miles) – allow two hours.

AT A GLANCE

POPULATION
598,830

**TRANSLATION OF
CITY'S NAME**
'Dear Green Place' in
Gaelic

**BEST TRADITIONAL
PUB**
Pot Still (p128)

**BEST LIVE-MUSIC
VENUE**
King Tut's Wah Wah
Hut (p131)

**BEST VINTAGE
SHOP**
Mr Ben (p133)

WHEN TO GO

Feb The drizzle won't
lift? Maroon yourself
in one of Glasgow's
fabulous pubs or
clubs.

Jun The Glasgow
Jazz Festival makes
the city music
heaven.

Aug Glasgow is
friendly at any time,
but when the sun is
shining it's Britain's
happiest city.

Glasgow Necropolis (p114)
TAKASHI IMAGES/SHUTTERSTOCK ©

Glasgow

Disarmingly blending sophistication and earthiness, Scotland's biggest city has evolved over the last couple of decades to become one of Britain's most intriguing metropolises.

The soberly handsome Victorian buildings, the legacy of manufacturing and trade, suggest a staid sort of place. Very wrong. There are stylish bars, top-notch restaurants and one of Britain's best live-music scenes. The combination of edgy urbanity and legendary friendliness equates to sheer vitality.

Glasgow also offers plenty by day, including famous shopping and fantastic museums and galleries. Charles Rennie Mackintosh's sublime designs dot the city, also displaying Glasgow's proud, working-class heritage.

Milngavie (4.5 miles)

River Kelvin

Firhill Basin

Great Western Rd

KELVINSIDE

Jordanhill

SCOTSTOUN

Hyndland

Botanic Gardens

See West End Map (p116)

Garscube Rd

Victoria Park

BROOMHILL

HILLHEAD

Ubiquitous Chip 5

Great Western Rd

Maryhill Rd

St Georges Rd

Dumbarton Rd

Byres Rd

University Ave

Inn Deep 6

Woodlands Rd

Partick

Clydeside Expressway

Kelvingrove Art Gallery & Museum 3

Kelvin Way

Kelvingrove Park

Mackintosh at the Willow 1

SHIELDHALL

Argyle St

KELVINGROVE

Charing Cross

Bath St

ANDERSTON

Glasgow (3 mi)

Shieldhall Rd

Exhibition Centre

Finnieston St

Anderston

Argyle St

Central Station

GOVAN

River Clyde

Cardonald

Lancefield Quay

Govan Rd

Paisley Rd

IBROX

Paisley Rd West

KINNING PARK

Shields Rd

Eglinton

Paisley Rd West

Paisley (3 mi)

SOUTH CARDONALD

Bellahouston Park

Mosspark Blvd

Dumbreck

POLLOKSHIELDS

Pollokshields East

Corkerhill

Maxwell Park

Pollokshields West

GOVANHIL

POLLOK

Pollok Country Park

Dumbreck Rd

Crossmyloof

Pollokshaws Rd

Queens Park

White Cart Water

Shawlands

Mount Florida

POLLOKSHAWS

Pollokshaws West

Pollokshaws East

Glasgow Highlights

1 Mackintosh at the Willow (p110) Sipping tea at Charles Rennie Mackintosh's original Willow tearoom.

2 The Lighthouse (p111) Gazing over Glasgow from the rooftop of Mackintosh's first building.

3 Kelvingrove Art Gallery & Museum (p114) Discovering Scottish and Renaissance art.

N 0 ——— 2 km
0 ——— 1 mile

FOSSILPARK

BARMULLOCH

🚇 Springburn

🚇 Barnhill

Hogganfield Loch

Sighthill Park

Hogganfield Park

RIDDRIE

See Central Glasgow Map (p112)

Cumbernauld Rd

owcaddens Rd

🚇 Queen St

Castle St

Cathedral St

Alexandra Pde

❹ Glasgow Necropolis

Alexandra Parade

Edinburgh Rd

George St

High St

CARNTYNE

❷ The Lighthouse

DENNISTOUN

Carntyne Rd

🚇 Argyle Street

Duke St

Clyde St

🚇 Bellgrove

🚇 Duke Street

Carntyne 🚇

The Barras

❼

Saltmarket

Gallowgate

Shettleston Rd

Gorbals St

London Rd

Glasgow Green

PARKHEAD

Westmuir St

BRIDGETON

Tollcross Rd

HUTCHESONTOWN

🚇 Bridgeton

uncart Rd

London Rd

Aikenhead Rd

POLMADIE

🚇 Dalmarnock

Dalmarnock Rd

) Crosshill

DALMARNOCK

ampden Park

🚇 Rutherglen

Cambuslang Rd

RUTHERGLEN Main St

BANKHEAD

Blantyre (4 mi)

❹ **Glasgow Necropolis** (p111) Strolling around peaceful greens and interesting tombstones.

❺ **Ubiquitous Chip** (p127) Savouring fresh Scottish

produce in a charming courtyard.

❻ **Inn Deep** (p130) Toasting craft beer on the Kelvin's riverside.

❼ **The Barras** (p132) Browsing the goods at Glasgow's favourite flea market.

History

The area where Glasgow now stands was bisected by the Romans in the 2nd century CE when they built the Antonine Wall to protect the fringes of their empire from the Caledonian wildlings beyond.

Glasgow grew around the religious site established in the 6th century by St Kentigern, better known as St Mungo (originally an affectionate nickname). It became an important bishop's seat, but the cathedral that was built here is one of the few remnants of the medieval city. It was swept away by the energies of a new age – the age of capitalism, the Industrial Revolution and the British Empire.

Glasgow's west-coast position led to it becoming an important port for trade with the Americas. In the 18th century much of the tobacco trade between Europe and the USA was routed through Glasgow, providing a great source of wealth. The tobacco barons were responsible for much construction around the city that remains today. Even after the tobacco trade declined in the 19th century, the city continued to prosper as a centre of textile manufacturing, shipbuilding and the coal and steel industries. Many of the city's major buildings and monuments were constructed during the Victorian period, when Glasgow was a byword for mercantile prosperity. The outward appearance, however, was tempered by the dire working conditions in the factories.

In the first half of the 20th century, Glasgow was the centre of Britain's munitions industry, supplying arms and ships for the two world wars, in the second of which the city was carpet-bombed. Post-WWII, the port and heavy industries began to dwindle, and by the early 1970s the city looked doomed. Glasgow became synonymous with unemployment, economic depression and urban violence, centred on high-rise housing schemes such as the infamous Gorbals.

More recently, gentrification and a booming cultural sector have injected style and confidence into the city. Though the standard of living remains low for Britain, and life continues to be tough for many, the ongoing regeneration process gives grounds for optimism. The successful hosting of the 2014 Commonwealth Games highlighted this regeneration to a wide global audience, as has the city's commitment to sustainable urban development. Glasgow is set to host the United Nations Climate Change Conference (COP26) in November 2021 and aims to be Britain's first carbon-neutral city by 2030.

◉ Sights

Glasgow's major sights are fairly evenly dispersed across the city. These include standout museums and galleries, the cathedral and a range of architecturally notable buildings, in particular those designed by Charles Rennie Mackintosh. The city's parks and green spaces are also a significant highlight.

◉ City Centre

★**Glasgow School of Art**   HISTORIC BUILDING
(Map p112; ☑ 0141-353 4500; www.gsa.ac.uk; 167 Renfrew St) In 2018, Charles Rennie Mackintosh's greatest building was gearing up for reopening after a devastating 2014 fire when, unbelievably, another blaze destroyed the painstakingly reconstructed interiors and severely damaged the building. The school has committed to reconstructing it, but it will be a lengthy process. At time of research, the visitor centre, shop and exhibitions in the neighbouring Reid building were closed to visitors; check the website to see if visits and tours have resumed.

★**City Chambers**   HISTORIC BUILDING
(Map p112; ☑ 0141-287 2000; www.glasgow.gov. uk; George Sq; ⊙ 9am-5pm Mon-Fri) FREE The grand seat of local government was built in the 1880s at the high point of Glasgow's wealth. The interior is even more extravagant than the exterior, and the chambers have sometimes been used as a movie location to represent the Kremlin or the Vatican. You can have a look at the opulent ground floor during opening hours. Free guided tours are held at 10.30am and 2.30pm Monday to Friday; it's worth popping in earlier in the day to prebook.

Mackintosh at the Willow   HISTORIC BUILDING
(Map p112; ☑ 0141-204 1903; www.mackin toshatthewillow.com; 217 Sauchiehall St; exhibition adult/child £5.50/4.50; ⊙ tearoom noon-5pm, exhibition 10am-4.45pm, last entry 1hr before closing) Opened in 2018, this reconstruction of the original Willow tearoom that Mackintosh designed and furnished in the early 20th century for restaurateur

Kate Cranston offers authentic design splendour in its original location. You can admire the architect's distinctive touch in just about every element; he had free rein and even the teaspoons were given his attention. Alongside the tearoom is a visitor centre, with a two-level interactive exhibition about the historical context and Cranston's collaboration with Mackintosh and Margaret Macdonald.

The tearoom offers afternoon teas, light bites and desserts. Tearoom tours (adult/child £7.50/5.50) run daily between 10am and 1pm every hour. They last 45 minutes and should be prebooked by emailing bookings@mackintoshatthewillow.com. More specialised architectural tours are also available.

The Lighthouse   HISTORIC BUILDING
(Map p112; ☑0141-276 5365; www.thelighthouse.co.uk; 11 Mitchell Lane; ◷10.30am-5pm Mon-Sat, from noon Sun) **FREE** Mackintosh's first building, designed in 1893, was a striking new headquarters for the *Glasgow Herald*. Tucked up a narrow lane off Buchanan St, it now serves as Scotland's Centre for Architecture and Design, with fairly technical temporary exhibitions (sometimes admission is payable for these), as well as the Mackintosh Interpretation Centre, a detailed (if slightly dry) overview of his life and work. On the top floor of the 'lighthouse', drink in great views over the rooftops and spires of the city centre.

Guided tours (adult/child £5/3) are offered on Saturday from 1pm on a first come, first served basis.

◉ **East End**

★**Glasgow Cathedral**   CATHEDRAL
(HES; Map p112; ☑0141-552 6891; www.historicenvironment.scot; Cathedral Sq; ◷9.30am-5.30pm Mon-Sat, 1-5pm Sun Apr-Sep, 10am-4pm Mon-Sat, from 1pm Sun Oct-Mar) Glasgow Cathedral has a rare timelessness. The dark, imposing interior conjures up medieval might and can send a shiver down the spine. It's a shining example of Gothic architecture, and unlike nearly all of Scotland's cathedrals, it survived the turmoil of the Reformation mobs almost intact. Most of the current building dates from the 15th century.

Entry is through a side door into the nave, hung with regimental colours. The wooden roof has been restored many times

since its original construction, but some of the timber dates from the 14th century; note the impressive shields. Many of the cathedral's stunning, narrow stained-glass windows are modern – to your left is Francis Spear's 1958 work *The Creation,* which fills the west window.

The cathedral is divided by a late-15th-century stone choir screen, decorated with seven pairs of figures perhaps representing the seven deadly sins. The four stained-glass panels of the east window, depicting the Apostles (also by Spear), are particularly evocative. At the northeastern corner is the entrance to the 15th-century upper chapter house, where the University of Glasgow was founded. It's now used as a sacristy.

The most interesting part of the cathedral, the lower church, is reached by a stairway. Its forest of pillars creates a powerful atmosphere around the tomb of St Mungo (who founded a monastic community here in the 6th century), the focus of a famous medieval pilgrimage that was believed to be as meritorious as a visit to Rome.

While here, don't miss a stroll in the necropolis.

★**Glasgow Necropolis**   CEMETERY
(www.glasgownecropolis.org; ◷7am-4.30pm) **FREE** Behind Glasgow Cathedral, this sizeable 19th-century necropolis stretches picturesquely up and over a green hill. The elaborate Victorian tombs of the city's wealthy industrialists, several of them designed by prominent architects of the day (including Alexander Thomson and Charles Rennie Mackintosh), make for an intriguing stroll and offer great views and a vague Gothic thrill. Walking tours run regularly at the weekend; contact tours@glasgownecropolis.org.

★**St Mungo's Museum of Religious Life & Art**   MUSEUM
(Map p112; ☑0141-276 1625; www.glasgowlife.org.uk; 2 Castle St; ◷check online/call ahead) **FREE** Set in a reconstruction of the bishop's palace that once stood in the cathedral forecourt, this museum audaciously attempts to capture the world's major religions in an artistic nutshell. A startling achievement, it presents the similarities and differences in how various religions approach common themes such as birth, marriage and death. The attraction is twofold: firstly, impressive art that blurs the lines between religion

Central Glasgow

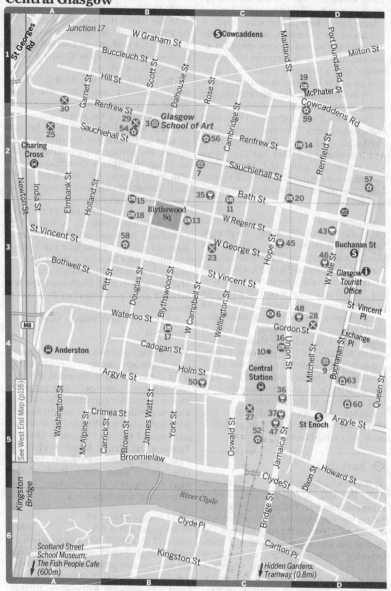

and culture; and secondly, the opportunity to delve into different faiths, as deeply or shallowly as you wish.

Provand's Lordship   HISTORIC BUILDING
(Map p112; ☎ 0141-276 1625; www.glasgowlife.org.
uk; 3 Castle St; ⊙ check online/call ahead) FREE

Near the cathedral is Provand's Lordship, the oldest house in Glasgow. This rare example of 15th-century domestic Scottish architecture was built in 1471 as a manse. The ceilings and doorways are low, and the rooms are furnished with period furniture and artefacts. Upstairs a room recreates

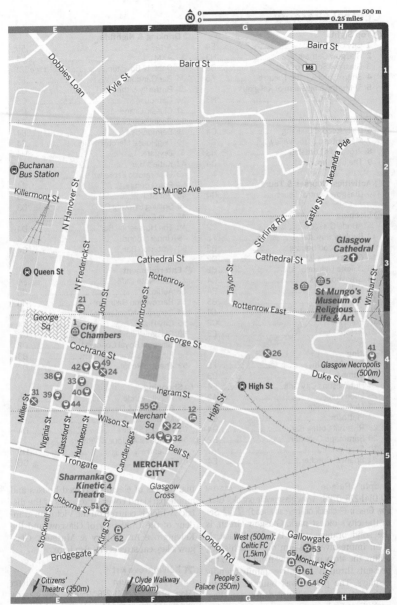

the living space of an early-16th-century chaplain. The building's biggest draw is its authentic feel, though it's a shame the original wooden floors have had to be covered for protection.

Provand's Lordship was once one of several dozen religious buildings in the immediate vicinity of the cathedral. It was built to house the master of the St Nicholas chapel and hospital, which once stood just to the south. Behind Provand's Lordship, the St Nicholas Garden recreates what a 15th-century hospital garden might have been like.

Central Glasgow

People's Palace   MUSEUM
(📞0141-276 0788; www.glasgowlife.org.uk; Glasgow Green; ⊙check online/call ahead) FREE Set in the city's oldest park, Glasgow Green, is the solid orange stone People's Palace. It is an impressive museum of social history, telling the story of Glasgow from 1750 to the present through inventive family-friendly displays. The palace was built in the late 19th century as a cultural centre for Glasgow's East End.

◉ West End

With its appealing studenty buzz, modish bars and cafes and bohemian swagger, the West End is for many the most engaging area of Glasgow – it's great for people-watch-ing. Streets of elegant terraced houses and ample parkland cover large areas of the district, which is centred on the Victorian grandeur of the University of Glasgow and the Kelvingrove Art Gallery & Museum. Glasgow's key eat streets are also here.

★**Kelvingrove Art
Gallery & Museum**   GALLERY
(Map p116; 📞0141-276 9599; www.glasgow museums.com; Argyle St; ⊙11am-4pm) FREE A magnificent sandstone building, this grand Victorian cathedral of culture is a fascinating and unusual museum, with a bewildering variety of exhibits. You'll find fine art alongside stuffed animals, and Micronesian shark-tooth swords alongside a Spitfire plane, but it's not mix 'n' match: rooms are

carefully and thoughtfully themed, and the collection is of a manageable size. It has an excellent room of Scottish art, a room of fine French impressionist works, and quality Renaissance paintings from Italy and Flanders.

Salvador Dalí's superb *Christ of St John of the Cross* is also here. Best of all, nearly everything, including the paintings, has an easy-reading paragraph of interpretation. You can learn a lot about art here, and it's excellent for children, with plenty to do and displays aimed at a variety of ages. Free hour-long guided tours begin at 11am and 2.30pm. Be here at 1pm to hear the impressive organ being played. Bus 17, among many others, runs here from Renfield St.

★ **Mackintosh House**   HISTORIC BUILDING
(Map p116; ☑0141-330 4221; www.hunt erian.gla.ac.uk; 82 Hillhead St; adult/child £6/3; ☉10am-5pm Tue-Sat, 11am-4pm Sun) Attached to the **Hunterian Art Gallery** (Map p116; ☑0141-330 4221; www.hunterian.gla.ac.uk; 82 Hillhead St; ☉10am-5pm Tue-Sat, 11am-4pm Sun) **FREE**, this is a reconstruction of the home that Charles Rennie Mackintosh shared with his wife, noted designer-artist Margaret Macdonald. It's fair to say that interior decoration was one of their strong points; Mackintosh House is startling even today. The quiet elegance of the hall and dining room on the ground floor give way to a stunning drawing room and bedroom upstairs. Visits are currently self-guided.

The visual highlight is the white-as-white drawing room. There's something other-worldly about the mannered style of the beaten silver panels, the long-backed chairs and the surface decorations echoing Celtic manuscript illuminations. You wouldn't have wanted to be the guest who spilled a glass of red on this carpet.

A new space, the Mackintosh Interpretation Centre, was due to open in the spring of 2021 with new insights into the Mackintoshes' daily life. The house will perhaps become part of the new museum at Kelvin Hall (p116), but likely not until at least 2025.

Hunterian Museum   MUSEUM
(Map p116; ☑0141-330 4221; www.hunterian. gla.ac.uk; University Ave; ☉10am-5pm Tue-Sat, 11am-4pm Sun) **FREE** Housed in the glorious sandstone university building, which is in itself reason enough to pay a visit, this quirky museum contains the collection of renowned one-time student William Hunter (1718–83). Hunter was primarily an anatomist and physician, but as one of those wonderfully well-rounded Enlightenment figures, he interested himself in everything the world had to offer.

Pickled organs in glass jars take their place alongside geological phenomena, potsherds gleaned from ancient brochs, dinosaur skeletons and a creepy case of deformed animals. The main halls of the exhibition, with their high vaulted roofs, are magnificent in themselves. Highlights include a display of artefacts from the

---

GLASGOW IN...

Two Days

On your first day, hit the East End for Glasgow Cathedral (p111), St Mungo's Museum (p111) and a wander through the hillside necropolis (p111). Later, take in one of the city's top museums: either the Burrell Collection (p119) or the Kelvingrove (p114). As evening falls, head to trendy Merchant City for a stroll and dinner; try Café Gandolfi (p125). Check out Artà (p130) for a pre- or post-meal drink. The next day, visit whichever museum you missed yesterday, and then it's Mackintosh time. Check out Mackintosh at the Willow (p110): if you like his style, head to the West End for Mackintosh House (p115). Hungry? Thirsty? Some of the city's best restaurants and bars are up this end of town, so you could make a night of it. Make sure to check out one of the numerous excellent music venues (p131) around the city.

Four Days

A four-day stay gives better scope to get to grips with Glasgow. Spend a day along the Clyde – the Riverside Museum (p117) and the Glasgow Science Centre (p118). Plan your weekend around a night out at the Cathouse (p130) or the legendary King Tut's Wah Wah Hut (p131), and a day strolling the stylish city-centre clothing emporia or attending a football game. Don't miss trying at least one of the city's classic curry houses.

West End

N 0 —————— 400 m
   0 —————— 0.2 miles

Hotel du Vin
(400m)

Kelvin Dr

Great Western Rd

Charles Rennie
Mackintosh
Society

Maryhill Rd

Ruthven La

Byres Rd

Cresswell La

Hillhead

Ashton Rd

Ashton La

Woodside Rd N

Kelvinbridge

Great Western Rd

W Princes St

Rupert St

Kelvinhall

Dumbarton Rd

River Kelvin

Byres Rd

WEST
END

Mackintosh
House

Hillhead St

Gibson St

University Ave

Otago La

Eldon St

Park Rd

Woodlands Rd

Park Quad

Kelvingrove
Art Gallery &
Museum

Kelvin Way

Kelvingrove
Park

Park Circus

Park Tce

Woodlands Tce

Lynedoch St

Woodside Tce

Woodside Pl

River Kelvin

Gray St

Royal Tce

Sauchiehall St

Berkeley St

Elderslie St

Kelvinhaugh St

St Vincent Cres

Argyle St

St Vincent St

Argyle St

Riverside
Museum;
Seaforce;
Tall Ship
(600m)

Clydeside Expressway

Exhibition
Centre

Minerva St

Finnieston St

St Vincent St

See Central Glasgow Map (p112)

Millennium
Bridge

Bell's
Bridge

River Clyde

Stobcross St

Elliot St

Lancefield St

Hydepark St

Govan Rd

Rangers FC (0.75mi);
House for an Art Lover (1mi)

Lancefield Quay

Antonine Wall and the beautiful 1674 Chinese *Map of the Whole World*, produced for the emperor by a Jesuit at the court.

This collection will perhaps become part of the new museum at Kelvin Hall, but probably not until at least 2025.

Kelvin Hall   MUSEUM
(Map p116; ☎ 0141-276 1450; www.glasgowlife.org.uk; 1445 Argyle St; ⊙ 6.30am-10pm Mon-Fri, 8am-5pm Sat, 8am-8pm Sun) FREE Opened in the 1920s as an exhibition centre, this enormous sandstone palace, renovated and reopened in 2016, is a mixed leisure-and-arts space.

West End

◎ Top Sights
1 Kelvingrove Art Gallery & Museum.......B4
2 Mackintosh House B3

◎ Sights
3 Botanic Gardens.....................................B1
4 Clydeside Distillery A5
5 Glasgow Science Centre.......................A6
6 Hunterian Art Gallery............................B2
7 Hunterian Museum.................................B3
8 Kelvin Hall...A3
9 Kelvingrove Park B3
10 Mackintosh Queen's Cross...................D1
11 National Library of Scotland................A4

◎ Activities, Courses & Tours
12 Glasgow Bike Tours B1
13 Waverley...A6

◎ Sleeping
14 15Glasgow..D4
15 Acorn Hotel..D4
16 Alamo Guest House................................B4
17 Amadeus Guest House...........................D2
18 Flower House..B5
19 Glasgow SYHA..C3
20 Heritage Hotel..B2
21 Sandyford Lodge.....................................C4

◎ Eating
22 78 Bar & Kitchen B4
23 Alchemilla...C4

24 Bay Tree..C2
25 Bothy..A2
26 Butchershop Bar & Grill.........................B4
27 Cail Bruich..B1
28 Gannet..B4
29 Left Bank...C3
30 Mother India...C4
31 Ox & Finch..C4
32 Stravaigin...B2
33 The Finnieston..C5
34 Ubiquitous Chip......................................B2

◎ Drinking & Nightlife
35 Brel...B2
36 Hillhead Bookclub..................................B2
37 Inn Deep...C2
38 Òran Mór...B1

◎ Entertainment
A Play, a Pie & a Pint....................(see 38)
39 Clyde Auditorium....................................B6
40 Grosvenor Cinema..................................A2
41 Hug & Pint...D3
42 Hydro..C6

◎ Shopping
43 Caledonia Books.....................................C2
44 De Courcy's Arcade................................B2
45 Glasgow Vintage Company...................C2
46 Hidden Lane C5

In addition to a gym and sports facilities, it hosts the audiovisual archive of the National Library of Scotland (Map p116; ✆0845-366 4600; www.nls.uk; ⊗10am-4pm Tue-Sat) FREE and also stores museum collections from the University of Glasgow and Glasgow Museums (available by appointment). The major exhibition halls are being developed and may end up holding the Hunterian collections as well as other city-related exhibits.

◉ The Clyde

Once a thriving shipbuilding area, the Clyde sank into dereliction during the postwar era but has been subject to extensive rejuvenation. There are noteworthy sights along the river, though the walk along its banks still isn't all that it could be.

★ Riverside Museum   MUSEUM
(✆0141-287 2720; www.glasgowmuseums.com; 100 Pointhouse Pl; ⊗11am-4pm; 🅿) FREE This visually impressive modern museum at Glasgow Harbour owes its striking curved forms to late British-Iraqi architect Zaha Hadid. A transport museum forms the collection's main part, featuring a fascinating series of cars made in Scotland, plus assorted railway locos, trams, bikes (including the world's first pedal-powered bicycle from 1847) and model Clyde-built ships. An atmospheric recreation of a Glasgow shopping street from the early 20th century puts the vintage vehicles into a social context. There's also a cafe.

It's west of the city centre. Get bus 100 from the north side of George Sq or walk (signposted) from the Kelvingrove Art Gallery & Museum – about half a mile.

The magnificent three-masted *Glenlee*, launched in 1896, is the tall ship (✆0141-357 3699; www.thetallship.com; ⊗10am-5pm Feb-Oct, to 4pm Nov-Jan; 🅿) FREE that's berthed alongside the museum. On board are family-friendly displays about the ship's history, restoration and shipboard life during its heyday. Upkeep costs are high, so make a donation or have a coffee below decks.

Glasgow Science Centre SCIENCE CENTRE
(Map p116; ☎0141-420 5000; www.glas
gowsciencecentre.org; 50 Pacific Quay; adult/
child £12/10, IMAX, Glasgow Tower or Planetari-
um extra £2.50-3.50; ⊙10am-5pm daily Apr-Oct,
to 3pm Wed-Fri, to 5pm Sat & Sun Nov-Mar; ▣)
This brilliant science centre will keep the
kids entertained for hours (middle-aged
kids, too!). It brings science and technology alive through hundreds of interactive
exhibits on four floors: a bounty of discovery for inquisitive minds. There's also
an **IMAX theatre** (see www.cineworld.
com for current screenings), a rotating
127m-high **observation tower**, a **plane-
tarium** and a **Science Theatre**, with live
science demonstrations. To get here, take
bus 89 or 90 from Union St.

Clydeside Distillery DISTILLERY
(Map p116; ☎0141-212 1401; www.theclydeside.
com; The Pumphouse, 100 Stobcross Rd; tour adult/
child £15/5; ⊙10am-4pm Sep-Jun, to 4.30pm Jul &
Aug) It's great to see this old pump-house by
the Clyde being put to good use as a new
malt whisky distillery run by proper whisky
folk. It's an impressive set-up, with the stills
overlooking the river (don't worry, the water
comes from Loch Katrine, not the Clyde).
The tour (1¼ hours) is engaging, with some
history of the Clyde. It includes a tasting of
three malts.

There's also a pleasant cafe and a well-
stocked whisky shop.

⊙ Southside

The Southside is an intriguingly multicultural part of Glasgow, with temples
and mosques alongside sturdy episcopal
churches. It's got an up-and-coming food
scene and thriving cultural centres. Several
excellent attractions are also dotted across
the area.

THE GENIUS OF CHARLES RENNIE MACKINTOSH

Great cities have great artists, designers and architects contributing to their urban
environment while expressing their soul and individuality. Charles Rennie Mackintosh's
quirky, linear and geometric designs have had an enormous influence on Glasgow. Many
of the buildings Mackintosh designed are open to the public, and you'll see his tall, thin,
art nouveau typeface repeatedly reproduced.

Born in 1868, Mackintosh studied at the Glasgow School of Art. It was there that he
met the influential artist and designer Margaret Macdonald, whom he married; they
collaborated on many projects and were major influences on each other's work. Together
with her sister Frances and Herbert MacNair, the artist who married her, they formed
'The Four', a pioneering group that developed the Glasgow Style. This contribution to
art nouveau incorporated influences from the Arts and Crafts movement and Japanese
design.

In 1896, aged 27, Mackintosh won a competition for his design for the new building
of the Glasgow School of Art (p110), where he had studied. This was his supreme architectural achievement. The first section was opened in 1899 and is considered to be the
earliest example of art nouveau in Britain. The second section, opened a decade later,
includes some of the earliest art deco. The building demonstrates his skill in combining
function and style.

Another of Mackintosh's finest works is Hill House (p245) in Helensburgh. Other
buildings around town include the **Daily Record Building** (Map p112; 20 Renfield Lane),
Scotland Street School, **Mackintosh Queen's Cross church** (Map p116; ☎0141-946
6600; www.mackintoshchurch.com; 870 Garscube Rd; adult/child £4/free; ⊙11am-4pm Mon-Fri
Apr-Oct, Mon, Wed & Fri Nov, Dec, Feb & Mar, closed Jan) and House for an Art Lover. At Mackintosh at the Willow (p110), you can see his design concept right down to the smallest
level.

Although Mackintosh's genius was quickly recognised in the rest of Europe, he did
not receive the same encouragement in Scotland. His architectural career here lasted
only until 1914, when he moved to England to concentrate on furniture design. He died in
1928, and it is only since the last decades of the 20th century that Mackintosh's genius
has been widely recognised. For more about the man and his work, contact the **Charles
Rennie Mackintosh Society** (Map p116; ☎0141-946 6600; www.crmsociety.com; Mackintosh Queen's Cross, 870 Garscube Rd).

Burrell Collection — GALLERY

(☎ 0141-287 2550; www.glasgowlife.org.uk; Pollok Country Park) FREE One of Glasgow's top attractions, this outstanding museum 3 miles out of town houses everything from Chinese porcelain and medieval furniture to paintings by Cézanne. The tapestry collection is a particular highlight. It's closed for refurbishment, and is due to reopen in the near future. The new building will have double the exhibition space as well as a cafe. Meanwhile, some items are on display at the Kelvingrove Art Gallery & Museum (p114).

Scotland Street School Museum — NOTABLE BUILDING

(☎ 0141-287 0500; www.glasgowlife.org.uk; 225 Scotland St; ⏱ check online/call ahead) FREE Mackintosh's Scotland Street School seems a bit forlorn these days, on a windswept industrial street with no babble of young voices filling its corridors. Nevertheless, it's worth a visit for its stunning facade and the interesting museum of education that occupies the interior. Reconstructions of classrooms from various points in the school's life, combined with grumbling headmaster and cleaner, will have older visitors recalling their own schooldays. It's right opposite Shields Road subway station and there's also an OK cafe.

House for an Art Lover — NOTABLE BUILDING

(☎ 0141-483 1600; www.houseforanartlover. co.uk; Bellahouston Park, Dumbreck Rd; adult/ child £6.50/5; ⏱ roughly 10am-4pm Sun-Fri, to noon Sat) Although designed in 1901 as an entry in a competition run by a German magazine, this house in Bellahouston Park was not built until the 1990s. Mackintosh worked closely with his wife on the design and her influence is evident, especially in the rose motif. The overall effect of this brilliant architect's ideas is one of space and light. Buses 9, 10 and 38 all run here from the city centre; check the website for opening hours, as it's regularly booked for events.

The house is the hub of an arts promotion programme and there are regular workshops, exhibitions and events.

Scottish Football Museum — MUSEUM

(The Hampden Experience; ☎ 0141-616 6139; www.scottishfootballmuseum.org.uk; Hampden Park; adult/child £8/3.50; ⏱ 10am-5pm Mon-Sat, from 11am Sun) At Hampden Park, the national stadium, this museum covers the history of the game in Scotland and the considerable influence of Scots on the world game. It's crammed full of impressive memorabilia, including a cap and match ticket from the very first international football game ever played, held in Glasgow in 1872. You can also take a tour of the stadium (adult/child £8/3.50; combined ticket with museum £13/5), home ground to both Scotland and lower-division outfit Queens Park.

The museum is at Hampden Park, off Aikenhead Rd. Take a train to Mount Florida station or take bus 5, 31 or 75 from Stockwell St.

Activities

There are numerous green spaces within the city. Pollok Country Park surrounds the Burrell Collection and has several woodland trails. Nearer the centre of the city, the **Kelvin Walkway** follows the River Kelvin through **Kelvingrove Park** (Map p116), the Botanic Gardens and on to Dawsholm Park.

The **Clyde Walkway** stretches from Glasgow upriver to the Falls of Clyde near New Lanark, about 40 miles away. The tourist office (p134) has information outlining different sections of this walk. The 10-mile section through Glasgow has interesting parts, though most of the old shipyards are no longer there. There are some beautiful sections further upstream.

The well-trodden, long-distance footpath **West Highland Way** begins in Milngavie, 8 miles north of Glasgow (you can walk to Milngavie from Glasgow along the River Kelvin), and runs for 95 spectacular miles to Fort William.

There are several long-distance pedestrian/cycle routes that begin in Glasgow and follow off-road routes for most of the way. Check www.sustrans.org.uk for more details.

The **Clyde–Loch Lomond route** traverses residential and industrial areas in a 20-mile ride from Bell's Bridge to Loch Lomond. This route continues to Inverness, part of the **Lochs and Glens National Cycle Route**.

The **Clyde to Forth cycle route** runs through Glasgow. One way takes you to Edinburgh via Bathgate, the other takes you via Paisley to Greenock and Gourock, the first section partly on roads. Another branch heads down to Irvine and Ardrossan, for the ferry to Arran. An extension via Ayr, Maybole and Glentrool leads to the Solway coast and Carlisle.

Tours

Glasgow

Central Tours   WALKING
(Map p112; 0773-464 7381; www.glasgow centraltours.co.uk; tour £13; check website for tour times) A passionate, entertaining guide takes you around, behind and under Glasgow Central station (p135). Hidden spaces, an abandoned Victorian platform and lots of intriguing information make this a fascinating experience even if railways don't get you excited. It lasts about an hour; check the website for dates. The minimum age is 12 years.

Rabbies   BUS
(0131-226 3133; www.rabbies.com) This popular outfit runs a range of minibus tours up to the Highlands, including popular day trips taking in Glencoe, Loch Ness and the Highlands.

Glasgow Bike Tours   CYCLING
(Map p116; 0778-668 3445; www.glasgowbike tours.co.uk; 28 Vinicombe St; adult/child £39/22) A friendly guide runs a three-hour circuit around the city. It takes in several key sights around the periphery of the city centre and gets you an especially good look at the Clyde and the West End.

Seaforce   BOATING
(0141-221 1070; www.seaforce.co.uk; Riverside Museum) Departing from the Riverside Museum, Seaforce offers speedy all-weather powerboat jaunts along the Clyde. There's a variety of trips, including a 20-minute 'Clyde Ride' around central Glasgow (adult/child £10/5). They run year-round but call ahead as they are weather dependent.

Waverley   BOATING
(Map p116; 0141-243 2224; www.waverleyex cursions.co.uk; mid-May–early Sep, plus some Oct departures) The world's last ocean-going paddle steamer (built in 1947) cruises Scotland's west coast in summer, with many different routes; the website details days of departure. It serves several towns and the islands of Bute, Great Cumbrae, Arran and more. Its Glasgow departures are from the Glasgow Science Centre, while it also has frequent departures from Largs and Ayr among other locations.

Festivals & Events

Celtic Connections   MUSIC
(0141-353 8000; www.celticconnections.com; Jan) This two-week music festival focuses on roots music and folk from Scotland and around the world.

Glasgow Film Festival   FILM
(www.glasgowfilm.org/glasgow-film-festival; Feb) Two-week film festival with screenings in various locations across the city.

Glasgow International Comedy Festival   COMEDY
(0844 873 7353; www.glasgowcomedyfestival. com; Mar) Two weeks of quality comedy, both home-grown and imported, enlivens stages across the city in March.

Glasgow Jazz Festival   MUSIC
(www.jazzfest.co.uk; Jun) Excellent festival sees big-name international acts come to town, with stages set up in George Sq and Merchant City.

TRNSMT   MUSIC
(www.trnsmtfest.com; Jul) This festival only started in 2017 but has been a huge success, drawing major indie rock acts to Glasgow Green.

Merchant City Festival   STREET CARNIVAL
(www.merchantcityfestival.com; late Jul) Lively weeklong street festival in the Merchant City quarter, with lots of performances and stalls.

Sleeping

Glasgow has plenty of accommodation but can still fill up at weekends; booking ahead for weekends is essential, as well as in high season July and August.

Most providers set prices according to demand. Rates shoot up at weekends and reach stratospheric levels, even at mediocre places, if there's a big-name concert on a Saturday. By the same token, you can get excellent deals on quieter nights out of season.

City Centre

Z Hotel   HOTEL ££
(Map p112; 0141-212 4550; www.thezhotels. com; 36 North Frederick St; r £55-125;) Just off George Sq the facade of a historic building conceals a stylish contemporary hotel. Chambers are modern but compact – the idea is that you sleep here and socialise

🚶 City Walk
West End

START KELVINBRIDGE SUBWAY STATION
END ARGYLE ST, FINNIESTON
LENGTH 3 MILES; 2 HOURS

From the subway, turn left across ❶ **Great Western Bridge (Kelvinbridge)**, emblazoned with the lion rampant of the Hillhead burgh on the south side and the city coat of arms on the north. It crosses the leafy course of the River Kelvin; note the riverside bar ❷ **Inn Deep** (p130) to come back to.

Continue along Great Western Rd, stopping for a browse in ❸ **Glasgow Vintage Company** (p133) and ❹ **Caledonia Books** (p133). At the corner of Byres Rd, a former church is now ❺ **Oràn Mór** (p130); consider attending its lunchtime theatre session ❻ **A Play, a Pie and a Pint** (p130). Across the road stretch the ❼ **Botanic Gardens**.

Turn left down Byres Rd; investigate interesting shops on the left. At Cresswell St, turn left then right down Cresswell Lane to check out tiny ❽ **De Courcy's Arcade** (p133). Further down is the bar-heavy ❾ **Ashton Lane**,

where ❿ **Ubiquitous Chip** (p127) is still one of Scotland's best places to eat. Turn right opposite Jinty McGuinty's to reach Byres Rd again. Cross and examine the quirky shops down ⓫ **Ruthven Lane**, directly opposite.

Back on Byres Rd, head south, then turn left up University Ave. The ugly 1960s ⓬ **Boyd Orr tower** is soon replaced by more typical sandstone terraces as you climb the hill. On the left is the ⓭ **Hunterian Art Gallery** (p115) and ⓮ **Mackintosh House** (p115); on the right, the University of Glasgow's main building is home to the ⓯ **Hunterian Museum** (p115).

At the bottom of University Ave, turn left then right onto Gibson St, home to quality lunch stops such as ⓰ **Stravaigin** (p127). Cross the bridge and turn right into the park, bearing right down to the river and the ⓱ **Kelvin Walkway**. Follow this for half a mile through lovely ⓲ **Kelvingrove Park** (p119) to reach the ⓳ **Kelvingrove Art Gallery & Museum** (p114). From here it's a short hop to the Finnieston eating strip on ⓴ **Argyle St**.

GLASGOW FOR CHILDREN

Glasgow is easy to visit with children due to its extensive public transport system and friendly locals. The city boasts excellent family attractions and there are several apartment-hotels around town. In general, restaurants are well geared for children, and lots of places serve food throughout the day.

Family-oriented venues include the following:

➡ Glasgow Science Centre (p118)

➡ Riverside Museum (p117)

➡ People's Palace (p114)

Need to Know

Childcare For suggestions for short-term child-care agencies, contact the council-run Glasgow Family Information Service (www.gfis.org.uk).

Playgrounds Most parks in Glasgow have playgrounds for children.

Shopping centres Major shopping complexes are handy stops, with baby-changing facilities and soft play areas.

Pubs In family-licensed pubs, accompanied children under 14 years old are admitted between 11am and 8pm.

in the bar area, especially during the afternoon wine-and-cheese session. Big flatscreens and pleasing showers add comfort to rooms that can be great value if booked in advance.

★ **Grasshoppers** HOTEL **££**
(Map p112; 0141-222 2666; www.grasshoppersglasgow.com; 87 Union St; r incl breakfast £60-125; 🅿🛜🖥) Discreetly hidden atop a time-worn railway administration building alongside Central station, this small, well-priced hotel is a modern, upbeat surprise. Rooms are compact (a few are larger) but well appointed, with unusual views over the station roof's glass sea. Numerous touches – friendly staff, interesting art, in-room cafetière, free cupcakes and ice cream, and weeknight suppers – make this one of the centre's homiest choices.

There's a very good parking deal available (£8 per day) at a car park a block away.

Citizen M HOTEL **££**
(Map p112; 020-3519 1111; www.citizenm.com; 60 Renfrew St; r £89-199; @🛜) This modern chain does away with some normal hotel accoutrements in favour of self-check-in terminals and minimalist, plasticky, modern rooms with just two features: a big, comfortable king-sized bed and a decent shower with mood lighting. The idea is that guests make liberal use of the public areas, and why wouldn't you, with upbeat,

super-comfortable designer furniture, a 24-hour cafe and iMacs.

Indigo HOTEL **££**
(Map p112; 0141-226 7700; www.hinglasgow.co.uk; 75 Waterloo St; r £100-160; 🅿@🛜) Once the power station for early trams, this boutique-chain conversion of an elegant building has resulted in a satisfying, surprisingly quiet city-centre option. Rooms have muralstyle artwork, great beds and a free minibar (the contents improve as you go up the room grades). Space is good, and bathrooms have rain showerheads. Prices vary; there are usually good online deals.

There's an upmarket grill restaurant attached.

Pipers' Tryst Hotel HOTEL **££**
(Map p112; 0141-353 5551; www.thepipingcentre.co.uk; 30-34 McPhater St; r with/without breakfast £120/96; 🛜) The name is no tartan tourist trap; rather this cosy hotel with only eight rooms is run by the adjacent bagpiping centre, and profits go towards maintaining it. Cheery staff, great value and a prime city-centre location make this a wise choice. You won't have far to migrate after a night of Celtic music and malts in the snug bar-restaurant.

Babbity Bowster INN **££**
(Map p112; 0141-552 5055; www.babbitybowster.com; 16-18 Blackfriars St; s/d incl

breakfast £75/110; P 🛜) Smack bang in the heart of vibrant Merchant City, this lively, pleasant pub (p129) has simple rooms with sleek furnishings and a minimalist design (room 3 is a good one). Staying here is an excellent Glaswegian experience – the building's design is attributed to Robert Adam. The price is a steal given that breakfast and parking are included.

Point A   HOTEL ££

(Map p112; ☑0141-352 2650; www.pointa hotels.com; 80 Bath St; r £75; ❋🛜) Delivering urban comfort without frills, Point A concentrates on doing the basics well, offering very comfortable beds and reliable showers in minimalist, functional modern rooms with mood lighting, big flat-screens and climate control. Prices vary hugely by demand; some chambers don't have windows but are cheaper. Rooms are only serviced every third day.

The location is good, just where Bath St morphs from down-at-heel to intriguing.

★ Dakota Deluxe   HOTEL £££

(Map p112; ☑0141-404 3680; www.dakotahotels. co.uk; 179 West Regent St; r £150-585; ❋🛜❋) Suave and seductive in dark wood and grey tones, Dakota carries a strong design concept, from low-lit basement restaurant to light-filled suites. Rooms are very spacious and feature appealing sitting areas as well as inviting beds. Service is excellent, and the bar area – see how many Jacks you can name – a delight.

Blythswood Square   HOTEL £££

(Map p112; ☑0141-248 8888; www.kimpton blythswoodsquare.com; 11 Blythswood Sq; r £195-300; P 🛜❋❋) In a gorgeous Georgian terrace, this elegant five-star offers inner-city luxury, with grey and cerise providing casual soft-toned style throughout. Rooms (recently refurbished) go from standard to penthouse, with corresponding increases in comfort – it's hard to resist the traditional 'classic' rooms with windows onto the delightful square, but at weekends you'll have a quieter sleep in the new wing at the back.

It has an excellent bar and a superb restaurant, as well as a very handsome floorboarded and colonnaded salon space on the 1st floor that functions as an evening spot for cocktails. Other facilities include valet parking and a seductive spa complex.

Malmaison   HOTEL £££

(Map p112; ☑0141-378 0384; www.malmaison. com; 278 West George St; r £130-250; 🛜) This former church is a long-time favourite for its decadent decor and plush lines. Stylish rooms with mood lighting have a dark, brooding tone and opulent furnishings. It's a hedonistic sort of place and can be cheerfully boisterous at weekends. It's best to book online, as it's cheaper and various suite offers can be mighty tempting.

ABode Glasgow   HOTEL £££

(Map p112; ☑0141-221 6789; www.abodeglas gow.co.uk; 129 Bath St; r £124-164; ❋@🛜) A characterful listed building dating from the mid-19th century holds this interesting hotel that features plenty of original art, sweet rooms with tartan blankets, period features all over the public areas and helpful staff. Bathrooms are compact, but this is a good deal in the heart of things and a far cry from your typical chain hotel.

🛏 West End

Glasgow SYHA   HOSTEL £

(Map p116; ☑0141-332 3004; www.hos tellingscotland.org.uk; 8 Park Tce; dm/s/tw £29/52/69; @🛜❋) Perched on a hill overlooking Kelvingrove Park in a charming town house, this is one of Scotland's best official hostels. Dorms are mostly four to six beds with padlocked lockers, and all have en suite. The common rooms are spacious, plush and good for lounging about in. There's no curfew, it has a good kitchen, and meals are available.

The prices listed reflect weekend maximums and are usually cheaper. Non-members pay £3 extra, but it's cheap to join. There's a good self-catering two-bedroom apartment that sleeps six and will appeal to families.

Flower House   B&B £

(Map p116; ☑0141-204 2846; www.theflower house.net; 33 St Vincent Cres; s £40-60, d from £60; 🛜) Cosy, old-style B&B in a pretty Victorian terraced house fronted by a riot of creepers and flowers – you can't miss it. Just off the Finnieston strip, its comfortably dignified interior features antiques, curios, striped wallpaper and noble furniture. Bathrooms are exterior but private: they are extraordinary, particularly the 'penny wall'. Hospitality is good humoured

GREEN GLASGOW

Glasgow means 'Dear Green Place' in Gaelic and truly lives up to the name. There are more than 90 parks and gardens, as well as excellent cycling and hiking trails. Now efforts are being made by Glasgow to even become the greenest city in Europe.

Glasgow aims to become Britain's first carbon-neutral city by 2030. City Council, in cooperation with ScottishPower, has made several promises, including the decarbonisation of heating and transport, a mass electric-car-charging scheme, installing LED street lights and expanding the renewable electricity grid.

If successful, Glasgow will beat the Scottish government's target of reaching net-zero carbon emissions by 2045.

With ecofriendly projects and initiatives in place, Glasgow is also primed to host the United Nations Climate Change Conference (COP26) in November 2021. The two-week international summit will be the largest Britain has ever held, with up to 30,000 delegates and heads of state expected to attend.

and exceptional, with homemade treats for breakfast (£5).

Guests have access to a kitchen and hosts are flexible about breakfast arrangements.

Amadeus Guest House
B&B ££

(Map p116; ☑0141-339 8257; www.amadeus guesthouse.co.uk; 411 North Woodside Rd; s £60-70, s without bathroom £42-45, d £80-100; ☎) Just off the bustle of Great Western Rd, a minute's walk from the subway but on a quiet street by the riverside pathway, this B&B has compact bright rooms, all distinct, with a cheerful, breezy feel. There's a variety of types, including several singles. It offers excellent value and a genuine welcome. A good continental breakfast is included.

A few doors down the street, the same owners have two apartments (£120 to £140). These are excellent, with smart kitchens, cute rooms for kids, a comfortable lounge and a master bedroom. They make great options for families. There's a three-night minimum stay.

★ Alamo Guest House
B&B ££

(Map p116; ☑0141-339 2395; www.alamoguest house.com; 46 Gray St; d £100-£169, d without bathroom £59-85; ☎) The Alamo may not sound like a peaceful spot, but that's exactly what this great place is. Opposite Kelvingrove Park, it feels miles from the city's hustle, but several of Glasgow's best museums and restaurants are right at hand. The decor blends antique furnishings and modern design, with excellent bathrooms, and the owners will make you very welcome.

The superior rooms are a sumptuous sight to behold and may be a cheap upgrade at quiet times. Breakfast is abundant and events such as whisky tastings are regularly offered.

Sandyford Lodge
GUESTHOUSE ££

(Map p116; ☑0141-332 9009; www.sandyford lodge.com; 21 Royal Cres; incl breakfast s £59-89, d £109-139; ☎) This elegant Victorian building is handy for the West End's museums and the Finnieston restaurant strip. Rooms, which vary in size, offer decent value – except on busy weekends – with good facilities and comfort, while staff go out of their way to be helpful. Don't confuse with the nearby Sandyford Hotel, run by the same owners.

Heritage Hotel
HOTEL £££

(Map p116; ☑0141-339 6955; www.theherit agehotel.net; 4 Alfred Tce, Great Western Rd; s/d incl breakfast £70/150; P ☎) A stone's throw from all the West End action, this friendly hotel has an open, airy feel despite the rather dilapidated raised terrace on which it's located. Generally, rooms on the 1st and 2nd floors are a bit more spacious and have a better outlook. The location, parking option and very fair prices mark it out.

Prices are very demand dependent; on a quiet weekday you can score a real bargain.

Acorn Hotel
HOTEL ££

(Map p116; ☑0141-332 6556; www.acorn-hotel. com; 140 Elderslie St; s £60-80, d £80-120; @ ☎) Enjoying a pretty location by a park, yet by a decent pub and just a block from Sauchiehall St, this smart little place has rooms that are compact but boast stylish colours and comfortable beds. Staff are very welcoming.

15Glasgow
B&B **£££**

(Map p116; ☑ 0141-332 1263; www.15glasgow. com; 15 Woodside Pl; d/ste £150/180; P 🛜) Glasgow's 19th-century merchants certainly knew how to build a beautiful house, and this 1840s terrace is a sumptuous example. Huge rooms with lofty ceilings have exquisite period detail complemented by attractive modern greys, striking bathrooms and well-chosen quality furniture. Your welcoming host makes everything easy: the in-room breakfast, overlooking the park, is a real treat. They prefer no under-five-year-olds.

Hotel du Vin
HOTEL **£££**

(☑ 0141-378 0385; www.hotelduvin.com; 1 Devonshire Gardens; r £169-519; P @ 🛜 🐾) Traditionally Glasgow's favoured hotel of the rich and famous, and the patriarch of sophistication and comfort. A study in elegance, it's sumptuously decorated and occupies three classical sandstone terrace houses. There's a bewildering array of room types, all different in style and size. The hospitality is old-school courteous, and there's an excellent restaurant on-site with a vast wine selection.

🍴 Eating

Glasgow is the best place to eat in Scotland, with a stupendous range of restaurants and cafes. The West End is a culinary centre, with Merchant City also boasting a high concentration of quality establishments. Pubs and bars (p128) are often good mealtime options, too.

The excellent *Eating & Drinking Guide*, published by *The List* every second April, covers both Glasgow and Edinburgh.

🍴 City Centre

★ Riverhill Coffee Bar
CAFE **£**

(Map p112; ☑ 0141-204 4762; www.riverhillcoffee.co.uk; 24 Gordon St; breakfast £3-6.50; ⊙ 7am-5pm Mon-Fri, from 8am Sat, from 10am Sun; 🛜) 🍃 Chain cafes plaster Glasgow's centre, so it's a joy to come across this tiny place, which offers great coffee and hot chocolate as well as delicious filled rolls and toasts. Ingredients are sustainably sourced and seriously tasty. It's extremely friendly; you'd come every day if you lived nearby.

★ Singl-end
CAFE **£**

(Map p112; ☑ 0141-353 1277; www.thesingl-end. co.uk; 265 Renfrew St; dishes £5.50-10; ⊙ 10am-4pm; 🛜 🍴) There's something glorious about this long basement cafe with its cheery service and air of brunchy bonhomie. It covers a lot of bases, with good coffee, generous breakfasts and lunches, booze and baking. Dietary requirements are superbly catered for, with fine vegan choices and clear labelling. On a diet? Avert your eyes from the 'eat-me' cornucopia of meringues and pastries by the door.

Platform
STREET FOOD **£**

(Map p112; ☑ 0345-241 6253; www.platformgla. co.uk; 253 Argyle St; light meals £5-8; ⊙ 5-11pm Thu, from noon Fri & Sat) This atmospheric series of brick-arched vaults under the railway lines at Central station comes into its own at weekends, when street-food vendors open up stalls and a bar doles out pints to those seeking an escape from the weather. It's family and dog friendly. During the week the cafe is still open.

★ Saramago Café Bar
VEGAN **£**

(Map p112; ☑ 0141-352 4920; www.cca-glasgow. com; 350 Sauchiehall St; mains £9-12; ⊙ 10am-10pm Mon-Sat; 🛜 🍴) In the airy atrium of the Centre for Contemporary Arts, this place does a great line in eclectic vegan fusion food, with a range of top flavour combinations from around the globe. The upstairs bar (open from 4pm Thursday and noon Friday and Saturday) has a great deck on steep Scott St and packs out inside with a friendly, arty crowd enjoying the DJ sets and quality tap beers.

Spanish Butcher
SPANISH **££**

(Map p112; ☑ 0141-406 9880; www.spanish butcher.com; 80 Miller St; mains £14-24; ⊙ noon-1am; 🛜) In a refined interior, moodily dark with industrial decor above retro wickerwork chairs, this is a fine venue for quality northern Spanish beef, with the best cuts designed for sharing. But there's plenty more to delight: whole baked fish, expertly deboned, are attractive and succulent, and whole roasted suckling pig available by preorder.

There are some good Spanish wines by the glass and a range of tasty bar snacks if you just want a drink.

Café Gandolfi
CAFE **££**

(Map p112; ☑ 0141-552 6813; www.cafegan dolfi.com; 64 Albion St; mains £12.50-17.50; ⊙ 8am-11pm Mon-Sat, from 9am Sun; 🛜) In Merchant City, this cafe was once part of the old cheese market. It's been pulling in the punters for years and attracts an interesting mix of die-hard Gandolfers, the upwardly mobile and tourists. It covers all bases with excellent breakfasts and coffee, an enticing upstairs bar (p129), and top-notch bistro food, including Scottish and continental options, in an atmospheric, medieval-like setting.

Loon Fung
CANTONESE ££

(Map p112; ☑ 0141-332 1240; www.loonfungglasgow.com; 417 Sauchiehall St; mains £11-15; ⊙ noon-11pm; �﷽) This elegant Cantonese oasis is one of Scotland's most authentic Chinese restaurants; indeed, it's quite a surprise after a traditional dining experience here to emerge to boisterous Sauchiehall St rather than Hong Kong. The dim-sum choices are toothsome, and the seafood – try the sea bass – really excellent.

Gamba
SEAFOOD £££

(Map p112; ☑ 0141-572 0899; www.gamba.co.uk; 225a West George St; mains £21-30; ⊙ noon-2.15pm & 5-9.30pm Mon-Fri, noon-9.30pm Sat; �﷽) This business-district basement is easily missed but is actually one of the city's premier seafood restaurants. Presentation is elegant, with carefully selected flavours allowing the fish, sustainably sourced from Scotland and beyond, to shine. Service is smart and solicitous. From Thursday to Saturday, there are good lunch and pre-theatre deals (£22/34 for two/three courses).

Hutchesons City Grill
STEAK £££

(Map p112; ☑ 0141 406 9880; www.hutchesonsglasgow.com; 158 Ingram St; mains £23-38; ⊙ food noon-10pm; ☑) This upstairs dining room in a historic Merchant City building has real wow factor with superhigh ceilings, leadlights, ornamental fireplaces and 19th-century boardroom-style seating. Steaks are the order of the day with various delicious aged options available, but oysters, duck and other dishes are served too. A good portion of the short menu is vegetarian. The bar downstairs is equally plush.

✖ East End

McCune Smith
CAFE £

(Map p112; ☑ 0141-548 1114; www.mccunesmith.co.uk; 3 Duke St; light meals £4-7.50; ⊙ 8am-4pm; ☎☑) This stellar cafe is named after a University of Glasgow graduate who was a noted abolitionist and the first African American to hold a medical degree. The hospitable owners take their coffee seriously and offer scrumptious breakfast and brunch fare, plus delicious sandwiches and soups in a luminous, high-ceilinged interior. They bake their own bread and at least half the menu is vegan.

✖ West End

In many ways, the West End is the powerhouse of Glasgow's foodie scene, with the area around Byres Rd a hub of quality eating and Argyle St in Finnieston a heartland of fashionable new eating options. Great Western Rd and Gibson St also offer excellent choice.

78 Bar & Kitchen
CAFE £

(Map p116; ☑ 0141-576 5018; www.the78barandkitchen.com; 10 Kelvinhaugh St; mains £5-10; ⊙ food noon-9pm; ☎☑) More a comfortable lounge than your typical veggie restaurant, this cafe offers cosy couch seating and reassuringly solid wooden tables, as well as an inviting range of ales. The low-priced vegan food includes hearty stews and curries, and there's regular live music in a very welcoming atmosphere.

★ Ox & Finch
FUSION ££

(Map p116; ☑ 0141-339 8627; www.oxandfinch.com; 920 Sauchiehall St; small plates £5-14.50; ⊙ noon-10pm; ☎☑) This fashionable place could almost sum up the thriving modern Glasgow eating scene, with a faux-pub name, sleek but comfortable contemporary decor and an open kitchen. Grab a cosy booth and be prepared to have your taste buds wowed by innovative, delicious sharing plates. Flavours draw on French and Mediterranean influences but focus on quality Scottish produce, with excellent vegetarian creations available.

★ Mother India
INDIAN ££

(Map p116; ☑ 0141-221 1663; www.motherindia.co.uk; 28 Westminster Tce, Sauchiehall St; mains £11-16; ⊙ 5-10pm Thu & Fri, from 1pm Sat & Sun; ☎☑♿) Glasgow curry buffs forever debate the merits of the city's numerous excellent South Asian restaurants; Mother India features in every discussion. It's been a stalwart for years, and the quality and innovation are superb. The three dining areas are all attractive.

There are various other innovative, distinct sister restaurants around town.

Alchemilla MEDITERRANEAN **££**
(Map p116; ☑0141-337 6060; www.thisisal
chemilla.com; 1126 Argyle St; plates £4-13.50;
☺5pm-midnight Thu, from noon Fri-Sun) The
number of quality eating options opening on the Finnieston strip is phenomenal, and this is a fine example. The casual
open-kitchen eatery offers sharing plates
with an eastern Mediterranean feel. Interesting ingredients and intriguing textures
are key. There are lots of meat-free options
and a list of hard-to-find natural wines.

Left Bank BISTRO **££**
(Map p116; ☑0141-339 5969; www.theleftbank.
co.uk; 33 Gibson St; mains £7-15; ☺food 9am-
10pm Mon-Fri, from 10am Sat & Sun; 🖎🖉) 🖉
Huge windows fronting the street reveal
this outstanding eatery specialising in
gastronomic delights and lazy afternoons.
Lots of little spaces filled with couches
and chunky tables make for intimacy. The
wide-ranging menu features delightful creations using seasonal and local produce,
with an eclectic variety of influences, including Asian and traditional Scottish fare.
Brunch is also a highlight.

The Finnieston SEAFOOD **££**
(Map p116; ☑0141-222 2884; www.thefinnieston
bar.com; 1125 Argyle St; plates £7-20; ☺5-10pm
Thu, from noon Fri-Sun; 🖎) 🖉 A flagship of
this increasingly vibrant strip, this gastropub recalls the area's sailing heritage with
a cosily romantic below-decks atmosphere
and artfully placed nautical motifs. It's been
well thought through, with a short menu
of high-quality upmarket pub fare focusing
on sustainable Scottish seafood. Excellent
G&Ts (slurp one in the little courtyard) and
cocktails.

Bay Tree CAFE **££**
(Map p116; ☑0141-334 5898; www.thebaytree
westend.co.uk; 403 Great Western Rd; mains £7-16;
☺11am-10pm Tue-Fri, from 10am Sat & Sun; 🖎🖉)
There are many good cafes along this section of Great Western Rd, but the Bay Tree
is still a solid choice. It has lots of vegan
and vegetarian options, smiling staff, filling
mains (mostly Middle Eastern and Greek),
and generous salads.

Bothy SCOTTISH **££**
(Map p116; ☑0845 166 6032; www.bothyglas
gow.co.uk; 11 Ruthven Lane; mains £13-23; ☺5-
10pm Wed & Thu, from noon Fri, from 11am Sat &
Sun; 🖎) This West End player, boasting a
combo of modern design and comfy ret-

ro furnishings, blows apart the myth that
Scottish food is stodgy and uninteresting.
The Bothy dishes out traditional home-
style fare with a modern twist. It's filling,
but leave room for dessert. Smaller lunch
plates are a good deal, and there's an attractive outdoor area.

★**Stravaigin** FUSION **£££**
(Map p116; ☑0141-334 2665; www.stravaigin.
co.uk; 28 Gibson St; breakfast £8-14, restaurant
mains £14-25; ☺9am-10pm; 🖎🖉) Stravaigin
is a serious foodie's delight, with a menu
constantly pushing the boundaries of
originality and offering creative culinary
excellence. With a range of eating spaces
across three levels, it's pleasingly casual
and easy-going. The entry level also has a
buzzing bar with a separate menu. Scottish
classics like haggis take their place alongside a range of Asian-influenced and vegetarian dishes.

★**Ubiquitous Chip** SCOTTISH **£££**
(Map p116; ☑0141-334 5007; www.ubiquitous
chip.co.uk; 12 Ashton Lane; mains £17-26, tasting
menu £60; ☺restaurant 11am-10pm Tue-Sun; 🖎)
🖉 The original champion of Scottish produce, Ubiquitous Chip is legendary for its
still-unparalleled cuisine and lengthy wine
list. Named to poke fun at Scotland's culinary reputation, it offers a French touch
but resolutely Scottish ingredients, carefully selected and following sustainable principles. The elegant courtyard space offers
some of Glasgow's best dining, while the
brasserie above offers a more laid-back
vibe.

Two bars, including the cute Wee Pub
down the side alley, offer plenty of drinking pleasure. There's always something going on at the Chip – check the website for
upcoming events.

Butchershop Bar & Grill STEAK **£££**
(Map p116; ☑0141-339 2999; www.butcher
shopglasgow.com; 1055 Sauchiehall St; steaks £17-
33; ☺noon-10pm Sun-Thu, to 1am Fri & Sat; 🖎)
Offering several different cuts of traceably
sourced, properly aged beef, this is one of
the best spots in Glasgow for a tasty, served-
as-you-want-it steak. It's a perfect lunch
venue after the Kelvingrove Art Gallery
& Museum (p114). There are seats out the
front if the weather happens to be fine. It
also has a little seafood on the menu and
decently mixed cocktails.

Cail Bruich
SCOTTISH £££

(Map p116; ☑0141-334 6265; www.cailbruich.co.uk; 725 Great Western Rd; 3-course lunch £35, dinner £65; ⊗6-10pm Wed, noon-4pm & 6-10pm Thu-Sat; ☎) In an elegant if rather nondescript dining room, the kitchen here turns out some memorable modern Scottish fare. The forage ethos brings surprising, tangy, herbal flavours to plates that are always interesting but never pretentious. Everything from the amuse-bouche to the homemade bread is top-notch – the degustation menu (£60) with optional wine flight (£90) combines the best on offer.

Gannet
SCOTTISH £££

(Map p116; ☑0141-204 2081; www.thegannetgla.com; 1155 Argyle St; menu £50; ⊗6-9.15pm Wed & Thu, noon-2pm & 5.30-9.15pm Fri & Sat, 1-2.30pm & 6-9pm Sun; ☎) 🍴 In vogue but not starchy, this jewel of the Finnieston strip offers a cosy wood-panelled ambience and gourmet food that excels on presentation and taste without venturing towards cutting-edge. The short, polished daily menu features quality produce sourced mostly from southern Scotland, and the interesting wine list backs it up very well indeed. Solicitous, professional service is another plus.

✖ Southside

Cafe Strange Brew
CAFE £

(☑0141-440 7290; www.facebook.com/cafestrangebrew; 1082 Pollokshaws Rd; dishes £5-11; ⊗9am-4pm Mon-Sat, to 3pm Sun) This has such cachet as the Southside's – if not the city's – best cafe that you'll be waiting in line most days. It's worth the enforced contemplation, with generous, vibrant, filling brunchy fare that draws on global influences as well as closer-to-home inspiration. Presentation is a high point; leave room for the sinfully sticky desserts.

Fish People Cafe
SEAFOOD £££

(☑0141-429 8787; www.thefishpeoplecafe.co.uk; 350 Scotland St; mains £18-23; ⊗noon-9pm Tue-Thu, to 10pm Fri & Sat, to 4pm Sun) A subway-station forecourt is an unlikely spot to find a seafood restaurant of such quality, but pop out of Shields Rd and here it is. The adjacent fish shop supplies the raw materials for simple but perfectly prepared dishes that shine with quality. Service is also exceptionally welcoming. It's opposite Scotland Street School (p119), but worth the trip from anywhere in town.

Drinking & Nightlife

Glaswegians are known to enjoy a beverage or two, and some of Britain's best nightlife is found in the din and sometimes roar of the city's pubs and bars. There are as many different styles of bar as there are punters to guzzle in them. Craft beer, single malt, Scottish gins: it's all here.

Glasgow's clubbing scene has been affected by closures in recent years due to various reasons, but it's still lively. Glaswegians usually hit clubs after the pubs have closed, so many clubs offer discounted admission and cheaper drinks if you go early. Entry costs £5 to £10 (up to £25 for big events), although bars often hand out free passes. There's a minimum age of 21 years to enter some of them. Clubs shut comparatively early, so ask around to find out where the after-parties are.

City Centre

★ DogHouse Merchant City
BAR

(Map p112; ☑0141-552 6363; www.brewdog.com; 99 Hutcheson St; ⊗11am-10pm; ☎) Brewdog's zingy beers are matched by its upbeat attitude, so this Merchant City spot was always going to be a fun place. An open kitchen doles out slidery, burgery, smoked-meat fare, while 25 taps run quality craft beer from morning till night.

Sub Club
CLUB

(Map p112; ☑0141-248 4600; www.subclub.co.uk; 22 Jamaica St; ⊗11pm-4am Fri & Sat) Scotland's most famous house club is still going strong several decades on. Saturday at the Sub Club is one of Glasgow's legendary nights, offering serious clubbing with a sound system that aficionados usually rate as the city's best. The claustrophobic, last-one-in vibe is not for the faint of heart. Check the website for other nights.

★ Pot Still
PUB

(Map p112; ☑0141-333 0980; www.thepotstill.co.uk; 154 Hope St; ⊗11am-midnight; ☎) The cheeriest and cosiest of places, the Pot Still has a time-warp feel with its creaky floor and old-style wrought-iron-legged tables. There's a superb whisky selection and knowledgeable staff – constantly up and down ladders to get at bottles – to back it up. Tasty pies (£2 to £4) are on hand for solid sustenance.

Shilling Brewing Co
MICROBREWERY

(Map p112; ☑0141-353 1654; www.shillingbrewingcompany.co.uk; 92 West George St; ⊗4-10pm

Wed-Fri, from noon Sat & Sun; 🐾) Drinking in former banks is a Glasgow thing and this central brewpub offers some of the best of it. The wooden, high-ceilinged space has huge windows out to the city centre and room to spare to try its beers; the almost grapefruity Unicorn IPA is a real palate cleanser. Another couple of dozen taps showcase guest craft brews from around Scotland.

Laboratorio Espresso CAFE
(Map p112; 📞0141-353 1111; www.laboratorioespresso.com; 93 West Nile St; ⏰7.30am-5.30pm Mon-Fri, from 9am Sat, from 11am Sun) A chic space, all concrete and glass, this cafe offers the best coffee we've tried in Glasgow. It's sourced properly, and served in delicious double-shot creations with authentically concentrated espresso; soy milk is available. There are a couple of tables outside even in the coldest weather. Pastries and biscotti are on hand, but it's all about the brew.

Babbity Bowster PUB
(Map p112; 📞0141-552 5055; www.babbitybowster.com; 16-18 Blackfriars St; ⏰noon-midnight; 🐾) In a quiet corner of Merchant City, this handsome spot is perfect for a tranquil daytime drink, particularly in the adjoining beer garden. Service is attentive, and the smell of sausages may tempt you to lunch; it also offers accommodation (p122). This is one of the city centre's most charming pubs, in one of its noblest buildings. There's a regular folk-music scene.

Bar Gandolfi COCKTAIL BAR
(Map p112; 📞0141-552 4462; www.cafegandolfi.com; 64 Albion St; ⏰noon-11pm; 🐾) Above the cafe of the same name, this little upstairs gem is far from the often-boisterous Merchant Sq pubs opposite. Pared-back, unvarnished wooden stools and tables, offbeat art exhibitions and a large kitchen-bar area – there's far more space behind it than on the patrons' side – create a relaxing space for a

---

LGBTIQ+ GLASGOW

Glasgow has a vibrant LGBTIQ+ scene, with the gay quarter found in and around Merchant City (particularly Virginia, Wilson and Glassford Sts). Many straight clubs and bars also have gay and lesbian nights.

Most Glaswegians are very tolerant, but you may encounter disapproval away from central areas. Same-sex marriage was legalised in Scotland in 2014.

Waterloo Bar (Map p112; 📞0141-248 7216; www.waterlooglasgow.wixsite.com/home; 306 Argyle St; ⏰noon-11pm Mon-Thu, to midnight Fri & Sat, 12.30-11pm Sun) This traditional pub is Scotland's oldest gay bar. It attracts punters of all ages. It's very friendly and, with a large group of regulars, a good place to meet people away from the scene.

Katie's Bar (Map p112; 📞0141-237 3030; www.katiesbar.co.uk; 17 John St; ⏰noon-midnight Wed-Sun; 🐾) With an easily missed entrance between a Spanish and an Italian restaurant, this basement bar is a friendly LGBTIQ+ pub with a pool table and regular gigs at weekends. It's a pleasant, low-key space to start off the night and especially popular with women.

Underground (Map p112; 📞0141-553 2456; www.facebook.com/undergroundglasgo; 6a John St; ⏰noon-midnight; 🐾) Downstairs on cosmopolitan John St, Underground sports a relaxed crowd and, crucially, a free jukebox. You'll be listening to indie rather than Abba here.

AXM (Map p112; 📞0141-552 5761; www.facebook.com/axmclubglasgow; 80 Glassford St; ⏰10.30pm-4am Thu-Sat) This popular Manchester club's Glasgow branch is a cheery spot, not too scene-y, with all welcome. It makes for a fun place to finish off a night out.

Delmonica's (Map p112; 📞0141-559 6594; www.delmonicas.co.uk; 68 Virginia St; ⏰5-10pm Tue-Thu, from 3pm Fri & Sun, from noon Sat) In the heart of the Pink Triangle, this is a popular bar with a good mix of ages and orientations. It packs out in the evenings when private karaoke booths, drag shows and other fun keep things lively, and it's a pleasant spot for a quiet drink earlier in the day. Come here before the adjacent **Polo Lounge** (Map p112; 📞0141-559 6593; www.pologlasgow.co.uk; 84 Wilson St; cover £3-7; ⏰9pm-3am), as you might get a free pass.

quality cocktail or spirit. Tasty, well-sourced food available.

The Horseshoe Bar   PUB
(Map p112; ☑0141-248 6368; www.thehorse shoebarglasgow.co.uk; 17 Drury St; ☉10am-10pm) This legendary city pub and popular meeting place dates from the late 19th century and is largely unchanged. It's a picturesque spot, with the longest continuous bar in the UK, but its main attraction is what's served over it – real ale and good cheer. Upstairs in the lounge is some of the best-value pub food (dishes £4 to £10) in town.

Artà   BAR, CLUB
(Map p112; ☑0141-552 2101; www.arta.co.uk; 62 Albion St; ☉5pm-midnight Thu, 5pm-3am Fri, 12.30pm-3am Sat; ☎) Set in a former cheese market, this place is very OTT with its Mediterranean-villa decor; it really does have to be seen to be believed. Despite the luxury, it's got a relaxed, chilled vibe and makes a decent cocktail. It also does Spanish-influenced food but it's better visited as a bar and nightclub.

Cathouse   CLUB
(Map p112; ☑0141-248 6606; www.cathouse. co.uk; 15 Union St; ☉10.30pm-3am Wed-Sun; ☎) It's mostly rock, alternative and metal with a touch of Goth and post-punk at this long-standing indie venue. There are two dance floors: upstairs is pretty intense with lots of metal and hard rock; downstairs is a little more tranquil. Admission ranges from free to £6.

Butterfly & the Pig   PUB
(Map p112; ☑0141-221 7711; www.thebutterfly andthepig.com; 153 Bath St; ☉restaurant 8.30am-8pm Mon-Sat, 10am-8pm Sun, bar noon-midnight; ☎) A breath of fresh air, this offbeat spot makes you feel comfortable as soon as you plunge into its basement depths. The decor is eclectic with a cosy retro feel. There's regular live jazz or similar and a sizeable menu – if you can decipher it – of pub grub (dishes £5 to £15), plus a rather wonderful tearoom upstairs. Great for breakfast before the pub opens.

Corinthian Club   BAR
(Map p112; ☑0141-552 1101; www.thecorin thianclub.co.uk; 191 Ingram St; ☉2-10pm Thu, noon-10pm Fri & Sat, noon-6pm Sun; ☎) A breathtaking domed ceiling and majestic chandeliers make this casino a special space. Originally a bank and later Glas-gow's High Court, this regal building's main bar is a stunner. Cosy wrap-around seating and room to spare are complemented by a restaurant, a nightclub, a piano bar, a roof terrace and a gin bar, as well as the casino area itself.

Classic Grand   CLUB
(Map p112; ☑0141-847 0820; www.classicgrand. com; 18 Jamaica St; ☉hours vary; ☎) Rock, industrial, electronic and powerpop grace the stage and the turntables at this unpretentious central venue. It doesn't take itself too seriously, drinks are cheap and the locals are welcoming. Hours vary according to events, but core opening is 11pm to 3am Thursday to Saturday.

🍷 East End

Drygate   MICROBREWERY
(Map p112; ☑0141-212 8815; www.drygate.com; 85 Drygate; ☉11am-midnight; ☎) Dwarfed by the lager megabrewery Tennents next door, Drygate is a proud craft brewery that makes a tempting East End pit stop. You can watch the beer being made on the factory floor as you sip one of two dozen on tap in the likeably convivial, industrially fitted interior or hit the excellent terrace. Burgers, sandwiches, fish and chips and more provide ballast.

🍷 West End

★Inn Deep   BAR
(Map p116; ☑0141-264 2777; www.inndeep.com; 445 Great Western Rd; ☉noon-midnight Mon-Sat, to 11pm Sun) Descend the stairs to find yourself in a fabulous spot on the banks of the Kelvin. It's glorious on a fine day (and Glaswegians set that bar pretty low) to grab a craft beer and spill out onto the riverside path in a happy throng. The vaulted interior spaces under the bridge are also characterful.

Òran Mór   BAR, CLUB
(Map p116; ☑0141-357 6200; www.oran-mor. co.uk; cnr Byres & Great Western Rds; ☉9am-2am Mon-Wed, to 3am Thu-Sat, 10am-3am Sun; ☎) Some may be uncomfortable with the thought of drinking in a church. But we say: the Lord giveth. This bar, restaurant, club and theatre venue is a likeable and versatile spot with an attractive interior and a fine whisky selection to replace the holy water. The lunchtime **A Play, a Pie and a Pint** (Map p116; www.playpiepint.com;

incl pie & pint £12.50-15; ⊙1pm Mon-Sat) is an excellent feature.

Brel
BAR

(Map p116; ☑0141-739 4830; www.brelbar.com; 39 Ashton Lane; ⊙noon-10pm; 🔊) Perhaps the best bar on Ashton Lane, Brel can seem tightly packed, but there's a conservatory for eating out the back so you can pretend you're sitting outside when it's raining, and when the sun does peek through, there's an appealing tiered beer garden. It's got a huge range of Belgian beers, and also does *moules frites* and lobster *frites* among other tasty fare.

Hillhead Bookclub
BAR

(Map p116; ☑0141-576 1700; www.hillhead bookclub.co.uk; 17 Vinicombe St; ⊙3-10pm Mon-Thu, from noon Fri, from 10am Sat & Sun; 🔊) Atmosphere in spades is the call sign of this easy-going bar. An ornate wooden ceiling overlooks two levels of well-mixed cocktails, seriously cheap drinks, comfort food and numerous intriguing decorative touches. There's even a ping-pong table in a cage.

☆ Entertainment

Glasgow is Scotland's entertainment city, from classical music, fine theatre and ballet to an amazing range of live-music venues. To tap into the scene, check out *The List* (www.list.co.uk), an invaluable free events guide.

For theatre tickets, book directly with the venue. For concerts, a useful booking centre is Tickets Scotland (www.tickets-scotland.com).

Live Music

Glasgow is the king of Scotland's live music scene. Year after year, touring musicians and travellers alike name Glasgow as one of their favourite cities in the world to enjoy live music. Much of Glasgow's character is encapsulated in the soul and humour of its inhabitants, and the main reason for the city's musical success lies within its audience and the musical community it has bred and nurtured for years.

★ King Tut's Wah Wah Hut
LIVE MUSIC

(Map p112; ☑0141-221 5279; www.kingtuts.co.uk; 272a St Vincent St; ⊙noon-1am) One of the city's premier live-music pub venues, hosting bands every night of the week. A staple of the local scene, and a real Glasgow highlight.

Hug & Pint
LIVE MUSIC

(Map p116; ☑07429 432713; www.thehugand pint.com; 171 Great Western Rd; ⊙noon-midnight; 🔊) With bands almost daily in the downstairs space, this comfortable local is a great destination, which it would be anyway for its excellent atmosphere, highly original Asian-influenced vegan food and colourful interior.

Hydro
CONCERT VENUE

(Map p116; ☑0141-248 3000; www.thessehydro. com; Finnieston Quay; 🔊) A spectacular modern building to keep the adjacent 'Armadillo' company, the Hydro amphitheatre is a phenomenally popular venue for big-name concerts and shows.

13th Note Café
LIVE MUSIC

(Map p112; ☑0141-553 1638; www.13thnote.co.uk; 50-60 King St; ⊙noon-9pm Mon-Wed, to midnight Thu-Sat, to 5pm Sun; 🔊) Cosy basement venue with small independent bands as well as weekend DJs and regular comedy and theatre performances. At street level the pleasant cafe does decent vegetarian and vegan food (£7 to £10, until 9pm).

Barrowland Ballroom
CONCERT VENUE

(The Barrowlands; Map p112; ☑0141-552 4601; www.barrowland-ballroom.co.uk; 244 Gallowgate) A down-at-heel but exceptional old dance hall above the Barras market, catering for some of the larger acts that visit the city. It's one of Scotland's most atmospheric venues with its sprung floor and authentic character.

Clyde Auditorium
LIVE PERFORMANCE

(Map p116; ☑0844 395 4000; www.sec.co.uk; Finnieston Quay) Also known as the Armadillo because of its bizarre shape, the Clyde adjoins the SEC Centre auditorium, and caters for big national and international acts.

Audio
CONCERT VENUE

(Map p112; www.audioglasgow.co.uk; 14 Midland St) In the bowels of Central station, this is an atmospheric venue for regular concerts by touring acts, particularly of the rock and metal varieties.

Cinemas

★ Glasgow Film Theatre
CINEMA

(Map p112; ☑0141-332 6535; www.glasgowfilm. org; 12 Rose St; adult/child £10.90/7.90) This much-loved three-screener off Sauchiehall St shows art-house cinema and classics.

GLASGOW ENTERTAINMENT

Grosvenor Cinema   CINEMA

(Map p116; ☑0845 166 6002; www.grosvenor westend.co.uk; Ashton Lane) This sweet cinema puts you in the heart of the West End eating and nightlife for post-movie debriefings.

Theatres & Concert Halls

Citizens' Theatre   THEATRE

(☑0141-429 0022; www.citz.co.uk; 119 Gorbals St) South of the Clyde, this is one of Scotland's top theatres. It's well worth trying to catch a performance here.

Tramway   PERFORMING ARTS

(☑0845 330 3501; www.tramway.org; 25 Albert Dr; ⊙9.30am-8pm Mon-Sat, noon-6pm Sun; ☎) Occupying a former tram depot, this buzzy cultural centre has performance and exhibition spaces as well as a popular cafe. It's a real Southside community hub, with an unusual **garden** (☑0141-433 2722; www. thehiddengardens.org.uk; 25a Albert Dr; ⊙10am-8pm Tue-Sat, noon-6pm Sun Apr-Sep, 10am-4pm Tue-Sat, noon-4pm Sun Oct-Mar) **FREE** out the back. It attracts cutting-edge theatrical groups, is the home of Scottish Ballet and hosts a varied range of artistic exhibitions. It's very close to Pollokshields East train station.

Theatre Royal   CONCERT VENUE

(Map p112; ☑0844 871 7677; www.glasgowthe atreroyal.org.uk; 282 Hope St) Proudly sporting an eye-catching modern facelift, Glasgow's oldest theatre is the home of Scottish Opera.

City Halls   CONCERT VENUE

(Map p112; ☑0141-353 8000; www.glasgowcon certhalls.com; Candleriggs) In the heart of Merchant City, there are regular performances in this beautiful rectangular auditorium by the Scottish Chamber Orchestra and the Scottish Symphony Orchestra.

Glasgow Royal Concert Hall   CONCERT VENUE

(Map p112; ☑0141-353 8000; www.glasgow concerthalls.com; 2 Sauchiehall St; ☎) A feast of classical music is showcased at this concert hall, the modern home of the Royal Scottish National Orchestra. There are also regular pop, folk and jazz performances, typically by big-name solo artists.

Centre for Contemporary Arts   ARTS CENTRE

(Map p112; ☑0141-352 4900; www.cca-glasgow. com; 350 Sauchiehall St; ⊙10am-10pm Mon-Sat) This is a chic venue making terrific use of space and light. It showcases the visual and performing arts, including movies, talks and galleries. There's a good cafe-bar here too.

Sport

Two football clubs – Rangers and Celtic – totally dominate the sporting scene in Scotland, having vastly more resources than other clubs and a long history (and rivalry). This runs along traditionally partisan lines, with Rangers representing Protestant supporters, and Celtic, Catholic. It's worth going to a game; both play in magnificent arenas with great atmosphere. Games between the two (normally four a year) are fiercely contested, but tickets aren't sold to the general public; you'll need to know a season-ticket holder.

Celtic FC   FOOTBALL

(☑0871 226 1888; www.celticfc.net; Celtic Park, Parkhead) Playing in green and white hoops, Celtic is one of Glasgow's big two football clubs and traditionally represents the Catholic side of the divide. There are daily stadium tours (adult/child £13.50/8). Catch bus 61 or 62 from outside St Enoch centre.

Rangers FC   FOOTBALL

(☑0871 702 1972; www.rangers.co.uk; Ibrox Stadium, 150 Edmiston Dr) One of Glasgow's big two football clubs, Rangers play in blue and traditionally represent the Protestant, pro-Union side of the divide. It recently returned to the top division after a financial meltdown. Tours of the stadium and trophy room run Friday to Sunday (adult/child £15/5). Take the subway to Ibrox station.

🔒 Shopping

With the UK's largest retail phalanx outside London, Glasgow is a shopaholic's paradise. The 'Style Mile' around Buchanan and Argyle Sts and Merchant City (particularly upmarket Ingram St) is a fashion hub, while the West End has quirkier, more bohemian shopping options: it's great for vintage clothing. The weekend Barras market in the East End is very worthwhile.

The Barras   MARKET

(Map p112; ☑0141-552 4601; www.theglas gowbarras.com; btwn Gallowgate & London Rd; ⊙10am-5pm Sat & Sun) Glasgow's legendary weekend flea market, the Barras on Gallowgate, is a fascinating mixture of on-trend openings and working-class Glasgow. Genuine old stalls flogging time-faded glasses,

VINTAGE & RETRO SHOPPING

Snag a bargain and bring out the hipster in you with Glasgow's fabulous range of retro rag stores.

Mr Ben (Map p112; ☎0141-553 1936; www.mrbenretroclothing.com; 101 King St; ☺10.30am-5.45pm) This cute place is one of Glasgow's best destinations for vintage clothing, with a great selection of brands like Fred Perry, as well as more glam choices and even outdoor gear.

Randall's Antique & Vintage Centre (Map p112; ☎0754-626 0727; www.facebook.com/randallsantiqueandvintagecentre; Stevenson St West; ☺9am-5pm Sat & Sun) This is a real treasure trove of the once loved, the tacky, the tawdry, the magnificent and the curious from the not-so-recent past. It's an excellent set-up with several sellers and a top spot to browse. Don't take the kids; they'll make you feel ancient with their incredulity at items that you remember using not so very long ago.

Glasgow Vintage Company (Map p116; ☎0141-338 6633; www.glasgowvintage.com; 453 Great Western Rd; ☺11am-6pm Mon-Sat, to 5pm Sun) With a little more breathing room than some of Glasgow's vintage shops, this one offers relaxed browsing.

Caledonia Books (Map p116; ☎0141-334 9663; www.caledoniabooks.co.uk; 483 Great Western Rd; ☺10.30am-6pm Mon-Sat) This characterful spot is just what a secondhand bookshop should be, with a smell of dust and venerability and a wide range of intriguing volumes on the slightly chaotic shelves.

De Courcy's Arcade (Map p116; www.facebook.com/decourcysarcade; Cresswell Lane; ☺10am-5.30pm Mon-Sat, noon-5pm Sun) Down a West End lane, this sweet, bijou two-level arcade has a selection of tiny boutiques offering vintage clothing, art, homewares and more. Opening hours of individual shops can vary.

posters and DVDs that you'd struggle to give away are juxtaposed with vintage classics, very earthy traders' pubs and a street scene where fake designer gear is marked down and dodgy characters peddle smuggled cigarettes.

It's an intriguing stroll, as much for the assortment of local characters as for what's on offer. People come here just to wander, and parts of it have a real feel of a nearly vanished Britain of whelk stalls and rag-and-bone merchants. Watch your wallet.

Barras Art & Design ARTS & CRAFTS
(BAaD; Map p112; ☎0141-237 9220; www.baadglasgow.com; Moncur St; ☺noon-midnight Tue-Sat, 11am-10pm Sun) This workshop zone for artists and designers in the heart of the Barras has helped pep up the area and bring a new wave of folk in. It's a lovely covered courtyard with a bar, cafe and restaurant, as well as pop-up and other shops. There are events on most weekends, including a monthly farmers market.

Adjacent to the main building, converted shipping containers hold more workshops and creative spaces.

Princes Square SHOPPING CENTRE
(Map p112; ☎0141-221 0324; www.princessquare.co.uk; 48 Buchanan St; ☺10am-7pm Mon-Fri, 9am-6pm Sat, 11am-5pm Sun) Set in a magnificent 1841 renovated square with elaborate ironwork and an exuberant metal leaf-and-peacock facade, this place has lots of beauty and fashion outlets, including Vivienne Westwood. There's a good selection of restaurants and cafes, as well as a bar with a roof terrace.

Argyll Arcade JEWELLERY
(Map p112; ☎0141-248 5257; www.argyll-arcade.com; Buchanan St; ☺10am-5pm Mon-Sat, from noon Sun) This splendid historic arcade doglegs between Buchanan and Argyle Sts and has done since before Victoria reigned. It's quite a sight with its end-to-end jewellery and watch shops. Top-hatted doorpeople greet nervously excited couples shopping for diamond rings.

Hidden Lane ARTS & CRAFTS
(Map p116; www.thehiddenlaneglasgow.com; 1103 Argyle St; ☺hours vary) Well concealed down a passageway off the Finnieston strip, these back alleys house a colourful mix of arty shops and studios well investigating.

There's a tearoom, jewellery store, yoga centre and plenty more.

❶ Information

INTERNET ACCESS

There's a free wi-fi zone across the city centre. You can get a local SIM card for about a pound and data packages are cheap.

Gallery of Modern Art (☑ 0141-229 1996; www.glasgowlife.org.uk; Royal Exchange Sq; ⊙10am-5pm Mon-Wed & Sat, to 8pm Thu, 11am-5pm Fri & Sun; ☎) Basement library; free internet access. Bookings recommended.

Hillhead Library (☑ 0141-276 1617; www. glasgowlife.org.uk; 348 Byres Rd; ⊙10am-8pm Mon-Thu, to 5pm Fri & Sat, noon-5pm Sun; ☎) Free internet terminals.

iCafe (☑ 0141-353 6469; www.icafe.uk.com; 250 Woodlands Rd; per hour £2; ⊙9am-9pm; ☎) Sip a coffee and munch on a pastry while you check your emails on superfast internet connections. There is wi-fi too. It's actually a very good cafe in its own right. Check the website for the other branches.

Mitchell Library (☑ 0141-287 2999; www. glasgowlife.org.uk; North St; ⊙9am-8pm Mon-Thu, to 5pm Fri & Sat) Free internet access; bookings recommended.

MEDICAL SERVICES

Glasgow Dental Hospital (☑ 0141-211 9600; www.nhsggc.org.uk; 378 Sauchiehall St)

Glasgow Royal Infirmary (☑ 0141-211 4000; www.nhsggc.org.uk; 84 Castle St) Medical emergencies and outpatient facilities.

Queen Elizabeth University Hospital (☑ 0141-201 1100; www.nhsggc.org.uk; 1345 Govan Rd) Modern; south of the river.

POST

Many shops across the city centre offer postal service, including some supermarkets that are open Sundays. Service is reliable.

Post Office (Map p112; ☑ 0345-722 3344; www.postoffice.co.uk; 136 West Nile St; ⊙9am-5.30pm Mon-Sat) The most central full-service post office.

TOURIST INFORMATION

Glasgow Tourist Office (Glasgow iCentre; Map p112; ☑ 0141-566 4083; www.visitscotland. com; 158 Buchanan St; ⊙10am-4pm; ☎) The city's tourist office is in the centre of town.

USEFUL WEBSITES

Glasgow Food Geek (www.glasgowfoodgeek. co.uk) Likeably unpretentious food blog with restaurant reviews and the odd recipe.

Herald Scotland (www.heraldscotland.com) Online edition of Glasgow's broadsheet, printed since 1783.

The List (www.list.co.uk) Comprehensive entertainment listings and restaurant reviews.

Lonely Planet (www.lonelyplanet.com/scotland/glasgow) Destination information, hotel bookings, traveller forum and more.

People Make Glasgow (www.peoplemakeglasgow.com) Good city-run website with events and more.

SPT (www.spt.co.uk) Glasgow public transport information.

❶ Getting There & Away

Glasgow is easily reached by air from many British and some European destinations. It's about an hour's flight from London.

GLASGOW'S TINY SUBWAY SYSTEM

Scotland's largest city is home to the world's third-oldest underground metro network after the London Underground and the Budapest Metro – and it's also one of the smallest.

Despite various proposals for extensions over the years, the Glasgow Subway is the exact same length as when it opened on 14 December 1896 with a single 6.5-mile circular line around the city centre.

Initially a cable railway, the subway was converted to electric power in 1935, but its two circular tracks were never expanded. In 2016, the subway underwent significant electrical and mechanical modernisations, making it a fascinating hybrid machine made of old-world and new technology. It is the only railway of its size still in regular operation with the trains squeezing through an internal diameter of just 3.35m – smaller than London's famously narrow tube lines which have a minimum internal diameter of 3.56m.

The 'Clockwork Orange', as the subway has been nicknamed over the years, spans only 15 stations and takes about 25 minutes from start to finish. As such, the so-called 'Sub Crawl' has become quite popular with youngsters who buy an all-day ticket, get out at each station and track down the nearest pub or bar for a drink.

Trains and buses reach the city from London, Edinburgh and numerous other British cities.

Flights, cars and tours can be booked online at lonelyplanet.com/bookings.

AIR

Ten miles west of the city in Paisley, **Glasgow International Airport** (GLA; ☑ 0344-481 5555; www.glasgowairport.com; ☎) handles international and domestic flights. Facilities include car hire, ATMs and a supermarket where you can buy SIM cards.

Thirty miles southwest of Glasgow near Ayr, **Glasgow Prestwick Airport** (PIK; ☑ 0871-223 0700; www.glasgowprestwick.com; ☎) is used by Ryanair and some other budget airlines, with connections mostly to southern Europe.

BUS

All long-distance buses arrive at and depart from **Buchanan bus station** (Map p112; ☑ 0141-333 3708; www.spt.co.uk; Killermont St; ☎), which has pricey lockers, ATMs and wi-fi.

Megabus (☑ 900-160 0900; www.megabus.com) Your first port of call if you're looking for the cheapest fare. Megabus offers very cheap demand-dependent prices on many bus routes, including to Edinburgh and London.

National Express (☑ 0871 781 8181; www.nationalexpress.com) Runs daily to several English cities.

Scottish Citylink (☑ 0871 266 3333; www.citylink.co.uk) Buses to Edinburgh (£8.50, 1¼ hours, every 15 minutes) and most major towns in Scotland.

There are also buses from Buchanan bus station direct to/from Edinburgh Airport (£13, one hour, half-hourly).

TRAIN

As a general rule, **Glasgow Central station** (www.scotrail.co.uk; Gordon St) serves southern Scotland, England and Wales, and **Queen Street station** (www.scotrail.co.uk; George St) serves the north and east (including Edinburgh). Buses run between the two stations every 10 minutes. There are direct trains more than hourly to London Euston station (advance/off peak/any time £31/105.70/191.50); they're much quicker (4½ hours) and more comfortable than the bus.

ScotRail (www.scotrail.co.uk) runs Scottish trains. Destinations include the following:

Aberdeen (£44.30, 2½ to 3½ hours, hourly)

Dundee (£24.60, 1½ hours, hourly)

Edinburgh (£15.30, 50 minutes, every 15 minutes)

Fort William (£32.70, 3¾ hours, three daily)

Inverness (£46, 3½ to four hours, five daily, three on Sunday)

Oban (£26.80, three hours, three to six daily)

❶ Getting Around

TO/FROM THE AIRPORT
Glasgow International Airport

Bus 500 runs every half-hour from Glasgow International Airport to Buchanan bus station via Central and Queen Street train stations (single/return £8.50/14, 25 minutes). This is a 24-hour service. You can include a day ticket on the bus network for £4.70, or a one-week ticket for £18.

Another bus, the 77, covers the same route via the West End twice hourly, taking longer.

Glasgow Prestwick Airport

There's a dedicated train station at the airport, with four trains an hour to Glasgow (£8.80, 40 to 55 minutes). You get a 50% discount from the airport by showing your boarding pass at a staffed counter.

You can also take the bus X77 (£6.30, 50 minutes, every 15 minutes).

A taxi to the centre of Glasgow costs £55 to £65.

BICYCLE

The **Nextbike** (www.nextbike.co.uk; per 20min £2) bike-sharing scheme is easy; download the app for the most convenient use.

There are several places to hire a bike including the **Gear Bikes** (☑ 0141-339 1179; www.gearbikes.com; 19 Gibson St; half-day/day/week £15/20/80; ☒10am-6pm Mon-Sat, noon-5pm Sun) shop. The tourist office has a full list.

BUS

City bus services, mostly run by **First Glasgow** (☑ 0345-646 0707; www.firstglasgow.com), are frequent. You can buy tickets when you board buses, but if you don't have a card for contactless payment you'll need exact change. Using the mobile app is recommended (and a little cheaper, too). Short journeys in town cost £1.70 or £2.30; a day ticket (£4.60) is good value and is valid until 1am, when a night network starts. Weekly tickets starts at £17. Check route maps online at www.spt.co.uk.

AROUND GLASGOW

Good transport connections mean it's easy to plan day trips out of Glasgow. Around the city are varied attractions – the noble abbey at Paisley, home of the eponymous patterned fabric; the estuary mouth twin towns of Greenock and Gourock; and Blantyre, home to an evocative castle and birthplace of David Livingstone.

Paisley

POP 76,830

Once a proud weaving town, but these days effectively a southwestern suburb of Glasgow, Paisley gave its name to the distinctive teardrop-patterned fabric. Though flanked by green countryside, it's not an engaging place, but has an ace up its sleeve in the shape of the magnificent abbey, which is well worth the short trip from Glasgow to see. The Paisley Museum is also recommendable, although closed for renovations until late 2022.

★ **Paisley Abbey** ABBEY
(📞0141-889 7654; www.paisleyabbey.org.uk; Abbey Close; ⊗10am-3.30pm Mon-Sat) FREE
Paisley Abbey is well worth the short trip from Glasgow. This majestic Gothic building was founded in 1163 by Walter Fitzalan, first high steward of Scotland and ancestor of the Stuart dynasty. Apart from the magnificent perspective down the nave, points of interest include royal tombs, some excellent 19th- and 20th-century stained glass, including three windows by Edward Burne-Jones, and the 10th-century Celtic Barochan Cross.

A monastery for Cluny monks, it was damaged by fire during the Wars of Independence in 1306 but rebuilt soon after. Most of the nave is 14th or 15th century. The building was mostly a ruin from the 16th century until the 19th-century restoration, completed in 1928. A window commemorates the fact that William Wallace was educated by monks from this monastery.

Guided tours are available on Tuesdays and Thursdays at 2pm; Sunday service takes place at 10.30am and 12.30pm.

Paisley Museum MUSEUM
(📞0300-300 1210; www.paisley.org.uk/attractions/paisley-museum; High St; ⊗11am-4pm Tue-Sat, 2-5pm Sun) FREE At the western end of High St, worthwhile Paisley Museum is housed in an elegant Victorian Grecian edifice and has a decent collection of 19th-century Scottish art as well as a bit of everything else, from dinosaur footprints to a stuffed terrier, and plenty of information on the town's textile history and the famous Paisley pattern's origins in ancient Mesopotamia.

The museum was closed for refurbishment at the time of research and due to reopen late 2022.

ℹ Getting There & Away

Trains run from Glasgow Central station to Paisley (£3.80, 10 minutes, six hourly).

Greenock & Gourock

POP 55,000

Fused together these days, the towns of Gourock and Greenock were always warming sights to a Glasgow mariner's heart as their ships rounded the point from the Firth of Clyde into the river proper and thence to home. Gourock's firthside views are spectacular, and Greenock's historical sandstone buildings – despite the scrappy shopping complexes in its centre – invite a stop. Before the Clyde was dredged, larger ships couldn't progress further than Greenock, which consequently raked in considerable customs dues. In summer and on fine days, these become little resort towns for Glasgow families looking for a day out.

McLean Museum & Art Gallery MUSEUM
(📞01475-715624; www.inverclyde.gov.uk; 15 Kelly St, Greenock; ⊗10am-4pm Wed-Sat) FREE In the historic centre of Greenock, the McLean holds quite an extensive collection, with displays charting the history of steam power and Clyde shipping. The art gallery has some fine pieces, and several canvases give you an idea of just how busy Greenock's harbour once was. There's also a pictorial history of Greenock through the ages, displays from China, Japan and Egypt, and a natural history section.

ℹ Getting There & Away

Greenock is 27 miles west of Glasgow, and Gourock is 3 miles further west. The Glasgow–Greenock–Gourock leg of the Clyde to Forth pedestrian and cycle route follows an old train track for 10 miles.

There are trains from Glasgow Central station (£7, 35 to 50 minutes, two to three hourly) and hourly buses stopping in both towns.

Gourock's train station is next to the ferry terminal. Gourock is an important ferry hub:

Argyll Ferries (📞0800-066 5000; www.argyllferries.co.uk) A passenger service to Dunoon (£4.20, 25 minutes, half-hourly Monday to Saturday, hourly Sunday) on Argyll's Cowal Peninsula.

Caledonian MacBrayne (Cal-Mac; 📞0800 066 5000; www.calmac.co.uk) From Wemyss Bay (pronounced 'weemz'), 8 miles south of Gourock, ferries run to Rothesay on Bute (passenger/car £3.25/11.60, 35 minutes, hourly or better). Trains from Glasgow (£8, 50 minutes, more than hourly) connect with ferries. The operator also offers ferries from Gourock to Kilcreggan (£3.60, 15 minutes, 12 to 13 daily Monday to Saturday).

Western Ferries (☎ 0136-970 4452; www.western-ferries.co.uk) Has a car service (adult/child/car £4.90/2.40/18.70, 20 minutes, two to three hourly) to Dunoon from McInroy's Point, 2 miles south from Gourock train station on the Irvine road; Scottish Citylink buses run here.

Blantyre

POP 17,240

Though technically part of Lanarkshire, Blantyre, birthplace of David Livingstone, is an outlying suburb of Glasgow these days. It was founded as a cotton mill in the late 18th century. Livingstone, a zealous and pious doctor, missionary and explorer, was raised in a one-room tenement and worked in the mill by day from the age of 10, going to the local school at night. Amazingly for a time in which most mill workers were barely able to write their names, he managed to get himself into university to study medicine.

David Livingstone Centre   MUSEUM
(www.david-livingstone-trust.org; 165 Station Rd; 🏠) This museum tells the story of David Livingstone's life from his early days in Blantyre to the 30 years he spent in Africa, where he named the Victoria Falls on one of his numerous journeys. At the time of research, the museum was closed for renovations and scheduled to reopen in spring 2021. The grassy park the museum is set in makes a perfect picnic spot. Head straight down the hill from the station to reach the museum.

Bothwell Castle   CASTLE
(HES; ☎ 01698-816 894; www.historicenvironment.scot; Castle Ave, Uddingston; adult/child £3/1.80; ⏰ 9.30am-5.30pm Apr-Sep, 10am-4pm Sat-Wed Oct-Mar) It's a 30-minute walk from Blantyre along the river to Bothwell Castle, regarded as the finest 13th-century castle in Scotland. The stark, roofless, red-sandstone ruins are substantial and, largely due to their beautiful green setting, romantic.

ℹ Getting There & Away

Trains run from Glasgow Central station to Blantyre (£3.90, 20 minutes, three hourly).

AT A GLANCE

POPULATION
955,000

NUMBER OF RECORDED ROBERT BURNS WORKS
559

BEST PUB
The Cobbles (p150)

BEST FISH 'N' CHIPS
MacCallum's (p158)

BEST WATERSPORTS
Galloway Activity Centre (p167)

WHEN TO GO

May Take a fortnight to cross the whole region, hiking the gorgeous Southern Upland Way.

Jun The perfect time to visit the region's numerous stately homes, with spectacular blooming gardens.

Oct Hit Galloway's forests to see red deer battling it out in the rutting season.

Southern Scotland

Though wise folk are well aware of its charms, for many people southern Scotland is just something to drive through on the way to northern Scotland. Big mistake. But it does mean you'll find breathing room here in summer, and peaceful corners.

Proximity to England brought raiding and strife. There was loot to be had in the Borders, where large prosperous abbeys ruled over agricultural communities. Regularly ransacked before their destruction in the Reformation, the ruins of these churches, linked by cycling and walking paths, are among Scotland's most atmospheric historic sites.

The rolling west enjoys extensive forest cover between bustling market towns. The hills cascade down to sandy stretches of coastline blessed with Scotland's sunniest weather.

Southern Scotland Highlights

1 **Border Abbeys** (p145) Exploring the noble, evocative ruins – Dryburgh is our favourite – and the area's other excellent historic sights.

2 **Culzean Castle** (p161) Admiring the 18th-century architectural genius of a castle perched on wild sea cliffs.

3 **Hermitage Castle** (p148) Pondering the tough old life on the England–Scotland frontier at this desolate castle.

4 **Kirkcudbright** (p169) Exploring this charming, dignified town, marvelling at the creative flair of its inhabitants.

5 **Robert Burns Birthplace Museum** (p159) Learning

BORDERS REGION

The Borders has had a rough history: centuries of war and plunder have left a battle-scarred landscape, exemplified by the magnificent ruins of the Border abbeys. Their wealth was an irresistible magnet during cross-frontier wars, and they were destroyed and rebuilt numerous times. Today these massive stone shells are the region's finest attraction. And don't miss Hermitage Castle: nothing encapsulates the region's turbulent history like this spooky stronghold.

But the Borders region is also genteel. Welcoming villages with ancient traditions pepper the countryside, and grandiose mansions await exploration. It's fine walking and cycling country too, the hills lush with shades of green. Offshore you'll find excellent cold-water diving.

Peebles

POP 8600

With a picturesque main street set on a ridge between the River Tweed and Eddleston Water, Peebles is one of the most handsome of the Border towns. The agreeable atmosphere and good walking options in the rolling, wooded hills hereabouts will entice you to linger.

◉ Sights & Activities

The lovely riverside walk along the Tweed has plenty of grassed areas ideal for a picnic, and there's a children's playground (near the main road bridge).

As well as the activities hub of Glentress, there are further mountain-biking trails at Innerleithen, 7 miles east of Peebles.

★ 7stanes Glentress MOUNTAIN BIKING
(www.7stanesmountainbiking.com) FREE Two miles east of Peebles off the A72, in Glentress forest, this is the busiest of the 7stanes mountain-biking hubs, and also offers osprey viewing and marked walking trails. The **shop** (☑ 01721-724522; www.tweedvalley bikehire.com; hardtail per day £30; ◷ 9am-5pm or 6pm) hires rigs and will put you on the right trail for your ability. You can arrange courses with **Dirt School** (☑ 07545 339938; www.dirt-school.co.uk). These are some of Britain's best biking routes.

You can also hire bikes from Bspoke in Peebles itself. There's on-site cabin accommodation at Glentress, too.

Go Ape ADVENTURE SPORTS
(www.goape.co.uk; Glentress Forest; adult/child £33/25; ◷ Feb-Nov) This forest-top adventure course features rope bridges, swings and a glorious long zip line over trees and a reservoir. Opening times and days vary widely through the season, so check the website and book ahead online. Twilight sessions in autumn add another dimension.

🛏 Sleeping

Lindores Guest House B&B ££
(☑ 01721-729040; www.lindoresgh.co.uk; 60 Old Town; s £55-60, d £75-85; 🛜) Run by an interesting, kind couple, this rather striking house offers commodious, flowery rooms. Both en-suite and shared bathrooms are available, and showers are great. Breakfast features delicious home-baked bread among other goodies. There's secure parking for bikes and motorbikes.

Cringletie House HOTEL £££
(☑ 01721-725750; www.cringletie.com; Edinburgh Rd/A703; r £180-220; 🅿 🛜 🐾) Luxury without snobbery is this hotel's hallmark, and more power to it. To call this a house is being coy: it's an elegant baronial mansion, 2 miles north of Peebles, set in lush, wooded grounds. Rooms are plush and feature genteel elegance and linen so soft you could wrap a newborn in it. There's an excellent restaurant on site.

A delightful cottage here sleeps six people and has a deck and a hot tub. Dogs are also exceptionally well catered for.

🍴 Eating

Cocoa Black CAFE £
(☑ 01721-723764; www.cocoablack.com; 1 Cuddy Bridge; sweets £2-5; ◷ 10am-4pm Sun-Fri, to 4.30pm Sat; 🛜 🏠) Chocaholics should make a beeline for this friendly cafe, where exquisite cakes and other patisserie offerings will satisfy any cacao-focused cravings. It also runs a school where you can learn to make them yourself.

★ Coltman's DELI ££
(☑ 01721-720405; www.coltmans.co.uk; 71 High St; mains £14-17; ◷ 10am-5pm Mon-Thu, to 10pm Fri & Sat, to 6pm Sun; 🛜 🍴) 🐾 This main-street deli has numerous temptations, such as excellent cheeses and Italian smallgoods, as well as perhaps Scotland's tastiest sausage roll, with an equally toothsome vegetarian equivalent. Behind the shop, the good-looking dining area serves up confident bistro fare and light

TRAQUAIR HOUSE

One of Scotland's great country houses, **Traquair House** (☑01896-830323; www.traquair.co.uk; Innerleithen; adult/child/family £10/5/27.50; ☺11am-5pm daily Easter-Sep, to 4pm daily Oct, to 3pm Sat & Sun Nov), has a powerful, ethereal beauty, and exploring it is like time travel. Odd, sloping floors and a musty odour bestow a genuine feel, and parts of the building are believed to have been constructed long before the first official record of its existence in 1107. The massive tower house was gradually expanded but has remained virtually unchanged since the 17th century. Traquair is about 6 miles southeast of Peebles.

Since the 15th century, the house has belonged to various branches of the Stuart family, and the family's unwavering Catholicism and loyalty to the Stuart cause led to famous visitors such as Mary, Queen of Scots and Bonnie Prince Charlie, but also to numerous problems after the deposal of James II of England in 1688. The family's estate, wealth and influence were gradually whittled away as life as a Jacobite became a furtive, clandestine affair.

One of Traquair's most interesting places is the concealed room where priests secretly lived and performed Mass up until 1829 when the Catholic Emancipation Act was finally passed. Other beautiful, time-worn rooms hold fascinating relics, including the cradle used by Mary for her son, James VI of Scotland (who also became James I of England), and fascinating letters from the Jacobite Earls of Traquair and their families, including a particularly moving one written from death row in the Tower of London.

The main gates to the house were locked by one earl in the 18th century until the day a Stuart king reclaimed the throne in London, so meanwhile you'll have to enter by a side gate.

In addition to the house, there's a garden **maze**, a small **brewery** producing the tasty Bear Ale, and a series of **craft workshops**. You can also stay here in one of three opulent B&B rooms (single/double £155/220).

Bus X62 runs from Edinburgh via Peebles to Innerleithen and on to Galashiels.

snacks with a variety of culinary influences, using top-notch local ingredients. Upstairs is a cosy bar.

Osso
BISTRO ££
(☑01721-724477; www.ossorestaurant.com; Innerleithen Rd; share plates £7-13; ☺11am-9pm Wed-Sat, to 6pm Sun) Osso makes a great stop for a bit of home baking or a sandwich but also for a quality meal based around small and large share plates. There are a number of influences from Asia and the Mediterranean at work here, but also solidly local offerings like slow-cooked lamb. The food is delicious and artfully presented, but the atmosphere is comfortably casual.

Tontine Hotel
SCOTTISH ££
(☑01721-720892; www.tontinehotel.com; High St; mains £12-20; ☺noon-2.30pm & 6-8.45pm; ☜) Glorious is the only word to describe the Georgian dining room here, complete with musicians' gallery, fireplace and fabulous windows. It'd be worth it even for cat food on mouldy bread, but luckily the meals – ranging from pub classics like steak-and-ale pie to more globally influenced fare

– are tasty and backed by very welcoming service. Afternoon tea is served between meal times.

❶ Getting There & Around

The bus stop is beside the post office on Eastgate. Bus X62 runs half-hourly (hourly on Sunday) to Edinburgh (£5.90, one hour). In the other direction it heads for Galashiels (£5.90, 1¼ hours), from where you can change to Melrose.

Bspoke Cycles (☑01721-723423; www.bspokepeebles.co.uk; Old Tweeddale Garage, Innerleithen Rd; bikes per day from £30; ☺9am-5pm Tue-Fri, to 4pm Sat) Rents a variety of bikes (including e-bikes) in Peebles.

Melrose

POP 2500

Tiny, charming Melrose is a polished village running on the well-greased wheels of tourism. Sitting at the feet of the three heather-covered Eildon Hills, Melrose has a classic market square and one of the great abbey ruins. Just outside town is

Abbotsford, the home of Sir Walter Scott, which makes a superb visit.

◉ Sights & Activities

There are many attractive walks in the **Eildon Hills**, accessible via a footpath off Dingleton Rd (the B6359) south of Melrose, or via the trail along the River Tweed.

The St Cuthbert's Way (p154) long-distance walking path starts in Melrose, while the coast-to-coast Southern Upland Way (p154) passes through town. You can do a day's walk along St Cuthbert's Way as far as Harestanes (16 miles), on the A68 near Jedburgh, and return to Melrose on the hourly Jedburgh–Galashiels bus. The Tweed Cycle Route (p154) also passes through Melrose.

★ Melrose Abbey   RUINS
(HES; 🖉 01896-822562; www.historicenvironment.scot; adult/child £6/3.60; ⊘ 9.30am-5.30pm Apr-Sep, 10am-4pm Oct-Mar) Perhaps the most interesting of the Border abbeys, red-sandstone Melrose was repeatedly destroyed by the English in the 14th century. The remaining broken shell is pure Gothic and the ruins are famous for their decorative stonework – look out for the pig gargoyle playing the bagpipes. Though Melrose had a monastery way back in the 7th century, this abbey was founded by David I in 1136 for Cistercian monks, and later rebuilt by Robert the Bruce, whose heart is buried here.

The ruins date from the 14th and 15th centuries, and were repaired by Sir Walter Scott in the 19th century. The adjoining museum has many fine examples of 12th- to 15th-century stonework and pottery found in the area. Note the impressive remains of the 'great drain' outside – a medieval sewerage system.

★⁎⁎ Festivals & Events

Melrose Rugby Sevens   SPORTS
(www.melrose7s.co.uk; ⊘ mid-Apr) Rugby followers fill the town to see this famous one-day sevens competition.

⛏ Sleeping & Eating

Dunfermline House   B&B ££
(🖉 01896-822411; www.dunfermlinehouse.co.uk; Buccleuch St; s/d £45/75; 🖘) Very close to Melrose Abbey, this place offers a genuinely warm welcome and comfortable, flowery rooms in classic B&B style. It's very walker- and cyclist-friendly and breakfast is well above average, with plenty of fruit on hand. For sale at time of research, so may change.

★ Townhouse   BOUTIQUE HOTEL £££
(🖉 01896-822645; www.thetownhousemelrose.co.uk; Market Sq; s/d/superior d £97/134/151; 🅿🖘) The classy Townhouse exudes warmth and professionalism, and has some of the best rooms in town, tastefully furnished with attention to detail. The superior rooms are enormous, with lavish furnishings and excellent en suites. Standard rooms are a fair bit smaller but they're refurbished and very comfortable. Well worth the price.

There is an excellent restaurant located on-site.

Burts Hotel   HOTEL £££
(🖉 01896-822285; www.burtshotel.co.uk; Market Sq; s/d/superior d £79/148/158; 🅿🖘🍽) Set in an early-18th-century house, Burts is a famously reliable central hotel that retains much of its period charm. Rooms vary – the renovated ones with modern plaid fabrics are very smart, and the superiors are extra spacious. There are plenty of singles too. The air of friendly formality makes it a favourite with older visitors. Appealing food is also on hand.

Provender   SCOTTISH ££
(🖉 01896-820319; www.provendermelrose.com; West End Lane; mains £15-20; ⊘ 11am-2.30pm & 6-9pm Mon-Fri, 10am-2.30pm & 6-9pm Sat, 10am-3pm & 6-8pm Sun; 🖉) Though a relative newcomer to the local scene, Provender feels very Melrose – classy but comfortable – already. It's a warmly decorated space with attractively low lighting, booth seating and solicitous service. Great seafood creations and other well-executed, appealing fare are complemented by a short but excellent wine list. Weekend brunches are another highlight.

Townhouse   SCOTTISH ££
(🖉 01896-822645; www.thetownhousemelrose.co.uk; Market Sq; mains £14-22; ⊘ noon-2pm & 6-8pm; 🖘) The brasserie and restaurant here turn out excellent upmarket cuisine and offer decent value. There's some rich, elaborate, beautifully presented fare, with plenty of venison and other game choices.

ⓘ Getting There & Away

The Borders Railway runs from Edinburgh to Tweedbank (£11.30, one hour, half-hourly), which is 1.5 miles from Melrose. Buses run half-hourly from here into Melrose.

For other Borders destinations, you'll most likely need to change in nearby Galashiels, served by regular buses from Edinburgh and elsewhere.

Around Melrose

★ **Abbotsford** HISTORIC BUILDING
(🖥 01896-752043; www.scottsabbotsford.com; visitor centre free, house adult/child £11.50/5; ⊗ 10am-5pm Apr-Oct, to 4pm Nov-Mar, house closed Dec-Feb) Just outside Melrose, this is where to discover the life and works of Sir Walter Scott, to whom we arguably owe both the modern novel and our mind's-eye view of Scotland. This whimsical, fabulous house where he lived – and which ruined him when his publishers went bust – really brings this 19th-century writer to life. The grounds on the banks of the Tweed are lovely, and Scott drew much inspiration from rambles in the surrounding countryside.

A modern visitor centre displays memorabilia and gives an intriguing overview of the man; the smart audio-guide system – with one designed for kids – will then show you round the house. In the house are some gloriously over-the-top features, with elaborate carvings, enough swords and dirks to equip a small army, a Chinese drawing room and a lovely study and library.

A wing of the house offers luxurious self-catering accommodation designed for large groups.

Abbotsford is 2 miles west of Melrose; buses between Galashiels and Melrose will drop you at the nearby Tweedbank roundabout. It's also an easy walk from Tweedbank station, reachable in under an hour from Edinburgh. You can also walk from Melrose along the southern bank of the Tweed. There's a cafe-restaurant atop the visitor centre.

★ **Dryburgh Abbey** RUINS
(HES; 🖥 01835-822381; www.historicenvironment. scot; adult/child £6/3.60; ⊗ 9.30am-5.30pm Apr-Sep, 10am-4pm Oct-Mar) This is the most beautiful and complete of the Border abbeys, partly because the neighbouring town of Dryburgh no longer exists (another victim of the wars) and partly because of its lovely site by the Tweed in a sheltered birdsong-filled valley. Dating from about 1150, the abbey belonged to the Premonstratensians, a religious order founded in France, and evokes 12th-century monastic life more successfully than its nearby counterparts. The pink-hued stone ruins are the burial place of Sir Walter Scott.

The abbey is 5 miles southeast of Melrose on the B6404, which passes the famous Scott's View outlook. Hike there along the southern bank of the River Tweed, or take a bus to the nearby village of Newtown St Boswells.

Selkirk

POP 5600
While the noisy throb of machinery once filled the valleys below Selkirk, a prosperous

---

SIR WALTER SCOTT

Sir Walter Scott (1771–1832) is one of Scotland's greatest literary figures. Born in Edinburgh, he spent time on his grandparents' farm at Sandyknowe in the Borders as a child. It was here, rambling around the countryside, that he developed a passion for historical ballads and Scottish heroes. After studying in Edinburgh he bought Abbotsford, a country house in the Borders.

The Lay of the Last Minstrel (1805) was an early critical success. Further works earning him an international reputation included *The Lady of the Lake* (1810), set around Loch Katrine and the Trossachs. He later turned his hand to novels and was instrumental in their development. His first novel, *Waverley* (1814), which dealt with the 1745 Jacobite rebellion, set the classical pattern of the historical novel. Other works included *Guy Mannering* (1815) and *Rob Roy* (1817). He became something of an international superstar, and heavily influenced writers and artists such as Austen, Dickens and Turner. His writings virtually single-handedly revived interest in Scottish history and legend, and much of our Scottish clichés of today – misty glens, fierce warriors, tartan – are largely down to him. His organisation of the visit of George IV to Edinburgh reintegrated Highland dress into society.

Later in life Scott wrote obsessively to stave off bankruptcy. Tourist offices stock a *Sir Walter Scott Trail* booklet, which details many places associated with him in the Borders.

mill town in the early 19th century, today it sits placid and pretty – apart from busy traffic through the centre – atop its steep ridge. Naughty millworkers who fell foul of the law would have come face to face in court with Sir Walter Scott, sheriff here for three decades.

Sights

Halliwell's House Museum MUSEUM
(📞01750-726456; www.liveborders.org.uk; Halliwell's Close; ⏰11am-4pm Mon-Sat, noon-3pm Sun Apr-Oct) **FREE** Halliwell's House Museum is the oldest building (1712) in Selkirk. The museum charts local history with an engrossing exhibition, and the **Robson Gallery** has changing exhibitions. There's some local information available here too.

Sir Walter Scott's Courtroom MUSEUM
(📞01750-726456; www.liveborders.org.uk; Market Sq; ⏰10am-4pm Mon-Fri, 11am-3pm Sat late Mar-Sep, plus 11am-3pm Sun May-Aug, noon-3pm Mon-Sat Oct) **FREE** Drop into Sir Walter Scott's Courtroom, where there's an exhibition on the man's life and writings, plus a fascinating account of the courageous explorer Mungo Park (born near Selkirk) and his search for the River Niger.

Sleeping & Eating

Philipburn Hotel HOTEL **££**
(📞01750-720747; www.bw-philipburnhouseho tel.co.uk; Linglie Rd/A708; s £110, d £160-200; 🅿🛜🐾) On the edge of town, this former dower house has a jazzy 21st-century look that hasn't ruined its historic features, as well as appealing renovated rooms and a snug bar and restaurant. The luxury rooms are particularly good – some have a Jacuzzi, while another is a split-level affair with a double balcony. Room-only rates are available.

Self-catering facilities are on offer in the separate lodges, where pets are also welcome.

Fleece BISTRO **££**
(📞01750-725501; www.thefleecebarandkitchen. co.uk; 1 Ettrick Tce; lunch mains £12-15, dinner mains £13-19; ⏰noon-2pm & 5-9pm Tue-Sat, 11am-3pm Sun) Selkirk's best place to eat is in the heart of things. It has a convivial bar as well as a well-thought-out range of classic Scottish and other British fare. Presentation is strong and it manages to cover both pub-style meals and more innovative combinations.

❶ Getting There & Away

Bus X95 runs at least hourly between Carlisle and Edinburgh (£8.20, 1¾ hours) via Hawick, Selkirk and Galashiels. It's usually faster to hop off a bus at Galashiels and catch the train into Edinburgh.

Hawick
POP 13,900

Straddling the River Teviot, Hawick (pronounced 'hoik') is one of the largest towns in the Borders and has long been a major production centre for knitwear. There are several large outlets to buy jumpers and other woollens around town. Hawick is also famous for rugby; the local club has produced dozens of Scotland internationals.

Sights

Heart of Hawick VISITOR CENTRE
(www.heartofhawick.co.uk; Kirkstile) Three buildings form the 'heart' of Hawick. A former mill holds a cafe and cinema. Opposite, historic **Drumlanrig's Tower**, once a major seat of the Douglas clan, now houses the **Borders Textile Towerhouse** (📞01450-377615; 1 Tower Knowe; ⏰10am-4.30pm Mon-Sat, noon-3pm Sun Apr-Oct, 10am-4pm Mon & Wed-Sat Nov-Mar) **FREE**. This tells the story of the town's knitwear-producing history. Behind the mill, the **Heritage Hub** (📞01450-360699; Kirkstile; ⏰9.30am-4.45pm Mon-Fri) **FREE** is a state-of-the-art facility open to anyone wishing to trace their Scottish heritage or explore other local archives.

Borders Distillery DISTILLERY
(📞01450-374330; www.thebordersdistillery.com; Commercial Rd; tours £12; ⏰10am-4.30pm Mon-Fri) Bringing whisky-making back to the Borders after more than a century's absence, this distillery produces a range of spirits that can be tasted on a good tour that should be prebooked. Expect it to be open weekends again too in the future.

Hawick Museum & Art Gallery MUSEUM
(📞01450-364747; www.liveborders.org.uk; Wilton Lodge Park; ⏰10am-noon & 1-5pm Mon-Fri, 2-5pm Sat & Sun Apr-Sep, noon-3pm Mon-Fri, 1-3pm Sun Oct-Mar) **FREE** This museum has an interesting collection of mostly 19th-century manufacturing and domestic memorabilia as well as details on a tragic pair of local motorcycling legends. There are usually a couple of temporary exhibitions on as well.

Cycling Tour
The Borders

START PEEBLES
END JEDBURGH
LENGTH 80 MILES; TWO TO THREE DAYS

With the exception of the main A-roads, traffic is sparse, which, along with the beauty of the countryside, makes the Borders ideal cycling country. This route takes you through classic Borders countryside, visiting abbey ruins and stately homes along the way.

1 Peebles (p142) is easily accessed on the bus from Edinburgh and offers bike hire. Check out the downhill routes at nearby **2 Glentress** (p142) before following the south bank of the Tweed eastwards on the B7062.

3 Traquair House (p143) is a great stop on this stretch. Continue on the south side, signposted as part of the National Cycle Network, before crossing the river, bearing right onto the A708 then turning left (B7060) before the river recrosses the Tweed at a bridge with traffic lights. Following signposts, this will eventually take you past **4 Abbotsford** (p145), home of Sir Walter Scott, into **5 Melrose** (p143), a good overnighting option. From Melrose, it's a short ride to **6 Scott's View**, where you can admire a marvellous vista, then descend back to river level and sublime **7 Dryburgh Abbey** (p145). Past the abbey, turn left on the B6404, then detour left for just over a mile to visit signposted **8 Smailholm Tower** (p151). From here it's an easy 6 miles into **9 Kelso** (p149), where you should leave time to see impressive **10 Floors Castle** (p150).

You've seen three of the four great ruined Border abbeys by now, so it's time to complete the set by heading south to the fourth. There are several possible routes, but a nice quiet, picturesque one (25 miles) heads out of Kelso southeast on the B6352. Have a pint in the twin walkers' villages of **11 Town Yetholm** and **12 Kirk Yetholm** then head west on the B6401 through the village of Morebattle, then left 1.5 miles down a rustic road signposted to Cessford/Crailinghall. Follow this south then west all the way to **13 Jedburgh** (p148). There are bus connections from here back to Peebles.

All the towns mentioned have good overnighting options. Other routes are also detailed at www.cyclescottishborders.com.

WORTH A TRIP

HERMITAGE CASTLE

Hermitage Castle (HES; ☑ 01387-376222; www.historicenvironment.scot; B6357; adult/child £6/3.60; ☺ 9.30am-5.30pm Apr-Sep) The 'guardhouse of the bloodiest valley in Britain', Hermitage Castle embodies the brutal history of the Scottish Borders. Desolate but proud with its massive squared stone walls, it looks more like a lair for orc raiding parties than a home for Scottish nobility, and is one of the bleakest and most stirring of Scottish ruins. The castle is about 12 miles south of Hawick.

Strategically crucial, the castle was the scene of many a dark deed and dirty deal with the English invaders, all of which rebounded heavily on the perfidious Scottish lord in question. Here, in 1338, Sir William Douglas imprisoned his enemy Sir Alexander Ramsay and deliberately starved him to death. Ramsay survived for 17 days by eating grain that trickled into his pit (which can still be seen) from the granary above. In 1566 Mary, Queen of Scots famously visited the wounded tenant of the castle, Lord Bothwell, here. Fortified, he recovered to (probably) murder her husband, marry her himself, then abandon her months later and flee into exile.

🛏 Sleeping & Eating

Bank Guest House
B&B ££

(☑ 01450-363760; www.thebankno12highst.com; 12 High St; s £65-75, d £90-110; P �🖥) This posh boutique B&B in the centre of Hawick brings out the best in this solid 19th-century building with modish wallpapers and designer furniture and fabrics. Modern comforts as well as numerous thoughtful extras make this a great place to stay.

Teviotside Guest House
B&B ££

(☑ 01450-363393; www.teviotsideguesthouse. co.uk; 1 Teviotside Tce; s £40-55, d £80-90; 🖥🖥) Alan runs a relaxed and cheerful ship at this six-room B&B near the river. Room 1 is especially lovely with a wraparound outlook and upmarket bathroom. Breakfast is an easygoing buffet affair. There's some noise at weekends from a nearby nightclub.

Damascus Drum
CAFE £

(☑ 07707-856123; www.damascusdrum.co.uk; 2 Silver St; light meals £4-10; ☺ 10am-3pm Mon-Sat; 🖥🖥) The Middle East meets the Borders in this enticing cafe behind the tourist office. Patterned rugs and a secondhand bookshop make for a relaxing environment to enjoy breakfasts, bagels, burgers and tasty Turkish-style meze options.

Night Safe Bistro
BISTRO ££

(☑ 01450-377045; www.facebook.com/hawicknightsafebistro; 12 High St; mains £14-18; ☺ 10am-8pm Mon-Sat, 11am-8pm Sun; 🖥) This attractive High St bistro occupies the ground level of a handsome bank building.

A recent makeover has given it a light and stylish contemporary feel, with antler motifs and a striking mural. Drop in for scones or enjoy quality produce like local lamb or halibut from Eyemouth.

Exchange Bar
PUB

(Dalton's; ☑ 01450-376067; 1 Silver St; ☺ 11am-11pm Mon-Thu,11am-1am Fri & Sat,12.30-11pm Sun) This unusually shaped pub by the river is cosy, with moulded ceilings and wooden panelling. There's a very convivial atmosphere and a few excellent craft ales on tap.

ℹ Getting There & Away

Hourly bus X95 connects Hawick with Galashiels, Selkirk and Edinburgh (£8.20, two hours). Buses leave from Mart St at the northern end of the town centre.

Jedburgh

POP 4000

Attractive Jedburgh, where many old buildings and wynds (narrow alleys) have been intelligently restored, invites exploration by foot. It's centred on the noble skeleton of its ruined abbey.

◉ Sights & Activities

The tourist office has handy booklets for walks around the town, including sections of the Southern Upland Way (p154) or Borders Abbeys Way (p154). Jedburgh is also a popular stop for walkers on St Cuthbert's Way (p154), which passes nearby.

★ **Jedburgh Abbey** RUINS
(HES; ☑ 01835-863925; www.historicenvironment.
scot; Abbey Rd; adult/child £6/3.60; ⊘ 9.30am-
5.30pm Apr-Sep, 10am-4pm Oct-Mar; ⛓) Domi-
nating the town skyline, this was the first
of the great Border abbeys to be passed into
state care, and it shows – audio and visual
presentations telling the abbey's story are
scattered throughout the carefully preserved
ruins (good for the kids). The red-sandstone
ruins are roofless but relatively intact, and
the ingenuity of the master mason can be
seen in some of the rich (if somewhat faded)
stone carvings in the nave.

The abbey was founded in 1138 by David
I as a priory for Augustinian canons.

Mary, Queen of
Scots' Visitor Centre HISTORIC BUILDING
(Queen St; ⊘ 9.30am-4.30pm Mon-Sat, 10.30am-
4pm Sun early Mar–late Nov) **FREE** Mary stayed
at this beautiful 16th-century tower house
in 1566 after her famous ride to visit the in-
jured Earl of Bothwell, her future husband,
at Hermitage Castle. The interesting exhibition evokes the sad saga of Mary's life and
death. Various objects associated with her,
including a lock of her hair, are on display.

Jedburgh
Castle Jail MUSEUM
(☑ 01835-864750; www.liveborders.org.uk; Castlegate; ⊘ 10am-4.30pm Mon-Sat, 1-4pm Sun
Easter-Oct) **FREE** Jedburgh Castle was a
victim of Scotland's wars for independence
but this smart 1820s prison was built on
the site as part of a jail reform program.
You can check out the original cells and
some prisoners' stories, and browse the
town museum here.

🎪 Festivals & Events

Jethart Callant's Festival CULTURAL
(www.jethartcallantsfestival.com; ⊘ late Jun–mid-
Jul) This two-week cavalcade recalls the
perilous time when people rode out on
horseback checking for English incursions.
It's perhaps the most notable of the Common Riding festivals of the Borders. There
are various rides and processions over the
fortnight, involving hundreds of costumed
horse riders. Other events continue for another week afterwards.

🛏 Sleeping & Eating

Maplebank B&B £
(☑ 01835-862051; maplebank3@btinternet.com;
3 Smiths Wynd; s/d £30/50; 🅿 🤶 😸) It's pleas-

ing to come across older-style B&Bs where
it feels like you're staying in someone's
home. Here, that someone is like your favourite aunt: friendly, chaotic and generous.
There's lots of clutter and it's very informal.
Rooms are comfortable and large, sharing a
good bathroom. Breakfast (including fruit,
yoghurts and homemade jams) is brilliant
– much better than at most posher places.

Meadhon Guest House B&B ££
(☑ 01835-862504; www.meadhon.co.uk; 48 Castlegate; s/d/f £61/75/145; 🤶) Very close to
castle and abbey, this historic house on Jedburgh's main street dates back to 1653 and
has lots of character. Bonnie Prince Charlie
once stabled his horses here but the genial
Danish owners offer more human comforts, with keypad locks, plush mattresses
and impeccable standards. Home-cooked
evening meals are available, as are attractive
hand-knitted scarves.

Capon Tree SCOTTISH ££
(☑ 01835-869596; www.thecapontree.com; 61
High St; mains £14-20; ⊘ food 6-9pm; 🤶) Attractively combining smart and casual, this
welcoming bistro and bar does modern Scottish cuisine. Plates are beautifully, though
not fussily, presented and ingredients are
of high quality. The overall package is appealing, the service good and the ambience
romantic.

ℹ Information

Jedburgh Tourist Office (☑ 01835-863170;
jedburgh@visitscotland.com; Murray's Green;
⊘ 9.30am-5pm Mon-Sat, 10am-4pm Sun
Apr-Jun, Sep & Oct, 9am-5.30pm Mon-Sat,
10am-4pm Sun Jul & Aug, 10am-4pm Mon-
Sat Nov-Mar; 🤶) Tourist office for the whole
Borders region. Very helpful.

ℹ Getting There & Away

Jedburgh has good bus connections to Hawick,
Melrose and Kelso (all around 25 minutes,
roughly hourly, two-hourly on Sunday). For
Edinburgh, change in St Boswells or Galashiels.

Kelso
POP 5600

Kelso, a prosperous market town with a
broad, cobbled square flanked by Georgian
buildings, has a cheery feel and historic appeal. During the day it's a busy little place,
but after 8pm you'll have the streets to
yourself. The town has a lovely site at the

junction of the Tweed and Teviot, and is one of the most enjoyable places in the Borders, particularly popular for fishing.

◉ Sights & Activities

The Kelso–Jedburgh section (12 miles) of the Borders Abbeys Way (p154) is a fairly easy walk, largely following the River Teviot. The tourist office has a free leaflet with map and route description.

For a shorter ramble, leave the Square by Roxburgh St and take the signposted alley to **Cobby Riverside Walk**, a pleasant stroll along the river to Floors Castle (rejoin Roxburgh St to gain admission to the castle).

Floors Castle   HISTORIC BUILDING
(☎01573-223333; www.floorscastle.com; adult/child castle & grounds £11.50/6; ⊙10.30am-5pm daily May-Sep, Sat & Sun Oct) Grandiose Floors Castle is Scotland's largest inhabited mansion, home to the Duke of Roxburghe, and overlooks the Tweed about a mile west of Kelso. Built by William Adam in the 1720s, the original Georgian simplicity was 'improved' in the 1840s with the addition of somewhat OTT battlements and turrets. Inside, view the vivid colours of 17th-century Brussels tapestries in the drawing room and intricate oak carvings in the ornate ballroom. The walled garden is a highlight of the extensive grounds.

Kelso Abbey   RUINS
(HES; www.historicenvironment.scot; Bridge St; ⊙9.30am-5.30pm daily Apr-Sep, 10am-4pm Sat-Wed Oct-Mar) FREE Once one of the richest abbeys in southern Scotland, Kelso Abbey was built by the Tironensians, an order founded in Picardy and brought to the Borders around 1113 by David I. English raids in the 16th century reduced it to ruins, though what little remains today is some of the finest surviving Romanesque architecture in Scotland.

River Tweed Salmon Fishing Museum   MUSEUM
(www.salmonfishingmuseum.com; Town Hall, Kelso Sq; ⊙10am-4pm Mon-Sat, 10am-1pm Sun) FREE This museum in the town hall on the square tells the history of salmon fishing on the Tweed. It's a labour of love with many historical objects as well as a sculpture of a 70lb (32kg) monster landed here in the 18th century.

🛏 Sleeping

★Old Priory   B&B ££
(☎01573-223030; www.theoldpriorykelso.com; 33 Woodmarket; s/d £80/90; 🅿🛜) Fantastic rooms here are allied with numerous personal details – genial host Robin turns down the beds at night and makes you feel very welcome. Doubles are top-notch and the family room really excellent. The huge windows flood the rooms with natural light. The wonderful library room (£120) is huge and luxurious, with a super bathroom. Top-class B&B.

Inglestone House   B&B ££
(☎01573-225800; www.inglestonehouse.co.uk; Abbey Row; s/d/f £75/90/155; 🛜) 🍃 Northumbrian hosts are welcoming and very cordial in this spot behind the main street. Rooms are a good size with firm mattresses and the owners are committed to running a sustainable business. There are good options for the less mobile and the general can-do attitude is very appealing.

🍴 Eating & Drinking

★Cobbles   BISTRO ££
(☎01573-223548; www.cobbleskelso.co.uk; 7 Bowmont St; mains £10-17; ⊙food noon-2.30pm & 5.45-9pm Mon-Fri, noon-9pm Sat, noon-8.30pm Sun; 🛜) This inn off the main square is so popular you will need to book a table at weekends. It's cheery, very welcoming and warm, and serves excellent upmarket pub food in generous portions. Pick and mix from bar menu, steaks, kebabs and gourmet options. Leave room for cheese and/or dessert. The bar's own microbrewed ales are excellent. A cracking place.

Contented Vine   SCOTTISH ££
(☎01573-224777; www.contentedvine.co.uk; 60 Horsemarket; mains £12-18; ⊙6-10pm Mon-Thu, 5-10pm Fri-Sun; 🛜) Upmarket pasta dishes take their place alongside quality dishes of Scottish produce with a Mediterranean inflection at this popular, welcoming central restaurant that has a real throwback vibe and a curious setting in a former cinema. Early evening dining deals are generous. The wine list could be a lot more inspiring.

ℹ Getting There & Away

There are regular bus routes to other Borders towns and Berwick-upon-Tweed. For Edinburgh, change at St Boswells.

Around Kelso

The area around Kelso has two starkly contrasting historic buildings to visit, and the twin walkers' villages of Town Yetholm and Kirk Yetholm.

Mellerstain House — HISTORIC BUILDING

(☑01573-410225; www.mellerstain.com; Gordon; adult/child £11/5.50; ⊙noon-5pm Fri-Mon Easter & May-Sep) Finished in 1778, this is considered to be Scotland's finest Robert Adam–designed mansion. It is huge and famous for its classic elegance, ornate interiors and plaster ceilings; the library in particular is outstanding. The upstairs bedrooms are less attractive, but have a peek at the bizarre puppet-and-doll collection in the gallery.

It's about 6 miles northwest of Kelso, near Gordon. There are concerts held here through the summer months.

Smailholm Tower — TOWER

(HES; ☑01573-460365; www.historicenvironment.scot; Sandyknowe Farm, Smailholm; adult/child £6/3.60; ⊙9.30am-5.30pm Apr-Sep) Perched on a rocky knoll above a small lake, this narrow stone tower provides one of the most evocative sights in the Borders and keeps its bloody history alive. Although displays inside are sparse, the view from the top is worth the climb. The tower is 6 miles west of Kelso, a mile south of Smailholm village on the B6397.

The nearby privately owned farm, **Sandyknowe**, was owned by Sir Walter Scott's grandfather. As Scott himself recognised, his imagination was fired by the ballads and stories he heard as a child at Sandyknowe, and by the ruined tower a stone's throw away.

Eyemouth

POP 3500

Eyemouth is a busy fishing port and popular domestic holiday destination. The harbour itself is very atmospheric – you may even spot seals frolicking in the water. The community here suffered its greatest catastrophe in October 1881, when a terrible storm destroyed the coastal fishing fleet, killing 189 fishermen, 129 of whom were locals. Peter Aitchison's *Black Friday* is a good book about the disaster.

◎ Sights & Activities

Gunsgreen House — MUSEUM

(☑01890-752062; www.gunsgreenhouse.org; Gunsgreen Quay; adult/child £7/4.60; ⊙11am-5pm Apr-Oct; ♿) Standing proud and four-square across the harbour, this elegant 18th-century John Adam mansion was built on the profits of smuggling: Eyemouth was an important landing point for illegal cargoes from northern Europe and the Baltic. The house has been beautifully restored to reflect this and other aspects of its varied past. The hands-on exhibition makes a special effort to keep the kids entertained. Both the house and the adjacent tower-like dovecote can be hired out as self-catering accommodation.

Eyemouth Museum — MUSEUM

(☑01890-751701; www.eyemouthmuseum.co.uk; Manse Rd; adult/child £3.50/free; ⊙11am-4pm Mon-Sat Apr-Oct) Set in a church, the town museum has intriguing local history displays, particularly relating to the town's fishing heritage. Its centrepiece is the tapestry commemorating the 1881 fishing disaster.

Eyemouth RIB Trips — BOATING

(☑07941-441995; www.eyemouthribtrips.co.uk; Harbour Rd; ⊙Apr-Oct; ♿) Provides a range of fun boat trips, some focused on coastal scenery and wildlife spotting (adult/child £20/15), others on giving you a thrill and a soaking from the spray (adult/child

---

THE RIDING OF THE MARCHES

The Riding of the Marches, also known as the Common Riding, takes place in early summer in the major Borders towns. Like many Scottish festivals, it has ancient origins, dating back to the Middle Ages when riders would be sent to the town boundary to check on the common lands. The colourful event normally involves extravagant convoys of horse riders following the town standard as it is paraded along a well-worn route. Festivities vary between towns but usually involve lots of singing, sport, pageants and concerts, and plenty of whisky. If you want to zero in on the largest of the Ridings, head to Jedburgh for the Jethart Callant's Festival (p149).

PAXTON HOUSE

The family friendly **Paxton House** (☑ 01289-386291; www.paxtonhouse.co.uk; B6461; adult/child £10/4; ⊙ 10am-5pm Easter-Oct, grounds 10am-sunset; 🏛), 6 miles west of Berwick-upon-Tweed, is beside the River Tweed and surrounded by parkland and gardens. It was built in 1758 by Patrick Home for his intended wife, the daughter of Prussia's Frederick the Great. Unfortunately she stood him up, but it was her loss; designed by the Adam family – brothers John, James and Robert – it's acknowledged as one of Britain's finest 18th-century Palladian houses. Four tours run daily; see the website for limited winter visiting.

It contains a large collection of Chippendale and Regency furniture, and its picture gallery houses paintings from the national galleries of Scotland. The nursery is a feature designed to provide insight into a child's 18th-century life. In the grounds are walking trails, a restored waterwheel and a riverside museum on salmon fishing. There's plenty to keep the kids entertained, including boat trips on the Tweed.

Bus 32 runs past here every couple of hours from Berwick.

£20/15, minimum age 10). It also offers shuttle services to St Abbs (£5 each way; you can walk back).

✗ Eating

Oblò   BISTRO ££
(☑ 01890-752527; www.oblobar.com; Manse Rd; mains £12-16; ⊙ food 10am-8pm Sun-Thu, to 9pm Fri & Sat; 🔊🚲) For a meal any time, find your way upstairs to this modern Mediterranean-fusion bar-bistro with comfy seating and a modish interior. It's just down from the museum, and it's got a great deck to lap up the sunshine. Service is attentive and the food is delicious. Try the local seafood.

❶ Getting There & Away

Eyemouth is 5 miles north of the Scotland–England border. Buses go to Berwick-upon-Tweed (£3.10, 15 minutes, frequent), which has a train station, and to Edinburgh (£11.60, two hours, six to eight daily Monday to Saturday, three Sunday).

Coldingham & St Abbs

This picturesque area is fantastic for those who love the great outdoors. Some of the UK's best diving is here, as well as excellent cycling, walking, angling and birdwatching. From the village of Coldingham, with its twisting streets, take the B6438 downhill to the small fishing village of St Abbs, a gorgeous, peaceful little community with a picture-perfect harbour nestled below the cliffs.

⊙ Sights & Activities

St Abbs & Eyemouth
Voluntary Marine Reserve   NATURE RESERVE
(☑ 01890-771443; www.marine-reserve.co.uk) 🚩 The clear, clean waters around St Abbs form part of St Abbs & Eyemouth Voluntary Marine Reserve, one of the best cold-water diving sites in Europe. The reserve is home to a variety of marine life, including grey seals and porpoises. Visibility is about 7m to 8m but has been recorded at up to 24m. Beds of brown kelp form a hypnotically undulating forest on the seabed.

St Abbs Visitor Centre   MUSEUM
(☑ 01890-771672; www.stabbsvisitorcentre.co.uk; Coldingham Rd, St Abbs; ⊙ 10am-5pm Easter–mid-Oct) FREE This modern exhibition in St Abbs has interesting interactive displays on the often stormy history of this harbour village. Spoken reminiscences from locals like a fisherman and lighthouse keeper are the highlight.

Coldingham Priory   RUINS
(⊙ cemetery 24hr, church 2-4pm Wed May-Sep, plus 2-4pm Sun Jul & Aug) FREE Little remains of what was once one of the region's most powerful monasteries before the Black Death then Oliver Cromwell reduced it to ruins. The current church was rebuilt in Victorian times, but is barely a fraction of the original size, which you can divine via some remaining foundations among the headstones of the cemetery. It's a pleasant, peaceful spot to stroll.

St Abb's Head
National Nature Reserve   BIRDWATCHING
(www.nts.org.uk) This 78-hectare reserve is an ornithologist's wonderland, with large colonies of guillemots, kittiwakes, herring gulls, fulmars, razorbills and some puffins. The clifftop walks here are spectacular. You get to the reserve by following the 2-mile circular trail from the car park on the road just west of St Abbs, where there's a good **nature exhibition** (www.nts.org.uk; Old Smiddy, St Abbs; ⊘10am-5pm Apr-Oct) FREE in the Old Smiddy complex.

Coldingham Bay   BEACH
In Coldingham, a signposted turn-off to the east leads just under a mile down to away-from-it-all Coldingham Bay, which has a sandy beach and a clifftop walking trail to Eyemouth (3 miles). At **St Vedas Surf Shop** (☑01890-771679; www.stvedas.co.uk; Coldingham Bay; surfboard hire per hr £6.50, 2 person kayaks per hr/half-/full day £14/32/49; ⊘9am-dusk) you can hire surfboards, sea kayaks and snorkelling gear; there's a hotel here that serves cheap food. Surfing lessons (£40) are also available.

Berwickshire Coastal Path   WALKING
(www.scotborders.gov.uk) Thirty miles of spectacular coastal walking link Berwick-upon-Tweed in the south with Cockburnspath in the north, where you can continue on the Southern Upland Way (p154). A pretty 3½-mile section links St Abbs and Eyemouth.

Scuba Diving
The sea around St Abbs forms part of the St Abbs & Eyemouth Voluntary Marine Reserve. Three dive boats operate out of St Abbs. You can charter them whole, or phone to book a spot on a boat; it costs around £40 to £50 per person for two dives.

The three operators are **Dive St Abbs** (Paul Crowe; ☑01890-771945, 07710 961050; www.divestabbs.com; Rock House), **St Abbs Diving** (Paul O'Callaghan; ☑01890-771525, 07780 980179; www.stabbsdiving.com; The Harbour) and **St Abbs Charters** (Barry White; ☑07990 800525; www.stabbscharters.com; The Harbour)

The St Abbs Visitor Centre can provide some diving advice. A guide to local dive sites costs £7.50.

🛏 Sleeping & Eating

Rock House   HOSTEL, B&B £
(☑01890-771945; www.divestabbs.com; Harbour, St Abbs; dm £24, d £65, cottage £75; 🐾) Right by St Abbs' harbour, this is run by a friendly dive skipper and family; you can almost roll out of bed onto the boat. The bunkhouse (usually booked up by groups at the weekend) sleeps a total of 10. There's also a pretty B&B room and a cute cottage with a little deck overlooking the heart of the village.

Priory View   B&B ££
(☑01890-771525; www.prioryview.com; Eyemouth Rd, Coldingham; d £70-80, f £110; P🐾🐾) Once a police station, this solid house offers five comfortable B&B rooms decked out in wood. There's a pleasant garden with a games room and a genuine welcome from the owners, who also have a dive boat in St Abbs.

Ebbcarrs Cafe   CAFE £
(☑01890-771302; Harbour, St Abbs; light meals £4-7; ⊘10am-5pm Apr-Oct, 10am-4pm Tue-Sun Nov-Mar) A stone cottage by the harbour in St Abbs, sweet Ebbcarrs does tasty rolls with local crab, cullen skink and other sweet and savoury bites. Grab one of the picnic tables outside or head upstairs for indoor seating.

ℹ Getting There & Away
Bus 235 runs seven to 10 times daily to Coldingham and St Abbs from Berwick (£4, 25 minutes) via Eyemouth (£2.20, 10 minutes). From Berwick you can jump on a train to Edinburgh.

SOUTH LANARKSHIRE
South Lanarkshire combines a highly urbanised area south of Glasgow with scenically gorgeous country around the Falls of Clyde and the World Heritage–listed area of New Lanark, by far the biggest drawcard of the region. The handsome town of Biggar is also worth a visit.

Lanark & New Lanark
POP 8900
Below the market town of Lanark, in an attractive gorge by the River Clyde, is the World Heritage Site of New Lanark – an intriguing collection of restored mill buildings and warehouses.

WALKING & CYCLING IN SOUTHERN SCOTLAND

Walking

The region's most famous walk is the challenging 214-mile **Southern Upland Way** (☎ 01387-273987; www.southernuplandway.gov.uk), which runs coast to coast from Portpatrick to Cockburnspath. If you want a sample, one of the best bits is the three- to four-day section from Dalry to Beattock.

Another long-distance walk is 62-mile **St Cuthbert's Way** (www.stcuthbertsway.info), inspired by the travels of St Cuthbert, a 7th-century saint who lived at the first Melrose monastery. It crosses some superb scenery between Melrose and Lindisfarne (in England).

From Glasgow to Galloway via Ayrshire, the 143-mile Whithorn Way (p173) follows in the footsteps of ancient pilgrims.

The **Borders Abbeys Way** (www.bordersabbeysway.com) links all the great Border abbeys in a 65-mile circuit. For shorter walks and especially circular loops in the hills, the towns of Melrose, Jedburgh and Kelso all make ideal bases. On the Borders coast, the Berwickshire Coastal Path (p153) takes in splendid scenery.

For baggage transfer on these walks, contact **Walking Support** (☎ 01896-822079; www.walkingsupport.co.uk). In early September, look out for the **Scottish Borders Walking Festival** (www.borderswalking.com), with a week of walks for all abilities and an instant social scene.

Cycling

With the exception of the main A-roads, traffic is sparse, which, along with the beauty of the countryside, makes this ideal cycling country (p147).

The **Tweed Cycle Route** is 95 waymarked miles along the beautiful Tweed Valley, following minor roads from Biggar to Peebles (22 miles), Melrose (25 miles), Coldstream (28 miles) and Berwick-upon-Tweed (20 miles). The **4 Abbeys Cycle Route** is a 55-mile circuit of the Border abbeys. Local tourist offices have route maps; these and other routes are also detailed at www.cyclescottishborders.com. Further west, the Whithorn Way (p173) is also a cycling route.

Once Britain's largest cotton-spinning complex, it's better known for the pioneering social experiments of Robert Owen, who managed the mill from 1800. New Lanark is really a memorial to this enlightened capitalist. He provided his workers with housing, a cooperative store, the world's first nursery school, adult-education classes, a sick-pay fund for workers and a social centre he called the New Institute for the Formation of Character. Devote half a day to exploring this site as there's plenty to see and do, including appealing walks along the riverside. What must once have been a thriving, noisy, industrial village is now a peaceful oasis with only the swishing of trees and the rushing of the River Clyde to be heard.

◉ Sights & Activities

★ **New Lanark Visitor Centre**   MUSEUM
(☎ 01555-661345; www.newlanark.org; adult/child/family £13/10/40; ⊙10am-5pm Apr-Oct,

to 4pm Nov-Mar; ⊛) The main attractions of this World Heritage mill town are accessed with a single ticket. These include a huge working spinning mule, producing woollen yarn, and the **historic schoolhouse**, which contains an innovative, high-tech journey to New Lanark's past via a 3D hologram of the spirit of Annie McLeod, a 10-year-old mill girl who describes life here in 1820. The kids will love it as it's very realistic, though the 'do good for all mankind' theme is a little overbearing.

Included in your admission is entrance to a millworker's house, Robert Owen's home and exhibitions on 'saving New Lanark'. There's also a 1920s-style village store.

Falls of Clyde   WALKING
From New Lanark, you can walk through the beautiful nature reserve up to **Corra Linn** (0.75 miles) and **Bonnington Linn** (1.5 miles), two of the Falls of Clyde that inspired Turner and Wordsworth. You could return

via the path on the opposite bank, pass New Lanark and cross the river downstream to make a circular walk (6 miles total).

🛏 Sleeping & Eating

Wee Row Hostel   HOSTEL £
(☑ 01555-666710; www.newlanarkhostel.co.uk; Rosedale St, New Lanark; tw/q/studio £56/80/90; ☺ Mar-Oct; 🅿 @ 🛜) This hostel has a great location in an old mill building in the heart of the New Lanark complex. It has comfortable en-suite rooms with both beds and bunks and a really good downstairs common area. Prices come down substantially outside high season. Closed between 11am and 3pm. You can use the nearby hotel spa for a small charge.

New Lanark Mill Hotel   HOTEL £££
(☑ 01555-667200; www.newlanarkhotel.co.uk; New Lanark; r £119-179; 🅿 @ 🛜 ♨ 🐕) Cleverly converted from an 18th-century mill, this hotel is full of character and is a stone's throw from the major attractions. It has smart rooms (the deluxe ones are quite a bit more spacious), with contemporary art and views (and sounds) of the churning Clyde below. There's also self-catering accommodation in charming cottages, and a pool, spa and fitness area.

There are good facilities for people with disabilities. The hotel also serves good meals (mains £11 to £18). Rooms are quite a bit cheaper midweek. It often packs out for weddings at weekends.

⭐ La Vigna   ITALIAN £££
(☑ 01555-664320; www.lavigna.co.uk; 40 Wellgate, Lanark; mains £20-26; ☺ noon-2.30pm & 5-10pm Mon-Sat, noon-3pm & 5-9.30pm Sun; 🛜) This long-established local favourite is a great spot, seemingly plucked from some bygone age with its quietly efficient service and classy, welcoming ambience. The food is distinctly Italian, albeit using Scottish venison, beef and fish, and there are also vegetarian options. Lunch and early dining specials are great value.

❶ Getting There & Away

Lanark is 25 miles southeast of Glasgow. Express bus 240X runs hourly Monday to Saturday (£6.80, one hour); trains from Glasgow Central also run (£7.70, 50 minutes, every 30 minutes, hourly on Sundays).

It's a pleasant walk to New Lanark, but there's also a half-hourly bus service from the train station (daily) and taxis.

Biggar

POP 2500

Biggar is a pleasant town in a rural setting overlooked by Tinto Hill. The town has a worthwhile heritage museum and a famous puppet theatre. It's also known for the nationalist, leftist poet Hugh MacDiarmid, who lived near here for nearly 30 years until his death in 1978.

Biggar & Upper Clydesdale Museum   MUSEUM
(☑ 01899-221050; www.biggarmuseumtrust.co.uk; 156 High St; adult/child £5/2; ☺ 10am-5pm Tue-Sat, 1-5pm Sun Apr-Dec, closed Mon-Fri Jan-Mar) This museum is an enthusiastic community project that is well worth a visit. The pièce de résistance is Gladstone Court, a reconstructed street with historic Victorian-era nook-and-cranny shops that you can pop into to steal a glimpse of the past. A working telephone exchange is an impressive highlight. Other displays cover the archaeology, geography and history of the area, with features both on the Covenanters and the Polish soldiers billeted in Biggar in WWII.

Biggar Puppet Theatre   THEATRE
(☑ 01899-220631; www.purvespuppets.com; Broughton Rd; adult/child £10/8; ☺ Easter-Sep) A well-loved local institution that runs matinée shows every couple of days throughout the summer using miniature Victorian puppets and bizarre glow-in-the-dark modern ones over 1m high. Different shows are suitable for varying age groups, so enquire before you take the kids along. Check the website for performance times.

Tinto Hill   WALKING
The 712m hill dominates the town from a distance. It is a straightforward ascent by the northern ridge from the car park, just off the A73 by Thankerton Crossroads. Look out for the Stone Age fort on your way up. Allow two hours for the return trip (4½ miles).

---

❶ ARDROSSAN

The coastal town of Ardrossan, between Largs and Troon, is the main ferry port for Arran and easily reached by train from Glasgow. There are also seasonal ferry services from here to Campbeltown on the Kintyre peninsula.

WORTH A TRIP

GREAT CUMBRAE

Walking or cycling is the best way to explore this accessible, hilly island (it's only 4 miles long), ideal for a day trip from Largs. **Millport** is the only town, strung out around the bay overlooking neighbouring Little Cumbrae.

The island's minor roads have well-marked walking and cycling routes. Take the **Inner Circle route** up to the island's highest point, **Glaid Stone**, where you get good views of Arran and Largs, and even as far as the Paps of Jura on a clear day. You can walk between the ferry and the town via here in about an hour. There are bike-hire places in Millport, which also boasts Britain's smallest cathedral, the lovely **Cathedral of the Isles** (☑01475-530353; www.cathedraloftheisles.org; College St; ☺8.30am-6pm) **FREE**, completed in 1851. It also offers guesthouse accommodation. Drop by the friendly **Dancing Midge** (☑01475-530548; www.facebook.com/thedancingmidge; 24 Glasgow St; light meals £3-8; ☺9am-4pm Thu-Tue; 🐾) cafe for coffee, home baking and hearty breakfast options.

A frequent CalMac (www.calmac.co.uk) ferry links Largs with Great Cumbrae (passenger/car return £3.40/12.95, 10 minutes). Buses meet the ferries for the 3.5-mile journey to Millport.

❶ Getting There & Away

Biggar is 33 miles southeast of Glasgow. There are hourly buses (four on Sunday) to/from Edinburgh (£5.40, 1¼ hours); some services continue to Dumfries (£7, 1¾ hours). For Glasgow, change at Lanark. Other buses run to Peebles (£4.90, 40 minutes).

AYRSHIRE

Ayrshire is synonymous with golf and Robert Burns – and there's plenty on offer here to satisfy both of these pursuits. Troon and Turnberry have world-famous links courses, and there's enough Burns memorabilia in the region to satisfy even his most fanatical admirers.

The best way to appreciate the Ayrshire coastline is on foot: the **Ayrshire Coastal Path** (www.ayrshirecoastalpath.org; 🐾) offers 100 miles of spectacular waterside walking.

Largs

POP 11,300

On a sunny day, there are few places in southern Scotland more beautiful than Largs, where green grass meets the sparkling water of the Firth of Clyde. It's a resort-style waterfront town that harks back to seaside days in times of gentler pleasures, and the minigolf, amusements, old-fashioned eateries and bouncy castle mean you should get into the spirit, buy an ice cream and stroll around this slice of retro Scotland.

◉ Sights & Activities

In summer, the *Waverley* (p120), the last ocean-going paddle steamer ever built, runs spectacular coastal voyages. There are usually several departures a week from Largs; book online.

Víkingar! MUSEUM
(☑01475-689777; www.kaleisure.com; Greenock Rd; adult/child £4.50/3.50; ☺11.30am-2.30pm Sat & Sun Feb & Nov, 11.30am-1.30pm daily Mar, 10.30am-2.30pm daily Apr-Jun, Sep & Oct, 10.30am-3.30pm Mon-Fri, 11.30-3.30pm Sat & Sun Jul & Aug; 🐾) The town's main attraction is a multimedia exhibition describing Viking influence in Scotland until its demise at the Battle of Largs in 1263. It's got a slightly downbeat municipal feel these days, but tours with staff in Viking outfits run every hour; ring ahead to check, though. It also has a swimming pool, soft play area and leisure centre. It's on the waterfront road; you can't miss it, as it's the only place with a longship outside.

⚔ Festivals & Events

Largs Viking Festival CULTURAL
(www.largsvikingfestival.org; ☺1st week Sep) This festival celebrates the Battle of Largs and the end of Viking political domination in Scotland. The highlights are the authentic Viking village peopled by costumed locals and the re-enactment of the battle, complete with longship aflame.

🛏 Sleeping & Eating

Glendarroch
B&B ££

(☑ 01475-676305; www.glendarrochlargs.com; 24 Irvine Rd; d £70; ℗ 🛜) This B&B on the main road through town has warm and friendly owners who keep their prices fair and their four lovely rooms very shipshape. All are en suite and the king-sized double is particularly desirable.

St Leonards Guest House
B&B ££

(☑ 01475-673318; www.stleonardsguesthouse. com; 9 Irvine Rd; d £65-75; ℗ 🛜) On the main road through town, but excellently soundproofed, this spot offers a cordial welcome and spotless, well-decorated rooms, two of which share a top-notch modern bathroom. Breakfast is a pleasure.

Lounge
BISTRO ££

(☑ 01475-689968; www.loungeatlargs.com; 33 Main St; mains £11-17, lunch dishes £6-12; ⊙ food noon-3.30pm & 5-9.30pm Mon-Fri, noon-4pm & 5-9.30pm Sat & Sun; 🛜) Tucked away above the Royal Bank of Scotland on the main road, this stunningly attractive bar and bistro comes as quite a surprise. Eating is done in an elegant tearoom space, with hardwood floor, ceramic fireplace and leather seats. Service is willing, and there's a nice range of classic Scottish pub fare alongside tasty seafood and a few fusion dishes.

There's also a roof terrace with gas heaters, a fine spot for a drink.

Nardini's
ICE CREAM £

(☑ 01475-675000; www.nardinis.co.uk; 2 Greenock Rd; ice creams £2-3.50; ⊙ 9am-9pm or 10pm Apr-Oct, to 8pm Nov-Mar; 🛜 ♿) Nothing typifies the old-time feel of Largs more than this giant art-deco gelateria. The ice creams are decadently delicious, with rich flavours that'll have parents licking more than their fair share from their kids' cones. It also has a cafe with outdoor seating, and a restaurant.

ℹ Getting There & Away

Largs is 32 miles west of Glasgow by road. There are trains from Glasgow Central (£8.90, one hour, hourly). Buses run the route more slowly via Greenock and Gourock. Buses also run once or twice hourly to Ayr (£7.30, 1¾ hours) via Ardrossan and Irvine. You can also reach these by rail, some with a change at Kilwinning.

Troon

POP 14,640

Troon, a major sailing centre on the coast 7 miles north of Ayr, has excellent sandy beaches and six golf courses, including one of the world's finest. Nearby Dundonald Castle is also well worth a visit.

Dundonald Castle
CASTLE

(HES; ☑ 01563-851489; www.dundonaldcastle.org. uk; Winehouse Yett, Dundonald; adult/child £6/4; ⊙ 9.30am-5.30pm Apr-Oct, 10am-4pm Nov-Mar) Dundonald Castle commands impressive

---

OFF THE BEATEN TRACK

IRVINE

Boat lovers should check out the **Scottish Maritime Museum** (☑ 01294-278283; www. scottishmaritimemuseum.org; Harbour Rd; adult/child £8.50/free; ⊙ 10am-5pm; ♿) by the train station in Irvine, which long ago was west Scotland's busiest port. In the massive Linthouse Engine Shop – an old hangar with a cast-iron framework – is an absorbing collection of boats and machinery. Displays cover ropeworking, the age of steam and the Clyde's shipbuilding industry. Every boat here has a story – some tragic. Nearby at the dock, guides will show you a couple more ships and a restored shipyard worker's flat.

Further along the appealing harbour road, be sure to drop into the **Ship Inn** (☑ 01294-279722; www.facebook.com/shipinnirvine; 120 Harbour St; mains £9-13; ⊙ food noon-2.30pm & 5-9pm Mon-Fri, 10am-9pm Sat & Sun; 🛜) if it has reopened after some complications at time of research. It's the oldest pub in Irvine and has bucket-loads of character. Nearby, brilliant **Gro Coffee** (☑ 07881 934732; www.facebook.com/grocoffee; Harbour St; light meals £5-11; ⊙ 9am-10pm Mon-Sat, to 9pm Sun; 🛜 🎵) 🌱 is an upbeat cafe, bakery and evening pizza stop run according to sustainable principles.

Irvine is 26 miles from Glasgow. There are frequent buses from Ayr (30 to 40 minutes) and Largs (one hour). Trains run to/from Glasgow Central station; the other way they go to Ayr.

views and, in its main hall, has one of the finest barrel-vaulted ceilings preserved in Scotland. It was the first home of the Stuart kings, built by Robert II in 1371, and reckoned to be the third most important castle in Scotland in its time, after Edinburgh and Stirling. The visitor centre has good information on prior settlements, and scale models of the castle and its predecessors. Buses running between Troon and Kilmarnock stop in Dundonald.

There are ongoing archaeological investigations here that, it is hoped, will reveal remains of an earlier castle.

Winter opening hours are changeable; call ahead.

★ **Royal Troon** GOLF
(☑ 01292-311555; www.royaltroon.co.uk; Craigend Rd; ⊗ mid-Apr–early Oct) The demanding championship Old Course here hosted the 2016 Open Championship and is one of golf's classic links challenges. The standard green fee is £260 but there are sometimes offers on the website. The second course, Portland, can be played for £90.

★ **MacCallum's** SEAFOOD ££
(☑ 01292-319339; www.maccallumsoftroon. co.uk; Harbour Rd; seafood mains £13-21, fried fish £4-7; ⊗ restaurant noon-2.30pm & 6.30-8.30pm Wed-Sat, noon-2.30pm Sun, chip shop noon-8pm Sun & Tue-Thu, noon-9pm Fri & Sat) Right at the end of the harbour road, where yachts have given way to fishing boats, this set-up has two parts, both worthwhile. The Oyster Bar offers excellent fresh seafood in a smart, uncluttered setting. Next door,

A DAY AT THE RACES

Ayr Racecourse (☑ 01292-264179; www.ayr-racecourse.co.uk; Whitletts Rd) Scotland's premier racecourse is a fun day out, with both flat and jump racing days and good facilities. The biggest event is the Scottish Grand National in April. Check the website for a list of race days. As well as racing, other events, including a popular car boot sale, are regularly held here.

Established in 1576 and in its current location since 1907, the racecourse is an easy 15-minute walk from Ayr town centre.

the Wee Hurrie does fish and chips, with tempting fish choices like sea bass. Order the delicious fritto misto to try different varieties.

🛈 **Getting There & Away**

There are half-hourly trains to Ayr (£3.60, 10 minutes) and Glasgow (£8.60, 40 to 55 minutes). The ferry service to Northern Ireland is no longer running.

Ayr & Alloway
POP 46,710

Ayr's long sandy beach has made it a popular family seaside resort since Victorian times, but the town has struggled in recent years. However, the pretty, lush village of Alloway (3 miles south of Ayr) should be on the itinerary of every Robert Burns fan – he was born here on 25 January 1759. Even if you haven't been seduced by Burnsmania, it's still well worth a visit, as the Burns-related exhibitions give a good impression of life in Ayrshire in the late 18th century.

◉ **Sights**

◉ **Ayr**

St John's Tower TOWER
(Eglinton Tce) This is the only remnant of the church that hosted a parliament in 1315, the year after the celebrated victory at the battle of Bannockburn. John Knox' son-in-law was the minister here, and Mary, Queen of Scots, stayed overnight in 1563. You can only admire it from the street, but it's very photogenic.

Auld Kirk CHURCH
(Old Church; www.auldkirk.org; Blackfriars Walk; ⊗ 1-2pm Tue Mar-Jun & Sep-Nov, 10.30am-12.30pm Sat Jul & Aug) FREE Robert Burns was baptised in the Auld Kirk. The atmospheric cemetery here overlooks the river and is good for a stroll, offering an escape from the bustle of High St.

Auld Brig BRIDGE
(Old Bridge) Several of Burns' poems are set here in Ayr; in *Twa Brigs,* Ayr's old and new bridges argue with one another. The Auld Brig was built in 1491 and spans the river just north of the church.

Ayr

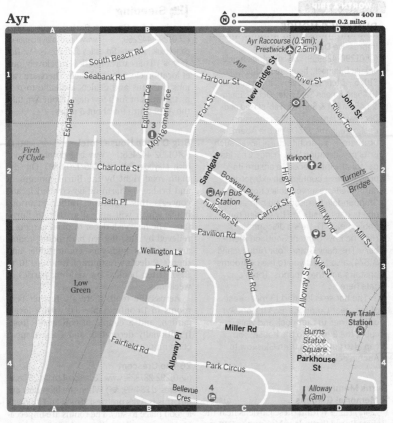

◉ Alloway

★ Robert Burns Birthplace Museum

MUSEUM

(NTS; ☎ 01292-443700; www.nts.org.uk; Murdoch's Lone; adult/child £10.50/7.50; ⊙ 10am-5.30pm Apr-Sep, to 5pm Oct-Mar) This impressive museum has collected a solid range of Burns memorabilia, including manuscripts and possessions of the poet, such as the pistols he packed for his work as a taxman. There's good biographical information, and a series of displays that bring to life poems via background snippets, translations and recitations. Appropriately the museum doesn't take itself too seriously: there's plenty of humour that the poet surely would have approved of, and entertaining audio and visual performances will keep the kids amused.

The admission ticket also covers the atmospheric **Burns Birthplace Cottage**

Ayr

◉ Sights

🛌 Sleeping

🍷 Drinking & Nightlife

(open 11am to 5pm), connected via a walkway to the Birthplace Museum. Born in the little box-bed in this cramped thatched dwelling, the poet spent the first seven years of his life here. It's an attractive display that gives you a context for reading plenty of his verse. Much-needed translation of some of the more obscure Scots farming terms he loved to use decorate the walls.

WORTH A TRIP

DUMFRIES HOUSE

Impressive **Dumfries House**
(☎01290-425959; www.dumfries-house.
org.uk; Cumnock; house tour adult/child
£10/5; ⊙tours 10.45am-3.30pm Sun-Fri,
10.45am & noon Sat Easter-Oct, 12.15pm
& 1.45pm Sat & Sun Nov-Feb, closed mid-
Dec-early Jan), a Palladian mansion
designed in the 1750s by the Adam
brothers, is an architectural jewel: such
is its preservation that Prince Charles
personally intervened to ensure its
protection. It contains an extraordi-
narily well-preserved collection of
Chippendale furniture and numerous
objets d'art. Visits are by guided tour;
book ahead. There's a discount for
Historic Environment Scotland members. The daily Grand Tour (adult/child
£13/4) also takes you to the bedrooms
upstairs and the grounds. There's a
cafe here.

The house is located 13 miles east
of Ayr, near Cumnock. Bus it from Ayr
or Dumfries to Cumnock and walk or
cab it the 2 miles to the house; you
can also get a train from Glasgow to
Auchinleck.

Burns Monument
& Memorial Gardens   GARDENS
(⊙24hr) FREE Within these gardens near the
Robert Burns Birthplace Museum (p159) is a
striking neo-Grecian monument to the poet,
completed in 1823. It affords a view of the
nearby 13th-century Brig o' Doon, another
Burns landmark.

Alloway Auld Kirk   RUINS
(Monument Rd; ⊙24hr) FREE Near the Robert
Burns Birthplace Museum (p159) are the ruins of the kirk, the setting for part of Burns'
verse tale 'Tam o' Shanter'. Burns' father,
William, is buried in the kirkyard; read the
poem on the back of the gravestone.

⁂ Festivals & Events

Burns an' a' That   CULTURAL
(www.burnsfestival.com) This festival encompasses several events that take place
throughout the year. There's a bit of
everything, from wine tasting and horse
racing to concerts, some of it Burns related.
Burnsfest is the major live-music event, held
on a Saturday in May.

🛌 Sleeping

Heads of Ayr Caravan Park   CAMPGROUND £
(☎01292-442269; www.headsofayr-caravan-
park.co.uk; Dunure Rd; sites £23-25; ⊙Mar-Oct;
P🅿🛜🐕) This caravan park is in a lovely, quiet location close to the beach. There are various caravans and chalets available to rent
by the week or for a few days. From Ayr, take
the A719 south for about 5 miles.

Brig O'Doon House Hotel   HOTEL ££
(☎01292-442466; www.brigodoonhouse.com;
High Maybole Rd; s/d £85/120; 🛜) On the
main road right by the Burns monument
and bridge, a charming ivy-covered facade
conceals this romantic, rather luxurious
hotel, which will appeal greatly to Burns
fans. The heavyish decor of plaid carpets is
relieved by slate-floored bathrooms; rooms
are spacious and very comfortable, and
there's a decent restaurant (mains £10 to
£14). Often booked by wedding parties at
weekends.

Across the road, there are further bedrooms in Doonbrae, blessed with a lovely
garden, and a couple of cottages – Rose,
traditionally decorated, and Gables, more
contemporary.

26 The Crescent   B&B ££
(☎01292-287329; www.26crescent.co.uk; 26 Belle-
vue Cres; d £84-99; 🛜) When the blossoms
are out, this is Ayr's prettiest street, and it boasts
a good place to stay. The rooms are impeccable – an upgrade to the spacious four-poster
room is a sound investment. Bathrooms are
excellent. Though there's more space on the
1st floor, we like the top-floor chambers with
sloping roof.

✕ Eating & Drinking

Tam O'Shanter   PUB
(☎01292-611684; 230 High St; ⊙11am-11pm Mon-
Sat, 12.30-11pm Sun; 🛜) In Robert Burns' poem
'Tam o' Shanter', Tam spends a boozy evening
in this pub, which now bears his name.
Opened in the mid-18th century, it's an atmospheric old place with a good vibe as well
as simple pub grub (served noon to 9pm).

ⓘ Getting There & Around

BUS
Ayr is 33 miles from Glasgow and is Ayrshire's
major transport hub. There are frequent express services to Glasgow (£6.80, one hour) via
Prestwick Airport, as well as services to Stran-

raer (£13.50, two hours, four to eight per day) and several Ayrshire towns. The bus station sits at the corner of Fullarton St and Sandgate.

Regular local and regional buses run south from Ayr to Alloway (10 minutes) and some X77 buses from Glasgow stop at Alloway. Otherwise you can walk or cycle to Alloway from Ayr.

TRAIN
There are at least two trains an hour that run between Ayr and Glasgow Central station (£9.30, 50 minutes), and some trains continue south from Ayr to Stranraer (£12.20, 1¼ hours).

Culzean Castle

★ **Culzean Castle & Country Park**   PALACE
(NTS; ☑01655-884455; www.nts.org.uk; Culzean; castle adult/child/family £17/12.65/42; ⊙castle 10.30am-5pm Apr-Oct, last entry 4pm, park 9.30am-sunset year-round; ♿) The Scottish National Trust's flagship property, magnificent Culzean (kull-*ane*) is one of the most impressive of Scotland's stately homes. On approach the castle floats into view like a mirage. Designed by Robert Adam, who was encouraged to exercise his romantic genius, the 18th-century mansion is perched dramatically on a clifftop. The sizeable grounds include a great kids' play area, which replicates the castle on a smaller scale, and a recreation of a Victorian vinery, an orangery, a deer park and an aviary.

Robert Adam was the most influential architect of his time, renowned for his meticulous attention to detail and the elegant classical embellishments with which he decorated his ceilings and fireplaces.

The beautiful oval staircase here is regarded as one of his finest achievements. On the 1st floor, the opulence of the circular saloon contrasts violently with the views of the wild sea below. Lord Cassillis' bedroom is said to be haunted by a lady in green, mourning for a lost baby. Even the bathrooms are palatial: the dressing room beside the state bedroom is equipped with a Victorian state-of-the-art shower.

Stagecoach buses running between Ayr and Girvan stop outside the gates, from where it's a 1-mile walk to the castle.

Culzean Camping & Caravanning Club   CAMPGROUND £
(☑01655-760627; www.campingandcaravanning-club.co.uk; Culzean Castle, Culzean; tent site for

1/2 £22.10/33.05; ⊙Apr-Oct; P✿☺) Right by the entrance to the Culzean country park (p161), this offers grassy pitches with great views. Pricing varies markedly and it's often cheaper to buy membership. Minimum two- or three-night stays apply here in high summer.

Crossraguel Abbey

Crossraguel Abbey   RUINS
(HES; ☑01655-883113; www.historicenvironment.scot; A77, near Maybole; adult/child £6/3.60; ⊙9.30am-5.30pm Sun-Wed Apr-Sep) Between the towns of Maybole and Kirkoswald, by the A77, Crossraguel Abbey is a substantial ruin dating back to the 13th century that's good fun to explore. The renovated 16th-century gatehouse is the best part – you'll find decorative stonework and superb views from the top. Inside, if you have the place to yourself, you'll hear only the whistling wind – an apt reflection of the abbey's long-deceased monastic tradition. Don't miss the echo in the chilly sacristy.

Ailsa Craig

The curiously shaped island of Ailsa Craig can be seen from much of southern Ayrshire. While its unusual blue-tinted granite – famous for making the best curling stones – has been used by geologists to trace the movements of the great Ice Age ice sheet, birdwatchers know Ailsa Craig as the world's second-largest gannet colony – around 10,000 pairs breed annually on the island's sheer cliffs.

To see the island close up, take a cruise from Girvan on the **MV Glorious** (☑07773 794358; www.ailsacraig.org.uk; 7 Harbour St; ⊙Apr-Oct). It's possible to land if the sea is reasonably calm; a four-hour trip costs £35/20 per adult/child.

Trains going to Girvan run approximately hourly (less frequently on Sundays) from Ayr (£6.10, 25 minutes).

DUMFRIES & GALLOWAY

Some of southern Scotland's finest attractions lie in the gentle hills and lush valleys of Dumfries and Galloway. It's an ideal destination for families, as there's plenty on offer for the kids. Galloway Forest – with its sublime views, mountain biking and walking trails, red deer, kites and other wildlife – is a highlight, as are the dream-like ruins of Caerlaverock Castle. Adding to the appeal of this enticing region is a string of southern Scotland's most idyllic towns, which are charming when the sun shines. And shine it does. This is the mildest region in Scotland and is warmed by the Gulf Stream, a phenomenon that has allowed the development of some famous gardens.

Dumfries

POP 32,900

Lovely, red-hued sandstone bridges crisscross the wide, grassy-banked River Nith, which runs through the centre of pleasant Dumfries. Historically the town held a strategic position in the path of vengeful English armies; consequently, though it has existed since Roman times, the oldest standing building dates from the 17th century. Plenty of famous names have passed through: Robert Burns lived here and worked as a tax collector, Peter Pan creator JM Barrie was schooled here and DJ Calvin Harris hails from the town.

◉ Sights

★ Burns House   MUSEUM

(☑ 01387-255297; www.dumgal.gov.uk; Burns St; ⊙10am-5pm Mon-Sat, 2-5pm Sun Apr-Sep, 10am-1pm & 2-5pm Tue-Sat Oct-Mar) FREE A place of pilgrimage for Burns enthusiasts. It's here that the poet spent the last years of his life, and there are various possessions of his in glass cases, as well as manuscripts and, entertainingly, letters: make sure you have a read.

Moat Brae   MUSEUM

(☑ 01387-255549; www.peterpanmoatbrae.org; 101 George St; adult/child £6.50/5, garden only £2; ⊙11am-5pm Tue-Sat, 10am-4pm Sun; ⊕) Wandering in this house and garden as a child inspired JM Barrie to write *Peter Pan*. This new attraction is a major project; a national centre for children's literacy and a great family visit run with heart-warming enthusiasm. The beautiful house has interactive exhibitions, reading rooms, actors and storytelling activities, while there's a cute shop, cafe and a great garden running down to the river featuring a pirate ship, crocodiles and other favourites from the book. Check the website for what's on each week.

Dumfries Museum
& Camera Obscura   MUSEUM

(☑ 01387-253374; www.dgculture.co.uk; Rotchell Rd; museum free, camera obscura adult/child £3.60/1.80; ⊙10am-5pm Mon-Sat, 2-5pm Sun Apr-Sep, 10am-1pm & 2-5pm Tue-Sat Oct-Mar) FREE This museum covers local history and prehistory with a wide range of displays from fossils to farm implements. In the tower is a camera obscura, built in 1836, giving an intriguing view, even in this digital age, of the surrounding area.

Devorgilla Bridge   BRIDGE

The red sandstone bridges arching over the River Nith are the most attractive feature of the town. Devorgilla Bridge (1431) is one of the oldest bridges in Scotland. Built into its southwestern end is the city's oldest extant house.

Robert Burns Centre   MUSEUM

(☑ 01387-264808; www.dgculture.co.uk; Mill Rd; audiovisual presentation £2.30; ⊙10am-5pm Mon-Sat, 2-5pm Sun Apr-Sep, 10am-1pm & 2-5pm Tue-Sat Oct-Mar) FREE A worthwhile Burns exhibition in an old mill on the banks of the River Nith; it tells the story of the poet and Dumfries in the 1790s. The optional audiovisual presentations give more background on Dumfries and explain the exhibition's contents. The centre functions as a cinema in the evenings.

Ellisland Farm   MUSEUM

(☑ 01387-740426; www.ellislandfarm.co.uk; Holywood Rd, Auldgirth; adult/child £5/free; ⊙10am-5pm Mon-Wed & Sat early Jan-Nov, plus 2-5pm Sun Apr-Sep) Six miles northwest of Dumfries, you can visit the farm that Robert Burns leased in 1788 by the River Nith. He had the house built for his family and lived here until 1791. The farmhouse still preserves plenty of atmosphere of the time. There's an exhibition and short film. Ellisland is signposted off the A76 to Kilmarnock; bus 246 will get you there too.

Robert Burns Mausoleum   TOMB

(Brooms Rd) FREE Burns' mausoleum is in the graveyard at **St Michael's Kirk**. It's in the far (eastern) corner from the entrance. There's a grisly account of his reburial on the information panel.

Dumfries

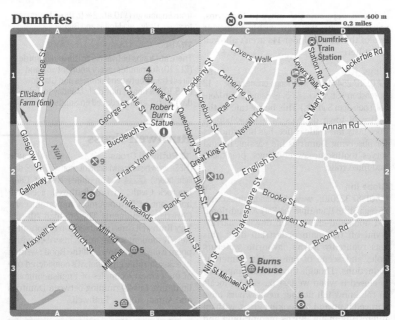

🛌 Sleeping

★ **Ferintosh Guest House**   B&B **££**
(📞 01387-252262; www.ferintosh.net; 30 Lovers Walk; s £38-42, d £70-72; 🛜 🐾) A typically lovely Dumfries sandstone Victorian villa opposite the train station, Ferintosh is a good-humoured place with excellent rooms and a warm welcome. These people have the right attitude towards hospitality, with comfortable plush beds, a free dram on arrival for LP readers, and plenty of good chat on distilleries. The owner's original artwork complements the decor.

Cyclists are welcomed with a shed and bike-washing facilities.

Huntingdon   B&B **££**
(📞 01387-249071; www.thehuntingdonbandb.co.uk; 32 Lovers Walk; r £79-90; 🅿 🛜) This smart modernisation of a sturdy sandstone former day hospital offers high-standard B&B in four attractive, very commodious rooms with good modern bathrooms right by the train station. There's a pleasant front lawn and a gracious host. Room-only rates are available.

🍴 Eating & Drinking

Cavens Arms   PUB FOOD **£**
(📞 01387-252896; www.cavensarms.com; 20 Buccleuch St; mains £9-15; ⏰ food 11am-9pm

Dumfries

Tue-Sat, noon-9pm Sun; 🛜 🍽) Engaging staff, 10 real ales on tap and a warm, contented buzz make this a legendary Dumfries pub. Generous portions of typical pub nosh backed by a long list of more adventurous daily specials make it one of the town's most enjoyable places to eat. Gets packed on weekends (but staff will still try to find you a table).

If you were going to move to Dumfries, you'd make sure you were within a block or two of this place. Under-14s aren't allowed to eat here.

Kings   CAFE £

(📞01387-254444; www.kings-online.co.uk; 12 Queensberry St; snacks £3-5; ⊘8am-5.30pm Mon-Sat, noon-4pm Sun; 🛜) This buzzy cafe in the centre of town doubles as a bookshop. It does tasty fair-trade coffee, has big windows for observing Dumfries life passing by and serves toothsome sweet things, breakfasts and filled rolls.

Globe Inn   PUB

(📞01387-323010; www.globeinndumfries.co.uk; 56 High St; ⊘11am-11pm Tue-Sat) A traditional old nook-and-cranny pub down a narrow wynd off the main pedestrian drag, this was reputedly Burns' favourite watering hole, and scene of one of his numerous seductions. Though Covid had temporarily closed it when we last passed by, locals in the know tell us that new owners have spruced it up and it's looking great, with an interesting menu, Burns memorabilia and some good beers.

❶ Information

Dumfries Tourist Office (📞01387-253862; 64 Whitesands; ⊘9.30am-4.30pm Mon-Sat, 10am-3pm Sun Nov-Mar, 9am-5pm Mon-Sat, 10am-4pm Sun Apr-Oct) By the river. Offers plenty of information on the region including a leaflet on the local Robert Burns trail. You can get a parking disc here to use in the riverside car park opposite.

❶ Getting There & Away

BUS

Buses run via towns along the A75 to Stranraer (£8, 2¼ hours, seven daily Monday to Saturday, three on Sunday), as well as to Castle Douglas and Kirkcudbright. Buses 101 and 102 run to/

DUMFRIES & GALLOWAY BUS PASS
....

Buses are the main mode of local transport, with **Stagecoach** (📞01387-253496; www.stagecoachbus.com) the primary operator. Its Megarider ticket costs £24.50 and gives you unlimited travel on Stagecoach buses within Dumfries and Galloway for a week – not a bad deal.

---

from Edinburgh (£10.40, 2¾ to three hours, four to seven daily), via Moffat and Biggar.

TRAIN

There are trains between Carlisle and Dumfries (£12.10, 40 minutes, every hour or two), and direct trains between Dumfries and Glasgow (£18.10, 1¾ hours, nine daily Monday to Saturday). Services are reduced on Sundays.

Ruthwell Cross

⭐**Ruthwell Cross**   MONUMENT

(HES; www.historicenvironment.scot; B724; ⊘daylight hours) FREE Seven miles east of Caerlaverock Castle, in tiny Ruthwell, a church holds one of Europe's most important early Christian monuments. The 6m-high 7th-century Ruthwell Cross is carved top to bottom in New Testament scenes and is inscribed with a poem called 'The Dream of the Rood'; written in a Saxon runic alphabet, it's considered one of the earliest examples of English-language literature. Bus 79 running between Dumfries and Annan stops in Ruthwell.

Caerlaverock

⭐**Caerlaverock Castle**   CASTLE

(HES; 📞01387-770244; www.historicenviron ment.scot; Glencaple; adult/child £6/3.60; ⊘9.30am-5.30pm Apr-Sep, 10am-4pm Oct-Mar) The ruins of Caerlaverock Castle, by Glencaple on a beautiful stretch of the Solway coast, are among the loveliest in Britain. Surrounded by a moat, lawns and stands of trees, the unusual pink-stoned triangular castle looks impregnable, though it fell several times, most famously when it was attacked in 1300 by Edward I: the siege became the subject of an epic poem, 'The Siege of Caerlaverock'.

The current castle dates from the late 13th century but, once defensive purposes were no longer a design necessity, it was refitted as a luxurious Scottish Renaissance mansion house in 1634. Ironically, the rampaging Covenanter militia sacked it a few years later. With nooks and crannies to explore, passageways and remnants of fireplaces, this castle is great for the whole family.

Caerlaverock Wetland Centre   NATURE RESERVE

(📞01387-770200; www.wwt.org.uk; Eastpark Farm; adult/child £8.27/4.72; ⊘10am-5pm; ♿) This protects 546 hectares of salt marsh and

THE SCOTTISH BARD

I see her in the dewy flowers,
I see her sweet and fair:
I hear her in the tunefu' birds,
I hear her charm the air:
There's not a bonnie flower that springs
By fountain, shaw, or green;
There's not a bonnie bird that sings,
But minds me o' my Jean.
(Robert Burns, 'Of a' the Airts', 1788)

Best remembered for penning the words of 'Auld Lang Syne', Robert Burns (1759–96) is Scotland's most famous poet and a popular hero; his birthday (25 January) is celebrated as Burns Night by Scots around the world.

Burns was born in Alloway to a poor family, who scraped a living gardening and farming. At school he soon showed an aptitude for literature and a fondness for the folk song. He later began writing his own songs and satires. When the problems of his arduous farming life were compounded by the threat of prosecution from the father of Jean Armour, with whom he'd had an affair, he decided to emigrate to Jamaica. He gave up his share of the family farm and published his poems to raise money for the journey.

The poems were so well reviewed in Edinburgh that Burns decided to remain in Scotland and devote himself to writing. He went to Edinburgh in 1787 to publish a 2nd edition, but the financial rewards were not enough to live on and he had to take a job as an excise man in Dumfriesshire. Though he worked well, he wasn't a taxman by nature, and described his job as 'the execrable office of whip-person to the bloodhounds of justice'. He contributed many songs to collections, and a 3rd edition of his poems was published in 1793. A prodigious writer, Burns composed more than 28,000 lines of verse over 22 years. He died (probably of heart disease) in Dumfries in 1796, aged 37, having fathered more than a dozen children to several different women. Generous-spirited Jean bore nine of them and took in another, remarking 'Oor Robbie should hae had twa wives'.

Many of the local landmarks mentioned in the verse tale 'Tam o' Shanter' can still be visited. Farmer Tam, riding home after a hard night's drinking in a pub in Ayr, sees witches dancing in Alloway churchyard. He calls out to the one pretty witch, but is pursued by them, and has to reach the other side of the River Doon to be safe. He just manages to cross the Brig o' Doon, but his mare loses her tail to the witches.

The Burns connection in southern Scotland is milked for all it's worth and tourist offices have a *Burns Heritage Trail* leaflet leading you to every place that can claim some link with the bard. Burns fans should have a look at www.robertburns.org. As well as Ayr and Alloway, there are worthwhile Burns attractionsin and around Dumfries (p162).

mudflats, the habitat for numerous birds, including barnacle geese. There are various activities, including badger watching, dawn goose flights and child-focused events. It also has a good bookshop for nature watchers, and a coffee shop that serves organic food.

New Abbey

The small, picturesque whitewashed village of New Abbey lies 7 miles south of Dumfries

and has several worthwhile things to see and do in and around it. The centre is dominated by the ruins of Sweetheart Abbey, while a working watermill is nearby. Outside town are a popular farm park and mountain biking trails.

Mabie Farm Park FARM
(📞 01387-259666; www.mabiefarmpark.co.uk; Burnside Farm, Mabie; adult/child £8.50/8; ⊙ 10am-5pm Apr-Oct, Sat & Sun Mar; 🚼) If your kids are complaining about historic sights and Robert Burns, pack up the clan and get

down to this spot, between Dumfries and New Abbey off the A710. It's a brilliantly run complex with plenty of animals and activities, including petting-and-feeding sessions, donkey rides, go-karting, slides, a soft play area, picnic spots...the list goes on. Put a full day aside.

New Abbey Corn Mill   NOTABLE BUILDING
(☑ 01387-850260; www.historicenvironment.scot; adult/child £6/3.60; ⊙ 9.30am-5.30pm Apr-Sep, 10am-4pm Sat-Wed Oct-Mar) This 18th-century watermill in the centre of the village is very well preserved. A video sets it in context, and cordial guides will show you the workings. On summer days it is often running.

Sweetheart Abbey   RUINS
(HES; ☑ 01387-850397; www.historicenvironment. scot; adult/child £6/3.60; ⊙ 9.30am-5.30pm Apr-Sep, 10am-4pm Sat-Wed Oct-Mar) The shattered red-sandstone remnants of this 13th-century Cistercian abbey stand in stark contrast to the manicured lawns surrounding them. The abbey, the last of Scotland's major monasteries to be established, was founded by Devorgilla of Galloway in 1273 in honour of her dead husband, John Balliol. On his death, she had his heart embalmed and carried it with her until she died 22 years later. She and the heart were buried by the altar: hence the name.

The couple founded Balliol College, Oxford.

7stanes Mabie   MOUNTAIN BIKING
(www.7stanesmountainbiking.com; A710) FREE Mabie Forest Park is one of southern Scotland's 7stanes mountain-biking hubs, set among forested hills a couple of miles north

of New Abbey. There are nearly 40 miles of trails for all levels; the closest bike hire is in Dumfries. It's very close to the Mabie Farm Park (p165), which is handy if you've got kids of different ages.

Annandale & Eskdale

These valleys, in Dumfries and Galloway's east, form part of two major routes that cut across Scotland's south. Away from the highways, the roads are quiet and there are some interesting places to visit, especially if you're looking to break up a road trip.

Gretna Green & Around
POP 3100

Firmly on the coach-tour circuit for its romantic associations, Gretna Green is on the outskirts of the town of Gretna, just across the river from Cumbria in England. Historically famous as a destination at which eloping couples get married, it's still one of Britain's most popular wedding venues.

Famous Blacksmith's Shop   MUSEUM
(☑ 01461-336001; www.gretnagreen.com; Gretna Green; exhibition adult/under-12 from £3.25/free; ⊙ 9am-5pm Oct-Mar, to 5.30pm Apr & May, to 7pm Jun-Sep) At the centre of the village of Gretna Green, the touristy Famous Blacksmith's Shop complex has a number of mediocre shops and eateries, a maze, and a quite entertaining multilingual exhibition on Gretna Green's history, with tales of intrigues, elopements, scoundrels and angry parents arriving minutes too late. There's a recreation of a blacksmith's forge, a collection of

---

TYING THE KNOT IN GRETNA GREEN

The *Marriage Act* that passed in England in 1754 suddenly required couples that did not have their parents' consent to be 21 years of age before they could marry. But cunning teenage sweethearts soon realised that the law didn't apply in Scotland, where a simple declaration in front of a pair of witnesses would suffice. As the first village in Scotland, Gretna Green's border location made it the most popular venue for eloping couples to get hitched.

Locals competed for the incoming trade, and marriages were performed by just about anyone who could round up a couple of witnesses from the nearest pub. One legendary Gretna vow-taker was the local blacksmith, who became known as the 'Anvil Priest'. In 1856 eloping was made more difficult when a law was passed obliging couples to have spent at least three weeks in Scotland prior to tying the knot, but Gretna Green remained popular. And it still is: some 5000 couples annually take or reaffirm their marriage vows in the village. If you want to get married over the famous anvil in the Old Blacksmith's Shop at Gretna Green, check out www.gretnagreen.com or www. gretnaweddings.co.uk.

handsome carriages and a few marriage rooms: you may well run into a modern-day wedding as you walk through.

Family-owned since 1885 when it was bought by Hugh Mackie, Gretna Green is now a fourth-generation business.

Devil's Porridge Museum MUSEUM
(☑ 01461-700021; www.devilsporridge.org.uk; Annan Rd, Eastriggs; adult/child £6/5; ☺ 10am-5pm Mon-Sat, 10am-4pm Sun) Between Annan and Gretna, make sure to visit this heart-on-sleeve museum on the site of an enormous WW1 cordite factory complex that once covered an astonishing 18 square miles. Beyond colourful anecdotes of the navvies' drinking exploits – the government had to nationalise the local pubs after the infamous 'night of 1000 whiskies' – this is really the fascinating story of the 12,000 women who worked here, driving the war effort with their physical labour and powerfully boosting the argument for suffrage.

Other focuses are on the Quintinshill railway disaster in 1915, while upstairs, displays cover WWII and the decommissioned Chapelcross nuclear reactor.

Castle Douglas & Around

POP 4100

Castle Douglas attracts a lot of day trippers but hasn't been 'spruced up' for tourism. It's an open, attractive, well-cared-for town, with some remarkably beautiful areas close to the centre, such as the small Carlingwark Loch. The town was laid out in the 18th century by Sir William Douglas, who had made a fortune in the Americas.

Northwest of the town, long Loch Ken is a good destination for water sports and, spotting red kites.

◉ Sights & Activities

Loch Ken LAKE
Stretching for 9 miles northwest of Castle Douglas between the A713 and A762, Loch Ken is a popular outdoor recreational area. The range of water sports includes windsurfing, sailing, canoeing, power-boating and kayaking. There are also walking trails and rich bird life. The Royal Society for the Protection of Birds (RSPB) has a **nature reserve** (☑ 01556-670464; www.rspb.org.uk) FREE on the western bank, north of Glenlochar. The eastern shore is great for watching red kites.

Threave Castle CASTLE
(HES; ☑ 07711 223101; www.historicenvironment. scot; adult/child incl ferry £6/3.60; ☺ 10am-5pm Apr-Sep, to 4pm Oct) Two miles west of Castle Douglas, this impressive tower sits on a small river island. Built in the late 14th century, it became a principal stronghold of the Black Douglases, including the excellently named Archibald the Grim. It's now basically a shell, having been badly damaged by the Covenanters in the 1640s, but it's a romantic ruin nonetheless. It's a 15-minute walk from the car park to the ferry landing, where you ring a bell to be taken across.

Also from the car park, where there's a small nature exhibition, a 1.5-mile circular **nature path** gives you the chance to spot deer and ospreys, as well as waterbirds from hides. At dusk it's good for batwatching.

★ **Galloway Activity Centre** WATER SPORTS
(☑ 01556-502011; www.lochken.co.uk; Parton; ☺ 10am-5pm, plus evening session Jun-Aug; ✚) 🏊 On the eastern bank of Loch Ken north of Parton, this excellent set-up runs a very wide range of activities on water and land, and also provides equipment and a variety of sustainable accommodation Activities run in sessions of 1½ hours; one session costs £22.50 each for two, and the price reduces substantially for further sessions. Best to book in advance.

Activities include but are not limited to windsurfing, foiling, sailing, kayaking, paddleboarding, archery and mountain biking. There's also a cafe here.

🛏 Sleeping & Eating

Lochside Caravan & Camping Site CAMPGROUND £
(☑ 01556-504682; www.dumgal.gov.uk/loch sidecs; Lochside Park; tent sites £12, plus car £4; ☺ Apr-Oct; P 🐾) Very central campsite attractively situated beside Carlingwark Loch; there's plenty of grass and fine trees provide shade.

Galloway Activity Centre CABIN £
(☑ 01556-502011; www.lochken.co.uk; Parton; dm £20.50, cabin for 2/6 people £46/90, yurt £105; P 🛜 🐾) 🏊 There's a wide range of intriguing accommodation at this waterside activity centre on Loch Ken. Solar-powered yurts sleep up to six; there's also a bunkhouse with en-suite dorms, cabins by the loch, a well-equipped safari tent, a campground and

very cosy eco-bothies, one with a wood-fired hot tub. It's all run along very sustainable lines.

★ **Douglas House** B&B ££
(☑ 01556-503262; www.douglas-house.com; 63 Queen St; s £43, d £80-87; 🛜🐾) This beautiful 200-year-old stone house has fabulous big bathrooms that complement the light, stylish chambers. The two upstairs doubles are lovely and the downstairs double is huge with a super-king-sized bed – it could sleep four! There are numerous little extras and prices are very fair for this high standard. Breakfast is recommended, with locally sourced produce.

★ **Designs** CAFE £
(☑ 01556-504552; www.designscafeonline.co.uk; 179 King St; lunches £7; ⊙ 10.30am-3.30pm Mon-Sat; 🛜) This excellent cafe under a gallery and shop is the best spot in town for a coffee, with cosy wood fittings offset by a garden space out the back. There's a nice line in ciabatta and bruschetta options complemented by chalkboard lunch specials. The carrot cake also comes warmly recommended.

Mr Pook's Kitchen BRITISH ££
(☑ 01556-504000; www.mrpooks.co.uk; 38 King St; mains £16-21; ⊙ 5-9pm Tue-Fri, noon-9pm Sat, 11am-4pm Sun) This converted bank on the main street is a convivial, colourful spot offering excellent local produce served with plenty of style and flair from its open kitchen. Though at last review it was serving a more limited menu due to virus restrictions, it was still a fun, delicious place to eat.

Nikos Greek Restaurant GREEK ££
(☑ 01556-504345; www.nikosgreekrestaurant. com; 139 King St; meze dishes £3-6; ⊙ 11am-2pm & 5-9pm Mon-Sat; 🛜🖉) On the main street, it's quite a surprise to find authentic Greek food here in provincial Castle Douglas. The charismatic, welcoming host prepares delicious, authentic meze, seafood and other dishes, with cheaper lunchtime specials and a variety of deals. It'll also open Sunday evenings if you book a table.

⊙ Getting There & Away

Buses run roughly hourly from Castle Douglas to Dumfries (from £3.50, 30 to 50 minutes); there are also services to Kirkcudbright (20 minutes), Stranraer, New Galloway and Ayr.

Gatehouse of Fleet
POP 1000

Gatehouse of Fleet is an attractive little town stretched along a sloping main street, in the middle of which sits an unusual castellated clock tower. The town lies on the banks of the Water of Fleet, off the beaten track, and is surrounded by partly wooded hills.

⊙ Sights

Cardoness Castle CASTLE
(HES; ☑ 01557-814427; www.historicenvironment. scot; adult/child £6/3.60; ⊙ 9.30am-5.30pm Apr-Sep) One mile southwest of Gatehouse of Fleet just off the A75, this well-preserved stronghold was the home of the McCulloch clan. It's a classic 15th-century tower house with great views from the top and a bloody history.

Mill on the Fleet VISITOR CENTRE
(☑ 01557-814099; www.millonthefleet.co.uk; High St; ⊙ 10am-5pm late Mar-Oct) FREE In the centre of town, in a converted 18th-century cotton mill, this centre has an exhibition on the history of the local industry and environment. The town was originally planned as millworkers' accommodation. It also has some visitor information, a cafe, a gallery and a likeably chaotic secondhand bookshop.

🛏 Sleeping & Eating

★ **Ship Inn** INN ££
(☑ 01557-814217, 07713 412030; www.theshipingatehouse.com; 1 Fleet St; s £80-89, d £97-119; 🛜🐾) This historic inn is now a boutique B&B with lovely rooms that are simply furnished in attractive contemporary style with plenty of space and excellent bathrooms. They are superbly presented. Upstairs ones are cute with attic ceilings. There's a restaurant serving meals plus a smart bar. The garden opposite rolls down to the river; a primo spot for a pint.

The same enthusiastic young owners run an upmarket self-catering property, Treetops, nearby.

⊙ Getting There & Away

Buses X75 and 500 between Dumfries (£5.20, 50 minutes to one hour) and Stranraer (£6.70, 1¼ hours) stop here nine times daily (three

MUSEUM OF LEAD MINING

Lead mining': even the phrase has a sort of dulling effect on the brain, and you'd think it'd be a tough ask to make the subject interesting. But the **Museum of Lead Mining** (☑ 01659-74387; www.leadminingmuseum.co.uk; Wanlockhead; adult/child £12.50/7.90, mine or cottages only £5.50/4.50; ☺ 11am-4.30pm Apr-Sep; ♿), signposted 10 miles off the motorway northwest of Moffat, manages to pull it off. The place is fascinating, and family friendly, offering a tour of a real mine, recreated miners' cottages, a remarkable 18th-century library, and a display on lead mining and other minerals.

It's apparently Scotland's highest village, set amid a striking landscape of treeless hills and burbling streams. In summer, the museum also runs gold-panning activities. The palpable enthusiasm and personableness of the staff bring the social history of the place alive. It's really rather special, and is one of our favourite museums in Scotland.

Buses running between Ayr and Dumfries stop in Sanquhar, from where there's a bus to Wanlockhead five times daily Monday to Saturday. Wanlockhead is also a stop on the Southern Upland Way (p154) walking route.

on Sunday). They also stop in Castle Douglas and Newton Stewart. Further buses run to Kirkcudbright.

Kirkcudbright

POP 3400

Kirkcudbright (kirk-*coo*-bree), with its dignified streets of 17th- and 18th-century merchants' houses and appealing harbour, is the ideal base from which to explore the south coast. Look for the nook-and-cranny closes and wynds in the elbow of beautifully restored High St. With its architecture and setting, it's easy to see why Kirkcudbright has been an artist colony since the late 19th century.

◉ Sights

Broughton House   GALLERY
(NTS; ☑ 01557-330437; www.nts.org.uk; 12 High St; adult/child £8/7; ☺ 10am-5pm Apr-Oct) Stately 18th-century Broughton House was once home and studio to Glasgow Boy EA Hornel, whose paintings, along with those of several of his contemporaries, grace the interior. Hornel was a great collector of books, and there's an important collection of Robert Burns works. The gallery room is a sumptuous space with wood panelling and a copy of the Parthenon marbles. Behind the house is an exuberant Japanese-inspired garden bristling with life (also opens during winter season; check website for hours).

Kirkcudbright Galleries   GALLERY
(☑ 01557-331276; www.kirkcudbrightgalleries. org.uk; St Mary St; ☺ 10am-5pm Tue-Sat) FREE This smart conversion of the town hall into a gallery gives enjoyable context to Kirkcudbright's artistic heritage. The permanent downstairs exhibition tells the story of the artists and designers who came to visit or reside here over the last century and a half, and displays some of their works. Two other galleries host high-quality temporary exhibitions. There's also a pretty cafe. Disabled facilities are excellent.

Tolbooth Art Centre   GALLERY
(☑ 01557-331556; www.dgculture.co.uk; High St; ☺ 10am-4pm Mon-Sat, 1-4pm Sun mid-Apr–Sep, 11am-4pm Mon-Sat Oct–mid-Apr) FREE As well as catering for today's local artists and holding a cinema, this centre has an exhibition on the history of the town's artistic development. The place is as interesting for the building itself as for the artistic works on display: it's one of the oldest and best-preserved tolbooths (a building that served as both town hall and courthouse in Scottish towns) in the country. There are interpretative signboards to explain its past.

MacLellan's Castle   CASTLE
(HES; ☑ 01557-331856; www.historicenvi ronment.scot; Castle St; adult/child £6/3.60; ☺ 9.30am-1pm & 2-5.30pm Apr-Sep) Near the harbour are the large, atmospheric remains of the castle built in 1577 by Thomas MacLellan, then provost of Kirkcudbright,

as his town residence. Inside, look for the 'lairds' lug', a 16th-century hidey-hole designed for the laird to eavesdrop on his guests.

✯✦ Festivals & Events

Thursdays in high summer are Scottish theme nights, with music, dancing and more in the centre of town.

Art & Crafts Trail   ART
(www.artandcraftstrail.com; ⊙ late Jul or early Aug) Each year the town revels in a four-day community artistic extravaganza with a theme that changes annually. There's something quirky – sculpture, music, handcraft workshops – going on all over the place in numerous venues: people's homes, improvised outdoor spaces, the castle. Infectious fun is guaranteed.

🛏 Sleeping

Silvercraigs Caravan & Camping Site   CAMPGROUND £
(☑ 01557-332050; www.silvercraigscaravanpark. co.uk; Silvercraigs Rd; tent sites £8-12; P 🐾) There are brilliant views from this year-round campsite; you feel like you're sleeping on top of the town. It's great for stargazing on clear nights, and there are good facilities, including a laundry. Both powered and unpowered sites are available. Call ahead in the low season.

★ Selkirk Arms Hotel   HOTEL ££
(☑ 01557-330402; www.selkirkarmshotel.co.uk; High St; s/d £90/120, compact d £99; P @ 🛜 🐾) What a haven of hospitality this is. Rooms look great, with a stylish purply finish and slate-floored bathrooms. Wood furnishings and views over the back garden give some an extra rustic appeal. There's a good restaurant as well as a cute gin and Prosecco bar.

Staff are happy to be there, and you will be, too.

Anchorlee   B&B ££
(☑ 01557-330197; www.anchorlee.co.uk; 95 St Mary St; s/d £70/82; ⊙ Easter-Dec; P 🛜 🐾) This elegant residence on the main road offers great hospitality from cordial hosts. Four lovely rooms offer plenty of space; No 4 is an appealing split-level affair overlooking the garden. Breakfast is excellent.

The Garret   BOUTIQUE HOTEL ££
(☑ 01557-332040; www.thegarrethotel.co.uk; 116 High St; s/d/f £85/95/105; 🛜) With a perfect

location on a lovely central street, this handsome Georgian town house has light, spacious rooms decorated in understated style. There's a pleasant cafe-bar with an amazingly large – positively Tardis-like – beer garden. Breakfast is excellent.

✗ Eating

★ Auld Alliance   SCOTTISH, FRENCH ££
(☑ 01557-330888; www.auldalliancekirkcudbright. co.uk; 29 St Cuthbert St; mains £14-23; ⊙ 5.30-8.30pm Thu-Sat, plus Wed & Sun Jul-Oct; 🕿) Overlooking the heart of town, this restaurant serves cuisine true to its name, which refers to the historic bond between Scotland and France. Local produce is given a Gallic and Mediterranean twist in a cosy, romantic interior.

Selkirk Arms Hotel   BISTRO ££
(☑ 01557-330402; www.selkirkarmshotel.co.uk; High St; mains £12-15; ⊙ noon-2pm & 6-9pm; P 🛜 🐾) Cheery servers and a wide-ranging menu of well-presented dishes give you plenty of options here – you can sit in the more formal restaurant area (dinner only) or the casual bar zone. Local scallops are a highlight, and some fairly elaborate mains can round out the meal, but you can also chow down on upmarket fish and chips. All positive.

ℹ Information

Check out www.kirkcudbright.town for heaps of information on the town.
Kirkcudbright Tourist Office (Harbour Sq; ⊙ 10am-4pm) Volunteer-run office with town information.

ℹ Getting There & Away

Kirkcudbright is 28 miles southwest of Dumfries. Buses run to Dumfries (£4.70 to £6, 1¼ hours) via (or changing in) Castle Douglas (£2.60, 15 minutes). Change at Ringford or Gatehouse of Fleet for Stranraer.

Galloway Forest Park

South and northwest of the small town of New Galloway is 300-sq-mile Galloway Forest Park, with numerous lochs and great whale-backed mountains covered in heather and pine. The highest point is **Merrick** (843m). The park is criss-crossed by off-road bike routes and some superb signposted walking trails, from gentle strolls to long-distance paths, including the Southern Upland Way (p154).

Walkers and cyclists should head for **Glentrool** in the park's west, accessed by the forest road east from Bargrennan off the A714, north of Newton Stewart. Located just over a mile from Bargrennan is the Glentrool Tourist Office (p172). The road then winds and climbs up to Loch Trool, where there are magnificent views.

The park is very family focused; look out for the booklet of annual events in tourist offices. It's also great for **stargazing**; it's been named a Dark Sky Park by the International Dark-Sky Association (www.darksky.org).

Activities

Pick up a copy of the *Galloway Kite Trail* leaflet at visitor centres, which details a circular route through impressive scenery that offers a good chance to spot the majestic reintroduced red kite.

Galloway Red Deer Range   WILDLIFE WATCHING
(☑0300 067 6900; www.forestryandland.gov.scot; A712) **FREE** Observe Britain's largest land-based beast from a hide and viewing area. During rutting season in autumn, it's a bit like watching a bullfight as snorting, charging stags compete for the harem. From April to September there are guided ranger-led visits (adult/child £8/5) to see these impressive beasts.

Nearby, the Wild Goat Range offers the chance to spot the namesake nimble creatures on a hillside.

Red Kite Feeding Station   BIRDWATCHING
(☑01644-450202; www.bellymackhillfarm.co.uk; Bellymack Hill Farm, Laurieston; adult/child £5/free;

⊙noon-4pm) Just off the B795, this farm has daily feedings of red kites at 2pm. There's a visitor centre (with cafe) here, from where you can observe these beautiful raptors, which congregate from about 1pm. There are often RSPB (Royal Society for the Protection of Birds) volunteers present who can inform you about the birds' lifestyles.

Raiders' Road   SCENIC DRIVE
(www.forestryandland.gov.scot; per vehicle £2; ⊙vehicles Apr-Oct; 🖢) About a mile west of Clatteringshaws Tourist Office, Raiders' Rd is a 10-mile drive through the forest with various picnic spots, child-friendly activities and short walks marked along the way. Drive slowly as there's plenty of wildlife about. One of the nicest spots is a cascade where you might spot otters. Walkers and cyclists can access the road year-round.

🛏 Sleeping & Eating

Several of the towns around the park's edges make appealing places to bed down for the night, and they certainly offer better lunching options than the park visitor centres. On the banks of the sparkling River Cree, **Newton Stewart** is popular with hikers and anglers and has good accommodation options such as **Stables Guest House** (☑01671-402157; www.stablesguesthouse.com; Corsbie Rd; s/d £50/80; [P] 🛜) .

St John's Town of Dalry, often just shortened to Dalry, is another charming place, hugging the hillside about 3 miles north of New Galloway on the A713 and on the Water of Ken. Here, the **Clachan Inn** (☑01644-430241; www.theclachaninn.co.uk; 8 Main St; s/d £55/85; [P] 🛜 🐾) is the heart of the village: an atmospheric pub with a fireplace and real

---

MOUNTAIN-BIKING HEAVEN

A brilliant way to experience southern Scotland's forests is by pedal power. The **7stanes** (stones) are seven mountain-biking centres around southern Scotland, featuring trails through some of the finest forest scenery you'll find in the country.

Glentrool (www.7stanesmountainbiking.com; Glentrool Tourist Office) **FREE** is one of these centres; the **Blue Route** here is 5.6 miles in length and is a lovely ride climbing up to Green Torr Ridge overlooking Loch Trool. If you've more serious intentions, the **Big Country Route** is 36 miles of challenging ascents and descents that afford magnificent views of the Galloway Forest. It takes a full day and is not for wimps.

Another of the trailheads is at Kirroughtree Tourist Office (p172), 3 miles southeast of Newton Stewart. This centre offers plenty of singletrack at four different skill levels. You can also **hire bikes here** (☑01671-401303; www.thebreakpad.com; Kirroughtree Tourist Office; bikes per half/full day from £22/30; ⊙10am-5pm). For more information on routes, see www.7stanesmountainbiking.com.

EXPLORING THE SOUTHWEST BY BIKE

It's not just mountain biking that is great in Dumfries and Galloway; there are some beautiful opportunities for road cycling too. The Machars is particularly good: scenic, flat roads with very little traffic. There are three colour-coded marked routes: check www.cycledumgal.wordpress.com for more details.

For in-depth exploration of the southwest on two wheels, **Galloway Cycling Holidays** (www.gallowaycycling.com) offers flexible self-guided tour packages in the region which can include bike hire and pickup, luggage transfer, accommodation booking and more.

ales. It serves an original and delicious bar menu (mains £11 to £17) and has luminous renovated rooms with light-wood furniture and good mattresses.

❶ Information

Clatteringshaws Tourist Office (☑ 0300 067 6800; www.forestryandland.gov.scot; A712; ⊙ 11am-4pm) On Clatteringshaws Loch's shore, 6 miles west of New Galloway, this is basically a cafe but it has the odd display panel. From here you can walk to a replica of a Romano-British homestead (0.5 miles), and to Bruce's Stone (1 mile), where Robert the Bruce is said to have rested after defeating the English at the Battle of Rapploch Moss.

Glentrool Tourist Office (☑ 0300 067 6800; www.forestryandland.gov.scot; ⊙ 10.30am-4pm) Located just over a mile from Bargrennan, this place stocks information on activities, including mountain biking, in the area. This is one of the 7stanes mountain-biking hubs (p171). There is a coffee shop with snacks.

Kirroughtree Tourist Office (☑ 0300 067 6800; www.forestryandland.gov.scot; off A75, Palnure; ⊙ 11am-4pm) This park tourist office, 3 miles east of Newton Stewart, has a cafe and a nature-watching hide, as well as walking trails from 400m to 4 miles. This is one of the 7stanes mountain-biking hubs, and there's a good bike shop (p171) that does hires and repairs.

❶ Getting There & Away

The scenic 19-mile A712 (Queen's Way) between New Galloway and Newton Stewart slices through the southern section of the park. It's the only road through the park, but no buses run

along it. The nearest public-transport point for the western part of this road is Newton Stewart, for the east New Galloway. There's **bike hire** (☑ 01671-401529; www.facebook.com/kirkcowancyclerepairs; Victoria Lane; half/full day £20/30, week £120; ⊙ 10am-4pm Mon-Fri, to 6pm Wed, to 2pm Sat, extended summer hours) available in Newton Stewart.

The Machars

South of Newton Stewart, the Galloway Hills give way to the softly rolling pastures of the triangular peninsula known as the Machars. The south has many early Christian sites and the 25-mile Pilgrims Way walk.

Bus 415 runs every hour or so (only twice on Sundays) between Newton Stewart and the Isle of Whithorn (£3.20, one hour) via Wigtown (15 minutes) and Whithorn. There are some intermediate services also.

Wigtown

POP 900

Little Wigtown, officially Scotland's National Book Town, has more than a dozen bookshops offering an astonishingly wide selection of volumes, giving book enthusiasts the opportunity to get lost here for days. A major **book festival** (www.wigtownbookfestival.com; ⊙ late Sep) is also held here.

Bladnoch Distillery DISTILLERY

(☑ 01988-402605; www.bladnoch.com; Bladnoch; tour £14; ⊙ 10am-5pm Tue-Sat) Browsing books can be thirsty work, so it's fortunate that Bladnoch Distillery is just a couple of miles away from Wigtown, in the village of Bladnoch. Now Australian-owned, it has had a serious facelift and offers friendly tours and a decent cafe.

Hillcrest House B&B ££

(☑ 01988-402018; www.hillcrest-wigtown.co.uk; Station Rd; d £88-95; 🅿 🛜 🐾) A noble stone building in a quiet part of town, this offers a genuine welcome and a lovely interior featuring high ceilings and huge windows. Spend the little extra for one of the superior rooms, which have stupendous views overlooking rolling green hills and the sea. This is all complemented by a ripper breakfast involving fresh local produce. Dinners also often available.

ReadingLasses CAFE £

(☑ 01988-403266; www.facebook.com/readinglasses; 17 South Main St; light meals £7; ⊙ 10am-

4pm Fri, Sat, Mon & Tue, noon-4pm Sun; 🛜📷) 📶
This bookshop is set around a brilliantly welcoming cafe serving decent coffee to prolong your reading time, as well as really delicious baking and other sweet treats. Soups, sandwiches and other light meals add a savoury side.

The Bookshop BOOKS
(📞01988-402499; www.the-bookshop.com; 17 North Main St; ⊙9am-5pm Mon-Sat) This claims to be Scotland's largest secondhand bookshop, and has a great collection of Scottish and regional titles. The owner's *Diary of a Bookseller* tells it like it is.

❶ Getting There & Away

Bus 415 runs every hour or so (thrice on Sundays) between Newton Stewart and Wigtown (£2.20, 15 minutes). Buses continue to Whithorn and Isle of Whithorn.

Whithorn

POP 800
Whithorn has a broad, attractive High St that is virtually closed at both ends (it was designed to enclose a medieval market). There are few facilities in town, but it's worth visiting because of its fascinating history.

In 397, while the Romans were still in Britain, St Ninian established the first Christian mission beyond Hadrian's Wall in Whithorn (pre-dating St Columba on Iona by 166 years). After his death, **Whithorn Priory**, the earliest recorded church in Scotland, was built to house his remains, and Whithorn became the focus of an important medieval pilgrimage.

★**Whithorn Timescape** MUSEUM
(The Whithorn Trust; 📞01988-500508; www.whithorn.com; 45 George St; adult/child £6/3.60; ⊙10.30am-5pm Apr-Oct) Ruined **Whithorn Priory** is part of this excellent complex, which introduces you to the history of the place with a very informative audiovisual and exhibition. A highlight is the brilliant replica Iron Age longhouse (three charismatic tours daily) based on nearby excavations. There's also a museum with some fascinating early Christian stone sculptures, including the **Latinus Stone** (c 450), reputedly Scotland's oldest Christian artefact.

Learn about the influences the carvers of these stones drew on, from around the British Isles and beyond.

Whithorn Way WALKING
(www.whithornway.org) This signposted route covers 149 miles of ancient pilgrimage trail from Glasgow's cathedral to Whithorn via Paisley and the Ayrshire coast.

Isle of Whithorn

POP 300
The Isle of Whithorn, once an island but now linked to the mainland by a causeway, is a curious place with an attractive natural harbour and colourful houses.

St Ninian's Chapel RUINS
(www.historicenvironment.scot; ⊙24hr) FREE
The roofless 13th-century St Ninian's Chapel, probably built for pilgrims who landed nearby on their way to the shrine at Whithorn, sits evocatively on the windswept rocky headland. Modern-day pilgrims are invited to add a stone to the Witness Cairn nearby.

St Ninian's Cave CAVE
(Physgill; ⊙24hr) FREE Around Burrow Head, to the southwest but accessed off the A747 before you enter the Isle of Whithorn, is St Ninian's Cave, where the saint apparently went to pray. You can walk here along the coast from the Isle of Whithorn.

Steam Packet Inn PUB
(📞01988-500334; www.thesteampacketinn.biz.co.uk; Harbour Row; ⊙food noon-2pm & 6.30-9pm; 🛜♿📶) The quayside Steam Packet Inn is a popular and friendly pub with real ales, seafood-focused meals and lodgings which are due to be upgraded.

Stranraer

POP 10,400
The friendly but somewhat ramshackle port of Stranraer has seen its tourist mainstay, the ferry traffic to Northern Ireland, move up the road to Cairnryan. The town's still wondering what to do with itself, but there are good places to stay and lots to explore in the surrounding area.

◉ Sights

Castle Kennedy Gardens GARDENS
(📞01776-702024; www.castlekennedygardens.com; Sheuchan; adult/child £6/2; ⊙10am-5pm Apr-Oct, Sat & Sun Feb & Mar) Three miles east of Stranraer, these magnificent gardens are among Scotland's most renowned. They cover 30 hectares and are set on an isthmus

WORTH A TRIP

CORSEWALL LIGHTHOUSE HOTEL

At the fabulously romantic 200-year-old **Corsewall Lighthouse Hotel** (☑01776-853220; www.lighthousehotel.co.uk; Kirkcolm; d £140-280; [P] [🖵]) it's just you and the cruel sea. On a sunny day, the water shimmers with light, and you can see Ireland, Kintyre, Arran and Ailsa Craig. But when wind and rain beat in, it's just great to be cosily holed up in the bar-restaurant or snuggling under the covers in your room.

It's right at the peninsula's northwest tip, 13 miles northwest of Stranraer, down a potholed road. Rooms in the lighthouse itself are attractive, if necessarily compact; chalets are also available. Five-course dinners are available for an extra £20 per person.

between two lochs and two castles. The landscaping was undertaken in 1730 by the Earl of Stair, who used unoccupied soldiers to do the work. Buses heading east from Stranraer stop at the gate on the main road; it's a pleasant 20-minute stroll from here to the gardens' entrance.

Some open-air cinema screenings are staged here during summer.

Stranraer Museum   MUSEUM

(☑01776-705088; www.dumgal.gov.uk; 55 George St; ⊙10am-5pm Mon-Fri, 10am-1pm & 1.30-4.30pm Sat) **FREE** This museum houses exhibits on local history and you can learn about Stranraer's polar explorers. The highlight is the carved stone pipe from Madagascar. Temporary exhibitions by local artists are also on display.

🛏 Sleeping & Eating

Ivy House   B&B £

(☑01776-704176; www.ivyhouse-ferrylink.co.uk; 3 Ivy Pl; s/d £40/60, s without bathroom £35; 🖵) This is a great guesthouse that does Scottish hospitality proud, with excellent facilities, tidy en-suite rooms and a smashing breakfast. Nothing is too much trouble for the genial host, who always has a smile for her guests. Prices are excellent. The room at the back overlooking the churchyard is particularly light and quiet.

★ **Thornbank House**   B&B ££

(☑01776-706168; www.thornbankhouse.co.uk; Thornbank Rd; r £80-90; [P] [🖵] [🐾] [🐾]) An excep-

tional place offering extremely comfortable and well-furnished modern rooms (one with a Jacuzzi), Thornbank also offers excellent breakfasts and friendly, casual hospitality. It's already well out of the ordinary before you even consider the large indoor swimming pool and absolutely sensational vista over the bay to Ailsa Craig. One room has an outdoor deck to enjoy the view.

Cairnryan B&B   B&B ££

(☑07759 498130; www.cairnryan-bb.co.uk; Cairnryan Rd; s/d £67/80; [P] 🖵) Overlooking the water in the centre of little Cairnryan, this is a modern bungalow with two comfortable en-suite rooms. The double has a lovely outlook over the bay, but it's the genuinely welcoming hosts – old hands at excellent B&B, and providing pick-up/drop-off at the nearby ferry – who make this a special experience. Breakfast features home-laid eggs.

Henrys Bay House   SCOTTISH ££

(☑01776-707388; www.henrysbayhouse.co.uk; Cairnryan Rd; mains £13-20; ⊙5-8pm Wed, noon-2pm & 5-8pm Thu-Sat, noon-8pm Sun) Just east of the centre, this is Stranraer's best place to eat, with hearty portions of well-sourced meat and seafood and a welcoming vibe. There's a pleasingly old-fashioned feel to some of the dishes, while others have a more contemporary style. If the weather's fine, the deck overlooking the bay is a great spot to be.

❶ Getting There & Away

Stranraer is 6 miles south of the ferry port of Cairnryan, which is on the eastern side of Loch Ryan. A bus service coinciding with Stena Line ferries runs between Stranraer and Cairnryan. Buses running frequently between Stranraer and Ayr also stop in Cairnryan. For a taxi (about £9), call **McLean's Taxis** (☑01776-703343; www.mcleanstaxis.com; 21 North Strand St; ⊙24hr).

BOAT

P&O (www.poferries.com) Runs six to eight fast ferries a day from Cairnryan to Larne (Northern Ireland). The crossing takes two hours.

Stena Line (☑03447 70 70 70; www.stenaline.co.uk) Runs five to six daily fast ferries from Cairnryan to Belfast (2¼ hours).

Prices for crossings vary but in the high season are around £35/105 per person/car.

BUS

Scottish Citylink (www.citylink.co.uk) buses run to Glasgow (£19.50, 2½ hours, four daily) and Edinburgh (£22.50, four hours, two daily).

There are also several daily local buses to Kirkcudbright and the towns along the A75, such as Newton Stewart (£4.30, 45 minutes, at least hourly) and Dumfries (£8, 2¼ hours, seven daily Monday to Saturday, three on Sunday).

TRAIN

Scotrail (www.scotrail.co.uk) runs to/from Glasgow (£14.40, 2¾ hours). There are four direct services Monday to Saturday and none on Sunday; more frequent daily connections (also a little quicker) change in Ayr.

The Rhinns of Galloway

The Rhinns (or Rhins) of Galloway is a hammerhead-shaped peninsula west of Stranraer that runs 25 miles from north to south. Its coastal scenery includes rugged cliffs, tiny harbours and sandy beaches. Dairy cattle graze on the greenest grass you've ever seen, and the warm waters of the Gulf Stream give the peninsula the mildest climate in Scotland.

Pretty Portpatrick, set around a harbour, is a big drawcard. Further south, sleepy Port Logan has an excellent sandy beach and a famous botanical garden. From Drummore, a fishing village on the east coast, it's another 5 miles to the spectacular Mull of Galloway, Scotland's most southerly point.

★Mull of Galloway   NATURE RESERVE
(www.mull-of-galloway.co.uk) Scotland's southernmost point is a spectacular spot, with windswept green grass and views of Scotland, England, the Isle of Man and Northern Ireland. The lighthouse here was built by Robert Stevenson, grandfather of the writer, in 1826. The Mull of Galloway RSPB nature reserve, home to thousands of seabirds, is also important for its wildflowers. At the entrance to the reserve is a spectacular clifftop cafe (☑01776-840558; www.galliecraig.co.uk; Mull of Galloway; light meals £4-9; ⊙11am-4pm Sat-Wed Feb & Mar, 10am-5pm daily Apr-Oct, 11am-4pm Sat & Sun Nov). The former homes of the lighthouse keepers are available as accommodation; check out www.lighthouseholidaycottages.co.uk.

Mull of Galloway Lighthouse   LIGHTHOUSE
(www.mull-of-galloway.co.uk; adult/child £3/1, with exhibition £5/1.50; ⊙10am-4pm Sat & Sun Apr-Oct, daily Jul & Aug) You can climb the lighthouse at the Mull of Galloway for views over four different political entities: Northern Ireland, Scotland, England and the Isle of Man. Check the website to coincide your visit with a blast on the newly restored foghorn (outside of seabird nesting season).

Logan Botanic Garden   GARDENS
(☑01776-860231; www.rbge.org.uk; Port Logan; adult/child £7/free; ⊙10am-5pm Mar-Oct, to 4pm early Nov) The mild climate in this southwestern part of Scotland is demonstrated at Logan Botanic Garden, a mile north of Port Logan, where an array of subtropical flora includes tree ferns and cabbage palms. The garden is an outpost of the Royal Botanic Garden in Edinburgh. There's a good cafe here.

Portpatrick

POP 500

Portpatrick is a charming harbour village on the rugged west coast of the Rhinns of Galloway peninsula. It is a good base from which to explore the area, and it's the starting or finishing point for the Southern Upland Way (p154). You can follow part of the Way to Stranraer (9 miles). It's a clifftop walk, with sections of farmland and heather moor.

Mount Stewart Hotel   BOUTIQUE HOTEL **££**
(☑01776-810291; www.themountstewarthotel.co.uk; South Cres; d without/with view £110/130; P⚡) If you thought the views harbourside were good, stroll up the hill to this hotel and they're even better. You can see Northern Ireland on a good day, or Belfast's lights at night. The rooms have been fitted out in modish urban style with lots of blacks and greys. The outlook from the front rooms is sensational. Downstairs is a bar serving adequate food.

There's also a sauna and hot tub available.

★Knockinaam Lodge   HOTEL **£££**
(☑01776-810471; www.knockinaamlodge.com; dinner & B&B s £225, d £380-480; P⚡⚡) For a real dose of luxury, head 3 miles southeast of Portpatrick to this former hunting lodge in a dramatic, secluded location with grassy lawns rolling down to a sandy cove. It's where Churchill plotted the endgame of WWII – you can stay in his suite – and it's a very romantic place to get away from it all.

Excellent French-influenced cuisine (lunch/dinner for nonguests £40/75) is backed up by a great range of wines and single malts, and breakfast features homemade jams.

ⓘ Getting There & Away

Bus 367 runs to Stranraer (£2, 20 minutes, hourly Monday to Saturday, three Sunday).

AT A GLANCE

POPULATION
764,000

NUMBER OF CASTLES
More than 100

BEST HOSTEL
Murray Library
Hostel (p199)

BEST GOLF COURSE
St Andrews Old
Course (p194)

BEST WALKING TRAIL
Loch Leven Heritage
Trail (p206)

WHEN TO GO

May A magical time
to explore before
summer crowds
arrive, and to enjoy
the Perth Festival of
the Arts.

Jul & Aug Seafood
feasts in Fife, and
fresh raspberries in
Blairgowrie.

Oct & Nov Autumn
colours enliven walks
in the Perthshire
woods around Crieff,
Comrie and
Blairgowrie.

Scone Palace (p202)
BINSON CALFORT/SHUTTERSTOCK ©

Central Scotland

The Scottish nation's historic roots are deeply embedded in central Scotland. Key battles around Stirling paved the road to independence; dramatic castles adorn the hilltops; and Perth, the former capital, is where kings were crowned on the Stone of Destiny.

Arriving from Glasgow or Edinburgh, visitors can get a sense of the country further north as the Lowland scenery ramps up towards Highland splendour. It's here that the landscape's majesty begins to unfold among woodlands, waterfalls, craggy hills and rivers, with silhouettes of soaring peaks on the northern horizon.

Whether in the softly wooded country of Perthshire or along the green Fife coastline, opportunities to enjoy the outdoors abound: walking, cycling and angling are all easy possibilities. The region also has some of the country's best pubs and restaurants.

STIRLING REGION

Covering Scotland's wasp-like waist, this region has always been a crucial strategic point connecting the Lowlands to the Highlands. Scotland's two most important independence battles were fought here, within sight of Stirling's hilltop castle. William Wallace's victory over the English at Stirling Bridge in 1297, followed by Robert the Bruce's triumph at Bannockburn in 1314, established Scottish nationhood, and the region remains a focus of much national pride.

Stirling

POP 36,150

With an impregnable position atop a mighty wooded crag (the plug of an extinct volcano), Stirling's beautifully preserved Old Town is a treasure trove of historic buildings and cobbled streets winding up to the ramparts of its impressive castle, which offer views for miles around. Clearly visible is the brooding Wallace Monument, a strange Victorian Gothic creation honouring the legendary freedom fighter of *Braveheart* fame. Nearby is Bannockburn, scene of Robert the Bruce's pivotal triumph over the English in 1314.

The castle makes a fascinating visit, but make sure you also spend time exploring the Old Town and the picturesque Back Walk footpath that encircles it. Below the Old Town, retail-oriented modern Stirling doesn't offer the same appeal; stick to the high ground as much as possible and you'll love the place.

◉ Sights

★ **Stirling Castle**   CASTLE
(HES; www.stirlingcastle.scot; Castle Wynd; adult/child £16/9.60; ⊙ 9.30am-6pm Apr-Sep, to 5pm Oct-Mar, last entry 45min before closing; ℗) Hold

Central Scotland Highlights

❶ **Stirling Castle** (p178) Admiring the views across ancient independence battlefields from this magnificent castle.

❷ **St Andrews** (p189) Pacing through the historic birthplace of golf to play the famous Old Course.

❸ **Scone Palace** (p202) Strutting with the peacocks at this elegant palace, near where Scottish kings were once crowned.

❹ **Falkirk Wheel** (p186) Taking a canal-boat trip through an engineering marvel.

❺ **East Neuk of Fife** (p195) Feasting on local seafood in picturesque fishing villages.

❻ **Culross** (p187) Exploring the set of TV series *Outlander* in this perfectly preserved medieval village.

❼ **Loch Leven Heritage Trail** (p206) Hiking or biking around lovely Loch Leven on a scenic all-abilities trail.

Stirling and you control Scotland. This maxim has ensured that a fortress of some kind has existed here since prehistoric times. You cannot help drawing parallels with Edinburgh Castle, but many find Stirling's fortress more atmospheric – the location, architecture, historical significance and commanding views combine to make it a grand and memorable sight. It's best to visit in the afternoon; many tourists come on day trips, so you may have the castle almost to yourself by about 4pm.

The current castle dates from the late 14th to the 16th century, when it was a residence of the Stuart monarchs. The undisputed highlight of a visit is the fabulous **Royal Palace**, which underwent a major restoration in 2011. The idea was that it should look brand new, just as when it was constructed by French masons under the orders of James V in the mid-16th century with the aim of impressing his new (also French) bride and other crowned heads of Europe.

The suite of six rooms – three for the king, three for the queen – is a sumptuous riot of colour. Particularly notable are the **Stirling Heads** – reproductions of painted oak roundels in the ceiling of the king's audience chamber (originals are in the Stirling Heads Gallery). The **Stirling tapestries** are modern reproductions, painstakingly woven by expert hands over many years, and based on 16th-century originals in New York's Metropolitan Museum. They depict the hunting of a unicorn – an event ripe with Christian metaphor – and are breathtakingly beautiful. An exhibition at the far end of the Nether Bailey (at the castle's northern end) describes their creation, often with a weaver on hand to demonstrate the techniques used.

The **Stirling Heads Gallery**, above the royal chambers, displays some of the original carved oak roundels that decorated the king's audience chamber – a real rogue's gallery of royals, courtiers, and biblical and classical figures. In the vaults beneath the palace is a child-friendly **exhibition** on various aspects of castle life.

The other buildings surrounding the main castle courtyard are the vast **Great Hall**, built by James IV; the **Royal Chapel**, remodelled in the early 17th century by James VI and with the colourful original mural painting intact; and the King's Old Building. The latter is now home to the **Argyll & Sutherland Highlanders Regimental Museum** (www.argylls.co.uk; Stirling Castle; with Stirling Castle entry free; ⊙9.30am-5pm Apr-Sep, 10am-4.15pm Oct-Mar).

Other displays include the **Great Kitchens**, bringing to life the bustle and scale of the enterprise of cooking for the king, and, near the entrance, the **Castle Exhibition**, which gives good background information on the Stuart kings and updates on current archaeological investigations. There are magnificent vistas from the ramparts towards the Highlands and the Ochil Hills.

Admission includes an audio guide, and free guided tours leave regularly from near the entrance.

★**Old Town Jail**   HISTORIC BUILDING
(www.oldtownjail.co.uk; St John St; adult/child £8/6; ⊙10.15am-5.15pm mid-Jul–Oct) This impressive Victorian prison building lay derelict from the 1960s until 2015, when it was reopened as a visitor attraction. Costumed guides lead tours around the former prison cells and up to the top of the observation tower, recounting gruesome tales of prisoners, punishments and executions along with fascinating facts about Stirling's history. Tours depart every 30 minutes.

Cowane's Hospital   HISTORIC BUILDING
(www.cowanes.org.uk; 49 John St) FREE Cowane's Hospital is one of Stirling's best-preserved medieval buildings, built in the mid-17th century as a home for elderly pensioners (it later served as a guild hall, and an isolation hospital during an outbreak of cholera in the 1830s). Following a major restoration it opened to the public in 2021 and houses an exhibition on the building's founder, local merchant John Cowane (1570–1633) – his statue adorns the tower above the main door – an artists' studio and a cafe.

National Wallace Monument   MONUMENT
(☎01786-472140; www.nationalwallacemonument.com; Abbey Craig; adult/child £10.75/6.75; ⊙9.30am-5pm Apr-Jun, Sep & Oct, to 6pm Jul & Aug, 10am-4pm Nov-Feb, 10am-5pm Mar; P⊞) Perched high on a crag above the floodplain of the River Forth, this Victorian monument in the shape of a medieval tower is so Gothic it deserves circling bats and croaking ravens. It commemorates William Wallace, the hero of the bid for Scottish independence depicted in the film *Braveheart*. The view from the top over the flat, green gorgeousness of the Forth Valley, including the site of Wallace's

1297 victory over the English at Stirling Bridge, almost justifies the steep entry fee.

The climb up the narrow staircase inside leads through a series of galleries, including the Hall of Heroes, a marble pantheon of lugubrious Scottish luminaries. Admire Wallace's 66 inches of broadsword and see the man himself recreated in a 3D audiovisual display.

Bus 52 runs from stance B across the road from Stirling train station to the visitor centre (£2.80, 10 minutes, every 30 minutes). From July to September, a hop-on, hop-off tourist bus links the bus station, castle and monument (£4.90 per day).

Battle of Bannockburn
Experience   MUSEUM
(NTS; www.battleofbannockburn.com; Glasgow; battle site free, Experience adult/child £7.50/5.50; ⊙10am-5.30pm Apr-Oct, to 5pm Nov-Mar; P 👶) Robert the Bruce's defeat of the English army on 24 June 1314 at Bannockburn established Scotland as a separate nation. The Battle of Bannockburn Experience uses interactive technology to bring the battle to life. The highlight is a digital projection of the battlefield onto a 3D landscape that shows the movements of infantry and cavalry (entry is by prebooked time slots). Bannockburn is 2 miles south of Stirling; buses run from Stirling bus station (£2.50, 10 minutes, three per hour).

Outside the centre, the 'battlefield' itself is no more than an expanse of neatly trimmed grass, crowned with a circular monument inscribed with a poem by Kathleen Jamie, and a Victorian statue of the victor astride his horse. There has been much debate over exactly where the Battle of Bannockburn took place, but it was definitely somewhere near here on the southern edge of Stirling's urban sprawl. Exploiting the marshy ground around the Bannock Burn, Bruce won a great tactical victory against a much larger and better-equipped force.

Stirling Old Bridge   BRIDGE
(HES; ⊙24hr) FREE Dating from the 15th century, this graceful arched stone bridge is one of the oldest in Scotland, and is now reserved for pedestrians and cyclists only. An earlier wooden bridge, which once lay a short distance upstream, was the site of the Battle of Stirling Bridge (1297), at which William Wallace defeated England's Edward I and laid the ground for Scottish independence.

🛏 Sleeping

Willy Wallace
Backpackers Hostel   HOSTEL £
(📞01786-446773; www.willywallacehostel.com; 77 Murray Pl; dm/tw from £15/44; @ 🛜) This highly convenient, central hostel is friendly, roomy and sociable – there's a piano and guitar in the common room. The colourful, spacious dormitories are clean and light, and it has free tea and coffee, a good kitchen and a laissez-faire atmosphere. Other amenities include bicycle hire and laundry service.

Stirling Youth Hostel   HOSTEL £
(HS; 📞01786-473442; www.hostellingscotland.org. uk; St John St; dm/tw £18/42; P @ 🛜) This hostel has an unbeatable location and great facilities. Though its facade is that of a former church, the interior is modern and efficient. The dorms are compact but comfortable, with lockers and en-suite bathrooms; other highlights include a pool table, bike shed and, at busy times, cheap meals on offer. Lack of atmosphere is a possible downside.

★ Friars Wynd   HOTEL ££
(📞01786-473390; www.friarswynd.co.uk; 17 Friars St; r from £89; 🛜) Set in a lovingly restored 19th-century town house just a short walk from the train station, Friars Wynd offers eight bedrooms of varying size, many with period features such as Victorian cast-iron fire surrounds or exposed patches of original red-brick walls. The 1st-floor rooms are directly above the bar and restaurant, so they can be a little noisy at weekends.

Munro Guesthouse   B&B ££
(📞01786-472685; www.munroguesthouse.co.uk; 14 Princes St; s/d from £65/75; 🛜🎿) Cosy and cheery, Munro Guesthouse is right in the centre of town but located on a quiet side street. Things are done with a smile, and the smallish rooms are most inviting, particularly the cute attic ones. The breakfast is also better than the norm, with fruit salad on hand. There's easy (pay) parking opposite.

★ Victoria Square
Guesthouse   B&B £££
(📞01786-473920; www.victoriasquare.scot; 12 Victoria Sq; s/d from £98/148; P 🛜) Though close to the centre of town, Victoria Sq is a quiet oasis of elegant Victorian buildings surrounding a verdant park. This luxury guesthouse's huge rooms, bay windows and period features make it a winner – there are two four-poster rooms (from £161) for

Stirling

Stirling

◎ Top Sights
1 Old Town Jail	B3
2 Stirling Castle	A2

◎ Sights
3 Argyll & Sutherland Highlanders Regimental Museum	A2
4 Cowane's Hospital	B3

🛏 Sleeping
5 Colessio Hotel	C3
6 Friars Wynd	C3
7 Munro Guesthouse	C3
8 Stirling Youth Hostel	B3
9 Victoria Square Guesthouse	B4
10 Willy Wallace Backpackers Hostel	C3

✖ Eating
11 Breá	C4
12 Darnley Coffee House	C3
13 Hermann's	B3

🍷 Drinking & Nightlife
Brewdog	(see 11)
14 Settle Inn	B2

🛍 Shopping
15 Stirling Bagpipes	B3

romantic getaways, and some bedrooms have views to the castle towering above. No children under 12.

Colessio Hotel   BOUTIQUE HOTEL £££
(📞01786-448880; www.hotelcolessio.com; 33 Spittal St; r from £148; 🛜) This luxury hotel and spa occupies a landmark neoclassical building (a former hospital) in the heart of the Old Town. The tasteful conversion includes sumptuous rooms and suites with a touch of designer decadence, and a sophisticated cocktail bar and restaurant.

Stirling Castle

A FORTRESS TOUR

Stirling's a sizeable fortress, but not so huge that you'll have to decide what to leave out – there's time to see it all. Unless you've got a working knowledge of Scottish monarchs, head to the ❶ **Castle Exhibition** first: it'll help you sort one James from another. That done, take on the sights at leisure. First, stop and look around you from the ❷ **ramparts**; the views high over this flat valley, a key strategic point in Scotland's history, are magnificent.

Track back towards the citadel's heart, stopping for a quick tour through the ❸ **Great Kitchens**; looking at all that fake food might make you seriously hungry, though. Then enter the main courtyard. Around you are the principal castle buildings, including the ❹ **Royal Chapel**. During summer there are events (such as Renaissance dancing) in the ❺ **Great Hall**; get details at the entrance. The ❻ **Argyll & Sutherland Highlanders Regimental Museum** is a treasure trove if you're interested in regimental history, but missable if you're not. Leave the best for last – crowds thin in the afternoon – and enter the sumptuous ❼ **Royal Palace**. Take time to admire the beautiful ❽ **Stirling Tapestries**, skillfully woven by hand on-site between 2001 and 2014.

THE WAY UP & DOWN

If you have time, take the atmospheric Back Walk, a peaceful, shady stroll around the Old Town's fortifications and up to the castle's imposing crag-top position. Afterwards, wander down through the Old Town to admire its facades.

FAST FACTS

➡ Admission is free for Historic Environment Scotland members. If you'll be visiting several Historic Environment Scotland sites a membership will save you plenty.

➡ Vital Statistics: first constructed before 1110; at least nine sieges; last besieger was Bonnie Prince Charlie (unsuccessful); £12 million spent refurbishing the Royal Palace.

MARCO BICCI/SHUTTERSTOCK ©

Argyll & Sutherland Highlanders Regimental Museum
The history of one of Scotland's legendary regiments – now subsumed into the Royal Regiment of Scotland – is on display here, featuring memorabilia, weapons and uniforms.

Prince's Tower

Guard Room Sq (Shop & Tickets)

Forework

❶

Entrance

Robert the Bruce statue

Castle Exhibition
A great overview of the Stuart dynasty here will get your facts straight, and also offers the latest archaeological titbits from the ongoing excavations under the citadel. Analysis of skeletons has revealed surprising amounts of biographical data.

Royal Palace
The impressive highlight of a visit to the castle is this recreation of the royal lodgings originally built by James V. The finely worked ceiling, ornate furniture and sumptuous unicorn tapestries dazzle.

Great Hall & Royal Chapel

Creations of James IV and VI, respectively, these elegant spaces around the central courtyard have been faithfully restored. The vast Great Hall, with its imposing beamed roof, was the largest medieval hall in Scotland.

King's Old Building

⑥ ④

⑦ ⑧

⑤

③

Nether Bailey

Grand Battery

②

Great Kitchens
Dive into this original display that brings home the massive enterprise of organising, preparing and cooking a feast fit for a Renaissance king. Your stomach may rumble at the lifelike haunches of meat, loaves of bread, fowl and fishes.

The Stirling Tapestries
Copies of an exquisite series of 16th-century tapestries hang in the Royal Palace. They were painstakingly reproduced by hand using medieval techniques – each one took four years to make – and depict a unicorn hunt rich with Christian symbolism.

Ramparts
Perched on the wall you can appreciate the utter dominance of the castle's position atop this lofty volcanic crag. From its vantage points, you can see the site of Robert the Bruce's victory at Bannockburn and the monument to William Wallace.

✗ Eating & Drinking

Darnley Coffee House
CAFE £

(☎01786-474468; www.facebook.com/darnley coffeehouse; 18 Bow St; mains £4-6; ⊙10am-4pm; 🛜🎐) Just down the hill from Stirling Castle, this is a good pit stop for home baking, soup, vegan food, tea and coffee (no espresso machine, though) during a walk around the Old Town. The cafe is in the vaulted cellars of a 16th-century house where Darnley, the lover and later husband of Mary, Queen of Scots, once stayed.

★ Hermann's
AUSTRIAN, SCOTTISH ££

(☎01786-450632; www.hermanns.co.uk; 58 Broad St; mains £14-20, 2-/3-course lunch £13/16; ⊙noon-3pm & 6-10pm; 🎐🏠) This elegant Scottish-Austrian restaurant is a reliable and popular choice, with conservative decor oddly offset by magazine-spread skiing photos, but the food doesn't miss a beat and ranges from Scottish favourites such as Cullen skink (smoked haddock soup) or scallops to Austrian schnitzel and spaetzle noodles. Vegetarian options are good, and quality Austrian wines provide an out-of-the-ordinary accompaniment.

Birds & Bees
PUB FOOD ££

(☎01786-473663; www.thebirdsandthebees-stir ling.com; Easter Cornton Rd, Causewayhead; mains £9-12, steaks £16-20; ⊙food served noon-2.30pm & 5-10pm; 🅿🛜🏠🐾) This pub is a bit of a local secret; it's in a converted farm steading hidden away on a back road on the city's northern fringes. There's faux-rustic decor and a crowd-pleasing pub-grub menu that runs from nachos and tempura king prawns to steaks, burgers, chilli con carne and fish and chips. There's outdoor seating and plenty of space for kids to run around.

Breá
SCOTTISH ££

(☎01786-446277; www.brea-stirling.co.uk; 5 Baker St; mains £16-27; ⊙noon-9pm Sun-Thu, to 10pm Fri & Sat; 🛜🎐🏠) 🍴 Bringing a bohemian touch to central Stirling, this busy bistro has pared-back contemporary decor and a short menu showcasing carefully sourced Scottish produce, including beef, venison, seafood, haggis and Brewdog beers, as well as gourmet burgers and a vegan menu.

Brewdog
BAR

(☎01786-440043; www.brewdog.com; 7 Baker St; ⊙noon-midnight Sun-Thu, to 1am Fri & Sat; 🛜) The Stirling outpost of the Brewdog empire has a cool bar, done out in designer-distressed timber, offering no fewer than 15 taps dispensing craft beers from all over the world, including several from its own famously crowdfunded brewery near Fraserburgh in Aberdeenshire.

Settle Inn
PUB

(☎01786-474609; 91 St Mary's Wynd; ⊙11am-11pm Mon-Sat, 12.30-11pm Sun; 🛜) A warm welcome is guaranteed at Stirling's oldest pub (1733), a spot strong on atmosphere, with its log fire, vaulted back room, low-slung ceilings and Friday-night folk-music sessions. Guest ales, atmospheric nooks where you can settle in for the night, and a blend of local characters make it a classic of its kind.

🔒 Shopping

Stirling Bagpipes
MUSIC

(☎01786-448886; www.stirlingbagpipes.com; 8 Broad St; ⊙10am-6pm Mon, Tue & Thu-Sat) Bagpipes are handmade and repaired in this combined shop and workshop, which also houses a collection of antique bagpipes and piping paraphernalia. The place is a focus

CENTRAL SCOTLAND STIRLING

STIRLING'S OLD TOWN

Sloping steeply down from Stirling Castle, the Old Town has a remarkably different feel to modern Stirling, its cobblestone streets packed with 15th- to 17th-century architectural gems and surrounded by Scotland's best-surviving town wall. Its growth began when Stirling became a royal burgh (about 1124), and reached a peak in the 15th and 16th centuries when rich merchants built their houses here.

Stirling's **town wall** was built around 1547 when Henry VIII of England began the 'Rough Wooing' – attacking Scottish towns in order to force Mary, Queen of Scots, to marry his son so the two kingdoms could be united. The wall can be explored on the **Back Walk**, which follows the line of the wall from Dumbarton Rd to the castle. You pass the town cemeteries (check out the **Star Pyramid**, an outsized affirmation of Reformation values dating from 1863), then continue around the back of the castle to Mote Hill and the **Beheading Stone**.

WILLIAM WALLACE – SCOTTISH PATRIOT

William Wallace is one of Scotland's best-known historical figures, a warrior whose exploits set the scene for Scotland's wars of independence. Born in 1270, he was cata-pulted to fame and a place in history as a highly successful guerrilla commander who harassed the English invaders for many years.

In the wake of his victory over the English at Stirling Bridge in 1297, Wallace was knighted by Robert the Bruce and proclaimed Guardian of Scotland. However, it was only a short time before English military superiority and the fickle loyalties of the Scots nobil-ity turned against the defender of Scottish independence.

Disaster struck in July 1298 when Edward I's forces defeated the Scots at the Battle of Falkirk. Wallace went into hiding and travelled throughout Europe to drum up support for the Scottish cause. But many Scottish nobles were prepared to side with Edward, and Wallace was betrayed after his return to Scotland in 1305. He was found guilty of treason at Westminster and hanged, beheaded and disembowelled at Smithfield, London.

for local pipers, and sells books and CDs of bagpipe music.

❶ Information

Stirling Health & Care Village (☑01786-434000; www.nhsforthvalley.com; Livilands Gate, FK8 2AU), with a minor injuries unit, is south of the town centre. The nearest emer-gency department is at Forth Valley Royal Hos-pital in Larbert, 9 miles southeast of Stirling.

Information can be found and accommodation booked at **Stirling Tourist Office** (☑01786-475019; www.yourstirling.com; Old Town Jail, St John St; ◷10am-5pm).

❶ Getting There & Away

BUS

From the **bus station** (Goosecroft Rd), **Citylink** (☑0871 266 3333; www.citylink.co.uk) offers a number of services to/from Stirling, including:

Dundee £15.70, 1¾ hours, hourly

Edinburgh £9.30, 1½ hours, hourly

Glasgow £9.30, 45 minutes, hourly

Perth £9.80, one hour, at least hourly

Some buses continue to Aberdeen, Inverness and Fort William; more frequently a change will be required.

TRAIN

ScotRail (www.scotrail.co.uk) has services to/from a number of destinations, including:

Aberdeen £37, 2¼ hours, hourly weekdays, every two hours Sunday

Dundee £15.90, one hour, hourly weekdays, every two hours Sunday

Edinburgh £9.70, 50 minutes, twice hourly Monday to Saturday, hourly Sunday

Glasgow £10, 40 minutes, twice hourly Mon-day to Saturday, hourly Sunday

Perth £14.60, 35 minutes, hourly weekdays, every two hours Sunday

---

Dunblane

POP 8800

Dunblane, 5 miles northwest of Stirling, is a pretty town with a notable cathedral. It's difficult not to remember the horrific mas-sacre that took place in the primary school in 1996, but happier headlines have come the town's way with the success of Dun-blane-born tennis star Andy Murray – a gold-painted letterbox at the north end of the High St commemorates his 2012 Olym-pic gold medal.

Dunblane Cathedral CHURCH
(HES; www.dunblanecathedral.org.uk; Cathe-dral Sq; ◷9.30am-5.30pm Mon-Sat, 2-5.30pm Sun Apr-Sep, 10am-4pm Mon-Sat, 2-4pm Sun Oct-Mar) FREE Dunblane Cathedral is a su-perbly elegant example of Gothic architec-ture – the lower parts of the bell tower date from the 11th century and the rest mainly from the 13th century, though it was all restored in late-Victorian times. There are fine 15th-century carved-wood misericord stalls in the chancel, and a 9th-century carved Celtic cross stands in the north aisle. A modern standing stone commemorates the children and teacher who died in the massacre.

Leighton Library LIBRARY
(www.leightonlibrary.org.uk; 61 High St; ◷11am-1pm Mon-Sat May-Sep) FREE The musty old Leighton Library, dating from 1684, is the oldest purpose-built library in Scotland. In the company of a guide, visitors get to handle and read books from the original

WORTH A TRIP

FALKIRK WHEEL & THE KELPIES

Scotland's canals were once vital avenues for goods transport, but the coming of the railway left them obsolete. A millennium project restored two of Scotland's major canals, the Union and the Forth & Clyde, which were once linked at Falkirk by an arduous series of 11 locks covering the difference in level of 115ft. The construction of the unique **Falkirk Wheel** (www.thefalkirkwheel.co.uk; Lime Rd, Falkirk; visitor centre free, boat trips adult/child £13.50/7.50; ⏲10am-5.30pm daily Mar-Oct, 11am-4pm Wed-Sun Nov-Feb; P) changed all that. Its arms literally scoop boats up and lift them to the higher waterway.

Completed in 2002, the wheel is a modern engineering marvel, a rotating boat lift that raises vessels the 115ft from the Forth & Clyde Canal to the Union Canal. Boat trips depart from the lower basin (eight daily March to October, three daily in winter) and travel into the wheel. After being lifted, the boats then go through Roughcastle Tunnel before the return descent on the wheel. Anyone with an interest in engineering should not miss this boat ride – it's great for kids, too.

There's also a water play park, a cafe and a visitor centre that explains the workings of the mighty wheel – it only takes the power of about eight toasters for a full rotation!

A pair of stunning equine statues graces the eastern entrance to the Forth & Clyde Canal, the **Kelpies** (☎01324-590600; www.thehelix.co.uk; The Helix, Falkirk; tours adult/child £7.50/free; ⏲visitor centre 9.30am-5pm, tours 11.30am, 1.20pm & 3.30pm; P), named after mythical Scottish water-horses. The two 30m-tall horse heads are fashioned out of stainless steel, and are a tribute to the working horses that once hauled barges along the canal. You can view them for free (indeed, they are clearly visible from the M9 motorway between Edinburgh and Stirling), but the 45-minute guided tour takes you inside the sculptures.

Falkirk is a large town about 10 miles southeast of Stirling. Regular buses and trains link the two, and also connect Falkirk with Glasgow and Edinburgh.

collection of Robert Leighton, the late 17th-century bishop of Dunblane. The oldest volume dates from 1504.

Cromlix House   HISTORIC HOTEL £££
(☎01786-822125; www.cromlix.com; Kinbuck; d/ste from £293/558; P📶) Wimbledon tennis champion Andy Murray (born in nearby Dunblane) has invested some of his winnings in this luxurious country-house hotel, signposted 4 miles north of Dunblane. Guests can enjoy walking and fishing in the extensive grounds; elegant, understated bedrooms; a restaurant overseen by legendary French chef Albert Roux; and – of course – a tennis court laid out in Wimbledon colours.

Riverside   PUB FOOD ££
(☎01786-823318; www.theriversidedunblane.co.uk; Stirling Rd; mains £13-24; ⏲food 10am-2.30pm & 5-9pm Mon-Fri, 10am-9pm Sat & Sun; 📶🅿♿) 🍴 The name describes the location of this pub-cafe-restaurant that champions local produce. It serves everything from free-range eggs Benedict for breakfast to seafood and chorizo risotto for lunch to beef bourguignon

for dinner – or just a glass of local beer on the terrace overlooking the Allan Water.

ⓘ Getting There & Away

There are frequent trains from Stirling to Dunblane (£3.80, 7 minutes, every 30 minutes). Bus services are slower and less convenient.

Doune
POP 1630

Doune is best known for its castle, which has been famously used as a film set. But it's a picturesque village in its own right, with a cluster of craft shops and some lovely walks along the River Teith.

Doune Castle   CASTLE
(HES; www.historicenvironment.scot; adult/child £6/3.60; ⏲9.30am-5.30pm Apr-Sep, 10am-4pm Oct-Mar; P) Magnificent Doune Castle is one of the best-preserved medieval fortresses in Scotland, having remained largely unchanged since it was built for the duke of Albany in the 14th century. It has been used as a set for the movie *Monty Python and the*

Holy Grail (1975) – the audio guide is narrated by Python member Terry Jones – and the TV series *Outlander* and *Game of Thrones*. Highlights include the cathedral-like Great Hall, and a kitchen fireplace big enough to roast a whole ox.

The castle was a favourite royal hunting lodge, but it was also of great strategic importance because it controlled the route between the Lowlands and Highlands. Mary, Queen of Scots, once stayed here, as did Bonnie Prince Charlie. There are great views from the castle walls, and the lofty gatehouse is very impressive, rising nearly 30m.

★ **Buttercup Cafe**   CAFE **£**
(📞 01786-842511; www.facebook.com/butter cupcafedoune; 7 Main St; mains £6-10; ⏱ 9am-4pm Mon-Fri, 9am-5pm Sat, 10am-4pm Sun; 🛜🍴♿) Right in the middle of the village, this cute cafe serves excellent breakfasts (including eggs Benedict, pancakes, fry-ups and vegetarian options; until 11.30am) and a range of lunch specials that includes a tempting vegetarian platter. There are outdoor tables in a courtyard at the back.

❶ Getting There & Away

Doune is 8 miles northwest of Stirling. Bus 59 runs from Stirling to Doune every hour or two (£5.10, 25 minutes) Monday to Saturday, less frequently on Sunday.

FIFE

The Kingdom of Fife (www.visitfife.com) as it calls itself – it was home to Scottish monarchs for 500 years – is a tongue of land protruding between the Firths of Forth and Tay that has managed to maintain an individual Lowland identity quite separate from the rest of the country. Though southern Fife is part of Edinburgh's commuter-belt territory, eastern Fife's rolling green farmland and quaint fishing villages are prime turf for exploration, and the fresh sea air feels like it's doing you a power of good. Fife's biggest attraction, St Andrews, has Scotland's most venerable university and a wealth of historic buildings. It's also, of course, the headquarters of golf and draws professionals and keen amateurs alike to take on the Old Course – the classic links experience.

❶ Getting Around

The main bus operator here is Stagecoach East Scotland (www.stagecoachbus.com). The Fife Dayrider ticket (£9.30) gives one day's unlimited travel around Fife on Stagecoach buses.

If you are driving from the Forth bridges to St Andrews, a slower but much more scenic route than the M90/A91 is along the signposted Fife Coastal Tourist Rte.

Culross

POP 400

Instantly familiar to fans of the TV series *Outlander*, in which it appears as the fictional village of Cranesmuir, Culross (*koo-ross*) is Scotland's best-preserved example of a 17th-century town. Limewashed white and yellow-ochre houses with red-tiled roofs stand amid a maze of cobbled streets, and the winding Back Causeway to the abbey is lined with whimsical cottages. The National Trust for Scotland (NTS) owns no fewer than 20 of the town's buildings.

As the birthplace of St Mungo, Glasgow's patron saint, Culross was an important religious centre from the 6th century. The burgh developed under local laird Sir George Bruce by extracting coal through ingenious tunnels extending under the seabed. When mining was ended by flooding of the tunnels, the town switched to making linen and shoes.

Culross Palace   HISTORIC SITE
(NTS; www.nts.org.uk; Low Causewayside; adult/child £10.50/7.50; ⏱ 11am-5pm Jul & Aug, to 4pm Apr-Jun, Sep & Oct) More large house than palace, the 17th-century residence of local laird Sir George Bruce features an interior largely unchanged since his time. The decorative wood panelling and painted timber ceilings are of national importance, particularly the allegorical scenes in the Painted Chamber, which survive from the early 1600s. Don't miss the recreation of a 17th-century garden at the back, with gorgeous views from the top terrace.

The Town House (with ticket and information desk downstairs) and the Study, both dating from the early 17th century, can be visited on a 45-minute guided tour of the town (£2 per person, available between 1pm and 3pm).

Culross Abbey   RUINS
(HES; www.historicenvironment.scot; Back Causeway; ⏱ dawn-dusk) 🆓 Ruined Culross Ab-

CENTRAL SCOTLAND CULROSS

bey, founded by the Cistercians in 1217, sits atop a hill in a lovely peaceful spot with vistas over the firth. The choir was converted into the parish church in the 16th century; it's worth a peek inside for the stained glass and the Gothic Argyll tomb.

Bessie's Cafe   CAFE £

(📞 07742-537301; www.facebook.com/culross palace; Main St; mains £5-9; ⊙ 9am-5pm Mon-Fri, 9am-6pm Sat & Sun; 🖋) This cute coffee shop in the medieval courtyard next to Culross Palace caters to vegetarian tastes with dishes such as halloumi herb cakes with salad, or avocado on sourdough toast, but also serves versions with organic bacon or smoked salmon.

ⓘ Getting There & Away

Culross is 16 miles east of Stirling, and 12 miles west of the Forth bridges. Buses run from Dunfermline (£3.30, 30 minutes, hourly) to Culross. Buses from Stirling (£8, 1½ hours, three daily) require a change at Alloa.

Dunfermline

POP 49,700

Dunfermline is rich in history. While it's a large and unlovely town, it's home to the evocative Dunfermline Abbey, its neighbouring palace and the attractive grounds of Pittencrieff Park, the last gifted to the city by local boy made good Andrew Carnegie (1835–1919), of US-steel-industry fame.

Dunfermline Abbey & Palace   RUINS

(HES; www.historicenvironment.scot; St Catherine's Wynd; adult/child £6/3.60; ⊙ 9.30am-5.30pm daily Apr-Sep, 10am-4pm Sat-Wed Oct-Mar) Dunfermline Abbey was founded by David I in the 12th century as a Benedictine monastery. The abbey and its neighbouring palace were already favoured by religious royals: Malcolm III married the exiled Saxon princess Margaret here in the 11th century, and both chose to be interred here. More royal burials followed, none more notable than that of Robert the Bruce, whose remains were interred here in 1329.

What remains of the abbey are the ruins of the impressive three-tiered refectory building, and the atmosphere-laden nave of the old church, endowed with geometrically patterned columns and fine Romanesque and Gothic windows. It adjoins the 19th-century **abbey church** (www.dunfermlineabbey.com; St Catherine's Wynd; ⊙ 10am-

4.30pm Mon-Sat, 2-4.30pm Sun Apr-Oct) **FREE** where Robert the Bruce lies entombed beneath the ornate pulpit.

Next to the refectory (and included in your abbey admission) is **Dunfermline Palace**. Once the abbey guesthouse, it was converted for James VI, whose son, the ill-fated Charles I, was born here in 1600. Below stretches the leafy, strollable **Pittencrieff Park**.

Andrew Carnegie
Birthplace Museum   MUSEUM

(📞 01383-724302; www.carnegiebirthplace.com; Moodie St; ⊙ 10am-5pm daily Jul & Aug, 10am-5pm Mon-Sat, 1-4pm Sun Mar-Jun, Sep & Oct, reduced hours Nov) **FREE** The cottage where the great American industrialist and philanthropist Andrew Carnegie was born in 1835 is now a museum. Carnegie emigrated to the US in 1848 and by the late 19th century had become the richest person in the world, but he gave away 90% of his wealth to build libraries, universities and schools all around the world. Dunfermline benefited by his purchase of Pittencrieff Park, beside the palace.

Dunfermline Carnegie
Library & Galleries   MUSEUM

(www.onfife.com/venues/dunfermline-carnegie-library-galleries; 1-7 Abbot St; ⊙ 10am-7pm Mon & Thu, 10am-5pm Tue & Fri, 10am-2pm Wed, 10am-4pm Sat, noon-4pm Sun) **FREE** This award-winning building houses a museum that charts the history of Dunfermline, with a massive Meldrum weaving loom as its centrepiece. There are also galleries that host art exhibitions, and a decent cafe.

ⓘ Getting There & Away

There are frequent buses between Dunfermline and Edinburgh (£6.80, 50 minutes), Stirling (£5.60, 1¼ hours) and St Andrews (£12, 1½ hours), plus trains to/from Edinburgh (£6, 35 minutes, half-hourly).

Aberdour

POP 1630

Aberdour is a popular seaside town with an impressive castle and a lovely family beach, known as the Silver Sands.

Aberdour Castle   CASTLE

(HES; www.historicenvironment.scot; adult/child £6/3.60; ⊙ 9.30am-5.30pm daily Apr-Sep, 10am-4pm Sat-Wed Oct-Mar; 🅿) Long a residence of the Douglases of Morton, this impressive structure exhibits several architectural phases, from tumbled 12th-century masonry with oyster shells poking from the mortar to a 17th-century painted timber ceiling. Most charming of all is the elaborate 16th-century *doocot* (dovecote) at the far end of the gardens. Be sure to pop into the beautiful Romanesque **church of St Fillan's**, next door to the castle.

Aberdour Hotel   PUB FOOD **££**
(☏01383-860325; www.aberdourhotel.co.uk; 38 High St; mains £11-16; ⊙food served noon-9pm; 🛜🍽) This family-run hotel on the main road not only is a good place to stay but also does bar meals with an emphasis on hearty, home-cooked food. There are real ales and good vegetarian choices on the menu.

❶ Getting There & Away

There are hourly trains to Edinburgh (£6.70, 35 minutes) and Dundee (£15.70, 1¼ hours) from Aberdour, as well as buses to nearby Dunfermline (£4.60, 45 minutes, twice hourly).

Falkland

POP 1100

Below the soft ridges of the Lomond Hills in the centre of Fife lies the charming village of Falkland, a cluster of whitewashed cottages with red pantile roofs and crowstep gables. A handful of tearooms and antique shops dot the narrow streets, and rising majestically over the village square is Falkland Palace.

Falkland Palace   PALACE
(NTS; www.nts.org.uk; High St; adult/child £13/9; ⊙11am-5pm Mon-Sat, noon-5pm Sun Mar-Oct) Falkland Palace, a 16th-century country residence of the Stuart monarchs, is prettier and in many ways more impressive and interesting than the Palace of Holyroodhouse (p65) in Edinburgh. Mary, Queen of Scots, is said to have spent the happiest days of her life here in the surrounding woods and parks, and James V, James VI and Charles II all stayed here on various occasions. Don't miss the world's oldest surviving **real tennis court**, dating from 1539.

The palace was built between 1501 and 1541 to replace a castle dating from the 12th century; French and Scottish craftspeople were employed to create a masterpiece of Scottish Gothic architecture. The

FIFE COASTAL PATH

The **Fife Coastal Path** (www.fifecoastandcountrysidetrust.co.uk) runs for 117 miles, following the entire Fife coastline from Kincardine to Newburgh. It's well waymarked, picturesque and not too rigorous, though winds can buffet. It's easily accessed for shorter sections or day walks, and long stretches of it can also be tackled on a mountain bike.

keeper's bedroom houses an extraordinary royal four-poster bed made for James VI in 1618, richly carved with figures of Faith, Hope, Justice and Prudence.

The **Chapel Royal**, an extravaganza of carved wood and painted ceilings, has been restored to its original glory (and still serves as a Roman Catholic place of worship), while the neighbouring hall is hung with prodigious 17th-century Flemish hunting **tapestries**. In the grounds, the real tennis court that was built in 1539 for James V is the oldest still in use anywhere in the world (the one at London's Hampton Court Palace was originally built in 1528 but was renovated for Charles II in the 17th century).

❶ Getting There & Away

Falkland village is 11 miles north of Kirkcaldy. Stagecoach (www.stagecoachbus.com) bus 36 links Perth to Falkland direct (£6.80, one hour, hourly Monday to Saturday, five on Sunday). If travelling from Edinburgh (£14.50, two hours, hourly Monday to Saturday, five on Sunday), change buses at Glenrothes.

St Andrews

POP 16,900

For a small town, St Andrews has made a big name for itself: first as a religious centre and place of pilgrimage, then as Scotland's oldest (and Britain's third-oldest) university town. But it is its status as the home of golf that has propelled it to even greater fame, and today's pilgrims mostly arrive with a set of clubs in hand. Nevertheless, it's a lovely place to visit even if you've no interest in the game, with impressive medieval ruins, stately university buildings, beautiful sandy beaches and excellent guesthouses and restaurants.

OUTLANDER TOURS

The worldwide popularity of *Outlander,* a historical fantasy TV series set in 18th-century Scotland, has seen a huge surge in visitors to the places where it was filmed. Numerous operators will take you on guided location tours that last anything from a day to a week or more. The main locations are listed by VisitScotland (www.visitscotland.com/outlander).

Top Five Outlander Locations

Doune Castle (p186) Stars as Castle Leoch, the main location in season 1.

Culross (p187) Doubles as the village of Cranesmuir.

Glasgow Cathedral (p111) Featured as L'Hôpital des Anges in Paris in season 2.

Hermitage (p324) Dunkeld beauty spot that puts in an appearance in season 5.

Highland Folk Museum (p316) The replicas of turf-roofed Highland cottages were used for several period scenes.

The Old Course, the world's most famous golf links, has a striking seaside location at the western end of town – it's a thrilling experience to stroll the hallowed turf. Nearby is magnificent West Sands beach, made famous by the film *Chariots of Fire*.

History

St Andrews is said to have been founded by St Regulus (also known as St Rule), who arrived from Greece in the 4th century, bringing with him the bones of St Andrew, Scotland's patron saint. The town grew into a major pilgrimage centre and later developed into the ecclesiastical capital of Scotland. The university, the oldest in Scotland, was founded in 1410.

Golf has been played at St Andrews for more than 600 years; the game's governing body, the Royal & Ancient Golf Club, was founded here in 1754 and the imposing Royal & Ancient Clubhouse was built 100 years later.

◉ Sights

St Andrews Cathedral   RUINS
(HES; www.historicenvironment.scot; The Pends; adult/child £6/3.60; ⊙9.30am-5.30pm Apr-Sep, 10am-4pm Oct-Mar) All that's left of one of Britain's most magnificent medieval buildings are ruined fragments of wall and arch, and a single towering gable, but you can still appreciate the scale and majesty of the edifice from these scant remains. There's also a **museum** with a collection of superb 17th- and 18th-century grave slabs, 9th- and 10th-century Celtic crosses, and the late-8th-century **St Andrews Sarcopha-**

gus, Europe's finest example of early medieval stone carving.

Founded in 1160 and consecrated in 1318, the cathedral stood as the focus of this important pilgrimage centre until 1559, when it was pillaged during the Reformation. The bones of St Andrew himself lie beneath the altar; until the cathedral was built, they had been enshrined in the nearby **Church of St Regulus** (or Rule). All that remains of this church is **St Rule's Tower**, worth the claustrophobic climb for the view across St Andrews. The admission fee only applies for the museum and tower; you can wander freely around the atmospheric ruins.

St Andrews Castle   CASTLE
(HES; www.historicenvironment.scot; The Scores; adult/child £9/5.40; ⊙9.30am-5.30pm Apr-Sep, 10am-4pm Oct-Mar) The castle is mainly in ruins, but the site itself is evocative and has dramatic coastline views. It was founded around 1200 as a fortified home for the bishop of St Andrews. After the execution of Protestant reformers in 1545, other reformers retaliated by murdering Cardinal Beaton and taking over the castle. They spent almost a year holed up, during which time they and their attackers dug a complex of **siege tunnels**; you can walk (or stoop) along their damp, mossy lengths.

The visitor centre gives a good audiovisual introduction and has a small collection of Pictish stones.

British Golf Museum   MUSEUM
(www.britishgolfmuseum.co.uk; Bruce Embankment; adult/child £10/free; ⊙9.30am-5pm Mon-Sat, 10am-5pm Sun Apr-Oct, 10am-4pm daily Nov-Mar) This museum provides a comprehensive

overview of the history and development of the game and the role of St Andrews in it. The huge collection ranges from the world's oldest set of clubs (late 17th century, used with feather-stuffed golf balls) to modern equipment, trophies and clothing, and there's a large collection of memorabilia from Open winners both male and female, including Tiger Woods' sweat-stained Nike cap.

🏌️ Activities

Apart from the obvious activity – golf (p193) – the tourist office has a list of local **walks** and also sells OS maps. **Fergus Cook** (✆07921 577137; www.guidedtoursofstandrews.co.uk; per person £10-30) offers guided walking tours of the town.

All the main East Neuk attractions are within reasonable **cycling** distance.

The section of the Fife Coastal Path (p187) between St Andrews and the East Neuk is fun, either on foot (return by bus) or by mountain bike. Parts of the track are tricky and can be covered by the tide, so check tide times before you go. The tourist office has a detailed map.

EatWalk St Andrews   FOOD
(✆07740 869359; www.eatwalkstandrews.co.uk; per person from £67; ⊙1pm daily) Three-hour guided food tours of the town, taking in five places where you stop to sample locally produced food and drink.

🎉 Festivals & Events

Open Championship   SPORTS
(www.theopen.com; ⊙Jul) One of international golf's four major championships. The tournament venue changes from year to year, and comes to St Andrews every five years (the 2020 event was postponed due to Covid-19) – the 150th Open will be held here in 2022. Check the website for future venues.

St Andrews Highland Games   CULTURAL
(www.standrewshighlandgames.co.uk; adult/child £8/4; ⊙Jul) Held on the North Haugh on the last Sunday in July.

🛏️ Sleeping

St Andrews' accommodation is expensive and often heavily booked, especially in summer, at weekends, and during golfing events and university graduations, so reserve well ahead. Almost every house on supercentral Murray Park and Murray Pl is a guesthouse.

Budget accommodation is thin on the ground, but during summer (June to August) three student residences are open to visitors – **Agnes Blackadder Hall** (✆01334-467000; North Haugh; s/d from £59/79; ⊙Jun-Aug; 🅿️@🛜) 🍴, **David Russell Hall** (✆01334-467100; Buchanan Gardens; s/d from £59/79; ⊙Jun-Aug; 🅿️@🛜) 🍴 and **McIntosh Hall** (✆01334-467035; Abbotsford Cres; s/tw from £52/72; ⊙Jun-Aug; 🅿️@🛜) 🍴. Prices are good value for the standard of accommodation on offer.

Cameron House   B&B ££
(✆01334-472306; www.cameronhouse-sta.co.uk; 11 Murray Park; s/d from £65/105; 🛜) Beautifully decorated rooms and warm, cheerful hosts make this a real home away from home. The two single rooms share a bathroom. Prices drop £10 per person outside peak season.

St Nicholas Farmhouse   B&B ££
(✆01334-473090; www.stnicholasfarmhouse.com; Albany Park, KY16 8LD; s/d from £75/85; 🛜) Tucked away amid leafy modern suburbs just a few paces from the south end of East Sands beach (look out for the inconspicuous gate on Albany Park opposite the brown tourist signpost), this 19th-century farmhouse offers a warm welcome, appealing bedrooms and hearty breakfasts (fun fact for golf fans – Tom Watson once rented the entire house during the Open Championship).

★ **34 Argyle St**   B&B £££
(✆07712 863139; www.34argylestreet.com; 34 Argyle St; r from £150; 🛜) Set in a fine old stone-built house just west of the town centre, the Argyle has four luxurious, hotel-quality bedrooms with huge modern bathrooms of dark tile, chrome and glass (two of the four have free-standing bath tubs). Little touches like drinks offered on arrival, fresh flowers and sweets add to the atmosphere of hospitality.

★ **Old Fishergate House**   B&B £££
(✆01334-470874; www.oldfishergatehouse.co.uk; North Castle St; r from £135; 🛜) This historic 17th-century town house, furnished with period pieces, is in the oldest part of town, close to the cathedral. The two twin rooms are very spacious and even have their own sitting room. On a scale of one to 10 for quaintness, we'd rate it a 9½. The cracking breakfast menu features pancakes with maple syrup, and smoked-haddock omelette.

Old Course Hotel   HOTEL £££
(✆01334-474371; www.oldcoursehotel.co.uk; Old Station Rd; r from £327; 🅿️🛜🏊) A byword for

St Andrews

200 m
0.1 miles

West Sands (200m)

West Sands Rd

North Sea

St Andrews Bay

Museum

The Pends

Crail (10mi);
Anstruther (10mi)

Abbey St

South St

West Burn La

Queen's Gdns

Church Sq

Holy Trinity Church

Church St

College St

Butts Wynd

South Castle St

North Castle St

The Scores

North St

Murray Park

Murray Pl

Greyfriars Gdn

St Mary's Pl

Market St

Bell St

Alexandra Pl

Argyle St

Doubledykes Rd

Station Rd

Bus Station

City Rd

Golf Pl

Hope St

The Links

Old Course

Old Pavilion

Old Course Hotel (350m);
Leuchars Train Station (5mi);
Dundee (13mi)

David Russell Hall (700m)

Kinburn Park

St Andrews

golfing luxury, this hotel is right alongside the famous 17th green (Road Hole) on the Old Course and has huge rooms, excellent service and a raft of facilities, including a spa complex. Fork out the extra £50 or so for a view over the Old Course. You can usually find good deals online.

Five Pilmour Place   B&B £££
(☑ 01334-478665; www.5pilmourplace.com; 5 Pilmour Pl; s/d from £100/140; 🛜) Just around the corner from the Old Course, this luxurious and intimate spot offers stylish, compact rooms with plenty of designer touches. The king-size beds are especially comfortable, and the lounge area is an Edwardian-style retreat of leather armchairs, polished wood and swagged curtains.

✖ Eating

Tailend   FISH & CHIPS £
(www.thetailend.co.uk; 130 Market St; takeaway £5-10; ⊘ noon-9.30pm) 🍴 Delicious fresh fish sourced from Arbroath, just up the coast, puts this place a class above most chippies; it cooks fries to order and the food's worth the wait. The array of exquisite smoked delicacies at the counter will have you planning a picnic or fighting for a table in the licensed cafe out the back.

Northpoint Cafe   CAFE £
(☑ 01334-473997; www.facebook.com/north pointcafe; 24 North St; mains £4-9; ⊘ 8.30am-5pm Mon-Fri, 9am-5pm Sat, 10am-4pm Sun; 🛜📷) The cafe where Prince William famously met his future wife, Kate Middleton, while they were both students at St

Andrews serves good coffee and a broad range of breakfast fare, from porridge topped with banana to toasted bagels, pancake stacks and classic fry-ups. It's a bit too busy for its own good these days, so get in early for lunch, which includes vegan specials.

★ Balgove Larder & Steak Barn   CAFE, BARBECUE ££
(☑ 01334-898145; www.balgove.com; Strathtyrum; mains cafe £6-9, barn £10-21; ⊘ cafe 9am-4.30pm; 🅿🛜🍴) A bright and spacious agricultural shed in a rural setting a mile west of St Andrews houses this farm shop and cafe, which serves good coffee, hearty breakfasts, and lunch dishes based around local produce. The neighbouring barn has been equipped with huge charcoal barbecues that turn out meltingly tender steaks and juicy burgers.

No bookings; first come, first served.

Adamson   BRASSERIE ££
(☑ 01334-479191; www.theadamson.com; 127 South St; mains £14-28; ⊘ noon-3pm & 5pm-midnight Mon-Fri, 11am-midnight Sat & Sun; 🛜🍴) Housed in the former post-office building, this loud and bustling brasserie panders to a youngish clientele of well-heeled students, local families and tourists with a crowd-pleasing menu of steaks and seafood. Service can be overeager or occasionally chaotic, but it all adds to the hectic buzz.

Mitchell's Deli   DELI, SCOTTISH ££
(☑ 01334-441396; www.mitchellsstandrews.co.uk; 110-112 Market St; mains £12-16; ⊘ 8am-10pm

DON'T MISS

PLAYING THE OLD COURSE

Pitch up at **St Andrews Old Course** (reception 01334-466666, reservations 01334-466718; www.standrews.com; Golf Pl; green fees £95-195; Mon-Sat), the oldest and most famous golf course in the world. Golf has been played here since the 15th century – by 1457 it was apparently so popular that James II had to ban it because it was interfering with his troops' archery practice. Although it lies beside the Royal & Ancient Golf Club, the Old Course is a public course.

To play the Old Course, you'll need to book in advance via the website, or by phoning the Reservations Department (or reception, if just one day in advance or on the day). Reservations open on the last Wednesday in August the year before you wish to play. Unless you've booked months in advance, getting a tee-off time is literally a lottery; enter the ballot at the **caddie office** (01334-466666; West Sands Rd) (or online, or by phoning reception) before 2pm two days before you hope to play (there's no Sunday play). Be warned that applications by ballot are normally heavily oversubscribed, and green fees are £195 from April to October.

A caddie for your round costs £55 plus tip. If you play on a windy day, expect those scores to balloon: Nick Faldo famously stated, 'When it blows here, even the seagulls walk'.

There are **guided walks** (www.standrews.com/walk; per person £12.50; 11am & 2pm daily Apr-Sep) of the Old Course, and you are free to walk over the course on Sunday or follow the footpaths around the edge at any time.

Sun-Thu, to 11pm Fri & Sat;) Railway-sleeper floors, cut-down-workbench tables and seats upholstered with recycled tweed jackets lend a utilitarian air to this excellent deli-cafe-restaurant where local produce is king. Brunch (served till 5pm) includes free-range eggs Benedict, and avocado on sourdough toast, while the evening menu runs to fish and chips, mac and cheese, and vegan haggis.

★**Haar** SCOTTISH £££
(01334-845750; www.haarrestaurant.com; 127 North St; 5-course tasting menu £60; 4-10pm Wed, noon-10pm Thu-Sun) Chef Dean Banks grew up in Arbroath, on the far side of the Tay estuary from St Andrews, and opened this atmospheric little restaurant after reaching the finals of *Masterchef* in 2018. Fresh local produce, with an emphasis on seafood, is treated to subtle Asian flavours – Dean's signature dish of lobster served with mirin butter is not to be missed.

Seafood Ristorante SEAFOOD £££
(01334-479475; www.theseafoodrestaurant. com; The Scores; mains £25-32; noon-9.30pm Wed-Sun) This stylish restaurant occupies a glass-walled room, built out over the sea, with polished wooden floors, crisp white linen, an open kitchen and panoramic views of St Andrews Bay. It offers top-notch seafood and an excellent wine list;

an all-day menu offers smaller dishes between lunch and dinner service. There's a two-/three-course set lunch menu (£25/30) available from noon till 2.30pm.

Vine Leaf SCOTTISH £££
(01334-477497; www.vineleafstandrews.co.uk; 131 South St; 2-/3-course dinner £28/33; 6-11pm Tue-Sat;) Classy, comfortable and well established, the friendly Vine Leaf offers a changing menu of sumptuous Scottish seafood, game and vegetarian dishes. There's a wide selection within the set-price menu, all well presented, and an interesting, mostly old-world wine list. Reservations recommended.

Drinking & Entertainment

St Andrews Brewing Co MICROBREWERY
(www.standrewsbrewingcompany.com; 177 South St; 11am-midnight;) Good beer, good food and good company are the order of the day in this friendly, modern brewpub, with 18 beers and ciders on tap (including several of its own brews), more than 170 varieties in bottles, and around 30 craft gins.

Eden Mill Distillery DISTILLERY
(01334-834038; www.edenmill.com; Main St, Guardbridge; tours per person £10; 10am-6pm) This brewery-distillery produces beer and whisky but is best known for its range of

craft gins made using locally grown botanicals. One-hour tours of the gin distillery depart from 11am to 4pm, beginning with a G&T and ending with a tasting session (there are whisky and beer tours, too). Eden Mill is 4 miles northwest of St Andrews, towards Leuchars.

Vic
BAR

(www.vicstandrews.co.uk; 1 St Mary's Pl; ☺ 10am-2am; ☎) Warehouse chic meets medieval conviviality in this strikingly restored student favourite. Walls plastered with black-and-white pop culture give way to a handsome, high-ceilinged bar with sociable long tables down the middle and an eclectic assortment of seating. Other spaces include a more romantic bar, a dance floor and a deck for smokers. There are regular events, including weekend club nights.

Byre Theatre
THEATRE

(☎ 01334-475000; www.byretheatre.com; Abbey St; ☎) This theatre company started life in a converted cow byre in the 1930s, but it now occupies flashy modern premises that make clever use of light and space.

🛍 Shopping

Topping & Co
BOOKS

(☎ 01334-585111; www.toppingbooks.co.uk; 7 Greyfriars Garden, KY16 9HG; ☺ 9am-8.30pm) As befits a university town, this is a classic old-school bookshop crammed floor to ceiling with a huge range of titles, with free tea and coffee, armchairs and sofas tucked into hidden corners, and a packed calendar of readings, signings and other literary events.

IJ Mellis
CHEESE

(☎ 01334-471410; www.mellischeese.net; 149 South St; ☺ 9am-6pm Mon-Sat, noon-5pm Sun) IJ Mellis has a wealth of mouth-watering Scottish, British, Irish and continental cheeses you can smell from halfway down the street.

ℹ Information

The helpful staff at St Andrews Tourist Office (☎ 01334-472021; www.visitscotland.com; 70 Market St; ☺ 9.15am-6pm Mon-Sat, 10am-5pm Sun Jul & Aug, reduced hours rest of year) have good knowledge of the city and Fife.

ℹ Getting There & Away

BUS

All buses leave from the **bus station** (Station Rd). Services include the following:

Anstruther £4.60, 40 minutes, hourly

Crail £4.60, 25 minutes, hourly

Dundee £5.20, 40 minutes, at least half-hourly

Edinburgh £13, two hours, hourly

Glasgow £13, 2½ hours, hourly

TRAIN

There is no train station in St Andrews itself, but you can take a train from Edinburgh (grab a seat on the right-hand side of the carriage for great sea views) to Leuchars (£15.60, one hour, half-hourly), 5 miles to the northwest. From here, buses leave regularly for St Andrews (£3.30, 10 minutes, every 10 minutes), or a taxi costs around £13.

ℹ Getting Around

To order a cab, call **Golf City Taxis** (☎ 0800 652 3552; www.golfcitytaxis.co.uk).

Spokes (☎ 01334-477835; www.spokescycles.com; 37 South St, KY16 9QR; per day/week £20/95; ☺ 8.45am-5.30pm Mon-Sat) hires out mountain bikes.

East Neuk

This charming stretch of coast runs south from St Andrews to the headland at Fife Ness, then as far west as Earlsferry. Neuk is an old Scots word for 'corner', and it's certainly an appealing corner of the country to investigate, with picturesque fishing villages whose distinctive red pantiled roofs and crowstep gables are a legacy of centuries-old trading links with the Low Countries.

The most scenic stretches are in this area. It's easily visited from St Andrews, or even as a day trip from Edinburgh, but also offers many pleasant places to stay.

ℹ Getting There & Away

The East Neuk is best explored with your own car, though finding a place to park in the villages on summer weekends can be difficult.

Stagecoach (www.stagecoachbus.com) bus 95 runs hourly from St Andrews to Leven along the coast via Crail, stopping at all the East Neuk villages on the way.

Crail
POP 1640

Pretty and peaceful, little Crail has a much-photographed stone-built harbour surrounded by quaint cottages with red-tiled roofs. The village's history is outlined in the Crail Museum, but the main attraction

Scottish Castles

Scotland is home to more than 1000 castles, ranging from bare-bones 12th-century ruins to magnificent Victorian mansions. They all began with one purpose: to serve as fortified homes for the landowning aristocracy. But as society became more settled and peaceful, defensive features gave way to ostentatious displays of wealth and status.

Curtain-Walled Castles

Norman castles of the 12th century were mainly of the 'motte-and-bailey' type, consisting of earthwork mounds and timber palisades. The first wave of stone-built castles emerged in the 13th century, characterised by massive curtain walls up to 3m thick and 30m tall to withstand sieges. Good examples are Dunstaffnage Castle and Caerlaverock Castle.

Tower Houses

The appearance of the tower house in the 14th century marked the beginning of the development of the castle as a residence. Clan feuds, cattle raiders and wars between Scotland and England meant that local lords built fortified stone towers in which to live, from diminutive Smailholm Tower in the Borders to impressive Doune Castle near Stirling.

1. Balmoral Castle (p318) 2. Caerlaverock Castle (p165)
3. Smailholm Tower (p151)

Artillery Castles

The arrival of gunpowder and cannon in the 15th century transformed castle design, with features such as gun loops, round towers, bulwarks and bastions making an appearance. Forbidding Hermitage Castle is a prime example of a castle adapted for artillery defence.

Status Symbols

The Scottish Baronial style of castle architecture, characterised by a profusion of pointy turrets, crenellations and stepped gables, had its origins in 16th- and 17th-century castles such as Craigievar and Castle Fraser, and reached its zenith in the royal residences of Glamis and Balmoral.

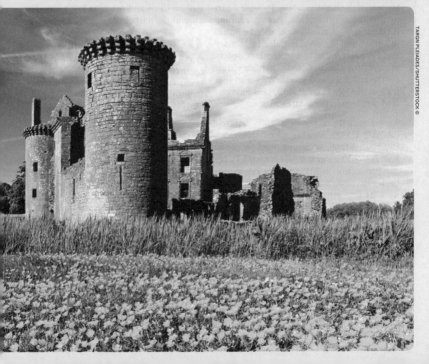

WORTH A TRIP

PEAT INN

The superb Michelin-starred **Peat Inn** (☑ 01334-840206; www.the peatinn.co.uk; KY15 5LH; 3-course lunch/dinner £29/65; ⊗12.30-2pm & 6.30-9pm Tue-Sat; P), backed by a commodious suite of bedrooms (singles/doubles from £220/240; pW), makes an ideal gourmet break. The chef makes a great effort to source premium-quality Scottish produce and presents it in innovative ways that never feel pretentious or overmodern. The inn is 6 miles from St Andrews; head southwest on the A915, then turn right onto the B940.

The split-level bedrooms look over the garden and fields beyond. Various all-inclusive offers are available.

is just wandering the winding streets and hanging out by the harbour. There are views across to the Isle of May.

Cambo Gardens GARDENS
(www.cambogardens.org.uk; Cambo Estate; adult/child £6.50/free; ⊗10am-5pm; P ⃟) Cambo Estate, 2.5 miles north of Crail, is the country seat of the Erskine family. Its walled garden, with an ornamental stream running through the middle, is famously beautiful in spring and summer, but also in January and February, when its spectacular displays of snowdrops are in flower. There's a visitor centre and cafe, and woodland walks that lead to the Fife Coastal Path, plus kids can feed potatoes to the estate's pigs.

Kingsbarns Distillery DISTILLERY
(☑ 01333-451300; www.kingsbarnsdistillery.com; East Newhall Farm, Kingsbarns; tours per person from £12; ⊗10am-5pm; P) This distillery began production in 2015 and uses Fife-grown barley to create a distinctive Lowland whisky – its first single malt, called Dream to Dram, won a slew of awards in 2020. Meanwhile, one-hour tours explain the process and offer tasting sessions, while the on-site cafe serves excellent tea and scones.

Crail Museum MUSEUM
(www.crailmuseum.org.uk; 62 Marketgate, KY10 3TL; ⊗11am-4pm Mon-Sat, 1.30-4pm Sun Jun-Oct, Sat & Sun only Apr & May) FREE Covers the village's history and involvement with the fishing industry, and provides tourist information.

Colstoncraig B&B ££
(☑ 01333-451013; www.colstoncraigbedandbreakfast.com; West End; s/d from £50/75; P) Nothing is too much trouble for the welcoming hosts at this semidetached B&B with a traditional red pantile roof and a view over the houses across the road to the Firth of Forth and the Isle of May. Ask for the ground-floor twin room with a glimpse of the sea from the bay window.

Crail Harbour Gallery & Tearoom CAFE £
(www.crailharbourgallery.co.uk; Shoregate; mains £6-12; ⊗10.15am-4.30pm) Set in an original 17th-century pantiled cottage, with a low ceiling and quirkily uneven stone floor, this cosy cafe goes beyond the usual coffee and cake by serving locally caught dressed crab, and hot-smoked salmon salad.

★**Lobster Store** SEAFOOD ££
(☑ 01333-450476; www.facebook.com/reillyshellfish; 34 Shoregate; mains £6-15; ⊗noon-4pm Sat & Sun Easter-Jun, noon-4pm Tue-Sun Jul-Sep) This quaint little shack overlooking Crail harbour serves dressed crab and freshly boiled lobster that has been caught locally. You can have a whole lobster (split) or lobster rolls. This is no-fuss takeaway – there's a single table out the front, but you can find a place to sit and eat your catch anywhere around the harbour.

❶ Getting There & Away

Crail is 10 miles southeast of St Andrews. Stagecoach (www.stagecoachbus.com) bus 95 linking Leven, Anstruther, Crail and St Andrews passes through Crail hourly every day (£4.60, 35 minutes to St Andrews).

Anstruther

POP 3450

Once among Scotland's busiest fishing ports, cheery Anstruther (pronounced *enster* by locals) has ridden the tribulations of the declining fishing industry better than some, and now offers a pleasant mixture of bobbing boats, historic streets, and visitors ambling around the harbour grazing on fish and chips or contemplating a boat trip to the Isle of May.

⊙ Sights & Activities

Scottish Fisheries Museum MUSEUM
(www.scotfishmuseum.org; East Shore; adult/child £9/free; ⊗10am-5.30pm Mon-Sat, 11am-5pm Sun Apr-Sep, 10am-4.30pm Mon-Sat,

noon-4.30pm Sun Oct-Mar; 🅐) This excellent museum covers the history of the Scottish fishing industry in fascinating detail, including plenty of hands-on exhibits for kids. Displays include the Zulu Gallery, which houses the huge, partly restored hull of a traditional 19th-century Zulu-class fishing boat, redolent with the scents of tar and timber. Afloat in the harbour outside the museum is the Reaper, a fully restored Fifie-class fishing boat built in 1902.

Isle of May
NATURE RESERVE

(www.nature.scot) The mile-long Isle of May, 6 miles southeast of Anstruther, is a spectacular nature reserve. Between April and July the island's cliffs are packed with breeding kittiwakes, razorbills, guillemots, shags and more than 80,000 puffins. Inland are the remains of the 12th-century St Adrian's Chapel, dedicated to a monk who was murdered on the island by the Danes in 875. Several boats operating out of Anstruther harbour offer trips to the island.

May Princess
BOATING

(☑ 07957 585200; www.isleofmayferry.com; Middle Pier; adult/child £28/14; ⊗ Apr-Sep) A five-hour boat trip to the Isle of May, including two to three hours ashore, sails three to seven times weekly from April to September (daily from July to September). You can make reservations and buy tickets at the harbour kiosk at least an hour before departure. Departure times vary depending on the tide – call, or check the website.

Osprey
BOATING

(☑ 07473 631671; www.isleofmayboattrips.co.uk; Middle Pier; adult/child non-landing trip £26/19, with time ashore £34/26; ⊗ Apr-Sep) The 12-seater high-speed rigid-hull inflatable *Osprey* offers one-hour non-landing circuits of the Isle of May as well as 4½-hour trips with time ashore.

🛏 Sleeping & Eating

★ Murray Library Hostel
HOSTEL £

(☑ 01333-311123; www.murraylibraryhostel.com; 7 Shore St; dm/d from £22/58; 🛜) Set in a handsome, red-sandstone waterfront building that once housed the local library, this hostel is beautifully furnished and equipped. There are four- to eight-bed dorms, many with sea views, plus private twins and doubles, a gorgeous modern kitchen and a comfortable lounge.

★ Spindrift
B&B ££

(☑ 01333-310573; www.thespindrift.co.uk; Pittenweem Rd; s/d/f £80/135/150; 🅿🛜🐾) Arriving from the west, there's no need to go further than Anstruther's first house on the left, a redoubt of Scottish cheer and warm hospitality. The rooms are elegant and extremely comfortable – some have views across to Edinburgh, and one is a wood-panelled recreation of a ship's cabin, courtesy of the sea captain who once owned the house.

There are DVD players and teddies for company, an honesty bar with local ales and malts, and fine company from your hosts. Breakfast includes porridge once voted the best in the kingdom.

Anstruther Fish Bar
FISH & CHIPS £

(☑ 01333-310518; www.anstrutherfishbar.co.uk; 42-44 Shore St; takeaway £6-10; ⊗ 11.30am-9.30pm Sun-Thu, to 10pm Fri & Sat; 🅐) An award-winning chippie famous for its deep-fried haddock and chips, this place also offers classy takes on traditional takeaway dishes, including dressed crab and battered prawns (both locally caught).

★ Cellar Restaurant
SCOTTISH £££

(☑ 01333-310378; www.thecellaranstruther.co.uk; 24 East Green; 5-course lunch/7-course dinner £45/75; ⊗ 6.30-9pm Wed, 12.30-1.45pm & 6.30-9pm Thu-Sun, no lunch Thu Oct-Mar) 🖉 Tucked away in an alley behind the Scottish Fisheries Museum, the elegant and upmarket Cellar has been famous for its superb food and fine wines since 1982. The recipient of a Michelin star in 2015, it is at the top of its game, offering a creative menu built around Scottish seafood, lamb, pork and beef. Advance booking essential.

❶ Getting There & Away

Stagecoach (www.stagecoachbus.com) bus X60 runs hourly from Edinburgh to Anstruther (£11.50, 2½ hours) and on to St Andrews (£4.60, 25 minutes). Bus 95 links Anstruther to all the other East Neuk villages, including Crail (£2.50, 15 minutes, hourly).

Around Anstruther

Scotland's Secret Bunker
MUSEUM

(www.secretbunker.co.uk; Troywood; adult/child £12.95/8.95; ⊗ 10am-5pm Feb-Nov; 🅿) This fascinating – and chilling – monument to Cold War paranoia was built in the 1950s to serve as one of Britain's regional command centres in the event of a nuclear war.

Driving Tour
The Fife Coast

START STIRLING
END ST ANDREWS
LENGTH 76 MILES; ONE DAY

This tour links two of the most popular tourist towns in central Scotland via the scenic delights of the Fife coast.

Head south from ① **Stirling** (p178) on the M9 and at Junction 7 turn east towards Kincardine Bridge. As you approach the bridge, follow signs for Kincardine and Kirkcaldy; then once across the Firth of Forth, follow the Fife Coastal Tourist Rte signposts to the historic village of ② **Culross** (p187). Spend an hour or so exploring the medieval buildings of Culross before continuing via the A994 to ③ **Dunfermline** (p188), for a look at its fine abbey and palace ruins.

From Dunfermline take the M90 towards the Forth Road Bridge, but leave at Junction 1 (signposted A921 Dalgety Bay) and continue to the attractive seaside village of ④ **Aberdour** for lunch at the Aberdour Hotel. Stay on the A921 as far as Kirkcaldy, then take the faster A915 (signposted St Andrews) as far as

Upper Largo, where you'll follow the A917 towards Elie; from here on, you will be following the brown Fife Coastal Tourist Rte signs.

⑤ **Elie**, with its sandy beaches and coastal footpaths, is a great place to stretch your legs and take in some bracing sea air before driving just a couple of miles further to explore the neighbouring fishing villages of ⑥ **St Monans** and ⑦ **Pittenweem**. Just 1 mile beyond Pittenweem, ⑧ **Anstruther** (p198) deserves a slightly longer stop for a visit to the Scottish Fisheries Museum, a stroll by the harbour and an ice cream. If time allows, you may want to detour inland a couple of miles to visit Kellie Castle or Scotland's Secret Bunker.

The final stop before St Andrews is the pretty fishing village of ⑨ **Crail** (p195), where the late-afternoon or early-evening light will provide ideal conditions for capturing one of Scotland's most photographed harbours. A brisk hike along the coastal path towards Fife Ness, keeping an eye out for seals and seabirds, will round off the day before you drive the last 10 miles into ⑩ **St Andrews** (p189).

Hidden 30m underground and encased in nearly 5m of reinforced concrete, it houses two levels of austere operations rooms, communication centres, broadcasting studios, weapons stores and dormitories, filled with period artefacts and museum displays. The bunker is 3 miles north of Anstruther, off the B9131 to St Andrews.

You can book a **Go-Flexi** (☑ 01382-540624; www.go-flexi.org) 'taxibus' from Anstruther (£2.30) or take a standard taxi (around £20) from St Andrews.

Kellie Castle   CASTLE

(NTS; www.nts.org.uk; adult/child £10.50/7.50; ⊙ 11am-5pm daily Jun-Aug, Sat-Thu Apr, May, Sep & Oct; ℗) An authentic example of Lowland Scottish domestic architecture, Kellie Castle has creaky floors, crooked little doorways, superb decorative plasterwork and some marvellous works of art. The original part of the building dates from 1360 but it was enlarged to its present dimensions around 1606. The castle is set amid beautiful gardens that are open year-round from 9.30am to 6pm or dusk.

It's 3 miles northwest of Pittenweem on the B9171.

Pittenweem

POP 1490

Pittenweem is the main fishing port on the East Neuk coast, and there are lively morning fish sales at its harbour. The village is a great place to wander, with boats bobbing along the harbour front, and art galleries, cafes and craft shops on the High St a block above – the two are linked by steep, narrow alleys.

The village name means 'place of the cave', referring to St Fillan's Cave.

St Fillan's Cave   CAVE

(Cove Wynd; adult/child £1/free; ⊙ 10am-6pm) St Fillan's Cave was used as a chapel by a 7th-century missionary who reputedly possessed miraculous powers – apparently, when he wrote his sermons in the dark cave, his arm would throw light on his work by emitting a luminous glow. The cave is protected by a locked gate, but a key and an information leaflet are available from the nearby Cocoa Tree Cafe.

Cocoa Tree Cafe   CAFE £

(www.pittenweemchocolate.co.uk; 9 High St; mains £5-9; ⊙ 10am-5pm Tue-Sun; 🛜🎫😊) This artisan chocolatier also houses a cafe that serves deliciously decadent hot chocolate, as well as freshly prepared focaccia sandwiches and salads.

St Monans

POP 450

This ancient fishing village is named after a cave-dwelling 7th-century saint who is said to have been killed by pirates. Apart from a historic **windmill** overlooking the sea, its main sight is the picturesque **parish church**, built in 1362 on the orders of a grateful King David II, who was rescued by villagers from a shipwreck in the Firth of Forth. It was burned by the English in 1544 but restored. The church commands sweeping views of the firth, and the past echoes inside its cold, whitewashed walls.

Craig Millar @ 16 West End   SEAFOOD £££

(☑ 01333-730327; www.16westend.com; 16 West End; 3-course lunch/4-course dinner £32/55; ⊙ 12.30-2pm & 6.30-9pm Wed-Sat, 12.30-2pm Sun) 🍴 The range of seafood on offer changes daily at this comfortable but classy restaurant on the harbour – it could include oysters, scallops, cod, turbot or monkfish (the menu details the provenance of these sustainable catches), so just swim with the tide.

Elie & Earlsferry

These two attractive villages mark the southwestern end of the East Neuk. There are great sandy beaches, two golf courses and good walks along the coast – seek out the **Chain Walk**, an adventurous scramble along the rocky shoreline at Kincraig Point, west of Earlsferry, using chains and steel rungs cemented into the rock (allow two hours, and ask local advice about tides before setting off). On a more relaxing note, there's nothing better than a lazy summer Sunday in Elie, watching the local team play cricket on the beach.

Elie Watersports   WATER SPORTS

(☑ 01333-330962; www.eliewatersports.com; Elie Harbour, Elie; ⊙ May-Sep, ring ahead other times) Hires out windsurfers (£30 per two hours), sailing dinghies (from £25 per hour), canoes (from £15 per hour) and mountain bikes (£20 per day), and offers instruction (at extra cost).

Ship Inn   PUB FOOD ££

(☑ 01333-330246; www.shipinn.scot; The Toft, Elie; mains £9-19, steak £30; ⊙ food served 11am-

9pm; 🅟🐾) Down by Elie harbour, this is a pleasant and popular place for a pint in the beer garden overlooking the wide sweep of the bay, but there's also a restaurant area with an above-average menu based on local seafood and steak.

LOWLAND PERTHSHIRE & KINROSS

For sheer scenic variety, Perthshire is the pick of Scotland's counties and a place where everyone will find a special, personal spot. The county straddles the Highland border, with Highland Perthshire stretching north from Dunkeld, while Lowland Perthshire ranges from the sedate streets of Perth itself, a fair city with a fabulous attraction in lavish Scone Palace, to the rural market towns of Crieff and Blairgowrie. Kinross, once one of Scotland's smallest counties, is famous for lovely Loch Leven, with a historic island castle, scenic walks and good trout fishing.

Perth

POP 46,970

Elegantly arranged along the Tay, Perth is a pleasant city with large tracts of parkland surrounding an easily navigated centre. The Scottish Parliament once sat here and, but for the murder of James I at Blackfriars monastery in 1437, Perth might have been the capital of Scotland. Instead it built its fortune on the weaving, dyeing, fishing and brewing industries, and gave the country some of its most famous brand names, including Pullars (dry cleaning), Dewars and Bells (both whisky). To learn more about the city's history, pick up the *Walks Around Historic Perth* booklet at the museum.

On the outskirts lies Scone Palace, a country house of staggering luxury built alongside the ancient crowning place of Scotland's kings. The palace is a must-see, and the town itself – known as the Fair City – is endowed with fine galleries and good restaurants, and is within easy striking distance of Edinburgh and Glasgow.

⊙ Sights

★ **Scone Palace**   PALACE
(🕿01738-552300; www.scone-palace.co.uk; Scone Estate; adult/child £20/13, grounds only £9/6; ⊙9.30am-6pm May-Sep, 10am-5pm Apr & Oct,

last entry 1hr before closing; 🅟) 'So thanks to all at once and to each one, whom we invite to see us crowned at Scone.' This line from *Macbeth* indicates the importance of Scone (pronounced 'skoon') as the coronation place of Scottish monarchs. The original palace of 1580, laying claim to this historic site, was rebuilt in the early 19th century as a Georgian mansion of extreme elegance and luxury. The guided tour takes you through a succession of sumptuous rooms filled with fine French furniture and noble portraits.

Scone has belonged for centuries to the Murray family, earls of Mansfield, and many of the objects have a fascinating history attached to them. Each room has comprehensive multilingual information; there are also panels relating histories of some of the Scottish kings crowned at Scone over the centuries. Outside, peacocks – each named after a monarch – shriek and strut around the magnificent grounds, which incorporate woods, a butterfly garden and a maze.

Ancient kings were crowned on **Moot Hill**, now topped by a chapel next to the palace. It's said that the hill was created by bootfuls of earth, brought by nobles attending the coronations as an acknowledgement of the king's rights over their lands, although it's more likely the site of an ancient motte-and-bailey castle. Here in 838 Kenneth MacAlpin became the first king of a united Scotland and brought to Scone the **Stone of Destiny**, on which Scottish kings were ceremonially invested. In 1296 Edward I of England carted this talisman off to Westminster Abbey, where it remained for 700 years before being returned to Scotland in 1997 (it now sits in Edinburgh Castle, but there are plans afoot to return it to Perth).

Scone Palace is 2 miles north of Perth; from the town centre, cross the bridge, turn left, and bear left along the footway beside the A93 until you reach the gates of the estate. From here, it's another half-mile to the palace (about 45 minutes' walk). Various buses from town stop here; the tourist office (p205) can advise.

Perth City Hall   MUSEUM
(www.culturepk.org.uk; King Edward St) Built in 1908, this squat neoclassical building in the heart of the city once hosted public events, but lay empty after the opening of Perth Concert Hall in 2005. A 2019 redevelopment programme will see the hall converted into a 'cultural and heritage attraction', opening by early 2022, that will tell the story of the

Stone of Destiny and the birth of Scottish nationhood. It may even see the Stone of Destiny returned to Perth from Edimburgh Castle.

Perth Museum & Art Gallery
MUSEUM

(www.culturepk.org.uk; 78 George St; ⊙10am-5pm Tue-Sat year-round, plus 10am-5pm Sun Apr-Oct) **FREE** This elegant neoclassical building, based on the Pantheon in Rome, houses one of the oldest purpose-built museums in Britain. There's a varied range of exhibits covering the city's history and natural environment, from portraits of dour lairds to carved Pictish stones and a plaster cast of Britain's record rod-caught salmon (29kg, hooked on the River Tay in 1922) along with an account of its capture by the angler, Georgina Ballantine.

Fergusson Gallery
GALLERY

(www.culturepk.org.uk; cnr Marshall Pl & Tay St; ⊙10am-5pm Tue-Sat year-round, plus noon-4.30pm Sun Apr-Oct) **FREE** Beautifully set in a circular cast-iron building that was once a waterworks, this gallery exhibits an extensive collection of paintings by the Scottish Colourist JD Fergusson in a most impressive display. Fergusson spent time in Paris, and the influence of artists such as Matisse on his work is evident; his voluptuous female portraits against a tropical-looking Riviera background are memorable, as is the story of his lifelong relationship with noted Scottish dancer Margaret Morris.

Black Watch Museum
MUSEUM

(☑01738-638152; www.theblackwatch.co.uk; Hay St; adult/child £8.75/3.60; ⊙9.30am-4.30pm Apr-Oct, 10am-4pm Nov-Mar; ℗) Housed in Balhousie Castle on the edge of North Inch park, this museum honours what was once Scotland's foremost army regiment (it was subsumed into the new Royal Regiment of Scotland in 2006). Formed in 1725 to control rebellious Highlanders following the Jacobite uprising of 1715, the Black Watch fought in numerous famous campaigns, recreated here with paintings, memorabilia and anecdotes.

There's justifiable pride in the regiment's role in the gruelling trench warfare of WWI, where it suffered nearly 30,000 casualties, but little sense of historical perspective on less glorious colonial engagements, such as those against the 'Fuzzy Wuzzies' of Sudan.

OFF THE BEATEN TRACK

LINDORES ABBEY DISTILLERY

Of the many new distilleries that have popped up all over Scotland in recent years, the **Lindores Abbey Distillery** (☑01337-842547; www.lindoresabbeydistillery.com; Abbey Rd, Newburgh KY14 6HH; tours per person £12.50; ⊙10am-4pm Apr-Sep, 11am-4pm Oct-Mar; ℗⊛) – opened in 2017 – has a unique historical claim. It's a stunning modern building (made using local stone and timber) that stands beside the ruins of Lindores Abbey, the site of the earliest written reference to Scotch whisky, which dates from 1494. The disillery is in northwest Fife, next to the small town of Newburgh, 20 minutes' drive from Perth.

St John's Kirk
CHURCH

(www.st-johns-kirk.co.uk; St John's St; ⊙10am-4pm Mon-Sat May-Sep) **FREE** Imposing St John's Kirk was founded in 1126 and is still the centrepiece of the town. In 1559 John Knox preached a powerful sermon here that helped begin the Reformation, inciting a frenzied destruction of Scone abbey and other religious sites. The church itself, restored in the 19th century, is a rare example of a surviving medieval Scottish kirk.

Perth used to be known as St John's Town after this church, and the local football team is still called St Johnstone.

🛏 Sleeping

Perth Youth Hostel
HOSTEL £

(HS; ☑01738-877800; www.hostellingscotland.org.uk; Crieff Rd; s/tw/apt from £23/46/99; ⊙mid-Jun–late Aug) A 20-minute stroll from the centre, this summer-only hostel is set in a student residence at Perth College. The rooms are all en-suite twins and five-bed apartments, with good shared kitchens and common rooms. Turn into the Brahan entrance on Crieff Rd; the hostel is by the large car park. Numerous buses stop outside.

★ Pitcullen Guest House
B&B ££

(☑01738-626506; www.pitcullen.co.uk; 17 Pitcullen Cres; d/f from £70/130; ℗⊛) This excellent B&B has a much more contemporary feel than other guesthouses on this strip. Great-looking fabrics and modern styling give the rooms an upbeat look, and lots of thought has gone into making your stay

Perth

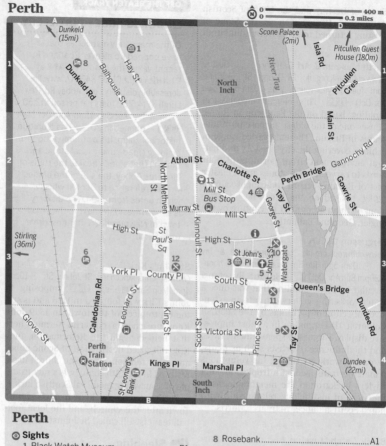

Perth

◎ Sights
1 Black Watch Museum	B1
2 Fergusson Gallery	C4
3 Perth City Hall	C3
4 Perth Museum & Art Gallery	C2
5 St John's Kirk	C3

◎ Sleeping
6 Heidl Guest House	A3
7 Parklands	B4

8 Rosebank	A1

◎ Eating
9 63 Tay Street	C4
10 Breizh	C3
11 Cardo	C3
12 Tabla	B3

◎ Drinking & Nightlife
13 King James	C2

more comfortable, with things like fridges with free drinks in the rooms, plenty of plugs to make recharging easy and handy maps on the walls.

Heidl Guest House B&B ££
(☎01738-635031; http://heidlguesthouse.co.uk; 43 York Pl; s/d/f from £45/70/105; [P][☎]) It may lack a little character from outside, but the Heidl is an excellent guesthouse, and the enthusiastic owners have renovated it well, leaving the seven bedrooms very spruce in-

deed. Most rooms are en suite; the two that aren't have separate but private bathrooms. Writer John Buchan (of *The Thirty-Nine Steps* fame) was born in the house opposite.

Rosebank B&B ££
(☎01738-301707; www.rosebankguesthousep erth.co.uk; 53 Dunkeld Rd; d/f from from £82/90; [P][☎]) One of several B&Bs on the northern approach to the city centre, the Rosebank impresses with its warm welcome and brightly decorated rooms. Hearty break-

fasts are served in an elegant dining room with original Victorian cornices and fireplace. Possible two-night minimum stay.

Parklands
HOTEL £££

(☑ 01738-622451; www.theparklandshotel.com; 2 St Leonard's Ban; s/d/f from £99/123/170; P 🛜) This relaxing hotel occupies a luxurious villa set amid lush hillside gardens overlooking the parklands of the South Inch. While the rooms preserve the character of this beautiful building, formerly the residence of the town's mayors, they also offer modern conveniences and plenty of style. There's a great terrace and garden area in which to lap up the Perthshire sun.

✗ Eating & Drinking

★ Tabla
INDIAN ££

(☑ 01738-444630; www.tablarestaurant.co.uk; 173 South St; mains £10-15; ⊙ noon-2pm & 5-10pm Mon-Sat, 5-10pm Sun) Tabla is one of the best Indian restaurants in the whole of central Scotland. Its bustling, modern dining room caters to a loyal clientele of locals tucking into authentic dishes such as *andhra wada* (lentil patties with chilli, coriander and cumin) and railway *boti* (curried lamb on the bone with curry leaves and star anise, as served on Indian trains).

Cardo
MEDITERRANEAN ££

(☑ 01738-248784; www.cardo.restaurant; 38 South St; mains £10-23; ⊙ 11.30am-9pm Tue-Sun; 🍴) Amid a lively atmosphere, this spacious bistro showcases the Mediterranean culinary background of the husband (French) and wife (Portuguese) owners in dishes that range from falafel with beetroot hummus or potted pork rillette to braised Iberico pork cheek or *choucroute de la mer* (seafood with pickled cabbage). There's also wood-fired pizza and a range of daily specials.

Breiz
BISTRO, FRENCH ££

(☑ 01738-444427; www.breizhrestaurant.com; 28 High St; mains £13-23; ⊙ noon-9pm Wed-Sun; 🍴) This funkily French bistro – the name is Breton for Brittany – is a treat. Dishes are served with real panache, and the salads, featuring all sorts of delicious ingredients, are a feast of colour, texture and subtle flavours. The blackboard specials offer great value and an authentic taste of northwestern France, including traditional *galettes* (Breton buckwheat pancakes with savoury fillings).

FAIR CITY FESTIVAL

If you're in Perth in the last two weeks of May you'll come across the low-profile but high-quality **Perth Festival of the Arts** (☑ 01738-621031; www.perthfestival. co.uk; ⊙ May). Various venues around town host a diverse range of cultural events; don't be surprised to see some big-name bands (Jools Holland is a regular) or a quality ballet company appearing at very reasonable prices.

★ 63 Tay Street
SCOTTISH £££

(☑ 01738-441451; www.63taystreet.com; 63 Tay St; mains lunch £13-14, dinner £17-25; ⊙ 6.30-9pm Tue & Wed, noon-2pm & 6.30-9pm Thu-Sat; 🍴) 🍷 Classy and warmly welcoming, this understated restaurant is Perth's best, featuring a lightly decorated dining area, excellent service and quality food. In a culinary Auld Alliance, French influence is applied to the best of Scottish produce to create memorable game, seafood, beef and vegetarian dishes.

King James
PUB

(www.kingjamespub.co.uk; 73 Kinnoull St; ⊙ 11am-11pm Mon-Wed, 11am-midnight Thu, 11am-12.30am Fri & Sat, noon-11.30pm Sun) The basement of this pub contains a crime scene – the medieval stonework here is all that survives of Blackfriars monastery, where James I of Scotland was murdered in 1437. A glass panel in the floor of the bar allows drinkers to look on this piece of Perth history, though most regulars will be watching sport on the large-screen TVs.

ℹ Information

Perth Tourist Office (☑ 01738-450600; www. perthshire.co.uk; 45 High St; ⊙ 10am-4pm Mon-Sat, 11am-4pm Sun, longer hours Jul & Aug)

ℹ Getting There & Away

BUS

Citylink (www.citylink.co.uk) and **Stagecoach** (www.stagecoachbus.com) intercity buses operate from the **bus station** (Leonard St, PH2 8ET), with services to/from the following:

Dundee £8.70, 35 minutes, hourly
Edinburgh £13.10, 1¾ hours, hourly
Glasgow £13.70, 1¾ hours, hourly
Inverness £23.50, three hours, five daily
Stirling £9.80, one hour, hourly
Further buses run from the Broxden Park & Ride on Glasgow Rd; this is connected regularly with

WORTH A TRIP

GLENEAGLES

Deep in rural Perthsire near the town of Aucherarder lies **Gleneagles Hotel** (☑01764-662231; www.gleneagles.com; r from £410; P @ 🛜 🛋), one of Scotland's most famous resorts. Not your typical bed-and-breakfast, this is a no-holds-barred luxury retreat with three championship **golf courses** (green fees £80-150; 🏌), Michelin-starred **Andrew Fairlie** – often referred to as Scotland's best restaurant (open for dinner Tuesday to Saturday) – and a variety of extravagantly elegant rooms and suites.

Despite the imposing building and kilted staff snapping to attention, it's welcoming to non-VIPs, and family friendly to boot, with lots of activities available. There's Gleneagles train station if you wish to arrive sustainably; if not, limousine transfers are available. Check the website for deals.

Phoenix Falconry (☑07715 691803; www.scottishfalconry.co.uk; Easterton Farm; per person £30-180), just along the road from Gleneagles Hotel, offers experiences that range from one-hour bird-handling sessions to all-day adventures, flying Harris's hawks and other raptors over the owner's estate.

the bus station by shuttle bus. These include **Megabus** (www.megabus.com) discount services to Aberdeen, Edinburgh, Glasgow, Dundee and Inverness.

Stagecoach buses serving local Perthshire destinations depart from **Mill St** (PH1 5EX). An East Scotland Dayrider ticket gives you one day of unlimited bus travel in Perthshire, Fife, Dundee and Angus for £16.

TRAIN

Trains run between Perth and various destinations, including the following:

Dundee £8.80, 20 minutes, hourly

Edinburgh £18.10, 1½ hours, at least hourly Monday to Saturday, every two hours Sunday

Glasgow £18.10, 1½ hours, at least hourly Monday to Saturday, every two hours Sunday

Pitlochry £15.30, 30 minutes, 10 daily

Stirling £14.60, 35 minutes, hourly weekdays, every two hours Sunday

Kinross & Loch Leven

The town of Kinross sits on the banks of pretty Loch Leven, a haven for walkers, cyclists and anglers. Just east of the town sits the gorgeously restored **Kinross House** (http://kinrosshouse.com), the finest Palladian mansion in Scotland, built by Sir William Bruce in 1693. Sadly, it's not open to the public (it can be rented for a princely sum), but you can get a glimpse of it from the loch-side trail.

Lochleven Castle   CASTLE

(HES; www.historicenvironment.scot; Kinross Pier; adult/child incl boat ride £9/5.40; ⏰10am-5.15pm Apr-Sep, to 4.15pm Oct, last sailing 1hr before closing; P) Evocative Lochleven Cas-

tle served as an island fortress and prison from the late 14th century; its most famous captive was Mary, Queen of Scots, who was incarcerated here in 1567. Her famous charms bewitched Willie Douglas, who managed to get hold of the cell keys to release her, then rowed her across to the shore. The castle is now roofless but basically intact and makes for an atmospheric destination; visitors cross to the island by boat (included in admission fee).

★ Loch Leven Heritage Trail   WALKING, CYCLING

(www.pkct.org) One of the best all-abilities hiking and biking routes in Scotland, this scenic 14-mile circuit of Loch Leven links Kinross Pier, the RSPB Loch Leven nature reserve, and Loch Leven's Larder. Allow two hours to cycle the trail or five hours to walk it; you can hire bikes and mobility scooters at Kinross Pier.

Loch Leven Fisheries   FISHING

(☑01577-863407; www.fishlochleven.co.uk; Kinross Pier; boat hire per day £20-50) World famous among anglers for more than 100 years for its hard-fighting, pink-fleshed brown trout, Loch Leven has been stocked in recent years with rainbow trout as well. Fishing is by fly only, from boats that can be hired at Kinross Pier (one to three anglers per boat).

★ Loch Leven's Larder   SCOTTISH £

(☑01592-841000; www.lochlevenslarder.com; Channel Farm; mains £6-11; ⏰9am-5pm; P 🛜 🏌 🐕) 🍴 Three miles east of Kinross, off the A911, this family-run farm shop and restaurant overlooking Loch Leven is the ideal place to enjoy fresh local food, much of it from the family's own farm, whether it's a breakfast of soft-boiled free-range eggs with hot buttered toast, a platter of Scottish cheeses, or a lunch of Arbroath smoked-haddock quiche with potato salad.

There's a terrace with a panorama over the loch, a children's playground, and a footpath that connects to the Loch Leven Heritage Trail, making it an ideal break on a walking or cycling circuit of the loch.

Upper Strathearn

The Highland villages of Comrie and St Fillans in Upper Strathearn are surrounded by forests and bare, craggy hilltops where deer and mountain hares live in abundance.

Comrie is a cute little village that has played its part in the history of science – on its western edge stands the tiny **Earthquake House** (www.strathearn.com/pl/earthquake.htm), the world's first seismic observatory. There are many excellent local walks, a favourite being to the spectacular gorge and waterfall known as the **Deil's Cauldron**, 1 mile north of the village.

St Fillans enjoys a scenic location at the eastern end of **Loch Earn**, which reflects the silhouettes of surrounding peaks. The loch has good **fishing** for brown trout and pike – you can buy permits (£12 for one day) from the village shop in St Fillans.

Four Seasons Hotel　　　HOTEL **££**
(📞 01764-685333; www.thefourseasonshotel.co.uk; St Fillans; d from £75; ⊗ closed Jan–mid-Feb; 🅿 🛜 🐾) The historic Four Seasons (the Beatles stayed here while on tour in 1964) has been given a classy modern makeover. Two beautifully appointed lounges and an atmospheric wee bar enjoy great views over the loch. The superior rooms – worth the upgrade – have the best vistas, and there are six chalets nestled in the slopes behind the hotel.

There are many activities to choose from, including waterskiing, quad biking and pony trekking, and a noted fine-dining restaurant.

⭐**Hansen's Kitchen**　　　DELI, CAFE **£**
(📞 01764-670253; www.facebook.com/hansenskitchen; Drummond St, Comrie; mains £4-6; ⊗ 8am-5pm Mon-Sat, 10am-4pm Sun; 📷) 🥗 The foodie epicentre of Upper Strathearn, Hansen's is a hugely popular delicatessen and cafe (there's barely a dozen seats crammed into the interior) serving superb coffee, cheese and charcuterie platters, and lunch dishes such as home-baked panini stuffed with salami,

mozzarella and pesto. If you can't get a table, grab some takeaway and head for the riverside benches beneath the church.

ℹ Getting There & Away

Comrie is 24 miles west of Perth, and St Fillans is about 5 miles further west. Buses run from Perth via Crieff (£3.30, 45 minutes) to Comrie (£4.30, one hour, hourly Monday to Saturday, every two hours Sunday).

Crieff

POP 7370

Elegant Crieff is an old resort-style town, known for golf, fishing and the Glenturret whisky distillery, and it's as popular with tourists today as it was in Victorian times. It sits in a valley amid some glorious Perthshire countryside and, with excellent eating and accommodation options, it's a fine base for exploring this part of the country.

⊙ Sights

Glenturret Distillery　　　DISTILLERY
(📞 01764-656565; www.theglenturret.com; Hosh; standard tour £11; ⊗ 10am-6pm Apr-Oct, 10am-5pm Nov-Mar; 🅿) At Glenturret – Scotland's oldest working distillery, in operation since at least 1763 – the better-than-average, one-hour tour

WORTH A TRIP

CASTLE CAMPBELL

One of central Scotland's most dramatically situated castles, **Castle Campbell** (HES; www.historicenvironment.scot; FK14 7PP; adult/child £6/3.60; ⊗ 9.30am-5.30pm daily Apr-Sep,10am-4pm daily Oct, 10am-4pm Sat-Wed Nov-Mar; 🅿) is on a spur between two deep, wooded ravines known as the Burn of Sorrow and the Burn of Care. A former stronghold of the dukes of Argyll, it was originally known as 'Castle Gloom'. There are interesting rooms in the 15th-century tower house, but the main attraction is the spectacular view from the top. The castle lies a mile north of charming Dollar village, about 11 miles west of Kinross.

There's a superb circular walk (30 minutes) from the lower car park, up the track to the castle and then back down via a walkway through the ravine.

CENTRAL SCOTLAND UPPER STRATHEARN

WORTH A TRIP

THE LIBRARY OF INNERPEFFRAY

The **Innerpeffray Library** (☑ 01764-652819; www.innerpeffraylibrary.co.uk; Innerpeffray PH7 3RF; adult/child £7.50/free; ☺ 10am-5pm Wed-Sat, 2-5pm Sun Mar-Oct, by appt Nov-Feb; ℙ) is Scotland's oldest lending library (founded in 1680) and houses a huge collection of rare, interesting and ancient books, some of them 500 years old. If you have any interest in books you could easily spend half a day here in the company of voluntary guides, who will point out interesting volumes or find books on subjects that interest you. The library is signposted along a farm road about 5 miles southeast of Crieff, off the B8062.

Next to the library is **Innerpeffray Chapel**, built in 1507 as a private Catholic chapel for the Drummond family (who also founded the library). It contains some fragments of painted plaster, and the remarkable **Faichney monument** (1707), an ornately carved gravestone that celebrates the mason's pride in his family.

is strong on how the different flavours are created during the making of its single malt whisky. Two tiny drams are included in the standard tour; more expensive tours offer more detailed tasting sessions. Look out for Glen and Turret, the distillery cats.

🛏 Sleeping

Comrie Croft　　　　HOSTEL, CAMPGROUND £
(☑ 01764-670140;　　　　www.comriecroft.com; Braincroft; campsites per person £11, dm £25; ℙ@☎☻) 🍴 A rustic, hospitable place that has a bit of everything: camping; a pleasant, airy hostel; and Nordic katas (£99 per night), with wood stoves, that sleep up to six. Activities include mountain biking (purpose-built trails; bike hire available), fishing, walking, and lots of games for the kids. It's 4 miles west of Crieff on the A85.

★ Merlindale　　　　B&B ££
(☑ 01764-655205; www.merlindale.co.uk; Perth Rd; s/d from £80/95; ☺ Mar-Nov; ℙ☎) Georgian architecture meets generous hospitality at this excellent guesthouse at the eastern end of town. The four fabulous rooms all have individual character, and two have sumptuous bathrooms with free-standing tubs. There's a comfy lounge-library, the owner is a Cordon Bleu–trained chef, and thoughtful touches abound.

Yann's at Glenearn House　　　　B&B ££
(☑ 01764-650111;　　　www.yannsatglenearnhouse.com; Perth Rd; r £105; ℙ☎☻) This luxury B&B is a most welcoming establishment, offering four large, bright rooms with plenty of understated style, an atmospheric lounge stuffed with armchairs, and French crêpes on the breakfast menu. The owner is a French chef, and there's an excellent

restaurant (mains £14-22; ☺ 6-9pm Wed-Sun; ℙ☎☻) on the premises.

Crieff Hydro　　　　HOTEL ££
(☑ 01764-655555; www.crieffhydro.com; Ferntower Rd; r from £109; ℙ@☎☻☻☻) This enormous spa hotel is nearly 150 years old, but apart from its monumental exterior it looks very different from its mannered Victorian past. It's attractively functional and really does have everything for a family holiday, from cinema and gym to restaurants, activities and pools. It's exceptionally child friendly, with free daily childcare.

Room rates vary substantially, so check the website. There are also self-catering cottages dotted around the extensive grounds offering a quieter stay in a cosier, more couple-focused environment (and you can still access all the leisure facilities at the hotel).

🍴 Eating

Delivino　　　　CAFE, DELI ££
(www.delivino.co.uk; 6 King St; mains £12-15, sharing platters £20; ☺ 9am-8pm Mon-Thu, 9am-9pm Fri & Sat, noon-4pm Sun; 👪) Just down from the square on the main street, elegant Delivino offers something for everyone, from Crieff locals to travellers looking for a light bite. An extensive selection of 'small plates' allows you to graze on several flavours at a time, while delicious bruschetta and pizza, accompanied by a glass of Italian red, make this a great lunch option.

Lounge　　　　BISTRO ££
(☑ 01764-654407; www.loungeincrieff.co.uk; 1 West High St; mains £11-22; ☺ noon-9pm Tue-Thu, noon-10.30pm Fri & Sat; ☎) Enter the romantic interior of this informal lounge bar and bistro for anything from a cup of tea to good wines by the glass to an interesting array of gour-

met sandwiches, tapas and other delights – notably *galettes au sarrasin* (delicious French buckwheat pancakes with savoury fillings). It's run by Delphine, sister of Yann, owner of Crieff's top restaurant.

★ **Barley Bree**   SCOTTISH £££
([phone] 01764-681451; www.barleybree.com; 6 Willoughby St, Muthill; mains lunch £13, dinner £25; [clock] noon-2pm & 6.45-9pm Wed-Sat, noon-3pm & 6-9pm Sun; [P] [child]) [reservation] Set in the pretty village of Muthill (*mooth*-il), 3 miles south of Crieff, the Barley Bree is a delightfully rustic restaurant with rooms. Wooden floorboards, stone fireplace, stacked logs and deer antlers set the scene for dishes of fine Scottish seafood, beef and game; half a dozen luxurious bedrooms (doubles from £110) tempt you to stay the night.

🛍 Shopping

Crieff Food Company   FOOD & DRINKS
([phone] 01764-655817; www.thecriefffoodco.co.uk; cnr High St & James Sq; [clock] 9am-5pm Mon-Sat, 10am-4pm Sun; [wifi]) This food hall and delicatessen is a showcase for local producers, and it's a great place to stock up on Scottish delicacies such as Heather Hills honey, Strathearn cheeses, Perthshire oatcakes and smoked venison from Rannoch Smokery. There's a good **cafe** here, too.

Gordon & Durward   FOOD
(www.scottishsweets.co.uk; 14 West High St; [clock] 9am-5pm Mon-Sat, 11am-5pm Sun) On the go since 1925, this old-fashioned sweet shop is lined with jars of traditional Scottish sweets (candies) such as boilings, macaroons, Edinburgh rock, sugar mice and tablet (a crumbly, buttery fudge).

ℹ Getting There & Away

Buses link Crieff with Perth (£3.30, 45 minutes, hourly Monday to Saturday, less frequently on Sunday) and Stirling (£3.60, one hour, four to 10 daily).

Blairgowrie & Around
POP 8950

Blairgowrie is a compact market town on the banks of the River Ericht, famed for its salmon fishing. Formerly a flax-spinning centre, the town today is the hub of Scotland's soft-fruits industry – the fields for miles around are ripe with raspberries and strawberries, for sale in season from kiosks on the edge of town.

About 5 miles east of Blairgowrie, **Alyth** is a charming historic village clustered along the banks of the Alyth Burn, which is crossed by a 15th-century stone bridge and a couple of modern footbridges.

Off the A94 and 8 miles east of Blairgowrie, **Meigle** is well worth the trip for those with a fascination for Pictish sculptured stones, which can be viewed at the **Meigle Museum** (HES; [phone] 01828-640612; www.historicenvironment.scot; Dundee Rd, Meigle; adult/child £6/3.60; [clock] 9.30am-5.30pm Apr-Sep, 10am-4pm Oct).

Cateran Trail   WALKING
(www.caterantrail.org) Blairgowrie is the start and finish point for the Cateran Trail, a circular 64-mile waymarked path that leads through the mountains around Glenshee on the southern fringes of the Cairngorms National Park. The first mile or so along the River Ericht, as far as the waterfall at **Cargill's Leap** and the former flax mill at Keathbank, makes an excellent short walk.

Dalmore Inn   SCOTTISH ££
([phone] 01250-871088; www.dalmoreinn.com; Perth Rd; mains £14-19, steaks £28-32; [clock] 10am-9pm; [P] [child]) [reservation] One of Blairgowrie's most popular eateries, the Dalmore finds inventive ways to present the best of local produce, with upmarket takes on old favourites such as loin of Scotch lamb with asparagus risotto, or steak, haggis and ale pie with creamy mashed potatoes. The inn is on the southern edge of town, on the A93 towards Perth.

ℹ Getting There & Away

Buses run to Blairgowrie from Perth (£3.90, 40 minutes, hourly) and from Dundee (£3.90, one hour, hourly), and there are buses every two hours between Blairgowrie and Alyth (£2, 16 minutes), and Blairgowrie and Meigle (£2.70, 25 minutes).

There is no public transport from Blairgowrie to Braemar.

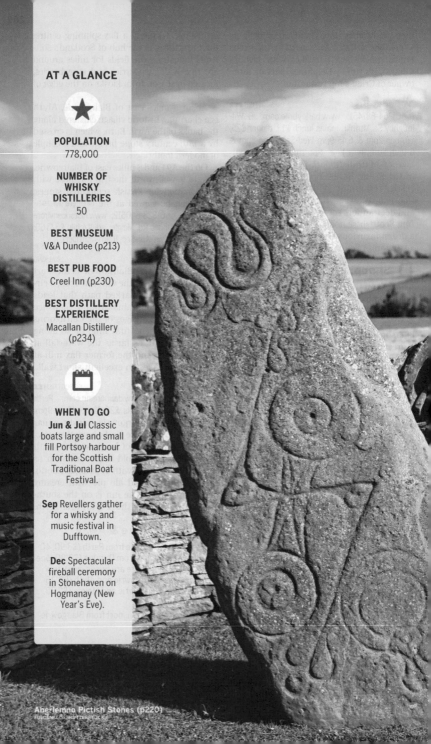

AT A GLANCE

★

POPULATION
778,000

**NUMBER OF
WHISKY
DISTILLERIES**
50

BEST MUSEUM
V&A Dundee (p213)

BEST PUB FOOD
Creel Inn (p230)

**BEST DISTILLERY
EXPERIENCE**
Macallan Distillery
(p234)

📅

WHEN TO GO
Jun & Jul Classic
boats large and small
fill Portsoy harbour
for the Scottish
Traditional Boat
Festival.

Sep Revellers gather
for a whisky and
music festival in
Dufftown.

Dec Spectacular
fireball ceremony
in Stonehaven on
Hogmanay (New
Year's Eve).

Aberlemno Pictish Stones (p220)
FULCANELLI/SHUTTERSTOCK ©

Northeast Scotland

Many visitors pass by this corner in their headlong rush to the tourist honeypots of Loch Ness and Skye. But they're missing out on a part of Scotland that's just as beautiful and diverse as the west.

Here are two of Scotland's four largest cities: Dundee, the city of jute, jam and journalism, home to Captain Scott's Antarctic research ship, the *Discovery*, and the stunning V&A Dundee museum of design; and Aberdeen, the granite city, an economic powerhouse fuelled by the riches of North Sea oil.

Angus is a region of rich farmland and scenic glens dotted with mysterious stones left by the ancient Picts, while Aberdeenshire and Moray hold the greatest concentration of Scottish Baronial castles and dozens of whisky distilleries along the River Spey.

Northeast Scotland Highlights

1 V&A Dundee (p213 Discovering the best of Scottish and international design at this architecturally stunning museum in the heart of Dundee's waterfront.

2 Aberlemno Stones (p220) Meditating on the meaning of these mysterious Pictish stones, carved with strange symbols and scenes of battle.

3 Silver Darling (p226) Tucking into the finest Scottish seafood at this classic Aberdeen restaurant.

4 Macallan Distillery (p234) Absorbing the history of Scotch whisky in this breathtaking visitor centre.

5 Scottish Dolphin Centre (p227) Learning about the Moray Firth's bottlenose dolphins at Spey Bay.

6 Scottish Lighthouse Museum (p230) Exploring the heritage of Scotland's maritime tradition and visiting the country's oldest lighthouse, set atop a 16th-century castle.

DUNDEE & ANGUS

Angus is a fertile farming region stretching north from Dundee – Scotland's fourth-largest city – to the Highland border. It's an attractive area of broad straths (valleys) and low, green hills contrasting with the rich, red-brown soil of freshly ploughed fields. The romantic Angus Glens finger their way into the foothills of the Grampian Mountains, while the scenic coastline ranges from the red-sandstone cliffs of Arbroath to the long, sandy beach of Lunan Bay. This was the Pictish heartland of the 7th and 8th centuries, and many interesting Pictish symbol stones survive here.

Apart from the crowds visiting newly confident Dundee and the coach parties shuffling through Glamis Castle, Angus is a bit of a tourism backwater and a good place to escape the crowds.

Dundee

POP 147,300

London's Trafalgar Sq has Nelson, Edinburgh's Princes St has Sir Walter Scott and Belfast has Queen Victoria outside City Hall. Dundee's City Sq, on the other hand, is graced – rather endearingly – by the bronze figure of Desperate Dan. Familiar to generations of British schoolchildren, Dan is one of the best-loved cartoon characters from the comic *Dandy*, published by Dundee firm DC Thomson since 1937.

Dundee enjoys perhaps the finest location of any Scottish city, spreading along the northern shore of the Firth of Tay, and has tourist attractions of national importance in V&A Dundee, Discovery Point and Verdant Works. Add attractive seaside town Broughty Ferry, and the Dundonians themselves – among the friendliest, most welcoming and entertaining people you'll meet – and Dundee is definitely worth a stopover.

The waterfront around Discovery Point has undergone a massive redevelopment, centred on the construction of the architecturally outstanding V&A Dundee museum of design.

History

During the 19th century Dundee grew from its trading-port origins to become a major player in the shipbuilding, whaling, textile and railway engineering industries. Dundonian firms owned and operated most of the jute mills in India (jute is a natural fi-

bre used to make ropes and sacking), and the city's textile industry employed as many as 43,000 people – little wonder Dundee earned the nickname 'Juteopolis'.

Dundee is often called the city of the 'Three Js' – jute, jam and journalism. According to legend, it was a Dundee woman, Janet Keillor, who invented marmalade in the late 18th century; her son founded the city's famous Keillor jam factory. Jute is no longer produced, and when the Keillor factory was taken over in 1988, production was transferred to England. Journalism still thrives, however, led by the family firm of DC Thomson. Best known for children's comics such as the *Beano* and the *Dandy*, and regional newspapers including the *Press and Journal*, Thomson is now the city's largest employer.

In the late 19th and early 20th centuries Dundee was one of the richest cities in the country – there were more millionaires per head of population here than anywhere else in Britain – but the textile and engineering industries declined in the second half of the 20th century, leading to high unemployment and urban decay.

In the 1960s and '70s Dundee's cityscape was scarred by ugly blocks of flats, office buildings and shopping centres linked by unsightly concrete walkways; most visitors passed it by. Since the mid-1990s, however, Dundee has reinvented itself as a tourist destination and a centre for the computer games industry (Grand Theft Auto was invented here), while its waterfront has undergone a major rejuvenation. It also has more university students – one in seven of the population – than any other town in Europe except Heidelberg.

🔘 Sights

★ **V&A Dundee**   MUSEUM
(📞01382-411611; www.vam.ac.uk/dundee; 1 Riverside Esplanade; ⊙10am-5pm) **FREE** The centrepiece of Dundee's revitalised waterfront is this stunning building designed by Japanese architect Kengo Kuma. Opened in late 2018, it houses an outpost of London's Victoria & Albert Museum of art and design. The permanent collections showcase the work of Scottish designers past and present, from famous names such as Charles Rennie Mackintosh to modern creatives such as fashion designer Holly Fulton, while temporary exhibitions celebrate the best of art and design from around the world.

Dundee

The distinctive horizontal panels on the building's exterior recall the layered ledges of the sea cliffs of Scotland's east coast, while the curved and overhanging corners call to mind the bows and sterns of sailing ships, echoing the shape of the RRS *Discovery* next door. The 1st-floor Tatha Restaurant offers stylish dining with a view across the Firth of Tay.

★ **Discovery Point**   MUSEUM
(www.rrsdiscovery.com; Discovery Quay; adult/child £11.50/6.40; ⊙ 10am-6pm Mon-Sat, 11am-6pm Sun Apr-Oct, to 5pm Nov-Mar; P ⛆) The three masts of Captain Robert Falcon Scott's famous polar expedition vessel the RRS *Discovery* provide a historic counterpoint to the modern architecture of the nearby V&A design museum. Exhibitions and audiovisual displays in the neighbouring visitor centre provide a fascinating history of both the ship and Antarctic exploration, but *Discovery* is the star attraction. You can visit the bridge, the

galley and the mahogany-panelled officers' wardroom, and poke your nose into the cabins used by Scott and his crew.

The ship was built in Dundee in 1900, with a wooden hull at least half a metre thick to survive the pack ice, and sailed for the Antarctic in 1901 where it spent two winters trapped in the ice. From 1931 it was laid up in London where its condition steadily deteriorated, until it was rescued by the efforts of Peter Scott (Robert's son) and the Maritime Trust, and restored to its 1925 condition. In 1986 the ship was given a berth in its home port of Dundee, where it became a symbol of the city's regeneration.

A joint ticket that gives entry to both Discovery Point and the Verdant Works costs £18.65/10.50/48 per adult/child/family.

★ **Verdant Works**   MUSEUM
(www.verdantworks.com; West Henderson's Wynd; adult/child £11.50/6.40; ⊙ 10am-6pm Mon-Sat, 11am-6pm Sun Apr-Oct, reduced hours Nov-Mar;

🔒) One of the finest industrial museums in Europe, the Verdant Works explores the history of Dundee's jute industry. Housed in a restored jute mill, complete with original machinery in working condition, the museum's exhibits follow the raw material from its origins in India through to the manufacture of a wide range of finished products, from sacking to sailcloth to wagon covers for the pioneers of the American West. The museum is 250m west of the city centre.

McManus Galleries   MUSEUM
(www.mcmanus.co.uk; Albert Sq; ⏰10am-5pm Mon-Sat, 12.30-4.30pm Sun) FREE Housed in a solid Victorian Gothic building designed by Gilbert Scott in 1867, the McManus Galleries are a city museum on a human scale – you can see everything there is to see in a single visit, without feeling rushed or overwhelmed. The exhibits cover the history of the city from the Iron Age to the present day,

including relics of the Tay Bridge Disaster and the Dundee whaling industry.

Computer geeks will enjoy the Sinclair ZX81 and Spectrum (pioneering personal computers with a whole 16Kb of memory!), which were made in Dundee in the early 1980s.

HMS Unicorn   MUSEUM
(www.frigateunicorn.org; Victoria Dock; adult/child £7.25/3.60; ⏰10am-5pm Apr-Oct, 10am-4pm Tue-Sun Nov-Mar) Dundee's second floating tourist attraction – unlike the polished and much-restored RRS *Discovery* – retains the authentic atmosphere of a salty old sailing ship. Built in 1824, the 46-gun *Unicorn* is the oldest British-built ship still afloat – it was mothballed soon after launching and never saw action. Wandering around below deck gives you an excellent impression of what it must have been like for the crew forced to live in such cramped conditions.

By the mid-19th century sailing ships were outclassed by steam and the *Unicorn* served as a gunpowder store, then later as a training vessel. When it was proposed to break up the ship for scrap in the 1960s, a preservation society was formed. The ship is berthed in Victoria Dock, just northeast of the Tay Road Bridge. The entry price includes a self-guided tour (also available in French and German).

Dundee Contemporary Arts ARTS CENTRE

(www.dca.org.uk; Nethergate; ⊙10am-6pm Fri-Wed, to 7pm Thu) FREE Pioneering the development of the city's Cultural Quarter from its opening in 1999, Dundee Contemporary Arts is a centre for modern art, design and cinema. The galleries here (closed Monday and Tuesday) exhibit work by contemporary UK and international artists, and there are printmakers' studios where you can watch artists at work, or even take part in craft demonstrations and workshops. There's also the Jute Café Bar.

City Square SQUARE

The heart of Dundee is City Sq, flanked to the south by the 1930s facade of **Caird Hall**, which was gifted to the city by a textile magnate and is now home to the City Chambers. A more recent addition to the square, unveiled in 2001, is a bronze statue of **Desperate Dan**, the lantern-jawed hero of children's comic the *Dandy* (he's clutching a copy in his right hand).

🛏 Sleeping

Most city-centre hotels are business-oriented and cheaper on weekends. B&Bs are concentrated along Broughty Ferry Rd and Arbroath Rd east of the city centre, and Perth Rd to the west. If you don't fancy a night in the city, consider nearby Broughty Ferry.

Dundee accommodation is usually booked solid during the Open golf tournament at Carnoustie or St Andrews – check www.theopen.com for dates (it's in St Andrews in 2022).

Dundee Backpackers HOSTEL £

(☑01382-224646; www.hoppo.com/dundee backpackershostel; 71 High St; dm £18, s/tw from £25/45; @ 🛜) This hostel is set in a beautifully converted historic building, with a clean, modern kitchen, a pool room and an ideal location right in the city centre. It can get a bit noisy at night, but that's because it's close to pubs and nightlife.

Aabalree B&B £

(☑01382-223867; www.aabalree.com; 20 Union St; s/tw/q £35/55/80; 🛜) 🌱 This is a pretty basic B&B, almost a hostel – there are no en suites, and no lift to the three floors – but it's bright and cheerful (don't be put off by the dark entrance), the owners are welcoming, and there are vegan breakfasts on offer. It

couldn't be more central, close to both train and bus stations, so book ahead.

★Malmaison BOUTIQUE HOTEL ££

(☑01382-339715; www.malmaison.com/locations/dundee; 44 Whitehall Cres; r from £87; 🛜) Housed in a Victorian hotel building, this place has been refurbished in typical Malmaison style with period features such as intricate wrought-iron balustrades complemented by delightfully over-the-top modern decor. The rooms on the south side overlook the redeveloped waterfront and the V&A museum. Room rates are excellent value; check the website for special offers.

Urban Quarters APARTMENT ££

(☑07876 450961; www.urbanquarters.co.uk; 26 South Tay St; 2-bedroom apt from £111; 🛜) This complex contains four two-bedroom apartments (sleeping up to four people), all stylishly decorated with clean, modern lines and kitted out with modern kitchens (including Nespresso coffee machines) and smart TVs with access to Netflix. There's a four-night minimum stay.

Shaftesbury Lodge HOTEL ££

(☑01382-669216; www.shaftesburylodge.co.uk; 1 Hyndford St; s/d from £63/85; 🛜) The family-run, 12-room Shaftesbury is set in a Victorian mansion that was built for a jute baron and has many authentic period features, including a fine marble fireplace in the dining room. It's 1.5 miles west of the city centre, just off Perth Rd.

Apex City Quay Hotel HOTEL ££

(☑01382-202404; www.apexhotels.co.uk/dundee-hotel; 1 West Victoria Dock Rd; r from £102; P🛜🐾) Though it looks plain and boxy from the outside, the Apex sports the sort of stylish, spacious, sofa-equipped rooms that make you want to lounge around all evening munching chocolate in front of the TV. If you can drag yourself away from your room, there are spa treatments, saunas and Japanese hot tubs to enjoy.

🍴 Eating

★Bach CAFE £

(www.the-bach.com; 31 Meadowside; mains £6-13; ⊙9am-5pm; 🛜🌱) Easily the best breakfast spot in town (brunch is served all day till 4pm), this place sports a mix of Scottish, New Zealand, Asian and Mexican influences with delightful dishes such as Hebridean eggs (with Stornoway black pudding), homemade Kiwi burgers and bao buns (soft Chinese buns filled with pork belly or tempeh), plus the best flat white in town.

Parlour Cafe   CAFE **£**
(☑ 01382-203588; 58 West Port; mains £6-9; ⊙ 8am-6pm Mon-Sat, 10am-3pm Sun; 🛜🚳) 🖊
Tiny but terrific, this friendly neighbourhood cafe is bursting with good things to eat including filled tortillas, savoury tarts, Mediterranean-style meze and homemade soup, all freshly prepared using seasonal produce. Great coffee and cakes, too, but be prepared to wait for a table.

Bridgeview Station   SCOTTISH **£**
(☑ 01382-660066; www.bridgeviewstation.com; Riverside Dr; lunch mains £10-15; ⊙ 8am-6pm Sun-Tue, 8am-10pm Wed-Sat; 🅿🚺) Bridgeview enjoys a lovely setting in a redbrick Victorian railway station building on the western fringes of Dundee, with a view across the Firth of Tay. Covering everything from breakfast to dinner, the menu majors on fresh local produce with the lunch platters (fish, vegetarian, or cheese and ploughman's) offering unbeatable value.

Agacán   TURKISH **££**
(☑ 01382-644227; https://agacan.co.uk; 113 Perth Rd; mains £11-19; ⊙ 5-9.30pm Tue-Sun; 🚺) With a charismatic owner, quirky decor and wonderfully aromatic Turkish specialities (İskender kebab is a favourite), it's no wonder that you have to book ahead at this colourful little restaurant, a 20-minute walk up Perth Rd from the centre. If you can't get a table, you can settle for takeaway.

Jute Café Bar   BISTRO **££**
(☑ 01382-909246; www.jutecafebar.co.uk; 152 Nethergate; mains £10-25; ⊙ food served noon-9pm; 🛜🚺) The industrial-chic cafe-bar in the Dundee Contemporary Arts centre serves excellent deli sandwiches and burgers, as well as more adventurous Mediterranean-Asian fusion cuisine. Tables spill out into the sunny courtyard in summer.

🍺 Drinking & Nightlife

Speedwell Bar   PUB
(www.facebook.com/thespeedwellbar; 165-167 Perth Rd; ⊙ 11am-midnight Mon-Sat, 12.30pm-midnight Sun; 🛜) Known to generations of Dundonians as 'Mennie's' (Mrs Mennie was a former barkeeper), this university district pub, 1.5 miles west of the city centre, is the city's best preserved Edwardian bar, com-

---

WORTH A TRIP

NEWPORT RESTAURANT

At the **Newport** (☑ 01382-541449; www.thenewportrestaurant.co.uk; 1 High St, Newport-on-Tay; 3-course lunch £32.50, tasting menu £65; ⊙ noon-2.30pm Thu-Sat, noon-3pm Sun, 6-9.30pm Wed-Sat; 🅿🚳) the setting is fabulous, with vast windows overlooking the Firth of Tay, and quirky 'recycled' decor that includes the clever use of an old piano to store cutlery and wine glasses. Linger over a lunch that showcases the best of local produce, or opt for the seven-course tasting menu; it has vegetarian and pescatarian options.

The restaurant is across the water from Dundee, a short drive (or just a 30-minute walk) away over the Tay Road Bridge.

---

plete with acres of polished mahogany, real ale on tap and a choice of 150 malt whiskies.

Braes   BAR
(☑ 01382-226344; www.braesdundee.co.uk; 14-18 Perth Rd; ⊙ 11am-midnight Sun-Thu, 11am-1am Fri & Sat; 🛜🚺🍽) Students from the nearby university crowd the tables at this modern bar with its cute, Scandinavian-style decor (lots of colourfully painted wood panelling) and views across the rooftops to the Tay Bridge. A good range of craft beers and coffee are complemented by a decent choice of pub grub (mains £8 to £15, good vegetarian options).

Empire State Coffee   COFFEE
(www.facebook.com/ESCartisanroasters; 28 Whitehall Cres; ⊙ 7.30am-6pm Mon-Sat, 9am-5pm Sun; 🛜) Get your morning caffeine hit at this small artisan roastery – if the street-level cafe looks full up, head to the back and down the stairs where you'll find a nifty basement lounge decorated to look like a railway carriage. Good hot chocolate too.

☆ Entertainment

Dundee Rep Theatre   THEATRE
(☑ 01382-223530; www.dundeerep.co.uk; Tay Sq.; ⊙ box office 9.30am-6pm Mon-Sat) Dundee's main venue for the performing arts, the Rep is home to Scotland's only full-time repertory company and to the Scottish Dance Theatre.

ℹ REGIONAL BUS PASSES

Stagecoach (www.stagecoachbus.com) offers a **Moray Coast Megarider ticket** (£39.50) that gives seven days unlimited bus travel around Elgin as far as Dufftown, Portsoy and Banff, and an **Aberdeen Zone 6 Megarider ticket** (£48.50) that allows seven days of unlimited travel on all its services in Aberdeenshire, as far as Braemar Strathdon and Banff.

ℹ Information

Dundee Tourist Office (☑ 01382-527527; www.angusanddundee.co.uk; 16 City Sq; ⊙ 10am-4pm Mon-Sat)

Ninewells Hospital (☑ 01382-660111; www.nhstayside.scot.nhs.uk) At Menzieshill, west of the city centre.

Post Office (30 Whitehall St; ⊙ 8.30am-6pm Mon-Fri, 9am-5.30pm Sat)

ℹ Getting There & Away

AIR

Located 2.5 miles west of the city centre, **Dundee Airport** (www.hial.co.uk/dundee-airport) has scheduled flights to London City (daily except Saturday) and Belfast City (twice weekly). A taxi from the city centre to the airport takes 10 minutes and costs around £6.

BUS

The bus station is northeast of the city centre. Some Aberdeen buses travel via Arbroath, others via Forfar.

Aberdeen £19.40, 1½ hours, hourly

Edinburgh £18.60, 1½ hours, hourly, some change at Perth

Glasgow £18.60, 1¾ hours, hourly

London (Megabus) £45, 11 to 12 hours, daily

Oban £44, 5½ hours, three daily, change at Glasgow

Perth £8.70, 35 minutes, hourly

TRAIN

Trains from Dundee to Aberdeen travel via Arbroath and Stonehaven.

Aberdeen £22, 1¼ hours, twice hourly

Edinburgh £20, 1¼ hours, at least hourly

Glasgow £20, 1½ hours, hourly

Perth £8.80, 20 minutes, hourly

ℹ Getting Around

The city centre is compact and easy to get around on foot. For information on local bus services, check **Xplore Dundee** (https://nxbus.co.uk/dundee).

BUS

City bus fares cost £1.80 to £2.30 depending on distance; buy your ticket from the driver (exact fare only – no change given).

CAR

Rental agencies include **Arnold Clark** (☑ 01382-225382; www.arnoldclarkrental.com; East Dock St, DD1 3HB; ⊙ 8am-6pm Mon-Sat, 9am-4pm Sun).

TAXI

Tele Taxis (☑ 01382-825825; https://teletaxisdundee.com)

Broughty Ferry

Dundee's attractive seaside suburb, known locally as 'the Ferry', lies 4 miles east of the city centre. It has a castle, a long, sandy beach and a number of good places to eat and drink. It's also handy for the golf courses at nearby **Carnoustie** (☑ 01241-802270; www.carnoustiegolflinks.co.uk; 20 Links Pde, Carnoustie, Angus; green fees £54-252).

Broughty Ferry is a more attractive place to stay than central Dundee, and has a good choice of B&Bs and hotels. There are campsites too, a few miles further east at Monifieth.

Ashley House　　　　B&B **££**

(☑ 01382-776109; www.ashleyhousebroughtyferry.com; 15 Monifieth Rd; s/d/f from £60/80/75; 🅿 🛜 🐾) This spacious and comfortable guesthouse has long been one of Broughty Ferry's best. Its five cheerfully decorated bedrooms come equipped with hotel-grade beds and DVD players; one has a particularly grand bathroom.

Fisherman's Tavern　　　　B&B **££**

(☑ 01382-775941; www.fishermanstavern-broughtyferry.co.uk; 10-16 Fort St; r from £86; 🛜) A delightful 17th-century terraced cottage just a few paces from the seafront, the Fisherman's was converted into a pub in 1827. It now has 12 stylishly modern rooms, most with en suite, and an atmospheric pub.

Ship Inn　　　　PUB FOOD **££**

(☑ 01382-779176; www.theshipinn-broughtyferry.co.uk; 121 Fisher St; mains £10-20; ⊙ food served noon-2.30pm & 5-9.30pm) This snug, wood-panelled, 19th-century pub on the waterfront serves top-notch dishes ranging from gourmet haddock and chips to venison steaks; you can eat in the upstairs restaurant, or down in the bar (bar meals £9 to £13). It's always busy, so get there early to grab a seat.

★**Tayberry**   MODERN SCOTTISH £££
(☑ 01382-698280; www.tayberryrestaurant.com; cnr Brook St & Esplanade; mains £25, 3-course lunch £27; ☺ noon-2pm & 6-9pm Tue-Sat) 🥢 Neutral decor enriched with splashes of berry purple create an understated atmosphere in which accomplished chef Adam Newth presents gorgeous and colourful confections using fresh and foraged local produce. Dishes such as smoked haddock beignet with mussels, creamed leek and Parmesan, or roast duck with beetroot, date purée, chicory and Earl Grey jus, delight the eye as much as the palate.

ⓘ Getting There & Away

Dundee city bus 5 and Stagecoach bus 73 run from Dundee High St to Broughty Ferry (£2.30, 20 minutes) several times an hour from Monday to Saturday, and hourly on Sunday.

There are eight to 10 trains daily from Dundee (£1.60, five to 10 minutes).

Arbroath

POP 23,900

Arbroath is an old-fashioned seaside resort and fishing harbour, home of the famous Arbroath smokie (a form of smoked haddock). The humble smokie achieved European Union 'Protected Geographical Indication' status in 2004 – the term 'Arbroath smokie' can only be used legally to describe haddock smoked in the traditional manner within an 8km radius of Arbroath.

⊙ Sights

Arbroath Abbey   HISTORIC BUILDING
(HES; www.historicenvironment.scot; Abbey St; adult/child £6/3.60; ☺ 9.30am-5.30pm Apr-Sep, 10am-4pm Oct-Mar) The picturesque, red-sandstone ruins of Arbroath Abbey, founded in 1178 by King William the Lion, dominate the town of Arbroath. It is thought that Bernard of Linton, the abbot here in the early 14th century, wrote the famous Declaration of Arbroath in 1320, asserting Scotland's right to independence; a new visitor centre, originally scheduled to open in 2020 to mark the 700th anniversary of the Declaration, will now open in 2021.

You can climb part way up one of the towers for a grand view over the ruins.

St Vigeans Museum   MUSEUM
(HES; ☑ 01241-878756; www.historicenvironment. scot; St Vigeans Lane; adult/child £6/3.60) About a mile north of Arbroath town centre, this cottage museum houses a superb collection of Pictish and medieval sculptured stones. The museum's masterpiece is the **Drosten Stone**, beautifully carved with animal figures and hunting scenes on one side, and an interlaced Celtic cross on the other (look for the devil perched in the top left corner). Check the website for open days; otherwise phone ahead or ask at Arbroath Abbey to arrange a visit.

🏃 Activities

The coast northeast of Arbroath consists of dramatic red-sandstone cliffs riven by inlets, caves and natural arches. An excellent **clifftop walk** follows the coast for 3 miles to the quaint fishing village of **Auchmithie**, which claims to have invented the Arbroath smokie; you can try it at the village's But'n'Ben Restaurant (p220).

If you fancy catching your own fish, the **Mari Dawn** (☑ 01241-873957, 07775 645091; ianswankie@yahoo.co.uk), **MV Ardent** (☑ 07543 005908; www.arbroathangling.co.uk) and **Girl Katherine II** (☑ 07752 470621; http://fishingarbroath.co.uk) offer three-hour sea-angling trips (usually from 2pm to 5pm) out of Arbroath harbour for around £15 to £20 per person, including tackle and bait.

🛏 Sleeping & Eating

Harbour Nights Guest House   B&B ££
(☑ 01241-434343; www.harbournights.co.uk; 4 The Shore; s/d from £55/75; 🖥) With a superb location overlooking the harbour, four stylishly decorated bedrooms and a gourmet breakfast menu, Harbour Nights is our favourite place to stay in Arbroath. Rooms 2 and 3, with harbour views, are a bit more expensive (from £80), but well worth asking for when booking.

Townhouse Hotel   HOTEL ££
(☑ 01241-431577; www.townhousehotelarbroath. co.uk; 99 High St; r from £70; 🖥) The Townhouse, set in a restored Georgian-style building on Arbroath's main street, offers stylishly decorated if smallish rooms in a superb location just a few minutes' walk from Arbroath Abbey.

Smithie's Deli
CAFE £

(www.facebook.com/smithiesdeli1; 16 Keptie St; mains £5-8; ⊙9.30am-4.30pm Mon-Fri, 9.30am-4pm Sat; 🕏🖉) 🍴 Housed in a former butcher's shop, with hand-painted tiles and meat hooks on the ceiling, Smithie's is a great little neighbourhood deli and cafe serving fair-trade coffee, pancakes, wraps and an Italian charcuterie and cheese platter. Sadly, no espresso or breakfast menu.

But'n'Ben Restaurant
SCOTTISH ££

(⎚01241-877223; www.thebutnben.com; 1 Auchmithie; mains £9-29; ⊙noon-2pm Wed-Mon, 6-9pm Wed-Sat, 4-5.30pm Sun; 🅿🖼) 🍴 Above the harbour in Auchmithie, this cosy cottage restaurant with open fireplace, rustic furniture and sea-themed art serves the best of local seafood – the Arbroath-smokie pancakes are recommended – plus great homemade cakes and desserts, and high teas on Sunday (£19). It's best to book.

Old Brewhouse
SCOTTISH ££

(⎚01241-879945; www.oldbrewhousearbroath. co.uk; 1 High St; mains £10-15, steaks £23-30; ⊙noon-8.30pm Mon-Fri, noon-9pm Sat, 12.30-8.30pm Sun; 🕏) Located on the seafront east of the harbour, the Old Brewhouse has the scent of the North Sea in its nostrils, and also on its menu – choose from a Cullen skink, scampi, haddock and chips, or Arbroath smokie done half a dozen ways (speciality of the house is a smokie gratin, topped with breadcrumbs and Gruyere cheese).

ABERLEMNO PICTISH STONES

The mysterious **Aberlemno Stones** (⊙Apr-Sep) are among Scotland's finest Pictish carved stones. By the roadside there are three 7th- to 9th-century slabs with various symbols, including the z-rod and double disc; in the churchyard at the bottom of the hill there's a magnificent 8th-century stone displaying a Celtic cross, interlace decoration, entwined beasts and, on the reverse, scenes of the Battle of Nechtansmere (where the Picts vanquished the Northumbrians in 685).

The site is 5 miles northeast of Forfar, on the B9134.

The stones are covered up from October to March, otherwise there's free access at all times.

Also offers B&B from £100 for a double room.

Gordon's Restaurant
SCOTTISH £££

(⎚01241-830364; www.gordonsrestaurant.co.uk; Main St, Inverkeillor; 3-course lunch £39, 4-course dinner £69; ⊙12.30-1.30pm Sun, 7-8.30pm Tue-Sun, closed Sun dinner Oct-Apr) 🍴 Six miles north of Arbroath, in the tiny and unpromising-looking village of Inverkeillor, lies this intimate and rustic restaurant serving gourmet-quality Scottish cuisine. There are five comfortable **bedrooms** (double £110 to £165) for those who don't want to drive after dinner.

ⓘ Getting There & Away

Bus 140 runs from Arbroath to Auchmithie (£1.80, 15 minutes, six daily Monday to Friday, three daily on Saturday and Sunday).

Trains from Dundee to Arbroath (£6.30, 25 minutes, two per hour) continue to Aberdeen (£22, 55 minutes) via Montrose and Stonehaven.

Glamis Castle

Looking every inch the Scottish Baronial castle, with its roofline sprouting a forest of pointed turrets and battlements, **Glamis Castle** (www.glamis-castle.co.uk; adult/child £15.50/10; ⊙10am-5.30pm Apr-Oct, last entry 4.30pm; 🅿🖼) claims to be the legendary setting for Shakespeare's *Macbeth*. A royal residence since 1372, it is the family home of the earls of Strathmore and Kinghorne – the Queen Mother (born Elizabeth Bowes-Lyon, 1900–2002) spent her childhood at Glamis (pronounced 'glams') and Princess Margaret (the Queen's sister, 1930–2002) was born here.

The five-storey, L-shaped castle was given to the Lyon family in 1372, but was significantly altered in the 17th century. Inside, the most impressive room is the **drawing room**, with its vaulted plasterwork ceiling. There's a display of armour and weaponry in the haunted crypt and frescoes in the chapel (also haunted). **Duncan's Hall** is named for the murdered King Duncan from *Macbeth* (though the scene actually takes place in Macbeth's castle in Inverness). As with Cawdor Castle, the claimed Shakespeare connection is fictitious – the real Macbeth had nothing to do with either castle, and died long before either was built.

You can also look around the **royal apartments**, including the Queen Mother's bedroom. Hour-long guided tours (included in admission) depart every 15 minutes; the last tour is at 4.30pm.

Glamis Castle is 12 miles north of Dundee, on the way to Kirriemuir.

Kirriemuir

POP 6100

Known as the Wee Red Town because of its close-packed, red-sandstone houses, Kirriemuir is famed as the birthplace of JM Barrie (1860–1937), writer and creator of the much-loved *Peter Pan*. A bronze statue of the 'boy who wouldn't grow up' graces the intersection of Bank and High Sts.

Tourist information is available in the Gateway to the Glens Museum (p320).

JM Barrie's Birthplace MUSEUM
(NTS; www.nts.org.uk; 9 Brechin Rd; adult/child £6.50/5.50; ⏰11am-4pm Thu-Mon Jul & Aug, Sat & Sun Apr-Jun & Sep) This is Kirriemuir's big attraction, a place of pilgrimage for *Peter Pan* fans from all over the world. The two-storey house where Barrie was born has been furnished in period style, and preserves his writing desk and the wash house at the back that served as his first 'theatre'.

Camera Obscura HISTORIC BUILDING
(www.kirriemuircameraobscura.com; by donation; ⏰11am-4pm Sat-Mon Apr-Sep) Kirriemuir Hill, northeast of the town centre, enjoys grand views towards the Angus Glens. The 1930s cricket pavilion here was gifted to the town by famous son JM Barrie, and is now managed by local volunteers. The camera obscura incorporated into its pointed turret uses a lens to project live images of the surrounding countryside on to a viewing table, and is one of only four in Scotland. Barrie is buried in the nearby cemetery – follow the signs to visit his grave.

★88 Degrees CAFE, DELI £
(📞01575-570888; www.facebook.com/88kirriemuir; 17 High St; mains £4-8; ⏰10am-4pm Wed-Sat, 10am-3pm Sun; 🍴) 🌱 This tiny deli serves the best cafe cuisine in the county – superb coffee (the cafe is named for the ideal temperature of an espresso), delicious cakes and tray bakes, and handmade chocolates. Lunch (served from 11.30am) includes mac'n'cheese made with Manchego cheese and red peppers.

Star Rock Shop FOOD & DRINKS
(📞01575-572579; https://starrockshop.com; 25 Roods; ⏰10am-4pm Tue-Sat) For generations of local school kids, the big treat when visiting Kirriemuir was a trip to the Star Rock Shop. Established in 1833, it specialises in traditional Scottish 'sweeties', arranged in colourful jars along the walls – including humbugs, cola cubes, pear drops and the original Star Rock candy, still made to an 1833 recipe.

❶ Getting There & Away

Stagecoach bus 20 runs from Dundee to Kirriemuir (£4.70, one hour, hourly Monday to Saturday, every two hours Sunday) via Forfar (25 minutes, change here for Glamis).

Edzell

POP 900

The picturesque village of Edzell, with its broad main street and grandiose **monumental arch**, dates from the early 19th century when Lord Panmure decided that the original medieval village, a mile to the west, spoiled the view from Edzell Castle. The old village was razed and the villagers moved to this pretty, planned settlement.

Two miles north of Edzell, the B966 to Fettercairn crosses the River North Esk at Gannochy Bridge. From the lay-by just over the bridge, a wooden door in the stone wall gives access to a delightful footpath that leads along the wooded river gorge for 1.5 miles to a picturesque spot known as the **Rocks of Solitude**.

Edzell Castle CASTLE
(HES; www.historicenvironment.scot; adult/child £6/3.60; ⏰9.30am-5.30pm Apr-Sep; 🅿) The Lindsay earls of Crawford, Lord Panmure's predecessors as owners of Edzell Castle, built the L-plan tower house in the 16th century. Sir David Lindsay, a cultured and well-travelled man, laid out this castle's beautiful **pleasance** in 1604 as a place of contemplation and learning. Unique in all of Scotland, this Renaissance walled garden is lined with niches for nesting birds, and sculptured plaques illustrating the cardinal virtues, the arts and the planetary deities.

Glenesk Hotel SLEEPING ££
(📞01356-647333; www.gleneskhotel.com; High St; s/d from £80/100; 🅿🛜) The Glenesk is a grand old country-house hotel with a solidly traditional atmosphere. The bedrooms range

from no-surprises standard to four-poster luxury (from £160), while the bar reflects the twin passions of the owner – commercial aviation (aircraft portraits on the walls) and malt whisky (one of Scotland's largest collections, with more than 1000 varieties).

ℹ Getting There & Away

Stagecoach buses 21 and 21A from Dundee (via Forfar and Brechin) stop at Edzell (£6.20, 1½ hours, seven daily Monday to Friday, five on Saturday).

ABERDEENSHIRE

Since medieval times Aberdeenshire and its northwestern neighbour Moray have been the richest and most fertile regions of the Highlands. Aberdeenshire is famed for its Aberdeen Angus beef cattle, its many fine castles and the prosperous 'granite city' of Aberdeen.

North of Aberdeen, the Grampian Mountains fall away to rolling agricultural plains pocked with small, craggy volcanic hills. This fertile Lowland corner of northeastern Scotland is known as Buchan; the old Scots dialect, the Doric, is in everyday use here (if you think the Glaswegian accent is difficult to understand, just try listening in on a conversation in Fraserburgh).

The Buchan coast alternates between rugged cliffs and long, long stretches of sand, dotted with picturesque little fishing villages such as Pennan, where parts of the film *Local Hero* were shot.

Aberdeen

POP 195,000

Aberdeen is northeast Scotland's powerhouse, fuelled by the North Sea petroleum industry. Oil money made the city as expensive as London, with prices charged to match the depth of oil-wealthy pockets, though regular downturns in the industry see prices fall. Happily, most cultural attractions, such as the Maritime Museum and Aberdeen Art Gallery, are free.

Known throughout Scotland as the 'granite city', much of the town was built using silvery-grey granite hewn from the now-abandoned Rubislaw Quarry, at one time the biggest artificial hole in the ground in Europe. On a sunny day the granite lends an attractive glitter to the city, but when low,

grey rain clouds scud in off the North Sea it can be hard to tell where the buildings stop and the sky begins.

Royal Deeside is easily accessible to the west, Dunnottar Castle to the south, sandy beaches to the north and whisky country northwest.

◉ Sights & Activities

◉ City Centre

Union St is the city's main thoroughfare, lined with solid, Victorian granite buildings. The oldest area is Castlegate, at the eastern end, where the castle once stood. When it was captured from the English for Robert the Bruce, the password used by the townspeople was 'Bon Accord' (good fellowship), which is now the city's motto.

In the centre of Castle St stands the 17th-century **Mercat Cross** (Castle St, AB11 5HP), bearing a sculpted frieze of portraits of Stuart monarchs. The Baronial heap towering over the eastern end of Castle St is the **Salvation Army Citadel** (www.salvationarmy. org.uk/aberdeen-citadel; Castle St), which was modelled on Balmoral Castle.

On the northern side of Union St, 200m west of Castlegate, is 17th-century **Provost Skene's House** (☑01224-641086; www.aagm. co.uk; Guestrow) FREE, one of the city's oldest buildings (reopened in 2021 after redevelopment). Another 100m to the west is **St Nicholas Church** (Back Wynd), the so-called 'Mither Kirk' (Mother Church) of Aberdeen. The granite spire dates from the 19th century, but there has been a church on this site since the 12th century; the early-15th-century **St Mary's Chapel** survives in the eastern part of the church.

★ **Aberdeen Art Gallery**   GALLERY
(☑01224-523700; www.aagm.co.uk; Schoolhill; ⊙10am-5pm Tue-Sat, 2-5pm Sun) FREE Fresh from a major refurbishment, Aberdeen's art gallery eschews the traditional arrangement of its collections by historical period in favour of themes. For example, Gallery 10 (French Impressions) compares and contrasts the works of French Impressionists with contemporary Scottish artists who were inspired by them – William McTaggart, Samuel Peploe, Francis Cadell – while Gallery 16 (Shoreline) looks at the influence of Scotland's coast on landscape artists such as Joan Eardley.

Other highlights include the wide-ranging works of larger-than-life Aberdeenshire artist-adventurer James McBey (1883–1959), and *Gallowgate Lard,* a chilling, ghostly self-portrait by Glaswegian painter Ken Currie (born 1960).

★ **Aberdeen Maritime Museum**   MUSEUM
(☑01224-337700; www.aagm.co.uk;   Shiprow; ⊙10am-5pm Mon-Sat, noon-3pm Sun) FREE
Overlooking the nautical bustle of Aberdeen harbour is the Maritime Museum, centred on a three-storey replica of a North Sea oil-production platform, which explains all you ever wanted to know about the petroleum industry. Other galleries, some situated in **Provost Ross's House**, the oldest building in the city and part of the museum, cover the shipbuilding, whaling and fishing industries.

Sleek and speedy **Aberdeen clippers** were a 19th-century shipyard speciality, used by British merchants to import tea, wool and exotic goods (opium, for instance) to Britain, and, on the return journey, transport emigrants to Australia.

Gordon Highlanders Museum   MUSEUM
(www.gordonhighlanders.com;   St Lukes, Viewfield Rd;   adult/child £8/4.50; ⊙10am-4.30pm Tue-Sat Feb-Nov; P⊞) This excellent museum records the history of one of the British Army's most famous fighting units, described by Winston Churchill as 'the finest regiment in the world'. Originally raised in the northeast of Scotland by the 4th Duke of Gordon in 1794, the regiment was amalgamated with the Seaforths and Camerons to form the Highlanders regiment in 1994. The museum is about a mile west of the western end of Union St – take bus 11 or X17 from Union St.

Marischal College   HISTORIC BUILDING
(Broad St, AB10 1AB) Marischal College, founded in 1593 by the 5th Earl Marischal, merged with King's College (founded 1495) in 1860 to create the modern University of Aberdeen. The college's huge and impressive facade overlooking Broad St, in perpendicular Gothic style – unusual in having such elaborate masonry hewn from notoriously hard-to-work granite – dates from 1906 and is the world's second-largest granite structure (after El Escorial near Madrid).

A renovation project saw the facade returned to its original silvery-grey glory, and the building now houses Aberdeen City Council's headquarters. Outside, Marischal

POTARCH'S DINNIE STONES

Granite boulders **Dinnie Stones** (www.thedinniestones.com; Potarch,), named after Donald Dinnie (1837–1916), a famous Aberdeenshire athlete and strongman, weigh 733lb (335.5kg) in total. Dinnie famously carried them (one in each hand) across Potarch Bridge in 1860, a feat of strength that went unrepeated until the 1970s. The current record for lifting and holding the stones sits at 41 seconds, set in 2019. The stones sit outside Potarch Lodge, 10 miles west of Crathes Castle.

There are pleasant forest and riverside walks nearby, and a good cafe (☑01339-884468; www.ballogie-estate.co.uk; Potarch Lodge; mains £10-20; ⊙10am-4pm Sun-Thu, 10am-10pm Fri & Sat; P⊛⊞) too.

Sq has been redeveloped as a pedestrian plaza, its modern architecture controversially juxtaposed with the college's neo-Gothic facade.

◉ Aberdeen Beach

Just 800m east of Castlegate is a spectacular 2-mile sweep of clean, golden sand stretching between the mouths of the Rivers Dee and Don. At one time Aberdeen Beach was a good, old-fashioned British seaside resort, but the availability of cheap package holidays has lured Scottish holidaymakers from its somewhat chilly delights. On a warm summer's day, though, it's still an excellent beach; when the waves are right, a small group of dedicated **surfers** ride the breaks at the south end.

Bus 15 (eastbound) from Union St goes to the beach, or you can walk from Castlegate in 10 minutes.

◉ Old Aberdeen

Just over a mile north of the city centre is the district called Old Aberdeen. The name is misleading – although Old Aberdeen is certainly old, the area around Castlegate in the city centre is older still. This part of the city was originally called Aulton, from the Gaelic for 'village by the stream', and this was Anglicised in the 17th century to Old Town.

Aberdeen

Bus 20 from Littlejohn St (just north of Marischal College) runs to Old Aberdeen every 15 to 20 minutes.

St Machar's Cathedral CATHEDRAL
(www.stmachar.com; The Chanonry; ⊙9.30am-4.30pm) FREE The 15th-century St Machar's, with its massive twin towers, is a rare example of a fortified cathedral. According to legend, St Machar was ordered to establish a church where the river takes the shape of a bishop's crook, which it does just here. The cathedral is best known for its impressive **heraldic ceiling**, dating from 1520, which has 48 shields of kings, nobles, archbishops and bishops. Sunday services are held at 11am and 6pm.

🎪 Festivals & Events

True North MUSIC
(www.aberdeenperformingarts.com/truenorth; ⊙Sep) Held over the last weekend in September, this four-day festival celebrates the balladeer tradition of northeast Scotland with a program devoted to singer-songwriters from Scotland and all around the world.

Sound Festival MUSIC
(http://sound-scotland.co.uk; ⊙Oct-Nov) Festival dedicated to new music – classical, elec-

um, and rates tend to be significantly lower at weekends.

★ Globe Inn
B&B ££

(☏ 01224-641171; www.the-globe-inn.com; 13-15 North Silver St; r from £63; 🛜) This popular pub has seven appealing, comfortable guest bedrooms upstairs, simply but tastefully decorated. There's live music in the pub on weekends so it's not a place for early-to-bed types, but the price versus location factor can't be beaten. There's no dining room, so breakfast is continental, served on a tray in your room. It's cheaper at weekends.

★ Dutch Mill Hotel
HOTEL ££

(☏ 01224-322555; www.dutchmill.co.uk; 7 Queen's Rd, ; s £65-85, d £75-95; 🅿🛜) The grand, granite-hewn, Victorian-era mansions that line Queen's Rd house financial offices, private schools, medical practices and the occasional hotel – this one has nine bedrooms with beautifully understated modern decor, a popular bar and a conservatory restaurant. Rates are cheaper at weekends.

tro-acoustic, improvised, experimental and jazz – performed at a range of venues large and small across Aberdeen and northeast Scotland, held over 10 days in late October/early November.

⬛ Sleeping

There are clusters of B&Bs on Bon Accord St and Springbank Tce (both 400m southwest of the train station) and along Great Western Rd (the A93, a 25-minute walk southwest of the city centre). With so many oil-industry workers staying the night before flying offshore, single rooms are at a premi-

NORTHEAST SCOTLAND ABERDEEN

Jays
B&B ££

(☎ 01224-638295; www.jaysguesthouse.co.uk; 422 King St; s/d from £70/100; ☺ Mon-Thu; P ☎) Located halfway between the city centre (a 15-minute walk) and Old Aberdeen (a 10-minute walk), this elegantly decorated Edwardian villa is a cosy nest of hospitality, with welcoming owners who seemingly can't do enough to help their guests enjoy their stay. It's popular, so book well in advance (note – open Monday to Thursday nights only).

Jurys Inn
HOTEL ££

(☎ 01224-381200; www.jurysinns.com; Union Sq, Guild St; r from £109; ☎) Conveniently located between the train and bus stations, this business-oriented hotel has stylish, spacious rooms with plenty of space for unpacking suitcases.

✕ Eating

Bonobo Cafe
VEGAN £

(www.facebook.com//bonoboaberdeen; 73-75 Skene St; mains £5-8; ☺ 8am-4pm Tue-Fri, 9am-5pm Sat, 10am-4pm Sun; ☑☎) ✦ Aberdeen has lagged behind a bit in the vegetarian-restaurant stakes, so it was good to see this 100% vegan cafe open in 2017. The menu runs from breakfast (served till noon, and all day on Sunday), of avocado on toast or smoked carrot and cream-cheese bagel, to lunch dishes, such as seitan 'chicken' kebabs.

★ Braided Fig
INTERNATIONAL ££

(☎ 01224-620333; www.thebraidedfig.co.uk; 39 Summer St; mains £13-18; ☺ food served noon-9pm Mon-Sat, 12.30-8pm Sun; ☎) ✦ An actual fig tree, draped in fairy lights, forms the focal point of this delightfully intimate and informal restaurant, its understated decor enlivened with shades of blackberry and avocado. The menu takes local produce and leads it on a journey around the globe, pairing crab cakes with chorizo, roast chicken with satay sauce, and langoustine scampi-style with *petit pois à la française*.

★ Café 52
BISTRO ££

(☎ 01224-590094; www.cafe52.co.uk; 52 The Green; mains lunch £7, dinner £12; ☺ noon-midnight Wed-Sat, 6pm-midnight Tue; ☎☑☎) This little haven of laid-back industrial chic – a high, narrow space lined with bare stonework, rough plaster and exposed ventilation ducts – serves some of the finest and best-value cuisine in the northeast (slow-cooked beef casserole with roasted root veggies, red wine and garlic), and at incredible prices considering the quality on offer.

★ Silver Darling
SEAFOOD ££

(☎ 01224-576229; www.thesilverdarling.co.uk; Pocra Quay, North Pier; mains £15-23, steaks £30-36; ☺ noon-2pm & 5.30-9.30pm Mon-Fri, noon-9.30pm Sat, noon-8pm Sun; ☒) ✦ The Silver Darling (an old Scottish nickname for herring) is the place for a special meal, housed in a former Customs office at the entrance to Aberdeen harbour with picture windows overlooking the sea. Here you can enjoy fresh Scottish seafood while you watch the porpoises playing in the harbour mouth. Bookings are recommended.

Sand Dollar Café
CAFE ££

(☎ 01224-572288; www.sanddollarcafe.com; 2 Beach Esplanade; mains £8-16; ☺ 9am-4pm Wed-Fri, 8.30am-4pm Sat & Sun; ☒) A cut above your usual seaside cafe – on sunny days you can sit at the wooden tables on the prom and share a bottle of chilled white wine, or choose from a menu that includes pancakes with maple syrup, homemade burgers and chocolate brownies with Orkney ice cream.

On the esplanade, 800m northeast of the city centre.

Moonfish Café
MODERN SCOTTISH £££

(☎ 01224-644166; www.moonfishcafe.co.uk; 9 Correction Wynd; 2-/3-course dinner £30/36; ☺ noon-2pm & 6-9.30pm Tue-Sat) ✦ The menu of this little place hidden on a backstreet concentrates on good-quality Scottish produce but draws its influences from cuisines all around the world, from butter-roasted hake with crab bisque, tomato and olives, to lamb neck fillet with potato gnocchi and pickled mushrooms. Two-course lunches are £17.

🍷 Drinking & Nightlife

Aberdeen is a great city for a pub crawl – it's more a question of knowing when to stop than where to start. There are lots of pre-club bars in and around Belmont St and Langstane Pl, with more traditional pubs scattered throughout the city centre.

★ Orchid
COCKTAIL BAR

(www.orchidaberdeen.com; 51 Langstane Pl; ☺ 6pm-2am Sun-Thu, 5pm-3am Fri, 6pm-3am Sat) This relaxed and welcoming spot is quietly confident in its wide-ranging knowledge and expertise – two of its bartenders were nominated in the UK Top 100 in 2020. It offers regular gin- and whisky-tasting sessions as well as mixology classes – the house cocktail is the Pink Orchid (vanilla vodka, black raspberry liqueur, cranberry and lime).

Globe Inn PUB
(www.the-globe-inn.com; 13-15 North Silver St; ⊙11am-midnight Sun-Thu, 11am-1am Fri & Sat) This lovely Edwardian-style pub with wood panelling, marble-topped tables and walls decorated with old musical instruments is a great place for a quiet afternoon drink. It serves good coffee, as well as real ales and malt whiskies, and has live music Friday and Saturday. It also has probably the poshest pub toilets in the country.

BrewDog BAR
(www.brewdog.com/bars/aberdeen; 17 Gallowgate; ⊙noon-midnight Mon-Thu, to 1am Fri & Sat, 12.30pm-midnight Sun; 🛜🐕) The original flagship bar of northeast Scotland's most innovative craft brewery brings a bit of industrial chic to Aberdeen's pub scene along with a vast range of guest beers from around the world.

Grape & Grain WINE BAR
(📞01224-633761; www.grapeandgrain.wine; 31 Thistle St; ⊙4-11pm Mon-Thu, noon-11pm Fri & Sat, noon-8pm Sun) The decadent decor of deep-blue-green panelling, designer copper light fittings and mirrored walls will entice you to linger in this classy wine bar – there are even wireless phone chargers built into the tabletops. The cellar is stocked with a wide but carefully curated selection of wines, plus craft beers and gins. It also serves tempting platters of Scottish cheeses.

Blue Lamp PUB
(www.jazzatthebluelamp.com; 121 Gallowgate; ⊙11am-midnight Mon-Thu, 11am-1am Fri & Sat, 12.30-11pm Sun) A long-standing feature of the Aberdeen pub scene, the Blue Lamp is a favourite student hang-out – a cosy drinking den with good beer and *craic* (lively conversation) and Sunday afternoon sessions of live jazz (admission £5). The pub is 150m north of the city centre, along Broad St.

☆ Entertainment

Belmont Filmhouse CINEMA
(www.belmontfilmhouse.com; 49 Belmont St; tickets £11; 🛜) A great little art-house cinema, with a lively program of cult classics, director's seasons, foreign films and mainstream movies.

WORTH A TRIP

PICTURESQUE PENNAN

Pennan is a picturesque harbour village tucked beneath red-sandstone cliffs, 12 miles west of Fraserburgh. It featured in the 1983 film *Local Hero*, and fans of the film still come to make a call from the red telephone box that played a prominent part in the plot (the box in the film was just a prop, and it was only later that film buffs and locals successfully campaigned for a real one to be installed).

The interior of the village hotel, the Pennan Inn, also appeared in the film, though one of the houses further along the seafront to the east doubled for the exterior of the fictional hotel. The beach scenes were filmed on the other side of the country, at **Camusdarach Beach** (🅿) in Arisaig.

His Majesty's Theatre BALLET, OPERA
(www.aberdeenperformingarts.com; Rosemount Viaduct) The main theatre in Aberdeen hosts everything from ballet and opera to pantomimes and musicals.

Lemon Tree Theatre PERFORMING ARTS
(www.aberdeenperformingarts.com; 5 West North St) Hosts an interesting program of dance, music and drama, and often has live rock, jazz and folk bands playing. There are also children's shows, ranging from comedy to drama to puppetry.

Tunnels LIVE MUSIC
(www.facebook.com/tunnelsaberdeen; Carnegie's Brae) This cavernous, subterranean club – the entrance is in a road tunnel beneath Union St – is a great live-music venue, with a packed program of up-and-coming Scottish bands. It also hosts regular DJ nights – check its Facebook page for the latest events.

Cafe Drummond LIVE MUSIC
(www.facebook.com/drummondsab10; 1 Belmont St) A long-established stalwart of Aberdeen's alternative music scene, Drummond's is a crowded, grungy student hang-out offering live gigs from up-and-coming local talent, and regular club nights extending into the wee hours.

ℹ Information

Aberdeen Royal Infirmary (📞0345 456 6000; www.nhsgrampian.org; Foresterhill) Medical services. About a mile northwest of the western end of Union St.

Aberdeen Tourist Office (☎ 01224-269180; www.aberdeen-grampian.com; 23 Union St; ⊙ 9am-6.30pm Mon-Sat, 10am-4pm Sun Jul & Aug, 10am-4pm Mon-Sat Sep-Jun; ☎)

Books & Beans (www.booksandbeans.co.uk; 22 Belmont St; per 15min £1; ⊙ 10am-4pm Mon-Sat, 10am-3pm Sun; ☎) Internet access; also fair-trade coffee and secondhand books.

Main Post Office (St Nicholas Shopping Centre, Upperkirkgate; ⊙ 9am-5.30pm Mon-Sat, noon-4pm Sun)

ℹ Getting There & Away

AIR

Aberdeen Airport (☎ 0344 481 6666; www.aberdeenairport.com) is at Dyce, 6 miles northwest of the city centre. There are regular flights to numerous Scottish and UK destinations, including London, Belfast, Orkney and Shetland, and international flights to several European countries.

Stagecoach Jet bus 727 runs regularly from Aberdeen bus station to the airport (single £3.50, 35 minutes). A taxi from the airport to the city centre takes 25 minutes and costs around £15.

BOAT

Car ferries from Aberdeen to Orkney and Shetland are run by **Northlink Ferries** (www.northlinkferries.co.uk). The ferry terminal is a short walk east of the train and bus stations.

BUS

The **bus station** (Guild St) is next to Jurys Inn, close to the train station.

Braemar £12.45, 2¼ hours, every two hours, via Ballater and Balmoral

Dundee £19.40, 1½ hours, hourly

Edinburgh £35, three hours, three daily direct, more frequent changing at Perth

Glasgow £35, three hours, at least hourly

Inverness £13.85, four hours, hourly, via Huntly, Keith, Fochabers, Elgin and Nairn

London (Megabus) £45, 12 to 14 hours, twice daily

Perth £27, two hours, hourly

TRAIN

The train station is south of the city centre, next to the massive Union Square shopping centre.

Dundee £22, 1¼ hours, twice an hour

Edinburgh £37, 2½ hours, hourly

Glasgow £37, 2¾ hours, hourly

Inverness £32, 2¼ hours, eight daily

London King's Cross £180, seven to 11 hours, hourly, some direct, most change at Edinburgh

ℹ Getting Around

BUS

The main city bus operator is **First Aberdeen** (www.firstgroup.com/aberdeen). Local fares cost from £1.70 to £2.90; pay the driver as you board the bus. A FirstDay ticket (£4.40) allows unlimited travel from the time of purchase until midnight on all First Aberdeen buses. Information, route maps and tickets are available from the **First Travel Centre** (47 Union St; ⊙ 9am-5.30pm Mon-Fri, 9am-4.30pm Sat).

The most useful services for visitors are buses 15 and 19 from Union St to Great Western Rd (for B&Bs); bus 11 from Union St to Aberdeen SYHA and the airport; and bus 20 from Marischal College to Old Aberdeen.

CAR

Car-rental companies include the following.

Arnold Clark (☎ 01224-622714; www.arnoldclarkrental.com; Canal Rd; ⊙ 8am-6pm Mon-Fri, 8am-5pm Sat, 9am-4pm Sun)

Enterprise Car Hire (☎ 01224-894679; www.enterprise.co.uk; 80 Skene Sq; ⊙ 8am-5pm Mon-Fri, 9am-noon Sat)

The Aberdeen Western Peripheral Route (AWPR), a new road that allows motorists heading north to bypass the city centre, opened in 2019.

TAXI

The main city-centre taxi ranks are at the train station and on Back Wynd, off Union St. To order a taxi, phone **ComCab** (☎ 01224-353535; www.comcab-aberdeen.co.uk) or **Rainbow City Taxis** (☎ 01224-878787; www.rainbowcitytaxis.com).

Around Aberdeen

Crathes Castle   CASTLE

(NTS; ☎ 01330-844525; www.nts.org.uk; adult/child £14.50/11; ⊙ 10.30am-5pm daily Apr-Oct, 11am-4pm Sat & Sun Nov-Mar; P ♿) This atmospheric, 16th-century castle is famous for its Jacobean painted ceilings, magnificently carved canopied beds, and the 'Horn of Leys', reputedly presented to the Burnett family by Robert the Bruce in the 14th century. The beautiful formal gardens include 300-year-old yew hedges and colourful herbaceous borders. The castle is signposted off the A93; Stagecoach buses 201 and 202 from Aberdeen stop at the castle entrance (£5.45, 45 minutes, every 30 minutes).

Haddo House   HISTORIC BUILDING

(NTS; ☎ 0844 493 2179; www.nts.org.uk; adult/child £14.50/11; ⊙ tours noon-2pm Mon-Fri,

11.30am-3.30pm Sat & Sun Apr-Oct; P) Designed in Georgian style by William Adam in 1732, Haddo House is best described as a classic English stately home transplanted to Scotland. Home to the Gordon family, it has sumptuous Victorian interiors with wood-panelled walls, Persian-rug-scattered floors and a wealth of period antiques. The beautiful grounds are open all year (10am to dusk) – walk the Scots Mile avenue down to the lake. The house is accessed by guided tour only.

Haddo is 19 miles north of Aberdeen, near Ellon.

Buses run hourly Monday to Saturday from Aberdeen to Tarves/Methlick (£6.60, 50 minutes), stopping at the end of the Haddo House driveway; it's a 1 mile walk from bus stop to house.

Fyvie Castle CASTLE
(NTS; www.nts.org.uk; adult/child £14.50/11; ⊙11am-5pm daily Jun-Aug, Sat-Wed Apr, May, Sep & Oct; P) Though a magnificent example of Scottish Baronial architecture, this castle is probably more famous for its ghosts, including a phantom trumpeter and the mysterious Green Lady, and its art collection, which displays portraits by Thomas Gainsborough and Sir Henry Raeburn. The grounds are open all year (9am to dusk).

The castle is 25 miles north of Aberdeen on the A947 towards Turriff. A bus runs hourly from Aberdeen to Banff and Elgin via Fyvie village (£8.60, 1¼ hours), a mile from the castle.

Stonehaven

POP 11,430
Originally a small fishing village, Stonehaven has been the county town of Kincardineshire since 1600 and is now a thriving family-friendly seaside resort.

⊙ Sights & Activities

A boardwalk and footpath leads around the shoreline of the bay from the town centre to the picturesque cliff-bound **harbour**. Here you'll find a couple of appealing pubs and the town's oldest building, the **Tolbooth**, built about 1600 by the Earl Marischal. It now houses a small local history **museum** (www.stonehaventolbooth.co.uk; Old Quay; ⊙1.30-4.30pm Wed-Mon Apr-Sep) FREE and a restaurant.

Dunnottar Castle CASTLE
(☑01569-766320; www.dunnottarcastle.co.uk; adult/child £8/4; ⊙9am-5.30pm Apr-Sep, 10am-4.30pm or dusk Oct-Mar; P) A pleasant, 20-minute walk along the clifftops south of Stonehaven harbour leads to the spectacular ruins of Dunnottar Castle, spread out across a grassy promontory 50m above the sea. As dramatic a filmset as any director could wish for, it provided the backdrop for Franco Zeffirelli's *Hamlet* (1990), starring Mel Gibson. The original fortress was built in the 9th century; the keep is the most substantial remnant, but the drawing room (restored in 1926) is more interesting.

Open-Air Swimming Pool SWIMMING
(☑01569-762134; www.stonehavenopenairpool.co.; adult/child £5.70/3.55; ⊙10am-6pm Sat & Sun late May–early Sep, see website for weekday hours; ⊕) This Olympic-size (50m), heated, seawater pool was built in 1934 in art-deco style, and sits on the seafront to the north of Stonehaven town centre. It is also open for 'midnight swims' from 10pm to midnight Wednesdays from the end of June to mid-August.

SAND DUNES & SAND TRAPS

At the **Forvie National Nature Reserve** (www.nature.scot; P), coastal sand dunes extend north from Aberdeen for more than 14 miles, one of the largest areas of dunes in the UK, and the least affected by human activity. This reserve has wildlife hides and way-marked trails through the dunes to an abandoned medieval village where only the ruins of a church survive. The dunes form an important nesting and feeding area for birds – don't wander off the trails during the nesting season (April to August).

Donald Trump sparked a major controversy when he opened Trump International Golf Links in 2012, amid a 'protected' area of sand dunes at Menie, 4 miles south of Forvie. Planning permission for a second course was granted in 2020, further splitting the community between those who welcome the potential economic benefits, and conservationists worried about the environmental damage.

WORTH A TRIP

LIGHTHOUSE MUSEUM

The fascinating **Scottish Lighthouse Museum** (☎01346-511022; www.lighthousemuseum.org.uk; Kinnaird Head; adult/child £9/4; ⊙10am-5pm daily Apr-Oct, 10am-4.30pm Wed-Sun Nov-Mar; P ♿) provides an insight into the network of lights that have safeguarded the Scottish coast for over 100 years, and the men and women who built and maintained them. A guided tour takes you to the top of the old Kinnaird Head lighthouse, built on top of a converted 16th-century castle; the engineering is so precise that the 4.5-ton light assembly can be rotated by pushing with a single finger.

The anemometer here measured the strongest sea-level wind speed ever recorded in the UK, with a gust of 123 knots (142mph) on 13 February 1989.

✤ Festivals & Events

Fireball Ceremony   CULTURAL
(www.stonehavenfireballs.co.uk; ⊙31 Dec) Stonehaven's famous Fireball Ceremony takes place on Hogmanay, when people parade along High St at midnight swinging blazing fireballs around their heads before throwing them into the harbour.

Stonehaven Midsummer Beer Happening   BEER
(www.midsummerbeerhappening.co.uk; ⊙late Jun) Home to the Six Degrees North craft brewery and several excellent real ale pubs, Stonehaven makes a great setting for this convivial three-day celebration of artisan beers.

Stonehaven Folk Festival   MUSIC
(www.stonehavenfolkfestival.co.uk; ⊙mid-Jul) The town fills with musicians for this lively four-day folk festival.

🍴 Sleeping & Eating

★**24 Shorehead**   B&B ££
(☎01569-767750; www.twentyfourshorehead.co.uk; 24 Shorehead; s/d £80/90; 🛜) Location makes all the difference, and the location of this former cooperage offering peaceful and very stylish B&B accommodation can't be beaten – it's the last house at the end of the road, overlooking the harbour with lovely sea views. Using the binoculars provided, you can even spot seals from your bedroom.

Bayview B&B   B&B ££
(☎07791 224227; www.bayviewbandb.co.uk; Beachgate Lane; d £45-95; 🛜) The two bedrooms at this stylish B&B are characterised by bright modern decor and original artwork, but the big selling point is that the more expensive Beachfront room has floor-to-ceiling windows and a terrace with views over the bay. Continental breakfast only.

The views are even better at the luxurious two-bedroom apartments upstairs (£160 a night, up to four persons), bookable through Airbnb.

★**Creel Inn**   SEAFOOD ££
(☎01569-750254; www.thecreelinn.co.uk; Catterline; mains £13-20, lobster £30; ⊙noon-2pm & 6-9pm Mon-Fri, noon-9.30pm Sat, noon-8.30pm Sun; P ♿) ✔ Set in the tiny fishing village of Catterline, 5 miles south of Stonehaven, the Creel is a rustic pub with thick stone walls, low ceilings and open fireplaces. It's famous for its menu of locally caught fish and shellfish – the lobster and crab come from the bay below the village.

Marine Hotel   SEAFOOD ££
(☎01569-762155; www.marinehotelstonehaven.co.uk; 9-10 The Shore; mains £7-16; ⊙food served noon-2.30pm & 6-9pm Mon-Sat, noon-9pm Sun; ♿) Polished wood, brass taps, bare stone and muted colours give this popular harbourside pub, run by Stonehaven's own Six Degrees North craft brewery, a trad-meets-boutique look. There are half a dozen real ales on tap, and a menu that includes fresh seafood specials served both in the bar and in the upstairs restaurant.

★**Tolbooth Restaurant**   SEAFOOD £££
(☎01569-762287; www.tolbooth-restaurant.co.uk; Old Pier; mains £18-33; ⊙noon-3pm & 6-9.30pm Wed-Sat & noon-3pm Sun Oct-Apr, lunch & dinner Tue-Sun May-Sep) ✔ Set in the 17th-century Tolbooth building overlooking the harbour, and decorated with local art and crisp white linen, this is one of the best seafood restaurants in the region. Daily specials include dishes such as scallops with crispy pork belly and burnt apple sauce. From Wednesday to Saturday you can get a two-/three-course lunch for £20/24. Reservations recommended.

❶ Getting There & Away

Stonehaven is 15 miles south of Aberdeen and is served by frequent buses travelling between Aberdeen (£5.45, 45 minutes, hourly) and Dundee (£8.20, 1¾ hours).

Hourly trains to Dundee (£17, 55 minutes) and Aberdeen (£5.80, 20 minutes) are faster and offer a more scenic journey.

Strathdon

Strathdon – the valley of the River Don – is home to several of Aberdeenshire's finest castles, and stretches westward from Kintore, 13 miles northwest of Aberdeen, taking in the villages of Kemnay, Monymusk, Alford (*ah*-ford) and the tiny hamlet of Strathdon. The A944 parallels the lower valley; west of Alford, the A944, A97 and A939 follow the river's upper reaches.

The A939, known as the **Cockbridge–Tomintoul road** – a magnificent roller coaster of a route much loved by motorcyclists – runs from Strathdon across the Lecht pass (637m), where there's a small skiing area with lots of short easy and intermediate runs.

Grampian Transport Museum   MUSEUM
(🖉 01975-562292; www.gtm.org.uk; Montgarrie Rd, Alford; adult/child £11/4; ⊙10am-5pm Apr-Sep,10am-4pm Oct; 🅿 🖻) This museum houses a fascinating collection of vintage vehicles, including a Triumph Bonneville in excellent nick, a couple of Model T Fords (including one used by Drambuie), a Ferrari F40 and an Aston Martin V8 Mk II. More unusual exhibits include a 19th-century horse-drawn sleigh from Russia, a 1942 Mack snowplough and a steam-powered tricycle built in 1895 by a local postman.

The museum's centrepiece is TV presenter Guy Martin's collection, which includes a Rolls Royce Merlin engine (from a WWII Spitfire fighter aircraft) and the pedal cycle on which he set the British cycle speed record of 112mph (drafting behind a racing truck) in 2014.

Castle Fraser   CASTLE
(NTS; www.nts.org.uk; adult/child £14.50/11; ⊙10am-4pm daily Jul & Aug, Wed-Sun Apr-Jun, Sep & Oct; 🅿) This impressive 16th- to 17th-century castle, 16 miles west of Aberdeen, is the ancestral home of the Fraser family. The largely Victorian interior includes the **great hall** (with a hidden opening where the laird could eavesdrop

on his guests), the library, bedrooms and an ancient kitchen, plus a secret room for storing valuables. Fraser family relics on display include needlework hangings and a 19th-century artificial leg. The 'Woodland Secrets' area in the castle grounds is designed as a kids' adventure playground.

Craigievar Castle   CASTLE
(NTS; www.nts.org.uk; adult/child £14.50/11; ⊙10.30am-5pm daily Jul-Sep, Fri-Tue Apr-Jun; 🅿) A superb example of the original Scottish Baronial style, Craigievar has managed to survive pretty much unchanged since its completion in the 17th century. The lower half is a plain tower house, the upper half sprouts corbelled turrets, cupolas and battlements – an extravagant statement of its builder's wealth and status.

It's 6 miles south of Alford and last admission is at 4pm.

Alford Bistro   CAFE £
(🖉 01975-563154;   thealfordbistro@btconnect. com; 40 Main St, Alford; mains £7-11; ⊙9am-4pm Mon, 10am-8pm Thu-Sat, 10am-7pm Sun; 🖻) 🌱 This great-value family bistro is always crowded, and it's easy to see why. Bright, modern decor in muted shades of pale green and grey, friendly service and a menu of lovingly prepared, classic comfort food such as yellow pea soup, macaroni cheese, beef stew with skirlie (oatmeal and onion fried in butter), homemade sausage rolls...wear trousers with an elastic waistband.

❶ Getting There & Away

Stagecoach bus X20 runs from Aberdeen to Alford (£10.25, 1¼ hours, six daily Monday to Friday, three on Saturday).

NORTHEAST 250 ROUTE

Encouraged by the success of the North Coast 500, local tourism bodies have come up with the **Northeast 250** (www.northeast250.com), a circular driving route that takes in the Aberdeenshire and Moray coastline, Speyside, Royal Deeside and the southern Cairngorms. Highlights include grand coastal scenery, picturesque fishing villages, Baronial castles and heather-clad mountains.

WORTH A TRIP

DOLPHIN SPOTTING

Based in a historic icehouse that used to store ice for preserving local salmon catches, the **Scottish Dolphin Centre** (☑01343-820339; https://dolphincentre.whales.org; Tugnet Ice House, Spey Bay; ☺10.30am-5pm Apr-Oct; P) is one of the best land-based dolphin-spotting places in the country. The indoor attractions include feeds from nearby wildlife cameras, a 'dry dive' audiovisual experience that takes you beneath the waves of the Moray Firth, and a pleasant cafe. Outdoors, you can watch for dolphins, seals and other marine creatures at the mouth of the River Spey, or join a guided wildlife walk.

The centre is in the tiny village of Spey Bay, 4 miles north of Fochabers, at the mouth of the River Spey.

Banff & Macduff

POP 9100

The handsome Georgian town of Banff and the busy fishing port of Macduff lie on either side of Banff Bay, separated only by the mouth of the River Deveron. **Banff Links** – 800m of clean golden sand stretching to the west – Duff House and Macduff's impressive aquarium pull in the holiday crowds.

★ **Duff House**   GALLERY
(HES; ☑01261-818181; www.nationalgalleries.org/visit/duff-house; Banff; adult/child £9/5.40; ☺9.30am-5.30pm daily Apr-Sep, 10am-4pm Fri-Sun Oct-Mar; P) One of Scotland's underappreciated treasures, this impressive baroque mansion is home to an art gallery with a superb collection of Scottish and European art, including important works by Raeburn and Gainsborough. Built between 1735 and 1740 as the seat of the Earls of Fife, it was designed by William Adam, and bears similarities to that other Adam masterpiece, Hopetoun House (p101) near Edinburgh. It's on the southern edge of Banff.

Macduff Marine Aquarium   AQUARIUM
(www.macduff-aquarium.org.uk; 11 High Shore, Macduff; adult/child £7.75/4.65; ☺10am-5pm Mon-Fri, 11am-5pm Sat & Sun Apr-Oct, 11am-4pm Sat-Wed Nov-Mar; P🖈) The centrepiece of Macduff's aquarium is a 400,000L open-air tank, complete with kelp-coated reef and

wave machine. Marine oddities on view include the brightly coloured cuckoo wrasse, the warty-skinned lumpsucker and the vicious-looking wolf fish. There's also a live CCTV feed from the seabird nesting colonies at the RSPB's Troup Head nature reserve.

ⓘ Getting There & Away

Bus 35 runs from Banff to Elgin (£11.70, 1¾ hours, every two hours) and Aberdeen (£13.85, two hours), while bus 272 runs to Fraserburgh (£9.50, 55 minutes, three daily) on weekdays only.

Portsoy

POP 1750

The pretty fishing village of Portsoy has an atmospheric **17th-century harbour** and a maze of narrow streets lined with picturesque cottages. An ornamental stone known as Portsoy marble – actually a beautifully patterned green-and-pale-pink serpentine – was quarried near Portsoy in the 17th and 18th centuries, and was reputedly used in the decoration of some rooms in the Palace of Versailles.

Portsoy Salmon Bothy   MUSEUM
(https://salmonbothy.org; Links Rd; ☺2-4pm Fri-Mon Apr-Sep) FREE Built in 1834 as a workshop, icehouse and storage space for nets and equipment, the bothy now houses a museum that records the history of salmon fishing in the local area.

Scottish Traditional Boat Festival CULTURAL
(www.stbfportsoy.com; ☺Jun or Jul) Each year on the last weekend in June or first weekend in July, Portsoy harbour is home to this lively gathering of historic wooden sailing boats accompanied by sailing races, live folk music, crafts demonstrations, street theatre and a food festival.

★ **Sail Loft Bunkhouse**   HOSTEL £
(☑01261-842222; http://portsoysailloft.org; Back Green; dm/tw £23/48; P🛜) Housed in a row of restored 18th-century cottages and a former sail-making loft, this bunkhouse offers luxurious accommodation in four- and six-bed dorms and a choice of private doubles and twins. There's a large modern kitchen, comfortable lounge with wood-burning stove, outdoor deck and barbecue, and even a wood-fired hot tub (£7.50 per person per hour).

Check in at the neighbouring caravan park.

ℹ Getting There & Away

Portsoy is 8 miles west of Banff; the hourly bus between Banff (£5.45, 25 minutes) and Elgin (£11.35, 1½ hours) stops here.

MORAY

The old county of Moray (*murr*-ay), centred on the county town of Elgin, lies at the heart of an ancient Celtic earldom and is famed for its mild climate and rich farmland – the barley fields of the 19th century once provided the raw material for the Speyside whisky distilleries, one of the region's main attractions for present-day visitors.

Elgin

POP 23,130

Elgin has been the provincial capital of Moray for over eight centuries and was an important town in medieval times. It's dominated by a hilltop monument to the 5th Duke of Gordon, and the main attractions are its impressive ruined cathedral, where the tombs of the duke's ancestors lie, and its fine museum.

◉ Sights

★ Elgin Museum
MUSEUM

(www.elginmuseum.org.uk; 1 High St; donations accepted; ◷ 10am-5pm Mon-Fri, 11am-4pm Sat Apr-Oct) **FREE** Scotland's oldest independent museum is an old-fashioned cabinet of curiosities, a captivating collection artfully displayed in a beautiful, purpose-built Victorian building. Exhibits range from Ecuadorian shrunken heads to Peruvian mummies, and include mysterious Pictish carved stones and internationally important fish and reptile fossils discovered in local rocks.

Elgin Cathedral
CATHEDRAL

(HES; www.historicenvironment.scot; King St; adult/child £9/5.40; ◷ 9.30am-5.30pm Apr-Sep, 10am-4pm Oct-Mar) Many people think that the ruins of Elgin Cathedral, known as the 'lantern of the north', are the most beautiful and evocative in Scotland; its octagonal chapter house is the finest in the country. Consecrated in 1224, the cathedral was burned down in 1390 by the infamous Wolf of Badenoch, the illegitimate son of Robert II, following his excommunication by the Bishop of Moray.

🛏 Sleeping & Eating

Moraydale
B&B ££

(☏ 01343-546381; www.moraydaleguesthouse.com; 276 High St; s/d/f from £60/80/100; Ⓟ 🛜 🐕) The Moraydale is a spacious Victorian mansion filled with period features – check out the stained glass and the cast-iron and tile fireplaces. The bedrooms are all en suite and equipped with modern bathrooms – the three large family rooms are particularly good value.

Southbank Guest House
B&B ££

(☏ 01343-547132; www.southbankguesthouse.co.uk; 36 Academy St; d/tr from £80/150; Ⓟ 🛜) The family-run, 15-room Southbank is set in a large Georgian town house in a quiet street south of Elgin's centre, just five minutes' walk from the cathedral and other sights. There may be a three-night minimum stay in high season.

★ Weavers
CAFE £

(www.johnstonsofelgin.com/visit-us/weavers-restaurant; Johnstons of Elgin, Newmill; mains £7-15; ◷ 10am-4pm; Ⓟ 🛜 🐕) The restaurant at Johnstons woollen mill is one of the best places to eat in town, serving breakfast till noon (including eggs Benedict and avocado toast), hot lunches from noon to 3pm (from steak pie to lobster ravioli) and afternoon teas from 2pm.

Batchen Street Coffee
CAFE £

(www.facebook.com/batchenstreetcoffee; 33 Batchen St; mains £4-7; ◷ 8.30am-4pm Mon-Fri, 9.30am-4.30pm Sat; 🛜) 🍴 A great little coffee shop that serves superb espresso (it roasts its own beans, and also offers Chemex brews), good-value breakfasts (scrambled eggs on toast), light lunches (soup, quiche) and excellent home baking.

🛍 Shopping

Gordon & MacPhail
FOOD & DRINKS

(☏ 01343-545110; www.gordonandmacphail.com; 58-60 South St; ◷ 8.30am-5pm Mon-Sat, alcohol on sale from 10am) The world's largest specialist malt-whisky dealer is more than a century old and offers around 1000 different varieties. Its Elgin shop is a place of pilgrimage for whisky connoisseurs, and also houses a mouthwatering delicatessen.

Johnstons of Elgin
FASHION & ACCESSORIES

(☏ 01343-554009; www.johnstonsofelgin.com/visit-us/elgin-mill; Newmill; ◷ 10am-4.30pm) Founded in 1797, Johnstons is famous for its cashmere clothing, and is the only UK woollen mill that still sees the manufacturing process through from raw fibre to finished garment. There's a retail outlet and restaurant (p233), and free guided tours of the works.

❶ Getting There & Away

The **bus station** (Alexandra Rd) is a block north of High St, and the train station is 900m south of the town centre.

BUS

Aberdeen £13.85, 2½ hours, hourly
Banff & Macduff £11.70, 1¾ hours, hourly
Dufftown £6.45, 50 minutes, hourly Monday to Saturday
Inverness £11.55, 1½ hours, hourly

TRAIN

Aberdeen £21, 1½ hours, five daily
Inverness £13.90, 45 minutes, five daily

Dufftown & Aberlour

Rome may be built on seven hills, but Dufftown's built on seven stills, say the locals. Founded in 1817 by James Duff, 4th Earl of Fife, Dufftown is 17 miles south of Elgin and lies at the heart of the Speyside whisky-distilling region. With seven working distilleries nearby, Dufftown has been dubbed Scotland's malt-whisky capital and is host to the biannual Spirit of Speyside whisky festival. Ask at the whisky museum about the **Malt Whisky Trail** (www.maltwhiskytrail.com), a self-guided tour around the local distilleries.

Aberlour (www.aboutaberlour.co.uk) – or Charlestown of Aberlour, to give it its full name – is prettier than Dufftown, straggling along the banks of the River Spey. It is famous as the home of Walkers Shortbread, and has the Aberlour Distillery right on the main street. Attractions include salmon fishing on the Spey, nearby Knockando Woolmill and some lovely walks along the Speyside Way.

◉ Sights

Knockando Woolmill   MUSEUM
(☏01340-810345; www.kwc.co.uk; Knockando; ⊙10am-4pm Tue-Sun Apr-Oct; 🅿🐕) 🌿FREE
Hidden in a fold of the hills 5 miles west of Aberlour, Knockando is a rare survival of an 18th-century woollen mill that has been

---

BLAZE YOUR OWN WHISKY TRAIL

Visiting a distillery can be memorable, but only hardcore malthounds will want to go to more than one or two. Here are the top five whisky sights in the area.

Aberlour (☏01340-881249; www.aberlour.com; tours from £20; ⊙9.30am-5pm daily Apr-Oct, 10am-4pm Mon-Fri Nov-Mar; 🅿) Has an excellent, detailed tour with a proper tasting session. It's on the main street in Aberlour.

Glenfarclas (☏01807-500345; www.glenfarclas.com; AB37 9BD; tours £7.50; ⊙10am-5pm Mon-Fri Apr-Sep, also to 4pm Sat Jul-Sep, Mon-Fri Oct-Mar; 🅿) Small, friendly and independent, Glenfarclas is 5 miles south of Aberlour on the Grantown road; the last tour leaves 90 minutes before closing. The in-depth Connoisseur's Tour (Fridays only July to September) is £40.

Glenfiddich (☏01340-820373; www.glenfiddich.co.uk; entry free, tours from £10; ⊙9.30am-4.30pm; 🅿) It's big and busy, but handiest for Dufftown and foreign-language tours are available. The standard tour (£10) starts with an overblown video, but it's fun and informative. The in-depth half-day Pioneer's Tour (£95) must be prebooked.

Macallan (☏01340-318000; www.themacallan.com; Easter Elchies, Craigellachie; visitor centre free, distillery tours from £50; ⊙10am-6pm; 🅿) This distillery enjoys a lovely location 1 mile west of Craigellachie and is housed in a spectacular turf-roofed visitor centre made from engineered timber.

Speyside Cooperage (☏01340-871108; www.speysidecooperage.co.uk; tours from £4; ⊙9am-5pm Mon-Fri, closed Christmas-early Jan; 🅿) Here you can see the fascinating art of barrel-making in action. It's a mile south of Craigellachie on the Dufftown road.

The biannual **Spirit of Speyside** (www.spiritofspeyside.com; ⊙early May & early Sep) whisky festival in Dufftown has a number of great events. Both accommodation and events should be booked well ahead.

lovingly restored to full working order. The ancient looms clank away Tuesday to Friday, turning out plaid and tweed textiles that can be purchased in the neighbouring shop. Guided tours cost £5; book in advance.

Whisky Museum   MUSEUM

(📞 01340-821097; www.whisky.dufftown.co.uk; 12 Conval St; ⊙10am-4pm Apr-Oct) **FREE** As well as housing a selection of distillery memorabilia (try saying that after a few drams), the museum holds 'nosing and tasting evenings' where you can learn what to look for in a fine single malt (£20 per person; 8pm Wednesdays July and August).

Test your new-found skills at the nearby Whisky Shop, which stocks hundreds of single malts.

Keith & Dufftown Railway   HERITAGE RAILWAY

(📞 01340-821181; www.keith-dufftown-railway. co.uk; Dufftown Station; adult/child return £11/5; 🅿️🎯) A line running for 11 miles from Dufftown to Keith sees trains hauled by 1950s diesel motor units running on weekends from Easter to September, plus Fridays from June onward. There are also two 1930s 'Brighton Belle' Pullman coaches, and a cafe housed in two 1950s British Railways coaches.

🛏️ Sleeping & Eating

Davaar B&B   B&B **££**

(📞 01340-820464; www.davaardufftown.co.uk; 17 Church St; d/f £70/85; 🛜) This sturdy Victorian villa has three smallish but comfy rooms. The breakfast menu is superb, offering the option of Portsoy kippers as well as the traditional fry-up (which uses eggs from the owner's own chickens).

Mash Tun   B&B **££**

(📞 01340-881771; www.mashtun-aberlour.com; 8 Broomfield Sq; s/d from £85/120; 🛜🎯) Housed in a curious stone building made for a sea captain in the outline of a ship, this luxurious B&B has a famous whisky bar – a place of pilgrimage for whisky enthusiasts – which has a collection of old and rare single malts. There's also an excellent restaurant (mains £12 to £25, lunch and dinner daily) that serves top-notch pub grub.

Craigellachie Hotel   HOTEL **£££**

(📞 01340-881204; www.craigellachiehotel.co.uk; Craigellachie; r from £150; 🅿️🛜) This country house hotel has been beautifully refurbished but retains a wonderful old-fashioned atmosphere, from the wood-panelled lobby to the opulent drawing room where you can sink into a sofa in front of the log fire. The big attraction for whisky connoisseurs is the **Quaich Bar**, a cosy nook filled with handcrafted furniture and lined with more than 900 varieties of single malt whisky.

It's a mile northeast of Aberlour, overlooking the River Spey.

Grouse Inn   PUB

(📞 01466-702200; Lower Cabrach; ⊙10am-11pm Easter-Oct) A resolutely old-fashioned pub famed for its whisky collection, the Grouse has an astounding 235 different malt whiskies on the optic behind the bar, and more than 700 to choose from. There's also a tearoom (open 10am to 6pm Saturday to Thursday, 1pm to 6pm Friday). The inn is 8 miles south of Dufftown on the A941 road.

🛍️ Shopping

Spey Larder   FOOD & DRINKS

(📞 01340-871243; www.speylarder.com; 96-98 High St; ⊙9.30am-5pm Mon-Sat) This deli is the place to shop for picnic goodies to eat on the banks of the River Spey. Choose from a great selection of Scottish artisan cheeses, smoked salmon, venison charcuterie, delicious home-baked bread and local craft beers.

Whisky Shop   FOOD & DRINKS

(📞 01340-821097; www.whiskyshopdufftown.co.uk; 1 Fife St; ⊙10am-6pm Mon-Sat year-round, plus Sun Easter-Oct) A fantastic shop that stocks hundreds of single malts and runs tasting sessions and other events.

ℹ️ Getting There & Away

Buses link Elgin to Dufftown (£6.45, 50 minutes) hourly Monday to Saturday, continuing to Huntly and Aberdeen.

On summer weekends you can take a train from Inverness or Aberdeen to Keith (£19, one hour, five daily), and then ride the Keith and Dufftown Railway to Dufftown.

There are hourly buses to Aberlour from Elgin (£6.15, 40 minutes), and from Dufftown (£3.05, 15 minutes).

AT A GLANCE

POPULATION
255,000

**LENGTH OF
COASTLINE**
3000 miles

**BEST
AWAY-FROM-IT-ALL
HOTEL**
Monachyle Mhor
(p249)

**BEST
PUFFIN-SPOTTING**
Staffa & Lunga
(p289)

BEST PIES
Aberfoyle Delicates-
sen (p245)

WHEN TO GO
May Fèis Ìle (Islay
Festival) celebrates
traditional Scottish
music and whisky.

Jun Roadsides and
gardens become a
blaze of colour with
deep-pink rhododen-
dron blooms.

Aug The best month
of the year for whale
watching off the west
coast.

Oban (p272)
TRAVELLIGHT/SHUTTERSTOCK ©

Southern Highlands & Islands

The complex coastline of Scotland's southwest harbours some of its most inspiring corners. Seagoing ferries allow you to island-hop from the scenic splendour of Arran to majestic Mull or Tiree's lonely sands, via the whisky distilleries of Islay, the wild mountains of Jura, the scenic delights of diminutive Colonsay and Oban's sustainable seafood scene.

On fresh water too, waterbuses, vintage steamboats, canoes and kayaks ply Loch Lomond and the Trossachs National Park, a memorable scenic concentration that's very accessible but possessed of a wild beauty.

Wildlife experiences are a highlight, from the rasping spout of a minke whale to the corncrake's 'krek-krek'. Spot otters tumbling in the kelp, watch sea eagles snatch fish from a lonely loch and thrill to the sight of dolphins riding the bow-wave of your boat.

Southern Highlands & Islands Highlights

1 **The Trossachs** (p244)
Exploring the lovely lochscapes and accessible walking and cycling routes.

2 **Islay** (p262) Visiting the smoky heavyweights of the whisky world on their peaty turf.

3 **Arran** (p250) Blowing away the cobwebs on this scenic, activity-packed island.

4 **Corryvreckan Whirlpool** (p270) Visiting the white waters of this maelstrom at the north end of lonely Jura.

5 **Iona** (p285) Journeying through wildlife-rich Mull to reach this holy emerald isle.

6 **West Highland Way** (p239) Hiking along the eastern shore of Loch Lomond.

7 **Seafood Restaurants** (p277) Tucking into a platter of fresh local langoustines at Ee-Usk or another one of Oban's eating establishments.

8 **Machrihanish** (p262) Teeing off on the great-value old and new golf courses down the Kintyre peninsula.

LOCH LOMOND & THE TROSSACHS

The 'bonnie banks' and 'bonnie braes' of Loch Lomond have long been Glasgow's rural retreat – a scenic region of hills, lochs and healthy fresh air within easy reach of Scotland's largest city. Today the loch's popularity shows no sign of decreasing. The picturesque Trossachs have likewise long been popular for their wild Highland beauty, set so close to the southern population centres. With the region covered by a large national park, it makes a fine destination for outdoor activity, with some excellent walking and cycling on offer and lots of high-quality accommodation and eating choices.

Loch Lomond

Loch Lomond is mainland Britain's largest lake and, after Loch Ness, the most famous of Scotland's lochs. Its proximity to Glasgow (20 miles away) means that the tourist honeypots of Balloch and Luss get pretty crowded in summer. The eastern shore, which is followed by the West Highland Way long-distance footpath, is quieter and offers a better chance to appreciate the loch away from the busy main road along the western shore.

Loch Lomond straddles the Highland border. The southern part is broad and is-land-studded, fringed by woods and Lowland meadows. However, north of Luss the loch narrows, occupying a deep trench gouged out by glaciers during the Ice Age, with 900m mountains crowding either side.

🏃 Activities & Tours

Walking

The **West Highland Way** (www.westhighland way.org) runs along the loch's eastern shore, while the **Rob Roy Way** (www.robroyway. com) heads from Drymen to Pitlochry via the Trossachs. The **Three Lochs Way** (www.threelochsway.co.uk) loops west from Balloch through Helensburgh and Arrochar before returning to Loch Lomond at Inveruglas. The **Great Trossachs Path** (www. lochlomond-trossachs.org) links the loch with the Trossachs. There are numerous shorter walks around: get further information from tourist offices.

Rowardennan is the starting point for ascents of Ben Lomond (p242) (974m), a popular and relatively straightforward (if strenuous) climb.

Cycling

The mostly traffic-free **Clyde and Loch Lomond Cycle Way** links Glasgow to Balloch (20 miles), where it joins the **West Loch Lomond Cycle Path**, which continues along the loch shore to Tarbet (10 miles). The park website (www.lochlomond-trossachs.org) details some other local routes.

🚣 Boating

Loch Lomond Leisure   WATER SPORTS
(☑ 0333 577 0715; www.lochlomond-scotland.com; Luss) From Luss pier, Loch Lomond Leisure runs speedboat tours of the loch (short trip £10/5 per adult/child) as well as waterskiing or wakeboarding (both £40/105 for one/three sets) and other splashy activities. Kayaks (£20/65 per hour/day) and various boats are also available for hire.

Cruise Loch Lomond   BOATING
(☑ 01301-702356;   www.cruiselochlomond.
co.uk; Tarbet; cruises adult/child from £12/7.50;
⏰ 8.30am-5.30pm late Mar-early Nov) With departures from Tarbet and Luss, this operator runs several cruises, including options exploring loch islands, Rob Roy's cave, the Arklet Falls, or walking a section of the West Highland Way from Inversnaid. The one-hour Northern Highlights cruise is a quick introduction from Tarbet (adult/child £12/7.50), while 90-minute circuits

---

ℹ GETTING AROUND THE PARK

Loch Lomond and the Trossachs are conjoined by the **Loch Lomond & the Trossachs National Park** (☑ 01389-722600; www.lochlomond-trossachs.org) – Scotland's first national park, created in 2002. The park extends over a huge area, from Balloch north to Tyndrum and Killin, and from Callander west to the forests of Cowal. The length of Loch Lomond means that access between the western part of the park and the Trossachs in the east is either in the far north of the region via Crianlarich or the far south via Drymen. Walkers and cyclists can link the two more easily via the waterbuses that criss-cross Loch Lomond.

Loch Lomond & the Trossachs NP

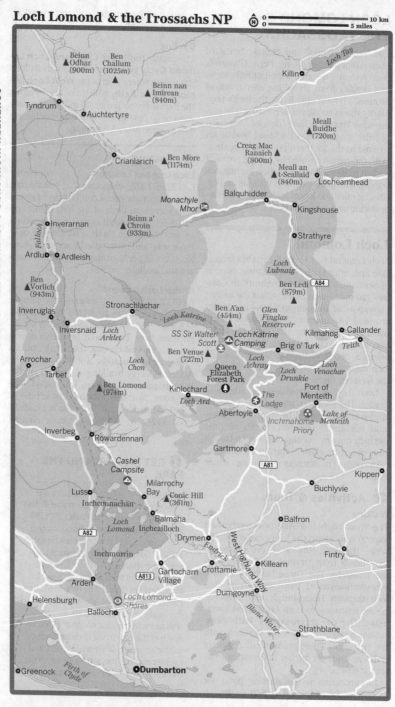

N

0   10 km
0   5 miles

Loch Tay

Beinn Odhar (900m)

Ben Challum (1025m)

Killin

Beinn nan Imirean (840m)

Tyndrum

Auchtertyre

Meall Buidhe (720m)

Creag Mac Ranaich (800m)

Crianlarich

Ben More (1174m)

Meall an t-Seallaid (840m)

Locheamhead

Monachyle Mhor

Balquhidder

Kingshouse

Inverarnan

Beinn a' Chroin (933m)

Strathyre

Falloch

Ardlu

Ardleish

Loch Lubnaig

Ben Ledi (879m)

A84

Ben Vorlich (943m)

Stronachlachar

Loch Katrine

Ben A'an (454m)

Glen Finglas Reservoir

Inveruglas

Loch Arklet

SS Sir Walter Scott

Loch Katrine Camping

Kilmahog

Callander

Inversnaid

Brig o' Turk

Teith

Arrochar

Loch Chon

Ben Venue (727m)

Queen Elizabeth Forest Park

Loch Achray

Loch Drunkie

Loch Venachar

Tarbet

Port of Menteith

Ben Lomond (974m)

Kinlochard

Loch Ard

The Lodge

Aberfoyle

Inchmahome Priory

Lake of Menteith

Inverbeg

Rowardennan

Gartmore

A81

Kippen

Cashel Campsite

Milarrochy Bay

Buchlyvie

Luss

Conic Hill (361m)

Inchconnachan

Balmaha

Balfron

Loch Lomond

Inchcailloch

A82

Drymen

West Highland Way

Inchmurrin

Endrick

Fintry

Arden

Gartocharn Village

Croftamie

Killearn

A813

Helensburgh

Loch Lomond Shores

Dumgoyne

Balloch

Blane Water

Strathblane

Greenock

Firth of Clyde

Dumbarton

from Luss or Tarbet run at adult/child £15/7.50.

From its Tarbet office it also rents out bikes.

Sweeney's Cruises BOATING
($\square$ 01389-752376; www.sweeneyscruiseco.com; Balloch Rd, Balloch) Offers a popular one-hour return cruise to Inchmurrin (adult/child £12.50/8, nine times daily April to September, twice daily October to March). The quay is directly opposite Balloch train station. It also runs summer trips from a dock at Loch Lomond Shores.

Piped commentary is by Neil Oliver.

❶ Information

Balloch Tourist Office ($\square$ 01389-753533; www.visitscotland.com; Balloch Rd, Balloch; $\odot$9.30am-6pm Jul & Aug, to 5.30pm Jun & Sep, 9.30am-4pm Oct-May) Opposite Balloch's train station.

Balmaha National Park Centre ($\square$ 01389-722100; www.lochlomond-trossachs.org; Balmaha; $\odot$9.30am-4pm Apr-Oct, 9.30am-4pm Sat & Sun Nov-Mar) Has maps showing local walking routes.

❶ Getting There & Away

BUS

First Glasgow (www.firstglasgow.com) Bus 1/1A runs from Argyle St in central Glasgow to Balloch (£5.40, 1½ hours, at least two per hour).

Scottish Citylink ($\square$ 0871 266 3333; www.citylink.co.uk) Coaches from Glasgow stop at Luss (£9.90, 55 minutes, nine to 18 daily), Tarbet (£10.10, 65 minutes, nine to 18 daily) and Ardlui (£18, 1½ hours, four to nine daily).

TRAIN

Glasgow–Balloch (£5.90, 45 minutes, every 30 minutes)

Glasgow–Arrochar & Tarbet (£13.20, 1¼ hours, four to seven daily)

Glasgow–Ardlui (£17.30, 1½ hours, four to seven daily, continuing to Oban or Fort William)

❶ Getting Around

Bus 309 runs from Balloch to Drymen (£2.85) and Balmaha (£3.15, 20 minutes, nine to 10 daily), while bus 305 heads to Luss (£3.10, 20 minutes, nine to 10 daily). Bus 207 connects Balloch with Loch Lomond Shores and Alexandria. An **SPT Daytripper ticket** gives a family group unlimited travel for a day on most bus and train services in the Glasgow, Loch Lomond and Helensburgh area. Buy the ticket (£13.10 for one adult and two children, £23.20 for two adults

and up to four children) from any train station or Glasgow bus station.

Tarbet and Ardlui are accessible by train and by Citylink buses between Glasgow and north-western destinations.

Local buses also run from Helensburgh to Arrochar (£3.15) via Luss and Tarbet (same price) four times daily Monday to Friday.

Western Shore

Balloch, straddling the River Leven at Loch Lomond's southern end, is the loch's main population centre and transport hub. A Victorian resort once thronged by day trippers transferring between the train station and the steamer quay, it is now a 'gateway centre' for Loch Lomond and the Trossachs National Park. Visitors still arrive in abundance. On its edge, the overblown Loch Lomond Shores complex provides family-friendly attractions, boat trips, eating establishments and lots of retail.

Leaving Balloch behind, the road along the western shore offers great views of Loch Lomond. There's also busy traffic along what is a major route to north and west Scotland. The western shore sees the bulk of Loch Lomond's tourists, but there are some pretty places and docks for boat trips and waterbuses to explore the loch.

Head first for the picture-postcard village of **Luss**. Stroll among the pretty cottages, built by the local laird in the 19th century for his estate workers, and admire the lochside vistas. You won't be alone: to live in one of these cute cottages must occasionally feel like being a celeb with paparazzi camped outside the door.

Beyond Luss, **Tarbet** sits at the junction where you choose between Argyll and Kintyre or Oban and the Highlands. Following the shore brings you to **Ardlui** and thence Crianlarich.

◉ Sights & Activities

Loch Lomond Sea Life AQUARIUM
($\square$ 01389-721500; www.visitsealife.com; Loch Lomond Shores; adult/child £15.95/10.95; $\odot$10am-5pm Mar-Oct, to 4pm Nov-Feb) The centrepiece of **Loch Lomond Shores** (www.lochlomond-shores.com; $\odot$9.30am-6pm) is this smallish aquarium, which has displays on the wildlife of Loch Lomond, an otter enclosure (housing short-clawed Asian otters, not Scottish ones), and other creatures ranging from sharks to stingrays to sea turtles. It's cheaper if you book in advance online.

CLIMBING BEN LOMOND

Standing guard over the eastern shore of Loch Lomond is **Ben Lomond** (www.nts.org.uk/visit/places/ben-lomond; 974m), Scotland's most southerly Munro. It's a popular climb: most follow the Tourist Route up and down from Rowardennan car park. It's a straight-forward route on a well-used and maintained path; allow five hours for the 7-mile round trip.

The Ptarmigan Route is less crowded and has better views, following a narrow but clearly defined path up the western flank, directly overlooking the loch, to a curving ridge leading to the summit. You can then descend via the Tourist Route, making this option a satisfying circuit.

To find the start of the Ptarmigan path, head north from Rowardennan car park 600m, past the youth hostel; cross the bridge after Ben Lomond Cottage and immediately turn right along a path through the trees. The route is then easy to follow.

Maid of the Loch   SHIP
(www.maidoftheloch.org; adult/child £3/free; ⊙11am-5pm Wed-Sun Easter-Oct) The vintage paddle steamer *Maid of the Loch,* built in 1953, is moored at Loch Lomond Shores while funds are raised for a full restoration – you can help out by nipping aboard for a look around.

🍴 Sleeping & Eating

Glenview   B&B **££**
(☑ 01389-528878; www.glenview-luss.co.uk; Luss; d £100-140; P🐾) In the centre of things on the road through Luss village, this white house offers a genuine welcome and three highly appealing suites. All are show-room-spotless: one comes with a full kitchen and dining area, the others with spacious lounge areas, with one also having a modish four-poster bed. Breakfast is continental, with a cooked option available in their cafe around the corner.

Drover's Inn   PUB FOOD **££**
(☑ 01301-704234; www.thedroversinn.co.uk; Inverarnan; bar meals £10-14; ⊙food 11.30am-10pm Mon-Sat, to 9.30pm or 10pm Sun; P🐾) Don't miss this low-ceilinged howff (drinking den), just north of Ardlui, with its smoke-black-ened stone, kilted bartenders, and walls adorned with moth-eaten stags' heads and stuffed birds. The convivial bar, where Rob Roy allegedly dropped by for pints, serves hearty hill-walking fuel and hosts live folk music on weekends.

Rooms could do with an upgrade but there are some newer ones in a separate building, the Stagger Inn.

Arrochar

The village of Arrochar, just west of Tarbet, has a wonderful location, looking across the head of Loch Long to the jagged peaks of the Cobbler (884m). The mountain takes its name from the shape of its north peak (the one on the right, seen from Arrochar), which looks like a cobbler hunched over his bench. The village makes a picturesque overnight stop.

Cobbler   HIKING
(Ben Arthur) To climb the Cobbler, start from the roadside car park at Succoth near the head of Loch Long. A steep uphill hike through woods is followed by an easier section heading into the valley below the triple peaks. Then it's steeply uphill again to the saddle between the north and central peaks.

The central peak is higher, but awkward to get to – scramble through the hole and along the ledge to reach the airy summit. The north peak to the right is an easy walk. Allow five to six hours for the 5-mile round trip.

Eastern Shore

Away from the busy western road, the loch's eastern shore is a quieter spot populated mostly by walkers and campers. Nevertheless, the narrow road gets busy. It runs from **Drymen** through attractive **Balmaha**, where you can hire boats.

There are several lochside picnic areas; **Milarrochy Bay** (1.5 miles north of Balmaha) has a nice gravel beach and superb views across the loch to the Luss hills.

The road ends at **Rowardennan**, where there's a hotel, hostels and boat hire, but the West Highland Way (p239) hiking trail continues north along the shore of the loch. It's 7 miles to **Inversnaid**, reachable by road from the Trossachs, and 15 miles to **Inverarnan** at the loch's northern end. Rowardennan is also the launchpad for climbing Ben Lomond.

🛏 Sleeping & Eating

Book your accommodation ahead in the walking season, as it packs out. There are hostel, hotel and camping options as well as B&Bs along this stretch.

From March to September, wild camping is restricted on the eastern shore of Loch Lomond between Drymen and Ptarmigan Lodge (just north of the Rowardennan Youth Hostel). There are campsites at Milarrochy, Cashel and Sallochy, and a hostel at Inversnaid.

Rowardennan Youth Hostel   HOSTEL £

(Hostelling Scotland; ☎01360-870259; www.hostellingscotland.org.uk; Rowardennan; dm/tw/q £24/54/99; ⊙mid-Mar–mid-Oct; P🖘) Where the road ends on the eastern side of Loch Lomond is this postcard-quality retreat in an elegant ex-hunting lodge, with lawns stretching right down to the water's edge. Whether you're walking the West Highland Way, climbing Ben Lomond or just putting your feet up, it's a great choice, with a huge lounge that has windows overlooking the loch.

Meals are available, including packed lunches for walkers, and there's a pub a short walk away. The wi-fi is a patchy satellite link.

Inversnaid Bunkhouse   HOSTEL £

(☎01877-386249; www.inversnaid.com; Inversnaid; dm £23, d without bathroom £52-62, tent site per person £10; ⊙Mar-Oct; P🖘🐾) This former church is now a remote, welcoming hostel in a peaceful streamside location. It's popular with walkers and offers simple accommodation in crowded dorms, very pleasant doubles and grassy campsites (pre-pitched tents available). It's 15 miles from Aberfoyle by road, or by ferry from Loch Lomond's western side, or via an 8-mile walk north from Rowardennan on the West Highland Way.

A hot tub is great for aching muscles and the cafe serves simple meals, packed lunches and decent beers; you can also self-cater evening meals. It's a 15-minute uphill trudge from the lakeshore and trail, but it offers free transfers. A modern self-catering cabin is also available.

Cashel Campsite   CAMPSITE £

(☎01360-870234; www.campingintheforest.co.uk; Rowardennan; site for 1/2 £20/28; ⊙Mar-late Oct; P🐾) The most attractive campsite in this eastern shore area is 3 miles north of Balmaha, on the loch shore.

Oak Tree Inn   INN ££

(☎01360-870357; www.theoaktreeinn.co.uk; Balmaha; s/d £85/110; P🖘) An attractive traditional inn built in slate and timber, this bustling place offers bright, modern bedrooms for pampered hikers, plus super-spacious superior chambers, self-catering cottages and glamping pods with their own deck. The rustic restaurant brings locals, tourists and walkers together and serves generously proportioned pub grub (mains £10 to £14; open noon to 9pm). There's plenty of outdoor seating.

But it doesn't end there; the Oak Tree is an impressive set-up that makes its own ice cream (and sells it in an adjacent cafe), and smokes its own fish. In fact, Balmaha basically *is* the Oak Tree these days.

Crianlarich & Tyndrum

POP 400

Surrounded by spectacular hillscapes at the northern edge of Loch Lomond and the Trossachs National Park, these villages are popular pit stops on the main A82 road for walkers on the West Highland Way and Munro-baggers. Crianlarich has a train station and more community atmosphere. Tyndrum (*tyne*-drum), 5 miles up the road, has two stations, a bus interchange, fuel, and late-opening motorists' cafes; it's popular for the ascent of Munros **Cruach Ardrain** (1046m), **Ben More** (1174m) and magnificent **Ben Lui** (1130m).

🛏 Sleeping & Eating

Strathfillan Wigwams   CAMPSITE, CABIN £

(☎01838-400251; www.wigwamholidays.com; A82, Strathfillan; sites per adult/child £8/4, wigwam d small/large/en suite £40/50/75, lodge d £70-80; P@🖘🐾) A working farm off the A82 between Crianlarich and Tyndrum, this place has heated 'wigwams': wooden A-frame cabins, with fridges and foam mattresses, that

---

> ### ⓘ LOCH LOMOND WATER BUS
>
> From mid-March to October a network of boats criss-crosses Loch Lomond, allowing you to explore the loch's hiking and biking trails using public transport. The Loch Lomond Water Bus timetable is available from tourist offices and online (www.lochlomond-trossachs.org).

can sleep four at a pinch. More upmarket are the self-contained lodges with their own bathrooms and kitchen facilities. It also has camping and a shop. There's a two-night minimum on summer weekends. Wi-fi costs extra.

Crianlarich Youth Hostel HOSTEL £

(Hostelling Scotland; ☑ 01838-300260; www. hostellingscotland.org.uk; Station Rd, Crianlarich; dm/tr/q £20/56/94; P ⊛ ⊛ ⊛) Well run and comfortable, with a spacious kitchen, dining area and lounge, this hostel is a real haven for walkers or anyone passing through. Dorms vary in size – there are some great en-suite family rooms that should be booked in advance – but all are clean and roomy.

Ewich Guest House B&B ££

(☑ 01838-300536; www.ewich.co.uk; A82, Strathfillan; s £45, d £75-85; P ⊛ ⊛) This lovely Swiss-run stone farmhouse is just below the main road between Crianlarich and Tyndrum, but has a fabulous outlook over a valley, with uplifting views and a large garden. It's very handy for walking and cycling routes and boasts enticing rooms with cheerful fabrics and floorboards. Breakfast has home-laid eggs and there's a personable pooch.

Walker-friendly features like packed lunches, laundry and a drying room are also available.

Real Food Café CAFE £

(☑ 01838-400235; www.therealfoodcafe.com; A82, Tyndrum; mains £7-11; ⊗ 7.30am-8pm Nov-Mar, to 9pm Apr-Oct; ⊛ ⊛ ⊛) ✐ Hungry hillwalkers throng the tables in this justifiably popular cafe. The menu looks familiar – fish and chips, soups, salads and burgers – but the owners make an effort to source sustainably and locally, and the quality shines through.

❶ Getting There & Away

Scottish Citylink (p241) runs several buses daily to Glasgow (£18.80, 1¾ hours), Fort William (£18.60, 1¼ hours) and Skye (£47.10, four to five hours) from both Crianlarich and Tyndrum.

Trains run to Tyndrum and Crianlarich from Fort William (£22.40, 1¾ hours, three to four daily Monday to Saturday, two on Sunday), Oban (£13.60, 1¼ hours, four or six daily) and Glasgow (£21.10, two hours, three to seven daily).

The Trossachs

The Trossachs region has long been a favourite weekend getaway, offering outstanding natural beauty and excellent walking and cycling routes within easy reach of the country's southern population centres. With thickly forested hills, romantic lochs, national-park status and an interesting selection of places to stay and eat, its popularity is sure to continue.

The Trossachs first gained cachet in the early 19th century, when curious visitors came from across Britain, drawn by the romantic language of Walter Scott's poem 'Lady of the Lake', inspired by Loch Katrine, and novel *Rob Roy,* about the derring-do of the region's famous outlaw.

In summer, the Trossachs can be overburdened with coach tours, but many of these are for day trippers – peaceful, long evenings gazing at the reflections in the nearest loch are still possible. If you can, it's worth timing your visit to avoid weekends.

Aberfoyle & Around

POP 700

Little Aberfoyle has lots to do close at hand and has great accommodation options nearby. It's also a stop on the Rob Roy Way (p239). However, it's overwhelmed with day-tripping visitors on most weekends and dominated by a huge car park. Callander or other Trossachs towns appeal more as a base.

◉ Sights & Activities

You can hire bikes at **Aberfoyle Bike Hire** (☑ 01877 382023; www.aberfoylebikehire.co.uk; bike 3hr/day/week £15/25/110; ⊗ 9am-5pm Wed-Mon, daily Jun-Aug).

Inchmahome Priory RUINS

(☑ 01877-385294; www.historicenvironment.scot; Lake of Menteith; incl ferry adult/child £9/5.40; ⊗ 10am-3.30pm Apr-Oct, last ferry to island 45min before closing) From the **Lake of Menteith** (called 'lake' not 'loch' due to a mistranslation from Gaelic), 3 miles east of Aberfoyle, a ferry takes visitors to these substantial ruins. It's best to book ahea as capacity is limited. Mary, Queen of Scots was kept safe here as a child during Henry VIII's 'Rough Wooing'. Henry attacked Stirling, trying to force Mary to marry his son in order to unite the kingdoms.

WORTH A TRIP

HILL HOUSE

The stylish **Hill House** (☎01436-673900; www.nts.org.uk; Upper Colquhoun St, Helensburgh; adult/child £12.50/5.50; ⏰10am-5pm Mar-Oct, Thu-Sun only Nov-Feb), built in 1902 for Glasgow publisher Walter Blackie, is perhaps architect Charles Rennie Mackintosh's finest creation – its timeless elegance still feels chic today. The interiors are stunning, with rose motifs and fabulous furniture. Water soaking through the rendered cement exterior means that you'll find the house enclosed in a giant covering structure. You can stay on the top floor – check the Holidays section of the NTS website. It's near Helensburgh Upper station, though not all trains stop there.

The house also has a beautiful garden. Mackintosh was very protective of his creation: he once chided Mrs Blackie for putting the wrong-coloured flowers in a vase in the hall.

If you're arriving at Helensburgh Central station, it's about a 1-mile uphill walk to Hill House. Buses 302 and 306 can get you close.

★**Loch Katrine Circuit** CYCLING

An excellent 20-mile circular cycle route from Aberfoyle starts on the **Lochs & Glens Cycle Way** on the forest trail. Then following the southern shore of Loch Achray, you reach the pier on Loch Katrine. The 10.30am boat (or afternoon sailings in summer) takes you to the western shore, from where you can follow the beautiful B829 via Loch Ard back to Aberfoyle.

Instead of getting the boat, you could bike it along the loch's northern shore, adding an extra 14 miles to the trip. An alternative to the forest trail from Aberfoyle is taking the A821 over Duke's Pass.

The Lodge Forest Visitor Centre OUTDOORS

(David Marshall Lodge; ☎0300 067 6615; www.forestryandland.gov.scot; A821; car park £1-3; ⏰10am-5pm Apr-Oct, to 4pm Nov, Dec, Feb & Mar, to 3pm Jan) Half a mile north of Aberfoyle, this nature centre has info about the many walks and cycle routes in and around the **Queen Elizabeth Forest Park**. There are live wildlife cameras offering a peek at osprey and barn-owl nests among others. The centre is worth visiting solely for the views.

Picturesque but busy waymarked trails start from here, ranging from a light 20-minute stroll to a nearby waterfall – with great interactive play options for kids – to a hilly 4-mile circuit. The centre has a popular cafe. Also here, **Go Ape!** (☎0333 920 4859; www.goape.co.uk; Queen Elizabeth Forest Park; adult/child £35/28; ⏰Sat & Sun Nov & Feb-Easter, Wed-Mon Easter-Oct) will bring out the monkey in you on its exhilarating adventure course of long zip lines, swings and rope bridges through the forest. Look out, too, for the spooky mirror sculptures by local artist Rob Mulholland.

🛏 Sleeping & Eating

Bield B&B **££**

(☎01877-382351; www.thebieldbnb; Trossachs Rd, Aberfoyle; s/d £60/80; P 🛜) With a kind, genuine welcome, the Bield is exactly the sort of place you want after a long day's walking or cycling. This striking sandstone house has large, comfortable rooms, a sociable breakfast table and views from its hillside location just above Aberfoyle's centre.

Mayfield Guest House B&B **££**

(☎01877-382962; www.mayfield-aberfoyle.co.uk; Main St, Aberfoyle; s £55, d £70-75; ⏰Mar-Oct; P 🛜 ⚙) Nothing is too much trouble for the friendly hosts at this guesthouse right in the heart of Aberfoyle. It has three compact, comfortable ground-floor rooms, all painted in cheerful colours and very well kept. There's a sweet little conservatory lounge and it's bike- and motorbike-friendly, with a garage out back.

★**Lake of Menteith Hotel** HOTEL **£££**

(☎01877-385258; www.lake-hotel.com; Port of Menteith; r £150-255; P 🛜 ⚙) Soothingly situated on a lake (yes, it's the only non-loch in Scotland) 3 miles east of Aberfoyle, this genteel retreat makes a great romantic getaway. Though all rooms are excellent, with a contemporary feel, it's worth an upgrade to the enormous 'lake heritage' ones with a view of the water: it really is a sensational outlook.

Even if you're not staying, head down to the waterside bar-restaurant (mains £15 to £19). Check the website for packages.

★**Aberfoyle Delicatessen & Trossachs Butcher** DELI **£**

(☎01877-382242; 3 Dukes Ct, Aberfoyle; pies £2.40; ⏰8.30am-5pm Mon-Fri, from 8am Sat, from 9.30am Sun) This main-street shop is a cut above most of Aberfoyle's culinary offerings. There's good produce for self-caterers and excellent sandwiches, but the pies are a step beyond even those. Steak and black pudding? Venison? It's all delicious, and ingredients are specified for those with dietary needs.

❶ Information

Aberfoyle Tourist Office (☑ 01877-381221; www.visitscotland.com; Main St, Aberfoyle; ☺10am-5pm Apr-Oct, to 4pm Nov-Mar; ☎) A large office with a good selection of walking information.

❶ Getting There & Away

First (www.firstgroup.com) has six daily buses (Monday to Saturday) from Stirling (£5.20, 55 minutes).

DRT (Demand Responsive Transport; ☑ 01786-404040; www.stirling.gov.uk/drt) operates in the Aberfoyle area.

Lochs Katrine & Achray

This rugged area, 7 miles north of Aberfoyle and 10 miles west of Callander, is the heart of the Trossachs. **Loch Katrine Cruises** (☑01877-376315; www.lochkatrine.com; Trossachs Pier, Loch Katrine; 1hr cruise adult £12-14, child £6.50-7.50) run from Trossachs Pier at the eastern tip of beautiful Loch Katrine. One of these is the fabulous centenarian steamship *Sir Walter Scott;* check the website for departures, as it's worth taking a trip on this veteran if possible. Things were a bit disrupted at the time of research while the *Sir Walter Scott* awaited funds for a major repair. Normal service includes various one-hour afternoon sailings, and at 10.30am (plus additional summer departures) there's a trip to Stronachlachar at the other end of the loch. From Stronachlachar (accessible by car via a 12-mile road from Aberfoyle), you can reach Loch Lomond's eastern shore at isolated Inversnaid. A tarmac path links Trossachs Pier

❶ TROSSACHS TRANSPORT

DRT covers the Trossachs area. It might sound complex, but basically it means for the price of a bus you get a taxi to where you want to go. There are various zones. It's easiest to book online.

with Stronachlachar, so you can take the boat out and walk/cycle back (14 miles). At Trossachs Pier, **Katrinewheelz** (☑01877-376366; www.katrinewheelz.co.uk; Trossachs Pier, Loch Katrine; bike hire per half-/full day from £15/20; ☺9am-5pm Apr-Oct, check for winter hours) hires out good bikes. There's a cafe here and a good one at Stronachlachar.

Loch Achray Walks   HIKING
The path to the rocky cone called **Ben A'an** (454m) begins at a car park just east of the Loch Katrine turn-off. It's easy to follow and the return trip is just under 4 miles. A tougher walk is up rugged **Ben Venue** (727m). Start walking from the signed car park just south of the Loch Katrine turn-off (7.5 miles return).

Loch Katrine Camping   CABIN £
(☑01877-376317; www.lochkatrine.com; Loch Katrine; pods £45-110; P ☎ 🐾) Just beyond the ferry pier on Loch Katrine, this is a pleasing place to stay, offering tent and motorhome pitches as well as cute camping pods with a little deck. They sleep two or four and come in three categories, one with underfloor heating and en-suite bathroom. Book them well ahead.

Callander

POP 3100

Callander, the principal Trossachs town, has been pulling in tourists for over 150 years, and has a laid-back ambience along its main thoroughfare that quickly lulls visitors into lazy pottering. There's an excellent array of accommodation options here, and some intriguing places to eat. Good walking and cycling routes are close at hand.

◉ Sights & Activities

★**Hamilton Toy Collection**   MUSEUM
(☑01877-330004; www.thehamiltontoycollection.co.uk; 111 Main St; adult/child £3/1; ☺10.30am-5pm Mon-Sat, noon-5pm Sun Apr-Oct; 👶) A powerhouse of 20th-century juvenile memorabilia, chock-full of dolls houses, puppets and toy soldiers. It's an amazing collection and a guaranteed nostalgia trip. Phone ahead in winter as it opens some weekends.

Bracklinn Falls &
Callander Crags   WALKING
Impressive Bracklinn Falls are reached by track and footpath from Bracklinn Rd (30 minutes each way from the car park). Also

off Bracklinn Rd, a woodland trail leads up to Callander Crags, with great views over the surroundings; a return trip from the car park is about 4 miles.

Wheels Cycling Centre CYCLING
(☑ 01877-331100; www.scottish-cycling.com; bike per hour/day/week from £8/20/90; ☺ 10am-6pm Mar-Oct) The Trossachs is a lovely area to cycle around. On a cycle route, excellent Wheels Cycling Centre has a wide range of hire bikes. To get here from the centre of Callander, take Bridge St off Main St, turn right onto Invertrossachs Rd and continue for a mile.

🛌 Sleeping

★ Callander Hostel HOSTEL £
(☑ 01877-330141; www.callanderhostel.co.uk; 6 Bridgend; dm/d £20/60; ⓟ@☺) 🏊 This hostel in a mock-Tudor building has been a major labour of love by a local youth project and is now a top-class facility. Well-furnished dorms (private at the time of research due to Covid-19) offer bunks with individual lights and USB charge ports, while en-suite doubles have super views. Staff are lovely, and it has a spacious common area and share kitchen as well as a cafe and garden.

White Shutters B&B £
(☑ 01877-330442; www.incallander.co.uk/white-shutters-bb; 6 South Church St; s/d £28/50; ☺) A cute little house just off the main street of Callander, White Shutters offers pleasing rooms with shared bathroom and a benevolent welcome. The large double is particularly appealing, but everything's clean and comfortable and offers exceptional value.

Abbotsford Lodge HOTEL ££
(☑ 01877-330066; www.abbotsfordlodge.com; Stirling Rd; d £95; ☺ mid-Feb–early Nov; ⓟ☺) Offering excellent value for stylish contemporary rooms in a handsome Victorian house, this main-road choice has energetic owners who provide first-class hospitality and have a real eye for design. There are fabulous, spacious superiors (£135) as well as cheaper (£75) top-floor rooms – with shared bathroom – that have lovably offbeat under-roof shapes. It caters to cyclists and walkers with bike storage and packed lunches.

Room-only rates are available, but breakfast is top-notch. There are some appealing options for families, though no under-6s are allowed.

Arden House B&B ££
(☑ 01877-339405; www.ardenhouse.org.uk; Bracklinn Rd; d £120-130; ☺ Mar-Oct; ⓟ☺) This elegant home has a fabulous hillside location with verdant garden and lovely vistas; it's close to Callander's centre but far from the crowds. The rooms are impeccable, with lots of natural light, and include large upstairs doubles with great views. Welcoming owners, noble architectural features – super bay windows – and a self-catering studio make this a top option. No children.

There's a two-night minimum stay in summer.

Callander Meadows B&B ££
(☑ 01877-330181; www.callandermeadows.co.uk; 24 Main St; s £65, d £80-100; ⓟ☺☺) Upstairs at this recommended restaurant (p248) are some very appealing chambers, elegantly kitted out with solid furniture and good modern shower rooms. One, which can serve as a family room, has a four-poster bed. The owners are very welcoming and you are right in the heart of Callander. Breakfast is excellent.

★ Roman Camp Hotel HOTEL £££
(☑ 01877-330003; www.romancamphotel.co.uk; off Main St; s/d/superior £135/180/290; ⓟ☺☺) Callander's best hotel is centrally located but feels rural, set by the river in beautiful grounds. Endearing features include a lounge with blazing fire and a library with a tiny secret chapel. It's an old-fashioned warren of a place with four grades of rooms; standards are certainly luxurious, but superiors are even more appealing, with period furniture, excellent bathrooms, armchairs and fireplace.

The upmarket restaurant and cute garden cafe-bistro are open to the public. Reassuringly, the name refers not to toga parties but to a ruin in the adjacent fields.

🍴 Eating & Drinking

Mhor Bread CAFE, BAKERY £
(☑ 01877-339518; www.mhorbread.net; 8 Main St; light meals £2-6; ☺ 9am-4pm Mon-Fri, 8am-5pm Sat & Sun; ☺) 🏊 Great traditional-recipe bread (sourdough, seeded, local) for picnics is baked at this high-street spot, which is also a good stop for decent coffee, pies and filled rolls. The steak and haggis pie is a treat.

★ **Callander Meadows** SCOTTISH ££

(☏ 01877-330181; www.callandermeadows.co.uk; 24 Main St; dinner mains £13-19; ☺ 10am-2.30pm & 6-8.30pm Thu-Sun year-round, plus Mon May-Sep; ☜) Informal and cosy, this well-loved restaurant in the centre of Callander occupies the front rooms of a Main St house. It's truly excellent; there's a contemporary flair for presentation and unusual flavour combinations, but a solidly British base underpins the cuisine. There's a great beer/coffee garden out the back, where you can also eat. Lighter lunches such as sandwiches are also available.

★ **Venachar Lochside** SCOTTISH ££

(☏ 01877-330011; www.venachar-lochside.com; Loch Venachar; mains £11-17; ☺ 11am-4pm Jan-Nov, plus 5.30-8.30pm Fri & Sat Jun-Sep; ☜⁜) On lovely Loch Venachar, 4.5 miles west of Callander, this cafe-restaurant has a stunning waterside setting and does a nice line in carefully sourced produce (including delicious local trout) prepared in innovative ways. You can also hire boats and tackle to go fishing for trout on the loch.

Check its Facebook page for dinner openings.

Mhor Fish SEAFOOD ££

(☏ 01877-330213; www.mhorfish.net; 75 Main St; mains £9-18; ☺ noon-9pm Tue-Sun, closed Tue Nov–mid-Feb; ☜) 🍴 This simply decorated spot, with Formica tables and a hodgepodge of chairs, sources brilliant sustainable seafood. Browse the fresh catch then eat it pan-seared in the dining area accompanied by a decent wine selection, or fried and wrapped in paper with chips to take away. It's all

great, and calamari and oysters are wonderfully toothsome starters.

Lade Inn PUB

(☏ 01877-330152; www.theladeinn.com; Kilmahog; ☺ noon-11pm Mon-Thu, to 1am Fri & Sat, 12.30-10.30pm Sun; ☜⁜) Callander's best pub isn't in Callander – it's a mile west of town. It pulls a good pint (with its own real ales), and next door it has a shop with a dazzling selection of Scottish beers. There's low-key live music here on weekends. The food is solid (mains £9 to £14; noon to 9pm, from 12.30pm Sunday).

❶ Getting There & Away

First (www.firstgroup.com) operates buses from Stirling (£6.30, 45 minutes, hourly Monday to Saturday, every two hours Sunday). **Kingshouse** (☏ 01877-384768; www.kingshousetravel.com) has buses between Callander and Killin (£5.60, 40 minutes, five to six Monday to Saturday).

For Aberfoyle, use DRT (p246) or get off a Stirling-bound bus at Blair Drummond safari park, cross the road and pick up an Aberfoyle-bound bus.

Balquhidder & Around

North of Callander, you'll skirt past the shores of gorgeous Loch Lubnaig. Not as famous as some of its cousins, it's still well worth a stop for its sublime views of forested hills. In the small village of Balquhidder (ball-whidder), 9 miles north of Callander off the A84, there's a churchyard with – perhaps – Rob Roy's grave. In the church itself is the 8th-century St Angus' stone, probably a marker to the original tomb of St Angus.

ROB ROY

Nicknamed Red ('*ruadh*' in Gaelic, anglicised to 'roy') for his ginger locks, Robert MacGregor (1671–1734) was the wild leader of the wildest of Scotland's clans, outlawed by powerful neighbours, hence their sobriquet, Children of the Mist. Incognito, Rob became a prosperous livestock trader, before a dodgy deal led to a warrant for his arrest.

A legendary swordsman, the fugitive from justice then became notorious for daring raids into the Lowlands to carry off cattle and sheep. Forever hiding from potential captors, he was twice imprisoned, but escaped dramatically on both occasions. He finally turned himself in and received his liberty and a pardon from the king. He lies buried – perhaps – in the churchyard at Balquhidder; his uncompromising later epitaph reads 'MacGregor despite them'. His life has been glorified over the years due to Walter Scott's novel and the 1995 film. Many Scots see his life as a symbol of the struggle of the common folk against the inequitable ownership of vast tracts of the country by landed aristocrats.

Mhor 84 INN ££

(☑ 01877-384646; www.mhor84.net; A84, Kingshouse; r without breakfast £90; P 🛜 😉) ⚑ At the A84 junction, this 18th-century inn has been given a modern-retro revamp and is an upbeat place with bags of facilities, simple, good-value rooms and a delicious menu of hearty, nourishing meals following the Mhor philosophy of local and sustainable. A great pit stop for drivers, walkers and cyclists. Some rooms are in a rear cottage; there's also a self-catering one.

Food is served 8am to 9pm.

★ Monachyle Mhor HOTEL £££

(☑ 01877-384622; www.monachylemhor.net; Balquhidder; d £195-360; ⊘ Feb-Dec; P 🛜 😉) ⚑ A luxury hideaway with a fantastically peaceful location overlooking two lochs, Monachyle Mhor is a great fusion of country Scotland and contemporary attitudes to design and food. Rooms are superb and feature quirkily original decor, particularly the fabulous 'feature rooms'. Otherwise, go glamping in a retro wagon (£130) or kip in a romantic...ferry waiting room (£145). The restaurant is excellent.

It's an enchanting combination of topclass hospitality with a relaxed rural atmosphere: dogs and kids happily romp on the lawns, and no one looks askance if you come in flushed and muddy after a day's fishing or walking.

ℹ Getting There & Away

Local buses between Callander and Killin stop at Kingshouse, the main-road turn-off to Balquhidder, as do daily buses with Scottish Citylink (p241) between Edinburgh and Oban/Fort William.

Balquhidder is part of the DRT scheme (p246), which you can use to get to Monachyle Mhor.

Killin

POP 800

A fine base for the Trossachs or Perthshire, this lovely village sits at the western end of Loch Tay and has a spread-out, relaxed feel, particularly around the scenic **Falls of Dochart**, which tumble through the centre. On a sunny day people sprawl over the rocks by the bridge, with pint or picnic in hand. Killin offers fine walking around the town, and there are mighty mountains and glens close by.

🏃 Activities

Five miles northeast of Killin, **Ben Lawers** (1214m) rises above Loch Tay. Walking routes abound; one rewarding **circular walk** heads up into the Acharn forest south of town, emerging above the treeline to great views of Loch Tay and Ben Lawers. **Killin Outdoor Centre** (☑ 01567-820652; www.killinoutdoor.co.uk; Main St; bike per 24hr £25, kayak/canoe per 2hr £25; ⊘ 8.45am-5.45pm, hires available roughly Apr-Oct) provides walking advice.

Glen Lochay runs westwards from Killin into the hills of Mamlorn. You can take a **mountain bike** up the glen; the scenery is impressive and the hills aren't too difficult. It's possible, on a nice summer day, to climb over the top of **Ben Challum** (1025m) and descend to Crianlarich, but it's hard work. A potholed road, not maintained and no longer suitable for cars, also connects Glen Lochay with Glen Lyon.

Killin is on the **Lochs & Glens Cycle Way** from Glasgow to Inverness. Hire bikes from helpful Killin Outdoor Centre (which also has canoes and kayaks and, in winter, crampons and snowshoes).

🛏 Sleeping

High Creagan CAMPSITE £

(☑ 01567-820449; www.facebook.com/highcreagancaravanpark; Aberfeldy Rd; per person tent/caravan sites £7/9; ⊘ Apr-Oct; P) High Creagan is a long-established favourite with a good-humoured boss and a well-kept, sheltered campsite with plenty of grass set high on the slopes overlooking sparkling Loch Tay, 3 miles east of Killin. Under-16s aren't allowed in the tent area (for insurance reasons), as there's a gorge running through it.

Courie Inn INN ££

(☑ 01567-831000; www.thecourieinn.com; Main St; d £109-140; P 🛜) An excellent all-round choice, Courie Inn has quality, comfortable rooms decorated with restrained modern elegance; they come in a variety of sizes, including a sumptuous suite with views. It artfully blends the traditional and contemporary. A smaller room is a little cheaper (£89). Downstairs, the restaurant does competent food like curries and fish and chips, and there's a cosy bar.

Old Bank B&B ££

(☑ 01567-829074; www.theoldbankkillin.co.uk; Manse Rd; s/d £60/85; P 🛜) This handsome four-square building with a pretty garden stands proud above the main street in Killin. The hosts are very welcoming and the five rooms are super-comfortable, with contemporary colours, hill views and thoughtful extras.

 Drinking & Nightlife

Falls of Dochart Inn PUB
(☑01567-820270; www.fallsofdochartinn.co.uk; mains £13-18; 🛜) In a prime position overlooking the falls, this pub is a snug, atmospheric space with a roaring fire, real ales and decent food. The outside tables are great spots on a sunny day.

ℹ️ **Getting There & Away**

Kingshouse (p248) runs five to six buses Monday to Saturday to Callander (£5.60, 40 minutes), where you can change for Stirling. Citylink buses between Edinburgh and Oban/Fort William stop at the main road junction 2½ miles southwest of town.

ARRAN

POP 4600

Enchanting Arran is a jewel in Scotland's scenic crown. The island is a visual feast, and boasts culinary delights, its own brewery and distilleries, and stacks of accommodation options. The variations in Scotland's dramatic landscape can all be experienced on this one island, best explored by pulling on the hiking boots or jumping on a bicycle. Arran offers some challenging walks in the mountainous north, while the island's circular coastal road is very popular with cyclists.

ℹ️ **Information**

The **tourist office** (☑01770-303774; www.visitscotland.com; ⊙9am-5pm Mon-Sat Mar-Oct, plus 10am-5pm Sun Apr-Sep, 11am-4pm Mon-Sat Nov-Feb) is in Brodick. The ferry from Ardrossan also has some tourist information. Useful websites include www.visitarran.com.

ℹ️ **Getting There & Away**

CalMac (p255) runs ferries between Ardrossan and Brodick (adult/car £4/15.95, 55 minutes, four to nine daily). From April to late October services also run between Claonaig on the Kintyre peninsula and Lochranza (adult/car £3/9.95, 30 minutes, seven to nine daily). In winter this service runs to Tarbert (1¼ hours) once daily and must be reserved.

ℹ️ **Getting Around**

BICYCLE

Several places hire out bicycles, including these in Brodick:

Arran Adventure Company (☑01770-303349; www.auchrannie.co.uk/adventure. html; Auchrannie Rd) Has good mountain bikes.

Arran Bike Hire (☑07825-160668; www.arranbikehire.com; Shorehouse, Shore Rd; per 24hr/week £20/80; ⊙10am-4pm Apr-Oct, by appointment Nov-Mar) On the waterfront in Brodick. Hires out trail bikes and hybrids and can offer advice on mountain-biking routes.

BUS

Four to seven buses daily go from Brodick pier to Lochranza (£3.25, 45 minutes), and many head the other way to Lamlash (£2.10) and Whiting Bay (£2.85, 30 minutes), then on to Kildonan and Blackwaterfoot. Pick up a timetable from the tourist office.

An Arran Dayrider costs £6.30 from the driver, giving a day's travel. Download a bus timetable from www.spt.co.uk.

CAR

Island of Arran Car Hire (☑01770-302839; www.arran-motors.com; car hire 24hr from £49; ⊙8am-5pm Mon-Sat, from 10am Sun) is at the service station by Brodick ferry pier.

Brodick & Around

POP 800

Most visitors arrive in Brodick, the beating heart of the island of Arran, and congregate along the coastal road to admire the town's long curving bay. On a clear day it's a spectacular vista, with Goatfell looming over the forested shore.

◉ **Sights & Activities**

Brodick Castle CASTLE
(NTS; ☑01770-302202; www.nts.org.uk; castle & park adult/child £13.50/9.50, park only £7/5; ⊙castle 11am-4pm Apr-Oct, park 9.30am-sunset year-round) This elegant castle 2 miles north of Brodick evolved from 13th-century origins into a stately home and hunting lodge for the Dukes of Hamilton. The interior is characterised by fabulous 19th-century wooden furniture and an array of horses 'n' hounds paintings. The hunting gallery is wallpapered with deer heads. Helpful guides and good information panels add background.

The extensive grounds, now a country park with various trails among the rhododendrons, justify the steep entry fee.

Arran Aromatics
WORKSHOP

(☑01770-303003; www.arran.com; ⊙9.30am-4.30pm, to 6pm summer; ♿) Near Brodick Castle is this popular shop and visitor centre where you can purchase any number of scented items and watch the production line at work (it operates from Monday to Thursday). It runs child-friendly activities such as soap-making and candle-dipping, too.

Isle of Arran Heritage Museum
MUSEUM

(☑01770-302636; www.arranmuseum.co.uk; Rosaburn; adult/child £5/3; ⊙10.30am-4.30pm Apr-Oct) This museum has a varied collection of historical and ethnographic items, from prehistoric stone tools to farming implements. There's quite a bit to see across several heritage buildings, with good background on the island and its people. Gardens and a cafe round out the experience. It's on the way to the castle from Brodick.

★ Goatfell
HIKING

The walk up and down Goatfell (874m), the island's highest point, is 8 miles return (up to eight hours), with trailheads at Brodick and Brodick Castle among others. In fine weather there are superb views to Ben Lomond and Northern Ireland. It can, however, be very cold and windy up here; take appropriate maps (available at the tourist office), waterproofing and a compass.

🎎 Festivals & Events

Arran Mountain Festival
SPORTS

(☑01770-303347; www.arranmountainfestival.co.uk; ⊙mid-May) This four-day event offers a wide range of walking and climbing activities led by experienced mountain guides, with events for all abilities. Most cost between £18 and £25 and can be booked online.

Arran Folk Festival
MUSIC

(www.arranfolkfestival.co.uk; ⊙Jun) A three-day festival with concerts and great atmosphere in Brodick. Free daytime sessions are usually in the Douglas hotel, with evening concerts (tickets around £20) in Brodick Hall.

Arran

🔺 N 0 ———— 5 km
0 ———— 2.5 miles

🛏 Sleeping

★ Glenartney
B&B ££

(☑01770-302220; www.glenartney-arran.co.uk; Mayish Rd; d £80-110; ⊙Easter-Oct; P🐕🛜🏠) Uplifting bay views and genuine, helpful hosts make this a cracking option. Airy, stylish rooms make the most of the natural light at the top of the town. Comfortable lounges, help-yourself home baking and pod coffee plus a sustainable ethos make for a very pleasurable stay. Top facilities for cyclists, plus drying rooms and trail advice for hikers are added bonuses.

Belvedere Guest House
B&B ££

(☑01770-302397; www.belvedere-guesthouse.co.uk; Alma Rd; s £60, d £95-110; P🛜) Overlooking town, bay and surrounding mountains, this place has very well-presented rooms with comfortable mattresses. Make sure you pay extra to grab room 1 or 2, each of which is spacious and has fabulous vistas over the water. Breakfast has plenty of choice; there's also a self-catering cottage. It's a likeable Brodick base with a laid-back and helpful host.

Douglas
HOTEL £££

(☑01770-302968; www.thedouglashotel.co.uk; Shore Rd; r £179-249; P🛜🏠) Opposite the ferry, the Douglas is a smart, stylish haven of island hospitality. The views are magnificent and luxurious rooms with smart contemporary fabrics make the most of them. There are numerous thoughtful touches such as binoculars to admire the vistas, and bathrooms are great. The downstairs **bar and bistro** (☑ 01770-302968; www.thedouglashotel.co.uk; Shore Rd; bistro mains £13-20, bar meals £10-15; ⊘ bistro 6-9.30pm, bar noon-9.30pm; 🛜✔) are also recommended. Prices drop midweek and in winter.

 Eating

Ormidale Hotel   PUB FOOD £
(☑ 01770-302293; www.ormidale-hotel.co.uk; Glen Cloy; mains £9-13; ⊘ food 5-9pm; 🛜✔🛝) This hotel serves as a local watering hole and has decent bar food. Dishes change regularly, but there are always some good vegetarian options, and daily specials. Quantities and value-for-money are high, and Arran beers are on tap.

Wineport   CAFE £
(☑ 01770-302101; www.wineport.co.uk; Cladach Centre; mains £9-14; ⊘ 11am-6pm Apr-Oct, check for off-season opening) Located 1.5 miles from Brodick, next to the Isle of Arran Brewery, whose ales are offered on tap, this cafe-bar has great outdoor tables for sunny days and does a nice line in pleasing pub-style fare, such as wings, wedges and soups. It opens for dinner some nights, but hours vary widely each year.

Brodick Bar & Brasserie   BRASSERIE £££
(☑ 01770-302169; www.brodickbar.co.uk; Alma Rd; mains £17-28; ⊘ noon-2.30pm & 5.30-8.30pm Tue-Sat; 🛜) A courteous host and excellent service characterise this upmarket Brodick choice. The menu changes seasonally and focuses on local produce, with particularly

tasty seafood and game dishes. Portions are small and elegantly presented.

🛍 Shopping

Arran Art Trail   ARTS & CRAFTS
(www.arranopenstudios.com) Arran is home to quite a few creatives making a wide variety of art and handicrafts. This trail maps out a couple of dozen studios that you can visit around the island; grab the brochure from the tourist office or see the website.

Corrie to Lochranza

The coast road heads north from Brodick to small, pretty Corrie, where there's a Goatfell trailhead. After **Sannox**, with a sandy beach and great mountain views, the road cuts inland. Heading to the very north, on the island's main road, visitors weave through lush glens flanked by Arran's towering mountain splendour. This is perhaps the most beautiful section of the whole Arran coastal circuit.

Lochranza

POP 200

The village of Lochranza has a stunning location in a small bay on Arran island's north coast. It's characterised by the photogenic 13th-century **Lochranza Castle** (www.historicenvironment.scot; ⊘ 24hr) FREE, a ruin standing proud on a little promontory. The nearby **Isle of Arran Distillery** (☑ 01770-830264; www.arranwhisky.com; tours adult/child £10/free; ⊘ 10am-5pm Mar-Oct, 10.30am-4pm Nov-Feb) produces a light, aromatic single malt. The Lochranza area bristles with red deer, who wander insouciantly into the village to crop the grass.

⭐**Lochranza Youth Hostel**   HOSTEL £
(Hostelling Scotland; ☑ 01770-830631; www.hostellingscotland.org.uk; dm/s/d/q £23.50/30/60/99; ⊘ mid-Mar–Oct, plus Sat & Sun year-round; 🅿@🛜🐾) ✔ An excellent hostel in a charming spot with lovely views. Rooms sport chunky wooden furniture, keycards and lockers. Rainwater toilets, energy-saving heating solutions and a wheelchair-accessible room show thoughtful design, while plush lounging areas, a kitchen you could run a restaurant out of, a laundry, a drying room, red deer in the garden and welcoming management combine for a top option.

Butt Lodge B&B ££

(☑ 01770-830333; www.buttlodge.co.uk; d £90-100, ste £120-135; ⊘ Mar–mid-Oct; P🕏) Down a short potholed road, this Victorian hunting lodge has been adapted to offer contemporary comfort with relaxed style and a genuine welcome. Rooms give perspectives over hills, garden and the rustic village golf course, with its red deer greenkeepers. The Castle suite is a fabulous space with views three ways and a mezzanine seating area. Evening meals are available for guests.

Sandwich Station SANDWICHES £

(☑ 07393 602806; https://thesandwichstation.weebly.com; sandwiches £5-6; ⊘ 8.45am-3.30pm Tue-Sun Mar-Sep; 🖉) Just by Lochranza's ferry slip, this spot does excellent artisanal sandwiches with creative fillings, as well as soups and coffees. The produce is top quality and you can eat at the picnic tables outside.

Stags Pavilion BISTRO ££

(☑ 01770-830600; www.stagspavilion.com; mains £12-20; ⊘ 5.30-8pm Thu-Tue; 🖉) The best restaurant up this end of Arran island, Stags Pavilion is unassumingly set in the former clubhouse of the rustic Lochranza golf course. There's a strong emphasis on local seafood, and dishes are created with a marked Italian influence. You'll likely see red deer munching the grass nearby. It's almost always booked out; reserve ahead if possible. BYO booze.

West Coast

Blackwaterfoot is the largest village on the west coast of Arran, with a shop and hotel. It's pleasant enough, though not the most scenic of the island's settlements. You can walk to **King's Cave** (⊘ 24hr) FREE from here (6 miles), and this walk can easily be extended to the **Machrie Moor Stone Circle** (Machrie; ⊘ 24hr) FREE, the highlight of the area.

⭐**Cafe Thyme** CAFE £

(☑ 01770-840227; www.oldbyre.co.uk; Old Byre Visitor Centre, Machrie; dishes £10-14; ⊘ 10am-5pm, reduced hours winter; 🕏🖉) At the Old Byre Visitor Centre, this is a very pleasant spot, with chunky wooden tables, outdoor seating and sweeping views from its elevated position. It has home baking, a wide tea selection and decent coffee. Less predictably, the food menu features great Turkish pizza, meze boards and smartly priced daily specials. Lunches are served from noon to 3pm.

South Coast

The landscape in the south of Arran is gentler than in the north; the road drops into little wooded valleys, and it's particularly lovely around **Kilmory** and **Lagg**, from where a 10-minute walk will take you to **Torrylinn Cairn**, a chambered tomb over 4000 years old. **Kildonan** has pleasant sandy beaches, a gorgeous water outlook, a hotel, a campsite and an ivy-clad ruined castle.

In genteel **Whiting Bay**, strung out along the water, you'll find small sandy beaches and easy one-hour walks through the forest to the **Giant's Graves** and **Glenashdale Falls** – keep an eye out for golden eagles and other birds of prey.

Lagg Distillery DISTILLERY

(☑ 01770-870565; www.laggwhisky.com; Lagg; tours adult/child £10/free; ⊘ 10am-5.30pm daily Apr-Sep, 10am-4pm Tue-Sat Oct-Mar) This new distillery has a spectacular coastal setting and makes an appealing stop along the road around the island. The squat stills produce a modern, robust, peaty whisky that is a good contrast to the more delicate malt from the sibling distillery in Lochranza. Tours run on the hour and tastings are available. A cafe does sandwiches and comfort food like burritos and poutine, while upstairs is a bistro.

⭐**Sealshore Campsite** CAMPSITE £

(☑ 01770-820320; www.campingarran.com; Kildonan; 1-/2-person tents £9/18, pods for 2 people £40; ⊘ Mar-Oct; P🕏🍴) Living up to its name, this excellent small campsite is right by the sea (and the Kildonan Hotel) and has one of Arran's finest views from its grassy camping area. There are good facilities, including barbecues, power showers and a day room; the breeze keeps the midges away. Camping pods offer a non-tent choice.

Viewbank House B&B ££

(☑ 01770-700326; www.viewbank-arran.co.uk; Whiting Bay; s £59-65, d £85-99; ⊘ Apr-Oct; P🕏🍴) Appropriately named, this quiet and relaxing place does indeed have tremendous views from its vantage point high above Whiting Bay. Rooms, of which there are a variety with and without bathrooms, are well kept; three have a vista. Owners are very hospitable; check out the Clapton guitar and blues memorabilia in the breakfast room. It's well signposted from the main road.

Lamlash

POP 1000

Lamlash, just 3 miles south of Brodick, is in a dazzling setting strung along the beachfront. The bay was used as a safe anchorage by the navy during WWI and WWII.

Holy Island   ISLAND
(www.holyisle.org) Just off Lamlash, this island is owned by the Samye Ling Tibetan Centre and used as a retreat, but day visits are allowed. A tide-dependent **ferry** (☑07970 771960, 01770-700463; tomin10@btinternet.com; return adult/child £12/6; ☉daily Apr-Oct, by arrangement Tue & Fri Nov-Mar) zips across from Lamlash. No dogs, bikes, alcohol or fires are allowed on the island. A good walk to the top of the hill (314m) takes two or three hours return. You can stay at the **Holy Island Centre for World Peace & Health** (☑01770-601100; www.holyisle.org; dm/s/d incl full board £32/55/80; ☉Apr-Oct). Prices include full (vegetarian) board.

Lilybank Guest House   B&B **££**
(☑01770-600230; www.lilybank-arran.co.uk; Shore Rd; s/d £65/90; ☉Apr-Sep; **P**@⑨) Built in the 17th century, Lilybank retains its heritage but has been refurbished for 21st-century needs. Rooms are clean and comfortable, with one that's good for those with limited mobility. The front rooms have great views over Holy Island. Breakfast includes organic porridge, oak-smoked kippers and other Arran goodies.

★**Glenisle Hotel**   HOTEL **£££**
(☑01770-600559; www.glenislehotel.com; Shore Rd; s/d/superior d £110/169/225; ⑨) This stylish hotel offers great service and high comfort levels. Rooms are decorated with contemporary fabrics; 'cosy' rooms under the sloping roof are a little cheaper. All feel fresh and include binoculars for scouring the seashore; upgrade to a 'superior' for the best water views. Downstairs is excellent **food** (☑01770-600559; www.glenislehotel.com; Shore Rd; mains £11-18; ☉noon-8.45pm; ⑨☑) and lovely outdoor seating by the garden.

SOUTH ARGYLL

The impossibly tortuous coastline of the mainland and islands of South Argyll would confuse the most adept geographer. Sea lochs slice the rugged land into peninsulas that offer some of Scotland's most spectacular coastal scenery. The archipelago of islands includes the whisky Shangri La of Islay, the brooding hills of lonely Jura and the retro charms of Bute.

Cowal

The remote and picturesque Cowal Peninsula is cut off from the rest of the country by the lengthy fjords of Loch Long and Loch Fyne. It comprises rugged hills and narrow lochs, with only a few small villages and the old-fashioned, down-at-heel holiday resort of Dunoon. It makes for great, off-the-beaten-track exploration at a very accessible range from busier Glasgow and Loch Lomond.

The attractive **Loch Lomond & Cowal Way** (www.lochlomondandcowalway.org) is a 57-mile walking path crossing the region from Portavadie to Loch Lomond or vice versa.

From Arrochar near Loch Lomond, the A83 to Inveraray loops around the head of Loch Long and climbs into spectacular Glen Croe. The pass at the head of the glen is called the **Rest and Be Thankful**. As you descend Glen Kinglas on the far side, the A815 forks to the left just before Cairndow; this is the main overland route into Cowal.

There are ferries to Cowal from Gourock and Tarbert. Buses run from Glasgow to Dunoon via the ferry. Other buses run by West Coast Motors head overland into and around the peninsula.

Dunoon & Around

Like Rothesay on Bute, Dunoon is a Victorian seaside resort that owes its existence to the steamers that once carried thousands of Glaswegians on pleasure trips 'doon the watter' in the 19th and 20th centuries. Fortunes declined when cheap foreign holidays stole the market and Dunoon is still a bit down in the dumps. Bypass its ugly town centre and take in the magnificent perspectives along the long waterfront.

The town's main attraction is still, as it was in the 1950s, strolling along the **promenade**, licking an ice-cream cone and watching the yachts at play in the Firth of Clyde.

Benmore Botanic Garden　　　GARDENS
(☎ 01369-706261; www.rbge.org.uk; A815; adult/child £7/free; ⊙10am-6pm Apr-Sep, to 5pm Mar & Oct) This garden, 7 miles north of Dunoon, contains Scotland's finest collection of flowering trees and shrubs, including impressive displays of rhododendrons and azaleas, and is entered along a spectacular avenue of giant redwoods. A highlight is the Victorian fernery, nestled in an unlikely fold in the crags. The cafe here (which also opens through some of the winter) appeals for lunch or coffee. Buses run between here and Dunoon.

❶ Getting There & Away

BOAT

Dunoon is served by two ferry services from Gourock (near Greenock). CalMac is passenger-only but better if you are travelling on foot and want to arrive in the town centre. Gourock is easily reached by train from Glasgow.

CalMac (www.calmac.co.uk; adult/child £4.20/2.10, 25 minutes, hourly or more)

Western Ferries (www.western-ferries.co.uk; adult/child/car £4.90/2.40/13.80, 20 minutes, two to three hourly) Arrives at a pier just over a mile from the centre of Dunoon. Departs from McInroy's Point, 2 miles south of Gourock train station on the Irvine road; Scottish Citylink buses run to here.

BUS

Buses around the Cowal Peninsula are operated by West Coast Motors. All ferry slips are served and there's also a run between Dunoon and Inveraray (£4.60, 1¼ hours, three daily Monday to Saturday).

Tighnabruaich

POP 200

Sleepy little seaside Tighnabruaich (tinna-broo-ah) is one of the most attractive villages on the Firth of Clyde and by far the most appealing place at which to overnight on the Cowal Peninsula.

Kames Hotel　　　INN **££**
(☎ 01700-811489;　　www.kames-hotel.com; Kames; s £70, d £90-140; ☎) A mile south of Tighnabruaich, in the village of Kames, this place has a variety of comfortable rooms, including cute ones under the sloping roof on the top floor. Friendly owners have given the place an excellent facelift.

The bar downstairs, popular with yachties and locals, has great atmosphere, killer water views and good-value bar meals.

Bute

POP 6500

The scenic island of Bute lies pinched between the thumb and forefinger of the Cowal Peninsula, separated from the mainland by a narrow, picturesque strait. The main town, Rothesay, is a Victorian resort with a long waterfront and noteworthy castle; south of here is the grand pile of Mount Stuart (p256), one of Scotland's finest stately homes. The west side of the island features dreamy outlooks across to the hills of Arran.

❶ Information

Isle of Bute Discovery Centre (☎ 01700-507043; www.visitscotland.com; Victoria St; ⊙9.30am-5.30pm Jul & Aug, to 5pm Apr-Jun & Sep, 10am-5pm Oct, 10am-4pm Mon-Sat & 11am-3pm Sun Nov-Mar; ☎) There's a free audiovisual display here that provides an upbeat introduction to the island. It's in Rothesay's restored Winter Gardens building – once an entertainment venue and still serving as a cinema.

❶ Getting There & Away

CalMac (☎ 0800 066 5000; www.calmac.co.uk) has ferries between Wemyss Bay and Rothesay (adult/car £3.25/11.60, 35 minutes, roughly hourly). Another crosses the short stretch of water between Rhubodach in the north of the island and Colintraive (adult/car £1.20/6.10, five minutes, half-hourly) in Cowal.

Buses run by **West Coast Motors** (☎ 01586-559135; www.westcoastmotors.co.uk) run around Bute and serve the Rhubodach–Colintraive ferry, also served by Cowal Peninsula buses on the other side.

Rothesay

POP 4500

From the mid-19th century until the 1960s, Rothesay was one of Scotland's most popular holiday resorts, bustling with day trippers disembarking from numerous steamers crowded around the pier. Its hotels were filled with elderly holidaymakers and convalescents taking advantage of the famously mild climate.

Cheap foreign holidays saw Rothesay's fortunes decline, but a nostalgia-fuelled

SOUTHERN HIGHLANDS & ISLANDS BUTE

resurgence of interest has seen many Victorian buildings restored. The grassy, flowery waterfront and row of noble villas make it a lovely place to be once again.

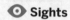 Sights

Rothesay Castle
CASTLE
(☑01700-502691; www.historicenvironment. scot; King St; adult/child £6/3.60; ⊗9.30am-5.30pm daily Apr-Sep, 10am-4pm Sat-Wed Oct-Mar) The splendid, ruined 13th-century Rothesay Castle, with seagulls and jackdaws nesting in the walls, was once a favourite residence of the Stuart kings. It is unique in Scotland in having a circular plan, with four stocky round towers. The landscaped moat, with manicured turf, flower gardens and lazily cruising ducks, makes a picturesque setting.

Victorian Toilets
HISTORIC BUILDING
(Rothesay Pier; adult/child 40p/free; ⊗9am-3.45pm Mon-Thu, to 4.45pm Fri-Sun Oct-Apr, 8am-5.45pm Mon-Thu, to 7.30pm Fri-Sun May-Sep) Dating from 1899, these toilets are a monument to lavatorial luxury – a disinfectant-scented temple of green and black marbled stoneware, glistening white enamel, glass-sided cisterns and gleaming copper pipes. It's the Gents that's the real eye-catcher; the attendant will escort women in for a look around when unoccupied.

🛏 Sleeping

★Boat House
B&B ££
(☑07737-097651; www.theboathouse-bute.co.uk; 15 Battery Pl; d £80-90; 🠾🠾) Boat House brings a touch of class to Rothesay's guesthouse scene, with quality fabrics and furnishings and an eye for design that makes it feel like a boutique hotel, without the expensive prices. Rooms are very swish, with a kitchenette and breakfast provided. Other features include a garden, sea views, a central location and a ground-floor room kitted out for wheelchair users.

Glendale Guest House
B&B ££
(☑01700-502329; www.glendale-guest-house. com; 20 Battery Pl; s £54, d £70-95, f £135; 🅿🠾) This grand Victorian waterfront villa, complete with turret, offers very generous rooms with plush furniture and good family options. Front-facing bedrooms have superb sea views from large windows, as do the lavishly elegant lounge and the breakfast room, where you'll find homemade smoked haddock fishcakes on the menu among oth-er interesting options. Genial hosts make for a pleasurable stay.

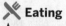 Eating

★Musicker
CAFE, VEGETARIAN £
(☑01700-502287; www.musicker.co.uk; 11 High St; mains £3-7; ⊗10am-5pm Mon-Sat; 🠾🠾) This cool little cafe serves Bute's best coffee, alongside a range of home baking, soups and sandwiches with imaginative fillings. It's very vegan-friendly and also sells CDs, books and guitars, and sports an old-fashioned jukebox.

Harry Haw's
BISTRO ££
(☑01700-505857; www.harryhawsbute.co.uk; 23 High St; mains £9-15; ⊗noon-8.30pm; 🠾🠾) There are great scenes at this welcoming modern bistro with an attractive interior and views over Rothesay Castle. Its moderate prices and pleasing range of deli-style fare plus burgers, pizza, local roast meat and tasty pastas make it a standout. The staff are very friendly and so cheerful you'll wonder if there's something in the water.

Around Rothesay

In the southern part of the island you'll find the haunting 12th-century ruin of **St Blane's Chapel** (⊗24hr) FREE, the nearby **Dunagoil Fort** (⊗24hr) FREE and a sandy beach at Kilchattan Bay. There are more good beaches: **Scalpsie Bay** has a fantastic outlook to Arran, while **Ettrick Bay** is bigger, and has a warmly welcoming **tearoom** (☑01700-500223; www.facebook.com/ettrickbay-tearoom; Ettrick Bay; light meals £3-9; ⊗9.30am-5.30pm, extended summer hours) and glamping pods.

★Mount Stuart
HISTORIC BUILDING
(☑01700-503877; www.mountstuart.com; adult/child £13/7.50; ⊗11am-4pm Apr, May & Oct, to 5pm Jun-Sep, see website for winter hours, grounds 10am-6pm Mar-Oct) The family seat of the Stuart Earls of Bute is one of Britain's more magnificent 19th-century stately homes, the first to have a telephone, underfloor heating and a heated pool. Its eclectic interior, with an imposing central hall and chapel in Italian marble, is heavily influenced by the third Marquess' interests in Greek mythology and astrology. The drawing room has paintings by Titian and Tintoretto among other masters. Mount Stuart is 5 miles south of Rothesay; bus 490 runs here hourly.

Buy tickets at the visitor centre (or book online), from where it's a 15-minute stroll (a courtesy bus is also available) through lovely grounds to the house. Entry is either by guided tour or free visit, depending on the time. Private tours (£20 or £40) offer glimpses of the pool and more bedrooms.

There's a cafe serving famously opulent afternoon teas (book ahead).

Discounted ferry-plus-entrance tickets are available from CalMac (p260).

Inveraray
POP 600

This historic planned village is all black and white – even logos of high-street chain shops conform. Spectacularly set on the shores of Loch Fyne, Inveraray was built by the Duke of Argyll in Georgian style when he revamped his nearby castle in the 18th century.

◉ Sights

Inveraray Castle   CASTLE
(☎01499-302203;   www.inveraray-castle.com; adult/child/family £12.50/8/35; ⊙10am-5.45pm Apr-Oct) This visually stunning castle on the north side of town has been the seat of the Dukes of Argyll – chiefs of Clan Campbell – since the 15th century. The 18th-century building, with its fairy-tale turrets and fake battlements, houses an impressive armoury hall, its walls patterned with more than 1000 pole arms, dirks, muskets and Lochaber axes. Entry is slightly cheaper if you book online.

Inveraray Jail   MUSEUM
(☎01499-302381;   www.inverarayjail.co.uk; Church Sq; adult/child £11.50/6.95; ⊙10am-5pm; ♿) At this entertaining interactive tourist attraction you can sit in on a trial, try out a cell and discover the harsh tortures that were meted out to unfortunate prisoners. The attention to detail – including a life-sized model of an inmate squatting on a 19th-century toilet – is excellent, and actors enliven things during busy periods. Last admission is an hour before closing.

🛏 Sleeping & Eating

★ George Hotel   INN ££
(☎01499-302111;   www.thegeorgehotel.co.uk; Main St E; d £100-145; P �...) The George boasts a magnificent choice of opulent, individual rooms decorated with sumptuous period furniture. Some feature four-poster beds, Victorian roll-top baths and/or private Jacuzzis (superior rooms and suites cost £165 to £225 per double; the library suite is quite a sight). Some rooms are in an annexe opposite and there are also self-catering options.

The cosy wood-panelled bar, with rough stone walls, flagstone floor and peat fires, is a delightful place to all-day bar meals, and has a beer garden.

Samphire   SEAFOOD ££
(☎01499-302321; www.samphireseafood.com; 6a Arkland; dinner mains £14-23; ⊙noon-2.30pm & 5-8.45pm Wed-Sun; ♥) ⌀ There's lots to like about this compact restaurant that makes an effort to source sustainable local seafood.

FYNE FOOD & DRINK

Eight miles north of Inveraray, at the head of Loch Fyne, it pays to stop by two great local establishments:

Loch Fyne Oyster Bar (☎01499-600482; www.lochfyne.com; Clachan, Cairndow; mains £15-26; ⊙9am-7pm Mon-Sat, 10am-7pm Sun, to 5pm Nov-Mar, restaurant noon-5pm or 6pm; ♥) The success of this cooperative is such that it now lends its name to dozens of restaurants throughout the UK. But the original is still the best, with large, salty, creamy oysters straight out of the lake, and fabulous salmon dishes. The atmosphere and decor is simple, friendly and unpretentious; it also has a shop and deli where you can eat casually.

Fyne Ales (☎01499-600120; www.fyneales.com; Achadunan, Cairndow; tours £7.50-10; ⊙10am-6pm) The friendly folk here do a great range of craft beers in this attractive modern brewery off the A83, 9 miles northeast of Inveraray. There's a lovely bar-cafe (with outdoor seating) where you can taste them all: the light, citrussy Jarl is a standout. Tours, which run for about 45 minutes, should be prebooked online. A range of walks tackle the pretty glen from a car park nearby.

It does a delicious seafood stew and you can expect to see lobster, oysters and langoustines from the loch regularly featuring as specials.

ⓘ Getting There & Away

Scottish Citylink (📞0871 266 3333; www.citylink.co.uk) has buses running from Glasgow to Inveraray (£13.90, 1¾ hours, up to nine daily). Some continue to Campbeltown (£15.10, 2¼ hours), others to Oban (£11.50, 1¼ hours). There are also buses to Dunoon (£4.60, 1¼ hours, three daily Monday to Saturday).

Crinan Canal

Completed in 1801, picturesque Crinan Canal runs for 9 miles from Ardrishaig to Crinan allowing seagoing vessels – mostly yachts, these days – to take a short cut from the Firth of Clyde and Loch Fyne to the west coast of Scotland, avoiding the long passage around the Mull of Kintyre. You can easily walk or cycle the **canal towpath** in an afternoon.

★**Venture West**   BOATING
(📞07789 071188; www.venture-west.co.uk; Crinan Harbour; 2½hr trip adult/child £45/30; ☺Mar-Oct) Venture West has really enjoyable boat trips from Crinan (other pick-up points are available) out to Jura, the Garvellach islands and the Corryvreckan Whirlpool. Highlights include sea eagles and (tide-dependent) landings on remote islands. Note that trips run from the old harbour, a little further west than the harbour at the end of the canal. Longer trips head to Iona and Staffa.

★**Crinan Hotel**   HOTEL £££
(📞01546-830261; www.crinanhotel.com; Crinan; s £155, d £230-290; ☺Mar-Dec; 🅿🀢🛜🍴) Romantic Crinan Hotel boasts one of the west coast's most spectacular views. All the bright, light rooms enjoy wonderful perspectives, and the somewhat faded old-world atmosphere is beguiling, with paintings throughout and a top-floor gallery. You're paying for the ambience and view here: don't expect five-star luxury. It's run with welcoming good humour and offers various eating options.

The restaurant **Westward** (mains £21-35; ☺7-8.30pm Mar-Dec; 🛜) does delicious up-market dinners, the cosy **Crinan Seafood Bar** (mains £13-22; ☺noon-2.30pm & 6-8.30pm; 🛜) does great fresh food, including excellent local mussels with white wine and garlic, and the nearby **Crinan Coffee Shop** (snacks £3-7; ☺9am-5pm Mar-Oct, 10am-4pm Sat & Sun Nov-Dec; 🛜) has tasty home baking. Upstairs, **Lock 16** opens for seafood dinners with spectacular views on summer weekends.

ⓘ Getting There & Away

West Coast Motors (p255) has the 425/426 service from Lochgilphead that runs along the canal to Crinan once or twice Monday to Friday. This allows you to walk the canal one way and get the bus back the other.

Kilmartin Glen

This magical glen is the focus of one of the biggest concentrations of prehistoric sites in Scotland. Burial cairns, standing stones, stone circles, hill forts and cup-and-ring-marked rocks litter the countryside. Within a 6-mile radius of Kilmartin village

---

RETURN OF THE BEAVER

Beavers had been extinct in Britain since the 16th century. But in 2009 they returned to Scotland, when a population of Norwegian beavers was released into the hill lochs of Knapdale, Argyll. After a broadly successful trial, the beavers are now here to stay; the first successful reintroduction of a previously extinct mammal to Britain.

You can try to get a glimpse of them on the **Beaver Detective Trail**. This circular walk starts from the Barnluasgan forestry car park on the B8025 road to Tayvallich, about 1.5 miles south of the Crinan Canal. There's an information hut here. The trail is 3 miles, but you might glimpse them at pretty Dubh Loch just half a mile down the track.

Near here, the **Argyll Beaver Centre** (📞01546-810218; www.argyllbeavercentre.co.uk; Barnluasgan; ☺10am-5pm Apr-Oct, reduced opening Nov-Mar) has a visitor centre and runs guided wildlife walks, including beaver-oriented ones.

there are 25 sites with standing stones and more than 100 rock carvings.

In the 6th century, Irish settlers arrived in this part of Argyll and founded the kingdom of Dál Riata (Dalriada), which eventually united with the Picts in 843 to create the first Scottish kingdom. Their capital was the hill fort of Dunadd, on the plain to the south of Kilmartin.

Kilmartin House Museum
MUSEUM
(☑01546-510278; www.kilmartin.org; Kilmartin) This museum, in Kilmartin village, is a fascinating interpretive centre that provides a context for the ancient monuments you can go on to explore, alongside displays of artefacts recovered from various sites. A major redevelopment of the museum is underway, and it's due to reopen in 2023. Meanwhile, it's still the best place to head for first, as an outdoors display gives information about all the sites to visit in the surrounding valley. There's a takeaway cafe too.

Dunadd Fort
ARCHAEOLOGICAL SITE
(⊘24hr) FREE This atmospheric hill fort, 3.5 miles south of Kilmartin village, was the seat of power of the first kings of Dál Riata, and may have been where the Stone of Destiny was originally located. Atop the hill, a footprint, faint rock carvings of a boar and an ogham inscription may have been used in inauguration ceremonies. The prominent little hill rises straight out of the boggy plain of Moine Mhor Nature Reserve.

A slippery path leads to the summit, where you can gaze out on much the same view that the kings of Dál Riata enjoyed 1300 years ago.

❶ Getting There & Away

Bus 423 between Oban and Ardrishaig (three to five Monday to Friday, two on Saturday) stops at Kilmartin (from Oban £6.60, 1¼ hours).

You can walk or cycle along the **Crinan Canal** from Ardrishaig, then turn north at Bellanoch on the minor B8025 road to reach Kilmartin (12 miles one way). It's a lovely journey.

Kintyre

The 40-mile-long Kintyre peninsula is almost an island, with only a narrow isthmus at Tarbert connecting it to Knapdale. During the Norse occupation of the Western Isles, the Scottish king decreed that

WALK KINTYRE

Tarbert is the starting point for the 103-mile **Kintyre Way** (www.thekintyreway.com), a walking route that meanders the length of the peninsula to Southend at the southern tip and around to Machrihanish. It's very scenic, with wonderful coastal views nearly the whole way.

the Vikings could claim as their own any island they circumnavigated in a longship. So in 1098 the wily Magnus Barefoot stood at the helm while his men dragged their boat across this neck of land, validating his claim to Kintyre.

The coastline is spectacular on both sides, with stirring views of Arran, Islay, Jura and Northern Ireland. On a sunny day the water shimmers beyond the stony shore. Hiking the Kintyre Way is a great means of experiencing the peninsula, which has a couple of cracking golf courses at Machrihanish near Campbeltown.

Tarbert
POP 1100
The attractive fishing village and yachting centre of Tarbert is the gateway to Kintyre, and is most scenic, with buildings strung around its excellent natural harbour. A crossroads for nearby ferry routes, it's a handy stepping stone to Arran or Islay, but is well worth a stopover on any itinerary.

The picturesque harbour is overlooked by the crumbling, ivy-covered ruins of **Tarbert Castle** (⊘24hr) FREE, rebuilt by Robert the Bruce in the 14th century. You can hike up via a signposted footpath beside **Loch Fyne Gallery** (☑01880-820390; www.facebook.com/LochFyneGallery; Harbour St; ⊘10am-5pm Mon-Sat, 11am-4pm Sun), which showcases the work of local artists.

🛏 Sleeping & Eating

★ **Knap Guest House**
B&B ££
(☑01880-820015; www.knapguesthouse.co.uk; Campbeltown Rd; d £90-99; 🐾) This cosy upstairs spot at the bend in the main road offers faultless hospitality, luxurious furnishings and an attractive blend of Scottish and Far Eastern decor, with wooden elephants especially prominent. The welcome is warm, and there are great harbour views from the breakfast room, where the

open kitchen allows you to admire the host at work. Prices drop in low season.

Rooms are plush, with the owner's years in hospitality paying dividends for guests. One is a suite (£135 to £180), which has an excellent, spacious lounge area with vistas.

Moorings B&B **££**
(☑ 01880-820756; www.themooringsbb.co.uk; Pier Rd; s £50-60, d £80-100; ⓟ⌃) Follow the harbour just past Tarbert's centre to this spot, which is beautifully maintained and decorated by one man and his dogs. It has great views over the water, an eclectic menagerie of ceramic and wooden animals plus offbeat artwork; you can't miss it from the street.

★ Starfish SEAFOOD **££**
(☑ 01880-820733; www.starfishtarbert.com; Castle St; mains £14-21; ⊙5-8.30pm Tue-Thu, 12.30-2pm & 5-8.30pm Fri & Sat Mar-Oct; ⌃⊘) ⊘ This attractive, very welcoming restaurant does simple, stylish seafood of brilliant quality. A great variety of specials – anything from classic French fish dishes to Thai curries – are prepared with whatever's fresh off the Tarbert boats that day. There are options for vegetarians and meat eaters, too, and decent cocktails. Closed Sunday and Monday early and late in the season.

ⓘ Getting There & Away

BOAT
CalMac (☑ 0800 066 5000; www.calmac. co.uk) operates a car ferry from Tarbert to Portavadie on the Cowal Peninsula (adult/car

£2.80/8.65, 25 minutes, six to 12 daily). From late October to March there are also ferries to Lochranza on Arran (adult/car £3/9.95, 1¼ hours, one daily) that must be booked in advance. In summer this leaves from Claonaig near Skipness, 13 miles south.

Ferries to Islay and Colonsay depart from Kennacraig ferry terminal, 5 miles southwest.

BUS
Tarbert is served by four to five daily coaches with Scottish Citylink (p258), between Campbeltown (£9, one hour) and Glasgow (£18.80, 3¼ hours).

Gigha

POP 200

Gigha (*ghee*-ah; www.gigha.org.uk) is a low-lying island, 6 miles long by about 1 mile wide, famous for its sandy beaches, pristine turquoise water and mild climate – subtropical plants thrive in **Achamore Gardens** (☑ 01583-505275; www.gigha.org.uk; Achamore House; suggested donation adult/child £6/3; ⊙dawn-dusk). Other highlights include the ruined **church** at Kilchattan, the **bible garden** at the manse, and Gigha's picturesque northern end.

The island was famously purchased by its residents in 2002, though they have had some financial problems since. Local **Gigha cheeses** include goats cheese and oak-smoked cheddar.

Gigha Hotel INN **££**
(☑ 01583-505254; www.gighahotel.com; Ardminish; s £80, d £85-135; ⓟ⌃⊗) The island's quirky hotel, just south of the central junction, has a variety of cosy rooms, some with views. It

OFF THE BEATEN TRACK

SKIPNESS

Tiny Skipness, 13 miles south of Tarbert, is pleasant and quiet with great views of Arran. Beyond the village rise the substantial remains of 13th-century **Skipness Castle** (www. historicenvironment.scot; ⊙castle & chapel 24hr, tower 9.30am-5.30pm Apr-Sep, 10am-4pm Oct) **FREE**, a former possession of the Lords of the Isles.

Skipness Seafood Cabin (☑ 01880-760207; www.skipnessseafoodcabin.co.uk; dishes £3-18; ⊙11am-7pm Sun-Fri late May-Sep) Attached to Skipness House, near the castle, this place has a great summer scene on a fine day, serving no-frills but delicious local fish and shellfish dishes at outdoor picnic tables that have grand views over the grassy coast across to Arran. It's famous for its crab rolls, which are on the small side: add on a pot of mussels or plate of gravadlax.

Skipness Smokehouse (☑ 01880-760378; www.skipnesssmokehouse.com; ⊙noon-5pm Sun-Fri Mar-Dec) The hot smoked salmon from these folk behind Skipness Castle is extremely succulent, along with other treats. There's usually somebody around even outside the official opening hours.

also serves breakfasts, bar meals and posher restaurant dishes.

★ The Boathouse
SEAFOOD ££

(☑ 01583-505123; www.boathouseongigha.com; Ardminish; mains £12-20; ⏱ 11.30am-9pm mid-Mar–Oct; 🛜) This picturesque stone cottage is right by the water near the ferry slip. It's *the* place to go for fresh seafood: local lobster, delicious oysters and sustainable, organic Gigha-farmed halibut are the highlights. Sit at the deck outside and admire the idyllic view. You can also camp here (£4/2 per adult/child), but space is limited so call in advance.

❶ Getting There & Away

CalMac (p255) runs from Tayinloan in Kintyre (adult/car £2.70/7.80, 20 minutes, roughly hourly). Stopping at the terminal are four to five daily buses with Scottish Citylink (p258), in each direction between Glasgow/Tarbert and Campbeltown

Campbeltown & Around
POP 4800

Blue-collar Campbeltown is set around a beautiful harbour. It still suffers from the decline of its fishing and whisky industries and the closure of the nearby air-force base, but is rebounding on the back of golf tourism, increased distillery action and a ferry link to Ayrshire. The spruced-up seafront backed by green hills lends the town a distinctly optimistic air.

⦿ Sights & Activities

Springbank
DISTILLERY

(☑ 01586-555468; www.springbank.scot; 85 Longrow; tours from £10; ⏱ tours Mon-Sat) There were once no fewer than 32 distilleries around Campbeltown, but most closed in the 1920s. Today this is one of only three still in operation. It is also one of the few around that distills, matures and bottles all its whisky on the one site, making for an interesting tour. It produces a quality malt, one of Scotland's finest. Various premium tours take you deeper into the process.

Davaar Cave
CAVE

(⏱ 24hr) FREE A very unusual sight awaits in this cave on the southern side of Davaar island, at the mouth of Campbeltown Loch. On the wall of the cave is an eerie painting of the Crucifixion by local artist Archibald MacKinnon, dating from 1887. You can walk

WORTH A TRIP

MULL OF KINTYRE

The **Mull of Kintyre** is narrow winding road, 15 miles long, leads south from Campbeltown to the Mull of Kintyre, passing good sandy beaches near Southend. This remote headland was immortalised in the famous song by Paul McCartney and Wings; the former Beatle owns a farmhouse in the area. From the road's end, a 30-minute steep downhill walk leads to a clifftop lighthouse, with Northern Ireland, only 12 miles away, visible across the channel. Don't leave the road when the frequent mists roll in; it's easy to become disoriented.

to the island at low tide: check tide times with the tourist office.

🛌 Sleeping & Eating

★ Campbeltown Backpackers
HOSTEL £

(☑ 01586-551188; www.campbeltownbackpackers.co.uk; Big Kiln St; dm £22; 🅿🛜) 🌿 This beautiful hostel occupies a central former school building: it's great, with a modern kitchen, state-of-the-art wooden bunks and access for people with disabilities. Profits go to maintain the Heritage Centre (opposite) that runs it. Rates are £2 cheaper if you book ahead.

Argyll Hotel
INN ££

(☑ 01583-421212; www.argyllhotelkintyre.co.uk; A83, Bellochantuy; s £65, d £85-100; 🅿🛜) Right on a fine stretch of beach with a magnificent outlook to Islay and Jura, this traditional inn 10 miles north of Campbeltown on the main road is run with cheery panache. Rooms are cosy and breakfast is a highlight, with creative egg dishes and a wealth of homemade jams, as you gaze over the water.

The restaurant does some inventive fusion fare. The water reaches the heady heights (for Scotland) of 11°C in summer if you fancy a dip. Don't confuse this place with the Argyll Arms Hotel in Campbeltown itself.

🍸 Drinking & Nightlife

Ardshiel Hotel
BAR

(☑ 01586-552133; www.ardshiel.co.uk; Kilkerran Rd; ⏱ noon-11pm Mon-Sat, from 12.30pm Sun; 🛜) This friendly hotel has one of Scotland's best

GOLF AT MACHRIHANISH

Machrihanish, 5 miles northwest of Campbeltown, is home to a couple of excellent golf courses:

Machrihanish Golf Club (01586-810277; www.machgolf.com; Machrihanish; green fee £75) Machrihanish Golf Club is a classic links course, designed by Old Tom Morris. It's remarkably good value compared to courses of a similar standard elsewhere in Scotland. The famous first hole requires a very decent drive across the bay, or you'll literally end up on the beach. Nearby is an upmarket hotel and restaurant, as well as self-catering villas.

Machrihanish Dunes (01586-810000; www.machrihanishdunes.com; Machrihanish; green fee £110) Much newer than its venerable neighbour Machrihanish Golf Club, the Dunes is an impressive seaside experience and commendably light on snobbery: the clubhouse is a convivial little hut, it's child-friendly and there are often website offers. Good packages including accommodation are available.

whisky bars, the perfect place to learn more about the Campbeltown distilling tradition and to taste the local malts. With over 700 whiskies to choose from, it's not a place for the indecisive.

ⓘ Getting There & Away

AIR

Loganair (www.loganair.co.uk) flies between Glasgow and Campbeltown's mighty runway at Machrihanish. Depending on the season, there may be other summer connections possible to Islay and Tiree.

BOAT

Kintyre Express (01586-555895; www.kintyreexpress.com; ⊘Apr-Sep) operates a small, high-speed passenger ferry from Campbeltown to Ballycastle in Northern Ireland (£50/90 one way/return, 1½ hours, daily May to August, Friday to Sunday April and September). You must book in advance. You can also get to Islay, and charters are available.

CalMac (p255) runs thrice weekly May to September between Ardrossan in Ayrshire and Campbeltown (adult/car £8.30/44.05, 2¾ hours); the Saturday return service stops at Brodick on Arran.

BUS

Scottish Citylink (p258) runs from Campbeltown to Glasgow (£22.90, 4¼ hours, four to five daily) via Tarbert, Inveraray and Loch Lomond. Change at Inveraray for Oban.

Islay

POP 3200

The home of some of the world's greatest and peatiest whiskies, whose names reverberate on the tongue like a pantheon of Celtic deities, Islay (*eye*-lah) is a wonderfully friendly place whose welcoming inhabitants offset its lack of scenic splendour compared to Mull or Skye. The distilleries are well geared-up for visits, but even if you're not a fan of single malt, the birdlife, fine seafood, turquoise bays and basking seals are ample reasons to visit. Locals are among Britain's most genial: a wave or cheerio to passers-by is mandatory, and you'll soon find yourself unwinding to relaxing island pace. The only drawback is that the waves of well-heeled whisky tourists have induced many sleeping options to raise prices to eye-watering levels.

☞ Tours

Islay Sea Adventures BOATING
(01496-300129; www.islay-sea-adventures.co.uk; Port Ellen) Leaving from Port Ellen, this set-up runs tours with a variety of small boats. A 2½-hour trip takes in the southern distilleries and lots of wildlife (adult/child £45/35), or you could head off to Jura and the Corryvreckan whirlpool (£80, four hours).

✯ Festivals & Events

Fèis Ìle MUSIC, FOOD & DRINK
(Islay Festival; www.islayfestival.com; ⊘late May) A weeklong celebration of traditional Scottish music and whisky: events include *ceilidhs* (evenings of traditional Scottish entertainment), pipe-band performances, barbecues and lots of whisky-related fun, with many distilleries releasing special bottlings for the event. The island packs out; book accommodation well in advance.

ℹ️ Information

Bowmore Tourist Office (📞 01496-305165; www.islayinfo.com; The Square; ⏱️10am-5pm Mon-Sat, noon-5pm Sun Mar-May, 9.30am-5.30pm Mon-Sat, noon-3pm Sun Jun-Aug, 10am-5pm Mon-Sat Sep & Oct, 10am-3pm Mon-Fri Nov-Feb) One of the nation's best tourist offices. The staff will bend over backwards to find you accommodation if things look full up.

ℹ️ Getting There & Away

There are two ferry terminals: Port Askaig on the east coast, and Port Ellen in the south. Islay airport lies midway between Port Ellen and Bowmore.

AIR

Loganair (www.loganair.co.uk) flies up to three times daily from Glasgow to Islay, sometimes via Campbeltown, while Hebridean Air Services (p277) operates twice daily on Thursday from Oban to Colonsay and Islay.

BOAT

CalMac (p255) runs ferries from Kennacraig to Port Ellen or Port Askaig (adult/car £6.90/34.30, two hours, three to five daily). On Wednesday and Saturday in summer you can usually travel to Colonsay (adult/car £4.25/17.75, 1¼ hours, day trip possible) and Oban (adult/car £10.05/54.30, four hours).

Book car space on ferries several days in advance.

ℹ️ Getting Around

BICYCLE

There are various places to hire bikes, including **Islay Cycles** (📞 07760 196592; www.islaycycles.co.uk; 2 Corrsgeir Pl, Port Ellen; bikes per day/week from £20/70) and **Port Charlotte Bicycle Hire** (📞 01496-850488; Main St, Port Charlotte; bike hire 1/3 days £15/35; ⏱️9am-6pm).

BUS

A bus links Ardbeg, Port Ellen, Bowmore, Port Charlotte, Portnahaven and Port Askaig (Monday to Saturday only). You can get unlimited travel for 24 hours for £10, but fares are low anyway. Pick up a copy of the *Islay & Jura Public Transport Guide* from the Bowmore tourist office or on the ferry on the way over.

CAR

Islay Car Hire (📞 01496-810544; www.islaycarhire.com; Islay Airport) offers car hire from £42 a day and can meet ferries.

TAXI

There are various taxi services on Islay; **Carol's Cabs** (📞 07775 782155, 01496-302155; www.carols-cabs.co.uk) is one that can take bikes.

Port Ellen & Around

Port Ellen is Islay's principal entry point. The coast stretching northeast is one of the loveliest parts of the island, where within 3 miles you'll find three of whisky's biggest names: Laphroaig, Lagavulin and Ardbeg.

The kelp-fringed skerries (small rocky islands or reefs) of the **Ardmore Islands**, near Kildalton, are a wildlife haven and home to Europe's second-largest colony of common seals.

⊙ Sights

The three southern distilleries of Laphroaig, Lagavulin and Ardbeg are arrayed in an easy succession east of town. There's an ongoing project to reopen the Port Ellen distillery, dismantled apart from its malting works in 1983.

Ardbeg DISTILLERY
(📞 01496-302244; www.ardbeg.com; tours from £8; ⏱️9.30am-5pm Mon-Fri year-round, plus Sat & Sun Apr-Oct) Ardbeg's iconic peaty whiskies start with their magnificent 10-year-old. The basic tour is good, and it also offers longer tours involving walks, stories and extended tastings. It's 3 miles northeast of Port Ellen; there's a good **cafe** (📞 01496-302244; www.ardbeg.com; Ardbeg; mains £8-13; ⏱️10am-4pm Mon-Fri year-round, plus Sat & Sun Apr-Oct; 🍴) for lunch here, too.

Lagavulin DISTILLERY
(📞 01496-302749; www.lagavulindistillery.com; tours from £15; ⏱️9.15am-5pm daily Mar-Sep,

---

GONE FISHIN'

A lifetime's experience of exploring his native rivers, lochs and coastline means there isn't much that professional guide Duncan Pepper, owner of **Fishinguide Scotland** (📞 07714 598848; www.fishinguide.co.uk; daily per person £200-400), doesn't know about Scottish fishing. Though based in Perthshire, he leads fishing trips all over Scotland for salmon, trout, pike, pollack and more. Packages include travel, instruction, permits, tackle and a lavish picnic lunch.

Islay, Jura & Colonsay

9.45am-5pm Mon-Sat Oct-Dec, 10.15am-4pm Mon-Sat Jan & Feb) Peaty and powerful whisky is made by Lagavulin, one of the triumvirate of southern distilleries near Port Ellen. The Lagavulin Tasting Experience (£15) is a good option, cutting out much of the distillery mechanics that you might have already seen elsewhere and replacing it with an extended tasting. The Warehouse Tour (£35) is also a lot of fun.

Laphroaig DISTILLERY
(☑ 01496-302418; www.laphroaig.com; tours from £10; ⊙ 9.45am-5pm daily Mar-Oct, to 4.30pm daily Nov & Dec, to 4.30pm Mon-Fri Jan & Feb) Laphroaig produces famously peaty whiskies just outside Port Ellen. Of the various premium tastings that it offers, the 'Water to Whisky' tour is recommended – you see the water source, dig peat, have a picnic and try plenty of drams.

Kildalton Cross MONUMENT
(Kildalton; ⊙ 24hr) FREE A pleasant drive or ride leads past the distilleries to ruined **Kildalton Chapel**, 8 miles from Port Ellen. In the kirkyard is the exceptional late-8th-century Kildalton Cross. There are carvings of biblical scenes on one side and animals on the other.

🛏 Sleeping & Eating

Kintra Farm CAMPSITE, B&B £
(☑ 01496-302051; www.kintrafarm-islay.co.uk; tent site £6-10, plus adult/child £5/3; ⊙ May-Sep; P 🐕) At the southern end of Laggan Bay, 3.5 miles northwest of Port Ellen, Kintra is a basic but beautiful campsite on buttercup-sprinkled turf amid the dunes, with sunset views across the beach. There are also self-catering cottages at this working farm.

Askernish B&B B&B ££
(☑ 01496-302536; www.askernishbandb.co.uk; 49 Frederick Cres, Port Ellen; s £70, d £90-110; 🛜) Very handy for the Port Ellen ferry slip, this dark-stone Victorian house was once the local medical practice; indeed, one of the rooms is in the former surgery, while another is the waiting room. Rooms are generous, with old-style flowery decor but modern bathroom fittings. The owner Joy takes real interest in her guests and is a delight.

★ SeaSalt BISTRO ££
(☑ 01496-300300; www.seasalt-bistro.co.uk; 57 Frederick Cres, Port Ellen; mains £10-16; ⊙ noon-2.30pm & 5-8.45pm) This buzzy modern place represents an unusual combination in Port Ellen: a takeaway doing kebabs, pizzas and bacon rolls, but also a classy bistro.

High-backed dining chairs are comfortable for devouring delicious local seafood off a menu of daily specials. The owner and staff are very friendly. It also opens from 10am to noon for coffee and breakfasty fare.

Bowmore

POP 700

Islay's attractive Georgian capital was built in 1768 to replace the village of Kilarrow, which just had to go – it was spoiling the view from the laird's house. Its centrepieces are the **Bowmore Distillery** (☑01496-810441; www.bowmore.com; School St; tours from £10; ⊙9.30am-6pm Mon-Sat, noon-4pm Sun Mar-Oct, 10am-5pm Mon-Sat Nov-Feb) and distinctive **Round Church** at the top of Main St, built in circular form to ensure that the devil had no corners to hide in. He was last seen in one of the island's distilleries.

🛏 Sleeping

⭐**Lambeth House**   B&B ££
(☑01496-810597; www.lambeth-guesthouse.co.uk; Jamieson St; s/d £75/100; 🕿) Cheerily welcoming, and with smart modern rooms with top-notch en-suite bathrooms, this is a sound option in the centre of town. The host is a long-time expert in making guests feel at home, and her breakfasts are reliably good. Rooms vary substantially in size but their prices are the same, so ask for a larger one when booking.

Dha Urlar   B&B ££
(☑07967 505991; www.dha-urlar-bed-and-breakfast.co.uk; Cruach; r £120-150; 🅿🕿) Just a mile out of Bowmore, this place sits in an elevated position granting spectacular perspectives across moorland to Jura, the Mull of Kintyre and the coast of Ireland. Rooms have lots of space, comfortable beds and modern bathrooms. Breakfast is served from an open kitchen while your hosts helpfully supply you with lots of local information.

Island Bear   B&B ££
(☑01496-301462; www.islandbear.co.uk; Shore St; s/d £75/100; 🕿) As central as you can be in Bowmore, this house is compact and built very vertically, though some ground-floor accommodation is on the way. Rooms are cosy and inviting, with modern decor and stylish en suite bathrooms. There are

views from two of the rooms, a kindly welcome and tasty breakfasts.

Bowmore House   B&B £££
(☑01496-810324; www.thebowmorehouse.co.uk; Shore St; s/d from £90/140; 🅿🕿) This stately former bank building has plenty of character and super water views. It's a top-level B&B, with coffee machines in the rooms, an honesty minibar with bottles of wine and local ales, and plush king-sized beds. Rooms are spacious, high-ceilinged and light. Further rooms are in adjacent cottages, also available on a self-catering basis.

Harbour Inn   BOUTIQUE HOTEL £££
(☑01496-810330; www.bowmore.com/harbour-inn; The Square; s/d from £120/145; 🕿) The plush seven-room Harbour Inn, owned by Bowmore Distillery, offers friendly service, a good restaurant, a snug bar and prime location a few steps from the water in Islay's capital. The chambers are well appointed with modern comforts, quality amenities – including whisky soaps and gels – and plush fabrics, though some are on the small side for the price.

Bowmore Distillery also offers various cottages around the centre, bookable via the same website.

🍴 Eating

Peatzeria   PIZZA ££
(☑01496-810810; www.peatzeria.com; 22 Shore St; pizzas £9-20; ⊙noon-10pm, closed Mon in winter; 🕿) This is one of those names that just had to be. Nice work, punsters! An impressively realised church conversion has created a warmly welcoming Italian restaurant that specialises in toothsome stone-baked pizzas with innovative toppings that include local seafood. The weatherproof conservatory seating area has special views over the bay.

Bridgend Hotel   SCOTTISH ££
(☑01496-810212; www.bridgend-hotel.com; Bridgend; mains £11-20; ⊙food noon-2pm & 6-9pm; 🕿♿) At Islay's major crossroads, 3 miles northeast of Bowmore, this hotel offers satisfying dining in an attractive slate-floored room on one side and a more formal dining room on the other. Exceptionally cheery service is allied with competent dishes of fish, venison and other local game, with fresh seafood specials adding to the options. There's also a decent bar menu.

Tobermory (p281), Mull **2.** Hermaness National Nature Reserve
»427) **3.** Ardbeg single malt Scotch from Corryvreckan (p270)

Scotland's Islands

Scotland's sweeping array of islands – more than 900 at last count, around 100 of which are inhabited – defines the country's complex coastline. Ruins, from prehistoric religious centres to staunch castles, overlook landscapes where sheep crop lush grass, the scant remaining fisherfolk take on powerful seas, and urban professionals looking for a quieter life battle with unreliable wi-fi.

Geography & History

Though in the modern world these islands might seem remote outposts, Scotland's complex geography has meant that, from Celts through to Vikings and the Lords of the Isles, transport, trade and power have been intimately tied to the sea. Today's lonely island stronghold was yesteryear's hub of connections spreading right across western and northern Britain and beyond.

Sights & Activities

For the visitor, there's bewildering scope. The once-Norse islands of Orkney and Shetland are Britain's northernmost parts, while the Hebrides guard the west coast like a storm shield against the mighty Atlantic. The choice is yours: for scenic splendour with hills to climb and memorable walks, you might choose spectacular Skye, diverse Mull, accessible Arran or lonely Jura. Neolithic villages, standing stones and evocative prehistoric monuments? Head to far-flung Orkney, Shetland or the Outer Hebrides. Abbeys, castles or stately homes? Magical Iona, Bute, Coll, Barra or Westray. Beaches? Pick Harris or Tiree. Birdlife? Unst, the Uists, Fair Isle, Noss, North Ronaldsay or Staffa. Whisky? It's got to be Islay. A convivial pub, local seafood and a warm welcome? Take your pick of any, finding yourself a snug cottage with a scent of the salty breeze, and call it home for a day or three.

DON'T MISS

ISLAY'S DISTILLERIES

Islay has nine working distilleries, with a 10th, the back-from-the-dead Port Ellen, on the way. All welcome visitors and run tours, which you should definitely book ahead by phone, as they have maximum numbers and can fill up days in advance. More expensive, specialised tours let you taste more malts and take you further behind the scenes. Pick up the invaluable pamphlet listing tour times from the Bowmore Tourist Office (p263). Five of the nine distilleries can be reached by the island's buses; a bit of walking, hitching or cabbing will easily get you to the others.

Harbour Inn
BRITISH ££

(☑ 01496-810330; www.bowmore.com; The Square; mains £15-24; ☺ noon-2.30pm & 6-9.30pm; ☎) Owned by the Bowmore Distillery, this restaurant at the Harbour Inn (p265) is the classiest in town. The conservatory-style dining area offers wonderful sunset views over the water. Islay oysters are a delicious and obvious choice; the rest of the menu could benefit from a little more seasonal and local focus, but is competently prepared and presented.

It's also open in the morning for pretty good breakfasts and all afternoon for sandwiches and light meals.

Port Charlotte & Around

On the opposite shore of Loch Indaal 11 miles from Bowmore is attractive Port Charlotte, a former distillery town that appeals as a base. Museums in town and distilleries close by mean there's plenty to do.

The road ends 6 miles southwest of Port Charlotte at **Portnahaven**, a picturesque fishing village. For seal-spotting, you can't do better; there are frequently dozens of the portly beasts basking in the small harbour.

◉ Sights

★ Bruichladdich
DISTILLERY

(☑ 01496-850190; www.bruichladdich.com; Bruichladdich; tours from £7.50; ☺ 9am-6pm Mon-Fri, to 5pm Sat, 10am-4pm Sun Apr-Sep, reduced hours Oct-Mar) A couple of miles from Port Charlotte, Bruichladdich (brook-*lad*-dy)

is an infectiously fun distillery to visit and produces a mind-boggling range of bottlings; there's always some new experiment cooking. The standard expression is lightly peated, but Bruichladdich turns out some phenolic monsters under the Port Charlotte and Octomore labels. It also makes a gin here, the Botanist, infused with local herbs. A generous attitude to tastings makes for an uplifting visit.

Kilchoman
DISTILLERY

(☑ 01496-850011; www.kilchomandistillery. com; Rockfield Farm, Kilchoman; tours from £10; ☺ 9.45am-5pm Apr-Oct, closed Sat & Sun Nov-Mar) ✐ Likable Kilchoman, set on a farm, is one of Scotland's smallest distilleries. It grows and malts some of its own barley here and does its own bottling by hand. It has a wide variety of attractively packaged expressions: the 100% Islay whiskies are the ones produced from the home-grown barley. The tour is informative and the tasting generous. There's also a good cafe.

Museum of Islay Life
MUSEUM

(☑ 01496-850358; www.islaymuseum.org; Port Charlotte; adult/child £4/1; ☺ 10.30am-4.30pm Mon-Fri Apr-Oct) Islay's long history is lovingly recorded in this museum, housed in the former Free Church. Prize exhibits include an illicit still, 19th-century crofters' furniture, and a set of leather boots once worn by the horse that pulled the lawnmower at Islay House (so it wouldn't leave hoof prints on the lawn!).

🛏 Sleeping & Eating

Islay Youth Hostel
HOSTEL £

(Hostelling Scotland; ☑ 01496-850385; www. hostellingscotland.org.uk; Main St, Port Charlotte; dm/tw/q £23.50/52/97; ☺ Apr-Oct; @☎) This clean and modern brick hostel has spotless dorms with washbasins and a large kitchen and living room. It's housed in a former distillery building with views over the loch. The bus stops nearby. Breakfast and heatable dinners are available. Have a crack at Islay Monopoly, one of the board games on hand.

Distillery House
B&B ££

(☑ 01496-850495; mamak@sky.com; Main St, Port Charlotte; s/d £40/84, tw without bathroom £80; P☎) For genuine islander hospitality at a fair price, head to this homely B&B, on the right as you enter Port Charlotte from the north. Set in part of the former Lochindaal distillery, it's run by a kindly local couple who make their own delicious marmalade and oatcakes. Rooms are well kept and most comfortable. The cute single has sea views. Minimum two-night stay.

Port Charlotte Hotel HOTEL £££
(📞01496-850360; www.portcharlottehotel.co.uk; Main St, Port Charlotte; s/d/f £180/250/300; 🅿🛜🐾) This lovely old Victorian hotel has individually decorated bedrooms – modern but classic in style – with crisp white sheets, good toiletries and sea views. It's a friendly place with a plush lounge, cosy bar and quality restaurant.

Port Askaig & Around

Port Askaig is set in a picturesque nook halfway along the Sound of Islay. It's little more than a hotel, shop (with ATM), petrol pump and ferry pier. There are three distilleries within reach and ferry connections to the mainland and Jura, just across the strait.

Three miles southwest, lush meadows swathed in buttercups and daisies slope down to reed-fringed **Loch Finlaggan**. This bucolic setting was once the most important settlement in the Hebrides, the central seat of power of the Lords of the Isles from the 12th to the 16th centuries.

⭐**Finlaggan** RUINS
(📞01496-840644; www.finlaggan.org; adult/child £4/2; ⏰ruins 24hr, museum 10.30am-4.15pm Mon-Sat Apr-Oct) Three miles from Port Askaig, tumbledown ruins of houses and a chapel on an islet in a shallow loch mark what remains of the stronghold of the Lords of the Isles. A wooden walkway leads over the reeds and water lilies to the island, where information boards describe the remains. Start your exploration at the visitor centre, which has some good explanations of the site's history and archaeology and a video featuring Tony Robinson. The island itself is open at all times.

The setting is beautiful and the history fascinating. The MacDonald clan, descendants of the legendary warrior Somerled, administered their island territories from here from the 12th to the 15th centuries and entertained visiting chieftains in their great hall. A smaller island, Eilean na Comhairle, was reserved for solemn councils. Though this unassuming inland loch seems a strange place from which to wield serious political power, it had likely been an important place since prehistoric times. A cran-

nog, fort and early Christian chapel were all located here, and the presence of ritual stones possibly aligned to the brooding Paps of Jura means the MacDonalds may have appropriated a place that already had strong ritual significance.

Buses between Bowmore and Port Askaig stop at the road junction, from where it's a 15-minute walk to the loch.

Ardnahoe DISTILLERY
(📞01496-840777; www.ardnahoedistillery.com; Ardnahoe; tours from £10; ⏰10am-5pm) Two miles down the narrow road towards Bunnahabhain, this independent distillery is Islay's newest. It's in a spectacular position gazing right across at the Paps of Jura. A light peaty kind of whisky is their style; tours are brisk and interesting and there's a likeable cafe-bistro space.

Jura

POP 200

Jura lies long, dark and low off the coast like a vast Viking longship, its billowing sail the distinctive triple peaks of the Paps of Jura. A magnificently wild and lonely island, it's the perfect place to get away from it all – as George Orwell did in 1948. Orwell wrote his masterpiece *Nineteen Eighty-Four* while living at the remote farmhouse of Barnhill in the north of the island.

Jura takes its name from the Old Norse *dyr-a* (deer island) – an apt appellation, as the island supports a population of around 6000 red deer, outnumbering their human cohabitants by about 30 to one.

There's a shop but no ATM on Jura; you can get cash back with debit cards at the Jura Hotel.

💿 Sights

Isle of Jura Distillery DISTILLERY
(📞01496-820385; www.jurawhisky.com; Craighouse; tours from £5; ⏰10am-5pm Mon-Sat Apr-Oct, to 4pm Mon-Fri Nov-Mar) There aren't a whole lot of indoor attractions on the island of Jura apart from a visit to the Isle of Jura Distillery. The standard tour runs twice a day, while specialist tours (£15 to £25) take you deeper into the production process and should be booked in advance.

Lussa Gin DISTILLERY
(📞01496-820196; www.lussagin.com; Ardlussa; ⏰10am-4.30pm Mon-Fri) At the northern end of Jura island, three local women have set

up this sweet little distillery in the former stables of the Ardlussa estate. It produces gin that's flavoured with local botanicals. Phone ahead to book a tour, which includes a taste of the refreshing lemony spirit.

 Activities

Walking Jura is an adventure. There are few proper footpaths, and off-path exploration often involves rough going through giant bracken, knee-deep bogs and thigh-high tussocks. Hill access may be restricted during the deer-stalking season (July to February); the Jura Hotel can provide details. Look out for adders – the island is infested with them, but they're shy snakes and will move away as you approach.

Corryvreckan Viewpoint   HIKING

A good Jura walk is to a viewpoint for the Corryvreckan Whirlpool. From the northern end of the public road (a 16-mile return trip from here) hike past Barnhill to Kinuachdrachd Farm (6 miles). Just before the farm a footpath forks left and climbs before traversing rough and boggy ground, a natural grandstand for viewing the turbulent waters of the **Gulf of Corryvreckan**.

If you've timed it right (check tide times at the Jura Hotel, you will see the whirlpool as a writhing mass of white water.

Evans' Walk   HIKING

This is a stalkers' path leading 6 miles from the main road through a pass in the hills to a hunting lodge above the remote sandy beach at Glenbatrick Bay. The path leaves the road 4 miles north of Craighouse (just under a mile north of the bridge over the River Corran). Allow six hours for the 12-mile round trip.

Paps of Jura   HIKING

Climbing the Paps is a truly tough hill-walk over ankle-breaking scree requiring good fitness and navigational skills. It's 11 hard miles (allow eight hours). The first peak you reach is **Beinn a'Chaolais** (734m), the second **Beinn an Oir** (784m), then **Beinn Shiantaidh** (755m). Most hikers also climb **Corra Bheinn** (569m), before joining Evans' Walk to return.

Sleeping & Eating

Places to stay are very limited, so book ahead. As well as the Jura Hotel, there's a handful of B&Bs and several self-catering cottages let by the week (see www.juradevelopment.co.uk). One of these is remote Barnhill, where Orwell stayed.

You can camp (£10/15 for two/four people) in the field below the Jura Hotel; there's a toilet and shower block that walkers, yachties and cyclists can also use.

THE SCOTTISH MAELSTROM

The Gulf of Corryvreckan – the channel (0.6 miles wide) between the northern end of Jura and the island of Scarba – is home to one of the most notorious tidal whirlpools in the world.

On Scotland's west coast, the rising tide – the flood tide – flows northwards. As it moves up the Sound of Jura, to the east of the island, it is forced into a narrowing bottleneck jammed with islands and builds up to a greater height than the open sea to the west of Jura. As a result, millions of tonnes of sea water pour westwards through the Gulf of Corryvreckan at speeds of up to 8 knots – an average sailing yacht is going fast at 6 knots.

The **Corryvreckan Whirlpool** forms where this mass of moving water hits an underwater pinnacle, which rises from the 200m-deep sea bed to within just 28m of the surface, and swirls over and around it. The turbulent waters create a magnificent spectacle, with white-capped breakers, standing waves, bulging boils and overfalls, and countless miniature maelstroms whirling around the main vortex.

Corryvreckan is at its most violent when a flooding spring tide, flowing west through the gulf, meets a westerly gale blowing in from the Atlantic. In these conditions, standing waves up to 5m high can form and dangerously rough seas extend more than 3 miles west of Corryvreckan, a phenomenon known as the Great Race.

You can see the whirlpool by making the long hike to the northern end of Jura, or by taking a boat trip from Islay, Ardfern or the Isle of Seil.

For tide times, see www.whirlpool-scotland.co.uk.

The Jura Hotel, a cafe and shop are basically the only places to get a bite to eat on the island. Some B&B providers offer evening meals.

Jura Hotel HOTEL ££
(☏ 01496-820243; www.jurahotel.co.uk; Craighouse; s £70, d £110-150; P 🛜) The heart of Jura's community is this hotel, which is warmly welcoming and efficiently run. Rooms vary in size and shape, but all are renovated and inviting. The premier rooms, which have sea views, are just lovely, with understated elegance and polished modern bathrooms. Eat in the restaurant or the convivial pub.

Ardlussa Estate B&B £££
(☏ 01496-820323; www.ardlussaestate.com; Ardlussa; d £130; P 🛜) This grand shooting lodge in Jura's north offers B&B accommodation in three plush rooms with beautiful vistas. Lavish four-course dinners made with estate produce cost £50 per head. There's also a substantial self-catering wing sleeping up to 10 people.

❶ Getting There & Away

A **car ferry** (☏ 01496-840681; www.argyll-bute. gov.uk) shuttles between Port Askaig on Islay and Feolin on Jura (adult/car/bicycle £2/8.20/ free, five minutes, hourly Monday to Saturday, every two hours Sunday). There is no direct car-ferry connection to the mainland.

From April to September, **Jura Passenger Ferry** (☏ 07768 450000; www.jurapassengerferry. com; one way £20; ⊘ Apr-Sep) runs from Tayvallich on the mainland to Craighouse on Jura (one hour, one or two daily except Wednesday). Booking is recommended (you can do this online).

❶ Getting Around

The island's only **bus service** (☏ 01436-810200; www.garelochheadcoaches.co.uk) runs between the ferry slip at Feolin and Craighouse (20 minutes, six to seven Monday to Saturday), timed to coincide with ferry arrivals and departures. Some of the runs continue north as far as Inverlussa.

Hire bikes from **Jura Cycles** (☏ 07436 886621; juracycles@outlook.com; bike hire per day £15) in Craighouse.

Colonsay

POP 130

Legend has it that when St Columba set out from Ireland in 563, his first landfall was Colonsay. But on climbing a hill he found he could still see the distant coast of his homeland, and pushed on north to Iona, leaving behind only his name (Colonsay means 'Columba's Isle').

Colonsay is a little jewel-box of varied delights, none exceptional but each exquisite – an ancient priory, a woodland garden, a golden beach – set amid a Highland landscape in miniature: rugged, rocky hills, cliffs and sandy strands, machair and birch woods, even a trout loch.

◎ Sights & Activities

There are several good sandy beaches, but **Kiloran Bay** in the northwest, a scimitar-shaped strand of dark golden sand, is outstanding. As well as natural attractions, there's a gin distillery and a brewery to visit on the island.

★ Oronsay Priory RUINS
(⊘ 24hr) 🆓 If the tide is right, don't miss walking across the half-mile of cockleshell-strewn sand linking Colonsay to smaller Oronsay. Here you can explore the 14th-century ruins of one of Scotland's best-preserved medieval priories. There are two beautiful 15th-century stone crosses in the kirkyard, but the highlight is the collection of superb carved grave slabs in the Prior's House. The island is accessible on foot for about 1½ hours either side of low tide; there are tide tables at the ferry terminal and hotel.

Colonsay House Gardens GARDENS
(☏ 01951-200316; www.colonsayholidays.co.uk; Kiloran; walled garden adult/child £3/1; ⊘ gardens dawn-dusk, walled garden noon-5pm Tue & Thu Apr-Oct) 🆓 Situated at Colonsay House, 1.5 miles north of Scalasaig, these gardens are tucked in an unexpected fold of the landscape and are famous for their outstanding collection of hybrid rhododendrons and unusual trees. The formal walled garden around the mansion has a terrace cafe.

🛏 Sleeping & Eating

Accommodation is limited and should be booked before coming to the island. Wild camping is allowed. See www.colonsay.org. uk for self-catering listings.

As well as the Colonsay Hotel, there are a couple of cafes on the island for food.

Backpackers Lodge HOSTEL £
(☏ 01951-200312; www.colonsayholidays.co.uk; Kiloran; dm/tw £25/60; P 🛜) Set in a former gamekeeper's house, this lodge is a 30-min-

ute walk from the ferry on Colonsay (you can arrange to be picked up). Smart refurbished twin rooms are a great deal and are set in the house, with bunk rooms in a smaller stone building alongside. There's a kitchen in another building.

★ **Colonsay Hotel** HOTEL **£££**
(☑ 01951-200316; www.colonsayholidays.co.uk; Scalasaig; s/d from £80/130; ☺ mid-Mar–Oct; P 🛜 🐾) ✔ This wonderfully laid-back hotel is set in an atmospheric old inn dating from 1750, a short walk uphill from the ferry pier in Scalasaig. It's a plush 18th-century place with well-appointed rooms, some with lovely views and four-poster beds. The bar and restaurant are the island's main social centres.

❶ Information

General information is available at www.colonsay.org.uk and at the ferry waiting room (the ferry pier is at Scalasaig, the main village, which has a shop but no ATM).

❶ Getting There & Around

AIR
Hebridean Air Services (p277) operates flights from Oban's airport (at North Connel) to Colonsay and Islay twice daily on Thursday.

BOAT
CalMac (☑ 0800 066 5000; www.calmac.co.uk) runs ferries from Oban to Colonsay (passenger/car £7.60/38.55, 2¼ hours, seven weekly in summer, three in winter). From April to October, on Wednesday and Saturday, the ferry from Kennacraig to Islay continues to Colonsay (adult/car £4.25/17.75, 1¼ hours) and on to Oban. A day trip from Islay allows you six to seven hours on the island.

OBAN & THE INNER HEBRIDES

The Victorian harbour town of Oban is a pretty place in its own right, with an excellent seafood scene, and is also a major gateway to the Hebrides. The big island drawcard is Mull, whose majestic scenery, birdlife and pretty capital Tobermory are complemented by the enchanting holy island of Iona just offshore. But the attributes of other islands really merit exploration: the strange rock formations of uninhabited Staffa, the walking on Kerrera, the intriguing slate-quarrying communities of Seil, the peace of Coll and the glorious windswept beaches of Tiree.

Oban

POP 8600

Oban, the main gateway to many of the Hebridean islands, is a waterfront town on a delightful bay, with sweeping views to Kerrera and Mull. It's peaceful in winter, but in summer the town centre is jammed with traffic and crowded with holidaymakers and travellers headed for the archipelago. But the setting is still lovely, and Oban's brilliant seafood restaurants are marvellous places to be as the sun sets over the bay. There's a real magic to the location.

◉ Sights

Note that Connel's attractions (p290) are just a short drive north from Oban.

Oban Distillery DISTILLERY
(☑ 01631-572004; www.malts.com; Stafford St; tours £10; ☺ noon or 12.30-4.30pm Dec-Feb, 9.30am-5pm Mar-Jun, Oct & Nov, 9.30am-7.30pm Mon-Fri, 9.30am-5pm Sat & Sun Jul-Sep) This handsome distillery has been in operation since 1794. The standard guided tour leaves regularly (worth booking) and includes a dram, a take-home glass and a taste straight from the cask. Specialist tours (£40) run once on Mondays to Fridays in summer. Even without a tour, it's still worth looking at the small exhibition in the foyer.

Dunollie Castle CASTLE
(☑ 01631-570550; www.dunollie.org; Dunollie Rd; adult/child £6/3; ☺ 10am-5pm Mon-Sat, noon-5pm Sun Apr-Oct) A pleasant 1-mile stroll north along the coast road leads to Dunollie Castle, built by the MacDougalls of Lorn in the 13th century and unsuccessfully besieged for a year during the 1715 Jacobite rebellion. It's ruined, but ongoing conservation work is offering increasing access. The nearby 1745 House – seat of Clan MacDougall – is an intriguing museum of local and clan history, and there are pleasant wooded grounds and a cafe. Free tours run twice daily.

McCaig's Tower HISTORIC BUILDING
(cnr Laurel & Duncraggan Rds; ☺ 24hr) Crowning the hill above town is this Colosseum-like Victorian folly, commissioned in

Driving Tour
The Trossachs to Mull

START CALLANDER
END TOBERMORY
LENGTH 240 MILES; TWO TO FOUR DAYS

Having explored the southern part of the Trossachs, head north out of Callander on the A84, following pretty Loch Lubnaig before optional detours of a few miles to see Rob Roy's grave at ➊ **Balquhidder** (p248) and the Falls of Dochart at pretty ➋ **Killin** (p249).

Continue on the A85 to ➌ **Crianlarich** (p243), surrounded by Highland majesty, then turn left on the A82 to follow the western shore of Loch Lomond. Stop for a look and/or pint at the quirky ➍ **Drover's Inn** (p242), then deviate right at Tarbet onto the A83 – shortly thereafter, ➎ **Arrochar** (p242) makes for a scenic lunch stop.

Head through picturesque Glen Croe, over the pass and into Glen Kinglas, then follow the shore of Loch Fyne – stops at the ➏ **Fyne Ales brewery** (p257) and/or oyster bar obligatory! – to picturesque ➐ **Inveraray** (p257). Go right through the arch here on the

A819, then left onto the B840, a lonely road following stiletto-like Loch Awe. You'll eventually reach ➑ **Kilmartin** (p258), with its great museum and evocative prehistoric sights.

Follow the A816 north to ➒ **Oban** (p272), where good accommodation options, a handsome harbour and delicious seafood await. You may want to deviate to see the island of ➓ **Seil** (p278) en route: from here, great boat trips can take you out to the Corryvreckan whirlpool. Catch a ferry from Oban to Mull and follow the A849 southwest via ⓫ **Duart Castle** (p281) to the island's tip at Fionnphort, where you cross to the emerald jewel of ⓬ **Iona** (p285) and can take a boat trip to the spectacular rock formations of Staffa.

Retrace your steps, then follow Mull's winding west coast on the B8035 and B8073 via spectacular coastline and the beach at Calgary to arrive at the colourful shorefront houses of the main town, ⓭ **Tobermory** (p281).

Oban

1890 by local worthy John Stuart McCaig, with the philanthropic intention of providing work for unemployed stonemasons. To reach it on foot, make the steep climb up Jacob's Ladder (a flight of stairs) from Argyll St; the bay views are worth the effort.

Activities

Hire a bike – try **Oban Cycles** (☑ 01631-566033; www.obancyclescotland.com; 87 George St; per day/week £28/150; ☺ 10am-5pm Tue-Sat Feb-Dec) – for the local bike rides listed in a leaflet at the tourist office, including a 16-mile route to Seil.

Oban

⦿ **Sights**

1	McCaig's Tower	D3
2	Oban Distillery	C4

➕ **Activities, Courses & Tours**

3	Coastal Connection	C3
4	Oban Cycles	C4
5	Sea Kayak Oban	C4

🛏 **Sleeping**

6	Backpackers Plus	C2
7	Fàilte	D4
8	Oban Backpackers	C2
9	Oban Youth Hostel	A1
10	Old Manse Guest House	C2
11	Sandvilla Guesthouse	C2

🍴 **Eating**

12	Coast	C3
13	Ee-Usk	B4
14	Oban Seafood Hut	B5
15	Waterfront Fishouse Restaurant	B5

🍷 **Drinking & Nightlife**

16	Aulay's Bar	C5
17	Oban Inn	C4

Various operators offer boat trips (adult/child £12/5) to spot seals and other marine wildlife, departing from North Pier.

Oban has lots of outdoor shops and is a good place to get kitted out for the Highlands and island outdoors.

Sea Kayak Oban   KAYAKING
(National Kayak School; ☑ 01631-565310; www.seakayakoban.com; Argyll St; ⊙ 10am-5pm Mon-Fri, 9am-5pm Sat, 10am-4pm Sun, winter hours greatly reduced) Sea Kayak Oban has a well-stocked shop, great route advice and sea-kayaking courses, including an all-inclusive two-day intro for beginners (£195 per person). It also has full equipment rental for experienced paddlers – trolley your kayak from the shop to the ferry (kayaks carried free) to visit the islands. Day trips (£80 to £95) leave regularly in season.

Puffin Adventures   DIVING
(☑ 01631-566088; www.puffin.org.uk; Port Gallanach) If you fancy exploring the underwater world, Puffin Adventures offers a two-hour package (£89) for complete beginners, often with same-day availability, as well as four-day diving courses. A serious professional set-up, it has training services and excursions for more experienced divers as well. It's located south of Oban near the Kerrera ferry.

🧭 Tours

★ **Basking Shark Scotland**   WILDLIFE
(☑ 07975-723140; www.baskingsharkscotland.co.uk; ⊙ Mar-Oct) Runs boat trips focused on finding and observing basking sharks – the world's second-largest fish – and other notable marine species. The one-day options (July to September) leave from Coll, synchronised with the ferry from Oban, and

cost £195. Multiday trips are available. It also offers diving and wildlife-watching. Book shark trips months in advance.

Coastal Connection   BOATING
(☑ 01631-565833; www.coastal-connection.co.uk) Runs wildlife-spotting trips (adult/child £30/20), fast day trips to Tobermory (£45/30) and custom excursions to many west coast islands in a speedy, comfortable boat.

🎉 Festivals & Events

Highlands & Islands Music & Dance Festival   MUSIC
(www.obanfestival.org; ⊙ early May) An exuberant celebration of traditional Scottish music and dance, when Oban packs out.

West Highland Yachting Week   SAILING
(www.whyw.co.uk; ⊙ late Jul or early Aug) Oban becomes the focus of one of Scotland's biggest yachting events, when hundreds of yachts cram into the harbour and the town's bars are jammed with thirsty sailors.

Oban Games   CULTURAL, SPORTS
(Argyllshire Gathering; www.obangames.com; adult/child £12/6; ⊙ late Aug) A key event in the Highland games calendar, the Oban Games include a prestigious pipe-band competition.

🛏 Sleeping

Despite having lots of B&B accommodation, Oban can still fill up quickly in July and August, so try to book ahead. Avoid the substandard, tourist-trap B&Bs south of the roundabout on Dunollie Rd. If you can't find a bed in Oban, consider Connel, 4 miles north.

★ Backpackers Plus HOSTEL £

(☏ 01631-567189; www.backpackersplus.com; Breadalbane St; dm/s/d £21.50/27/54; @ ⬤) This is a friendly place in an old church with a good vibe and a large and attractive communal lounge with lots of sofas and armchairs. A buffet breakfast is included, plus there's free tea and coffee, a laundry service and powerful showers. Private rooms are available in adjacent buildings: they are a very good deal.

Modern en suite doubles (£60) are in the old church hall, while a former guesthouse has sweet shared-bathroom options with a good common kitchen.

Oban Backpackers HOSTEL £

(☏ 01631-562107; www.obanbackpackers.com; Breadalbane St; dm £18.50-20.50; @ ⬤) Simple, colourful, relaxed and casual, this hostel has plenty of atmosphere. Dorms are basic, with high ceilings and plenty of space; prices vary according to size. Top bunks are wall-mounted. There's a sociable downstairs lounge with big windows and zebra-patterned couches, plus a sizeable kitchen. Breakfast is available for £3 and a safe is on hand (no lockers).

Oban
Youth Hostel HOSTEL £

(Hostelling Scotland; ☏ 01631-562025; www.hostellingscotland.org.uk; Corran Esplanade; dm/tw/q £25/69/109; P ⬤) Set in a grand Victorian villa on the Esplanade, 0.75 miles north of Oban's train station, this hostel is modernised to a high standard, with comfy wooden bunks, lockers, good showers and a lounge with great views across Oban Bay. All dorms are en suite; the neighbouring lodge has three- and four-bed rooms. Breakfast is available. Dorm rates drop substantially in low season.

★ Elderslie
Guest House B&B ££

(☏ 01631-570651; www.obanbandb.com; Soroba Rd; s £55, d £78-92; ☉ Apr–mid-Oct; P ⬤) A B&B can be a difficult balancing act: making things modern without losing cosiness, being friendly and approachable without sacrificing privacy. At this spot a mile south of Oban, the balance is absolutely right, with a variety of commodious rooms with big showers, large towels and lovely outlooks over greenery. Breakfast is great, there's outdoor lounging space and the hosts are excellent.

Old Manse
Guest House B&B ££

(☏ 01631-564886; www.obanguesthouse.co.uk; Dalriach Rd; s/d £80/100; ☉ Mar-Oct; P ⬤) Set on the hillside above town, this Oban B&B commands magnificent views over to Kerrera and Mull. It's run with genuine enthusiasm, and the owners are constantly adding thoughtful new features to the bright, cheerful rooms, such as binoculars, DVDs, poetry, corkscrews and tartan hot-water bottles. There are breakfast menus, with special diets catered for.

Fàilte B&B ££

(☏ 01631-570219; www.failtebandb.com; Rockfield Rd; s £55, d £90-100; ☉ Feb-Nov; P ⬤) Solicitous host Thomas knows a thing or two about guest comfort and the thoughtful extras here (powerpoints, disposable razors, real milk in the mini-fridge) make for a very comfortable stay. Rooms are pleasingly contemporary, with a white-and-blond Scandinavian feel and modern showers. The family's quality artworks decorate the building and breakfast features fresh fruit and homemade breads and jams.

Kathmore
Guest House B&B ££

(☏ 01631-562104; www.kathmore.co.uk; Soroba Rd; s £68, d £77-98; P ⬤) A 10-minute stroll from Oban's centre, this warmly welcoming place mixes traditional Highland hospitality and hearty breakfasts with a wee touch of boutique flair in its stylish bedspreads and colourful artwork. It's actually two adjacent houses combined. There's a comfortable lounge and outdoor garden deck where you can enjoy a glass of wine on long summer evenings.

Sandvilla Guesthouse B&B ££

(☏ 01631-564483; www.holidayoban.co.uk; Breadalbane St; d £75-95; P ⬤) Upbeat, bright and modern, this well kept B&B is our favourite of several options on this street. Enthusiastic owners guarantee a personal welcome and service with a smile. No young children are allowed.

Manor House HOTEL £££

(☏ 01631-562087; www.manorhouseoban.com; Gallanach Rd; r £174-251; P ⬤⬤) Built in 1780 for the Duke of Argyll, the old-fashioned Manor House is Oban's finest hotel. It has small but elegant Georgian-style rooms – the majority with lovely sea views – with antiques and period-style wallpaper, plus a classy restaurant serving Scottish/French cuisine (table d'hôte dinner £42). Rates include access to a local gym and golf course. No under-12s.

Eating

Oban

Seafood Hut   SEAFOOD **£**
(☑ 07881-418565; www.facebook.com/obanseafood.hut.9; Railway Pier; mains £3-14; ☺10am-6pm mid-Mar–Oct) If you want to savour superb Scottish seafood without the expense of an upmarket restaurant, head for Oban's famous seafood stall – it's the green shack on the quayside near the ferry terminal. Here you can buy fresh and cooked seafood to take away, such as excellent prawn sandwiches, dressed crab and fresh oysters, for a pittance.

Ee-Usk   SEAFOOD **££**
(☑ 01631-565666; www.eeusk.com; North Pier; mains £14-24; ☺noon-3pm & 5.45-9.30pm Apr-Oct, noon-2.30pm & 5.45-9pm Nov-Mar; ☎) 🍽 Bright and modern Ee-Usk (how you pronounce *iasg*, Gaelic for fish) occupies a prime pier location. Floor-to-ceiling windows allow diners on two levels to enjoy sweeping views while sampling local sustainable seafood ranging from fragrant fish cakes to langoustines. A bevy of serving staff make it swift and efficient, and they'll try to give you the best view available.

Waterfront
Fishouse Restaurant   SEAFOOD **££**
(☑ 01631-563110; www.waterfrontfishouse.co.uk; 1 Railway Pier; mains £15-23; ☺noon-2pm & 5.30-9pm, extended hours Jun-Aug; ☎♿) Waterfront is housed on the top floor of a converted seamen's mission, and the stylish, unfussy decor, bathed by the summer evening sun, does little to distract from the seafood freshly landed at the quay just a few metres away. The menu ranges from classic haddock and chips to fresh oysters, scallops and langoustines. It's best to book for dinner.

Coast
    SCOTTISH **££**
(☑ 01631-569900; www.coastoban.co.uk; 104 George St; mains £17-22; ☺noon-2pm & 5.30-9pm Mon-Sat, 5.30-9pm Sun Feb-late Dec; ☎) With a stylishly casual contemporary interior, this place in a former bank offers well-integrated plates with a focus on local game and seafood. Dishes are presented with flair but don't stray into pretension; the flavours are trusty and quality combinations that work very well.

Drinking & Nightlife

Oban Inn   PUB
(☑ 01631-567441; www.facebook.com/theobaninn; 1 Stafford St; ☺11am-1am; ☎) It's a pleasure to drop by this 18th-century pub, with its solid walls, flagstone floor and roof beams in the front bar. It has Fyne Ales on tap, making it a prime spot for a waterfront pint, with a good mix of locals, visitors and yachties.

Aulay's Bar   PUB
(☑ 01631-562596; 8 Airds Cres; ☺11.30am-midnight; ☎) An authentic Scottish pub, Aulay's is cosy and low-ceilinged, its walls covered with old photographs of Oban ferries and other ships. It pulls in a mixed crowd of locals and visitors with its warm atmosphere and wide range of malt whiskies. There are two sides: the left door leads to a quieter lounge bar.

ℹ Information

Oban Tourist Office (☑ 01631-563122; www.oban.org.uk; 3 North Pier; ☺10am-5pm Mon-Sat, 11am-3pm Sun Nov-Mar, 9am-5.30pm Mon-Sat, 10am-5pm Sun Apr-Oct) Helpful; on the waterfront.

ℹ Getting There & Away

AIR
Hebridean Air Services (☑ 0845 805 7465; www.hebrideanair.co.uk; Oban Airport, North Connel) Flies from North Connel airfield to the islands of Coll, Tiree, Colonsay and Islay.

BOAT
Oban is a major gateway to the Hebrides. The **CalMac Ferry Terminal** (☑ 01631-562244; www.calmac.co.uk; Railway Pier) is in the centre, close to the train station, with ferries running from here to Mull, Islay, Colonsay, Coll, Tiree, Barra and Lismore.

BUS
Scottish Citylink (p258) has two to five buses connecting Glasgow (£21.80, three hours) with Oban. Most of these travel via Tarbet and Inveraray; in summer, one goes via Crianlarich. Two buses Monday to Saturday head north to Fort William (£9.40, 1½ hours).

TRAIN
ScotRail trains run to Oban from Glasgow (£26.80, three hours, three to six daily). Change at Crianlarich for Fort William.

ARGYLL SEA KAYAK TRAIL

The **Argyll Sea Kayak Trail** (www.pad dle-argyll.org.uk) is a 96-mile route promoted by the local government that runs from Oban to Helensburgh via sea lochs and the Crinan canal. It's a spectacular paddle; the only annoyance is not being able to traverse the canal's locks: bookable trolleys are provided for easy portage. Paddlers are encouraged to register online.

Around Oban

Kerrera

POP 50

Some of the area's best **walking** is on Kerrera, which faces Oban across the bay. There's a 6-mile circuit (allow three hours), which follows tracks or paths and offers the chance to spot wildlife such as Soay sheep, wild goats, otters, golden eagles, peregrine falcons, seals and porpoises. At the island's southern end, there's a **ruined castle**.

Two miles from the ferry, **Kerrera Tea Garden** (☑01631-566367; www.kerrerabunk house.co.uk; Lower Gylen; light meals £3-10; ⊙10.30am-4.30pm Apr-Sep) 🍴 is a friendly cafe doing snacks and light meals. It has a charming **bunkhouse** in a converted stable that is available for exclusive use only (£100 to £130, March to October, sleeps seven); ask about tent accommodation. If you're staying, they'll pick up your bags from the ferry.

❶ Getting There & Away

CalMac (p272) runs a daily passenger ferry to Kerrera from Gallanach, 2 miles southwest of the Oban town centre (adult return £3.20, five minutes, half-hourly in summer, eight to nine daily in winter).

Seil

POP 600

The small island of Seil, 10 miles southwest of Oban, is best known for its connection to the mainland – the graceful **Bridge over the Atlantic**, designed by Thomas Telford and opened in 1793.

On the west coast is the pretty conservation village of **Ellenabeich**, with white-washed cottages and rainwater barrels backed by a wee harbour and rocky cliffs. It was built to house local slate workers, but the industry collapsed in 1881 when the sea broke into the main quarry – the flooded pit can still be seen. The **Scottish Slate Islands Heritage Trust** (☑01852-300449; www.slateislands.org.uk; Ellenabeich; ⊙10.30am-4.30pm Apr-Oct) **FREE** displays fascinating old photographs illustrating life in the village in the 19th and early 20th centuries.

Just offshore is small **Easdale Island**, which has more old slate-workers' cottages and the interesting **Easdale Island Folk Museum** (☑01852-300370; www.easdalemu seum.org; Easdale; suggested donation £3; ⊙11am-4pm Apr–mid-Oct). The island once housed 450 people, but the population fell to just seven old-timers by 1950. It now has a healthier 50-odd after a program welcoming incomers.

Confusingly Ellenabeich is also referred to as Easdale, so 'Easdale Harbour', for example, is on the Seil side.

🏃 Activities

⭐ **Sealife Adventures** BOATING

(☑01631-571010; www.sealife-adventures.com; B844; 3/4/5hr trip £59/73/84) Sealife Adventures, based on the eastern side of Seil island near the bridge, has a large, comfortable boat offering wildlife cruises with knowledgable guides and trips to the Corryvreckan whirlpool.

⭐ **Seafari Adventures** BOATING

(☑01852-300003; www.seafari.co.uk; Ellenabeich; ⊙Apr-Oct) Runs a series of exciting boat trips in high-speed rigid inflatables to Corryvreckan whirlpool (adult/child £48/38; call about dates for 'Whirlpool Specials', when the tide is strongest). There are also three-hour summer whale-watching trips (£59/46), day-long cruises to Iona and Staffa (£90/68) and private charters available to other islands. There's a minimum of six passengers required for low-season departures.

Sea Kayak Scotland KAYAKING

(☑01852-300770; www.seakayakscotland.com; courses for 1/2/4 people per person £125/90/70) Year-round hire, instruction and guided sea-kayaking trips run by an experienced operator.

✨ Festivals & Events

World Stone-Skimming
Championships SPORTS
(www.stoneskimming.com; ☺ Sep) Anyone who fancies their hand at ducks and drakes should try to attend a flooded slate quarry in Easdale on a Sunday in late September. There's no use boasting about the number of skips: once it's hit the water a minimum of three times it's all about the distance reached.

🛏 Sleeping & Eating

An Lionadh RENTAL HOUSE ££
(✆ 01688-400388; www.anlionadh.co.uk; Easdale; per week £920; 🛜 🐾) Occupying a comparatively lofty position on the tranquil island of Easdale, this is a standout self-catering option with views both ways: over the village and out to the west, where a grassy lawn lets you contemplate the vistas at great leisure. There are four bedrooms, a lounge and a very attractive kitchen/dining area.

★ Puffer CAFE ££
(✆ 01852-300022; www.pufferbarandrestaurant. co.uk; Easdale; mains £8-17; ☺ food 11am-4pm & 6-7.30pm Mon-Sat, 12.30-4pm Sun Easter-Oct, call for winter opening; 🛜 🐾) 🍴 Easdale Island is fed and watered by the Puffer, named after the boats that once served the community. It combines pub, tearoom and restaurant. There are front and back decks, both very pleasant, and all-day sandwiches, burgers, and deli platters (appropriately served on a slate). Evening meals step it up a notch, with quality dishes based on regional produce.

❶ Getting There & Around

West Coast Motors (✆ 01586-555885; www. westcoastmotors.co.uk) Bus 418 runs four to five times a day, except Sunday, from Oban to Ellenabeich (£2.40, one hour).
Easdale Ferry (✆ 01631-569167; www.ar-gyll-bute.gov.uk) Has a daily passenger-only ferry service from Ellenabeich to Easdale Island (£2.30 return, bicycles free, five minutes, shuttle service at busy times, otherwise every 30 minutes).

Mull

POP 2800
From the rugged ridges of Ben More and the black basalt crags of Burg to the blinding white sand, rose-pink granite and emerald waters that fringe the Ross, Mull can lay claim to some of the finest and most varied scenery in the Inner Hebrides. Noble birds of prey soar over mountain and coast, while the western waters provide good whale watching. Add a lovely waterfront 'capital', an impressive castle, the sacred island of Iona and easy access from Oban, and you can see why it's sometimes impossible to find a spare bed on the island.

☞ Tours

Mull's varied landscapes and habitats offer the chance to spot some of Scotland's rarest and most dramatic wildlife, including sea eagles, golden eagles, otters, dolphins and whales. Numerous operators offer walking or road trips to see them; email mull@vis-itscotland.com for a full list.

Nature Scotland WILDLIFE
(✆ 07743 956380; www.naturescotland.com) Enthusiastic, expert guides offer a range of excellent wildlife tours, including afternoon trips that can link to ferries (adult/child £40/30, four hours), evening otter-spotting trips (£50/45, three to four hours), all-day driving/walking trips (£60/50, seven hours) and winter stargazing excursions (£60/50, four hours).

Mull Eagle Watch BIRDWATCHING
(✆ 01680-812556; www.mulleaglewatch.com; adult/child £10/5; ☺ Apr-Sep) Britain's largest bird of prey, the white-tailed eagle, or sea eagle, has been successfully reintroduced to Mull, and the island is crowded with bird-watchers raptly observing the raptor. Two-hour tours to observe this bird are held in the mornings and afternoons, and must be booked in advance.

Turus Mara BOATING
(✆ 01688-400242; www.turusmara.com; ☺ Apr–mid-Oct) Offers trips from Ulva Ferry in central Mull to Staffa and the Treshnish Isles (adult/child £70/35, six hours), with plenty of time ashore on Staffa and Lunga, where you can see seals, puffins, kittiwakes, razorbills and many other species of seabird. There are also trips to Staffa alone (£25/17.50, 3¾ hours) and birdwatching-focused trips (£80/40, eight hours).

Transfer is also available from the Craignure ferry terminal, allowing you to visit as a day trip from Oban.

Mull, Coll & Tiree

Mull Magic
WALKING
(☎01688-301213; www.mullmagic.com) Offers guided walking tours in the Mull countryside to spot eagles, otters, butterflies and other wildlife. Customised tours are also available; check the website for the different itineraries.

Staffa Tours
BOATING
(☎07831 885985; www.staffatours.com; ☺Apr–mid-Oct) Runs boat trips from Fionnphort and Iona to Staffa (adult/child £25/15, 2½ hours), or Staffa plus the Treshnish Isles (also available from Tobermory and Ardnamurchan; £65/35, six hours). Before and after the seabird season, the trip is shorter (£45/25, four hours), not landing on Lunga. There are also connection-plus-tour options leaving from Oban.

🎸 Festivals & Events

Mull Music Festival
MUSIC
(www.facebook.com/mullmusicfestival; ☺last weekend Apr) Four days of foot-stomping traditional Scottish and Irish folk music at Tobermory's pubs.

Mendelssohn on Mull
MUSIC
(www.mendelssohnonmull.com; ☺Sep) A week-long festival of chamber music, with performances around Mull island. The month can vary, so check ahead.

ℹ Information
There's a bank with an ATM in Tobermory; otherwise you can get cash back with a purchase from Co-op food stores.

Craignure Tourist Office (☎01680-812377; www.visitscotland.com; Craignure; ☺9am-5pm Mon, 8.30am-5pm Tue-Sat, 10am-5pm Sun Sep-Jun, 9am-6.15pm Mon, 8.30am-6.15pm Tue-Sat, 10am-4.15pm Sun Jul & Aug) Opposite the ferry slip.

Explore Mull (☎01688-302875; www.isle-of-mull.net; Ledaig; ☺9am-5pm Easter-Jun & Sep–mid-Oct, to 7pm Jul & Aug; 🛜) In Tobermory car park. Has local information, can book all manner of island tours and hires bikes.

ℹ Getting There & Away
CalMac (☎0800 066 5000; www.calmac.co.uk) has three car ferries that link Mull with the mainland:

Oban to Craignure (adult/car £3.70/13.75, 40 minutes, every two hours) The busiest route – bookings are advised if you have a car.

Lochaline to Fishnish (adult/car £2.50/7.35, 15 minutes, at least hourly, except four daily on winter Sundays) On the east coast of Mull.

Tobermory to Kilchoan (adult/car £2.85/8.90, 35 minutes, seven daily Monday to Saturday, five Sunday April to October, three Monday to Saturday November to March) Links to the Ardnamurchan peninsula.

❶ Getting Around

BICYCLE
You can hire bikes for around £20 per day from various places around the island, including Explore Mull in Tobermory.

BUS
West Coast Motors (🗹 01680-812313; www.westcoastmotors.co.uk) connects ferry ports and main villages. Its Discovery Day Pass (adult/child £15/7.50) is available from April to October and grants a day's unlimited bus travel.

The routes useful for visitors are bus 95/495 from Craignure to Tobermory (£12.50 return), bus 96/496 from Craignure to Fionnphort (£17.50 return), and bus 494 from Tobermory to Dervaig and Calgary.

Craignure & Around

Duart Castle
CASTLE
(🗹 01680-812309; www.duartcastle.com; adult/child £8/4; ⊙10.30am-5pm daily May–mid-Oct, 11am-4pm Sun-Thu Apr) The ancestral seat of the Maclean clan enjoys a spectacular position on a rocky outcrop overlooking the Sound of Mull. Originally built in the 13th century, it was abandoned for 160 years before a 1912 restoration. As well as dungeons, courtyard and battlements with memorable views, there's lots of clan history – none worse than the story of Lachlan Cattanach, who took his wife on an outing to an island in the strait, then left her there to drown when the tide came in.

A bus to the castle meets some of the incoming ferries at Craignure (£13 return including castle entrance), but it's a pretty walk to get here, too.

★Craignure Bunkhouse
HOSTEL £
(🗹 01680-812043; www.craignure-bunkhouse.co.uk; Craignure; dm/q £24/90; ℗🛜) 🏵 An excellent hostel near the ferry slip, this purpose-built accommodation features top en-suite dorms fetchingly decked out in wood. Bunks have lots of headroom and individual USB chargers, lamps and power points. There are also double bunks for families. The ecologically minded design means sustainable sleeping, and the hostel

has a great kitchen, sociable common area and enthusiastic staff.

Tobermory

Mull's main town is a very picturesque little fishing and yachting port with brightly painted houses arranged around a sheltered harbour. It's a great base, with good places to eat, inviting pubs and an array of quality accommodation both along the harbourfront and on the hill behind.

◉ Sights & Activities

Whale-watching boat trips run out of Tobermory harbour. A range of tours can be booked at Explore Mull in the waterfront car park.

Hebridean Whale & Dolphin Trust
MUSEUM
(🗹 01688-302620; www.hwdt.org; 28 Main St; ⊙10.30am-4.30pm Mar-Nov) 🏵**FREE** This place has displays, videos and interactive exhibits on whale and dolphin biology and ecology, and is a great place for kids to learn about sea mammals. It also provides information about volunteering and reporting sightings of whales and dolphins. Opening times are rather variable.

Mull Aquarium
AQUARIUM
(🗹 01688-302876; www.mullaquarium.co.uk; Ledaig; adult/child £5.50/4; ⊙9.30am-5pm Easter-Oct; 🖚) 🏵 By the harbour car park, this aquarium has good information on the local marine environment, and little touch pools with crabs, starfish and the like for kids. All the creatures are returned to the sea after they've done a four-week shift here.

Mull Museum
MUSEUM
(🗹 01688-301100; www.mullmuseum.org.uk; Main St; ⊙10am-4pm Mon-Sat Easter-Oct) **FREE** Mull Museum, which records the history of the island, is a good place to go on a rainy day. There are interesting exhibits on crofting, and on the *Tobermory Galleon*, a ship from the Spanish Armada that sank in Tobermory Bay in 1588 and has been the object of treasure seekers ever since. Donations are appreciated in this volunteer-run set-up.

Tobermory Distillery
DISTILLERY
(🗹 01688-302647; www.tobermorymalt.com; Ledaig; ⊙11am-5pm) This bijou distillery was established in 1798. It doesn't always open on

winter weekends; phone ahead to check or book. There are two whisky lines here: the standard Tobermory and the lightly peated Ledaig. At time of research it was running in-depth tasting sessions for £25, but there will likely be a £10 tour back on offer in the future.

Sea Life Surveys
WILDLIFE

(☑ 01688-302916; www.sealifesurveys.com; Ledaig; ☉ Apr-Oct) Whale-watching trips head from Tobermory harbour to the waters north and west of Mull. The four-hour Wildlife Adventure cruise (adult/child £60/30) is your best chance of seeing a whale. Shorter Ecocruz excursions (adult/child £20/10, 1½ hours) are good for seal-spotting.

🛏 Sleeping

Tobermory has dozens of B&Bs, but the place can still be booked solid any time from May through to September, especially at weekends. Many apply minimum stays and most options close in winter.

Tobermory Youth Hostel
HOSTEL £

(Hostelling Scotland; ☑ 01688-302481; www.hostellingscotland.org.uk; Main St; dm/tw/q from £18/50/90; ☉ Apr-Oct; @☎) This hostel has a great location in a Victorian house right on the waterfront. It's got an excellent kitchen and spotless if somewhat austere dorms, as well as good triples and quads for families. It books out fast in summer.

★ Sonas House
B&B ££

(☑ 01688-302304; www.sonashouse.co.uk; Fairways, Erray Rd; s/d £90/130, apt for 2 excl/incl breakfast £100/130; 🅿☎🏊) Here's a treat: a B&B with a heated, indoor 10m swimming pool! Sonas is a large, modern house (follow signs to the golf course) offering luxury in a beautiful setting with superb Tobermory Bay views. Both rooms are beautifully done out with blond wood and other colours; 'Blue Poppy' has its own balcony. There's also a self-contained studio apartment. Hospitality is faultless.

Harbour Guesthouse
B&B ££

(☑ 01688-302209; www.harbourguesthousetobermory.com; 59 Main St; s £70-75, d £100-120; ☉ Easter–mid-Oct; ☎) On the harbourfront, this is a cute Tobermory base that offers rooms varying in size and shape that have been refurbished and are most comfortable. Great harbour views and cordial hosts.

★ Highland Cottage
BOUTIQUE HOTEL £££

(☑ 01688-302030; www.highlandcottage.co.uk; Breadalbane St; d £175-190; ☉ Apr–mid-Oct; 🅿☎🏊🐾) Antique furniture, four-poster beds, embroidered bedspreads, fresh flowers and candlelight lend this small hotel (with only six rooms) an appealingly old-fashioned cottage atmosphere, but with all mod cons, including full-size baths and room service. There's also an excellent restaurant (dinner £49.50), and the personable owners are experts in guest comfort.

🍴 Eating

Pier Café
CAFE £

(☑ 07786 197377; www.facebook.com/thepiercafetobermory; The Pier; light meals £7-11; ☉ noon-7pm Wed-Sun mid-Mar–Oct, extended hours in summer; ☎🐾) A cosy wee corner with local art on the walls, tucked beneath Café Fish at the north end of Tobermory village, the Pier serves great coffee and breakfast rolls, top baguettes that may feature local squat lobster or other seafood, plus tasty lunches such as scallops and chips, pasta and sandwiches.

Fish & Chip Van
FISH & CHIPS £

(☑ 01688-301109; www.tobermoryfishandchipvan.co.uk; Main St; fish & chips £6-10; ☉ 12.30-9pm Mon-Sat Apr & May, 12.30-9pm daily Jun-Sep, 12.30-7pm Mon-Thu, to 8pm Fri & Sat Oct-Mar) If it's takeaway you're after, you can tuck into some of Scotland's best gourmet fish and chips down on the Tobermory waterfront. And where else will you find a chip van selling freshly cooked scallops?

★ Café Fish
SEAFOOD ££

(☑ 01688-301253; www.thecafefish.com; The Pier; mains £12-26; ☉ noon-3pm & 5.30-11pm mid-Mar–Oct; ☎) 🐟 Seafood doesn't come much fresher than the stuff served at this warm and welcoming little restaurant overlooking Tobermory harbour. Crustaceans go straight from boat to kitchen to join rich seafood stew, fat scallops, fish pie and catch-of-the-day on the daily-changing menu, where confident use of Asian ingredients adds an extra dimension. Book ahead.

Hebridean Lodge
SCOTTISH ££

(☑ 01688-301207; www.hebrideanlodge.co.uk; Salen Rd, Baliscate; mains £17-22; ☉ 6.30-8.30pm Wed-Fri Easter-Dec) Above a gallery and shop, this mezzanine restaurant offers delicious local produce at chunky wooden tables. There's a warm welcome and fine, fresh seafood and lamb, with daily specials complementing the short menu of generous-spirited Scottish cuisine. Book ahead.

Drinking & Entertainment

★ Mishnish Hotel
PUB

(☑ 01688-302500; www.themishnish.co.uk; Main St; ⊙ 11am-1am; 🐾) 'The Mish', near the pier on the harbourfront, is a favourite hang-out for visiting yachties and a great place for a pint, with a very convivial atmosphere. Wood-panelled and flag-draped, this is a good old traditional pub where you can listen to live folk music, toast your toes by the open fire or challenge locals to a game of pool.

There are also pub meals and good local seafood available, plus (in summer) Italian upstairs.

★ Comar
PERFORMING ARTS

(☑ 01688-302211; www.comar.co.uk) Mull's lively arts scene includes a famous theatre group, regular art exhibitions and concerts. This arts organisation puts on exhibitions, plays and concerts in Tobermory's **An Tobar Arts Centre** (☑ 01688-302211; www.comar.co.uk; Argyll Tce; ⊙ 11am-4pm or 5pm Tue-Sat) FREE and elsewhere. Check its website for upcoming events.

🛍 Shopping

Tobermory Fish Co
FOOD

(☑ 01688-302120; www.tobermoryfish.co.uk; Unit 7, Baliscate; ⊙ 9am-5pm Mon-Sat) In a small commercial complex just outside Tobermory on the Salen road, this worthwhile smokehouse and shop offers very toothsome cold-smoked salmon and trout as well as a range of hot-smoked flavours, fresh seafood and other goodies.

North Mull

The road from Tobermory west to Calgary cuts inland, leaving most of Mull's north coast wild and inaccessible. It continues through the settlement of Dervaig to the glorious beach at Calgary. From here onwards you are treated to spectacular coastal views; it's worth doing the route in reverse from Gruline for the best vistas.

⊙ Sights

Calgary Beach
BEACH

Mull's best (and busiest) silver-sand beach, flanked by cliffs and with views out to Coll and Tiree, is about 12 miles west of Tobermory. And yes – this is the place from which Canada's more famous Calgary takes its name.

Glengorm Castle
GALLERY, PARK

(☑ 01688-302321; www.glengormcastle.co.uk; Glengorm; ⊙ buildings 10am-5pm Easter-Oct) FREE A long, single-track road leads north for 4 miles from Tobermory to majestic Glengorm Castle, with views across the sea to Ardnamurchan, Rum and the Outer Hebrides. The castle outbuildings house a **nature centre** and the excellent **Glengorm Coffee Shop** (☑ 01688-302321; www.glengormcastle.co.uk; Glengorm Castle; light meals £5-10; ⊙ 10am-5pm Easter-Oct; 🐾🅿) 🐾. The castle, which also has upmarket B&B acccommodation (p284), is not open to the public, but you're free to explore the beautiful grounds, where several good walks are signposted. Guided nature walks also run from here; check the website for times.

Calgary Art in Nature
GALLERY

(☑ 01688-400256; www.calgary.co.uk; Calgary; entry by donation; ⊙ 10am-5pm Mar-Nov) 🐾 Run with enthusiasm and vision, this place just back from Calgary beach is an excellent art space, and also has great self-catering accommodation. On-site silversmiths and wood sculptors ply their trade in their workshops, while a luminous gallery exhibits high-quality work from local artists. Other pieces dot the woodland ramble on the hill behind. There's also the good **Calgary Farmhouse Tearoom** (☑ 01688-400256; www.calgary.co.uk; Calgary; light meals £5-9; ⊙ 10am-5pm Easter-Oct, to 2pm Mon-Fri Nov-Mar; 🐾🅿) 🐾 here.

🛏 Sleeping & Eating

Calgary Bay Campsite
CAMPSITE £

(Calgary) You can camp for free in a lovely setting at the southern end of the beach at Calgary Bay. There are no facilities other than the public toilets across the road; water comes from the stream.

Dervaig Bunkrooms
HOSTEL £

(☑ 07435 656420; www.dervaigbunkrooms.co.uk; Dervaig; dm/q £23/70; ⊙ Apr-Oct; 🅿🐾) Comfortable bunkhouse accommodation in Dervaig's village hall, with a self-catering kitchen and sitting room. The dorms have good en-suite bathrooms and comfortable bunks.

ULVA

Ulva, meaning 'Wolf's Island' in Norse, is a sizeable island off the west coast of Mull. A peaceful place to escape the crowds thronging Mull in the summer, it has good walking and off-road biking, a 9th-century Viking fort, and a wee 19th-century church built to a Thomas Telford design. It is linked by a bridge to the even more remote island of Gometra.

Once Scotland's main centre for kelp gathering, Ulva formerly had a population approaching 1000; kelp was an essential ingredient in soap production. Today the population has fallen to six, with many removed from the area in the Clearances of 1850. You can still see many of the derelict cottages used by crofters in centuries past. Nevertheless, the community bought the island from its private owner in 2018.

The two-minute ferry crossing to Ulva on the west coast of Mull runs on demand during certain hours; check www.ulva.scot for up-to-date information.

★ **Calgary Farmhouse** COTTAGE **££**

(☑ 01688-400256; www.calgary.co.uk; Calgary; per week summer apt & cottages £675-1900, per 3 days studios & cabin £180-250; P 🕾 🕸) 🌶 This brilliant complex near Calgary beach offers a number of fantastic apartments, cottages and houses, beautifully designed and fitted out with timber furniture and wood-burning stoves. The Hayloft is spectacular, with noble oak and local art, while the wood-clad long-hall-like Beach House has luxury and dreamy views. Romantic Kittiwake, a beautiful wooden camping cabin among trees, has bay views and a boat ceiling.

There are options sleeping from two to nine. The larger ones go by the week in summer, but smaller ones are available for shorter stays. There's a good on-site cafe that sells some foodstuffs too. Bikes are available for hire.

Bellachroy INN **££**

(☑ 01688-400314; www.thebellachroy.co.uk; Dervaig; s/d £90/129; 🕙 Easter-Oct; P 🕾 🕸) The Bellachroy is an atmospheric 17th-century droving inn with seven comfortable bedrooms with stripy carpets; they vary in size. The bar is a focus for local social life and serves decent food (noon to 2.30pm and 6pm to 8.30pm). Management are very helpful.

Glengorm Castle B&B **£££**

(☑ 01688-302321; www.glengormcastle.co.uk; r £160-300; P 🕾 🕸) Bristling with turrets as a real castle should, this accommodation enjoys an unforgettable location, with huge windows framing green fields sloping down to the water. The attractive interior has 20th-century art instead of stags' heads. Bedrooms are all different, with lots of space and character. It's got lively, genuinely friendly owners, and kids will have a ball running around the grounds.

There are also serviced apartments and self-catering cottages around the grounds.

Am Birlinn SCOTTISH **££**

(☑ 01688-400619; www.ambirlinn.com; Penmore, Dervaig; mains £12-20; 🕙 noon-2.30pm & 5-9pm Wed-Sun mid-Mar–Oct; 🕾) 🌶 Occupying a spacious and modern wooden building between Dervaig and Calgary, this is an interesting dining option. Locally caught crustaceans and molluscs are the way to go here, though there are also tasty modern Scottish-style meat dishes available. Free pick-up and drop-off from Tobermory or other nearby spots is offered. There's also a bar.

South Mull

The road from Craignure to Fionnphort climbs through wild and desolate scenery before reaching the southwestern part of the island, which consists of a long peninsula called the **Ross of Mull**. The Ross has a spectacular south coast lined with black basalt cliffs that give way further west to white-sand beaches and pink granite crags. The cliffs are highest at Malcolm's Point, near the superb **Carsaig Arches**.

The village of **Bunessan** is home to a cottage museum; a minor road leads south from here to the beautiful white-sand bay of **Uisken**, with views of the Paps of Jura.

At the western end of the Ross, 35 miles from Craignure, is **Fionnphort** (*finn*-a-fort) and the Iona ferry. The coast here is a beautiful blend of pink granite rocks, white sandy beaches and vivid turquoise sea.

◉ Sights

Ardalanish Weavers   WORKSHOP
(☑ 01681-700265; www.ardalanish.com; ⊙10am-5pm Mon-Sat Easter–mid-Oct, 10am-4pm Mon-Fri mid-Oct–Easter) ✦ Fleeces from the Hebridean sheep on this farm are woven into fine woollen products using venerable looms, which you can see at work in the old cowshed. Hot drinks and snacks are available at the shop, which sells weaving and farm produce. You can also feed the Highland cattle here. It's on a remote rural back road 2 miles south of Bunessan.

🛏️ Sleeping & Eating

★ Seaview   B&B ££
(☑ 01681-700235; www.iona-bed-breakfast-mull.com; Fionnphort; s £65, d £90-110; ⊙mid-Mar-Oct; P 🛜 🐾) ✦ Just up from the ferry, Seaview has beautifully decorated bedrooms and a breakfast conservatory with grand views across to Iona. The rooms are compact and charming, with gleaming modern bathrooms. The owners are incredibly helpful and also offer tasty three-course dinners (outside of summer), often based around local seafood, while breakfasts include locally sourced produce.

Achaban House   B&B ££
(☑ 01681-700205; www.achabanhouse.co.uk; Fionnphort; s/d £49/79; P 🛜) This super refurbished rural house has very pleasing contemporary rooms with modern fabrics and a light, uncluttered feel. Some rooms look over the loch below. It's casual and friendly, and the ideal base for visiting Iona with the ferry less than a mile away. Guests have use of an excellent kitchen and a lounge with woodburning stove. Continental breakfasts feature homemade bread.

It's also available as a whole hire. On the same property the owners run an excellent exclusive-use bunkhouse, great value for families and groups. See www.rossofmullbunkrooms.co.uk.

Staffa House   B&B ££
(☑ 01681-700677; www.staffahouse.co.uk; Fionnphort; s/d £75/90; ⊙Mar-Oct; P 🛜 🐾) ✦ This charming and hospitable B&B is packed with antiques and period features, and offers breakfast in a conservatory with a view of Iona. Solar panels top up the hot-water supply, and the hearty breakfasts and packed lunches make use of homegrown and organic produce where possible. Rooms are designed for relaxation, with no TVs. Ex-

cellent chef-cooked evening meals are available (£25 to £40).

Tiroran Hotel   HOTEL £££
(☑ 01681-705232; www.tiroran.com; r £160-250; P 🛜 🐾) Secluded comfort and elegance are the key concepts at this hotel, which feels a world away from anywhere. Set 4 miles off the Craignure–Fionnphort road, it offers substantial country comfort in its plush, almost French-style rooms, and has a seasonal restaurant that takes food seriously. The gardens and grounds are lovely, and there are also self-catering cottages.

Just beyond the hotel, they've also got the Whitetail gin distillery.

★ Ninth Wave   SCOTTISH £££
(☑ 01681-700757; www.ninthwaverestaurant.co.uk; Bruach Mhor, Fionnphort; 3-/4-/5-course dinner £50/58/70; ⊙ sittings 7-7.30pm Wed-Sun May-Oct) ✦ This excellent croft restaurant is owned and operated by a Canadian chef and her lobster fisherman husband. The daily menu makes use of locally landed shellfish and crustaceans, vegetables and salad grown in the garden, and quality meats with a nose-to-tail ethos. It's all served in a stylishly converted bothy. Advance bookings (a couple of weeks at least) are essential. No under-12s.

It's worth going all-in and taking on the superb cheeseboard if you've got room. Don't miss the handmade chocolates infused with locally foraged flavours.

Iona
POP 200

Like an emerald teardrop off Mull's western shore, enchanting, idyllic Iona, holy island and burial ground of kings, is a magical place that lives up to its lofty reputation. From the moment you embark on the ferry towards its sandy shores and green fields, you'll notice something different about it. To appreciate its charms, spend the night: there are some excellent places to stay. Iona has declared itself a fair-trade island and actively promotes ecotourism.

History

St Columba sailed from Ireland and landed on Iona in 563, establishing a monastic community with the aim of Christianising Scotland. It was here that the *Book of Kells* – the prize attraction of Dublin's Trinity College – is believed to have been transcribed. It was taken to Ireland for safekeeping from 9th-century Viking raids.

The community was re-founded as a Benedictine monastery in the early 13th century and prospered until its destruction during the Reformation. The ruins were given to the Church of Scotland in 1899, and by 1910 a group of enthusiasts called the Iona Community Council had reconstructed the abbey. It's still a flourishing spiritual community offering regular courses and retreats.

Sights

Past the abbey, look for a footpath on the left signposted Dun I (dun-ee). An easy 15-minute walk leads to Iona's highest point, with fantastic 360-degree views, with the hills of Rum and Jura prominent on clear days.

★ Iona Abbey   HISTORIC BUILDING
(☑ 01681-700512; www.historicenvironment. scot; adult/child £9/5.40; ☉ 9.30am-5.30pm Apr-Sep, 10am-4pm Oct-Mar) Iona's ancient but heavily reconstructed abbey is the spiritual heart of the island. The spectacular nave, dominated by Romanesque and early Gothic vaults and columns, is a powerful space; a door on the left leads to the beautiful cloister, where medieval grave slabs sit alongside modern religious sculptures. Out the back, the museum displays fabulous carved high crosses and other inscribed stones, along with lots of background information. A replica of the intricately carved St John's Cross stands outside the abbey.

Next to the abbey is an ancient graveyard where there's an evocative 12th-century Romanesque chapel, as well as a mound that marks the burial place of 48 of Scotland's early kings, including Macbeth. Former Labour party leader John Smith is also buried in this cemetery. The atmospheric ruined nunnery closer to the ferry was established at the same time as the Benedictine abbey. The museum is closed Sundays in winter.

Tours

Alternative Boat Hire   BOATING
(☑ 01681-700537;   www.boattripsiona.com; ☉ Mon-Thu Apr–mid-Oct) Offers cruises in a traditional wooden sailing boat for fishing, birdwatching, picnicking or just admiring the scenery. Three-hour afternoon trips cost £35/15 per adult/child; on Wednesday there's a full-day cruise (£50/20). Bookings are essential.

Staffa Trips   BOATING
(☑ 01681-700755; www.staffatrips.co.uk; ☉ Apr–mid-Oct) Runs three-hour boat trips to Staffa (adult/child £35/17.50) on the MV Iolaire, departing Iona pier at 9.45am and 1.45pm, and from Fionnphort at 10am and 2pm, with one hour ashore on Staffa.

Sleeping & Eating

There are B&B options, camping, a hostel and a pair of hotels on the island. It's imperative to book accommodation well ahead in spring and summer. Very little is open in winter apart from the hostel.

There are a couple of hotel restaurants, and the abbey has a cafe, as does the heritage centre. There's also a supermarket.

WHALE WATCHING ON MULL

The North Atlantic Drift – a swirling tendril of the Gulf Stream – carries warm water into the cold, nutrient-rich seas off the Scottish coast, resulting in huge plankton blooms. Small fish feed on the plankton, and bigger fish feed on the smaller fish; this huge seafood smorgasbord attracts large numbers of marine mammals, from harbour porpoises and dolphins to minke whales and even – though sightings are rare – humpback and sperm whales.

There are dozens of operators around the coast offering whale-watching boat trips lasting from a couple of hours to all day; some have sighting success rates of 95% in summer.

While seals, porpoises and dolphins can be seen year-round, minke whales are migratory. The best time to see them is from June to August, with August being the peak month for sightings. The website of the Hebridean Whale & Dolphin Trust (www.hwdt.org) has lots of information on the species you are likely to see, and how to identify them.

★ **Iona Hostel** HOSTEL £
(📱01681-700781; www.ionahostel.co.uk; dm £22, snug or bothy s/d £75/90; 🅿🛜) 🍴 This working ecological croft and environmentally sensitive hostel is one of Scotland's most rewarding and tranquil places to stay. Black Hebridean sheep surround the building, which features pretty, practical and comfy dorms and an excellent kitchen-lounge. There's a fabulous beach nearby, and a hill to climb for views. It's just over a mile from the ferry on Iona, past the abbey.

There's also a cute wheeled bothy nearby, perfect for a bit of solitude. At the time of research Covid-19 meant that the hostel was only being rented for exclusive use, with a two-person adjoining snug also available.

★ **Argyll Hotel** HOTEL ££
(📱01681-700334; www.argyllhoteliona.co.uk; s £80, d £100-118; ⊙mid-Mar–mid-Oct; 🛜🐾) 🍴 This lovable, higgledy-piggledy warren of a hotel has great service and appealing snug rooms (those with sea views cost more – £176 for a double), including good-value family options. The rooms offers simple comfort and relaxation rather than luxury. Most look out to the rear, where a huge organic garden supplies the restaurant. This is a relaxing and amiably run Iona haven.

St Columba Hotel HOTEL ££
(📱01681-700304; www.stcolumba-hotel.co.uk; s £70, d £118-197; ⊙Mar-Oct; 🛜) Near the abbey, cosy modernised rooms offer plenty of comfort at this peaceful place, with a good guest lounge adding to the appeal of the sun-dappled restaurant and beer garden that offer sweeping views over fields and down to the water.

Iona Pods CABIN ££
(📱07935 219079; www.ionapods.com; pods £80; 🅿🛜) Sleeping up to four, these pods on a working croft have a simple kitchen. There's power, but washing and toilet facilities are separate.

🛍 **Shopping**

Aosdàna JEWELLERY
(📱01681-700121; www.aosdanaiona.com; ⊙10am-5pm mid-Mar–Oct) This shop between the ferry and the abbey makes rather beautiful jewellery pieces using (in many cases) symbols drawn from Iona and its history.

ℹ **Getting There & Away**

The ferry from Fionnphort to Iona (£3.50 adult return, five minutes, hourly) runs daily. Cars can only be taken with a permit. There are also various day trips available to Iona from Tobermory and Oban.

Tiree

POP 700

Low-lying Tiree (tye-*ree;* from the Gaelic *tiriodh,* meaning 'land of corn') is a fertile sward of lush, green machair liberally sprinkled with yellow buttercups, much of it so flat that, from a distance, the houses seem to rise out of the sea. It's one of the sunniest places in Scotland, but also one of the windiest – cyclists soon find that, although it's flat, heading west usually feels like going uphill. One major benefit – the constant breeze keeps away the midges.

The surf-lashed coastline here is scalloped with broad, sweeping beaches of white sand, hugely popular with windsurfers and kite-surfers. Most visitors, however, come for the birdwatching, beachcombing and lonely coastal walks.

👁 **Sights & Activities**

Skerryvore Lighthouse Museum MUSEUM
(📱01879-220045; www.hebrideantrust.org; Hynish; ⊙9am-5pm May-Sep) FREE The picturesque harbour and hamlet of Hynish, near Tiree's southern tip, was built in the 19th century to house workers and supplies for the construction of lonely Skerryvore Lighthouse, 10 miles offshore. This museum occupies the old workshops by the sand-filled but flushable harbour; up the hill is the signal tower once used to communicate by semaphore with the lighthouse.

Wild Diamond WATER SPORTS
(📱07712 159205; www.wilddiamond.co.uk; Cornaig; ⊙Apr-Oct) Professional and friendly, this outfit runs courses in windsurfing (£35/100 per session/day), kitesurfing (£70/120 per half-/full day), surfing, sand-yachting and stand-up paddleboarding, and rents out equipment including surfboards.

Blackhouse Watersports WATER SPORTS
(📱07711 807976; www.blackhouse-watersports. co.uk; Gott Bay; ⊙Mar-Nov) Operating out of a beach hut at the far end of Gott Bay, this welcoming set-up runs kitesurfing (£110) and surf (£40) lessons, hires kayaks (£25 for

three hours, including wetsuit), lends out fishing tackle and rents bikes (£10 per day).

Festivals & Events

Tiree Music Festival   MUSIC
(www.tireemusicfestival.co.uk; ⊙ mid-Jul) Held over a weekend in mid-July, this is a very likeable festival with a range of folksy, bluesy and rootsy music. They like to keep it small so limit the capacity; book ahead. Campsites are set up around the festival area in Crossapol.

Tiree Wave Classic   SPORTS
(www.tireewaveclassic.co.uk; ⊙ Oct) Reliable wind and big waves have made Tiree one of Scotland's top windsurfing venues. The annual Tiree Wave Classic competition has been held here since 1986, making it one of the world's longest-standing windsurfing championships.

Sleeping & Eating

Millhouse Hostel   HOSTEL £
(☑ 01879-220802; www.tireemillhouse.co.uk; Cornaig; dm/s/tw £25/43/58; P 🖥) Housed in a converted barn next to an old ruined water mill, this small but comfortable hostel is 5 miles west of the Tiree ferry pier. The dorms have beds rather than bunks, there's a common area and it's cheaper if you stay more than one night.

★ Rockvale Guest House   B&B ££
(☑ 01879-220675; www.rockvaletiree.co.uk; Balephetrish; s £100, d £110-120; P 🖥 🖥) Smart, comfortable, modern accommodation and a genuine welcome make this easily Tiree's best midrange accommodation choice. It's situated in the north of the island and does things with real panache. Breakfast is way above average, and features smoothies, fruit skewers, poached egg with spinach and pesto or banana mash.

Ceàbhar   SCOTTISH ££
(☑ 01879-220684; www.facebook.com/Ceabhar; Sandaig; mains £8-15; ⊙ 7-8.30pm Wed-Sat Easter-Oct, plus Tue Jul & Aug; 🖥 🖥 🖥) ✿ At Tiree's western end, this attractive restaurant looks out over the Atlantic towards the sunset. The cordial owners have the right attitude; they grow their own salads, eschew chips, and brew craft beer. Reopening plans were uncertain: check the Facebook page for updates.

ℹ Information

There's a bank (without an ATM), post office and supermarket in Scarinish, the main village on Tiree, half a mile south of the ferry pier. You can get cash back with debit-card purchases at the Co-op.

Some tourist information is available at the ferry terminal. A useful website is www.isleoftiree.com.

ℹ Getting There & Away

AIR

Loganair flies from Glasgow to Tiree daily. Hebridean Air Services (p277) operates from Oban to Tiree via Coll twice on Wednesdays.

BOAT

CalMac (p272) has a ferry from Oban to Tiree (adult/car £10.90/58.55, four hours, one daily) via Coll, except for a weekly service when the boat calls at Tiree first (three hours 20 minutes). The one-way fare from Coll to Tiree (one hour) is £3.55/16 per adult/car.

Coll

POP 200

Coll is more rugged and less populous than Tiree, its neighbour. The northern part of the island is a mix of bare rock, bog and lochans (small lochs), while the south is swathed in golden shell-sand beaches and machair dunes up to 30m high. It's a gloriously relaxing place.

The island's main attraction is the peace and quiet – empty beaches, bird-haunted coastlines, and long walks along the shore. The biggest and most beautiful sandy beaches are at **Crossapol** in the south, and **Hogh Bay** and **Cliad** on the west coast.

In summer the corncrake's 'krek-krek' is heard at the **RSPB Coll** (☑ 01879-230301; www.rspb.org.uk; Totronald; ⊙ 24hr) at Totronald in the southwest of the island. From Totronald a sandy 4WD track runs north past the dunes backing Hogh Bay to the road at Totamore, allowing walkers and cyclists to make a circuit back to Arinagour rather than backtracking.

Sleeping & Eating

There's a handful of places to stay, several of them excellent. You can wild camp for free on the hill above the Coll Hotel; ask at the hotel first.

STAFFA

Felix Mendelssohn, who visited the uninhabited island of Staffa, off Mull, in 1829, was inspired to compose his 'Hebrides Overture' after hearing waves echoing in the impressive and cathedral-like **Fingal's Cave**. The cave walls, an adjacent cave and the surrounding cliffs are composed of vertical, hexagonal basalt columns that look like pillars (Staffa is Norse for 'pillar island'). It's a striking sight. Various boat trips land you on the island, where you can walk along the shoreline and into Fingal's Cave as well as climb up to the grassy expanses above, with top views in all directions. The trip is good for spotting diving gannets and other seabirds and you can see puffins in season (mid-April to early August). There's also a fine chance of seeing cetaceans and seals.

Northwest of Staffa lies a chain of uninhabited islands called the Treshnish Isles. The two main islands are the curiously shaped **Dutchman's Cap** and **Lunga**. You can land on Lunga, walk to the top of the hill, and visit the spectacular seabird colonies on the west coast at Harp Rock. Here, puffins, guillemots, kittiwakes, storm petrels and shags breed in raucous splendour.

Unless you have your own boat, the only way to reach Staffa and the Treshnish Isles is on an organised boat trip from Fionnphort, Iona, Tobermory, Ardnamurchan, Seil or the Ulva ferry slip. Operators include Turus Mara (p279), Staffa Tours (p280), Staffa Trips (p286) and Seafari Adventures (p278).

★ **Coll Bunkhouse** HOSTEL £
(☑ 01879-230217; www.collbunkhouse.com; Arinagour; dm/tw £24/60; ⓟ🛜🐕) This gorgeous modern bunkhouse is in Coll's main settlement, just a 10- to 15-minute walk from the ferry pier. It's a great facility, with a kitchen, good showers and access for travellers with disabilities.

Tigh-na-Mara B&B ££
(☑ 01879-230354; www.tnmcoll.com; Arinagour; d £80-100; ⓟ🛜) The first building you reach coming from the ferry on Coll is this lovely B&B, with a large front garden and magnificent views over the water. The owners are relaxed and welcoming, and the rooms have bird books and planispheres, so you can do some spotting from your window. There's also a self-catering option.

ⓘ Information

For information on Coll, visit www.visitcoll.co.uk. Arinagour, half a mile from the ferry pier, is Coll's only village, home to a shop, post office (with ATM), craft shops and aged petrol station. Pride of the island is the phone mast; there was virtually no signal until 2015.

ⓘ Getting There & Away

AIR
Hebridean Air Services (p277) operates from Oban to Coll (twice daily Wednesday) and on to Tiree.

BOAT
Ferries with CalMac (p255) run from Oban to Coll (adult/car £9.05/47.40, 2¾ hours, one daily) and on to Tiree, except one weekly service when the ferry calls at Tiree first. The one-way fare between Coll and Tiree (one hour) is £3.55/16 per adult/car.

NORTH ARGYLL

The northern parts of Argyll harbour a diverse range of attractions, including two of Scotland's most photogenic castles and an island made for exploration by bike. Though it's often traversed rapidly by folk heading for the northern Highlands, it's worth slowing down to appreciate its many charms.

Loch Awe

Loch Awe is one of Scotland's most beautiful lochs, with rolling forested hills around its southern end and spectacular mountains in the north. It lies between Oban and Inveraray and is the longest loch in Scotland – about 24 miles – but is less than 1 mile wide for most of its length. At its northern end, it escapes to the sea through the narrow **Pass of Brander**, where Robert the Bruce defeated the MacDougalls in 1309.

WORTH A TRIP

LISMORE

The island of Lismore (in Gaelic *Lios Mór* means 'Big Garden') is all lush grassland sprinkled with wildflowers, with grey blades of limestone breaking through the soil. And that's the secret – limestone is rare in the Highlands, but it weathers to a very fertile soil.

Lismore is long and narrow – 10 miles long by 1 mile wide – with a road running almost its full length. It's a lovely place that appeals for off-the-beaten-track relaxation and picturesque walking.

CalMac (p272) has car ferries from Oban to Achnacroish, with four to five sailings Monday to Saturday, two on Sunday (adult/car £2.85/12.15, 55 minutes).

Argyll & Bute Council operates the **passenger ferry** (☑01631-730356; www.argyll-bute.gov.uk) from Port Appin to Point, Lismore (£2.10, 10 minutes, hourly). Bicycles can be carried for free.

★**Kilchurn Castle** CASTLE
(www.historicenvironment.scot; Dalmally; ⊙9.30am-5.30pm Apr-Sep) FREE At the northern end of Loch Awe are the scenic ruins of the strategically situated and much-photographed Kilchurn Castle. Built in 1440, it enjoys one of Scotland's finest settings. Even when it's not open, it's worth visiting for the scenic stroll to it. It's a half-mile walk from an unmarked car park on the A85, just west of the Inveraray turnoff between Dalmally and Lochawe.

Cruachan Power Station NOTABLE BUILDING
(☑01866-962630; www.visitcruachan.co.uk; A85; adult/child £7.50/2.50; ⊙9.15am-4.45pm Mon-Fri Apr-Oct, to 3.45pm Mon-Fri Nov-Mar) In the Pass of Brander, by the A85, you can visit this power station. Electric buses take you more than half a mile inside Ben Cruachan, allowing you to see the pump-storage hydroelectric scheme, which occupies a vast cavern hollowed out of the mountain. The tour takes half an hour. Falls of Cruachan railway station (seasonal) is very close by.

Brander Lodge HOTEL ££
(☑01866-822243; www.branderlodge.com; A85, Bridge of Awe; d £110, superior d £140-160; P ⧖) Midway between Loch Etive and Loch Awe

and set among imposing Highland scenery, Brander Lodge makes a good base for exploring the area. An enthusiastic owner has transformed the place into a comfortable modern hotel, with continuing improvements being rolled out. Upstairs standard rooms are compact but comfortable, with good beds and big screens. Downstairs king-size-bedded rooms open to the garden.

The bar has a fine selection of malts, while food covers a few pub classics along with a short menu of tasty meat and fish dishes.

❶ Getting There & Away

Trains from Glasgow to Oban stop at Dalmally and Lochawe villages.

In summer three daily buses with Scottish Citylink (p258) from Glasgow to Oban go via Dalmally, Lochawe village and Cruachan Power Station.

Connel & Taynuilt

Hemmed in by dramatic mountain scenery, **Loch Etive** stretches 17 miles from Connel to Kinlochetive (accessible by road from Glencoe). Some very different but worthwhile sights complement the beautiful scenery around here.

★**Bonawe Iron Furnace** HISTORIC SITE
(☑01866-822432; www.historicenvironment. scot; Taynuilt; adult/child £6/3.60; ⊙9.30am-5.30pm Apr-Sep) Bonawe Iron Furnace is one of the region's most unusual historical sights. Near Taynuilt (not Bonawe), and dating from 1753, it was built by an iron-smelting company from Cumbria because of the abundance of birch and oak in the area. The coppiced wood was made into the charcoal that was needed for smelting the iron. It's now a tranquil, beautiful place, with the old buildings picturesquely arranged around a green hillside, and there's great background information on the iron industry. Take a picnic!

Falls of Lora WATERFALL
(Connel) At Connel Bridge, 5 miles north of Oban, the loch joins the sea via a channel partly blocked by an underwater rock ledge. When the tide flows in and out, water pours through this bottleneck, creating spectacular white-water rapids known as the Falls of Lora. Park near the north end of the bridge

and walk back into the middle to have a look.

Dunstaffnage Castle CASTLE
(☏ 01631-562465; www.historicenvironment. scot; adult/child £6/3.60; ⊙ 9.30am-5.30pm Apr-Sep, 10am-4pm Oct, 10am-4pm Sat-Wed Nov-Mar) Dunstaffnage, 2 miles west of Connel, looks like a child's drawing of what a castle should be – square and massive, with towers at the corners, and perched on top of a rocky outcrop. It was built around 1260 and was captured by Robert the Bruce during the Wars of Independence in 1309. The haunted ruins of the nearby 13th-century chapel contain lots of Campbell tombs decorated with skull-and-crossbone carvings.

ⓘ Getting There & Away

Trains from Glasgow to Oban stop at Taynuilt and Connel.

In summer one daily bus with Scottish Citylink (p258) bus from Glasgow to Oban goes via Taynuilt and Connel. Citylink services between Oban and Fort William also stop in Connel.

Appin & Around

The Appin region, once ruled over by the Stewarts from their stronghold at Castle Stalker, stretches north from the rocky shores of Loch Creran to the hills of Glencoe. Port Appin, a couple of miles off the main road, is a pleasant spot with a passenger ferry to the beautiful island of Lismore.

Castle Stalker CASTLE
(☏ 01631-730354; www.castlestalker.com; Portnacroish; adult/child/family £20/10/50; ⊙ tours Apr-Oct) One of Scotland's most spectacularly sited castles, Castle Stalker perches on a tiny offshore island – Monty Python buffs will recognise it as the castle that appears in the final scenes of the film *Monty Python and the Holy Grail*. Visits are by two-hour guided tour by a family member. Dates are limited so book well ahead online.

Pierhouse Hotel HOTEL £££
(☏ 01631-730302; www.pierhousehotel.co.uk; Port Appin; r £195-295; P🐾📶🍽️) The delightful Pierhouse Hotel sits on the waterfront above the pier for the Lismore ferry, and has stylish modern rooms, a sauna and an excellent restaurant. There are great views across the water to Lismore (rooms that enjoy them do come at a premium) and a relaxing, end-of-the-road feel. It has bikes available for guests to hire.

AT A GLANCE

POPULATION
149,420

LARGEST CITY
Inverness (p296)

BEST MOUNTAIN BIKING
Nevis Range (p339)

BEST WILDLIFE ENCOUNTERS
Aigas Field Centre (p303)

BEST SEAFOOD
Lochleven Seafood Cafe (p334)

WHEN TO GO
Apr & May Mountain scenery is at its most spectacular, with snow lingering on the higher peaks.

Jun Fort William hosts the UCI Mountain Bike World Cup.

Sep Ideal for hiking and hill walking: midges are dying off, but weather is still reasonably good.

Glen Coe (p331)

Inverness & the Central Highlands

From the sub-Arctic plateau of the Cairngorms to the hills of Highland Perthshire and the rocky peaks of Glen Coe, the central mountain ranges of the Scottish Highlands are testimony to the sculpting power of ice and weather. Here the landscape is at its grandest, with soaring hills of rock and heather bounded by wooded glens and waterfalls.

Aviemore, Glen Coe and Fort William draw hill walkers and climbers in summer, and skiers, snowboarders and ice climbers in winter. Inverness, the Highland capital, provides urban rest and relaxation, while nearby Loch Ness and its elusive monster add a hint of mystery.

From Fort William, base camp for climbing Ben Nevis, the Road to the Isles leads past the beaches of Arisaig and Morar to Mallaig, jumping-off point for the Small Isles.

The Little Minch

Loch Snizort

Uig
Trotternish

Rona

Loch Torridon

Achnasheen

Bran

Meig

A87

Torridon

Loch Dunvegan

Sound of Raasay

Loch Damh

Carron

Orrin Reservo

Dunvegan

Ose

Portree

Skye

Raasay

Inner Sound

Loch Kishorn

Lochcarron

Loch Carron

Loch Monar

Farrar

Sligachan

Kyle More
Scalpay

Kyle of Lochalsh

Loch Mullardoch

Cannich

Luib

Kyleakin

Loch Alsh

Dornie

Coruisk

Bealach Ratagain (339m)

Loch Duich

Five Sisters of Kintail (1068m)

Loch Affric

Glen Affric ❾

Loch na Cuilce

Glenelg

Shiel Bridge

A887

A87

Canna

Sleat

Loch Hourn

Arnisdale

Cluanie Inn

Loch Cluanie

A87

Loc Oic

Kinloch Castle

Armadale

Knoydart Peninsula ❸

Ladhar Bheinn (1020m)

Kinloch Hourn

Invergarry

Rum

Sound of Sleat

Inverie

Loch Quoich

Loch Lochy

Glen R

Askival (812m)

Mallaig

Loch Nevis

Strathan

Loch Arkaig

Achnacarry

Ro

Morar

Loch Morar

Tarbet

Gairlochy

Roy Bridge

Eigg

Arisaig

Lochailort

A830

Glenfinnan

Maltie

Loch Lochy

Spean Bridge

Spe

Sea of the Hebrides

Sound of Arisaig

Loch Moidart

Glenuig

Loch Shiel

Corpach

Loch Eil

Fort William

Nevis Range ✈

❹

Loch Treig

Muck

Castle Tioram

Ardmolich

Cona

Ben Nevis

Corrour Station

Coll

Ardnamurchan Point

Portuairk

Acharacle

Salen

Strontian

Ardgour

Corran

Kinlochleven

Loch Leven

Ardnamurchan ❷

Kilchoan

Loch Sunart

A861

Ballachulish

Glencoe

Kings Hous Hote

Uig

Tobermory

Bonnavoulin

A884

Appin

Glen Coe ❽

A82

Kinlochetive

Coupall

Mull

Loch Aline

Lochaline

West Highland Way

Bridge of Orchy

Loch Tuath

Salen

Lismore

Loch Etive

Loch na Keal

Kilchenan

Beinn a' Bhùiridh (896m)

Tyndrum

Craignure

Connel

Taynuilt

Ben (1130

Fionnphort

Oban

Lochawe

Ardbrecknish

Kilmelford

Inveruglas

Inverness & the Central Highlands Highlights

❶ **Rothiemurchus Estate** (p312) Wandering through ancient Caledonian forest in the heart of the Cairngorms.

❷ **Ardnamurchan** (p339) Taking the winding, single-

track road past stunning vistas to Ardnamurchan Point.

❸ **Knoydart Peninsula** (p342) Venturing into the country's most remote and rugged wilderness.

❹ **Ben Nevis** (p338) Making it to the summit of the UK's highest mountain.

❺ **Inverness** (p296) Eating at the region's best restaurants, strolling along the River Ness and dolphin spotting in the Moray Firth.

6 Glen Lyon (p331) Exploring the woods and mountains around this gorgeous and romantic glen.

7 Rannoch Moor (p328) Keeping right on to the end of the road at this bleak but beautiful moor.

8 Glen Coe (p331) Soaking up the moody but magnificent scenery (when you can see it!).

9 Glen Affric (p303) Hiking among the hills, lochs and forests of this wild and enchanting glen.

❶ Getting There & Around

For timetable information, check Traveline (www.travelinescotland.com).

BUS

Scottish Citylink (www.citylink.co.uk) Runs buses from Perth and Glasgow to Inverness and Fort William, and links Inverness to Fort William along the Great Glen.

Stagecoach (www.stagecoachbus.com) The main regional bus company, with an office in Inverness. Dayrider tickets are valid for a day's unlimited travel on Stagecoach buses in various regions, including Inverness (£7) and Aviemore (£7.50).

TRAIN

Two railway lines serve the region: the Perth–Aviemore–Inverness line in the east, and the Glasgow–Fort William–Mallaig line in the west.

INVERNESS & THE GREAT GLEN

Inverness, one of Britain's fastest growing cities, is the capital of the Highlands. It's a transport hub and jumping-off point for the central, western and northern Highlands, the Moray Firth coast and the Great Glen.

The Great Glen is a geological fault running in a line across Scotland from Fort William to Inverness. The glaciers of the last Ice Age eroded a deep trough along the fault line, which is now filled by four lochs – Linnhe, Lochy, Oich and Ness. The glen has always been an important communication route – General George Wade built a military road along the southern side of Loch Ness in the early 18th century, and in 1822 the various lochs were linked by the Caledonian Canal to create a cross-country waterway. The A82 road along the glen was completed in 1933 – a date that coincides neatly with the first modern sightings of the Loch Ness Monster.

Inverness

📞 01463 / POP 61,235

Inverness has a great location astride the River Ness at the northern end of the Great Glen. In summer it overflows with visitors intent on monster hunting (p306) at nearby Loch Ness, but it's worth a visit in its own right for a stroll along the picturesque River Ness, a cruise on Loch Ness and a meal in one of the city's excellent restaurants.

Inverness was probably founded by King David in the 12th century, but thanks to its often violent history, few buildings of real age or historical significance have survived – much of the older part of the city dates from the period following the completion of the Caledonian Canal in 1822. The broad and shallow River Ness, famed for its salmon fishing, runs through the heart of the city.

◉ Sights & Activities

★**Ness Islands**   PARK

The main attraction in Inverness is a stroll along the river to the Ness Islands. Planted with mature Scots pine, fir, beech and sycamore, and linked to the riverbanks and each other by elegant Victorian footbridges, the islands make an appealing picnic spot. They're a 20-minute walk south of the castle – head upstream on either side of the river and return on the opposite bank. The path on the eastern bank is the start of the Great Glen Way.

On the west bank you'll pass the red-sandstone towers of **St Andrew's Cathedral** (11 Ardross St), dating from 1869, and the modern Eden Court Theatre (p300), which hosts regular art exhibits.

Inverness Botanic Gardens   GARDENS
(📞 01463-713553; Bught Lane; ⊙10am-4pm)
FREE These peaceful gardens feature a cactus house and a steamy tropical house, with plenty of benches to take a rest among the flowers. It's a short detour to visit the gardens if you're walking to Ness Islands from the castle. There's a cafe here too.

Inverness Museum & Art Gallery   MUSEUM
(📞 01463-237114; www.inverness.highland.museum; Castle Wynd; ⊙10.30am-4pm Tue-Sat Apr-Oct, noon-4pm Thu-Sat Nov-Mar) **FREE** Inverness Museum and Art Gallery covers Highland history and culture with wildlife dioramas, geological displays, period rooms with historic weapons, Pictish stones, and exhibitions of contemporary Highland arts and crafts.

Dolphin Spirit   WILDLIFE WATCHING
(📞 07544 800620; www.dolphinspirit.co.uk; Inverness Marina, Stadium Rd; adult/child £19.50/12; ⊙Easter-Oct) This outfit runs recommended cruises from Inverness into the Moray Firth to spot the UK's largest pod of

Inverness

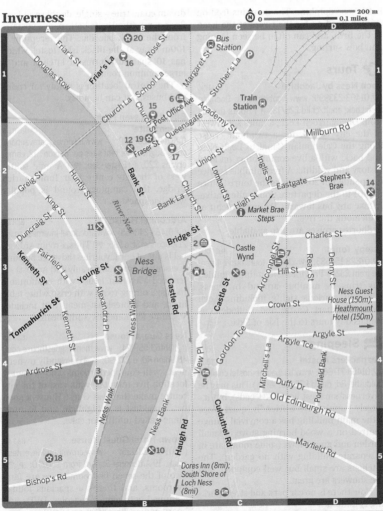

Inverness

◎ Sights
1 Inverness Castle	C3
2 Inverness Museum & Art Gallery	C3
3 St Andrew's Cathedral	B4

🛌 Sleeping
4 Ardconnel House	C3
5 Bazpackers Hostel	C4
6 Black Isle Rooms & Hostel	B1
7 Crown Hotel Guest House	C3
8 Rocpool Reserve	C5

✖ Eating
9 Café 1	C3
10 Contrast Brasserie	B5
11 Kitchen Brasserie	B3
12 Mustard Seed	B2
13 Rocpool	B3
14 Velocity Cafe	D2

🍷 Drinking & Nightlife
15 Black Isle Bar	B1
16 MacGregor's	B1
17 Malt Room	B2

⊛ Entertainment
18 Eden Court Theatre	A5
19 Hootananny	B2
20 Ironworks	B1

bottlenose dolphins. The dolphins feed on salmon heading for the rivers at the head of the firth, and can often be seen leaping and bow surfing.

Tours

Loch Ness by Jacobite
BOATING

(☑01463-233999; www.jacobite.co.uk; Dochgarroch Lock; adult/child £25/18; ♿) Boats depart from Dochgarroch Lock, 5 miles southwest of the city centre, for a two-hour cruise along the Caledonian Canal to Loch Ness and back, with a live commentary on local history and wildlife. A free minibus service (suspended in 2020) links the tourist office (p300) to the departure point; alternatively take any bus towards Drumnadrochit or walk along the river.

Shorter cruises are also available.

Happy Tours
BUS TOUR

(☑07828 154683; www.happy-tours.biz; 1-4 people from £320) Provides entertaining guided day trips by minibus around Inverness, taking in various sights including Loch Ness, Urquhart Castle and Culloden, as well as day tours to the Isle of Skye.

🛏 Sleeping

Bazpackers Hostel
HOSTEL £

(☑01463-717663; www.bazpackershostel.co.uk; 4 Culduthel Rd; dm/d £26/65; @🛜) This may be Inverness' smallest hostel (34 beds), but it's hugely popular. It's a friendly, quiet place – the main building has a convivial lounge centred on a wood-burning stove, a small garden and great views (some rooms are in a separate building with no garden). The kitchens are small but well equipped, and the showers are great.

Note there is no car park and street parking is limited.

Inverness Youth Hostel
HOSTEL £

(HS; ☑01463-231771; www.hostellingscotland.org.uk; Victoria Dr; d/tr/q £43/60/69; P@🛜) Inverness' modern 166-bed hostel is 10 minutes' walk northeast of the city centre. It's clean and well equipped, with comfy beds and a flashy stainless-steel kitchen. Booking is essential, especially at Easter and in July and August. In 2020 only private rooms were available (no shared dorms).

Black Isle Rooms & Hostel
HOSTEL £

(☑01463-229920; www.blackislebar.com; 47-49 Academy St; dm/s/d/f £26/60/95/110; 🛜) Black Isle Bar rooms are a beer drinker's dream come true – single, double and family rooms with private bathrooms, upstairs from the Black Isle Bar. The reception is 100m away at the Black Isle Hostel, which has 10 spacious dorms, a kitchen and a large common room.

The central location is handy for trains and buses, but can be noisy.

Bught Caravan Park & Campsite
CAMPSITE £

(☑01463-236920; www.invernesscaravanpark.com; Bught Lane; tent sites per person £12, campervans £20; ⊙Easter-Sep; 🛜) A mile southwest of the city centre near Tomnahurich Bridge, this camping ground is popular with backpackers.

Ardconnel House
B&B ££

(☑01463-240455; www.ardconnel-inverness.co.uk; 21 Ardconnel St; d £95; 🛜) The six-room Ardconnel is one of our favourites (advance booking is essential, especially in July and August) – a terraced Victorian house with comfortable rooms, a dining room with crisp white table linen, and a breakfast menu that includes Vegemite for homesick Antipodeans.

Ness Guest House
B&B ££

(☑01463-559174; www.thenessguesthouse.com; 48 Union Rd; d £72-90; P🛜) Friendly owners, neat, well-equipped rooms and a handy location five minutes' walk east of the city centre make the Ness Guest House a good bet. Breakfast is a highlight and features home-baked muffins or cake.

Crown Hotel Guest House
B&B ££

(☑01463-231135; www.crownhotel-inverness.co.uk; 19 Ardconnel St; s/d from £50/70; P🛜) Two of the seven bedrooms here are family rooms, and there's a spacious lounge equipped with games consoles, DVDs and board games. Breakfast costs £10.

★ Heathmount Hotel
BOUTIQUE HOTEL £££

(☑01463-235877; www.heathmounthotel.com; Kingsmills Rd; d from £170; P🛜) Small and friendly, the Heathmount combines a popular local bar and restaurant with eight designer hotel rooms, each one different, ranging from a boldly coloured family room in purple and gold to a slinky black velvet four-poster double. Five minutes' walk east of the city centre.

★ Trafford Bank
B&B £££

(☑01463-241414; www.traffordbankguesthouse.co.uk; 96 Fairfield Rd; d £135-170; P🛜) Lots of rave reviews for this elegant Victorian villa, which was once home to a bishop, just a mitre's-toss from the Caledonian Canal and 10 minutes' walk west from the city centre. The luxurious rooms include fresh flowers and fruit, bathrobes and fluffy towels – ask for the Tartan Room, which has a wrought-iron king bed and Victorian roll-top bath.

Rocpool Reserve BOUTIQUE HOTEL £££
(01463-240089; www.rocpool.com; Culduthel Rd; s £265, d £285-485; P) Boutique chic meets the Highlands in this slick and sophisticated little hotel, where an elegant Georgian exterior conceals an oasis of contemporary cool. A gleaming white entrance hall lined with red carpet and contemporary art leads to designer rooms in shades of chocolate, cream and gold.

Expect lots of decadent extras in the more expensive rooms, ranging from two-person showers to balcony hot tubs with aquavision TV.

✕ Eating

Velocity Cafe CAFE £
(01463-419956; www.velocitylove.co.uk; 1 Crown Ave; mains £3.50-6; 9am-4pm Tue-Sat) This cyclists' cafe serves vegetarian soups, sandwiches and salads prepared with organic, locally sourced produce, as well as yummy cakes and coffee. There's also a workshop where you can repair your bike or book a session with a mechanic.

★ Café 1 BISTRO ££
(01463-226200; www.cafe1.net; 75 Castle St; mains lunch £9-11, dinner £12-30; noon-2.30pm & 5-9.30pm Mon-Fri, 12.30-2.45pm & 5.30-9.30pm Sat) Café 1 is a friendly, appealing bistro with candlelit tables amid elegant blond-wood and wrought-iron decor. There's an international menu based on quality Scottish produce, from Aberdeen Angus steaks to crisp pan-fried sea bass and pappardelle pasta with local wild chanterelles.

Mustard Seed BISTRO ££
(01463-220220; www.mustardseedrestaurant.co.uk; 16 Fraser St; mains £14-25; noon-3pm & 5.30-10pm) The menu at this bright and bustling bistro changes weekly, but focuses on Scottish and French cuisine with a modern twist. Grab a table on the upstairs balcony if you can – it's the best outdoor lunch spot in Inverness, with a great view

across the river. And a two-course lunch for £12.95 is hard to beat.

On the opposite bank of the river, Mustard Seed's spectacular, glass-fronted sister restaurant **Kitchen Brasserie** (01463-259119; www.kitchenrestaurant.co.uk; 15 Huntly St; mains £11-25; noon-3pm & 5-10pm;) offers a similar menu. Ask for a table upstairs, by the window.

★ Rocpool MEDITERRANEAN £££
(01463-717274; www.rocpoolrestaurant.com; 1 Ness Walk; mains £15-30; noon-2.30pm & 5.45-10pm Mon-Sat) Lots of polished wood, crisp white linen and leather booths and banquettes lend a sophisticated nautical air to this relaxed bistro, which offers a Mediterranean-influenced menu that makes the most of quality Scottish produce, especially seafood. The two-course lunch is £18.95.

Contrast Brasserie BRASSERIE £££
(01463-223777; www.glenmoristontownhouse.com; 20 Ness Bank; mains £17-27; noon-2.30pm & 5-9pm Mon-Sat, 1-6.30pm Sun) At the Glenmoriston Town House Hotel, Contrast Brasserie drips designer style, with truly delicious food prepared using fresh Scottish produce. The two-/three-course lunch menu (£14.95/18.95) and three-course pre-theatre menu (£20.95, 5pm to 6.30pm) are good value.

🍷 Drinking & Nightlife

★ Malt Room BAR
(01463-221888; www.themaltroom.co.uk; 34 Church St; 5pm-1am Sun-Fri, noon-1am Sat) Tucked inside the entrance to the Victorian Market, this cosy little whisky bar is the best place in town for a dram. The carefully curated menu lists a number of themed whisky flights for guided tastings, or customise your own from a selection of more than 200 malts. Whisky cocktails include an excellent Smoky Amaretto Sour made with Lagavulin 16.

Black Isle Bar BAR
(www.blackislebrewery.com; 68 Church St; noon-midnight) Shared wooden tables and a rustic-industrial decor make for a convivial atmosphere at Black Isle Bar, where you'll find 18 beers from the nearby Black Isle Brewery (p304) on tap, along with a selection of ales from other craft breweries, organic wines and wood-fired pizzas (£10 to £14).

MacGregor's BAR

(www.macgregorsbars.com; 113 Academy St; ⊙11am-midnight Mon-Thu, to 1am Fri & Sat, noon-midnight Sun) Decked out in timber and tweed, this bar strikes a distinctly modern chord. There's a huge selection of Scottish craft beers on tap, and even a beer 'set menu' described as 'a journey through the basics of craft beer'. The beer nerdiness extends to the gents' toilets, where urinals and washbasins have been fashioned out of beer kegs.

☆ Entertainment

Hootananny LIVE MUSIC

(☑01463-233651; www.hootananny inverness. co.uk; 67 Church St; ⊙noon-1am Mon-Thu, to 3am Fri & Sat, 4pm-midnight Sun) Hootananny is the city's best live-music venue, with traditional folk and/or rock sessions nightly, including big-name bands from all over Scotland (and, indeed, the world). The bar is well stocked with a range of beers from the local Black Isle Brewery.

Ironworks LIVE MUSIC

(☑01463-718555; www.ironworksvenue.com; 122 Academy St) With live bands (rock, pop, tribute) and comedy shows two or three times a week, the Ironworks is the town's main venue for big-name acts.

Eden Court Theatre THEATRE

(☑01463-234234; www.eden-court.co.uk; Bishop's Rd; ⊙box office 11am-3pm Mon-Fri; ☎) The Highlands' main cultural venue – with theatre, art house cinema and a conference centre – Eden Court stages a busy programme of drama, dance, comedy, music, film and children's events. Pick up a programme from the foyer or check the website.

❶ Information

Inverness Tourist Office (☑01463-252401; wwww.visitscotland.com; 36 High St; ⊙9am-5pm; ☎) Accommodation booking service; also sells tickets for tours and cruises.

❶ Getting There & Away

AIR

Inverness Airport (INV; ☑01667-464000; www.invernessairport.co.uk) is at Dalcross, 10 miles east of the city, off the A96 towards Aberdeen. There are scheduled flights to Amsterdam, London, Manchester, Dublin, Orkney, Shetland and the Outer Hebrides, as well as other places in the UK.

Stagecoach (☑01463-233371; www.stage-coachbus.com) bus 11/11A runs from the airport to Inverness bus station (£4.50, 30 minutes, every 30 minutes).

BUS

Services depart from **Inverness bus station** (Margaret St). Most intercity routes are served by **Scottish Citylink** (www.citylink.co.uk) and Stagecoach. Destinations include the following:

Aberdeen (Stagecoach) £13.85, four hours, hourly

Aviemore £11.50, 45 minutes, eight daily

Edinburgh £34.30, four hours, eight daily

Fort William £11.60, two hours, eight daily

Glasgow £34.30, 3½ to four hours, hourly

Portree £28.10, 3¼ hours, two daily

Thurso (Stagecoach) £21.60, 3½ hours, two daily

Ullapool £14.90, 1½ hours, two daily except Sunday

If you book far enough in advance, **Megabus** (☑0900 1600 900; www.megabus.com) offers fares from as little as £3 for buses from Inverness to Glasgow and Edinburgh, and £32 to London.

TRAIN

The **Caledonian Sleeper** (☑0330 060 0500; www.sleeper.scot) to London (from £120 sharing a two-berth cabin; book well in advance) departs at 8.45pm Monday to Friday, 8.26pm Sunday. Other services:

Aberdeen £31.60, 2¼ hours, 11 daily

Edinburgh £47.40, 3½ hours, eight daily

Glasgow £46, 3½ hours, eight daily

Kyle of Lochalsh £25.60, 2½ hours, four daily Monday to Saturday, two Sunday; one of Britain's great scenic train journeys

London £180, eight hours, one daily direct (others require a change at Edinburgh)

Wick £22.40, 4½ hours, four daily Monday to Saturday, one or two on Sunday; via Thurso

❶ Getting Around

BICYCLE

Ticket to Ride (☑01463-419160; www. tickettoridehighlands.co.uk; Bellfield Park; per day from £30; ⊙9am-5.30pm Apr-Oct) Hires out mountain bikes, road bikes, hybrids and tandems; bikes can be dropped off in Fort William.

BUS

City services and buses to places around Inverness, including Nairn, Forres, the Culloden battlefield, Beauly, Dingwall and Lairg, are operated by Stagecoach. An Inverness Zone 2 Dayrider ticket costs £7 and gives unlimited travel for a day on buses as far afield as Culloden, Fortrose and Drumnadrochit.

CAR
Focus Vehicle Rental (✆ 01463-709517; www.focusvehiclerental.co.uk; 6 Harbour Rd) Rates start at £40 per day.

Parking is limited in and around the city centre. **Old Town Rose Street** (Rose St; ⊗24hr) is a secure multistorey car park that charges £7 for the first 24 hours, then £5 per subsequent day.

TAXI
Inverness Taxis (✆ 01463-222222; www.inverness-taxis.com) There's a taxi rank outside the train station.

Around Inverness

Culloden Battlefield
The Battle of Culloden in 1746 – the last pitched battle ever fought on British soil – saw the defeat of Bonnie Prince Charlie and the end of the Jacobite dream when 1200 Highlanders were slaughtered by government forces in a 68-minute rout. The Duke of Cumberland, son of the reigning King George II and leader of the Hanoverian army, earned the nickname 'Butcher' for his brutal treatment of the defeated Jacobite forces. The battle sounded the death knell for the old clan system, and the horrors of the Clearances, when tenants were evicted from their lands, soon followed.

The sombre moor where the conflict took place has scarcely changed in the ensuing 275 years. The battlefield has been preserved and enemy lines marked by coloured flags; admission is free.

Culloden Visitor Centre   MUSEUM
(NTS; www.nts.org.uk; adult/child £11/9.50; ⊗10am-4pm Wed-Sun; P) This impressive visitor centre has everything you need to know about the Battle of Culloden in 1746, including the lead-up and the aftermath, with perspectives from both sides. An innovative film puts you on the battlefield in the middle of the mayhem, and a wealth of other audio presentations must have kept Inverness' entire acting community in business for weeks. Pick up a leaflet for a self-guided tour of the battlefield, where you can see the newly restored 18th-century Leanach Cottage.

In 2020 the visitor centre reopened with limited hours and an online advance booking system.

❶ Getting There & Away
Culloden is 6 miles east of Inverness. Bus 2 runs from Eastgate shopping centre in Inverness to Culloden battlefield (£3.15, 30 minutes, hourly except Sunday).

Fort George
The headland guarding the narrows in the Moray Firth opposite Fortrose is occupied by the magnificent and virtually unaltered 18th-century artillery fortification of **Fort George** (HES; ✆ 01667-462777; www.historicenvironment.scot; adult/child £9/5.40; ⊗10am-4pm; P).

One of the finest artillery fortifications in Europe, Fort George was established in 1748 in the aftermath of the Battle of Culloden, as a base for George II's army of occupation in the Highlands. By the time of its completion in 1769 it had cost the equivalent of around £1 billion in today's money. It still functions as a military barracks; public areas have exhibitions on 18th-century soldiery.

The mile-plus walk around the ramparts offers fine views; look out for dolphins in the surrounding waters. Given its size, you'll need at least two hours to do the place justice. The fort is off the A96 about 11 miles northeast of Inverness; there is no public transport. The fort reopened in September 2020 with reduced opening hours and an online advance booking system.

Nairn
✆ 01667 / POP 9770
Nairn is a popular golfing and seaside resort with good sandy beaches. You can spend many pleasant hours wandering along the **East Beach**, one of the finest in Scotland.

The most interesting part of town is the old fishing village of **Fishertown**, down by the harbour, a maze of narrow streets lined with picturesque cottages.

The big events in the town's calendar are the **Nairn Highland Games** (www.nairnhighlandgames.co.uk; ⊗mid-Aug) and the **Nairn Book & Arts Festival** (www.nairnfestival.co.uk; ⊗Sep).

Boath House Hotel   HOTEL £££
(✆ 01667-454896; www.boath-house.com; Auldearn; d £220-290; P🛜) This beautifully

restored Regency mansion, set in private woodland gardens 2 miles east of Nairn on the A96, is one of Scotland's most luxurious country-house hotels. The grounds include an ornamental lake and a walled garden with free-range hens, beehives and the Kale Yard cafe-restaurant, serving wood-fired pizzas, risottos and pastas made with fresh produce from the kitchen garden.

Classroom GASTROPUB ££

(☑ 01667-455999; www.theclassroombistro.com; 1 Cawdor St; mains £12-25; ⊙ 10am-10pm Wed-Sat, 11am-10pm Sun; 🛜🚻) Done up in an appealing mixture of modern and traditional styles – lots of richly glowing wood with designer detailing – Classroom doubles as cocktail bar and gastropub, with a tempting menu that ranges from Seafood linguine to Highland steak with peppercorn sauce.

❶ Getting There & Away

Buses run hourly (less frequently on Sunday) from Inverness to Nairn (£6.25, 30 minutes) and on to Aberdeen. The bus station is just west of the town centre.

The town also lies on the Inverness–Aberdeen railway line, with five to seven trains a day from Inverness (£6.70, 15 minutes).

National Cycle Route 1 links Nairn and Inverness (20 miles).

Cawdor

Cawdor Castle CASTLE

(☑ 01667-404615; www.cawdorcastle.com; gardens & grounds adult/child £8/4; ⊙ 10am-5pm May-Sep; 🅿) This castle, 5 miles southwest of Nairn, was once the seat of the Thane of Cawdor, one of the titles bestowed on Shakespeare's Macbeth. The real Macbeth – an ancient Scottish king – couldn't have lived here though, since he died in 1057, 300 years before the castle was begun. Nevertheless the castle tour (not available in 2020) gives a fascinating insight into the lives of the Scottish aristocracy.

Even if the castle interior is closed, as it was in 2020, the walled gardens, maze and woodland trails through the grounds are worth a visit, and the courtyard cafe and shop provide a glimpse inside the castle walls. To get here, take bus 2 from Eastgate shopping centre in Inverness to Cawdor village (50 minutes, hourly except

Sunday), from where it's a 1-mile walk to the castle.

Cawdor Tavern PUB FOOD ££

(www.cawdortavern.co.uk; mains lunch £7-20, dinner £15-24; ⊙ noon-10pm Mon-Thu, noon-11pm Fri & Sat, 12.30-10pm Sun; 🅿🛜🚻) Cawdor Tavern, in the pretty village close to Cawdor Castle, is a cosy pub with wood panelling, open fires and an impressive whisky selection. There's also excellent pub food, including tempting daily specials.

West of Inverness

Beauly

☑ 01463 / POP 1370

Mary, Queen of Scots is said to have given this village its name in 1564 when she visited, exclaiming: *'Quel beau lieu!'* (What a beautiful place!) Founded in 1230, the red-sandstone Beauly Priory is now an impressive ruin, haunted by the cries of rooks nesting in a magnificent centuries-old sycamore tree.

Priory Hotel HOTEL ££

(☑ 01463-782309; www.priory-hotel.com; The Square; s/d from £69/79; 🅿🛜) The Priory Hotel, on Beauly's central square, has bright, modern rooms and serves good bar meals.

★**Corner on the Square** CAFE £

(☑ 01463-783000; www.corneronthesquare.co.uk; 1 High St; dishes £2.50-8.50; ⊙ 8.30am-5pm Mon-Fri, to 8pm Sat, 9am-5pm Sun) Beauly's best lunch spot is this superb little delicatessen and cafe that serves breakfast (till 11.30am), daily lunch specials (11.30am to 4.30pm) and excellent coffee.

❶ Getting There & Away

Bus 28X (express) and 28A from Inverness run to Beauly (£5.45, 25 to 45 minutes, hourly Monday to Saturday, five on Sunday), and the town lies on the railway lines connecting Inverness (£3.80, 15 minutes) to Thurso and Wick (£22.10, four hours) and Kyle of Lochalsh (£25.30, 2½ hours).

Strathglass & Glen Affric

The broad valley of Strathglass extends about 18 miles inland from Beauly, and is followed by the A831 to Cannich (the only village in the area), where there's a grocery store and a post office.

Glen Affric, one of the most beautiful glens in Scotland, extends deep into the hills beyond Cannich. The upper reaches of the glen are designated as the **Glen Affric National Nature Reserve** (www.nnr.scot), a scenic wonderland of shimmering lochs, rugged mountains and native Scots pines, home to pine martens, otters, red squirrels and golden eagles.

🏃 Activities

About 4 miles southwest of Cannich is **Dog Falls**, a scenic spot where the River Affric squeezes through a narrow, rocky gorge. A circular walking trail (red waymarks) leads from Dog Falls car park to a footbridge below the falls and back on the far side of the river (2 miles, allow one hour).

The road continues beyond Dog Falls to a parking area and picnic site at the eastern end of **Loch Affric**, where there are several short walks along the river and the loch shore. The circuit of Loch Affric (10 miles, allow five hours walking, two hours by mountain bike) follows good paths right around the loch and takes you deep into the heart of some very wild scenery.

It's possible to walk all the way from Cannich to Glen Shiel on the west coast (35 miles) in two days, spending the night at the remote **Glen Affric Youth Hostel** (HS; ☑ bookings 0845 293 7373; www.hostellingscotland.org.uk; Allt Beithe; r £61; ⊘ Apr–mid-Sep). The route is now part of the waymarked **Affric-Kintail Way** (www.affrickintailway.com), a 44-mile walking or mountain-biking trail leading from Drumnadrochit to Morvich via Cannich.

A minor road on the east side of the River Glass leads to the pretty little conservation village of **Tomich**, 3 miles southwest of Cannich, built in Victorian times as accommodation for estate workers. The road continues (unsurfaced for the last 2 miles) to a forestry car park, the starting point for a short (800m) walk to **Plodda Falls**. Here a restored Victorian viewing platform extends over the top of the falls like a diving board, giving a dizzying view straight down the cascade into a remote and thickly forested river gorge. Keep your eyes peeled for red squirrels and crossbills.

🛏 Sleeping & Eating

Cannich Caravan & Camping Park   CAMPSITE £
(☑ 01456-415364; www.highlandcamping.co.uk; sites per adult/child £9/5, pods s/d £26/36; 🐾) Good, sheltered spot, with on-site cafe and the option of wooden camping 'pods'. Mountain bikes for hire from £17 a day.

Tomich Hotel   HOTEL ££
(☑ 01456-415399; www.tomichhotel.co.uk; Tomich; d £120-140; ⊘ closed Dec & Jan; 🅿🐾🐶) About 3 miles southwest of Cannich on the southern side of the River Glass, this Victorian hunting lodge has a dog-friendly bar with blazing log fire that serves food from noon to 9pm; an intimate, candlelit restaurant; and eight comfortable rooms. It can organise trout fishing on local waters.

★ **Aigas Field Centre**   B&B £££
(☑ 01463-782443; www.aigas.co.uk; A831, IV4 7AD; s/d £140/320, lodge per person £135, round house d £320; ⊘ Apr–Oct; 🅿🐾) This grand Victorian estate is a centre for nature studies and wildlife holidays, and the family home of naturalist Sir John Lister-Kaye. B&B accommodation is available in two rooms in Aigas House, seven wooden cabins in the grounds and a round house. Breakfast and dinner (three courses £32) are at a shared table in the banquet hall of the house.

The 80-hectare grounds are home to pine martens, badgers, otters and beavers, which can be observed from hides strategically placed around a loch, plus a wildcat enclosure that's part of a conservation breeding programme. The centre also runs a number of week-long holidays that include a programme of activities such as ranger-led wildlife-watching trips, birdwatching expeditions and photography courses. Aigas is 6 miles southwest of Beauly.

★ **Struy Inn**   SCOTTISH £££
(☑ 01463-761308; www.thestruy.co.uk; Struy Village; mains £25-30; ⊘ 5.30-9.30pm Wed-Sun Apr-Oct, Thu-Sat Nov-Mar; 🅿🐾) Set in the heart of lovely Strathglass, on the road between Cannich and Beauly, this fine Victorian inn is a haven of old-fashioned charm. It houses a top-quality restaurant serving the finest Scottish cuisine; with just 18 seats, booking is essential.

❶ Getting There & Away

Stagecoach (p300) bus 17 runs from Inverness to Cannich (£6.10, 50 minutes, five daily Monday to Saturday) and Tomich (£6.10, 1¼ hours) via Drumnadrochit (£3.60, 25 minutes).

Black Isle

The Black Isle – a peninsula rather than an island – is linked to Inverness by the Kessock Bridge. Bypassed by the main A9 road, it's a peaceful backwater of wooded hills, picturesque villages and dramatic coastlines, with the added attraction of Scotland's best mainland dolphin-watching spot.

Black Isle Brewery
BREWERY

(☑ 01463-811871; www.blackislebrewery.com; Old Allangrange; ⏰ 10am-5pm Mon-Sat) 🏷 FREE One of Britain's best artisan breweries, Black Isle has won many awards for its organically produced ales. Free brewery tours are usually available but weren't running in 2020, so check ahead; the shop remained open. It's a few miles north of the Kessock Bridge.

Fortrose & Rosemarkie

The neighbouring towns of Fortrose and Rosemarkie make up the main population centre of the Black Isle. Between the two, the long gravel spit of **Chanonry Point** is the best land-based dolphin-spotting area in the country; the lighthouse is a prime spot. One-hour **dolphin-watching cruises** (☑ 01381-622383; www.dolphintripsavoch.co.uk; adult/child £18/12; ⏰ Apr-Sep) depart from the harbour at Avoch (pronounced 'auch'), 3 miles southwest.

From the northern end of Rosemarkie's High St, a short but pleasant signposted walk leads you through the gorges and waterfalls of the **Fairy Glen**. There are forest mountain-biking trails just north of Rosemarkie at **Learnie Red Rocks** (☑ 0300 067 6100; www.scotland.forestry.gov.uk/visit/learnie-red-rocks) FREE .

Fortrose Cathedral
HISTORIC BUILDING

(HES; Cathedral Sq, Fortrose; ⏰ 9.30am-5.30pm Apr-Sep, 10am-4pm Oct-Mar) FREE Here you'll find the vaulted crypt of a 13th-century chapter house and sacristy, and the remains of the 14th-century south aisle and chapel.

Groam House Museum
MUSEUM

(☑ 01381-620961; www.groamhouse.org.uk; High St, Rosemarkie; ⏰ 11am-4.30pm Mon-Fri, 2-4.30pm Sat & Sun Apr-Oct) FREE This museum has a superb collection of Pictish stones found in the village, engraved with designs similar to those on Celtic Irish stones. Book online in advance.

Anderson
PUB

(☑ 01381-620236; www.theanderson.co.uk; Union St, Fortrose; ⏰ 4-11pm, closed Sun-Tue Nov-Mar) The Anderson hotel serves good pub grub (mains £10 to £25), a range of real ales and craft beers (including several from the local Cromarty Brewing Company), and more than 200 single malt whiskies.

ℹ Getting There & Away

Stagecoach (p300) buses 26 and 26A run from Inverness to Fortrose and Rosemarkie (£3.25, 30 minutes, twice hourly Monday to Saturday, three on Sunday).

Cromarty

☑ 01381 / POP 730

The pretty village of Cromarty at the northeastern tip of the Black Isle has lots of 18th-century red-sandstone houses, and a lovely green park beside the sea for picnics and games. An excellent walk, known as the **100 Steps**, leads from the north end of the village to the headland viewpoint of South Sutor (4 miles round trip).

Hugh Miller's Cottage & Museum
MUSEUM

(NTS; www.nts.org.uk; Church St; adult/child £6.50/5.50; ⏰ 1-5pm Mar-Oct) This thatch-roofed cottage is the birthplace of Hugh Miller (1802–56), a local stonemason and amateur geologist who pioneered the study of fossil fishes in Scotland; he later moved to Edinburgh and became a famous journalist and newspaper editor. The Georgian villa next door is home to a museum celebrating his life and achievements.

Ecoventures
WILDLIFE WATCHING

(☑ 01381-600323; www.ecoventures.co.uk; Cromarty Harbour; adult/child £32/25) Ecoventures runs two-hour boat trips from Cromarty harbour into the Moray Firth to see bottlenose dolphins and other wildlife.

Sutor Creek
CAFE ££

(☑ 01381-600855; www.sutorcreek.co.uk; 21 Bank St; mains £9-14; ⏰ 10am-8pm Wed-Sun; 🖶) 🍴 This excellent little cafe and deli serves wood-fired pizzas and fresh local seafood including mussels and haddock, as well as burgers and cakes.

ℹ Getting There & Away

Stagecoach (p300) buses 26 and 26A run from Inverness to Cromarty (£4.70, one hour, hourly Monday to Saturday).

WORTH A TRIP

DORES INN

While crowded tour coaches pour down the west side of Loch Ness to the hot spots of Drumnadrochit and Urquhart Castle, the narrow B862 road along the eastern shore is relatively peaceful. It leads to the village of Foyers, where you can enjoy a pleasant hike to the **Falls of Foyers**.

But it's worth making the trip just for the **Dores Inn** (☎01463-751203; www.the-doresinn.co.uk; Dores; mains £10-28; ⊙noon-9pm Wed-Sun; 🅿 🛜), a beautifully restored country pub furnished with recycled furniture, local landscape paintings and fresh flowers. The menu specialises in quality Scottish produce, from haggis, turnips and tatties (potatoes), and haddock and chips, to steaks, scallops and seafood platters.

The pub garden enjoys a stunning view along Loch Ness, and even has a dedicated monster-spotting vantage point. The nearby campervan, emblazoned with Nessie-Serry Independent Research, has been home to dedicated Nessie hunter Steve Feltham (www.nessiehunter.co.uk) since 1991; in 2015 he concluded that Nessie could, in fact, be a giant catfish.

National Cycle Route 1 connects Inverness with Cromarty (26 miles).

Loch Ness

Deep, dark and narrow, Loch Ness stretches for 23 miles between Inverness and Fort Augustus. Its bitterly cold waters have been extensively explored in search of Nessie, the elusive Loch Ness Monster, but most visitors see her only in the form of a cardboard cut-out at Drumnadrochit's monster exhibitions. The busy A82 road runs along the northwestern shore, while the more tranquil and picturesque B862 follows the southeastern shore. A complete circuit of the loch is about 70 miles – travel anticlockwise for the better views.

 Activities

Walking

The 79-mile **Great Glen Way** (www.highland.gov.uk/greatglenway) long-distance footpath stretches from Inverness to Fort William, where walkers can connect with the **West Highland Way**. The Great Glen Way is split into stages of various lengths so that the full walk can be completed in four to seven days. Book accommodation in advance.

The area's newest waymarked trail is the **Loch Ness 360°** (www.lochness360.com), which loops for 80 miles around the circumference of the loch from Inverness and back. The trail is divided into six day-long sections, with stops in Drumnadrochit, Invermoriston, Fort Augustus, Foyers and Dores.

The climb to the summit of **Meall Fuar-mhonaidh** (699m), on the northwestern shore of Loch Ness, makes an excellent short hill walk: the views along the Great Glen from the top are superb. It's a 6-mile round trip, so allow about three hours. Start from the car park at the end of the minor road leading south from Drumnadrochit to Bunloit.

Cycling

The Great Glen can also be cycled via the **Route 78 Caledonia Way**, which runs for 234 miles from Campbeltown to Inverness (www.sustrans.org.uk). The 66-mile stretch from Fort William to Inverness runs alongside the Caledonian Canal via a mostly traffic-free path to Fort Augustus, then follows the B852 along the quieter eastern side of Loch Ness via Foyers to Inverness. There's a climb out of Fort Augustus up to the Suidhe Viewpoint but the views are worth it.

It's also possible to cycle the Great Glen Way and Loch Ness 360º trails by mountain bike.

You can hire a mountain bike in Fort William (p337) and drop it off in Inverness (p300), and vice versa.

Canoeing

The **Great Glen Canoe Trail** (www.greatglencanoetrail.info), a series of access points, waymarks and informal campsites, allows you to travel the length of the glen by canoe or kayak.

✦ Festivals & Events

Loch Ness
Marathon SPORTS
(www.lochnessmarathon.com; from £54; ☉Oct)
Runners can look out for Nessie as they
take the high road along the eastern shore
of Loch Ness from Fort Augustus to Dores,
finishing in Inverness.

Drumnadrochit

☑ 01456 // POP 1100

Seized by Loch Ness Monster madness, its
gift shops bulging with Nessie cuddly toys,
Drumnadrochit is a hotbed of beastie fever.

◉ Sights & Activities

Urquhart Castle CASTLE
(HES; ☑01456-450551; www.historicenviron-
ment.scot; adult/child £9.60/5.80; ☉9.30am-
6pm Apr-Oct, to 4.30pm Nov-Mar; ℙ)
Commanding a superb location 1.5 miles
east of Drumnadrochit, with outstanding
views (on a clear day), Urquhart Castle is a
popular Nessie-hunting hot spot. The castle was repeatedly sacked and rebuilt (and
sacked and rebuilt) over the centuries; in
1692 it was blown up to prevent the Jacobites from using it. The five-storey tower
house at the northern point is the most
impressive remaining fragment and offers

MONSTERS, MYTHS & LOCH NESS

Highland folklore is filled with tales of strange creatures living in lochs and rivers,
notably the kelpie (water horse) that lures unwary travellers to their doom. The use of
the term 'monster', however, is a relatively recent phenomenon, its origins lying in an
article published in the *Inverness Courier* on 2 May 1933, entitled 'Strange Spectacle
on Loch Ness'.

The article recounted the sighting of a disturbance in the loch by Mrs Aldie Mackay
and her husband: 'There the creature disported itself, rolling and plunging for fully a
minute, its body resembling that of a whale, and the water cascading and churning
like a simmering cauldron.'

The story was taken up by the London press and sparked a flurry of sightings that
year, including a notorious on-land encounter with London tourists Mr and Mrs Spicer
on 22 July 1933, again reported in the *Inverness Courier:* 'It was horrible, an abomina-
tion. About 50 yards ahead, we saw an undulating sort of neck, and quickly followed
by a large, ponderous body. I estimated the length to be 25ft to 30ft, its colour was
dark elephant grey. It crossed the road in a series of jerks, but because of the slope we
could not see its limbs. Although I accelerated quickly towards it, it had disappeared
into the loch by the time I reached the spot. There was no sign of it in the water. I am
a temperate man, but I am willing to take any oath that we saw this Loch Ness beast. I
am certain that this creature was of a prehistoric species.'

The London newspapers couldn't resist. In December 1933 the *Daily Mail* sent
Marmaduke Wetherell, a film director and big-game hunter, to Loch Ness to track
down the beast. Within days he found 'reptilian' footprints in the shoreline mud (soon
revealed to have been made with a stuffed hippopotamus foot). Then in April 1934
came the famous long-necked monster photograph taken by the seemingly reputable
Harley St surgeon Robert Kenneth Wilson. The press went into overdrive and the rest,
as they say, is history.

In 1994, however, Christian Spurling – Wetherell's stepson, by then 90 years old
– revealed that the most famous photo of Nessie ever taken was in fact a hoax, perpe-
trated by his stepfather with Wilson's help. Today, of course, there are those who claim
that Spurling's confession is itself a hoax. And, ironically, the researcher who exposed
the surgeon's photo as a fake still believes wholeheartedly in the monster's existence.

There have been regular sightings of the monster through the years (see www.
lochnesssightings.com), with a peak in 1996–97 (the Hollywood movie *Loch Ness* was
released in 1996). Reports have tailed off in recent years, though 2019 saw an uptick
in sightings, with the highest number reported since 1983.

Hoax or not, the bizarre mini-industry that has grown up around Loch Ness and its
mysterious monster since that eventful summer last century is a spectacle in itself.

wonderful views across the water. Book tickets at least one day in advance.

The visitor centre includes displays of medieval items discovered in the castle and a video theatre: the film, with a dramatic 'reveal' of the castle at the end, can be downloaded onto your phone using a QR code if the visitor centre is closed. The site also includes a gift shop and cafe.

Loch Ness Centre & Exhibition MUSEUM
(📞 01456-450573; www.lochness.com; adult/child £8.45/4.95; ⏰ 9.30am-6pm Jul & Aug, to 5pm Easter-Jun, Sep & Oct, 10am-4pm Nov-Easter; 🅿️�íl) This Nessie-themed attraction adopts a scientific approach that allows you to weigh the evidence for yourself. Exhibits include original equipment – sonar survey vessels, miniature submarines, cameras and sediment coring tools – used in various monster hunts, plus original photographs and film footage of sightings. You'll find out about hoaxes and optical illusions, as well as learning a lot about the ecology of Loch Ness – is there enough food in the loch to support even one 'monster', let alone a breeding population?

Nessie Hunter CRUISE
(📞 01456-450395; www.lochness-cruises.com; adult/child £16/10; ⏰ Apr-Oct) One-hour monster-hunting cruises, complete with sonar and underwater cameras. Cruises depart from Drumnadrochit hourly from 10am to 6pm daily, with additional sailings at 9am and 7pm from June to August.

🛏️ Sleeping

BCC Loch Ness Hostel HOSTEL £
(📞 07780 603045; www.bcclochnesshostel.co.uk; Glen Urquhart; s/d/q £30/46/68, tent sites per person £5, 2-person pods from £40; 🅿️🚀) Clean, modern, high-quality budget accommodation located 6.5 miles west of Drumnadrochit, halfway between Cannich and Loch Ness; booking well in advance is recommended. All rooms have en-suite bathrooms. There's also a good campsite with the option of glamping in wooden Hobbit houses.

Drumbuie Farm B&B ££
(📞 01456-450634; www.loch-ness-farm.co.uk; d from £75; 🅿️🚀) A B&B in a modern house on a working farm surrounded by fields full of sheep and Highland cattle, with views over Urquhart Castle and Loch Ness. Walkers and cyclists are welcome.

★ Loch Ness Inn INN £££
(📞 01456-450991; www.staylochness.co.uk; Lewiston; inn s/d/f £120/140/170, bunkhouse q £135; 🅿️🚀) Loch Ness Inn ticks all the weary traveller's boxes, with comfortable bedrooms (the family suite sleeps two adults and two children), a cosy bar pouring real ales from the local Loch Ness Brewery, and a restaurant (mains £13.50 to £26) serving wholesome fare. It's conveniently located in the quiet hamlet of Lewiston, between Drumnadrochit and Urquhart Castle.

In 2020 a new **bunkhouse** opened with dorm beds and family rooms as well as a kitchen, drying room and bike storage. Only private rooms (no shared dorms) were available in the summer of 2020.

🍴 Eating & Drinking

Fiddler's Restaurant CAFE ££
(www.fiddledrum.co.uk; Village Green; mains £7-17.50; ⏰ noon-11pm; 🚀) The coffee shop here serves cappuccino and croissants, while the restaurant dishes up traditional Highland fare, such as venison and haggis, and a range of bottled Scottish beers. There's also a whisky bar with a huge selection of single malts. In 2020 a beer garden food truck serving fish and chips was operating in place of the cafe and restaurant.

Benleva Hotel MICROBREWERY
(📞 01456-450080; www.benleva.co.uk; Kilmore Rd; ⏰ noon-midnight Mon-Thu, to 1am Fri, to 12.45am Sat, 12.30-11pm Sun) Set in an 18th-century manse a half-mile east of the main road, the Benleva is a rough diamond of a pub. The beer is the main event, with a selection of real ales from around the country, including those from its own Hanging Tree Brewery, located in the garden.

ℹ️ Getting There & Away

Stagecoach (p300) buses run from Inverness to Drumnadrochit (£3.80, 30 minutes, six to eight daily, five on Sunday) and Urquhart Castle car park (£4, 35 minutes).

Fort Augustus

📞 01320 / POP 620

Fort Augustus, at the junction of four old military roads, was originally a government garrison and the headquarters of General George Wade's road-building operations in the early 18th century. Today it's a neat and picturesque little place bisected

Driving Tour
A Loch Ness Circuit

START INVERNESS
END INVERNESS
LENGTH 130 MILES; SIX TO SEVEN HOURS

Head out of Inverness on the A862 to Beauly and breakfast at ❶**Corner on the Square** (p302). Backtrack a mile and turn right on the A831 to Cannich, passing ❷**Kilmorack Gallery**, which exhibits contemporary art in a converted church. The scenery gets wilder as you approach ❸**Cannich**; turn right and follow the single-track road to the ❹**Dog Falls** car park. Stroll along the rushing river, or hike to the viewpoint (about one-hour round trip; 2.5 miles) for a glimpse of remote Glen Affric.

Return to Cannich and turn right on the A831 to Drumnadrochit, then right on the A82 past picturesque ❺**Urquhart Castle** (p306) and along the shores of Loch Ness. At ❻**Invermoriston**, pause to look at the old bridge, built by Thomas Telford in 1813, then head west on the A887 towards Kyle

of Lochalsh; after 16 miles go left on the A87 towards Invergarry. You are now among some of the Highlands' finest mountain scenery; as the road turns east above Loch Garry, stop at the famous ❼**viewpoint** (layby on right, signposted Glengarry Viewpoint). Through a quirk of perspective, the lochs to the west appear to form the map outline of Scotland.

At Invergarry, turn left on the A82 to reach ❽**Fort Augustus** and a late lunch at the Lock Inn. Take the B862, following the line of General Wade's 18th-century military road, to the ❾**Suidhe Viewpoint**. A short (800m) walk up the well-worn path to the summit affords an even better panorama.

Ahead, you can choose the low road via the impressive ❿**Falls of Foyers**, or stay on the high road (B862) for more views; both converge on Loch Ness at ⓫**Dores** and the Dores Inn (p305), where you can sip a pint with a view along Loch Ness, and even stay for dinner before returning to Inverness.

by the Caledonian Canal and often overrun by coach-tour crowds in summer.

◉ Sights & Activities

Caledonian Canal   CANAL
(www.scottishcanals.co.uk) At Fort Augustus, boats using the Caledonian Canal are raised and lowered 13m by a 'ladder' of five consecutive locks. It's fun to watch, and the neatly landscaped canal banks are a great place to soak up the sun or compare accents with fellow tourists. The **Caledonian Canal Centre** (Ardchattan House, Canal Side; ⊘10am-4pm Wed-Sun) FREE, beside the lowest lock, has information on the history of the canal and a cafe.

Cruise Loch Ness   BOATING
(📞01320-366277; www.cruiselochness.com; adult/child £15/9; ⊘10am, noon, 2pm & 4pm daily Apr-Nov, fewer sailings Dec-Mar) One-hour cruises on Loch Ness are accompanied by the latest high-tech sonar equipment so you can keep an underwater eye open for Nessie. There are also one-hour evening cruises departing 8pm daily April to August.

🛏 Sleeping & Eating

★Morag's Lodge   HOSTEL £
(📞01320-366289; www.moragslodge.com; Bunoich Brae; dm/d/f from £25/62/81; P@🛜🐾) This large, well-run hostel is based in a big Victorian house with great views of Fort Augustus' hilly surrounds, and has a convivial bar with an open fire. It's hidden away in the trees up the steep side road just north of the tourist office car park. Breakfast (£5), packed lunches (£5) and dinner (£10) are also available.

Lorien House   B&B ££
(📞01320-366576; www.lorien-house.co.uk; Station Rd; s/d £75/85; P🛜) Lorien is a cut above your usual B&B – the bedrooms are spick and span, the house is set up to accommodate walkers and cyclists, the breakfasts include smoked salmon, and there's a library of walking, cycling and climbing guides in the lounge. No children under 10 years.

★Lovat   HOTEL £££
(📞01456-459250; www.thelovat.com; Main Rd; d from £140; P🛜🐾) 🌿 A boutique-style makeover has transformed this former huntin'-and-shootin' hotel into a luxurious but eco-conscious retreat set apart from the tourist crush around the canal. The bedrooms are spacious and stylishly furnished, while the lounge is equipped with a log fire, comfy armchairs and grand piano: perfect for a rainy evening.

Its highly acclaimed restaurant, **Station Road** (6.30pm to 8.30pm Tuesday to Saturday, one/three courses £27/42), serves an innovative tasting menu (£65) of beautifully presented plates prepared with home-grown, locally foraged and other seasonal produce; book ahead.

Lock Inn   PUB FOOD ££
(📞01320-366302; www.the-lockinn.co.uk; Canal Side; mains £10-16; ⊘kitchen noon-8pm) A superb little pub right on the canal bank, the Lock Inn has a vast range of malt whiskies and a tempting menu of bar meals, which includes Orkney salmon, homemade steak pie and daily seafood specials – the house speciality is beer-battered haddock and chips.

❶ Getting There & Away

Scottish Citylink (p296) and Stagecoach (p300) buses run to Fort Augustus from Fort William (£10.80, one hour, seven daily), continuing on to Inverness (£10.60, one hour).

THE CAIRNGORMS

The **Cairngorms National Park** (www.cairngorms.co.uk) is the largest national park in the UK, more than twice the size of the Lake District. It stretches from Aviemore in the north to the Angus Glens in the south, and from Dalwhinnie in the west to Ballater and Royal Deeside in the east.

The park encompasses the highest landmass in Britain – a broad mountain plateau, riven only by the deep valleys of the Lairig Ghru and Loch Avon, with an average altitude of more than 1000m and including five of the six highest summits in the UK. This wild mountain landscape of granite and heather has a sub-Arctic climate and supports rare alpine tundra vegetation and high-altitude bird species, such as snow bunting, ptarmigan and dotterel.

Aviemore

📞01479 / POP 3616

The gateway to the Cairngorms, Aviemore is the region's main centre for transport, accommodation, restaurants and shops. It's

The Cairngorms

not the prettiest town in Scotland by a long stretch – the main attractions are in the surrounding area – but when bad weather puts the hills off limits, Aviemore fills up with hikers, cyclists and climbers (plus skiers and snowboarders in winter) cruising the outdoor-equipment shops or recounting their latest adventures in the cafes and bars. Add in tourists and locals, and the eclectic mix makes for a lively little town.

Aviemore is on a loop off the A9 Perth–Inverness road. Almost everything of note is to be found along the main drag, Grampian Rd; the train station and bus stop are towards its southern end.

Cairngorm Mountain lies 10 miles southeast of Aviemore along the B970 (Ski Rd) and its continuation, past Rothiemurchus, Coylumbridge and Glenmore.

◎ Sights & Activities

Craigellachie
Nature Reserve　　　NATURE RESERVE
(www.nnr.scot; Grampian Rd) FREE This reserve is a great place for short hikes across steep hillsides covered in natural birch forest where you can spot wildlife such as the peregrine falcons that nest on the crags from April to July. A trail leads west from Aviemore Youth Hostel and passes under the A9 into the reserve.

Strathspey Steam Railway　HERITAGE RAILWAY
(☏01479-810725; www.strathspeyrailway.co.uk; Station Sq; adult/child return £16.25/8.10) The Strathspey railway runs steam trains on a section of restored line between Aviemore and Broomhill, 10 miles to the northeast, via Boat of Garten. There are four or five trains daily from June to August, and a more limited service in April, May, September, October and December, with the option of afternoon tea, Sunday lunch or a three-course dinner on board.

Cairngorm Brewery　　　　BREWERY
(☏01479-813303; www.cairngormbrewery.com; Dalfaber Industrial Estate; tastings per person £7; ⊙10am-5.30pm Tue-Sat, to 4.30pm Nov & Jan) Creator of multi-award-winning Trade Winds and Black Gold ales. In 2020 brewery tours were replaced with tasting sessions, including an explanation of the brewing process and the history of the brewery, to be booked in advance.

🛏 Sleeping

Aviemore Youth Hostel　　HOSTEL £
(HS; ☏01479-810345; www.hostellingscotland.org.uk; 25 Grampian Rd; s/d/tr £40/52/77; P@🛜) Upmarket hostelling in a spacious, well-equipped modern building, five minutes' walk south of the village centre. There are

four- and six-bed rooms, and a comfortable lounge with views of the mountains. Bookings for 2021 were for private rooms only (no shared dorms).

Aviemore Bunkhouse HOSTEL **£**
(📞 01479-811181; www.aviemore-bunkhouse.com; Dalfaber Rd; s/d/f £45/55/75; 🅿 @ 🛜) This independent hostel provides accommodation in modern six- or eight-bed dorms (available as private rooms only in 2020), each with private bathroom, and one family room. It has a drying room, secure bike storage and wheelchair-accessible dorms. From the train station, cross the pedestrian bridge over the tracks, turn right and walk south on Dalfaber Rd.

Cairngorm Hotel HOTEL **££**
(📞 01479-810233; www.cairngorm.com; Grampian Rd; s/d £75/110; 🅿 🛜) Better known as 'the Cairn', this long-established hotel is set in the fine old granite building with the pointy turret opposite the train station. It's a welcoming place with comfortable rooms and a determinedly Scottish atmosphere, with tartan carpets and stags' antlers. There's live music on weekends, so it can get a bit noisy – not for early-to-bedders.

The restaurant serves traditional Highland comfort food such as fish pie, fillet of venison and haggis, neeps and tatties (£10 to £23).

Ardlogie Guest House B&B **££**
(📞 01479-810747; www.ardlogie.co.uk; Dalfaber Rd; s/d/tr £90/110/150; 🅿 🛜) Handy to the train station, the welcoming five-room Ardlogie has great views over the River Spey towards the Cairngorms, and the chance of spotting red squirrels from your bedroom window. Two-night minimum stay.

Ravenscraig Guest House B&B **££**
(📞 01479-810278; www.ravenscraighouse.co.uk; Grampian Rd; s/d from £65/90; 🅿 🛜) Ravenscraig is a large, flower-bedecked Victorian villa with seven spacious and elegantly decorated en-suite rooms, plus another six in a modern chalet at the back (one is wheelchair accessible). It serves traditional and veggie breakfasts in an attractive conservatory dining room.

✖ Eating & Drinking

⭐ **Route 7 Cafe** CAFE **£**
(📞 01479-812433; http://highlandhomecentre.com/route-7-cafe.html; 18 Dalfaber Industrial Estate; mains £6-13; ⊙ 9am-4.30pm; 🅿 🛜 ♿) This

place, named for the cycle route that passes the door, takes a bit of finding (at the end of the side road that passes Cairngorm Brewery), but is well worth seeking out for its hearty menu of burgers, sandwiches, salads and soups. Cyclists can use the power washer and tools outside.

Rowan Tree SCOTTISH **££**
(📞 01479-810207; www.rowantreehotel.com; B9152, Loch Alvie; mains £15-28; ⊙ 6-8.30pm; 🅿 🛜 ✖) The menu at this relaxed country hotel ranges from traditional Highland cooking (fillet of beef with homemade haggis; beer-battered haddock and chips) to more innovative dishes (duck dumplings with a cornflake crumb; button mushroom and blue-cheese fricassee), with an emphasis on local seasonal ingredients. It's located in a pretty spot 2 miles south of Aviemore next to Loch Alvie.

Winking Owl PUB
(www.thewinkingowl.co; Grampian Rd; ⊙ noon-10pm Wed & Thu, to 11pm Fri & Sat, 12.30-10pm Sun; 🛜) Lively local pub that operates under the wing of the Cairngorm Brewery. It's popular with hikers and climbers, and serves a good range of real ales and malt whiskies. The menu (mains £10 to £14) features burgers, nachos and pizzas.

ℹ Information

There are ATMs outside the Tesco supermarket on Grampian Rd.

Tourist office (📞 01479-810930; www.visitaviemore.com; The Mall, Grampian Rd; ⊙ 10am-4pm Sep-Jun, longer hours Jul & Aug)

ℹ Getting There & Away

BUS
Buses stop on Grampian Rd opposite the train station; buy tickets at the tourist office. Services include the following:

Edinburgh £30.40, three to 3½ hours, six daily
Glasgow £30.40, 2¾ hours, six daily
Grantown-on-Spey £4.15, 35 minutes, 10 daily weekdays, two daily weekends
Inverness £11.50, 45 minutes, eight daily
Perth £22.20, 2¼ hours, eight daily

Bus 31 links Aviemore to Cairngorm Mountain car park (£3, 20 minutes, hourly) via Coylumbridge and Glenmore. A Strathspey Dayrider/Megarider ticket (£7.50/18.90) gives one/seven days unlimited bus travel from Aviemore as far as Cairngorm, Carrbridge and Kingussie; buy it from the bus driver.

TRAIN

The train station is on Grampian Rd. Services include the following:

Edinburgh £45, three hours, six daily
Glasgow £45, three hours, six daily
Inverness £3.60, 40 minutes, 12 daily

ⓘ Getting Around

Several places in Aviemore, Rothiemurchus Estate and Glenmore have mountain bikes for hire. Easy off-road cycle tracks link Aviemore with Glenmore and Loch Morlich to the east, and Boat of Garten to the north

Bothy Bikes (☑ 01479-810111; www.bothybikes.co.uk; 5 Granish Way, Dalfaber; per half-/full day £20/25; ⊙ 9am-5pm) Located in northern Aviemore, this place rents out mountain bikes and can also advise on routes and trails. Children's bikes (per day £12), child seats (per day £5) and trailers (per day £10) also available. Booking recommended.

Around Aviemore

Rothiemurchus Estate

The **Rothiemurchus Estate** (www.rothiemurchus.net), which extends from the River Spey at Aviemore to the Cairngorm summit plateau, is famous for having one of Scotland's largest remnants of Caledonian forest, the ancient forest of Scots pine that once covered most of the country. The forest is home to a large population of red squirrels, and is one of the last bastions of the capercaillie and the Scottish wildcat.

Activities, including quad and Segway tours, gorge swimming, paddleboarding and clay pigeon shooting, can be booked online or at the **Rothiemurchus Centre** (☑ 01479-812345; www.rothiemurchus.net; Ski Rd, Inverdruie; ⊙ 9.30am-5.30pm; ℙ) FREE, a mile southeast of Aviemore along the B970. The centre sells a map detailing more than 50 miles of footpaths and cycling trails.

Loch an Eilein   LAKE
(www.rothiemurchus.net; adult/child £1.50/50p parking £4.50; ♿) An even, 3-mile trail follows the shoreline of Loch an Eilein, with its ruined castle and ancient pine woods. Admission includes a map.

In Your Element   MOUNTAIN BIKING
(☑ 01479-810284; www.rothiemurchus.net; Rothiemurchus Estate; per day adult/child £23/15) Mountain-biking trails include the beautiful Old Logging Way to Glenmore, from where you can continue to the other-worldly Green Lochan and make a circuit of Loch Morlich before returning along the peaceful Ancient Forest Track.

Strathspey Highland Ponies   HORSE RIDING
(☑ 01479-812345; www.rothiemurchus.net; Rothiemurchus Estate) Hacks through the spectacular Rothiemurchus forests on Highland ponies range from 45-minute beginner rides (£29) to 90-minute rides for experienced riders (£45).

Rothiemurchus Fishery   FISHING
(☑ 01479-812915; www.rothiemurchus.net; Rothiemurchus Estate; ⊙ 9.30am-5pm Thu-Mon; ♿) Cast for rainbow trout at this loch at the southern end of the village; buy permits (from £10 for one hour, plus £7 for tackle hire) at the Fish Farm Shop. For experienced anglers, permits are available for the River Spey.

**Rothiemurchus Camp
& Caravan Park**   CAMPSITE £
(☑ 01479-812800; www.rothiemurchus.net; Coylumbridge; tent sites per adult/child £14/3) The nearest campsite to Aviemore is this year-round park, beautifully sited among Scots pines at Coylumbridge, 1.5 miles along the B970.

Loch Morlich

Six miles east of Aviemore, Loch Morlich is surrounded by some 8 sq miles of pine and spruce forest that make up the **Glenmore Forest Park**. Its attractions include a sandy beach (at the east end) and a water-sports centre.

The visitor centre at Glenmore has a small exhibition on the Caledonian forest and copies of Glenmore Forest Park maps, detailing local walks. The **circuit of Loch Morlich** (3.5 miles) makes a pleasant outing; the trail is along a mostly flat, wide gravel path.

🏃 Activities

★**Glenmore Lodge**   ADVENTURE SPORTS
(☑ 01479-861256; www.glenmorelodge.org.uk; Glenmore; 1-day courses from £90) One of Britain's leading adventure-sports training centres, offering courses in hill walking, rock climbing, ice climbing, canoeing, mountain biking and mountaineering. The centre's comfortable **B&B accommodation** (☑ 01479-861256; www.glenmorelodge.org.uk;

CYCLING IN THE CAIRNGORMS

Rothiemurchus Old Logging Way Off-road route through ancient Caledonian pine forest (6.5 miles each way). The route connects with further trails around Lochs Morlich and an Eilein.

Speyside Way The easy Route 7 off-road path connects Boat of Garten and Aviemore (6 miles each way).

Abernethy Forest Excellent cycling options along forest trails and quiet roads from Boat of Garten to Nethy Bridge via Loch Garten (6 miles each way).

Cairngorm Hill Climb The tough, 10-mile ride from Aviemore to Cairngorm Mountain upper car park is considered a classic by serious cyclists.

Kincraig Loop Starting at the Rothiemurchus Centre, this route follows the minor B970 road via Feshiebridge and Loch Insh to Kincraig village, returning along the B1952 (14 miles).

Bikes can be hired from In Your Element (p312), Bothy Bikes (p312) and Ride Cairngorm (p315).

Glenmore; s/tw £67/88; P 🐾 🛜 🐕) is available to all, even if you're not taking a course, as are the indoor climbing wall and gym.

Loch Morlich
Watersports Centre WATER SPORTS
(☑ 01479-861221; www.lochmorlich.com; ⊙ 9am-5pm Easter-Oct) This popular outfit rents out canoes (£20 an hour), kayaks (£10), rowing boats (£35), sailing dinghies (£35) and stand-up paddleboards (£15), and also offers instruction. Book in advance.

Cairngorm Reindeer Centre TOUR
(☑ 01479-861228; www.cairngormreindeer.co.uk; Glenmore; adult/child £17.50/12.50; 🐕) The warden here leads guided walks to see and feed Britain's only herd of reindeer, which are free-ranging but very tame. Walks take place at 11am daily (weather dependent), plus another at 2.30pm from May to September. Book tickets in advance by phone.

🛏 Sleeping

Glenmore Campsite CAMPSITE £
(☑ 01479-861271; www.campingintheforest.co.uk; Cairngorm Rd; tent & campervan sites for 2 people £17.50-30.30; ⊙ year-round; 🐕) Campers can set up base at this attractive lochside site with pitches amid the Scots pines. Family sites cost £21 to £37 for two adults and two children.

Cairngorm Lodge Hostel HOSTEL £
(HS; ☑ 01479-861238; www.hostellingscotland.org.uk; Glenmore; tw/tr/q £44/54/64; ⊙ closed Nov & Dec; P @ 🛜 🐕) Set in a former shooting lodge that enjoys a great location at the east end of Loch Morlich; prebooking is essential. In 2020 only private rooms were available (no dorm beds).

❶ Getting There & Away

Bus 31 links Aviemore with Loch Morlich and Glenmore (£3, 20 minutes, hourly).

Cairngorm Mountain

Cairn Gorm, 10 miles southeast of Aviemore, is the sixth-highest summit in the UK and home to the Cairngorm Mountain ski area. In 2018 the Cairngorm Mountain Funicular Railway was closed indefinitely due to structural problems, but the cafe, shop and ranger's station remain open. A number of short, waymarked trails start at the Coire Cas car park, including a mile-long family trail.

The climb from the car park at the Coire Cas ski area to the summit of **Cairn Gorm** (1245m) is 2 miles and takes about two hours (one way). To the south, across the high-level plateau, lies **Ben Macdui** (1309m), Britain's second-highest peak. If climbing Ben Macdui, it's best to ascend via the path to the west of the ski centre (across a footbridge) and descend Cairn Gorm mountain via the windy ridge path. From the car park to the peak and back is 11 miles and takes six to eight hours. It's a serious undertaking and is for experienced and well-equipped mountain walkers only.

The **Lairig Ghru trail**, which can take eight to 10 hours, is a demanding 19-mile walk from Aviemore through the Lairig Ghru pass (840m) to Braemar. The path starts from Ski Rd, a mile east of Coylumbridge, and involves some very rough going.

Warning: the Cairngorm plateau is a sub-Arctic environment where navigation is difficult and weather conditions can be severe, even in midsummer. Hikers must have proper hill-walking equipment, and know how to use a map and compass. In winter it is a place for experienced mountaineers only.

Cairngorm Mountain Ski Area
SNOW SPORTS

(www.cairngormmountain.org; 1-day ski pass per adult/child £28/17) Aspen or Val d'Isère it ain't, but with 19 runs, 23 miles of piste and 11 lifts, Cairngorm is Scotland's most popular ski area. When the snow is at its best and the sun is shining, you can close your eyes and imagine you're in the Alps; sadly, low cloud, high winds and horizontal sleet are more likely.

Ski or snowboard hire is around £26/19 per adult/child per day; there are lots of hire outlets at Coire Cas, Glenmore and Aviemore.

The season usually runs from December until the snow melts, which may be as late as the end of April, though snowfall here is unpredictable. You can check the latest snow conditions at www.winterhighland.info.

Kincraig & Glen Feshie

At Kincraig, 6 miles southwest of Aviemore, the Spey widens into Loch Insh, home of the **Loch Insh Outdoor Centre** (☑01540-651272; www.lochinsh.com; Kincraig; day ticket incl all activities adult/child £40/30; ☺8.30am-5.30pm; ⛨), which offers canoeing, windsurfing, sailing, mountain biking and fishing, as well as B&B accommodation.

Beautiful, tranquil Glen Feshie extends south from Kincraig, deep into the Cairngorms, with Scots pine woods in its upper reaches surrounded by big, heathery hills. The 4WD track to the head of the glen makes a great mountain-bike excursion (25-mile round trip).

★Highland Wildlife Park
ZOO

(☑01540-651270; www.highlandwildlifepark.org; Kincraig; adult/child £18.50/12.50; ☺10am-6pm Jul & Aug, to 5pm Apr-Jun, Sep & Oct, to 4pm Nov-Mar; ⓟ) This place features a drive-through safari park as well as animal enclosures, offering the chance to view rarely seen native wildlife, such as wildcats, capercaillies, pine martens, white-tailed sea eagles and red squirrels. It's also home to species that once roamed the Scottish hills but have long since disappeared, including wolf, lynx, wild boar, beaver and European bison.

There are also iconic species from around the world – snow leopard, red panda, Amur tiger and polar bear. Last entry is two hours before closing.

★Old Post Office Cafe
CAFE £

(☑01540-651779; www.kincraigartcafe.com; The Brae, Kincraig; mains £6-10, pizzas £12-13; ☺10am-5pm Thu, to 8pm Fri & Sat, 10.30am-5pm Sun; ⓟ⛨⛨) This cute little cafe-cum-artgallery serves top-notch coffee and cake plus comfort food with an Italian touch – focaccia filled with aubergine and hummus or Parma ham and pecorino, for example. Pizzas are available on Friday and Saturday evenings. Tables spill outdoors in summer.

Carrbridge

☑01479 / POP 700

Carrbridge, 7 miles north of Aviemore, is a good alternative base for exploring the region. It takes its name from the graceful **old bridge** (spotlit at night), built in 1717, over the thundering rapids of the River Dulnain.

Landmark Forest Adventure Park
AMUSEMENT PARK

(☑0800 731 3446; www.landmarkpark.co.uk; adult/child £23/21; ☺10am-6pm; ⛨) Set in a forest of Scots pines, this is a theme park with a difference: the theme is timber. The main attractions are the Ropeworx highwire adventure course, the Red Squirrel Nature Trail (a raised walkway through the forest canopy that allows you to view red squirrels, crossbills and crested tits), and the view from the Fire Lookout Tower. Rides include a small roller coaster and water slides.

❶ Getting There & Away

Bus 34 runs from Inverness to Carrbridge (£5.50, 45 minutes, six daily Monday to Friday, four on Saturday, one Sunday) and onwards to Grantown-on-Spey (£3, 20 minutes). Bus 32 links with Aviemore (£2.75, 15 minutes, five daily except Sunday).

Boat of Garten

Boat of Garten is known as the Osprey Village because these rare and beautiful birds of prey nest nearby at the **RSPB Loch Garten Osprey Centre** (☑01479-831694; www.rspb. org.uk/lochgarten; Tulloch; osprey hide adult/child £5/2.50; ☺osprey hide 10am-6pm Apr-Aug). The ospreys migrate here each spring from Africa and nest in a tall pine tree.

Loch Garten lies within the **Abernethy National Nature Reserve** (www.nature.scot), a spectacular tract of ancient Caledonian pine forest, sweeping moorland, wetlands and mountains that extends from the slopes of Ben Macdui to the village of Nethy Bridge.

There is flexible, good-quality homestay accommodation at **Fraoch Lodge** (☑01479-831331; www.scotmountainholidays.com; Deshar Rd; per person £50; ☑P☜), which can help arrange and guide a wide range of outdoor activities, while the **Boat Hotel** (☑01479-831258; www.boathotel.co.uk; Spey Ave; s/d from £140/150, mains £13-25; ☑P☜☖) offers country-style accommodation and serves decent pub grub.

❶ Getting There & Away

Boat of Garten is 5 miles northeast of Aviemore. The most interesting way to get here is on the Strathspey Steam Railway (p310) from Aviemore, or you can ride or walk along National Cycle Network Route 7 (allow 30 to 40 minutes by bike, two hours on foot). At Boat of Garten station, **Ride Cairngorm** (☑01479-831729; www.ridecairngorm.com; adult/child per day £20/12; ☺9am-5pm Tue-Sat) rents mountain bikes and gives advice on local trails.

Grantown-on-Spey

☑01479 / POP 2470

Grantown (*gran*-ton) is an elegant Georgian town with a grid of streets and a broad, tree-lined main square. It is a fine example of a planned settlement, founded by Sir Ludovic Grant in 1766 as a centre for the linen industry, and later becoming a tourist town after Queen Victoria's visit in 1860.

A favoured haunt of anglers and the tweed-cap-and-green-wellies brigade, Grantown is thronged with visitors in summer, but it reverts to a quiet backwater in winter. Most hotels can kit you out for a day of fly-fishing on the Spey, or put you in touch with someone who can.

Grantown Museum MUSEUM
(☑01479-872478; www.grantownmuseum.co.uk; Burnfield Ave; adult/child £4/free; ☺10am-5pm

Mon-Sat Apr-Oct; ☑P☖) A small museum that chronicles the history of the town and its relationship to Clan Grant; also houses a **tourist office** (☑01479-870477; Burnfield Ave; ☺10am-5pm Mon-Sat Apr-Oct).

Brooklynn B&B ££
(☑01479-873113; www.brooklynn.co.uk; Grant Rd; d/tr £100/140; ☑P☜) 🌿 This beautiful Victorian villa features original stained glass and wood panelling, and four spacious, luxurious rooms, all named after local whiskies. There's a guest sitting room with a wood-burning stove and the breakfast is superb.

Muckrach Country House Hotel HOTEL £££
(☑01479-851227; www.muckrach.com; Dulnain Bridge; d £100-270; ☑P☜☖) Built as a Victorian shooting lodge in 1860, Muckrach has been tastefully converted into a luxurious country house hotel with a relaxed and informal atmosphere. The lounge, complete with grand piano, serves coffee, cake and snacks through the day, and the restaurant serves a brasserie-style menu. Two-night minimum stay.

High Street Merchants CAFE £
(www.thehighstmerchants.com; 74 High St; mains £7-12.50; ☺10am-5pm Wed-Thu, 10am-5pm & 5.30-10pm Fri & Sat, 10am-4pm Sun; ☜☑) This artsy cafe serves breakfast (sourdough toast, granola, Earl Grey–soaked chia seeds with roasted nuts and yoghurt) until noon, lunch (bagels, hot sandwiches and salad bowls) until 3pm, and excellent coffee and cakes all day. On Friday and Saturday evenings it transforms into a cosy bistro serving pizzas and salads.

❶ Getting There & Away

Bus 34X runs from Inverness to Grantown-on-Spey (£6.90, 1¼ hours, six daily Monday to Friday, three Saturday) and on to Aviemore (£4.15, 35 minutes).

Kingussie & Newtonmore

The old Speyside towns of Kingussie (kin-*yew*-see) and Newtonmore sit at the foot of the great heather-clad humps known as the Monadhliath Mountains. Newtonmore is best known as the home of the excellent Highland Folk Museum; Kingussie for one of the Highlands' best restaurants.

The road west from Newtonmore to Spean Bridge passes Ardverikie Estate and Loch Laggan.

Sights & Activities

Ruthven Barracks RUIN
(HES; ⊙24hr; P) FREE Ruthven Barracks was one of four garrisons built by the British government after the first Jacobite rebellion of 1715, as part of a Hanoverian scheme to take control of the Highlands. Ironically the barracks were last occupied by Jacobite troops awaiting the return of Bonnie Prince Charlie after the Battle of Culloden. Perched dramatically on a river terrace and clearly visible from the main A9 road near Kingussie, the ruins are spectacularly floodlit at night.

Highland Folk Museum MUSEUM
(☑01540-673551; www.highlandfolk.com; Kingussie Rd, Newtonmore; ⊙10.30am-4pm Wed-Sun; P) FREE This open-air museum comprises a collection of historical buildings and artefacts revealing many aspects of Highland culture and lifestyle. Laid out like a farming township, it has a community of traditional thatch-roofed cottages, a sawmill, a schoolhouse, a shepherd's bothy (hut) and a rural post office. Actors in period costume give demonstrations of woodcarving, wool-spinning and peat-fire baking. You'll need two to three hours to make the most of a visit. In 2020 advance booking was required.

The thatch-roofed structures of the museum's Baile Gean township were used as a filming location for the TV series *Outlander*.

Laggan Wolftrax MOUNTAIN BIKING
(http://scotland.forestry.gov.uk/visit/laggan-wolftrax; Strathmashie Forest; trails free, parking per day £3; ⊙office 10am-5pm; 🛈) Ten miles southwest of Newtonmore, on the A86 road towards Spean Bridge, this is one of Scotland's top mountain-biking centres, with five purpose-built, graded trails ranging from family-friendly routes to black-diamond downhills with rock slabs and drop-offs. Has a **bike hire outlet and repairs shop** (☑01528-544751; www.facebook.com/weebikehub; Laggan Wolftrax; adult/child per day £25/18; ⊙10am-5pm Wed-Sun) – advance booking recommended – and a good cafe (open 10am to 5pm April to October).

Sleeping & Eating

Eagleview Guest House B&B ££
(☑01540-673675; www.eagleview-guesthouse.co.uk; Perth Rd, Newtonmore; r £90-105; P🐾) Welcoming Eagleview is one of the most pleasant places to stay in the area, with beautifully decorated bedrooms and nice little touches such as cafetières (coffee plungers) with real coffee – and fresh milk – on your hospitality tray. Breakfast is bountiful and delicious.

★ Restaurant at the Cross SCOTTISH £££
(☑01540-661166; www.thecross.co.uk; Tweed Mill Brae, off Ardbroilach Rd, Kingussie; 3-course lunch/dinner £26.50/48.50, tasting menu £57; ⊙noon-2pm & 7-8.30pm; P🐾) 🍴 Housed in a converted watermill, the Cross is one of the finest restaurants in the Highlands. The intimate, low-raftered dining room has an open fire and a patio overlooking the stream, and serves a daily-changing menu of fresh Scottish produce accompanied by a superb wine list (booking essential).

If you want to stay the night, there are eight stylish rooms (double or twin £130 to £200) to choose from.

THE SNOW ROADS

The Snow Roads (www.snowroads.com) is a 90-mile scenic driving route between Blairgowrie in Perthshire and Grantown-on-Spey, by way of Braemar and Ballater. It takes in two high mountain passes that are often snow-covered in winter – Glenshee (p321) and the Lecht. The route is marked by a series of landscape artworks at particularly picturesque viewpoints.

The stretch from Cockbridge to Tomintoul – a magnificent roller coaster of a route much loved by motorcyclists – passes **Corgarff Castle** (HES; ☑01975-651460; www.historicenvironment.scot; adult/child £6/3.60; ⊙9.30am-5.30pm Apr-Sep; P), an impressive fortress with a tower house that dates from the 16th century, before crossing the Lecht pass (637m), where there's a small **skiing area** (www.lecht.co.uk; Strathdon; 1-day lift pass adult/child £32/16; ⊙8.30am-4pm) with lots of short easy and intermediate runs.

ℹ Getting There & Away

BUS
Kingussie and Newtonmore are served by Scottish Citylink (p296) and Stagecoach buses. Services include the following:

Aviemore £3.70, 25 minutes, hourly
Inverness £10.70, 1½ hours, three daily, change at Carrbridge
Perth £17.10, 1¾ hours, one daily

TRAIN
Kingussie and Newtonmore are on the Edinburgh/Glasgow–Inverness railway line. Services include the following:

Edinburgh £39.80, 2¾ hours, seven daily Monday to Saturday, five Sunday
Inverness £13.60, one hour, 12 daily Monday to Saturday, seven Sunday

Tomintoul & Around

☎ 01807 / POP 320

Tomintoul (tom-in-towel) is a pretty, stone-built village with a grassy, tree-lined main square. It was built by the Duke of Gordon in 1775 on the old military road that leads over the Lecht pass from Corgarff, a route now followed by the A939. The duke hoped that settling the dispersed population of his estates in a proper village would help to stamp out cattle stealing and illegal distilling.

The village is part of the **Tomintoul and Glenlivet Cairngorms Dark Sky Park** (www.cairngormsdarkskypark.org), a designated dark sky reserve. Stargazing and astronomy events are held at least monthly from August to April.

◉ Sights & Activities

The **Glenlivet Estate** (now the property of the Crown) has lots of walking and cycling trails – the estate's **information centre** (☎ 01479-870070; www.glenlivetestate. co.uk; Main St; ⊙ 9am-5pm Mon-Fri) distributes free maps of the area – and a spur of the Speyside Way long-distance footpath runs between Tomintoul and Ballindalloch, 15 miles to the north.

Tomintoul & Glenlivet
Discovery Centre   MUSEUM
(☎ 01807-580760; discovery@tgdt.org.uk; The Square, Tomintoul; ⊙ 10am-5pm Apr-Oct) **FREE** This visitor centre and rural museum celebrates local history, with reconstructions of a crofter's kitchen and a blacksmith's forge.

BikeGlenlivet   MOUNTAIN BIKING
(www.glenlivetestate.co.uk; trails free, parking £3) There's excellent mountain biking at this trail centre, 4.5 miles north of Tomintoul, off the B9136 road. Custom-built trails include a 5.5-mile blue run for beginners, a 13.5-mile red route for more experienced riders, and an orange free-ride trail with 0.6 mile of jumps. There's a wonderful **cafe** (mains £6-9; ⊙ 10am-4pm Thu-Mon; P ✷) and bike hire on-site.

Whisky Castle   WHISKY
(☎ 01807-580213; www.whiskycastle.com; 6 Main St, Tomintoul; ⊙ 9.30am-5pm Mon-Sat, noon-5pm Sun) As well as stocking over 600 malts, this shop offers free guided whisky tastings, including from their own range of single cask whiskies.

🍴 Sleeping & Eating

For something to eat in town, try **Clockhouse Restaurant** (☎ 01807-580378; www. clockhouserestaurant.com; The Square, Tomintoul; mains £13-24; ⊙ 11am-9pm Apr-Oct).

Argyle Guest House   B&B ££
(☎ 01807-580766; www.argyletomintoul.co.uk; 7 Main St, Tomintoul; s/d/f £45/72/99; 🛜 ✷) Well-run B&B offers six comfortable rooms of varying sizes (two rooms share a bathroom) and the best porridge in the Cairngorms.

Royal Deeside

The upper valley of the River Dee stretches west from Aboyne and Ballater to Braemar, closely paralleled by the A93 road. Made famous by its long association with the monarchy – today's royal family still holidays at Balmoral Castle (p318), built for Queen Victoria in 1855 – the region is often called Royal Deeside.

The River Dee, renowned the world over for its salmon fishing, has its source in the Cairngorm Mountains west of Braemar, the starting point for long walks into the hills. The FishDee website (www.fishdee.co.uk) has all you need to know about fishing on the river.

Ballater

☎ 01339 / POP 1530

The attractive little village of Ballater owes its 18th-century origins to the curative waters of nearby Pannanich Springs (now bottled commercially as Deeside Natural

Mineral Water), and its prosperity to near-by Balmoral Castle – note the crests on the shopfronts along the main street proclaiming 'By Royal Appointment'.

Old Royal Station   HISTORIC BUILDING

(☑01339-755306; Station Sq; ☺tourist office 10am-3pm) After the original station was destroyed by fire in 2015, the Old Royal Station building – newly restored to exactly replicate the one built in 1866 to receive Queen Victoria when she visited Balmoral by train – reopened in 2018. It houses a tourist office, a tearoom and a cafe-bistro (www.thecarriageballater.co.uk).

Behind the tourist office is a replica of Queen Victoria's carriage, which survived the fire (the original is at the National Railway Museum in York).

🏃 Activities

As you approach Ballater from the east, the hills start to close in, and there are many pleasant walks in the surrounding area. The steep woodland walk up **Craigendarroch** (400m) takes just over one hour. **Morven** (871m) is a more serious prospect, taking about six hours return, but offers good views from the top.

You can hire bikes from **CycleHighlands** (☑01339-755864; www.cyclehighlands. com; The Pavilion, Victoria Rd; Santa Cruz mountain bike hire per day £80; ☺9am-5pm Mon-Thu & Sat, to 4pm Fri & Sun) and **Bike Station** (☑01339-754004; www.bikestationballater. co.uk; Station Sq; bicycle hire per day adult/child £20/10; ☺9am-6pm), which also offer guided bike rides and advice on local trails.

🛏 Sleeping & Eating

Ballater Hostel   HOSTEL £

(☑01339-753752; www.ballater-hostel.com; Bridge Sq; r £30-64; 🛜) 🍴 Tucked up a lane near the bridge over the River Dee, this is an attractive hostel with seven en-suite rooms, sleeping two to eight. Dorm beds (usually £18.70) were not available in 2020. Rooms have personal lockers and reading lamps, and there's a comfortable lounge with big, soft sofas and a wood-burning stove.

Auld Kirk   B&B £££

(☑01339-755762; www.theauldkirk.com; Braemar Rd; s/d from £130/140; 🅿🛜🐾) Here's something a little out of the ordinary – a seven-bedroom B&B and coffee lounge housed in a converted 19th-century church. The interior blends original features with sleek modern decor – the pulpit now serves as the reception desk, while the lounge is bathed in light from leaded Gothic windows.

Rock Salt & Snails   CAFE £

(☑07834 452583; www.facebook.com/rock-saltandsnailsballater; 2 Bridge St; mains £4-9; ☺10am-5pm Thu-Tue; 🛜♿🐾) A great little cafe serving excellent coffee and tempting lunch platters featuring locally sourced deli products (cheese, ham, salads etc), including a kids' platter.

❶ Getting There & Away

Bus 201 runs from Aberdeen to Ballater (£12.45, 1¾ hours, hourly Monday to Saturday, six on Sunday) via Crathes Castle, and continues to Braemar (£6.45, 30 minutes) every two hours.

Balmoral Castle

Built for Queen Victoria in 1855 as a private residence for the Royal Family, **Balmoral Castle** (☑01339-742534; www.balmoralcastle.com; Crathie; guided tour adult/child £15/6; ☺10am-5pm Apr-Jul, limited dates Oct-Dec; 🅿) kicked off the revival of the Scottish Baronial style of architecture that characterises so many of Scotland's 19th-century country houses. In 2020 admission was by advance booking only for an hour-long guided tour of the grounds and the castle ballroom. After the tour there is time to further explore the grounds and gardens without a guide.

Inside the castle only the ballroom, which displays a collection of Landseer paintings and royal silver, is open to the public. Don't expect to see the Queen's private quarters! The main attraction is learning about Highland estate management, rather than royal revelations.

You can buy a booklet that details several waymarked walks within Balmoral Estate; the best is the climb to **Prince Albert's Cairn**, a huge granite pyramid that bears the inscription 'To the beloved memory of Albert the great and good, Prince Consort. Erected by his broken hearted widow Victoria R. 21st August 1862'. The walk to Albert's pyramid is open to the public even when the castle is not, starting from the car park by the A93 at Crathie; directions are available on the castle website.

The massive pointy-topped mountain that looms to the south of Balmoral is **Lochnagar** (1155m), immortalised in verse by Lord Byron, who spent his childhood years in Aberdeenshire.

Balmoral is eight miles west of Ballater, and can be reached on the Aberdeen–Braemar bus.

Braemar

📞 01339 / POP 450

Braemar is a pretty little village with a grand location on a broad plain ringed by mountains where the Dee valley and Glen Clunie meet. In winter this is one of the coldest places in the country – temperatures as low as -27°C have been recorded – and during spells of severe cold, hungry deer wander the streets looking for a bite to eat. Braemar is an excellent base for hill walking, and there's also skiing at nearby Glenshee.

Sights & Activities

Braemar's new **Highland Games Centre** (www.highlandgamescentre.org) is open daily March to December (it was closed in 2020) and contains an exhibition on the Highland Games and a cafe. It's housed in a smart green pavilion at the Princess Royal and Duke of Fife Memorial Park, where the Braemar Gathering is held.

Signs in the village centre give details of a number of waymarked walks along the river and up nearby hills. An easy walk from Braemar is up **Creag Choinnich** (538m; 2-mile round trip), a hill to the east of the village above the A93. For a longer walk (6 miles, about three hours return) and superb views of the Cairngorms, head for the summit of **Morrone** (859m), southwest of Braemar.

Braemar Castle CASTLE
(www.braemarcastle.co.uk; adult/child £10/4; ⊙10am-5pm daily Jul & Aug, Wed-Sun Apr-Jun, Sep & Oct; 🅿) Just north of Braemar village, turreted Braemar Castle dates from 1628 and served as a government garrison after the 1745 Jacobite rebellion. In 2007 it was taken over by the local community, which now offers guided tours of the historic castle apartments. The castle interior was closed in 2020, but the grounds were open for walks and picnics.

Braemar Mountain Sports CYCLING
(📞01339-741242; www.braemarmountainsports. com; 5 Invercauld Rd; bike hire per 4hr/day £15/20; ⊙9am-6pm) You can hire bikes from Braemar Mountain Sports. It also rents skiing and mountaineering equipment.

🎉 Festivals & Events

Braemar Gathering SPORTS
(📞01339-755377; www.braemargathering.org; Princess Royal & Duke of Fife Memorial Pk; adult/child from £12/2; ⊙Sep) There are Highland Games in many towns and villages throughout the summer, but the best known is the Braemar Gathering, which takes place on the first Saturday in September. It's a major occasion, organised every year since 1817 by the Braemar Royal Highland Society. In 2020 a Virtual Highland Games was held without spectators and broadcast online.

Events include Highland dancing, pipers, tug of war, a hill race up Morrone, tossing the caber, hammer- and stone-throwing and the long jump. International athletes are among those who take part.

These kinds of events took place informally in the Highlands for many centuries as tests of skill and strength, but they were formalised around 1820 as part of the rise of Highland romanticism initiated by Sir Walter Scott and King George IV. Queen Victoria attended the Braemar Gathering in 1848, starting a tradition of royal patronage that continues to this day.

🛏 Sleeping

Rucksacks Bunkhouse HOSTEL £
(📞01339-741517; 15 Mar Rd; per person £20; 🅿) This appealing cottage has a comfy dorm and cheaper beds in an alpine-style bothy (shared sleeping platform for 10 people; bring your own sleeping bag). Extras include a drying room (for wet-weather gear), a laundry and even a sauna. The friendly owner is a fount of knowledge about the local area.

In 2020 bookings could be made for individuals, couples and families, but not groups, due to social-distancing measures.

Braemar Caravan Park CAMPSITE £
(📞01339-741373; www.braemarcaravanpark. co.uk; Glenshee Rd; tent sites incl 2 people £22.50, camping pods £68; ⊙closed mid-Oct–mid-Dec; 🛜) There is good camping here, in a sheltered spot surrounded by mountains, with hot showers and a laundry. There are also heated camping pods with mattresses, a kettle and a microwave (bedding not provided).

Craiglea B&B ££
(☎01339-741641; www.craigleabraemar.com; Hillside Rd; d/tr £90/115; 🅿🛜) Craiglea is a homely B&B set in a pretty stone cottage with double, twin and family rooms, all en suite. Packed lunches are available for a day in the hills and the owners can give advice on local walks. Minimum stay of two nights.

Braemar Lodge Hotel HOTEL £££
(☎01339-741627; www.braemarlodge.co.uk; Glenshee Rd; dm/s/d from £25/85/140, 3-bed cabin per wk from £770; 🅿🛜) This Victorian shooting lodge on the southern outskirts of Braemar has bags of character, not least in the wood-panelled Malt Room bar, which is as well stocked with mounted deer heads as it is with single malt whiskies. There's a good restaurant with views of the hills (mains £11 to £35), plus a 12-bed hikers' bunkhouse (book in advance).

The nine self-catering log cabins in the grounds sleep up to six people and are pet friendly.

✖ Eating

Bothy CAFE £
(☎01339-741019; Invercauld Rd; mains £4-10; ⏱9am-5.30pm Sun-Thu, to 6pm Fri & Sat; 🛜👶) An appealing cafe for breakfast, lunch and cakes. It's tucked behind the Mountain Sports shop, with a sunny terrace out front and a balcony at the back overhanging the river.

Taste CAFE £
(☎01339-741425; www.taste-braemar.co.uk; Airlie House, Mar Rd; sandwiches £4; ⏱10am-5pm Tue-Sat; 👶) 🍃 Taste is a relaxed little cafe which has armchairs in the window bays, and serves homemade soups, sandwiches, coffee and cakes.

❶ Getting There & Away

Bus 201 runs from Aberdeen to Braemar (£12.45, 2¼ hours, every two hours Monday to Saturday, five on Sunday). The 50-mile drive from Perth to Braemar is beautiful, but there's no public transport on this route.

The Angus Glens

Five scenic glens – Isla, Prosen, Clova, Lethnot and Esk – cut into the hills along the southern fringes of the Cairngorms National Park, accessible from Kirriemuir in Angus. All have attractive scenery, though each glen has its own distinct personality: Glen Clova and Glenesk are the most beautiful, while Glen Lethnot is the least frequented. You can get detailed information on walks in the Angus Glens from the **Gateway to the Glens Museum** (☎01575-526006; kirriemuirmuseum@angusalive.scot; 32 High St; ⏱10am-5pm Tue-Sat) FREE in Kirriemuir and from the Glen Clova Hotel in Glen Clova.

❶ Getting There & Away

There is no public transport to the Angus Glens other than a limited school-bus service along Glen Clova; ask at the Gateway to the Glens Museum in Kirriemuir for details.

Glen Clova

The longest and loveliest of the Angus Glens stretches north from Kirriemuir for 20 miles, broad and pastoral in its lower reaches but growing narrower and craggier as the steep, heather-clad Highland hills close in around its head.

The minor road beyond the Glen Clova Hotel ends at a Forestry Commission car park at Glen Doll with a **ranger centre** (☎01575-550233; www.forestryandland.gov.scot; Glen Doll; parking £2; ⏱9am-4.30pm) and picnic area, which is the trailhead for a number of strenuous walks through the hills to the north.

Jock's Road is an ancient footpath that was much used by cattle drovers, soldiers, smugglers and shepherds in the 18th and 19th centuries; 700 Jacobite soldiers passed this way during their retreat in 1746, en route to defeat at Culloden. From the car park, the path strikes west along Glen Doll, then north across a high plateau (900m) before descending steeply into Glen Callater and on to Braemar (15 miles; allow five to seven hours). The route is hard going and should not be attempted in winter; you'll need OS Landranger maps numbers 43 and 44.

An easier walk leads from Glen Doll car park to **Corrie Fee**, a spectacular glacial hollow in the edge of the mountain plateau (4.5-mile round trip, waymarked).

Glen Clova Hotel HOTEL ££
(☎01575-550350; www.clova.com; s £80-120, d £115-170; 🅿🛜) The Glen Clova Hotel is a lovely old drover's inn near the head of the glen, and a great place to get away from it all. As well as 18 comfortable, country-style,

en-suite rooms (one with a four-poster bed), it has a rustic, stone-floored climbers' bar with a roaring log fire, and a good **restaurant** (☑01575-550350; mains £10-18; ⊙noon-7.45pm Sun-Thu, to 8.45pm Fri & Sat, shorter hours Nov-Mar; Ⓟ🐾). No mobile phone reception.

Glenesk

The most easterly of the Angus Glens, Glenesk runs for 15 miles from Edzell to lovely **Loch Lee**, surrounded by beetling cliffs and waterfalls.

Fifteen miles up the glen from Edzell, the public road ends near **Invermark Castle**, an impressive ruined tower. From the car park, good hiking trails lead to a 17th-century kirkyard beside Loch Lee (1 mile), the monument at **Queen's Well** (a spring once visited by Queen Victoria; 2 miles) and the summit of **Mount Keen** (939m; 5.5 miles).

Glenesk Retreat & Folk Museum   MUSEUM
(www.gleneskretreat.scot; admission by donation; ⊙10am-5pm Mon-Fri, to 6pm Sat & Sun Apr-Oct; Ⓟ🐾) 🐾 Ten miles up Glenesk from Edzell is a former shooting lodge that houses a fascinating collection of antiques and artefacts documenting everyday life in the glen from the 17th to the early 20th centuries – 860 people once lived here; today the population is less than 100.

There's also a cafe (mains £6.50 to £9.50).

HIGHLAND PERTHSHIRE

The Highland border cuts diagonally across Scotland from Dumbarton to Stonehaven, dividing the county of Perthshire into two distinctive regions. Highland Perthshire, spreading north of a line from Comrie to Blairgowrie, is a land of mountains, forest and lochs, with some of the finest scenery in the UK. The ancient city of Dunkeld, on the main A9 road from Perth to Inverness, is the main gateway to the region.

❶ Getting There & Around

Citylink (p296) buses from Edinburgh or Glasgow to Inverness stop at Birnam and Pitlochry. There are regular buses from Perth to most of the towns in the area. Trains running between Perth and Inverness stop at Blair Atholl and Pitlochry.

GLENSHEE

The route along the A93 from Braemar to Blairgowrie through the ski area of Glenshee is one of the most scenic drives in the country. It's fantastic walking country in summer, and has some of Scotland's best skiing in winter. There's a car park, ticket office, cafe and uplift here but no other services or accommodation.

With 22 lifts and 36 runs, **Glenshee Ski Resort** (☑01339-741320; www.ski-glenshee.co.uk; Old Military Rd, A93; 1-day ski pass per adult/child £32/21) is Scotland's largest skiing area. When the sun burns through the clouds after a good fall of snow, you'll be in a unique position to drink in the beauty of the country; the skiing isn't half bad either. Equipment hire available (skis, boots and poles per adult/child £24/20; book in advance).

Dunkeld & Birnam

☑01350 / POP 1280

The Tay runs like a storybook river through the heart of Perthshire's Big Tree Country, where the twin towns of Dunkeld and Birnam are linked by Thomas Telford's graceful bridge of 1808. As well as Dunkeld's ancient cathedral, there's much walking to be done in this area of magnificent forested hills. These same walks were one of the inspirations for Beatrix Potter to create her children's tales.

There's less to see in Birnam, a name made famous by *Macbeth*. There's not much left of Birnam Wood, but a riverside path leads to the **Birnam Oak**, a venerable 500-year-old survivor from Shakespeare's time, its ageing boughs propped up with timber supports. Nearby is the 300-year-old Birnam Sycamore.

◉ Sights & Activities

Dunkeld Cathedral   CHURCH
(HS; www.dunkeldcathedral.org.uk; Cathedral St, Dunkeld; ⊙9.30am-5.30pm Apr-Sep, 10am-4pm Oct-Mar) Situated on the grassy banks of the River Tay, Dunkeld Cathedral is one of the most beautifully sited churches in Scotland; don't miss it on a sunny day, when there are few lovelier places to be. Half the cathedral is still in use as a church; the rest is a romantic ruin. It partly dates from the

Lochs & Mountains

Since the 19th century, when the first tourists started to arrive, the Scottish Highlands have been famed for their wild nature and majestic scenery, and today the country's biggest draw remains its magnificent landscape. At almost every turn is a vista that will stop you in your tracks – keep your camera close at hand.

Ben Nevis

Scotland's highest peak is a perennial magnet for hillwalkers and ice climbers, but it's also one of the country's most photographed mountains. The classic viewpoints for the Ben include Corpach at the entrance to the Caledonian Canal, and the B8004 road between Banavie and Gairlochy, from where you can see the precipitous north face.

Loch Ness

Scotland's largest loch by volume (it contains more water than all the lakes in England and Wales added together) may be most famous for its legendary monster, but it is also one of Scotland's most scenic. The minor road along the southeastern shore reveals a series of classic views.

Schiehallion

From the Gaelic *Sìdh Chailleann* (Fairy Hill of the Caledonians), this is one of Scotland's most distinctive mountains, its conical peak a prominent feature of views along Loch Tummel and Loch Rannoch. It's also one of the easier Munros, and a hike to the summit is rewarded with a superb panorama of hills and lochs.

Loch Awe

Loch Awe is a little off the beaten track, but it's well worth seeking out for its gorgeous scenery. It's dotted with islands and draped with native woodlands of oak, birch and alder. Its northern end is dominated by the evocative ruins of Kilchurn Castle, with the pointed peaks of mighty Ben Cruachan reflected in its shifting waters.

1. Kilchurn Castle (p290), Loch Awe 2. Ben A'an (p246)
3. Loch Ness (p305) 4. Schiehallion (p328)

CLOUDVISUAL/SHUTTERSTOCK ©

PETER BURNETT/GETTY IMAGES ©

14th century, having suffered damage during the Reformation and the battle of Dunkeld (Jacobites versus the government) in 1689.

The Wolf of Badenoch, a fierce 14th-century noble who burned towns and abbeys to the ground in protest at his excommunication, is buried here – undeservedly – in a fine medieval tomb behind the wooden screen in the church.

Dunkeld House Grounds GARDENS
(⊙24hr) FREE Waymarked walks lead upstream from Dunkeld Cathedral through the gorgeous grounds of Dunkeld House Hotel, formerly a seat of the dukes of Atholl. In the 18th and early 19th centuries the 'planting dukes', as they became known, planted more than 27 million conifers on their estates 'for beauty and profit', introducing species such as larch, Douglas fir and sequoia, and sowing the seeds of Scottish forestry.

The abundance of vast, ancient trees here has given rise to the name Big Tree Country (www.perthshirebigtreecountry.co.uk). Just west of the cathedral is the 280-year-old '**parent larch**', the lone survivor of several planted in 1738, and said to have provided the seed stock for all Scottish larch trees.

Loch of the Lowes
Wildlife Centre WILDLIFE RESERVE
(☑01350-727337; www.swt.org.uk; adult/child £4.50/free; ⊙10am-5pm Mar-Oct, 10.30am-4pm Fri-Sun Nov-Feb; P) Loch of the Lowes, 2 miles east of Dunkeld off the A923, has a visitor centre devoted to red squirrels and the majestic osprey. There's a birdwatching hide (with binoculars provided), where you can see the birds nesting during breeding season (late April to August), complete with a live video link to the nest. In 2020 advance booking was required.

Hermitage WALKING
(NTS; www.nts.org.uk; parking £3) One of the most popular walks near Dunkeld is the Hermitage, where a well-marked trail follows the River Braan to Ossian's Hall, a quaint folly built by the Duke of Atholl in 1758 overlooking the spectacular Falls of Braan (salmon can be seen leaping here, especially in September and October). It's signposted off the A9 just west of the village.

🛏 Sleeping & Eating

⭐ **Jessie Mac's** HOSTEL £
(☑01350-727324; www.jessiemacs.co.uk; Murthly Tce, Birnam; dm/s/d/f £23/37/61/85; 🛜👶) 🅿
Set in a Victorian manse complete with baronial turret, Jessie Mac's is a glorious cross between B&B and luxury hostel, with three gorgeous doubles and four shared or family rooms with bunks. Guests make good use of the country-style lounge, sunny dining room and well-equipped kitchen.

Breakfast (£6 to £9) is made with local produce, from organic eggs to Dunkeld smoked salmon.

⭐ **Taybank** PUB FOOD ££
(☑01350-727340; www.thetaybank.co.uk; Tay Tce, Dunkeld; mains £12-15; ⊙food served noon-9pm; P) 🅿 Top choice for a sun-kissed pub lunch by the river is the Taybank, a regular meeting place and performance space for folk musicians and a wonderfully welcoming bar. The menu features fresh produce from the kitchen garden in dishes such as cured mackerel with fennel, and wood pigeon with beetroot, blackberries and dukkah.

B&B accommodation is available in two newly renovated Scandi-style rooms (single/double from £120/150).

ℹ Getting There & Away

Citylink (p300) buses running between Glasgow/Edinburgh (£19.20, two hours, two or three daily) and Inverness (£22.40, 2½ hours) stop at the Birnam Hotel. Stagecoach (p300) runs hourly buses (seven on Sunday) between Perth and Dunkeld (£2.90, 45 minutes), continuing to Aberfeldy (£3.60, 40 minutes).

Pitlochry
☑01796 / POP 2780

Pitlochry, with the scent of the Highlands already in the air, is a popular stop on the way north. In summer the main street can be a conga line of tour groups, but linger a while and it can still charm – on a quiet spring evening it's a pretty place, with salmon leaping in the Tummel and good things brewing at the Moulin Hotel.

◉ Sights & Activities

One of Pitlochry's attractions is its beautiful riverside – the River Tummel is dammed here, and if you're lucky you might see salmon swimming up the **fish ladder** to

Loch Faskally above (May to November; best month is October).

Pitlochry Dam Visitor Centre   VISITOR CENTRE
(www.pitlochrydam.com; Armoury Rd; ⊙10am-4.30pm; P) FREE Opened in 2017, this architecturally stunning visitor centre is perched above the dam on the River Tummel, and houses an exhibition (closed in 2020) that details the history of hydroelectricity in Scotland, alongside the life cycle of Atlantic salmon (all hydro stations need a fish ladder to allow salmon to migrate upstream past the dams).

The centre's excellent **Salmon Leap Cafe** serves sandwiches, pizzas and cakes (mains £6 to £9), with tables overlooking the river.

Edradour Distillery   DISTILLERY
(☑01796-472095; www.edradour.com; Moulin Rd; tour & tasting £25, tasting only £10; ⊙tours 10am-5pm Mon-Fri Apr-Oct, shorter hours Nov-Mar; P) This is proudly Scotland's smallest and most picturesque distillery and one of the best to visit: you can see the whole process, easily explained, in one building. It's 2.5 miles east of Pitlochry by car, along the Moulin road, or a pleasant 1-mile walk. The distillery was closed to the public in 2020.

Blair Athol Distillery   DISTILLERY
(☑01796-482003; www.malts.com; Perth Rd; tour & tasting £16, tasting only £12; ⊙10am-5pm; P) Tours here focus on whisky making and the blending of this well-known dram; book in advance. More expensive private tours give you greater insights and superior tastings (per person £40).

Explorers Garden   GARDENS
(☑01796-484600; www.explorersgarden.com; Foss Rd; adult/child £4/1; ⊙10am-5pm Apr-Oct; P) This gem of a garden is based around plants brought to Scotland by 18th- and 19th-century Scottish botanists and explorers such as David Douglas (after whom the Douglas fir is named), and celebrates 300 years of collecting and the 'plant hunters' who tracked down these exotic species. It's behind the Pitlochry Festival Theatre (p326), south of the river. The garden was closed in 2020.

Pass of Killiecrankie   HISTORIC SITE
(NTS; www.nts.org.uk; parking £3; ⊙24hr; P⊞) FREE The beautiful, rugged Pass of Killiecrankie, 3.5 miles north of Pitlochry, where the River Garry tumbles through a narrow gorge, was the site of the 1689 **Battle of Killiecrankie** that ignited the Jacobite rebellion. The visitor centre (closed in 2020) has great interactive displays on Jacobite history and local flora and fauna. There are some stunning walks along the wooded gorge, too; keep an eye out for red squirrels.

Highland Fling Bungee   ADVENTURE SPORTS
(☑0845 366 5844; www.bungeejumpscotland.co.uk; Killiecrankie; per person £79, repeat jumps £30) Based at Killiecrankie, 3.5 miles north of Pitlochry, Highland Fling offers breathtaking 130ft bungee jumps off the bridge over the River Garry gorge on weekends year-round, plus selected weekdays from March to October.

★ Festivals & Events

Enchanted Forest   LIGHT SHOW
(www.enchantedforest.org.uk; adult/child £22/12; ⊙Oct) This spectacular month-long sound-and-light show staged in Faskally Wood near Pitlochry is a major family hit.

Winter Words   LITERATURE
(www.pitlochryfestivaltheatre.com; ⊙Feb) A 10-day literary festival, with a packed programme of talks by authors, poets and broadcasters. Past guests have ranged from novelist Louis de Bernières to mountaineer and author Sir Chris Bonington.

🛏 Sleeping

Pitlochry Backpackers Hotel   HOSTEL £
(☑01796-470044; www.pitlochrybackpackershotel.com; 134 Atholl Rd; dm £22-24, d/f £56/82; ⊙Apr–mid-Nov; P@🛜) Friendly, laid-back and very comfortable, this is a cracking hostel smack bang in the middle of town, with three- to eight-bed dorms that are in mint condition. There are also good-value en-suite twins and doubles, with beds, not bunks. Cheap breakfast and a pool table add to the convivial party atmosphere. No extra charge for linen.

Pitlochry Youth Hostel   HOSTEL £
(HS; ☑01796-472308; www.hostellingscotland.org.uk; Knockard Rd; tw/tr/q £44/54/64; ⊙Apr-Oct; P@🛜🕿) Great location overlooking the town centre, with a large self-catering kitchen (closed in 2020) and lounge. Popular with families and walkers. In 2020 only private rooms could be booked (no shared dorms).

★ **Craigatin House** B&B ££

(01796-472478; www.craigatinhouse.co.uk; 165 Atholl Rd; d/ste £115/145; P@) Several times more tasteful than the average Scottish B&B, this elegant house and garden is set back from the main road. Chic contemporary fabrics covering expansive beds offer a standard of comfort above and beyond the reasonable price; the rooms in the converted stable block are particularly inviting. A fabulous breakfast and lounge area gives views over the lush garden.

Breakfast choices include whisky-laced porridge, smoked-fish omelettes and apple pancakes. No children under 13 years.

★ **Fonab Castle Hotel** HISTORIC HOTEL £££

(01796-470140; www.fonabcastlehotel.com; Foss Rd; d from £329; P) This Scottish Baronial fantasy in red sandstone was built in 1892 as the country house of Lieutenant Colonel George Sandeman, a scion of the famous port and sherry merchants. Now a luxury hotel and spa, it has a tasteful modern extension with commanding views over Loch Faskally, and a superb restaurant serving the finest Scottish venison, beef and seafood.

Knockendarroch House HOTEL £££

(01796-473473; www.knockendarroch.co.uk; Higher Oakfield Rd; d incl dinner from £270; P) Top of the town and boasting the best views, this genteel, well-run hotel has a range of luxurious rooms with huge windows that take advantage of the Highland light. The standard rooms have better views than the larger, slightly pricier superior ones; a couple have great little balconies, perfect for a sundowner. Meals are excellent.

✕ Eating & Drinking

Port-na-Craig Inn BISTRO ££

(01796-472777; www.portnacraig.com; Port-na-Craig; mains £11-15; 11am-8.30pm; P) Across the river from the town centre, this cute little cottage sits in what was once a separate hamlet. Top-quality main meals are prepared with confidence and panache; there are also simpler sandwiches, kids' meals and light lunches. Or you could just sit outdoors by the river with a pint and watch the salmon anglers.

Moulin Hotel PUB FOOD ££

(01796-472196; www.moulinhotel.co.uk; Kirkmichael Rd; mains £11-16; food served noon-9.30pm; P) A mile away from town but a world apart, this atmospheric inn has low ceilings, ageing wood and snug booths. It's a wonderfully romantic spot for a home-brewed ale (there's a microbrewery out back) and some Highland comfort food: try the haggis, neeps and tatties. It's a pleasant uphill stroll from Pitlochry, and an easy roll down afterwards.

★ **Saorsa 1875** VEGAN £££

(01796-475217; www.saorsahotel.com; 2 E Moulin Rd; lunch mains £11-14, 5-course dinner per person £50; noon-3pm & 7.30pm; P) Britain's first vegan hotel can be found in an elegant Victorian building in little Pitlochry. The outstanding five-course dinner menu is served at a communal dining table, where the chef presents each of the dishes made with ingredients such as locally foraged mushrooms. Call in for lunch (banana blossom 'fish', salads, smoothies) in the beautifully styled bar; dinner is by reservation only.

From the drinks list to the cleaning products, everything at Saorsa is carefully sourced to be vegan friendly. Its 11 rooms (doubles £140 to £230) are individually styled with statement wallpaper and upcycled furniture. Yoga classes are held in a yurt in the hotel grounds, which include just under a hectare of woodland.

☆ Entertainment

★ **Pitlochry Festival Theatre** THEATRE

(01796-484626; www.pitlochryfestivaltheatre. com; Port-na-Craig; tickets £17-37) Founded in 1951 (in a tent!), this famous and much-loved theatre is the focus of Highland Perthshire's cultural life. The summer season, from May to mid-October, stages a different production each night of the week except Sunday.

🔒 Shopping

Melt Gallery ARTS & CRAFTS

(01796-472358; www.meltgallery.com; 14 Bonnethill Rd; 10am-5pm Thu-Sat) This gallery is a treasure trove of quality Scottish arts and crafts, including polished aluminium jewellery that is handmade in the owner's workshop at the back. Potential purchases include paintings, photography, bronzes and ceramics.

ℹ Information

Pitlochry Tourist Office (01796-472215; www.perthshire.co.uk; 22 Atholl Rd; 10am-

3pm, longer hours Jul & Aug) Free maps and good information on local walks.

❶ Getting There & Away

BUS

Scottish Citylink (p296) buses run two to five times daily to Inverness (£19.20, 1¾ hours), Perth (£12.30, 50 minutes), Edinburgh (£19.20, two to 2½ hours) and Glasgow (£19.20, 1¾ to two hours).

Megabus (☑ 0871 266 3333; www.megabus. com) offers discounted fares to Inverness, Perth, Edinburgh and Glasgow.

Stagecoach (p300) buses run via a change in Ballinluig to Aberfeldy (£3.90, 45 minutes, hourly Monday to Saturday, three Sunday), Dunkeld (£2.70, 40 minutes, hourly Monday to Saturday) and Perth (£4.30, 1¼ hours, hourly Monday to Saturday).

TRAIN

Pitlochry is on the main railway line from Perth (£15.30, 30 minutes, 12 daily Monday to Saturday, seven on Sunday) to Inverness (£24.80, 1¾ hours, same frequency).

❶ Getting Around

Local buses between Pitlochry and Blair Atholl stop at Killiecrankie (£1.75, 10 minutes, three to seven daily).

Blair Atholl

The village of Blair Atholl dates only from the early 19th century, springing up along the main road to the north after a new bridge was thrown across the River Tilt in 1822 (the original 16th-century Black Bridge, upgraded by General Wade in 1730, still stands just under a mile upstream at Old Bridge of Tilt).

Blair Castle is the main attraction here, but there's also the **Atholl Country Life Museum** (☑01796-473035; www.facebook. com/athollcountrylifemuseum; Main Rd; adult/child £4/free; ⊙1-5pm Apr-Oct; ℗), the old watermill, and many superb walks in the surrounding countryside, from short strolls through the castle grounds and longer walks to various viewpoints, to day-long hikes along Glen Tilt and up into the surrounding mountains (details from the information point near the museum).

★**Blair Castle**   CASTLE
(☑01796-481207; www.blair-castle.co.uk; house & gardens adult/child £14/8.50, gardens only £7.70/3.50; ⊙10am-5.30pm Easter-Oct, to 4pm

Sat & Sun Nov-Easter; ℗ ♿) One of the most popular tourist attractions in Scotland, magnificent Blair Castle – and its surrounding estates – is the seat of the Duke of Atholl, head of the Murray clan. It's an impressive white heap set beneath forested slopes above the River Garry. Thirty rooms are open to the public and they present a wonderful picture of upper-class Highland life from the 16th century on. In 2020 admission to the castle was by prebooked guided tour only.

The original tower was built in 1269, but the castle underwent significant remodelling in the 18th and 19th centuries. Highlights include the 2nd-floor **drawing room** with its ornate Georgian plasterwork and Zoffany portrait of the fourth duke's family, complete with a pet lemur (yes, you read that correctly) called Tommy; and the **tapestry room** draped with 17th-century wall hangings created for Charles I. The **dining room** is sumptuous – check out the nine-pint wine glasses.

In May, the Duke of Atholl visits to review the Atholl Highlanders, Britain's only private army, and attend the **Atholl Gathering and Highland Games.**

Blair Atholl Bike Hire   CYCLING
(☑0845 548 2270; www.segway-ecosse.com/bike-hire; Blair Castle Caravan Park; per day adult/child £28/20; ⊙9am-6pm) Atholl Estates has more than 50 miles of cycling trails through woodlands and open moorland; a map of graded off-road routes can be downloaded from www.atholl-estates.co.uk. This outfit, based at the caravan park reception, has mountain bikes for hire. Book online in advance; photo ID required.

Blair Atholl Watermill   CAFE £
(☑01796-481321; www.blairathollwatermill.com; Ford Rd; mains £4-7; ⊙9.30am-4pm Apr-Oct; ℗ 🛜 ♿) ✐ This working watermill grinds its own flour and bakes its own bread, and serves it up in this atmospheric cafe as deliciously fresh sandwiches. You can watch the mill at work, and even sign up for bakery courses.

Lochs Tummel & Rannoch

The scenic route along Lochs Tummel and Rannoch (www.rannochandtummel.co.uk) is worth doing any way you can – by foot, bicycle or car. Hillsides shrouded with ancient birch woods and forests of spruce,

RANNOCH MOOR

Beyond Rannoch Station, civilisation fades away and Rannoch Moor begins. This is the largest area of moorland in Britain, stretching west for eight barren, bleak and uninhabited miles to the A82 Glasgow–Fort William road. A triangular plateau of blanket bog occupying more than 50 sq miles, the moor is ringed by high mountains and puddled with countless lochs, ponds and peat hags. Water covers 10% of the surface, and it has been canoed across, swum across, and even skated across in winter.

Despite the appearance of desolation, the moor is rich in wildlife, with curlew, golden plover and snipe darting among the tussocks, black-throated diver, goosander and merganser on the lochs, and – if you're lucky – osprey and golden eagle overhead. Herds of red deer forage alongside the railway, and otters patrol the loch shores. Keep an eye out for the sundew, a tiny, insect-eating plant with sticky-fingered leaves.

A couple of excellent (and challenging) walks start from Rannoch Station – north to Corrour Station (11 miles, four to five hours) from where you can return by train; and west along the northern edge of the moor to the Kings House Hotel (p333) at the eastern end of Glen Coe (11 miles, four hours).

pine and larch make up the fabulous **Tay Forest Park**, whose wooded hills roll into the glittering waters of the lochs; a visit in autumn, when the birch leaves are at their finest, is recommended.

Eighteen miles west of Kinloch Rannoch the road ends at romantic and isolated **Rannoch Station**, which lies on the Glasgow–Fort William railway line. Beyond sprawls the desolate expanse of Rannoch Moor. There's an excellent tearoom on the station platform, and a welcoming small hotel alongside. Be aware that Rannoch Station is a dead-end, and the nearest service station is at Aberfeldy.

The **Queen's View** at the eastern end of Loch Tummel is a magnificent viewpoint with a vista along the loch to the prominent mountain of Schiehallion. The nearby **visitor centre** (www.forestry.gov.uk; parking £2; ⊙10am-4pm; ℗) provides parking and houses a cafe and gift shop.

Kinloch Rannoch is a great base for walks and cycle trips, or for fishing on Loch Rannoch for brown trout, Arctic char and pike; you can get permits (£8 per day) at the Country Store in the village.

Three miles west of Kinloch Rannoch near Carie, on the south shore of the loch, walking trails lead into the wildlife-rich **Black Wood of Rannoch**, a remnant of ancient Caledonian pine forest. There is a basic but beautiful forestry department **campsite** (☑0131-3705436; www.scotland. forestry.gov.uk; Kilvrecht; tent sites £10; ⊙Apr–mid-Oct) here.

Schiehallion (1083m), whose conical peak dominates views from Loch Rannoch,

is a relatively straightforward climb from Braes of Foss car park (6.5 miles return), and is rewarded by spectacular views. See www.johnmuirtrust.org/trust-land/east-schiehallion for more information.

🛏 Sleeping & Eating

Moor of Rannoch
Restaurant & Rooms HOTEL £££
(☑01882-633238; www.moorofrannoch.co.uk; Rannoch Station; s/d incl dinner £248/305; ⊙Thu-Mon Feb-Nov; ℗🐾) The end of the road beside Rannoch train station is one of Scotland's most isolated places (no internet, no TV, only fleeting mobile-phone reception), but luckily this beautifully renovated hotel is here to keep your spirits up – it's a magical getaway. It does excellent dinners (three courses £49; booking essential for non-residents). The hotel closes on Tuesday and Wednesday.

Rannoch Station Tea Room CAFE £
(☑01882-633247; www.rannochstationtearoom. co.uk; Rannoch Station; mains £3.50-9; ⊙8am-4.30pm Mon-Thu & Sat, 10am-4.30pm Sun; ℗🐾) This superb little tearoom sits on the platform at remote Rannoch Station, serving breakfast, lunchtime soup and sandwiches and afternoon coffee and cake to visiting hikers, mountain bikers and railway excursionists. Next door, in the former waiting room, is a fascinating exhibition on Rannoch Moor and the history of the railway.

ℹ Getting There & Around

A demand-responsive **minibus service** (☑Broons Buses & Taxis 01882-632418, Highland Travel 01882-633398; www.pkc.gov.uk; ☉7am-10pm Mon-Sat) – ie you have to phone and book it at least 24 hours in advance – runs between Kinloch Rannoch and Rannoch Station (£3, 35 minutes).

Elizabeth Yule Coaches (☑01796-472290; www.elizabethyulecoaches.co.uk) operates a bus service from Pitlochry to Kinloch Rannoch (£4.10, 50 minutes, three to five daily Monday to Saturday) via Queen's View and the Inn at Loch Tummel.

There are three trains daily (two on Sunday) from Rannoch Station north to Fort William (£11.80, one hour) and Mallaig (2½ hours, £26.50), and south to Glasgow (£26.80, 2¾ hours).

Aberfeldy

☑ 01887 / POP 2290

Aberfeldy is the gateway to Breadalbane (the historic region surrounding Loch Tay), and a good base: adventure sports, angling, art and castles all feature on the menu here. It's a peaceful, pretty place on the banks of the Tay, but if it's moody lochs and glens that steal your heart, you may want to push a little further west.

The B846 road towards Fortingall crosses the Tay via the elegant **Wade's Bridge**, built in 1733 as part of the network of military roads designed to tame the Highlands.

◉ Sights & Activities

The **Birks of Aberfeldy**, made famous by a Robert Burns poem, offer a great short walk from the centre of town, following a vigorous burn upstream past several picturesque cascades.

Aberfeldy Distillery   DISTILLERY
(www.dewarsaberfeldydistillery.com; tours adult/child from £9/free; ☉10am-6pm Mon-Sat, noon-4pm Sun Apr-Oct, 10am-4pm Mon-Sat Nov-Mar; P) At the eastern end of Aberfeldy, the home of the famous Dewar's blend offers a good 90-minute tour. After the usual overblown film, there's a museum section with audio guide, and an entertaining tour of the whisky-making process, followed by a tasting of venerable Aberfeldy single malts and others. Book in advance.

Castle Menzies   CASTLE
(www.castlemenzies.org; adult/child £8/4; ☉10.30am-4pm Mon-Sat, 2-4pm Sun Mar-Nov; P) Castle Menzies is the 16th-century seat of the chief of Clan Menzies (*ming*-iss), magnificently set against a forest back-

drop. Inside it reeks of authenticity, despite extensive restoration work. Check out the fireplace in the dungeon-like kitchens, and the gaudy Great Hall with windows revealing a ribbon of lush, green countryside extending into wooded hills beyond the estate. It's about 1.5 miles west of Aberfeldy, off the B846.

Watermill   GALLERY
(www.aberfeldywatermill.com; Mill St; ☉10am-5pm Mon-Sat, 11am-5pm Sun) FREE You could while away several hours at this converted watermill, which houses a **cafe** (☑01887-822896; www.aberfeldywatermill.com; Mill St; mains £5-7; ☉10am-5pm Mon-Sat, 11am-5pm Sun; ☝) ☛, bookshop and art gallery exhibiting contemporary works of art. The shop has the biggest range of titles in the Highlands, with a great selection of books on Scottish history, landscape and wildlife.

Splash   RAFTING
(☑01887-829706; www.rafting.co.uk; Dunkeld Rd; ☉office 9am-5pm Wed-Sun; ☝) Splash offers family-friendly white-water rafting on the River Tay (adult/child £49/30, Wednesday to Sunday year-round) and more advanced adult trips on the Tummel (Grade III/IV, June to September) and the Orchy (Grade III/V, October to March). It also offers pulse-racing descents on river bugs (£50) and canyoning (from £50).

Highland Safaris   TOUR
(☑01887-820071; www.highlandsafaris.net; ☉9am-5pm; ☝) This outfit offers an ideal way to spot some wildlife or simply enjoy Perthshire's magnificent countryside. Standard trips include the 2½-hour Mountain Safari (adult/child £45/25), which includes whisky and shortbread in a mountain bothy; and the four-hour Mountain Safari Trek (adult/child £80/45), culminating in a walk in the mountains and a picnic.

You may spot wildlife such as golden eagles, osprey and red deer. There's also mountain-bike hire (£30 per day).

🛌 Sleeping

Tigh'n Eilean Guest House   B&B **££**
(☑01887-820109; www.tighneilean.co.uk; Taybridge Dr; s/d from £48/80; P 🕙 🐾) Everything about this property screams comfort. It's a gorgeous place overlooking the Tay, with individually designed rooms – one has a Jacuzzi, while another is set on its own in

a cheery yellow summer house in the garden, giving you a bit of privacy. The garden itself is fabulous and the riverbank setting is delightful.

Balnearn Guest House B&B ££
(☑ 01887-820431; www.balnearnhouse.com; Crieff Rd; s/d from £70/80; P☎) Balnearn is a sedate and luxurious mansion near the centre of town, with space to spare. Most rooms have great natural light, and there's a particularly good family room downstairs. Breakfast has been lavishly praised by guests, and the attentive, cordial hosts are helpful while respecting your privacy.

✕ Eating & Drinking

★ **Inn on the Tay** PUB FOOD ££
(☑ 01887-840760; www.theinnonthetay.co.uk; Grandtully; mains £7-23; ⊙ food 1-8pm; P☎⊞) This convivial pub, with its modern bistro-style dining room, makes a great pit stop on the way west to Loch Tay. The menu is simple – salads, burgers, fish and chips – but top quality, and there's an outdoor deck above the river, where you can enjoy a drink while watching rafters descend the Grandtully rapids, 5 miles east of Aberfeldy.

Glen Lyon Coffee COFFEE
(www.glenlyoncoffee.co.uk; Aberfeldy Business Park; ⊙9.30am-4.30pm Mon-Fri, to 2pm Sat) Glen Lyon coffee roasters supplies many of the area's best cafes with their ethically sourced beans. The roasting takes place in Aberfeldy, where there are usually around seven single origins and blends available to take away or sample in the industrial-style coffee shop, warmed with rugs and a wood-burning stove.

❶ Getting There & Away

Stagecoach bus 23 runs from Perth to Aberfeldy (£4.30, 1½ hours, hourly Monday to Saturday, fewer on Sunday) via Dunkeld; from Pitlochry (£3.90, 45 minutes), you'll need to change buses at Ballinluig. There's no bus link west to Killin.

Local buses run a circular route from Aberfeldy through Kenmore, Fortingall and back to Aberfeldy once each way on school days only.

Loch Tay & Ben Lawers

Loch Tay is the heart of the ancient region known as Breadalbane (from the Gaelic Bràghad Albainn, 'the heights of Scotland') – mighty **Ben Lawers** (1214m), looming over the loch, is the highest peak outside the Ben Nevis and Cairngorms regions. Much of the land to the north of Loch Tay falls within the **Ben Lawers National Nature Reserve** (www.nts.org.uk), known for its rare alpine flora.

The main access point for the ascent of Ben Lawers is the car park 1.5 miles north of the A827, on the minor road from Loch Tay to Bridge of Balgie. The climb is 6.5 miles and can take up to five hours (return): pack wet-weather gear, water, food and a map and compass. There's also an easier nature trail here.

Loch Tay is famous for its fishing – salmon, trout and pike are all caught here. **Loch Tay Fish 'n' Trips** (☑ 07967 567347; www.lochtayfishntrips.co.uk) can kit you out for a day's fishing with boat, tackle and guide for £130 for two people, or rent you a boat for £65 a day.

The main road from Kenmore to Killin runs along the north shore of Loch Tay. The minor road along the south shore is narrow and twisting (unsuitable for large vehicles), but offers great views of the hills to the north.

★ **Scottish Crannog Centre** MUSEUM
(☑ 01887-830583; www.crannog.co.uk; adult/child £10/7; ⊙10am-5.30pm Apr-Oct; P⊞) Less than a mile south of Kenmore, on the banks of Loch Tay, is the fascinating Scottish Crannog Centre, perched on stilts above the loch. Crannogs – effectively artificial islands – were a favoured form of defensive dwelling from the 3rd millennium BCE onwards. This superb re-creation (based on studies of Oakbank crannog, one of 18 discovered in Loch Tay) offers a guided tour that includes an impressive demonstration of fire making and Iron Age crafts. Book tours in advance.

Fortingall

Fortingall is one of the prettiest villages in Scotland, with 19th-century thatched cottages in a tranquil setting beside an ancient church with impressive wooden beams and a 7th-century monk's bell.

The famous **Fortingall Yew Tree** in the churchyard is estimated to be between 2000 and 3000 years old, one of the oldest living organisms in Europe. Its girth was measured at 16m in 1769, but since then souvenir hunters and natural decay have reduced it to a few gnarly but thriving boughs – in 2015 it produced berries for the first time on record. It was almost certainly around when the Romans camped in the meadows by the River Lyon in the 1st century CE; popular, if unlikely, tradition says that Pontius Pilate was born here.

Glen Lyon

The 'longest, loneliest and loveliest glen in Scotland', according to Sir Walter Scott, stretches for 32 unforgettable miles of rickety stone bridges, native woodland and heather-clad hills, becoming wilder and less populated as it snakes its way west. The ancients believed it to be a gateway to Faerieland, and even the most sceptical of visitors will be entranced by the valley's magic.

From Fortingall, a narrow road winds up the glen, while another steep and spectacular route from Loch Tay crosses the hills to meet it at **Bridge of Balgie**. The road continues west as far as the dam on Loch Lyon, passing a memorial to Robert Campbell (1808–94; a Canadian explorer and fur trader, born in the glen).

There are no villages in the glen – the majestic scenery is the main reason to be here – just a cluster of houses and a tearoom at Bridge of Balgie.

There are several waymarked **woodland walks** beginning from a car park a short distance beyond Bridge of Balgie, and more challenging hill walks into the surrounding mountains (see www.walkhighlands.co.uk/perthshire). **Cycling** is an ideal way to explore the glen, and fit riders can complete a loop over to Glen Lochay via a potholed road (motor vehicles not permitted) leading south from the Loch Lyon dam.

★ **Milton Cottage**　　　　　B&B **££**
(Milton Eonan; ☑01887-866337; www.facebook.com/GlenlyonCroft; Bridge of Balgie; d/tr £80/110; P🐕🐾🐾) 🐾 Milton Cottage is a must for those seeking tranquillity. On a bubbling stream where a watermill once stood, it's a working rare-breed croft with a romantic one-bedroom cottage at the bottom of the garden (available as B&B or self-catering). It can sleep three at a pinch. The cottage can be booked on Airbnb.com.

The helpful owners offer packed lunches and evening meals using local and home-grown produce. After crossing the bridge

at Bridge of Balgie, you'll see Milton Eonan signposted to the right.

Glenlyon Tearoom　　　　　CAFE **£**
(☑01887-866221; Bridge of Balgie; snacks £3-4; ⊙10am-5pm Apr-Oct; P🐕) This cafe, with a suntrap of a terrace overlooking the river, is the beating heart of Glen Lyon, a hub for walkers, cyclists and motorists. The owner is a fount of knowledge about the glen, and her pistachio and almond cake is legendary. The coffee comes from a local roastery, and the soups, sausage rolls and sandwiches are homemade.

WEST HIGHLANDS

This region extends from the bleak blanket-bog of the Moor of Rannoch to the west coast beyond Glen Coe and Fort William, and includes the southern reaches of the Great Glen. The scenery is grand throughout, with high, rocky mountains rising above wild glens. Great expanses of moor alternate with lochs and patches of commercial forest. Fort William, at the inner end of Loch Linnhe, is the only sizeable town in the area.

Since 2007 the region has been promoted as Lochaber Geopark (www.lochabergeopark.org.uk), an area of outstanding geology and scenery.

Glen Coe

Scotland's most famous glen is also one of its grandest and – in bad weather – its grimmest. The approach to the glen from the east is guarded by the rocky pyramid of **Buachaille Etive Mor** – the Great Shepherd of Etive – and the lonely Kings House Hotel (p333). After the Battle of Culloden in 1745, the inn was used as a Hanoverian garrison – hence the name.

The A82 road leads over the Pass of Glencoe and into the narrow upper glen. The southern side is dominated by three massive, brooding spurs, known as the **Three Sisters**, while the northern side is enclosed by the continuous steep wall of the knife-edged **Aonach Eagach** ridge, a classic mountaineering challenge. The road threads its way past deep gorges and crashing waterfalls to the more pastoral lower reaches of the glen around Loch Achtriochtan and **Glencoe village**.

⊙ Sights

Glencoe Visitor Centre   MUSEUM

(NTS; ☑ 01855-811307; www.nts.org.uk; parking £4; ⏱ 9.30am-4pm; P) **FREE** This newly renovated centre provides comprehensive information on the geological, environmental and cultural history of Glen Coe via audiovisual displays, charts the history of mountaineering in the glen, and tells the story of the Glencoe Massacre in all its gory detail. There's an excellent 3D map of the glen and an information hub, and a ranger can give advice on local walks. It's 1.5 miles southeast of Glencoe village.

Glencoe Folk Museum   MUSEUM

(☑ 01855-811664; www.glencoemuseum.com; adult/child £3/free; ⏱ 10am-4.30pm Tue-Sat Apr-Oct) This small, thatched cottage houses a varied collection of farm equipment, tools of the woodworking, blacksmithing and slate-quarrying trades, and military memorabilia, including a riding boot that once belonged to Robert Campbell of Glen Lyon, who took part in the Glencoe Massacre.

🏃 Activities

There are several short, pleasant walks around **Glencoe Lochan**, near the village. To get there, turn left off the minor road to Glencoe Youth Hostel, just beyond the bridge over the River Coe. There are three walks (40 minutes to an hour), all detailed on a signboard at the car park. The artificial lochan was created by Lord Strathcona in 1895 for his homesick Canadian wife, Isabella, and is surrounded by a North American–style forest.

A more strenuous hike, but well worth the effort on a fine day, is the climb to the **Lost Valley**, a magical mountain sanctuary still haunted by the ghosts of MacDonalds who died here while escaping the Glencoe Massacre in 1692 (only 2.5 miles round trip, but allow three hours). A rough path from the car park at Allt na Reigh (on the A82, 6 miles east of Glencoe village) bears left down to a footbridge over the river, then climbs up the wooded valley between Beinn Fhada and Gearr Aonach. The route leads steeply up through a maze of giant, jumbled, moss-coated boulders before emerging – quite unexpectedly – into a broad, open valley with a half-mile-long meadow as flat as a football pitch. Back in the days of clan warfare, the valley – invisible from below – was used for hiding sto-

len cattle; its Gaelic name, Coire Gabhail, means 'corrie of capture'.

The summits of Glen Coe's mountains are for experienced mountaineers only. The Cicerone guidebook *Ben Nevis & Glen Coe* by Ronald Turnbull details everything from short easy walks to challenging mountain climbs.

Steven Fallon Mountain Guides   OUTDOORS

(☑ 0131-466 8152; www.stevenfallon.co.uk; per person from £69) If you lack the experience or confidence to tackle Scotland's challenging mountains alone, then you can join a guided hill walk or hire a private guide from this outfit.

Glencoe Mountain Resort   OUTDOORS

(☑ 01855-851226; www.glencoemountain.com; Kingshouse; chairlift adult/child £12/8; ⏱ 9am-4.30pm) Scotland's oldest ski area (eight lifts and 20 runs), established in the 1950s, is also one of the best, with grand views across the wild expanse of Rannoch Moor. The lower chairlift continues to operate in summer providing access to mountain-biking trails. In winter, a lift pass costs £35 a day; equipment hire is £25.

The Lodge Café-Bar (open 9am to 8.30pm) at the base station has comfy sofas where you can soak up the view through floor-to-ceiling windows.

There are tent pitches (per person £8), camping pods (£60 to £80 a night) and campervan hook-ups (£20 a night) beside the car park.

🛏 Sleeping

There are several campsites, B&Bs and hotels in and around Glencoe village at the western end of the glen, plus camping at Glencoe Mountain Resort at the eastern end.

Invercoe Caravan
& Camping Park   CAMPSITE £

(☑ 01855-811210; www.invercoe.co.uk; tent site without car per person £11, tent site with car £26; 🐕) This place has great views of the surrounding mountains and is equipped with anti-midge machines. There's a covered cooking area for campers.

Glencoe
Independent Hostel   HOSTEL £

(☑ 01855-811906; www.glencoehostel.co.uk; hostel/bunkhouse dm £25/20; P @ 🛜) This handily located hostel, just 1.5 miles southeast of Glencoe village, is set in an old farm-

THE CALEDONIAN CANAL

Running for 59 miles from Corpach, near Fort William, to Inverness via Lochs Lochy, Oich and Ness, the Caledonian Canal (www.scottishcanals.co.uk) links the east and west coasts of Scotland, avoiding the long and dangerous sea passage around Cape Wrath and through the turbulent Pentland Firth. Designed by Thomas Telford and completed in 1822 at a cost of £900,000 – a staggering sum then – the canal took 20 years to build, including 29 locks, four aqueducts and 10 bridges.

Conceived as a project to ease unemployment and bring prosperity to the Highlands in the aftermath of the Jacobite rebellions and the Clearances, the canal proved to be a commercial failure – the locks were too small for the new breed of steamships that came into use soon after its completion. But it proved to be a success in terms of tourism, especially after it was popularised by Queen Victoria's cruise along the canal in 1873. Today the canal is used mainly by yachts and pleasure cruisers. Much of the Great Glen Way (p305) follows the line of the canal.

house with six- and eight-bed dorms, and a newly renovated bunkhouse with another 16 spaces in communal, alpine-style bunks. There's also a wooden cabin that sleeps up to three (£73 per night).

Glencoe

Youth Hostel HOSTEL £
(HS; ☑ 08155-811219; www.hostellingscotland. org.uk; tr/q £81/108; P @ ☏ ☎) Very popular with hikers, though the atmosphere can be a little institutional. It's a 1.5-mile walk from Glencoe village along the minor road on the northern side of the river. Bookings for 2021 are for private rooms only (no dorm beds).

Clachaig Inn HOTEL £££
(☑ 01855-811252; www.clachaig.com; s/d £78/155; P ☏ ☎) The Clachaig, 2 miles southeast of Glencoe village, has long been a favourite haunt of hill walkers and climbers. As well as comfortable accommodation (opt for a room with a Glen Coe view), there's a lounge bar with snug booths and high refectory tables serving good food (mains £11 to £20) from noon to 9pm.

Climbers usually head for the lively Boots Bar on the other side of the hotel – it has log fires, serves real ale, and has live Scottish music on Saturday nights.

Kings House Hotel HOTEL £££
(☑ 01855-851259; www.kingshousehotel.co.uk; Kingshouse; r £210-290, bunkhouse dm £35; ☏ restaurant 6-8.30pm; P ☏ ☎) A major redevelopment has transformed this remote inn into a luxurious modern hotel, with 57 sleek but cosy rooms sleeping up to four people (two have large balconies with views of the hills) and a large bar and restaurant (mains £10 to £30). A purpose-built wooden chalet

houses a 35-bed bunkhouse, with laundry facilities and a drying room.

Dating from the 17th century, the Kings House claims to be one of Scotland's oldest licensed inns and has long been a favourite meeting place for climbers, skiers and walkers (it's on the West Highland Way). The old inn building is now the **Way Inn**, a pub serving breakfast and light meals during the day. Wild camping is permitted behind the bunkhouse.

✖ Eating

Glencoe Café CAFE £
(☑ 01855-811168; www.glencoecafe.co.uk; Lorn Dr, Glencoe Village; mains £4.50-10; ☏ 11am-5pm Fri-Wed May-Oct, to 4pm Nov-Apr; P ☏) This friendly cafe is the social hub of Glencoe village, serving breakfast fry-ups (including vegetarian versions) till 11.30am, light lunches based on local produce and the best cappuccino in the glen.

Crafts & Things CAFE £
(☑ 01855-811325; www.craftsandthings.co.uk; A82; mains £5-8; ☏ 9.30am-5pm; P ☏ ♿) Just off the main road between Glencoe village and Ballachulish, the tearoom in this craft shop is a good spot for a lunch of homemade lentil soup with crusty rolls, ciabatta sandwiches, or just coffee and carrot cake. There are tables outdoors and a box of toys to keep little ones occupied.

★ Laroch SCOTTISH ££
(☑ 01855-811940; www.thelarochrestaurantand bar.co.uk; Loanfern, Ballachulish; mains £12-22; ☏ noon-2.45pm & 6-8.45pm Tue-Sun; P ☏) This friendly restaurant and bar in Ballachulish village, 1 mile west of Glencoe village, is highly recommended for its excellent food.

Local ingredients are cooked with finesse and burst with flavour: the menu changes regularly but features dishes such as Mallaig halibut with roasted scallops and Loch Leven mussels, and wild mushroom and sweet potato risotto. Book ahead.

ⓘ Getting There & Away

Scottish Citylink (p296) buses run between Fort William and Glencoe (£13.60, 30 minutes, four to eight daily) and from Glencoe to Glasgow (£24.20, 2¾ hours, four to eight daily). Buses stop at Glencoe village (at the crossroads), Glencoe Visitor Centre and Glencoe Mountain Resort.

Shiel Buses (p337) route 44 links Glencoe village with Fort William (£4.50, 40 minutes, seven daily Monday to Saturday, four on Sunday) and Kinlochleven (£2.40, 15 minutes).

Kinlochleven

📞 01855 / POP 900

Kinlochleven is hemmed in by high mountains at the head of beautiful Loch Leven, about 7 miles east of Glencoe village. The aluminium smelter that led to the town's development in the early 20th century has long since closed, and the opening of the Ballachulish Bridge in the 1970s allowed the main road to bypass it completely. Decline was halted by the opening of the **West Highland Way**, which now brings a steady stream of hikers through the village.

The final section of the West Highland Way stretches for 14 miles from Kinlochleven to Fort William. The village is also the starting point for easier walks up the glen of the River Leven, through pleasant woods to the **Grey Mare's Tail** waterfall, and harder mountain hikes into the **Mamores**.

🏃 Activities

Via Ferrata   ADVENTURE SPORTS
(📞 01397-747111; www.verticaldescents.com; Unit 3, Kinlochleven Business Park; per person/family £65/240) Scotland's first via ferrata – a 500m climbing route equipped with steel ladders, cables and bridges – snakes through the crags around the Grey Mare's Tail waterfall, allowing non-climbers to experience the thrill of climbing (you'll need a head for heights, though!).

Ice Factor   ADVENTURE SPORTS
(📞 01855-831100; www.ice-factor.co.uk; Leven Rd; ⊗ 9am-10pm Tue & Thu, to 6pm Mon, Wed & Fri-Sun; 🐾) If you fancy trying your hand at ice-climbing, even in the middle of summer, the world's biggest indoor ice-climbing wall offers a one-hour beginner's 'taster' session for £30. You'll also find a rock-climbing wall, an aerial adventure course, a soft-play area for kids, and a cafe (open 9am to 5.30pm) and bar-bistro (food served 5pm to 9.30pm).

🛏 Sleeping & Eating

Blackwater Hostel & Campsite   HOSTEL £
(📞 01855-831253; www.blackwaterhostel.co.uk; Lab Rd; tw/tr £65/75, tent sites £30, pods from £45; 🅿 🛜) This 39-bed hostel (preference given to groups – individual travellers should check availability in advance) has spotless dorms with en-suite bathrooms and TV, and a well-sheltered campsite with the option of wooden glamping pods for two or four people.

★ Lochleven Seafood Cafe   SEAFOOD ££
(📞 01855-821048; www.lochlevenseafoodcafe.co.uk; mains £11-40, whole lobster £40; ⊗ meals noon-3pm & 6-9pm, coffee & cake 10am-noon & 3-5pm mid-Mar–Oct; 🅿 🐾) This place serves superb shellfish freshly plucked from live tanks – oysters, razor clams, scallops, lobster and crab – plus a daily fish special and some non-seafood dishes. For warm days, there's an outdoor terrace with a view across the loch to the Pap of Glencoe. The cafe is 5 miles west of Kinlochleven, on the north shore of the loch.

ⓘ Getting There & Away

Shiel Buses (p337) bus 44 runs from Fort William to Kinlochleven (£5.80, one hour, seven daily Monday to Saturday, four on Sunday) via Ballachulish and Glencoe village.

Fort William

📞 01397 / POP 10,460

Basking on Loch Linnhe's shores amid magnificent mountain scenery, Fort William has one of the most enviable settings in all of Scotland. If it weren't for the busy dual carriageway crammed between the less-than-attractive town centre and the loch, and one of the highest rainfall records in the country, it would be almost idyllic. Even so, the town has carved out a reputation as the 'Outdoor Capital of the UK' (www.outdoor-capital.co.uk), and easy access by rail and bus makes it a good base for exploring the surrounding mountains and glens.

Magical Glen Nevis (p337) begins near the northern end of the town and wraps itself around the southern flanks of Ben Nevis (1345m) – Britain's highest mountain and a magnet for hikers and climbers.

◉ Sights

★ Jacobite Steam Train   HERITAGE RAILWAY
(☑ 0844 850 4685; www.westcoastrailways.co.uk; day return adult/child from £43/26; ⊙ mid-May–Oct) The Jacobite Steam Train, hauled by a former LNER K1 or LMS Class 5MT locomotive, travels the scenic two-hour run between Fort William and Mallaig. Classed as one of the great railway journeys of the world, the route crosses the historic Glenfinnan Viaduct, made famous in the *Harry Potter* films – the Jacobite's owners supplied the steam locomotive and rolling stock used in the film.

Trains depart from Fort William train station at 10.15am and (in peak season only) 2.40pm, and return from Mallaig at 2.10pm and 6.40pm. There's a brief stop at Glenfinnan station, and you get 1½ hours in Mallaig (two hours on the afternoon service).

West Highland Museum   MUSEUM
(☑ 01397-702169; www.westhighlandmuseum.org. uk; Cameron Sq; ⊙ 10am-2pm Tue-Fri) FREE This small but fascinating museum is packed with all manner of Highland memorabilia. Look out for the secret portrait of Bonnie Prince Charlie – after the Jacobite rebellions, all things Highland were banned, including pictures of the exiled leader, and this tiny painting looks like nothing more than a smear of paint until viewed in a cylindrical mirror, which reflects a credible likeness of the prince. In 2020 the museum operated with limited opening hours and an advance booking system.

☆ Activities

3 Wise Monkeys Climbing   CLIMBING
(☑ 01397-600200; www.threewisemonkeysclimbing.com; Fassifern Rd; 1-day climbing £10; ⊙ 10am-10pm Mon-Fri, to 6pm Sat & Sun; ⛹) When the weather on the mountains keeps you off the crags, you can keep your fingers in trim at this popular indoor climbing wall. Instruction is available. There's a cafe here too.

Crannog Cruises   WILDLIFE
(☑ 01397-700714; www.crannog.net/cruises; adult/child £17.50/8; ⊙ 11am, 1pm & 3pm Easter-Oct) Operates 1½-hour wildlife cruises on Loch Linnhe, visiting a seal colony and a salmon farm.

☆☆ Festivals & Events

UCI Mountain Bike World Cup   SPORTS
(www.fortwilliamworldcup.co.uk; ⊙ Jun) In June, Fort William pulls in crowds of more than 18,000 spectators for this World Cup downhill mountain-biking event. The gruelling downhill course is at nearby Nevis Range ski area.

▙ Sleeping

Fort William Backpackers   HOSTEL £
(☑ 01397-700711; www.fortwilliambackpackers.com; Alma Rd; dm/tw £21/50; P@⚪) A 10-minute walk from the bus and train stations, this lively and welcoming hostel is set in a grand Victorian villa, perched on a hillside with great views over Loch Linnhe.

6 Caberfeidh   B&B ££
(☑ 01397-703756; www.6caberfeidh.com; 6 Caberfeidh, Fassifern Rd; d/f £90/120; ⚪) Friendly owners and comfortable accommodation make a great combination; add a good central location and you're all set. Choose from one of two family rooms (one double and one single bed) or a romantic double with four-poster.

★ Grange   B&B £££
(☑ 01397-705516; www.grangefortwilliam.com; Grange Rd; d £195-225; ⊙ closed Sun; P⚪) An exceptional 19th-century villa set in its own landscaped grounds, the Grange is crammed with antiques and warmed by log fires. It has two luxury suites fitted with leather sofas, handcrafted furniture and roll-top baths, one situated in a charming self-contained cottage in the sprawling gardens, all with a view over Loch Linnhe. No children.

Lime Tree   HOTEL £££
(☑ 01397-701806; www.limetreefortwilliam.co.uk; Achintore Rd; d £155-175; P⚪) Much more interesting than your average guesthouse, this former Victorian manse overlooking Loch Linnhe is an 'art gallery with rooms', decorated throughout with the artist-owner's atmospheric Highland landscapes. Foodies rave about the restaurant (p336), and the gallery space – a triumph of sensitive design – stages everything from serious exhibitions (works by David Hockney and Andy Goldsworthy have appeared) to folk concerts.

Crolinnhe   B&B £££
(☑ 01397-703795; www.crolinnhe.co.uk; Grange Rd; d £170-200; ⊙ Easter-Oct; P⚪) This grand 19th-century villa enjoys a lochside location,

beautiful gardens and sumptuous accommodation – a welcome dose of luxury at the end of the West Highland Way. Breakfast porridge comes with cream and a wee jug of whisky.

✕ Eating & Drinking

Wildcat
VEGAN £

(www.wildcatcafe.co.uk; 21 High St; mains £4-9; ☉8am-5.30pm Wed-Sat; ☑) ✔ This vegan cafe serves sourdough sandwiches, salads, soups and brunches made with mainly local produce, as well as coffee and cakes. All the ingredients used – nut butters, curry pastes, pesto etc – are made from scratch in the cafe's kitchen. At the back is a small store selling Fair Trade, organic snacks and plastic-free produce by weight.

★ Lime Tree
SCOTTISH ££

(☑01397-701806; www.limetreefortwilliam.co.uk; Achintore Rd; mains £19-22.50, set menu £30; ☉6.30-9.30pm; ℗☎) ✔ The restaurant at this small hotel (p335) and art gallery has put the UK's Outdoor Capital on the gastronomic map. The chef turns out delicious dishes built around fresh Scottish produce, such as Loch Fyne oysters, Loch Awe trout and Ardnamurchan venison.

★ Crannog
Seafood Restaurant
SEAFOOD ££

(☑01397-705589; www.crannog.net; Town Pier; mains £10-22.50; ☉noon-9pm) The Crannog wins the prize for the best location in town – perched on the Town Pier, giving window-table diners an uninterrupted view down Loch Linnhe. Informal and unfussy, it specialises in fresh local fish (there are three or four daily fish specials plus the main menu) though there are lamb, venison and vegetarian dishes, too.

At research time Crannog Seafood was operating at Garrison West while the pier was closed for repairs.

Garrison West
PUB FOOD ££

(☑01397-701873; www.garrisonwest.co.uk; 4 Cameron Sq; mains £11-22.50; ☎☑) A warm and inviting pub with log fires, stone walls and dining tables in a bright, modern extension. The menu features excellent pub food – burgers, steaks, fish and chips – as well as a good selection of fresh local seafood, while the bar is well stocked with local whiskies, gins and beers.

Geographer
INTERNATIONAL ££

(☑01397-705011; www.geographerrestaurant. co.uk; 88 High St; mains lunch £5-10, dinner £10-21; ☉noon-2pm & 5-9.30pm Mon-Sat; ☎☑☑) This bright, modern restaurant takes its inspiration from the owner's travels with a menu that includes local ingredients – shellfish, beef, North Sea haddock – as well as dishes from around the globe, such as Mediterranean falafel, salad and hummus bowls and Southern US-style spiced chicken. There's also a selection of Scottish gins and bottled craft beers.

Black Isle Bar
BAR

(www.blackislebrewery.com; Gordon Sq; ☉bar noon-11pm, food noon-9pm; ☎☒) In a grand granite building that was once a church, this pub serves craft beers from the Black Isle Brewery (p304) as well as organic wine and local whisky. There are also wood-fired pizzas (£11.50 to £13) with Scottish toppings such as haggis and venison salami.

Grog & Gruel
PUB

(☑01397-705078; www.grogandgruel.co.uk; 66 High St; ☉noon-midnight; ☎) The Grog & Gruel is a traditional-style, wood-panelled pub with an excellent range of cask ales from regional Scottish and English microbreweries.

🔒 Shopping

★ Highland Bookshop
BOOKS

(www.highlandbookshop.com; 60 High St; ☉10am-5.30pm Mon-Sat, noon-4pm Sun) As well as a good selection of fiction and children's books, this shop stocks a superb range of outdoor-related books and maps covering climbing, walking, cycling, canoeing and other subjects. The upstairs lounge hosts regular literary events.

Highland Soap Co
BEAUTY

(www.highlandsoaps.com; 48 High St; ☉10am-6pm Mon-Sat, 11am-4pm Sun) This local company specialises in soaps made with natural ingredients using traditional cold-batch processes, as well as scented candles and other toiletries. In addition to the High St shop, a new visitor centre offering soap-making classes is scheduled to open in late 2020 in Inverlochy, 2 miles east of Fort William town centre.

ℹ Information

Fort William Tourist Office (☑01397-701801; www.visithighlands.com; 15 High St; ☉9am-4pm, longer hours Jun-Aug)

ⓘ Getting There & Away

BUS

Scottish Citylink (www.citylink.co.uk) buses link Fort William with other major towns and cities. Services include the following:

Edinburgh £39.40, 5¼ hours, three daily with a change at Glasgow; via Glencoe and Crianlarich

Glasgow £26.40, three hours, four daily

Inverness £11.60, two hours, six daily

Oban £9.40, 1½ hours, two daily

Portree £34.40, three hours, three daily

Shiel Buses (✆ 01397-700700; www.shiel-buses.co.uk) service 500 runs to Mallaig (£6.60, 1½ hours, four daily Monday to Friday, one daily Saturday) via Glenfinnan (£3.50, 30 minutes) and Arisaig (£5.70, one hour).

TRAIN

The spectacular West Highland line runs from Glasgow to Mallaig via Fort William. The overnight **Caledonian Sleeper** (www.sleeper.scot) service connects Fort William and London Euston (from £117 sharing a twin-berth cabin, 13 hours).

There's no direct rail connection between Oban and Fort William – you have to change at Crianlarich, so it's faster to use the bus. Rail services include the following:

Edinburgh £55.20, five hours; change at Glasgow's Queen St station, three daily, two on Sunday

Glasgow £32.70, 3¾ hours, three daily, two on Sunday

Mallaig £13.80, 1½ hours, four daily, three on Sunday

ⓘ Getting Around

BICYCLE

Offbeat Bikes (✆ 01397-704008; www.offbeatbikes.co.uk; 177 High St; bike hire per day adult/child from £30/18; ⊙ 10am-5pm Tue-Sat) Rents road, mountain and electronic bikes, and offers advice on local routes.

Nevis Cycles (✆ 01397-705555; www.nevis-cycles.com; cnr Montrose Ave & Locheil Rd, Inverlochy; per day from £35; ⊙ 9am-5pm) Located a half-mile northeast of the town centre, this place rents everything from hybrid bikes and mountain bikes to full-suspension downhill racers. Bikes can be hired here and dropped off in Inverness. Book in advance.

BUS

Shiel Buses route 41 links Fort William with Nevis Range (£2.70, 20 minutes) and Glen Nevis (£2.20, 15 minutes).

DON'T MISS

COMMANDO MEMORIAL

Near Spean Bridge, at the junction of the B8004 and A82, 2.5 miles east of Gairlochy, stands the **Commando Memorial** (P), which commemorates the WWII special forces soldiers who trained in this area.

The Commandos were an elite unit of the British armed forces, formed in 1940 to carry out raids behind enemy lines in German-occupied Europe. In 1942 a centre was set up at Achnacarry, 6 miles west of Spean Bridge, where Commando units were trained in secrecy. This memorial was erected in 1952, in a glorious setting with superb views of Ben Nevis and its neighbouring mountains.

CAR

Fort William is 146 miles from Edinburgh, 104 miles from Glasgow and 66 miles from Inverness. The tourist office has listings of car-hire companies.

Easydrive Car Hire (✆ 01397-701616; www.easydrivescotland.co.uk; North Rd; ⊙ 8am-5.30pm Mon-Fri, to 5pm Sat, to 4pm Sun) Hires out small cars from £65/280 a day/week.

Around Fort William

Glen Nevis

Scenic Glen Nevis, used as a filming location for *Braveheart* and the *Harry Potter* movies, lies just an hour's walk from Fort William town centre. The **Glen Nevis Tourist Office** (✆ 01349-781401; parking £4; ⊙ 8.30am-4pm, longer hours Jul & Aug) is situated 1.5 miles up the glen, and provides information on hiking, weather forecasts, and specific advice on climbing Ben Nevis (p338).

From the Glen Nevis Visitor Centre, the road follows the river up the glen for 5 miles to reach a car park, where the road ends. This is the starting point for an excellent 1.5-mile walk through the spectacular, verdant Nevis Gorge valley to **Steall Falls**, a 100m-high bridal-veil waterfall. You can reach the foot of the falls by crossing the river on a wobbly, three-cable wire bridge – one cable for your feet and one for each hand – which is a real test of balance!

CLIMBING BEN NEVIS

As the highest peak in the British Isles, Ben Nevis (1345m) attracts many would-be ascensionists who would not normally think of climbing a Scottish mountain – a staggering (often literally) 100,000 people reach the summit each year.

Although anyone who is reasonably fit should have no problem climbing Ben Nevis on a fine summer's day, an ascent should not be undertaken lightly; every year people have to be rescued from the mountain. You will need proper walking boots (the path is rough and stony, and there may be snow on the summit), warm clothing, waterproofs, a map and compass, and plenty of food and water. And don't forget to check the weather forecast.

Here are a few facts to mull over before you go racing up the tourist track: the summit plateau is bounded by 700m-high cliffs and has a sub-Arctic climate; at the summit it can snow on any day of the year; the summit is wrapped in cloud nine days out of 10; in thick cloud, visibility at the summit can be 10m or less; and in such conditions the only safe way off the mountain requires careful use of a map and compass to avoid walking over those 700m cliffs.

The tourist track (the easiest route to the top) was originally called the Pony Track. It was built in the 19th century for the pack ponies that carried supplies to a meteorological observatory on the summit (now in ruins), which was in use continuously from 1883 to 1904.

There are three possible starting points for the tourist track ascent: Achintee Farm; the footbridge at Glen Nevis Youth Hostel; and, if you have a car, the car park at Glen Nevis Tourist Office (p337). The path climbs gradually to the shoulder at Lochan Meall an t-Suidhe (known as the Halfway Lochan), then zigzags steeply up beside the Red Burn to the summit plateau. The highest point is marked by a trig point on top of a huge cairn beside the ruins of the old observatory. The plateau is scattered with countless smaller cairns, stones arranged in the shape of people's names and, sadly, a fair bit of litter.

The total distance to the summit and back is 8 miles; allow at least four or five hours to reach the top, and another 2½ to three hours for the descent. Afterwards, as you celebrate in the pub with a pint, consider the fact that the record time for the annual Ben Nevis Hill Race is just under 1½ hours – up and down. Then have another pint.

🛏 Sleeping & Eating

★ Glen Nevis Youth Hostel
HOSTEL £

(HS; 📞 01397-702336; www.hostellingscotland. org.uk; tw/q £50/70; 🅿 @ 🛜) A modern, well-equipped hostel located 3 miles from Fort William, right beside one of the starting points for the tourist track up Ben Nevis. Breakfasts (£4.50) and packed lunches (£6.50) are available, and the small shop at reception sells local craft beers and snacks. In 2020 only private rooms were available (no shared dorms).

Glen Nevis
Caravan & Camping Park
CAMPSITE £

(📞 01397-702191; www.glen-nevis.co.uk; tent sites per person £10.50, campervan from £25; 🕗 mid-Mar–Nov; 🛜) This big, well-equipped site is a popular base camp for Ben Nevis and the surrounding mountains. The site is 2.5 miles from Fort William, along the Glen Nevis road. Advance booking required.

Achintee Farm
B&B ££

(📞 01397-702240; www.achinteefarm.com; Achintee; B&B d £115-135, self-catering tw/d from £56/90; 🕗 B&B May-Oct, self-catering year-round; 🅿 🛜) This attractive farmhouse offers excellent B&B accommodation and also has a small self-catered apartment attached. It's at the start of the path up Ben Nevis.

★ Ben Nevis Inn
SCOTTISH ££

(📞 01397-701227; www.ben-nevis-inn.co.uk; Achintee; mains £12-14.50; 🕗 noon-11pm Mar-Oct, Thu-Sun only Nov-Feb; 🅿 🛜 ♿) This great barn of a pub serves real ale and tasty bar meals (noon to 9pm), and has a comfy bunkhouse downstairs (£18 to £20 per person). It's at the start of the path from Achintee up Ben Nevis, and only a mile from the end of the West Highland Way.

ℹ Getting There & Away

Bus 41 runs from Fort William bus station to Glen Nevis Youth Hostel (£2.20, 15 minutes, two daily Monday to Saturday).

Neptune's Staircase

Three miles north of Fort William, at Banavie, is Neptune's Staircase, an impressive flight of eight locks that allows boats to climb 20m to the main reach of the Caledonian Canal (p333). The B8004 road runs along the west side of the canal to Gairlochy at the south end of Loch Lochy, offering superb views of Ben Nevis; the **canal towpath** on the east side makes a great walk or bike ride (6.5 miles).

Nevis Range

Six miles to the north of Fort William lies **Nevis Range ski area** (☑ 01397-705825; www.nevisrange.co.uk; gondola day ticket adult/child £19.50/11; ⊙ 9.30am-4pm Thu-Mon), where a gondola gives access to the upper part of Aonach Mor mountain (1221m). At the top there's a restaurant and a couple of hiking trails through nearby Leanachan Forest. The facility operates year-round, allowing visitors to access mountain paths and downhill mountain-biking trails outside of the ski season.

The gondola takes 15 minutes each way; tickets are valid for multiple trips. During the ski season a one-day lift pass costs £35.50/23.50 per adult/child.

Shiel Buses (p337) route 41 runs from Fort William bus station to Nevis Range (£2.70, 25 minutes, four daily Monday to Saturday).

Nevis Range
Downhill & Witch's Trails   MOUNTAIN BIKING

(☑ 01397-705825; www.nevisrange.co.uk/bike; single/multitrip ticket £20.50/33.50; ⊙ downhill course 10.15am-3.45pm Apr-Oct, forest trails 24hr year-round) Nevis Range ski area has a world championship downhill mountain-bike trail – for experienced riders only. Bikes are carried up on the gondola cabin. There's also a 4-mile XC red trail that begins at the ski area's Snowgoose restaurant, and the Witch's Trails – 25 miles of waymarked forest road and single-track, including a 5-mile world championship loop, in the nearby forest.

Mountain-bike hire is available on-site from **Nevis Cycles** (☑ 01397-705555; www.neviscycles.com; full-suspension bike per day from £65; ⊙ 9am-7.30pm Mar-Oct); advance booking advised.

Ardnamurchan

Ten miles south of Fort William, the Corran Ferry makes the short crossing to Ardgour. The drive (or cycle) from here to **Ardnamurchan Point**, the most westerly point on the British mainland, is one of the most beautiful in the western Highlands, especially in late spring and early summer when much of the narrow, twisting road is lined with the bright pink and purple blooms of rhododendrons.

The road clings to the northern shore of Loch Sunart, going through the pretty villages of **Strontian** – which gave its name to the element strontium, first discovered in ore from nearby lead mines in 1790 – and **Salen**.

The mostly single-track road from Salen to Ardnamurchan Point is only 25 miles long, but it'll take you 1½ hours each way. It's a dipping, twisting, low-speed roller coaster of a ride through sun-dappled native woodlands draped with lichen and fern. Just when you're getting used to the views of Morvern and Mull to the south, it makes a quick detour to the north for a panorama over the islands of Rum and Eigg.

⊙ Sights

Ardnamurchan Lighthouse   LIGHTHOUSE
(☑ 01972-510210; www.ardnamurchanlighthouse.com; Ardnamurchan Point; ⊙ 10am-5pm Apr-Oct; P ♿) The final 6 miles of road from Kilchoan to Ardnamurchan Point end at this 36m-high, grey granite tower, built in 1849 by the 'Lighthouse Stevensons' – family of Robert Louis – on the westernmost point of the British mainland. There's a tearoom, and the visitor centre (closed due to social distancing requirements in 2020) will tell you more than you'll ever need to know about lighthouses. The main attraction here is the expansive view over the ocean.

Ardnamurchan Natural
History & Visitor Centre   MUSEUM
(☑ 01972-500209; www.ardnamurchannaturalhistorycentre.com; Glenmore; ⊙ 8.30am-5pm Sun-Fri; ♿) **FREE** This fascinating centre – midway between Salen and Kilchoan – was originally devised by a wildlife photographer and tries to bring you face to face with the flora and fauna of the Ardnamurchan peninsula. The Living Building exhibit is designed to attract local wildlife, with a mammal den that is occasionally occupied by hedgehogs or pine martens, an owl nest-box, a mouse nest and

a pond. There's also a good **cafe** (🕽01972-500209; mains £6-10.50; ⊙8.30am-4.30pm Sun-Fri; P🛜♿) here.

🛏 Sleeping & Eating

Ardnamurchan Campsite   CAMPSITE £
(🕽01972-510766; www.ardnamurchanstudycentre.co.uk; Kilchoan; sites per adult/child £10/5; ⊙Mar-Oct; 🛜🐾) Basic but beautifully situated campsite, with the chance of seeing otters from your tent. It's along the Ormsaig road, 2 miles west of Kilchoan village.

Ard Daraich   COTTAGE ££
(🕽01855-841384; www.ardgour-selfcatering.co.uk; Sallachan, Ardgour; studio 3 nights £420; P🛜🐾) 🐾 About 3 miles southwest of Corran Ferry, this handsome West Highland house once belonged to florist Constance Spry (who arranged flowers for Queen Elizabeth II's coronation), and is set in beautiful gardens filled with rhododendrons, azaleas and heathers; there's a chance of seeing otters and pine martens nearby. Let as a two-person garden studio, and five-person cottage.

Salen Hotel   INN ££
(🕽01967-431661; www.salenhotel.co.uk; Salen; d £100-120; P🛜🐾) A traditional Highland inn with views over Loch Sunart, the Salen Hotel has three rooms in the pub (two with sea views). The cosy lounge has a roaring fire and comfy sofa, and the bar meals, including fish and chips, steak and pizzas, are very good (mains £10.50 to £18.50).

❶ Getting There & Away

Shiel Buses (p337) service 506 runs from Fort William to Acharacle, Salen and Kilchoan (£8.30, 2½ hours, one daily Monday to Saturday) via **Corran Ferry** (www.lochabertransport.org.uk; car £8.80, bicycle & foot passenger free; ⊙ every 20-30min, 6.30am-9.30pm Mon-Sat, 8.30am-9.30pm Sun). There's a car ferry between Kilchoan and Tobermory on the Isle of Mull.

Road to the Isles

The 46-mile A830 road from Fort William to Mallaig is traditionally known as the Road to the Isles, as it leads to the jumping-off point for ferries to the Small Isles and Skye, itself a stepping stone to the Outer Hebrides. This is a region steeped in Jacobite history, having witnessed both the beginning and the end of Bonnie Prince Charlie's doomed attempt to regain the British throne in 1745–46.

The final section of this scenic route, between Arisaig and Mallaig, has been upgraded to a fast straight road; the scenic old road is signposted 'Alternative Coastal Route'.

Between the A830 and the A87 far to the north lie Knoydart and Glenelg – Scotland's 'Empty Quarter'.

❶ Getting There & Around

Shiel Buses (p337) service 500 runs from Fort William to Mallaig (£6.60, 1½ hours, four daily Monday to Friday, one on Saturday) via Glenfinnan (£4.10, 30 minutes), Arisaig (£5.70, one hour) and Morar (£6.20, 1¼ hours).

The Fort William–Mallaig railway line has four trains a day (three on Sunday), with stops at many points along the way, including Corpach, Glenfinnan, Lochailort, Arisaig and Morar.

Glenfinnan

🕽01397 / POP 100

Glenfinnan is hallowed ground for fans of Bonnie Prince Charlie; the monument here marks where he raised his Highland army. It's also a place of pilgrimage for steam train enthusiasts and *Harry Potter* fans – the famous railway viaduct features in the *Potter* films, and is regularly traversed by the Jacobite Steam Train (p335).

◉ Sights & Activities

Glenfinnan Monument   MONUMENT
(NTS; www.nts.org.uk; parking £3) This tall column, topped by a statue of a kilted Highlander, was erected in 1815 on the spot where Bonnie Prince Charlie first raised his standard and rallied the Jacobite clans on 19 August 1745, marking the start of his ill-fated campaign, which would end in disaster at Culloden 14 months later. The setting, at the north end of Loch Shiel, is hauntingly beautiful. It's possible to climb the monument on a prebooked tour (adult/child £4/3); check times online.

The **visitor centre** (NTS; www.nts.org.uk; parking £3; ⊙9.30am-4.30pm; P) FREE here recounts the story of the '45, as the Jacobite rebellion of 1745 is known, when Bonnie Prince Charlie's loyal clansmen marched and fought their way from Glenfinnan south via Edinburgh to Derby, then back north to final defeat at Culloden.

Glenfinnan Station Museum　MUSEUM
(www.glenfinnanstationmuseum.co.uk; admission by donation; ⊙9am-5pm Easter-Oct; P) This fascinating little museum records the epic tale of building the West Highland railway line. The famous 21-arch **Glenfinnan viaduct**, just east of the station, was built in 1901, and featured in several *Harry Potter* movies. A pleasant walk of around 1200m east from the station (signposted) leads to a viewpoint for the viaduct and for Loch Shiel.

Loch Shiel Cruises　CRUISE
(📋07801 537617; www.highlandcruises.co.uk; 1hr cruise adult/child £15/7.50; ⊙Apr-Sep) Boat trips along Loch Shiel, with the opportunity of spotting golden eagles and other wildlife. There are one- to two-hour cruises offering fabulous views. Twice a week the boat goes the full length of the loch to Acharacle (one way/return £23/35), calling at Polloch and Dalilea, allowing for walks and bike rides using the forestry track on the eastern shore.

The boat departs from a jetty near Glenfinnan House Hotel.

🛏 Sleeping & Eating

Prince's House Hotel　INN **£££**
(📋01397-722246; www.glenfinnan.co.uk; s/d from £115/190; P🖵) A delightful old coaching inn dating from 1658, the Prince's House is a great place to pamper yourself – ask for the spacious, tartan-draped Stuart Room (£250), complete with four-poster bed, if you want to stay in the oldest part of the hotel. The relaxed but well-regarded restaurant specialises in Scottish produce; there's also a more casual bistro.

There's no documented evidence that Bonnie Prince Charlie actually stayed here in 1745, but it was the only sizeable house in Glenfinnan at that time, so...

Arisaig & Morar

The 5 miles of coast between the tiny villages of Arisaig and Morar is a fretwork of rocky islets, inlets and gorgeous silver-sand beaches backed by dunes and machair, with stunning sunset views across the sea to the silhouetted peaks of Eigg and Rum. The **Silver Sands of Morar**, as they are known, draw crowds of bucket-and-spade holidaymakers in July and August, when the many campsites scattered along the coast are filled to overflowing.

🏃 Activities

Arisaig Marine　WILDLIFE WATCHING
(📋01687-450224; www.arisaig.co.uk; Arisaig Harbour; ⊙late Apr-Sep) In summer Arisaig Marine operates wildlife-watching cruises (minke whales, basking sharks, porpoises, dolphins) from Arisaig harbour to Eigg (£18, one hour, six weekly), Rum (£25, 2½ hours, two or three weekly) and Muck (£20, two hours, three weekly). Sailing times allow five hours ashore on Eigg, and two or three hours on Muck or Rum.

There are also twice-weekly three-hour scenic boat trips (£22.50) that return to Arisaig harbour without docking elsewhere. In 2020 there were no boat trips to the Small Isles, which were closed to tourists.

🛏 Sleeping & Eating

Camusdarach Campsite　CAMPSITE **£**
(📋01687-450221; www.camusdarach.co.uk; Arisaig; tent/campervan sites £15/25, plus per person £5, glamping pods £60; ⊙Apr-Oct; 🖵🌂) 🅿 A small and nicely landscaped site with good facilities, only three minutes' walk from beautiful Camusdarach Beach via a gate in the northwest corner. It's popular so be sure to book in advance.

Old Library Lodge
& Restaurant　SCOTTISH **££**
(📋01687-450651; www.oldlibrary.co.uk; Arisaig; mains £10.50-17; ⊙noon-2pm & 6-8.30pm; P🖵) The Old Library is a charming restaurant with rooms (doubles £120) set in converted 200-year-old stables overlooking the waterfront in Arisaig village. The lunch menu concentrates on soups, burgers and smoked fish or meat platters, while dinner is a more sophisticated affair offering local seafood, beef and lamb.

Mallaig

📋01687 / POP 810
If you're travelling between Fort William and Skye, you may find yourself staying overnight in the bustling fishing and ferry port of Mallaig (*mahl*-ig). Indeed, it makes a good base for a series of day trips by ferry to the Small Isles and Knoydart.

Mallaig has a post office, a bank with an ATM and a co-op supermarket.

◉ Sights & Activities

Mallaig Heritage Centre　MUSEUM
(📋01687-462085; www.mallaigheritage.org.uk; Station Rd; adult/child £2.50/free; ⊙11am-5pm

WORTH A TRIP

GLENUIG INN

Set on a peaceful bay, halfway between Lochailort and Acharacle on the A861, the **Glenuig Inn** ([☎]01687-470219; www.glenuig.com; Glenuig; s/d/tr/q £85/130/170/200; [P][🖦][🐕]) [🏊] is a great place to get away from it all. As well as offering comfortable accommodation, good food (mains £13 to £19, served noon to 9pm) and real ale on tap, it's a great base for exploring Arisaig, Morar and the Loch Shiel area.

The inn runs on 100% renewable energy (even the wood-burners in the bar use local waste wood) and the bar is stocked with Scottish spirits from independent distilleries.

The owner offers guided **sea-kayaking trips** along the wild and beautiful coastline (www.seakayakarisaig.co.uk; per day adult/child £95/65).

Mon-Sun) The village's rainy-day attractions are limited to this heritage centre, which covers the archaeology and history of the region, including the heart-rending tale of the Highland Clearances in Knoydart.

Wildlife Boat Trips   CRUISE
(www.westernislescruises.co.uk; Mallaig Harbour; adult/child £13/6.50; [⊙]12.45pm & 5pm Apr-Oct; [👶][🐕]) These one-hour wildlife-spotting trips offer the chance to sight seals, porpoises, dolphins, whales and basking sharks, as well as seabirds. Sailings are timed to fit with the Jacobite Steam Train (p335) and Scotrail services from Fort William.

[🛏️] Sleeping & Eating

Seaview Guest House   B&B ££
([☎]01687-462059; www.seaviewguesthousemallaig.com; Main St; s/d £65/90, cottage per week £600; [P][🖦]) This comfortable B&B has grand views over the harbour, not only from the upstairs bedrooms but from the breakfast room, too. There's also a cute little cottage next door that offers self-catering accommodation (www.selfcateringmallaig.com; one double and one twin room).

Springbank Guest House   B&B ££
([☎]01687-462459; www.springbank-mallaig.co.uk; East Bay; d £90-95; [🖦]) The Springbank is a traditional West Highland house with four

homely guest bedrooms, with superb views across the harbour to the Cuillin of Skye.

Jaffy's   FISH & CHIPS £
(www.jaffys.co.uk; Station Rd; mains £4-8; [⊙]noon-2pm & 4.30-7.30pm Mon-Sat) [🏊] Owned by a third-generation fish merchant's family, Mallaig's chippy serves superbly fresh fish and chips, as well as kippers, prawns and other seafood.

[★]**Cabin**   SEAFOOD ££
([☎]01687-462207; Davies Brae; mains £5.50-18; [⊙]noon-7.30pm) The lobster, langoustines and calamari served at this fabulous family-run restaurant and takeaway might have been caught that day by your server's father. Local haddock, monkfish and scallops also feature on the menu, served with homemade aioli, salad and chips.

[ℹ️] Getting There & Away

BOAT

A passenger ferry operated by Western Isles Cruises links Mallaig to Inverie on the Knoydart Peninsula (25 to 40 minutes) four times daily Monday to Saturday (three on Sunday) from April to October.

CalMac ([☎]0800 066 5000; www.calmac.co.uk) operates the passenger-only ferry from Mallaig to the following destinations in the Small Isles:

Canna £11.20 return, two hours, three weekly

Eigg £8.20 return, 1¼ hours, three weekly

Muck £9.50 return, 1½ hours, four weekly

Rum £8.90 return, 1¼ hours, four weekly

There are CalMac car ferry services to Armadale in Skye (car/passenger £9.95/3, 30 minutes, five daily Monday to Saturday, three on Sunday), and Lochboisdale in South Uist (car/passenger £59.05/10.75, 3½ hours, one daily).

BUS

Shiel Buses (p337) service 500 runs between Fort William and Mallaig (£6.60, 1½ hours, four daily Monday to Friday, one daily Saturday and Sunday) via Arisaig (£2.80, 25 minutes) and Glenfinnan (£4.10, 55 minutes).

TRAIN

The West Highland line runs between Fort William and Mallaig (£13.80, 1½ hours, four daily, three on Sunday).

Knoydart

[☎]01687 / POP 110

The Knoydart peninsula – a rugged landscape of wild mountains and lonely sea lochs – is the only sizeable area in Britain that remains inaccessible to the motor car, cut off by miles of rough country and the embracing arms of Lochs Nevis and Hourn (Gaelic for the Lochs of Heaven and Hell). Walkers come to climb the 1020m peak of **Ladhar Bheinn** (laar-ven), but it's worth visiting just to enjoy the feeling of remoteness.

No road penetrates this wilderness of rugged hills – **Inverie**, its sole village, can only be reached by ferry from Mallaig, or on foot from the remote road's end at Kinloch Hourn (a tough 16-mile hike that affords walk-in bragging rights). A 4WD track leads northwest from Inverie for 7 miles to the outposts of **Doune** and **Airor**, which offer even more remote accommodation options.

🛏 Sleeping & Eating

Inverie has a pub and tearoom, and there's a small community shop (www.knoydart shop.org) stocked with canned and dry goods. Opposite the shop is the **Table** (www. facebook.com/thetableknoydart), a wooden shed with a fire pit, disco ball and seating area that was set up by the community as a social space for people to gather for a drink and a chat.

All accommodation is listed on www.visit-knoydart.co.uk.

Knoydart Foundation Bunkhouse   HOSTEL £
(✆ 01687-462163; www.knoydart-foundation. com; Inverie; 1-week 1-6 people £600; @ 🖥) 🏊
A 15-minute walk east of Inverie ferry pier, this is a cosy hostel with wood-burning stove, kitchen and drying room. In 2020 the bunkhouse could only be rented by one group at a time.

Long Beach Campsite   CAMPSITE £
(✆ 01687-462242; www.knoydart-foundation.com; Inverie; per person £5) A basic but beautiful campsite, a 10-minute walk east of the ferry; there's a water supply, fire pits and composting toilet, but no showers. Firewood is available for £5 a bundle. Pay online or at the village shop.

★ **Old Forge**   PUB FOOD ££
(✆ 01687-462267; www.theoldforge.co.uk; Inverie; mains £16-24; ⏰ kitchen 12.30-2.30pm & 5.30-9pm Thu-Tue Mar-Oct; 🖥🚗) The Old Forge is listed in *Guinness World Records* as Britain's most remote pub. It's surprisingly sophisticated – there's real ale on tap, including the Belgian owner's own brew, Remoteness, as

well as an Italian coffee machine. The house special is a seafood platter (£38); all ingredients are sourced within 7 miles of the pub.

In the evening you can sit by the fire, pint of beer in hand and join the *ceilidh* (an evening of traditional Scottish entertainment including music, song and dance) that seems to take place just about nightly (in pre-coronavirus times, at least).

There's also a shower here (with a hair-dryer) that can be used for £4.

ℹ Getting There & Away

Western Isles Cruises (✆ 01687-462233; www.westernislescruises.co.uk; Mallaig to Knoydart adult/child £11/5.50) Passenger ferry linking Mallaig to Inverie (25 to 40 minutes) four times daily Monday to Saturday and three on Sunday from April to October. Taking the morning boat gives you up to 10 hours ashore in Knoydart before the return trip (first and last boats of the day should be booked in advance). There's also an afternoon sailing between Inverie and Tarbet on the south side of Loch Nevis, allowing walkers to hike along the northern shore of Loch Morar to Tarbet and return by boat (£10 Inverie–Tarbet–Inverie).

SMALL ISLES

The scattered jewels of the Small Isles – Rum, Eigg, Muck and Canna – lie strewn across the silvery-blue Cuillin Sound to the south of Skye. Their distinctive outlines enliven the glorious views from the beaches of Arisaig and Morar.

Rum is the biggest and boldest of the four, a miniature Skye of pointed peaks and dramatic sunset silhouettes. Eigg is the most pastoral and populous, dominated by the miniature sugarloaf mountain of the Sgurr. Muck is a botanist's delight with its wildflowers and unusual alpine plants, and Canna is a craggy bird sanctuary made of magnetic rocks.

If your time is limited and you can only visit one island, choose Eigg or Rum; they have the most to offer on a day trip.

During the 2020 pandemic, the island communities requested that tourists didn't visit; all attractions and all but a handful of self-catering accommodations remained closed.

ℹ Getting There & Away

The main ferry operator is CalMac, which runs the passenger-only ferry from Mallaig.

Canna £11.20 return, two hours, three weekly
Eigg £8.20 return, 1¼ hours, three weekly
Muck £9.50 return, 1½ hours, four weekly

INVERNESS & THE CENTRAL HIGHLANDS KNOYDART

Rum £8.90 return, 1¼ hours, four weekly

You can also hop between the islands without returning to Mallaig, but the timetable is complicated and it requires a bit of planning. Bicycles are carried for free.

Arisaig Marine (p341) runs wildlife watching trips from Arisaig to Eigg, Muck and Rum. Sailing times allow five hours ashore on Eigg, and two or three hours on Muck or Rum.

Rum

☑ 01687 / POP 22

The Isle of Rum (www.isleofrum.com) – the biggest and most spectacular of the Small Isles – was once known as the Forbidden Island. Cleared of its crofters in the early 19th century to make way for sheep, from 1888 to 1957 it was the private sporting estate of the Bulloughs, a Lancashire family who made their fortune in the textile industry. Curious outsiders who ventured too close were liable to find themselves staring down the wrong end of a gamekeeper's shotgun.

The island was sold to the Nature Conservancy in 1957 and has since been a wildlife reserve with deer, wild goats, ponies, golden and white-tailed eagles, and a 120,000-strong colony of Manx shearwaters. Its dramatic, rocky mountains, known as the Rum Cuillin for their similarity to the peaks on neighbouring Skye, draw hill walkers and climbers.

Kinloch, with ferry landing, shop, post office and public telephone, is the island's only settlement.

◉ Sights & Activities

There's some great coastal and mountain walking on the island, including a couple of easy, waymarked nature trails in the woods around Kinloch. The first path on the left after leaving the pier leads to an **otter hide** (signposted).

The climb to the island's highest point, **Askival** (812m), is a strenuous hike and involves a bit of rock scrambling (allow six hours for the round trip from Kinloch).

★**Kinloch Castle**   CASTLE
(☑ 01687-462037; www.isleofrum.com; adult/child £9/4.50; ⊙ guided tours Mon-Sat Apr-Oct, to coincide with ferry times) When George Bullough, a dashing, Harrow-educated cavalry officer, inherited Rum along with half his father's fortune in 1891, he became one of the wealthiest bachelors in Britain. Bullough blew half his inheritance on building his dream bachelor pad – the ostentatious Kinloch Castle. Since the Bulloughs left, the castle has survived as a perfect time capsule of upper-class Edwardian eccentricity – the guided tour should not be missed. Castle tours were not available in 2020.

🛏 Sleeping & Eating

Accommodation on Rum is strictly limited – there is only one B&B, the **campsite** (www.is leofrum.com; sites per adult/child £6/3, cabins from £35; ☀) and a beautiful, Scandinavian-style timber **bunkhouse** (☑ 01687-460318; www. isleofrum.com; Kinloch; dm/tw £23/50; ☎) that overlooks the sea. Booking is essential, except for campers. There are also two bothies (unlocked cottages with no facilities, for the use of hikers) on the island, and wild camping is permitted.

Bring plenty of food supplies, as there is only one **tearoom** (www.kimskitchen.scot; Kinloch; mains £12-15, 3 courses £25-31; ⊙ 10am-4pm & 6-7.30pm Mon-Sat Apr-Sep; ☎) – in the village hall; evening meals must be booked in advance – and the grocery **shop** (☑ 01687-460328; ⊙ 5-8pm, also 10am-noon on ferry days) opening times are limited.

Eigg

☑ 01687 / POP 83

The island of Eigg (www.isleofeigg.org) made history in 1997 when it became the first Highland estate to be bought out by its inhabitants. The island is now owned and managed by the Isle of Eigg Heritage Trust, a partnership among the islanders, Highland Council and the Scottish Wildlife Trust.

It takes its name from the Old Norse *egg* (meaning 'edge'), a reference to the **Sgurr of Eigg** (393m), an impressive mini-mountain that towers over **Galmisdale**, the main settlement. Ringed by vertical cliffs on three sides, it's composed of pitchstone lava with columnar jointing similar to that seen on the Isle of Staffa and at the Giant's Causeway in Northern Ireland.

The climb to the summit of the Sgurr of Eigg (4.5 miles round trip; allow three to four hours) affords magnificent views – Rum and Skye to the north, Muck and Coll to the south, Ardnamurchan Lighthouse to the southeast and Ben Nevis shouldering above the eastern horizon. Take binoculars – there's a good chance of seeing minke whales feeding down below in the Sound of Muck. A shorter walk (2 miles; allow 1½ hours round trip, and bring a torch) leads west from the pier to the spooky and claustrophobic **Uamh Fraing** (Massacre Cave).

🛏 Sleeping & Eating

Sleeping options include **Eigg Organics** (01687-482480; www.eiggorganics.co.uk; Cleadale; tent sites per person £7, yurt £60-70, bothy £60-70; 🕾) campsite, where there is accommodation for two in a Mongolian yurt, and **Glebe Barn** (01687-315099; www.glebebarn. co.uk; Galmisdale; dm/tw £21/47; ⊘ Mar-Nov; 🕾). Wild camping is allowed. For a full listing of accommodation, see www.isleofeigg.org.

Eating out is limited to **Galmisdale Bay** (01687-482487; www.galmisdale-bay.com; The Pier, Galmisdale; sandwiches £3-5, mains £10.50-13.50; ⊘ check website, closed Wed & Sun) 🍴 and the restaurant at **Lageorna B&B** (01687-460081; www.lageorna.com; Cleadale; s/d £85/110, 3-course dinner £30; 🕾) 🍴, which must be booked in advance.

Canna

01687 / POP 12

The island of Canna (www.theisleofcanna. com) is a moorland plateau of black basalt rock, just 5 miles long and 1.25 miles wide; it was given to the National Trust for Scotland in 1981 by its owner, the Gaelic scholar and author John Lorne Campbell.

The ferry arrives at the hamlet of **A'Chill** at the eastern end of the island, where visiting sailors have left extensive graffiti on the rock face south of the harbour. There's a tearoom and craft shop by the harbour, and a tiny post office in a hut. There is no mobile-phone reception.

You can walk to **An Coroghon**, just east of the ferry pier, a medieval stone tower perched atop a sea cliff, and continue to **Compass Hill** (143m), which contains enough magnetite (an iron oxide mineral) to deflect the navigation compasses in passing yachts, or take a longer hike along the southern shore past **Canna House** (the former home of John Lorne Campbell) and an ornately decorated **early Christian stone cross**.

Facilities are limited. **Tighard** (01687-462474; www.tighard.com; tw/d £90/110; 🕾🕾) is the only B&B, while **Canna Campsite** (01687-462477; www.cannacampsite.com; tent sites £12, pods £35-40, caravans £50; 🕾) has tent pitches and glamping pods.

The only restaurant is **Cafe Canna** (01687-482488; www.cafecanna.co.uk; mains £14-17; ⊘ 11am-10pm Wed-Mon May-Sep; 🕾) 🍴, serving local fish, seafood and wild rabbit stew (booking recommended).

Muck

01687 / POP 27

The tiny island of Muck (www.isleofmuck. com), measuring just 2 miles by 1 mile, has exceptionally fertile soil, and the island is carpeted with wildflowers in spring and early summer. It takes its name from the Gaelic *muc* (pig), and pigs are still raised here.

Ferries call at the southern settlement of **Port Mor**. There's a tearoom and craft shop above the pier, which also acts as a tourist office.

It's an easy 15-minute walk along the island's only road from the pier to the sandy beach at **Gallanach** on the northern side of the island. A longer and rougher hike (3.5 miles; 1½ hours round trip) goes to the top of **Beinn Airein** (137m) for the best views. Puffins nest on the cliffs at the western end of Camas Mor, the bay to the south of the hill.

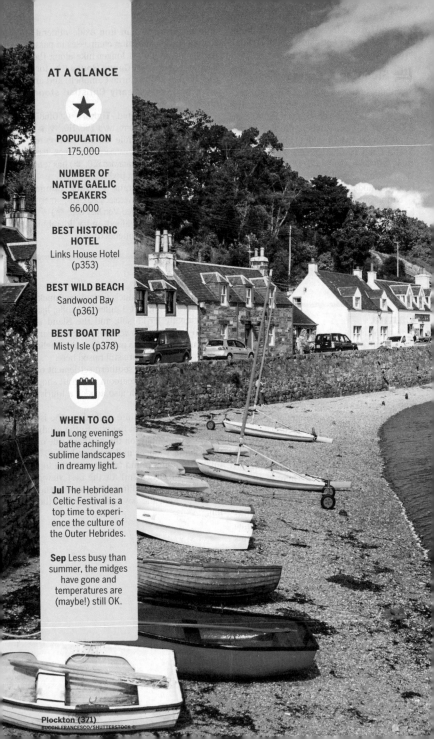

POPULATION
175,000

**NUMBER OF
NATIVE GAELIC
SPEAKERS**
66,000

**BEST HISTORIC
HOTEL**
Links House Hotel
(p353)

BEST WILD BEACH
Sandwood Bay
(p361)

BEST BOAT TRIP
Misty Isle (p378)

WHEN TO GO

Jun Long evenings
bathe achingly
sublime landscapes
in dreamy light.

Jul The Hebridean
Celtic Festival is a
top time to experi-
ence the culture of
the Outer Hebrides.

Sep Less busy than
summer, the midges
have gone and
temperatures are
(maybe!) still OK.

Plockton (371)
BUCCHI FRANCESCO/SHUTTERSTOCK ©

Northern Highlands & Islands

Swirling mist and looming mountains, naked rock and wind-raked water – Scotland's vast and melancholy soul is here: an epic land with a stark beauty that imprints itself on the hearts of those who journey through it.

The chambered cairns of Caithness and the stone circles of the Western Isles are testament to the skills of prehistoric builders; cragtop castles and the broken walls of abandoned crofts tell of the Highlands' turbulent history.

Outdoors is the place to be; there's nothing like comparing windburn or mud-ruined boots beside the crackling fire of a Highland pub. The landscape lends itself to activity, from woodland strolls to thrilling mountain-bike descents, from sea kayaking to Munro bagging. Best are the locals, big-hearted and straight-talking; make it your business to get to know them.

Northern Highlands & Islands Highlights

1 St Kilda (p392) Taking a white-knuckle boat trip to these spectacular islands, the remotest part of the British Isles.

2 Ullapool (p364) Gorging on fresh, succulent seafood in this delightful town with its picture-perfect harbour.

3 Harris (p388) Dipping your toes in the water at some of the world's most beautiful beaches in the Western Isles.

4 Cuillin Hills (p379) Shouldering the challenge of these hills, with their rugged silhouettes brooding over the skyscape of Skye.

5 Far Northwest (p361) Picking your jaw up off the ground as you marvel at the epic Highland scenery.

6 Cape Wrath (p363) Riding the ferry out to Britain's gloriously remote northwestern shoulder.

7 Plockton (p371) Relaxing in a postcard-pretty village where the Highlands meet the Caribbean.

8 Strathnaver (p360) Learning the sad history of the Highland Clearances on the Strathnaver Trail.

EAST COAST

In both landscape and character, the east coast is where the real barrenness of the Highlands begins to unfold. A gentle splendour and a sense of escapism mark the route along the twisting A9, as it heads north for the last of Scotland's far-flung, mainland population outposts. With only a few exceptions the tourism frenzy is left behind once the road traverses Cromarty Firth and snakes its way along wild and pristine coastline.

While the interior is dominated by vast and mournful peat bogs, along the coast great heather-clad hills heave themselves out of the wild North Sea. Rolling farmland drops suddenly into the chilly waters, and small, historic fishing villages are moored precariously on the coast's edge.

Strathpeffer

☑ 01997 / POP 1100

Strathpeffer is a charming old Highland spa town, with creaking pavilions and grandiose hotels dripping with faded grandeur. It rose to prominence during Victorian times, when the fashionable flocked here in huge numbers to bathe in, wash with and drink the sulphurous waters. The tourist influx led to the construction of grand buildings and architectural follies.

◉ Sights & Activities

There are many good signposted walking trails around Strathpeffer.

Highland Museum of Childhood   MUSEUM

(☑ 01997-421031; www.highlandmuseumofchildhood.org.uk; Old Train Station; adult/child £5/2.50; ☺ 11am-4pm Tue-Sat; ♿) Strathpeffer's former train station houses a wide range of social-history displays about childhood and also has activities for children, including a dressing-up box and toy train. In the complex there's also a gift shop to buy presents for a little somebody and a peaceful cafe.

Spa Pavilion & Upper Pump Room   HISTORIC BUILDING

(☑ 01997-420124; www.strathpefferpavilion.org; Golf Course Rd; ☺ Pump Room 10am-5pm Jun-Aug, 10am-5pm Tue-Thu & Sat, 1-5pm Mon, Fri & Sun Sep-Dec & Mar-May) FREE In Strathpeffer's heyday, the Pavilion was the social centre and venue for dances, lectures and concerts. These

days it's a renovated performing-arts venue. The neighbouring Upper Pump Room has some splendid displays showing the bizarre lengths Victorians went to for a healthy glow. There are also local art exhibitions, as well as artisanal sweets and tourist information in the friendly shop. Opening hours vary.

Eagle Stone   ARCHAEOLOGICAL SITE

The Eagle Stone is well worth a look. It's a pre-7th-century Pictish stone connected to a figure from local history – the Brahan Seer, who predicted many future events. The impressive carved eagle is topped by an arc dotted with symbols. It's a short, well-signposted stroll from the centre of town.

🛏 Sleeping & Eating

★ Craigvar   B&B ££

(☑ 01997-421622; www.craigvar.com; The Square; r from £115; ℗ 🛜) Luxury living with a refined touch is what you'll find in this delightful Georgian house in Strathpeffer's heart. Classy little extras are all here, including a welcome drink, Highland-Belgian chocolates, bathrobes, mini-fridges and fresh fruit. The owners offer wonderfully genuine hospitality with guest comfort paramount. The two light, elegant rooms are great, with fabulous modern bathrooms and thoughtful extras.

Beds are extremely comfortable and the downstairs lounge area is very elegant and commodious. The gourmet breakfasts, with lots of fish options, are a real highlight. It's hard to conceive how this place could improve, yet every time we visit it has done just that. A standout.

Coul House Hotel   HOTEL £££

(☑ 01997-421487; www.coulhousehotel.com; Contin; r from £265; ℗ @ 🛜 🐾) 🍃 South of Strathpeffer on the A835, Coul House dates from 1821 but has a light, airy feel in contrast to many country houses of this vintage. It's family run, and very cordial. Beautiful dining and lounge areas are complemented by elegant rooms with views over the lovely gardens; superior bedrooms look up the glen to the mountains beyond.

There's a fairy trail in the garden, forest paths for walking or mountain biking right on the doorstep, and a good restaurant. You can often find lower prices or multiday offers on the website.

Red Poppy BISTRO **££**
(☑ 01997-423332; www.redpoppyrestaurant.co.uk; Main Rd; mains £12-24; ⊗ 11.30am-8.30pm Tue-Sat, 12.30-3pm Sun; 🐾) On the main road opposite the spa buildings, this is comfortably Strathpeffer's best eating establishment. The casual modern interior with its bright red chairs is the venue for confident, well-presented dishes covering game and other classic British ingredients. It's a little cheaper at lunchtime, when set-price menus are available, and for traditional hot-meal high teas from 5pm.

❶ Getting There & Away

Stagecoach operates from Inverness to Strathpeffer (£5.90, 55 minutes, hourly Monday to Saturday, five on Sunday) via Dingwall (£2.20, 15 minutes). Services from Inverness to Gairloch and Durness, plus some buses from Inverness to Ullapool, also drop in.

Tain

☑ 01862 / POP 3700

Scotland's oldest royal burgh, Tain is a proud sandstone-built town that rose to prominence as pilgrims descended to venerate the relics of St Duthac, who is commemorated by the 12th-century ruins of St Duthac's Chapel, and St Duthus Church. It makes a fine stop on the way north.

Glenmorangie DISTILLERY
(☑ 01862-892477; www.glenmorangie.com; tours per person from £8; ⊗ tours 10am-4pm Jun-Aug, 10am-3pm Mon-Sat Apr-May & Sep-Oct, 10am & 2pm Mon-Fri Nov-Mar) Located on Tain's northern outskirts, Glenmorangie (emphasis on the second syllable) produces a fine lightish malt, subjected to a number of different cask finishes for variation. The tour is less in-depth than some but finishes with a free dram. There's a more comprehensive Signet tour (£40) and, for real whisky geeks, a full-day Heritage Tour (£150, April to October).

Tain Through Time MUSEUM
(☑ 01862-894089; www.tainmuseum.org.uk; Tower St; adult/child £3.50/2.50, museum only £1.50/50p; ⊗ 10am-5pm Mon-Fri Apr-Oct, plus Sat Jun-Aug) Set in the grounds of St Duthus Church is Tain Through Time, an entertaining heritage centre with a colourful and educational display on St Duthac, King James IV and key moments in Scottish history. Another building focuses on the town's fine

The **Sleeperzzz** (☑ 01408-641343; www.sleeperzzz.com; Rogart Station; s/tw/q £46/58/88, B&B s/d with bathroom £55/69; ⊗ Easter-Oct; 🅿🐾), an unusual hostel run on a sustainable basis, is set in two caringly converted railway carriages and a railway goods van parked in a siding by Rogart station. They contain cute two-person bedrooms, kitchenettes and shower rooms. There's also B&B (open all year) in the former waiting room, now an en-suite bedroom with kitchen; light breakfast is supplied.

It's on the A839, 11 miles east of Lairg, but is also easily reached by train on the Inverness–Wick line (small discount if you arrive this way or by bike). There's beautifully lonely Highland scenery in the vicinity, and a handy grocery store nearby.

silversmithing tradition and this is also a centre for Clan Ross. Admission includes an audio-guided walk around town.

Platform 1864 BISTRO **££**
(☑ 01862-894181; www.platform1864.com; 1 Station Rd; mains £12-23; ⊗ food 10am-3pm & 5-9.30pm, to 8pm Nov-Feb; 🐾🖐) 🍴 Real love has gone into this excellent restoration of Tain's train station building, which has become a handsome wood-clad bar and restaurant, open all day. The menu features hearty pub-style fare with a few flourishes. The enthusiastic owner and a beer garden make it a fine place to drop by for a drink or coffee at any time, too.

Bonar Bridge & Around

While the main road north crosses Dornoch Firth near Tain, an alternative scenic route loops west to the almost-joined villages of Ardgay and Bonar Bridge. This is an area worth exploring, with reminders of the Clearances, fine old-growth forest and good scope for outdoor activities. The A836 to Lairg branches west at Bonar Bridge.

Croick Church CHURCH
(www.croickchurch.com; Croick) From Ardgay, a single-track road leads 10 miles up Strathcarron to Croick, the scene of notorious evictions during the Clearances of 1845. You can

still see the evocative messages scratched by refugee crofters from nearby Glencalvie on the eastern windows of early-19th-century Croick Church.

Kyle of Sutherland Trails   MOUNTAIN BIKING
(www.scotland.forestry.gov.uk/visit/balblair; Balblair) At Balblair, a mile northwest of Bonar Bridge off the Lairg road, there are two mountain-biking trails. A 2-mile blue trail winds through the forest, while a 4.5-mile black track will test expert bikers with a stiff climb and an adrenalin-surging rock-slab descent.

Alladale Wilderness Reserve   LODGE £££
(☑ 01863-755338; www.alladale.com; Ardgay; r with full board from £445; P 🛜 🐾) In deep wilderness near Croick, this Victorian hunting lodge is part of a notable rewilding project. Sumptuous rooms in the main lodge (which includes meals) are available from October to May only (minimum two-night stay). The superbly remote Deanich lodge accommodates up to eight (£2750 a week self-catering). The scope for outdoor activities here is superb.

Crannag   BISTRO ££
(☑ 01863-766111; www.crannag.com; Bonar Bridge; mains £14-20; ☺ 6-8.30pm Tue-Sat; ☑) Classic casual dining fare from various parts of the world comes together at this likeable Highland bistro, an unlikely find in Bonar Bridge. The menu varies but you might find a classic French cut of steak alongside an Indian thali platter. The genial owner is full of ideas in the kitchen and they mostly work.

Lairg & Around
☑ 01549 / POP 900
Lairg is an attractive village, although the tranquillity can be rudely interrupted by the sound of military jets roaring overhead (the valley is frequently used by the RAF for low-flying exercises). Located at the southern end of Loch Shin, it's a remote but important Highland crossroads, gateway to central Sutherland's remote mountains and loch-speckled bogs.

Falls of Shin   WATERFALL
(www.kyleofsutherlanddevelopmenttrust.org/falls-of-shin-visitor-attraction; IV27 4EE; ☺ visitor centre approx 10am-3pm late Oct-Feb, 9am-8pm Mar-late Oct; 🐾) FREE Four miles south of Lairg, the picturesque Falls of Shin provide

one of the best places in the Highlands to see salmon leaping on their way upstream to spawn (best after heavy rain from June to October). A short, easy footpath leads to a viewing terrace overlooking the waterfall; there are waymarked forest trails here. There's also a gift shop and a pleasant community-run cafe in a salmon-shaped structure, with information panels on the fish.

★ Pier Café   CAFE, BISTRO ££
(☑ 01549-402971; www.pier-cafe.co.uk; Lochside, Lairg; lunch mains £6-15, dinner £12-19; ☺ 10am-4pm Mon-Sat, plus 5.30-9pm Fri & Sat, 10am-6pm Sun; 🛜 🐾) A very worthwhile stop, this bustling cafe by the loch has pleasant views, art exhibitions on the walls and real flair. Great chalkboard specials augment a Mediterranean-influenced bistro menu that draws on local produce. The coffee is the best for some distance around and the cafe is licensed. There's a little craft shop too.

Dornoch
☑ 01862 / POP 1200
On the northern shore of Dornoch Firth, 2 miles off the A9, this attractive old market town is one of the east coast's most pleasant settlements. Dornoch is best known for its championship golf course, but there's a fine cathedral among other noble buildings. Other historical oddities: the last witch to be executed in Scotland was boiled alive in hot tar here in 1722, and Madonna married Guy Ritchie here in 2000.

⊙ Sights & Activities
Have a walk along Dornoch's golden-sand beach, which stretches for miles. South of Dornoch, seals are often visible on the sandbars of Dornoch Firth.

Dornoch Cathedral   CHURCH
(www.dornoch-cathedral.com; St Gilbert St; ☺ 9am-7pm or later) FREE Consecrated in the 13th century, beautiful Dornoch Cathedral, one of the Highlands' loveliest churches, is an elegant Gothic edifice with an interior softly illuminated by modern stained-glass windows. The controversial first Duke of Sutherland, whose wife restored the church in the 1830s, lies in a sealed burial vault beneath the chancel.

By the western door is the sarcophagus of Sir Richard de Moravia, who died fighting the Danes at the battle of Embo in the 1260s. Until then, the battle had been going rather well for him; he'd managed to slay the Danish commander using the unattached leg of a horse that was to hand.

Royal Dornoch
GOLF

(☑01862-810219; www.royaldornoch.com; Golf Rd; green fees Apr-Oct £50-195, Nov-Mar £35-105) Royal Dornoch is one of Scotland's most famous links golf courses, described by Tom Watson as 'the most fun I ever had playing golf'. Online booking is straightforward; twilight rates (post 6pm May to July, post 5.30pm August) are the most economical. A golf pass (www.dornochfirthgolf.co.uk) lets you play five local courses at a discount.

🛏 Sleeping & Eating

★ 2 Quail
B&B ££

(☑01862-811811; www.2quail.com; Castle St; r £90-140; 🖻) Intimate and upmarket, 2 Quail offers a warm main-street welcome. Tasteful, spacious bedrooms are full of old-world comfort, with sturdy metal bed frames, plump duvets and plenty of books. The downstairs guest lounge is an absolute delight, with comfy armchairs, open fireplace and an extensive library. It's best to book ahead.

★ Links House Hotel
HOTEL £££

(☑01862-810279; www.linkshousedornoch.com; Golf Rd; r from £225; ℗🖻) Set in a 19th-century manse (a spacious house built for the minister of the local church), this small (15-room) hotel offers an authentic Scottish country-house experience, from the wood-panelled drawing room with its library of vintage angling books, to the whisky-focused cocktail bar and private putting green, plus the first hole of Royal Dornoch just along the road.

Courtroom
SCOTTISH ££

(☑01862-810279; www.linkshousedornoch.com/the-courtroom; Castle St; mains lunch £8-12, dinner £15-24; ⊙10am-11pm; 🖻) 🍴 Beautifully set in the former town courtroom, which dates from 1849, this is an atmospheric spot for breakfast, lunch or dinner, with a menu that's heavy on Scottish produce enlivened with flourishes of French, Mediterranean and Asian flavours. The modern mural on the wall above the bar celebrates figures from Dornoch's past (and present – see if you can spot Madonna!).

Luigi
CAFE ££

(☑01862-810893; www.luigidornoch.com; Castle St; lunch £10-13, dinner mains £17-22; ⊙10am-5pm daily, plus 6.45-9pm Fri & Sat Mar-Oct, daily Jul & Aug; 🖻) The clean lines of this contemporary Italian-American cafe make a break from the omnipresent heritage and history of the coastline. Ciabattas and salads stuffed with tasty deli ingredients make it a good lunch stop; more elaborate dinners usually include fine seafood choices. The coffee is the best in town.

ℹ Information

There's visitor information at https://visitdornoch.com.

ℹ Getting There & Away

Stagecoach Highland bus X99 runs twice daily from Inverness to Dornoch (£11.40, one hour), continuing north to Wick and Thurso (£17.10, 2½ hours).

Golspie

☑01408 / POP 1400

Golspie is a pretty little village most visited for nearby Dunrobin Castle. It's a congenial place to stop for a night or two, with good facilities and a pleasant beach.

There are several good local walks, including the classic 3.75-mile (return) hike that climbs steeply to the summit of **Ben Bhraggie** (394m), crowned by a massive monument to the Duke of Sutherland, notorious for his leading role in the Highland Clearances.

On the same slopes, **Highland Wildcat** (www.highlandwildcat.com; KW10 6TH; per day £3; ⊙dawn-dusk) offers excellent mountain biking.

★ Dunrobin Castle
CASTLE

(☑01408-633177; www.dunrobincastle.co.uk; adult/child £11/6; ⊙10.30am-4.30pm Apr, May & Oct, 10am-5pm Jun-Sep; ℗) Magnificent Dunrobin Castle, a mile past Golspie, is the Highlands' largest house. Although it dates to 1275, most of what you see was built in French style between 1845 and 1850. A seat of the dukes of Sutherland, it's richly furnished and offers an intriguing insight into the aristocratic lifestyle. The castle inspires mixed feelings locally; it was once the Sutherland home of the first duke, responsible for some of the cruellest episodes of the Highland Clearances.

In the first half of the 19th century the duke's estate was, at over 6000 sq km, the largest privately owned area of land in Europe. Between 1811 and 1821, he and his family spent most of their time in London, but they were still responsible for the eviction of around 15,000 people from their Sutherland farms to make way for sheep, sometimes burning their homes to prevent them being reoccupied.

The classic fairy-tale castle is adorned with towers and turrets, but only 22 of its 187 rooms are on display, with hunting trophies much to the fore. Beautiful formal gardens, where impressive falconry displays take place two or three times a day, extend down to the sea. In the gardens is a museum with an eclectic mix of archaeological finds, natural-history exhibits, more non-PC animal remains and an excellent collection of Pictish stones.

❶ Getting There & Away

Trains (£21.10, 2¼ hours) and buses (£12.90, 1½ hours) from Inverness towards Wick/Thurso stop in Golspie and at Dunrobin Castle.

Helmsdale

🖉 01431 / POP 700

Surrounded by hills whose gorse explodes mad yellow in springtime, this sheltered fishing town, like many settlements on the east coast, was created to house farming families displaced by the Highland Clearances; it later became a booming herring port. It's surrounded by stunning, undulating coastline, and the River Helmsdale is one of the best salmon rivers in the Highlands.

Timespan   MUSEUM
(🖉01431-821327; www.timespan.org.uk; Dunrobin St; adult/child £4/2; ⊙10am-5pm Easter-Oct, 2-4pm Tue, 10am-3pm Sat & Sun Nov-Easter; 🚻) In the heart of Helmsdale, this heritage centre has an impressive display covering local history, including the Clearances, the fishing industry and the 1869 gold rush; look out also for the impressive audiovisual content. Up the back are recreations of a traditional croft house, smithy, shop and byre (cowshed). There are also local art exhibitions upstairs, a geology garden and an attractive riverside cafe.

CAITHNESS

Once you pass Helmsdale, you are entering Caithness, a place of endless peat bogs and jagged gorse-and-grass-topped sea cliffs hiding tiny fishing harbours. Scotland's top corner was once Viking territory, historically more connected to Orkney and Shetland than the rest of the mainland. It's a mystical, ancient land dotted with old monuments and peopled by folk who are proud of their Norse heritage.

Helmsdale to Lybster

This spectacular stretch of coast follows the folds of the undulating landscape through villages established on the shoreline when communities were evicted from the interior in the Highland Clearances of the early 19th century.

The village of **Dunbeath** is spectacularly set in a deep glen. **Lybster** is a purpose-built fishing village dating from 1810, with a stunning harbour area surrounded by grassy cliffs. In its heyday, it was Scotland's third-busiest port. Things have changed – now there are only a couple of boats – but there are several interesting prehistoric sites in the area.

Grey Cairns
of Camster   ARCHAEOLOGICAL SITE
(⊙24hr) FREE Dating from between 4000 BCE and 2500 BCE, these burial chambers are hidden in long, low mounds rising from an evocatively lonely moor. The Long Cairn measures 60m by 21m. You can enter the main chamber, but must first crawl into the well-preserved Round Cairn, which has a corbelled ceiling. From a turn-off a mile east of Lybster on the A99, the cairns are 4 miles north. You can continue 7 further miles to approach Wick on the A882.

Whaligoe Steps   HISTORIC SITE
(Ulbster; ⊙24hr) FREE This staircase cut into the cliff 5 miles north of Lybster provides access to a tiny natural harbour, with an ideal grassy picnic spot, ringed by vertical cliffs and echoing with the cackle of nesting fulmars. The path begins at the end of the minor road opposite the road signposted 'Cairn of Get'. There's a good cafe (🖉01955-651702; www.whaligoesteps.co.uk; The Square, Whaligoe, Ulbster; mains £5-15; ⊙10.30am-5.30pm Thu-Sun mid-Mar–Sep, 11am-5pm Sat & Sun Oct-Dec) at the top.

CROFTING & THE CLEARANCES

The wild empty spaces of the northern Highlands are among Europe's least populated regions, but this wasn't always so. Ruins of cottages in desolate areas are mute witnesses to one of the most heartless episodes of Scottish history: the Highland Clearances.

Until the 19th century the most common form of farming settlement here was the *baile*, a group of a dozen or so families who farmed the land granted to them by the local chieftain in return for military service and a portion of the harvest. The arable land was divided into strips called *rigs*, which were allocated to different families by annual ballot so that each took turns at getting the poorer soils; this system was known as *runrig*. The families worked the land communally and their cattle shared the grazing land.

After the Battle of Culloden (1746), however, the king banned private armies and new laws made the clan chiefs actual owners of their traditional lands, often vast tracts of territory. With the prospect of unimagined riches allied to a depressing failure of imagination, the landlords (who now spent much of their time in London) decided that sheep were more profitable than agriculture and, in the late 18th and early 19th century, proceeded to evict tens of thousands of farmers.

These desperate folk were driven to head for the cities in the hope of finding work or to emigrate to the Americas or the southern hemisphere. Those who stayed were forced to eke out a living from narrow plots of marginal agricultural land, often close to the coast. This form of smallholding became known as crofting. The small patch of land barely provided a living and had to be supplemented by other work such as fishing and kelp-gathering. It was always precarious, as rights were granted on a year-by-year basis, so at any moment a crofter could lose not only the farm but also the house they'd built on it.

The late-19th-century economic depression meant many couldn't pay their rent. This time, however, the crofters resisted expulsion, instead forming the Highland Land Reform Association and their own political party. Their resistance led the government to accede to several demands, including security of tenure, fair rents and eventually the supply of land for new crofts. Crofters now have the right to purchase their farmland and 2004 laws finally abolished the feudal system, which had created so much misery.

Wick

☎ 01955 / POP 7100

Wick is worth a visit, particularly for its excellent museum and attractive, spruced-up harbour area, and it has some very good places to stay. More gritty than pretty, however, it's been a little down on its luck since the collapse of the herring industry. It was once the world's largest fishing port for the 'silver darlings', but when the market dropped off after WWII, job losses were huge and the town hasn't ever totally recovered.

Sights & Activities

★ **Wick Heritage Centre**   MUSEUM
(☎01955-605393; www.wickheritage.org; 20 Bank Row; adult/child £4/50p; ⊙10am-5pm Apr-Oct, last entry 3.45pm) Tracking the rise and fall of the herring industry, this great museum displays everything from fishing equipment to complete herring boats. It's absolutely huge inside, and is crammed with memorabilia and extensive displays describing Wick's heyday in the mid-19th century. The Johnston collection is the star exhibit – from 1863 to 1977 three generations of the family photographed everything that happened around Wick, and the 70,000 images constitute an amazing legacy.

Old Pulteney   DISTILLERY
(☎01955-602371; www.oldpulteney.com; Huddart St; tours £10; ⊙10am-4pm Mon-Fri Oct-Apr, 10am-5pm Mon-Fri, 10am-4pm Sat May-Sep) Though it can no longer claim to be the most northerly whisky distillery on mainland Scotland (that goes to the upstart Wolfburn in Thurso), friendly Pulteney still runs excellent tours twice or more daily (normally at 11am and 2pm), with more expensive visits available

for aficionados. Its Stroma whisky liqueur is dangerously moreish.

Caithness Seacoast   BOATING

(☑ 01955-609200; www.caithness-seacoast.co.uk; South Quay; ☺ Apr-Oct) This outfit will take you out to sea to inspect the rugged coastline of the northeast. Various options include a half-hour jaunt (adult/child £21/13), a 1½-hour tour (£33/24) and a three-hour return trip down to Lybster (£55/43).

🛏 Sleeping & Eating

Bank Guesthouse   B&B ££

(☑ 01955-604001; www.riversideapartments.scot; 28 Bridge St; s/d/f £65/85/125; P 🕿) In the very centre of Wick, this striking Victorian building contains a warmly welcoming B&B run by a local family. Rooms have plenty of space and feature attractive carpets, wallpaper and fabrics along with modern bathrooms with great showers. Breakfast is well above average. Stairs might be a problem for the less mobile.

Mackays Hotel   HOTEL £££

(☑ 01955-602323; www.mackayshotel.co.uk; Union St; s/d/f from £90/125/136; 🕿🍽) Hospitable Mackays is Wick's best hotel by a long stretch. Attractive, mostly refurbished rooms vary in layout and size, so ask to see a few; prices are usually lower than the rack rates. On-site **No 1 Bistro** (mains £15-22; ☺ noon-2pm & 5-9pm; 🕿) is a fine option for lunch or dinner. The world's shortest street, 2.06m-long Ebenezer Pl, is one side of the hotel.

Guests get free use of a local gym and pool. The hotel also has some self-catering apartments and town houses nearby.

Bord de l'Eau   FRENCH ££

(☑ 01955-604400; 2 Market St; mains £17-25; ☺ noon-2pm & 6-9pm Tue-Sat, 6-9pm Sun) This serene, relaxed French restaurant is Wick's best place to eat. It overlooks the river and serves a changing menu of mostly French meat and game classics, backed up by daily fish specials. Starters are great value, and mains include a huge assortment of vegetables. The conservatory dining room with water views is lovely on a sunny evening.

❶ Getting There & Away

BUS

Stagecoach buses run to/from Inverness (£21.60, three hours, twice daily), and from Wick to Thurso (£4.25, 45 minutes, five to eight daily).

There's also a connecting service to Gills Bay and John O'Groats (£3.75, 30 minutes, four to five Monday to Saturday) for the car and passenger ferries to Orkney.

TRAIN

Trains service Wick from Inverness (£22.40, 4¼ hours, four daily Monday to Saturday, one on Sunday).

John O'Groats

📞 01955 / POP 300

Though not actually the northernmost point of the British mainland (that's Dunnet Head), John O'Groats is famous as the end point of the 874-mile trek from Land's End in Cornwall, a popular if arduous route for cyclists and walkers, many of whom raise money for charitable causes. Most of the settlement is taken up by a stylish modern self-catering complex. There's a passenger ferry from here to Orkney.

Duncansby Head   VIEWPOINT

Two miles east of John O'Groats, Duncansby Head has a small lighthouse and 60m-high cliffs sheltering nesting fulmars. A 15-minute walk through a sheep paddock yields spectacular views of the sea-surrounded monoliths known as Duncansby Stacks.

Wildlife Cruises   BOATING

(☑ 01955-611353; www.jogferry.co.uk; adult/child £19/9.50; ☺ mid-Jun–Aug) The friendly folk who run the Orkney ferry also offer 1½-hour wildlife cruises to the island of Stroma or Duncansby Head. There are also **day tours** (☺ May-Sep) of Orkney available.

❶ Information

John O'Groats Tourist Office (☑ 01955-611373; www.visitjohnogroats.com; ☺ 10am-4pm Nov-Apr, to 5pm May & Sep-Oct, 9am-6pm Jun-Aug) This locally run tourist office at the John O'Groats car park is helpful and, as well as information and souvenirs, has a fine selection of local novels and nonfiction titles.

❶ Getting There & Away

Stagecoach runs between John O'Groats and Wick (£3.75, 30 minutes, four to five Monday to Saturday) or Thurso (£4.75, one hour, five to eight Monday to Saturday).

From May to September, a passenger ferry (p400) shuttles across to Burwick in Orkney. Three miles west, a car ferry (p400) runs all year from Gills Bay to St Margaret's Hope in Orkney.

Mey

☑ 01847 / POP 200

West of John O'Groats, the small village of Mey has a major drawcard for fans of the Royal Family in its pretty castle, formerly a residence of the late Queen Mother.

Castle of Mey   CASTLE
(☑ 01847-851473;   www.castleofmey.org.uk; adult/child £11.75/6.50; ⊘ 10.20am-5pm May-Sep, last entry 4pm) The Castle of Mey, a big crowd-puller for its Queen Mother connections, is 6 miles west of John O'Groats. The exterior is grand but inside it feels domestic and everything is imbued with the Queen Mum's character. The highlight is the genteel guided tour, with various anecdotes recounted by staff who once worked for her. In the grounds there's a farm zoo, an unusual walled garden that's worth a stroll and lovely views over the Pentland Firth.

The castle normally closes for a couple of weeks at the end of July for royal visits; Prince Charles often comes here in summer. There may also be limited April openings; check the website.

Hawthorns   B&B ££
(☑ 01847-851444; www.meybandb.co.uk; s/d £60/90; P🐾🖥🕮) On the main road near the Castle of Mey, the Hawthorns has five very spruce, super-spacious ground-floor rooms with mini-fridges. There are two triple rooms, good for families and groups, and one room with disabled access. It's open in the winter months, but only takes bookings, not walk-ups.

Thurso & Scrabster

☑ 01847 / POP 7600

Britain's most northerly mainland town, Thurso makes a handy overnight stop if you're heading west or across to Orkney. There's a pretty town beach, riverside strolls and a good museum. Ferries for Orkney leave from Scrabster, 2.5 miles away.

◉ Sights & Activities

Thurso is an unlikely surfing centre but the nearby coast has arguably the best and most consistent surf on mainland Britain. There's an excellent right-hand reef break on the eastern side of town, directly in front of the castle (closed to the public), and another

---

WORTH A TRIP

DUNNET HEAD

Eight miles east of Thurso, a minor road leads to dramatic Dunnet Head, the most northerly point on the British mainland. There are majestic cliffs dropping into the turbulent Pentland Firth, inspiring views of Orkney with basking seals and nesting seabirds below (it's a Royal Society for the Protection of Birds reserve), and a lighthouse built by Robert Louis Stevenson's grandad. Two cottages are available for rent (see www.dunnetheadlight house.com).

---

shallow reef break 5 miles west at Brimms Ness. You'll want to wear 6mm cover outside the summer season. Conditions are best in autumn.

🛏 Sleeping & Eating

★**Pennyland House**   B&B ££
(☑ 01847-891194; www.pennylandhouse.co.uk; s £80, d £90-100; P🐾🖥🕮) A historic house on the western edge of town, Pennyland is a standout B&B. It offers phenomenal value for this level of accommodation, with huge oak-furnished rooms named after golf courses: we especially loved St Andrews – super-spacious, with a great chessboard-tiled bathroom. Hospitality is enthusiastic and helpful, and there's an inviting breakfast space, garden and terraced area with views across to Hoy.

Two-night minimum stay in summer.

Camfield House   B&B ££
(☑ 07711 215823; www.riversideaccommodation. co.uk; Janet St, Thurso; r £125-145; P🕮) A Narnia-style portal leads from central Thurso through a gate and you're suddenly in what feels like an opulent rural estate. The garden is sumptuous, and extravagantly features a manicured par-3 golf hole, complete with bunker and water hazard. The interior lacks nothing by comparison, featuring spacious rooms with huge TVs, quality linen and excellent bathrooms. There's even a full-sized billiard table.

Possible three-night minimum stay.

Marine   B&B ££
(☑ 01847-890676; www.themarinethurso.co.uk; 38 Shore St, Thurso; s £104, d £110-115; P🕮) Tucked away in Thurso's most appealing

corner you'll find a top spot right by the town beach, offering spectacular vistas over to Orkney. Rooms are just fabulous, with a designer's touch and a subtle maritime feel, and surfers can study the breakers from the stunning conservatory lounge. Two-night minimum stay.

Forss House Hotel HOTEL **£££**
(☑01847-861201; www.forsshousehotel.co.uk; r from £215; P 🛜 🐾) Tucked into woodland alongside a beautiful salmon river 5 miles west of Thurso, this Georgian mansion offers elegant accommodation with both character and style. Sumptuous upstairs rooms are preferable to basement rooms as they have lovely garden views. There are also beautifully appointed suites in the garden itself, providing both privacy and tranquillity. Thoughtful extras like magazines and books in every room add appeal.

★ **Captain's Galley** SEAFOOD **£££**
(☑01847-894999; www.captainsgalley.co.uk; The Harbour, Scrabster; 5-course dinner £55, with wine flight £80; ⊙6.30-9pm Thu-Sat) 🍽 Classy but friendly Captain's Galley, by the Scrabster ferry, offers a short, seafood-based menu featuring local and sustainably sourced produce prepared in delicious ways that let the natural flavours shine through. The chef picks the best fish off the local boats, and the menu describes exactly which fishing grounds your morsel came from. It's worth scheduling a night in Thurso to eat here.

If you can't get a table, or just want a quick meal while waiting for the Orkney ferry, you can feast on fresh takeaway seafood – haddock, scallops, langoustines, crab and lobster – at the neighbouring **Seafood Bar** (☑07470 004625; www.scrabsterseafoodbar.co.uk; The Harbour, Scrabster; mains £9-13, lobster £25; ⊙4.30-6.30pm Tue-Sat) 🍽.

❶ Getting There & Away

BUS
Stagecoach buses link Thurso/Scrabster with Inverness (£21.60, 3½ hours, twice daily). There are also buses to Wick (£4.25, 45 minutes, five to eight daily), as well as every couple of hours to John O'Groats (£4.75, one hour, five to eight Monday to Saturday).

TRAIN
There are four daily trains (one on Sunday) from Inverness (£22.40, 3¾ hours), with a connecting bus to Scrabster.

NORTH & WEST COAST

Quintessential Highland country such as this, with breathtaking emptiness, a wild, fragile beauty and single-track roads, is a rarity on the modern, crowded, highly urbanised island of Britain. You could get lost up here for weeks – and that still wouldn't be enough time.

Carving its way from Thurso to Kyle of Lochalsh, the north and northwest coastline is a feast of fjord-like sea lochs, forgotten beaches and surging peninsulas. Within the rugged confines, the interior is home to vast, empty spaces, enormous lochs and some of Scotland's shapeliest peaks.

Whether in blazing sunshine or murky greyness, the character of the land is constantly changing – for that window of time in which you can glimpse it, you'll capture an exclusive snapshot of this ancient area in your mind. Stop the car and gaze. This northernmost slab of the Highlands is the stuff of coastal-drive dreams.

Thurso to Durness

It's 80 winding – and utterly spectacular – coastal miles from Thurso to Durness.

Ten miles west of Thurso, the **Dounreay** nuclear power station was the first in the world to supply mains electricity. It's currently being decommissioned; the clean-up is planned to be finished by 2025. Meanwhile it's still a major source of employment for the region.

Beyond, Melvich overlooks a fine beach and there are great views from **Strathy Point** (a 2-mile drive from the coast road, then a 15-minute walk).

Bettyhill is a pretty village that overlooks a magnificent stretch of coastline, and the scenery just improves as you head west through Coldbackie and Tongue, with a succession of gorgeous sea lochs, stunning beaches and striking rock formations backed by imposing hills and mountains.

❶ Getting Around

Public transport along the north coast is thin on the ground. Stagecoach buses only run as far west as Dounreay (from £2.30, 20 minutes, four a day).

Beyond that, there's the Far North Bus (p361), which runs minibus services around the remote northwest. Route 803 runs from Thurso to Tongue (£9, 1½ hours) on Tuesday, Thursday and Saturday, stopping at all villages on the way and continuing to Durness (£11, 2¼ hours) on Saturday only. Best to book in advance.

Transport for Tongue (www.transportfor-tongue.co.uk) is a community-run, on-demand taxi service that operates a handful of scheduled routes, notably between Lairg and Tongue on Wednesdays, and Inverness and Tongue on the last Saturday of the month. Must be booked in advance.

Bettyhill

🌐 01641 / POP 500

Bettyhill is a crofting community of resettled tenant farmers kicked off their land during the Clearances. The spectacular panorama of a sweeping, sandy beach backed by velvety green hills with rocky outcrops makes a sharp contrast to that tragic history.

Strathnaver Museum　　　　MUSEUM
(☏ 01641-521418; www.strathnavermuseum.org. uk; Clachan; adult/child £3/free; ⊙ 10am-5pm Mon-Sat Apr-Oct) Housed in an old church, this museum tells the sad story of the Strathnaver Clearances through posters created by local kids. The museum contains memorabilia of Clan Mackay, various items of crofting equipment and a 'St Kilda mailboat', a small wooden boat-shaped container bearing a letter that was used by St Kildans to send messages to the mainland.

Outside the back door of the church is the **Farr Stone**, a fine carved Pictish cross-slab.

Bettyhill Hotel　　　　INN £££
(☏ 01641-521202; www.bettyhillhotel.com; s/d without bathroom £65/95, d with bathroom from £130; ⊙ Apr-Oct, check for winter opening; 🅿 🛜 🐾) This former coaching inn has a fabulous position overlooking the sandy beach fringing Torrisdale Bay. The owners have completed a great renovation and the updated bedrooms are bright, with top-grade mattresses. Rooms come in many different types (some have sea or river views) with lots of singles, as well as a two-bedroom holiday cottage. Bar and restaurant meals are available.

★ Côte du Nord　　　　MODERN SCOTTISH £££
(☏ 01641-521773; www.cotedunord.co.uk; The School House, Kirtomy; tasting menu £55, paired wines £35; ⊙ 7.30pm Wed, Fri & Sat Apr-Sep; 🍴)
🍽 Brilliantly innovative cuisine, wonderfully whimsical presentation and an emphasis on local ingredients are the highlights of the gastronomic tasting menu here. It's an unlikely spot to find such a gourmet experience – the chef is none other than the local GP who forages for wild herbs and flavours in between surgery hours. Top value. It's tiny, so reserve well ahead.

NORTH COAST 500

The drive around Scotland's far northern coastline is one of Europe's finest road trips. Words fail to describe the sheer variety of scenic splendour which unfolds as you cross this empty landscape of desolate moorlands, brooding mountains, fertile coastal meadows and stunning white-sand beaches.

In a clever piece of marketing it's been dubbed the North Coast 500, as the round trip from Inverness is roughly that many miles, though you'll surely clock up a few more if you follow your heart down narrow byroads and seek perfect coastal panoramas.

In our opinion, the scenery is best viewed by travelling anticlockwise, heading north from Inverness up the east coast then turning west across the top of Scotland before returning down the west coast. This way, you'll make the most of the coastal vistas, the light and the awesome backdrop of the Assynt mountains.

Much of the drive is along single-track road, so it's important to pull over to let both oncoming vehicles and faster traffic behind you pass.

In recent years the North Coast 500 has become something of a victim of its own success. Visitor numbers are well up, which has led to traffic congestion on narrow roads (particularly around Applecross) and shortages of accommodation, so it's well worth booking everything in advance, even campsites.

FORSINARD & STRATHNAVER

Though it's tough to tear yourself away from the coast, we recommend plunging down the A897 just east of Melvich. After 14 miles you reach the railway at Forsinard. On the platform is **Forsinard Flows Visitor Centre** (☑01641-571225; www.rspb.org.uk; Forsinard; ⊗visitor centre 9am-5pm Apr-Oct, trails open all year; ℗) FREE, a small nature exhibition. There's a live hen-harrier cam, plus guided walks and 4WD excursions available – phone for dates. A 1-mile trail and an impressive viewing tower introduce you to the Flows peatland; 4 miles north is a 4-mile trail crossing golden plover and dunlin nesting grounds. The deep peat blanket bog is a rare and important habitat, at risk from climate change.

Past here, the epic peaty moorscapes stir the heart with their desolate beauty. Take a right at Kinbrace onto the B871, which covers more jaw-dropping scenery before arriving at Syre. Turn right to follow the valley of Strathnaver back to the coast near Bettyhill. Strathnaver saw some of the worst of the Highland Clearances; the **Strathnaver Trail** (www.strathnavermuseum.org.uk/strathnaver-trail) is a series of numbered points of interest along the valley relating to the Clearances and to various prehistoric sites.

Accommodation options on this lonely detour include **Cornmill Bunkhouse** (☑01641-571219; www.achumore.co.uk; A897; dm £18; ℗), a comfortable, modern hostel occupying a picturesque old mill on a working croft in the middle of nowhere; it's on the A897, 4 miles south of the coast road. Turning left instead of right at Syre, you'll eventually reach the remote **Altnaharra Hotel** (☑01549-411222; www.altnaharra.com; Altnaharra IV27 4UF; s/d from £110/165; ⊗Mar-Dec; ℗🅿🛜🐾).

Kirtomy is signposted off the main road about 2.5 miles east of Bettyhill; the restaurant is about a mile down this road.

Durness

☑01971 / POP 400

Durness (www.durness.org) is wonderfully located, strung out along cliffs rising from a series of pristine beaches. When the sun shines, the effects of blinding white sand, the cry of seabirds and the spring-green-coloured seas combine in a magical way.

⊙ Sights & Activities

Walking the sensational sandy coastline is a highlight, as is a visit to Cape Wrath (p363). Durness' beautiful beaches include **Rispond** (also known as Ceannabeinne) to the east, **Sango Sands** below town and **Balnakeil** to the west. At Balnakeil, a craft village occupies a one-time early-warning radar station. A northerly beach walk leads to **Faraid Head**, where there are puffins in early summer.

Bikes can be hired from a shed on the square.

Smoo Cave   CAVE
FREE A mile east of Durness is a path down to Smoo Cave. From the vast main chamber,

you can head through to a smaller flooded cavern where a waterfall sometimes cascades from the roof. There's evidence the cave was inhabited about 6000 years ago. You can take a **tour** (☑01971-511704; www.smoocavetours.weebly.com; adult/child £6/3; ⊗11am-4pm Apr, May, Sep & Oct, 10am-5pm Jun-Aug) to explore a little further into the interior.

🛏 Sleeping

Sango Sands Oasis   CAMPSITE £
(☑07838 381065; www.sangosands.com; sites per adult/child £9.50/6, 2nd child £3, others free; ℗🛜🐾) You couldn't imagine a better location for a campsite: pleasant grassy pitches on the top of the cliffs, with paths descending to two lovely sandy beaches. Facilities are good and very clean and there's a pub next door. Electric hook-up is an extra £4.50. You can camp for £9 per site from November to March.

Lazy Crofter Bunkhouse   HOSTEL £
(☑01971-511202; www.visitdurness.com/bunkhouse; dm from £22; 🛜) Durness' best budget accommodation is here, opposite the supermarket. A bothy vibe gives it a very Highland feel, and inviting dorms have lockers and plenty of space. There's also a sociable shared table for meals and board games,

and a great wooden deck with sea views, perfect for midge-free evenings.

Morven   B&B £££
(☑ 01971-511252; morven69@hotmail.com; s/d/f from £50/70/90; P🐾🛜🐾) Cheery owners, a handy next-to-pub location and a serious border-collie theme are key features of this ultra-cosy place. Rooms, which are upstairs and share a downstairs bathroom, have been renovated and feel new and super-comfortable. One is especially spacious and has a top coastal vista.

★ **Mackays Rooms**   HOTEL £££
(☑ 01971-511202; www.visitdurness.com; d standard £149, deluxe £169-210; ⊘May-Oct; P🛜🐾) You really feel you're at the furthest-flung corner of Scotland here, where the road turns through 90 degrees. But whether heading south or east, you'll go far before you find a better place to stay than this haven of Highland hospitality. With its big beds, soft fabrics and contemporary colours, it's a romantic spot with top-notch service.

There's also a self-contained cabin, which can be rented on a self-catering or B&B basis. With two rooms, it sleeps up to four (from £190 per night).

✖ Eating

★ **Cocoa Mountain**   CAFE £
(☑ 01971-511233; www.cocoamountain.co.uk; Balnakeil; mains £4-8; ⊘9am-6pm Easter-Oct) 🍴 At the Balnakeil craft village, this upbeat cafe and chocolate maker offers handmade treats, including a chilli, lemongrass and coconut white-chocolate truffle, plus many more unique flavours. Tasty espresso and hot chocolate warm the cockles on those blowy horizontal-drizzle days. It offers light lunches and home-baking too, plus chocolate-making workshops.

Smoo Cave Hotel   PUB FOOD ££
(☑ 01971-511227; www.smoocavehotel.co.uk; mains £9-15; ⊘food served noon-9pm; 🛜) Signposted off the main road at the eastern end of Durness, this amiable local has quality bar food in hefty portions. Haddock or daily seafood specials – plump scallops are a highlight – are an obvious and worthwhile choice; there's also a restaurant area with clifftop views.

ℹ Information

Durness has full services, including an ATM, shops and petrol.

ℹ Getting There & Away

A year-round **Far North Bus** (☑ 07782 110007; www.thedurnessbus.com) service heads to Lairg (£10, 2½ hours, Monday to Friday), where there is a train station.

On Saturday minibuses head to Inverness (£14, three hours) and Thurso (£11, 2¼ hours). In summer school holidays, there's also an Ullapool service (£11, 2½ hours).

All these services should be prebooked; some have bicycle capacity.

Durness to Ullapool

Perhaps Scotland's most spectacular road, the 69 miles connecting Durness to Ullapool is a smorgasbord of dramatic scenery – almost too much to take in. From Durness you pass through a broad heathered valley with the looming grey bulk of Foinaven and Arkle to the southeast. Heather gives way to a rockier landscape pockmarked with hundreds of lochans (small lochs).

Here you'll find some of the most interesting geology in the UK, including Britain's oldest rock – three-billion-year-old Lewisian gneiss. Next come the magnificent Torridonian sandstone mountains of Assynt and Coigach, including Suilven's distinctive sugarloaf, many-peaked Quinag and pinnacled Stac Pollaidh. The area has been designated as the **Northwest Highlands Geopark** (www.nwhgeopark.com).

WORTH A TRIP

SANDWOOD BAY

South of Cape Wrath, **Sandwood Bay** (www.johnmuirtrust.org/trust-land/sandwood) boasts one of Scotland's best and most isolated beaches, guarded at one end by the spectacular rock pinnacle Am Buachaille. A 9-mile round-trip hike from Blairmore car park, northwest of Kinlochbervie, follows a former peat track across bleak moorland puddled with lochans before arriving, almost unexpectedly, at this coastal jewel. Few people walk all the way to the beach's northern end, so if you've packed a picnic, that's the spot to aim for.

Scourie & Handa Island

Scourie is a pretty crofting community famous for its hill-loch trout fishing, halfway between Durness and Ullapool.

Handa Island
Nature Reserve
NATURE RESERVE

(www.scottishwildlifetrust.org.uk) A few miles north of Scourie Bay lies this nature reserve run by the Scottish Wildlife Trust. The island's spectacular western sea cliffs provide nesting sites for important breeding populations of great skuas, Arctic skuas, puffins, kittiwakes, razorbills and guillemots. Reach the island from Tarbet, 6 miles north of Scourie, via the **Handa Island Ferry** (📱07780 967800; www.handa-ferry.com; Tarbet Pier; adult/child return £15/5; ⊘outbound 9am-2pm Mon-Sat Apr-Aug, last ferry back 5pm); call for times and to book your spot.

★ Shorehouse
SeafoodRestaurant
SEAFOOD ££

(📱01971-502251; www.shorehousetarbet.co.uk; Tarbet Pier; mains £12-19; ⊘noon-7pm Mon-Sat Easter-Sep) By the ferry pier for Handa Island Nature Reserve, Shorehouse is a restaurant and cafe in a lovely setting, looking across the sound to the sandy beach on Handa Island. There's a conservatory and outdoor terrace that make the most of the view, and a menu that concentrates on local seafood including Handa crab and prawn salads and South Uist smoked salmon.

Kylesku & Loch Glencoul

Hidden away on the shores of Loch Glencoul, tiny Kylesku served as a ferry crossing on the route north until it was made redundant by elegant Kylesku Bridge in 1984. It's a good base for walks; you can hire bikes, too.

Eas a'Chual Aluinn
WATERFALL

Five miles southeast of Kylesku, in wild, remote country, lies 213m-high Eas a'Chual Aluinn, Britain's highest waterfall. You can hike to the top of the falls from a parking area at a sharp bend in the main road 3 miles south of Kylesku; allow five hours for the 6-mile return trip. It can also be seen on **boat trips** (📱01971-502231; www.kyleskuboattours.com; Kylesku; adult/child £30/20; ⊘Apr-Sep) from Kylesku.

★ Kylesku Hotel
SEAFOOD ££

(📱01971-502231; www.kyleskuhotel.co.uk; Kylesku; mains £15-26; ⊘noon-2.30pm & 6-9pm mid-Feb–Apr, Oct & Nov, noon-9pm May-Sep; 🛜📶🐾) 🍴 In this remote lochside location, it's a real pleasure to gorge yourself on delicious sustainable seafood. Local langoustines grilled on a skewer, squat lobsters and mussels are the specialities at this convivial restaurant, where you have the option of eating outdoors with a view of the sea. There's a good atmosphere of mingling locals and visitors at the bar.

Lochinver & Assynt

With its otherworldly scenery of isolated peaks rising above a sea of crumpled, lochan-spattered gneiss, Assynt epitomises the northwest's wild magnificence. Glaciers have sculpted the hills of Suilven (731m), Canisp (846m), Quinag (808m) and Ben More Assynt (998m) into strange and wonderful silhouettes.

Lochinver is the main settlement, a busy little fishing port that's a popular port of call with its laid-back atmosphere, good facilities and striking scenery. Just north of Lochinver (or if coming from the north, not far south of Kylesku), a 23-mile detour on the narrow B869 rewards with spectacular views and fine beaches. From the lighthouse at Point of Stoer, a one-hour cliff walk leads to the **Old Man of Stoer**, a spectacular sea stack.

🏃 Activities

The hills around Inchnadamph are famous for their limestone caves. There's some excellent walking in the area – check out the **Bone Caves** hike (www.walkhighlands.co.uk/ullapool/bonecaves.shtml).

Summer Isles Sea Kayaking
KAYAKING

(📱07900 641860; www.summerislesseakayaking.com; half-/full day £55/85) This outfit offers introductory sea-kayaking courses and guided kayaking tours around the Summer Isles and in the Lochinver and Ullapool areas. It also hires kayaks and will do pick-ups and drop-offs.

🛏 Sleeping & Eating

Clachtoll Beach Campsite
CAMPSITE £

(📱01571-855377; www.clachtollbeachcampsite.co.uk; B869, Clachtoll; site incl 1 adult £10-21, per extra adult/child £5/2; ⊘Apr–mid-Oct; 🅿🛜🐾) Set among the machair beside a lovely white-

WORTH A TRIP

CAPE WRATH

Though its name actually comes from the Norse word *hvarf* ('turning point'), there is something daunting and primal about Cape Wrath, the remote northwesternmost point of the British mainland.

The hazardous, stormy seas around the cape led to the building of the lighthouse here by Robert and Alan Stevenson in 1828. The last keepers had left by 1998, when humans were replaced by automation. Three miles to the east are the seabird colonies of Clo Mor, the British mainland's highest vertical sea cliffs (195m).

Part of the moorland here has served for decades as a bombing range. The island of An Garbh-Eilean, 5 miles from the cape, has the misfortune to be around the same size as an aircraft carrier and is regularly ripped up by RAF bombs and missiles. There is no public access when the range is in use; times are displayed at www.visitcape-wrath.com.

A cafe at the lighthouse serves soup and sandwiches. It's open year-round and John, the owner, will never turn anyone away whatever the time of day.

Getting to Cape Wrath involves taking a **ferry** (☑ 07719 678729; www.capewrathferry.wordpress.com; return £10, bike £15; ☺ 10am-4.30pm May-Sep) – passengers and bikes only – across the Kyle of Durness (10 minutes). It connects with the **Cape Wrath Minibus** (☑ 07742 670196; www.visitcapewrath.com; return £13; ☺ May-Sep), which runs the very slow and bumpy 11 miles to the cape (50 minutes).

This combination is a friendly but eccentric and sometimes shambolic service with limited capacity, so plan on waiting in high season, and call ahead to make sure the ferry is running. The ferry leaves from 2 miles southwest of Durness, and runs twice or more daily from May to September. If you eschew the minibus, it's a spectacular 11-mile bike ride or hike from boat to cape through bleak scenery.

An increasingly popular but serious and challenging walking route, the **Cape Wrath Trail** (www.capewrathtrail.org.uk) runs from Fort William up to Cape Wrath (230 miles). It's unmarked so buy the *Cape Wrath Trail* guidebook (www.cicerone.co.uk) or go with a guide – **C-n-Do** (☑ 01786-445703; www.cndoscotland.com) is one operator.

sand beach and emerald seas, Clachtoll is a divine coastal camping spot, though somewhat overwhelmed by the adjacent self-catering development. It's 6 miles northwest of Lochinver by road.

Achmelvich Beach
Youth Hostel HOSTEL £
(HS; ☑ 01571-844480; www.hostellingscotland.org.uk; Achmelvich; dm/tw £22.50/55; ☺ Apr-Sep; 🐾) Off the B869, this whitewashed cottage is set beside a great beach at the end of a side road. Dorms are simple, and there's a sociable common kitchen and eating area. Heat-up meals are available, as is a basic shop in summer; otherwise, there's a chip van at the adjacent campsite, or you can take the 4-mile walk to Lochinver.

Davar B&B ££
(☑ 01571-844501; www.davar-lochinver.co.uk; Baddidarroch, Lochinver; s/d from £85/110; 🅿️🛜) Run with a genuine welcome and enthusiasm, this is a beautiful house with a garden and a fabulous outlook across the bay to Suilven and the Assynt mountainscape.

The four rooms are well appointed and have plenty of space; it's the ideal base for exploring the region. To find it, turn west at the northern end of Lochinver.

⭐**Lochinver Larder**
& Riverside Bistro BISTRO £
(☑ 01571-844356; www.lochinverlarder.com; 3 Main St, Lochinver; pies £5-6, mains £7-13; ☺ 10am-7.45pm Mon-Sat, to 5.30pm Sun Apr-Oct, 10am-4pm Mon-Sat Nov-Mar; 🛜) An outstanding menu of inventive food made with local produce is on offer here. The bistro turns out delicious seafood dishes in the evening, while the takeaway counter sells tasty pies with a wide range of gourmet fillings (try the venison and cranberry). It also does quality meals to take away and heat up: great for hostellers and campers.

ⓘ Getting There & Away

Rapsons bus 809 goes from Ullapool to Lochinver (£5.50, one hour, two to four Monday to Saturday).

THE SUMMER ISLES

The dozen islands scattered in the sea to the west of Achiltibuie are known as the Summer Isles. There's a superb view of the islands, with the hills of Wester Ross in the background, from the minor road between Altandhu and Achnahaird – look out for a layby with a bench and a signpost, where a short path leads to the viewpoint.

In the late 19th century the Summer Isles were home to 120 people working at the herring fishery, but now the permanent population is only half a dozen, augmented by holiday visitors. The largest island, Tanera Mòr, has self-catering cottages.

You can visit the Summer Isles on boat trips from Ullapool; tour operators include **Seascape** (☑ 07511 290081; www.sea-scape.co.uk; adult/child £30/20; ⊗ May-Sep) and Shearwater Cruises. Otherwise, there are cruises with Summer Isles Seatours and other boat transport from Old Dornie pier, northwest of Achiltibuie, available in summer by prior arrangement.

Coigach

The region south of Assynt, west of the main A835 road from Ullapool to Ledmore Junction, is known as Coigach (www.coigach. com). A lone, single-track road penetrates this wilderness, leading through gloriously wild scenery to remote settlements. At the western end of Loch Lurgainn, a branch leads north to Lochinver, a scenic back road so narrow and twisting that it's nicknamed the **Wee Mad Road** (warning – not suitable for caravans or large motorhomes).

Coigach is a wonderland for walkers and wildlife enthusiasts, with a patchwork of sinuous silver lochs dominated by the isolated peaks of Cul Mor (849m), Cul Beag (769m), Ben More Coigach (743m) and Stac Pollaidh (613m). The main settlement is the straggling township of **Achiltibuie**, 15 miles from the main road, with the gorgeous Summer Isles moored just off the coast, and silhouettes of mountains skirting the bay.

Stac Pollaidh   HIKING
Despite its diminutive size, Stac Pollaidh provides one of the most exciting hill walks in the Highlands, with some good scrambling on its narrow sandstone crest.

Begin at the car park overlooking Loch Lurgainn, 5 miles west of the A835, and follow a clearly marked and well-made footpath around the eastern end of the hill to ascend from the far side; return by the same route (3 miles return, two to four hours).

Summer Isles Seatours   CRUISE
(☑ 07927 920592; www.summerisles-seatours. co.uk; adult/child £30/15; ⊗ Mon-Sat May-Sep) Cruises to the Summer Isles from Badentar-bat pier, northwest of Achiltibuie. You get to spend some time ashore on Tanera Mòr.

Acheninver Hostel   HOSTEL £
(☑ 01854-622283; www.acheninverhostel.com; dm £22, pod £80-90; ⊗ Apr-Sep) A quarter-mile (five-minute) hike from the road a couple of miles southeast of Achiltibuie, this off-the-beaten-track hostel has a remote, serene location that's one of the country's best. It's a cosy spot, and has a female dorm with single beds, a male dorm with bunks and three en-suite pods sleeping three or four. There's a kitchen, and some limited supplies are available.

★ Summer Isles Hotel   HOTEL £££
(☑ 01854-622282; www.summerisleshotel. com; Achiltibuie; r/ste from £190/310; ⊗ Easter-Oct; P ⚹ ⚹) This is a special place, with cracking views and wonderfully romantic rooms (one themed on Charlie Chaplin, who stayed here in the 1970s), plus suites in separate cottages and a snug bar with outdoor seating. 'Courtyard view' rooms are darkish; it's worth upgrading to one with sea views. It's the perfect spot for a romantic getaway or some quality time off the grid.

The restaurant (noon to 3pm and 6pm to 9pm; mains £23 to £40) is of high quality, with local lobster usually featuring in addition to renowned cheese and dessert trolleys. There's also a great wine list considering you're in the middle of nowhere.

Ullapool

☑ 01854 / POP 1500
This pretty harbour town on the shores of Loch Broom, purpose-built as a fishing

port in 1788, is the largest settlement in Wester Ross and one of the most alluring spots in the Highlands. It's a wonderful destination in itself, as well as a gateway to the Western Isles. Offering a row of whitewashed cottages arrayed along the loch shore and special views of the loch and its flanking hills, the town has a very distinctive appeal. The harbour served as an emigration point during the Clearances, with thousands of Scots watching Ullapool recede behind as they began the journey to a new continent.

◎ Sights & Activities

Ullapool is a great centre for hill walking. A good path up Gleann na Sguaib heads for the top of Beinn Dearg from Inverlael, at the inner end of Loch Broom. Ridge walking on the Fannichs (south of the A835) is relatively straightforward, if strenuous, and many different routes are possible.

The Ullapool Tourist Office (p366) can supply you with all the information and maps you need. Good walking books are also sold there, and at **Ullapool Bookshop** (☑01854-612918; www.ullapoolbookshop.co.uk; Quay St; ⊙10am-6pm Mon-Sat, noon-5pm Sun), or you can pick up a copy of the freebie guide to local woodland walks.

Ullapool Museum   MUSEUM
(☑01854-612987; www.ullapoolmuseum.co.uk; 7 West Argyle St; adult/child £5/free; ⊙11am-4pm Mon, Tue, Thu & Fri, 10am-5pm Sat Apr-Oct) Housed in a converted Telford church, this museum relates the prehistoric, natural and social history of the town and Lochbroom area, with a particular focus on Highland emigration to Nova Scotia and other places. There's also a genealogy section if you want to trace your Scottish roots.

Shearwater Cruises   BOATING
(☑01854-612472; www.summerqueen.co.uk; Harbour; adult/child £35/30; ⊙Mon-Sat May-Sep) Weather permitting, the catamaran *Shearwater* takes you out to the Summer Isles for a 2¼-hour cruise. They leave twice a day.

🛏 Sleeping

There's a good selection of B&Bs, with some standout options. Note that during summer Ullapool is very busy and finding accommodation can be tricky – book

ahead. Several places don't accept single-night stays.

Ullapool Youth Hostel   HOSTEL £
(HS; ☑01854-612254; www.hostellingscotland. org.uk; Shore St; dm/tw/q £23/59/103; ⊙Apr-Oct; 🛜) You've got to hand it to Hostelling Scotland – it's chosen some very sweet locations for its hostels. This one is right in the heart of town on the pretty waterfront; some rooms have harbour views and the busy dining area and little lounge are also good spots for contemplating the water.

★**Tamarin Lodge**   B&B ££
(☑01854-612667; www.tamarinullapool.com; 9 The Braes; s/d from £49/98; 🅿🛜🐾) Effortlessly elegant modern architecture in its own right, but the glorious vistas over the water far below to the hills opposite are unforgettable. All rooms face the view; some have a balcony, and all are spacious, quiet and relaxing, with unexpected features and gadgets. The great lounge and benevolent hosts are a delight.

Follow signs for Braes from the Inverness road.

Waterside House   B&B ££
(☑01854-612140; www.waterside.uk.net; 6 West Shore St; d from £90; ⊙Apr-Oct; 🅿🛜) This typical whitewashed West Highland house is right on the waterfront – so close to the ferry that you can watch it docking from your window. There are three compact but beautifully appointed rooms with excellent modern bathrooms. The location and the friendly welcome are fabulous, and your hosts go the extra mile at breakfast time – delicious. Minimum two-night stay in summer.

★**Ceilidh Place**   HOTEL £££
(☑01854-612103; www.theceilidhplace.com; 14 West Argyle St; r £130-180; 🅿🛜🐾) This hotel is a celebration of Scottish culture: we're talking literature and traditional music, not tartan and Nessie dolls. Rooms go for character over modernity; instead of TVs they come with a selection of books chosen by Scottish literati, plus eclectic artwork and cosy touches. The sumptuous lounge has sofas, chaises longues and an honesty bar. There's a bookshop here, too.

It's not luxurious but it's one of the Highlands' more unusual and delightful places to stay.

✕ Eating

West Coast Delicatessen
CAFE £

(📞 01854-613450; www.westcoastdeli.co.uk; 5 Argyle St; light meals £3-7; ⊙ 9am-5pm Mon-Sat; 🛜) A likeable venue for a coffee or snack, this upbeat modern place has sub rolls, decent coffee and a variety of deli produce, including some very tasty cheeses. It also does a good soup, perfect for chillier Ullapool days.

Seafood Shack
SEAFOOD £

(📞 07876 142623; www.seafoodshack.co.uk; West Argyle St; mains £5-10, half lobster £20; ⊙ noon-6pm Apr-late Oct) High-quality fresh seafood is served out of a trailer in this vacant lot by two cheery lasses, Kirsty and Fenella. There's a wide range of tasty fare available, from hand-dived scallops to calamari, mussels, crab, oysters and lobster.

Ceilidh Place
SCOTTISH ££

(📞 01854-612103; www.theceilidhplace.com; 14 West Argyle St; mains £7-22; ⊙ 8am-9pm Feb-Dec; 🛜) The restaurant in this hub of culture and good cheer serves inventive dishes that focus on fresh local seafood backed up by venison casserole, plus lighter meals like pies and burgers during the day. Quality depends a bit on staffing, but it's an atmospheric, cosy place with outdoor seating, good wines by the glass and regular live music and events.

❶ Information

Ullapool Tourist Office (📞 01854-612486; ullapool@visitscotland.com; 6 Argyle St; ⊙ 9am-6pm Mon-Sat, 9.30am-4.30pm Sun Jul & Aug, 10am-4pm Mon-Sat, 10am-3pm Sep-Jun, closed 12.45-1.30pm Nov-Easter) Can book ferries and buses.

Ullapool Library (📞 01854-612543; www. highlifehighland.com; Mill St; ⊙ 9am-5pm Mon-Fri, plus 6-8pm Tue & Thu, shorter hours & closed Mon & Wed during holidays; 🛜) Free internet access.

❶ Getting There & Away

Citylink has buses from Inverness to Ullapool (£14.90, 1½ hours, one to three daily), connecting with the Stornoway ferry.

Two daily CalMac (p464) ferries run from Ullapool to Stornoway on Lewis in the Outer Hebrides (adult/car £9.75/53, 2½ hours).

Ullapool to Kyle of Lochalsh

Although it's less than 50 miles as the crow flies from Ullapool to Kyle of Lochalsh, it's more like 150 miles along the circuitous coastal road – but don't let that put you off. It's a delightfully remote region and there are fine views of beaches and bays backed by mountains all the way along.

Twelve miles southeast of Ullapool at Braemore, the A832 doubles back towards the coast as it heads for Gairloch (the A835 continues southeast across the wild, sometimes snowbound, Dirrie More pass to Garve and Inverness). If you're hurrying to Skye, use the A835 and catch up with the A832 further south, near Garve.

Falls of Measach
WATERFALL

Just west of the junction of the A835 and A832, 2 miles south of Braemore, a car park gives access to the Falls of Measach, which spill 45m into the spectacularly deep and narrow Corrieshalloch Gorge. You can cross the gorge on a swaying suspension bridge, and walk west for 250m to a viewing platform that juts out dizzyingly above a sheer drop. The thundering falls and misty vapours rising from the gorge are very impressive.

Gairloch & Around

📞 01445 / POP 1000

Gairloch is a group of villages (comprising Achtercairn, Strath and Charlestown) around the inner end of a loch of the same name. It's a good base for whale- and dolphin-watching excursions, and the surrounding area has beautiful sandy beaches, good trout fishing and birdwatching. Hill walkers also use Gairloch as a base for the Torridon hills and An Teallach.

◉ Sights & Activities

The B8056 runs along Loch Gairloch's southern shore, past the cute little harbour of Badachro, to end at the gorgeous pink-sand beach of Red Point – a perfect picnic spot. Another coastal road leads north from Gairloch 11 miles to the settlement of Melvaig. From here a private road (open to walkers and cyclists) continues 3 miles to Rua Reidh Lighthouse (building and grounds off-limits to nonguests).

Driving Tour
Wee Roads & Mighty Mountains

START ULLAPOOL
END PORTREE
LENGTH 320 MILES; THREE TO FOUR DAYS

Starting in photogenic harbourside Ullapool, this drive takes in some of the lesser-known roads and most majestic Highland scenery, finishing on the Isle of Skye.

Leave your bags in the hotel, because the first day is a long round trip from Ullapool. Head north on the A835, and turn left to **1 Achiltibuie** (p364), where, after gaping at impressive lochside Stac Pollaidh en route, you can admire the outlook over the Summer Isles. From here, backtrack 6 miles then turn left up the Wee Mad Rd, a narrow, tortuous but scenic drive north to pretty **2 Lochinver** (p362). From here, the B869 winds north past spectacular beaches at Achmelvich and Clachtoll to **3 Kylesku** (p362), where the hotel makes a great lunch stop. Return south to Ullapool on the main road (A894–A837–A835), with things to see along the way, including the Inchnadamph Caves, Ardvreck Castle and Knockan Crag.

The next day head inland along the A835 before taking the A832 **4 Gairloch** (p366) turn-off, following the coast road with plenty of activity options, from whale watching to a botanic garden and hiking on Loch Maree. At **5 Kinlochewe** (p369) turn back coastwards on the A896, descending a spectacular pass to **6 Torridon** (p369), where the rugged beauty is simply breathtaking. There are good overnight stops all along this route.

From **7 Shieldaig** (p369), take the coastal road to sublime little **8 Applecross** (p370), then brave the Bealach na Bà pass to get you back to the main road. A loop around Loch Carron will eventually bring you to the A87. Turn left, passing **9 Eilean Donan Castle** (p373) and, reaching Glen Shiel, take the right turn to **10 Glenelg** (p373), a scenic, out-of-the-way place with a wonderfully rustic summer ferry crossing to Skye. Disembark at **11 Kylerhea** (p376) and enjoy the vistas on one of the island's least-trafficked roads before hitting the A87 again. From here, **12 Portree** (p381) is an easy drive, but numerous picturesque detours – to Sleat or Elgol, for example – mean you might take a while to reach it.

★ Inverewe Garden

GARDENS

(NTS; ☑ 01445-712952; www.nts.org.uk; adult/concession £13/11.50; ⊙ 9.30am-6pm Jun-Aug, to 5pm Mar, Apr & Sep, to 5.30pm May, to 4pm Oct, 10am-4pm Nov-Feb) Six miles north of Gairloch, this splendid place is a welcome splash of colour on the otherwise bleak coast. The climate here is warmed by the Gulf Stream, which allowed Osgood Mac-Kenzie to create this exotic woodland garden in 1862. There are free guided tours on weekdays at 1.30pm from March to October. The licensed cafe-restaurant serves great cakes.

Parking for non-members is £2.

Russian Arctic
Convoy Exhibition Centre

MUSEUM

(☑ 01445-731137; www.russianarcticconvoymuseum.org; Birchburn, Aultbea; adult/child £4/3; ⊙ 10am-4pm Mon-Sat Apr–mid-Dec, 11am-3pm Fri-Sun Jan-Mar) The Arctic convoys were a vital supply line for Russia during WWII; these merchant ships escorted by Allied warships brought supplies into the northern ports through a gauntlet of German ships and submarines. Many left from Loch Ewe, and this volunteer project tells the fascinating stories of those tough trips. There's also a small shop.

It's on the A832, 12 miles north of Gairloch. Winter opening hours may vary according to volunteer availability.

Gairloch Marine
Wildlife Centre & Cruises

WILDLIFE

(☑ 07751 992666; www.porpoise-gairloch.co.uk; Pier Rd, Gairloch; cruises adult/child £30/25; ⊙ 10am-6pm Easter-Oct) ✿ This small visitor centre has audiovisual and interactive displays, lots of charts, photos and knowledgeable staff. From here, cruises run three times daily (weather permitting) – during the two-hour trips you may see basking sharks, porpoises and minke whales. The crew collects data on water temperature and conditions, and monitors cetacean populations, so you are subsidising important research.

Hebridean Whale Cruises

WILDLIFE

(☑ 01445-712458; www.hebridean-whale-cruises.com; Pier Rd, Gairloch; ⊙ Apr-Oct) Based at Gairloch's harbour, this set-up runs three trips: a standard 2½-hour whale-watching excursion (£53; from May), a three-hour visit to the seabird-rich Shiant Islands (£57) and a four-hour excursion to further-flung feeding grounds in search of orcas (£84). Other wildlife it's possible to see includes otters, dolphins and seals. Trips are in a zippy rigid inflatable boat (RIB).

🛏 Sleeping & Eating

Gairloch Sands Youth Hostel

HOSTEL £

(HS; ☑ 01445-712219; www.hostellingscotland.org.uk; Carn Dearg; dm/tw/q £22.50/57/99; ⊙ Apr-Sep; 🅿🛜🐾) Located 2.5 miles west of Gairloch in a stunning coastal position, this hostel is close to beaches and well set up for walkers. Wood-panelled rooms and a large dining room/lounge offer comfort, but the real star is that view...magic!

Rua Reidh Lighthouse

LODGE £££

(☑ 01445-771263; www.stayatalighthouse.co.uk; Melvaig; r £130-140; ⊙ Easter-Oct; 🅿🐾) Three miles along a narrow private road beyond Melvaig (11 miles north of Gairloch), this simple yet excellent lodge gives a taste of a lighthouse-keeper's life. It's a wild, lonely location, great for walking and bird-watching. Breakfast is included and tasty evening meals are available. There's no TV or wi-fi and only a flaky mobile-phone signal. Two-night minimum stay.

There's a separate self-catering apartment that's available year-round.

Shieldaig Lodge

HOTEL £££

(☑ 01445-741333; www.shieldaiglodge.com; Badachro; s £180, d from £215; 🅿🛜) This refurbished hunting lodge has a super waterside position on a sizeable estate offering good walking and fishing as well as falconry and archery. It's a cosy place – think drams and a log fire – with a good restaurant, a very well stocked bar and tasteful rooms, the best of which have water views. There's also a snooker table and a lovely library.

Mountain Coffee Company

CAFE £

(☑ 01445-712316; www.facebook.com/mountaincoffee.gairloch; Strath Sq, Strath; light meals £4-7; ⊙ 9am-5.30pm, reduced hours low season) ✿ More the sort of place you'd expect to find on the gringo trail in the Andes, this offbeat and cosy (if occasionally brusque) spot is a shrine to mountaineering and travelling. It serves tasty savoury bagels, home baking and sustainably sourced coffees. The conservatory is the place to lap up the sun, while the attached Hillbillies Bookshop is well worth a browse.

There are rather sweet en-suite bedrooms available, too.

ℹ Information

Gairloch Tourist Office (☎ 01445-712071; www.galeactionforum.co.uk; Achtercairn; ⊙ 9.30am-5.30pm Mon-Sat, 10.30am-5pm Sun Jun-Sep, 10am-5.30pm Mon-Sat, 10.30am-4.30pm Sun Oct-May) Community-run information centre in the Gale Centre, on the road through town. Has good walking pamphlets; there's also a cafe.

ℹ Getting There & Away

Public transport to Gairloch is very limited. **Westerbus** (☎ 01445-712255) runs direct to/from Inverness (£11, 2¼ hours) twice weekly (Tuesday and Saturday), but the future of this service was in doubt at time of research.

Loch Maree & Around

Stretching 12 miles between Poolewe and Kinlochewe, Loch Maree is considered one of Scotland's prettiest lochs, with the imposing bulk of Slioch on its northeastern side and Beinn Eighe on the southwestern. Look out for black-throated divers on the lake in summer. At its southern end, tiny Kinlochewe makes a good base for outdoor activities.

Beinn Eighe Mountain Trail   WALKING
This waymarked 4-mile loop walk to a plateau and cairn on the side of Beinn Eighe has magnificent views over Loch Maree. It's quite exposed up there, so take some warm clothing. The walk starts from a car park on the A832 about 1.5 miles northwest of the Beinn Eighe Tourist Office.

From the same trailhead there's a shorter 1-mile trail through Scots pine forest.

Torridon

The road southwest from Kinlochewe passes through Glen Torridon, amid some of Britain's most beautiful scenery. Carved by ice from massive layers of ancient sandstone that takes its name from the region, the mountains here are steep, shapely and imposing, whether flirting with autumn mists, draped in dazzling winter snows, or reflected in the calm blue waters of Loch Clair on a summer day.

The road reaches the sea at spectacularly sited Torridon village, then continues westwards to lovely Shieldaig, which boasts an attractive main street of whitewashed houses right on the water.

🏃 Activities

The Torridon Munros – Liathach (1054m; pronounced 'lee-agakh', Gaelic for 'the Grey One'), **Beinn Eighe** (1010m; 'ben *ay*', 'the File') and **Beinn Alligin** (986m; 'the Jewelled Mountain') – are big, serious mountains for experienced hill walkers only. Though not technically difficult, their ascents are long and committing, often over rough and rocky terrain. Further information is available at the **Torridon Countryside Centre** (NTS; ☎ 01445-791221; www.nts.org.uk; Torridon Village; ⊙ 10am-5pm Sun-Fri Easter-Sep).

Torridon Outdoors (☎ 01445-791242; www.thetorridon.com/torridon-outdoors; The Stables; 2 adults half-/full day £150/250) runs a number of outdoor pursuits, including sea kayaking and mountain biking.

🍴 Sleeping & Eating

Torridon Youth Hostel   HOSTEL **£**
(HS; ☎ 01445-791284; www.hostellingscotland.org.uk; Torridon Village; dm/tw £23/59; ⊙ daily Mar-Oct, Fri & Sat nights Nov-Feb; P @ 🛜 🐾) This spacious modern hostel has enthusiastic, can-do management and sits in a magnificent location, surrounded by spectacular mountains. Roomy dorms and privates (twins have single beds) are allied to a huge kitchen and convivial lounge area, with ales on sale. It's a very popular walking base, with great advice from the in-house mountain-rescue team, so book ahead.

As well as breakfast, there are packed lunches and heat-up dinners on offer.

Stables   INN **£££**
(☎ 01445-791242; www.thetorridon.com/stay/the-stables; d/f from £155/245; ⊙ daily Easter-Oct, Thu-Sun mid-Feb–Easter & Nov, closed Dec–mid-Feb; P 🛜 🐾) This convivial but upmarket hikers' hang-out has excellent modern rooms that vary substantially in size and layout. Rooms for groups of up to six (from £285) offer more value than the commodious but overpriced doubles. The sociable bar serves all-day food and there are numerous activities on offer.

⭐ **Torridon**   HOTEL **£££**
(☎ 01445-791242; www.thetorridon.com/stay/hotel; r/ste from £350/425; ⊙ closed Jan, plus Mon & Tue Feb, Mar, Nov & Dec; P @ 🛜 🐾) If you prefer the lap of luxury to the sound of rain beating on your tent, head for this lavish Victorian hunting lodge with a romantic

lochside location. Sumptuous contemporary rooms with awe-inspiring views, top bathrooms and a cheery Highland cow atop the counterpane couldn't be more inviting. It's one of Scotland's top country hotels, always luxurious but never pretentious.

Master suites are lavish in size and comfort, with bay windows making the most of the panoramas. Service is excellent, with muddy boots positively welcomed, and dinners are splendid affairs and also open to nonguests. Friendly staff can organise any number of activities (p369) on land or water.

Tigh an Eilean
HOTEL £££

(☑ 01520-755251; www.tighaneilean.co.uk; Shieldaig; s/d £80/160; ☺ Feb-Dec; ☎) With a lovely waterfront location in the pretty village of Shieldaig, this is an appealing destination for a relaxing stay, offering old-style rooms that are comfortable rather than luxurious. Loch-view rooms – with gloriously soothing vistas – are allocated on a first-booked basis, so it's worth reserving ahead. Service is very helpful, and there's a cosy lounge with an honesty bar.

Prices drop for stays of three or more nights.

Wee Whistle Stop Cafe
CAFE £

(☑ 01445-791361; www.facebook.com/WeeWhistleStop; Loch Torridon Community Hall; meals £7-15; ☺ 9am-6pm Sat-Thu, to 7pm Fri) This is a tempting place to drop by for anything from a coffee to enticing bistro fare – the outdoor terrace has glorious views across Loch Torridon. There are great daily specials and delicious home baking, juices and smoothies. It's very friendly, and used to pumping life back into chilly walkers and cyclists. Opening hours may vary by season; check its Facebook page.

★ Shieldaig Bar & Coastal Kitchen
SEAFOOD ££

(☑ 01520-755251; www.tighaneilean.co.uk/coastal_kitchen.asp; Shieldaig; mains £13-25; ☺ food noon-2.30pm & 6-8.30pm or 9pm, closed some winter lunchtimes; ☎) This attractive pub has real ales and waterside tables plus a great upstairs dining room with an outdoor deck. There's an emphasis on quality local seafood as well as wood-fired pizzas and bistro-style meat dishes such as steak-frites or sausages and mash. Blackboard specials feature the daily catch – the superb seafood platter costs £32.

Applecross

☑ 01520 / POP 200

The remote seaside village of Applecross feels like an island retreat due to its isolation and the magnificent views of Raasay and the hills of Skye that set the pulse racing, particularly at sunset. On a clear day it's an unforgettable place. The campsite and pub fill to the brim in school holidays.

Twenty-five winding miles of single-track road lead here from Shieldaig, but more spectacular (accessed from further south on the A896) is the magnificent **Bealach na Bà** (626m; Pass of the Cattle), the third-highest motor road in the UK, and the longest continuous climb (not suitable for caravans or large motorhomes). Originally built in 1822, it climbs steeply and hair-raisingly via hairpin bends perched over sheer drops, with gradients of up to 25%, then plunges dramatically to the village with views of Skye ahead.

Hartfield House
HOSTEL £

(☑ 01520-744333; www.hartfieldhouse.org.uk; Hartfield Rd; dm/s/tw/d £27/35/55/70; ☺ Mar-Oct; P ☎ ☺) This former hunting lodge on the Applecross estate is about a mile off the road in a lovely rural location. With lots of beds across two separate buildings in both dorms and private rooms, plus good common areas, it offers plenty of space and comfort. Walkers and cyclists have decent facilities and a help-yourself continental breakfast is included.

★ Applecross Inn
INN £££

(☑ 01520-744262; www.applecrossinn.co.uk; Shore St; s/d from £100/150; P ☎ ☺) ✎ The hub of the spread-out Applecross community, this inn is a great spot to hole up, but you'll need to book ahead. Seven snug bedrooms all have a view of the Skye hills and the sea. It's a magical spot and there's a cracking pub and **restaurant** (☑ 01520-744262; www.applecrossinn.co.uk; Shore St; mains £12-22; ☺ noon-9pm; ☎) ✎. It also some cottage accommodation along the waterfront.

ⓘ Getting There & Away

There are two buses a week (Wednesday and Saturday) with **Lochcarron Garage** (☑ 01520-722997; www.lochcarrongarage.co.uk/bus) from Inverness to Applecross (£11.10, 3½ hours) via Shieldaig (ie around the north coast, not over the Bealach na Bà).

Lochcarron

📞 01520 / POP 900

Appealing, whitewashed Lochcarron is a veritable metropolis for this part of Scotland, with two supermarkets, a bank with an ATM and a petrol station. A long shoreline footpath at the loch's edge provides the perfect opportunity for a stroll to walk off breakfast.

Old Manse
B&B ££

(📞 01520-722208; www.theoldmanselochcarron.com; Church St; s/d from £45/75, tw with loch view £85; P 🛜 🐾) The Old Manse is a top-notch Scottish guesthouse, beautifully appointed and in a prime, quiet lochside position. Rooms are traditional in style and simply gorgeous, with elegant furniture. Those overlooking the water are larger and well worth the extra tenner. Follow signs for the West End.

⭐ Kishorn Seafood Bar
SEAFOOD ££

(📞 01520-733240; www.kishornseafoodbar.co.uk; Kishorn; mains £10-20; ⏰ 11am-5pm Mon-Sat, noon-4pm Sun, 6-9pm Thu-Sat Mar-Oct, plus 6-9pm Tue & Wed Jul & Aug, call for winter hours) 🍴 Four miles west of Lochcarron, the Kishorn Seafood Bar is a cute, pale blue bungalow that serves the freshest of local seafood simply and well, with very fair prices. The views are spectacular, and you've got the satisfaction of knowing that much of what you eat was caught in Loch Kishorn just below. Book for dinner.

Plockton

📞 01599 / POP 400

Idyllic little Plockton, with its perfect cottages lining a perfect bay, looks like it was designed as a film set. And it indeed served as just that – scenes from *The Wicker Man* (1973) were filmed here, and the village became famous as the location for the 1990s TV series *Hamish Macbeth*.

With all this picture-postcard perfection, it's hardly surprising that Plockton is a tourist hot spot, crammed with day trippers and holidaymakers in summer. But there's no denying its appeal, with 'palm trees' (actually hardy New Zealand cabbage palms) lining the waterfront, a thriving small-boat sailing scene and several good places to stay, eat and drink. The big event of the year is the **Plockton Regatta** (https://visitplockton.com/event/plockton-small-boat-regatta; ⏰ Jul/Aug).

The website www.visitplockton.com is a useful source of local information.

🏃 Activities

Hire canoes and rowboats on the waterfront to explore the bay.

Calum's Seal Trips
TOUR

(📞 07761 263828; www.calums-sealtrips.com; adult/child £14/6; ⏰ Apr-Oct) Wildlife-watching cruises visit a seal colony just outside the harbour. There's excellent commentary and you may even spot otters as well. Trips leave several times daily, and offer your money back if you don't see any seals.

Sea Kayak Plockton
KAYAKING

(📞 01599-544422; www.seakayakplockton.co.uk; 1-day beginner course adult/child £85/65) Sea Kayak Plockton offers everything from beginner lessons and family days out, to multi-day trips around Skye and the Outer Hebrides.

🛏 Sleeping

Plockton Station Bunkhouse
HOSTEL £

(📞 01599-544235; www.visitplockton.com/stay/bunkhouse; dm £18; P 🛜) Airily set in the former train station (the new one is opposite), this hostel has cosy four-bed dorms, a garden and kitchen-lounge with plenty of light, and good views over the frenetic comings and goings of the platforms below (OK, that last bit's a lie). The owners also have good-value B&B accommodation (single/double £35/60) next door in the inaccurately named 'Nessun Dorma'.

Seabank
CABIN ££

(📞 01599-544221; www.seabank-plockton.co.uk; 6 Bank St; per week £525; ⏰ Apr-Oct; 🛜) Centrally located but a little removed from the main-street bustle, this peaceful cabin offers a self-contained one-bed apartment overlooking the bay. There's a kitchenette and sitting area, and a double bed on a mezzanine floor, plus a little garden by the water where you can sit and absorb the tranquillity. Available for £80 a night (three-night minimum) November to March.

⭐ Plockton Hotel
INN £££

(📞 01599-544274; www.plocktonhotel.co.uk; 41 Harbour St; s/d £100/150, cottage s/d £65/100; 🛜) 🍴 The Plockton Hotel is one of those classic Highland spots that manages to make everyone happy, whether it's thirst, hunger or weariness that brings people knocking. Assiduously tended rooms are a real delight, with a homely atmosphere and thoughtful touches. Those without a sea view are consoled with more space and a balcony with rock-garden perspectives. The cottage nearby offers simpler comfort.

✖ Eating

Plockton Inn
SEAFOOD ££

(☑ 01599-544222; www.plocktoninn.co.uk; Innes St; mains £12-23; ⏱ noon-2.15pm & 6-9pm; 🛜) Offering a wide range of anything from haggis to toothsome local langoustines (Plockton prawns) and daily seafood specials, Plockton Inn covers lots of bases and has genuinely welcoming service. A range of rooms – some substantially more spacious than others, and some in an annexe – are also available (double £140).

★ Plockton Shores
SEAFOOD £££

(☑ 01599-544263; www.facebook.com/The ShoresPlockton; 30 Harbour St; restaurant mains £16-35; ⏱ cafe 9am-5.30pm Mon-Sat, noon-4pm Sun, restaurant 5-9pm Tue-Sat; 🅿) 🍴 This restaurant (attached to a shop) has a tempting menu of local seafood, including good-value platters with langoustines, mussels, crab, squat lobster and more, and succulent hand-dived tempura scallops. There's also a very tasty line in venison, steaks and a small selection of good vegetarian dishes that are more than an afterthought. The licensed cafe does home baking and light lunches.

Hours are reduced in winter but it's open year-round.

ℹ Getting There & Away

Trains running between Kyle of Lochalsh (£3, 15 minutes) and Inverness (£24.50, 2½ hours) stop in Plockton up to four times daily each way.

Kyle of Lochalsh

☑ 01599 / POP 700

Before the connecting bridge was opened in 1995, this was Skye's principal mainland ferry port. Visitors now tend to buzz through town, but Kyle has some good boat trips if you're interested in marine life, and there's some great seafood eating here. The railway trip from Inverness is spectacular.

Seaprobe Atlantis
BOATING

(☑ 0800 980 4846; www.seaprobeatlantis.com; adult/child from £15/9; ⏱ Easter-Oct) A glass-hulled boat takes you on a spin along the coast to spot seabirds, seals and maybe an otter. The basic trip includes entertaining commentary and plenty of beautiful jellyfish; longer trips also take in a WWII shipwreck.

The boat departs from Kyleakin across on Skye but the ticket office is in the main car park in Kyle.

★ Buth Bheag
SEAFOOD £

(☑ 01599-534002; www.buthbheag.co.uk; Kyel Prospect Rd; mains £6-10; ⏱ 10am-5pm Tue-Fri, to 3pm Sat Easter-Oct, 10am-3pm Tue-Fri Nov–mid-Dec & mid-Jan–Easter) This tiny shed by the water below the central car park sells excellent fresh fish and chips and seafood salads at great prices – the haddock wrap with pesto mayo is sublime. Get food to go and munch away while sitting by the harbour.

Waterside
SEAFOOD ££

(☑ 01599-534813; www.watersideseafoodrestaurant.co.uk; Train Station; mains £15-23; ⏱ 5.30-9pm mid-Mar–mid-Oct) 🍴 In a former waiting room on Kyle's train station platform, this quaint little spot serves reliably delicious fresh fish and shellfish. A big effort is made to source sustainably from local producers, and the quality is sky-high. A great list of specials is chalked up nightly on the blackboard.

In summer you nearly always have to book ahead.

ℹ Information

The website www.lochalsh.co.uk contains local tourist information.

ℹ Getting There & Away

Citylink runs two to three daily buses from Inverness (£23.10, two hours) and three from Glasgow (£44, five to six hours).

The train route between Kyle of Lochalsh and Inverness (£25.60, 2¾ hours, up to four daily) is marvellously scenic.

Kyle to the Great Glen

It's 55 miles southeast via the A87 from Kyle to Invergarry, which lies between Fort William and Fort Augustus, on Loch Oich. The road passes one of Scotland's most famous castles and through picturesque Glen Shiel, while a detour leads to the off-the-beaten-track Glenelg area.

Eilean Donan Castle

Photogenically perched on an island at the entrance to Loch Duich, and elegantly linked to the mainland by a stone-arched bridge, **Eilean Donan Castle** (☑01599-555202; www.eileandonancastle.com; Dornie; adult/child/family £10/6/29; ⊙10am-6pm Apr-Sep, to 5pm Oct, to 4pm Feb, Nov & Dec, closed Jan; ℗) is one of Scotland's most evocative castles. Although it looks venerable it's very much a reproduction, having been completed in the 1930s. There's an excellent introductory exhibition, photos of castle scenes from the movie *Highlander*, and a sword used at the battle of Culloden in 1746. Citylink buses from Fort William and Inverness to Portree stop opposite the castle.

The original 13th-century castle here was bombarded into ruins by government ships in 1719 when Jacobite forces were defeated at the Battle of Glen Shiel; it was rebuilt in its present form between 1912 and 1932.

Glen Shiel & Glenelg

From Eilean Donan Castle, the A87 follows Loch Duich towards spectacular Glen Shiel, with 1000m-high peaks soaring on either side of the road. Here, in 1719, a Jacobite army was defeated by Hanoverian government forces. Among those fighting on the rebel side were clansmen led by famous outlaw Rob Roy MacGregor and 300 soldiers loaned by the king of Spain; the mountain above the battlefield is still called Sgurr nan Spainteach (Peak of the Spaniard).

At Shiel Bridge, home to a famous wild-goat colony, a narrow side road goes over the Bealach Ratagain (pass), with great views of the Five Sisters of Kintail peaks, to Glenelg, where there's a community-run ferry to Skye. From Glenelg round to the road-end at Arnisdale, the scenery becomes even more spectacular, with great views across Loch Hourn to the remote Knoydart peninsula. A few miles south of Glenelg village a side road leads to two of the best-preserved **Iron Age brochs** in Scotland.

There are several good walks in the area, including the two-day, cross-country hike from Morvich to Cannich via scenic **Gleann Lichd** and Glen Affric Youth Hostel (35 miles). The **Five Sisters of Kintail** expedition is a classic but seriously challenging mountain-walk.

★ **Glenelg Inn**   GASTROPUB ££
(☑01599-522273; www.glenelg-inn.com; Glenelg; mains £12-19; ⊙kitchen 12.30-3pm daily, plus 6.15-8.15pm Thu-Sun Easter-Oct; ℗ 🛜 🐕) One of the Highlands' most picturesque places for a pint or a romantic away-from-it-all stay (doubles from £120), the Glenelg Inn has tables in a lovely garden with cracking views of Skye. The elegant dining room and cosy bar area serve posh pub grub, with local langoustines, scallops and fish usually featuring. Winter opening is sporadic; check the website.

❶ Getting There & Away

BOAT

A picturesque community-owned **vehicle ferry** (http://skyeferry.co.uk; foot passenger/bike/car with passengers £3/4/15; ⊙10am-6pm Easter–mid-Oct, to 7pm Jun-Aug) – the last manually operated turntable ferry in the country – runs from Glenelg across to Kylerhea on Skye, with crossings every 20 minutes. Booking not required.

BUS

Citylink buses between Fort William/Inverness and Skye travel along the A87.

Macrae Kintail (☑01599-511384; www.macraekintailbus.co.uk) minibuses run on request Monday, Tuesday and Friday from Kyle of Lochalsh to Arnisdale, via Shiel Bridge, Ratagan and Glenelg (£8, 1¼ hours). Must be booked in advance.

SKYE

POP 10,000

The Isle of Skye (an t-Eilean Sgiathanach in Gaelic) takes its name from the old Norse *sky-a,* meaning 'cloud island', a Viking reference to the often-mist-enshrouded Cuillin Hills. It's the second-largest of Scotland's islands, a 50-mile-long patchwork of velvet moors, jagged mountains, sparkling lochs and towering sea cliffs.

The stunning scenery is the main attraction, but when the mist closes in there are plenty of castles, crofting museums and cosy pubs and restaurants; there are also dozens of art galleries and craft studios.

Along with Edinburgh and Loch Ness, Skye is one of Scotland's top-three tourist destinations, and as a result can suffer from overcrowding at hot spots such as the Quiraing, the Old Man of Storr and the Fairy Pools. However, it's almost always possible to find peace and quiet in the island's further-flung corners. Come prepared for changeable weather: when it's fine it's very fine indeed, but all too often it isn't.

🏃 Activities

Walking

Skye offers some of the finest – and in places, the roughest and most difficult – walking in Scotland. There are many detailed guidebooks available, including a series of four walking guides by Charles Rhodes, available from the Aros Centre (p381) and the tourist office (p382) in Portree. You'll need Ordnance Survey (OS) 1:50,000 maps 23 and 32, or Harvey's 1:25,000 *Superwalker – The Cuillin*. Don't attempt the longer walks in bad weather or in winter.

Easy, low-level routes include: through **Strath Mor** from Luib (on the Broadford–Sligachan road) and on to Torrin (on the Broadford–Elgol road; allow 1½ hours, 4 miles); from **Sligachan to Kilmarie** via Camasunary (four hours, 11 miles); and from **Elgol to Kilmarie** via Camasunary (2½ hours, 6.5 miles). The walk from Kilmarie to Coruisk and back via Camasunary and the 'Bad Step' is superb but slightly harder (11 miles round trip; allow at least six hours).

The **Bad Step** is a rocky slab poised above the sea that you have to scramble across; it's easy in fine, dry weather, but some walkers find it intimidating.

Skye Wilderness Safaris runs one-day guided hiking trips for small groups (four to six people) through the Cuillin Hills, into the Quiraing or along the Trotternish ridge; transport to/from Portree is included.

Climbing

The Cuillin Hills are a playground for rock climbers, and the two-day traverse of the **Cuillin Ridge** is the finest mountaineering expedition in the British Isles. There are several mountain guides in the area who can provide instruction and safely introduce inexperienced climbers to the more difficult routes.

Skye Guides (☑ 01471-822116; www. skyeguides.co.uk) offers a one-day introduction-to-rock-climbing course for around £285; a private mountain guide can be hired for £295 a day (both rates are for two clients).

Sea Kayaking

The sheltered coves and sea lochs around the coast of Skye provide enthusiasts with magnificent sea-kayaking opportunities.

Whitewave Outdoor Centre   KAYAKING
(☑ 01470-542414; www.white-wave.co.uk; 19 Linicro, Kilmuir; half-day kayak session per person £40-50; ⊙ Mar-Oct) Provides sea-kayaking instruction and guiding for both beginners and experts; prices include equipment hire. Other activities include mountain boarding, bushcraft and rock climbing.

👉 Tours

There are several operators who offer guided minibus tours of Skye, covering history, culture and wildlife. Rates are from £150 to £200 for a six-hour tour for up to six people.

Skye Wilderness Safaris   WALKING
(☑ 01470-542229; www.skye-wilderness-safaris. com; per person £95-120, group of 4 from £250; ⊙ May-Sep) Runs one-day guided hiking trips for small groups through the Cuillin Hills, into the Quiraing or along the Trotternish ridge; transport to/from Portree included.

Also runs Skye Photo Academy (www. skyephotoacademy.com), which offers photography tuition (workshops from £230 per person) and photo tours around Skye, Glencoe and the Outer Hebrides.

Skye Tours   BUS
(☑ 01471-822716; www.skye-tours.co.uk; adult/ child £50/40; ⊙ Mon-Sat) Five-hour sightseeing tours of Skye in a minibus, taking in the Old Man of Storr (p383), Kilt Rock and Dunvegan Castle (p382). Tours depart from Kyle of Lochalsh train station at 11.30am (connects with the 8.55am train from Inverness, and returns to Kyle by 4.45pm in time to catch the return train at 5.13pm).

ℹ Information

Only Portree and Broadford have banks and ATMs.

Portree Tourist Office (p382) is the only tourist office on the island. It provides internet access and an accommodation booking service. Ask for the free *Art Skye – Gallery &*

Skye & Outer Hebrides

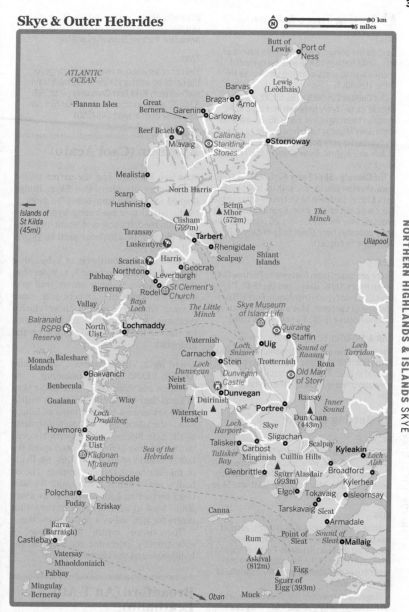

Studio Trails booklet, or download it from www.art-skye.co.uk.

Columba 1400 Community Centre
(☎01478-611410; www.columba1400.com; Staffin IV51 9JY; per hour £1; ⊙10am-8pm Mon-Sat Apr-Oct; 🕾) Internet access.

Portree Community Hospital (☎01478-613200; www.nhshighland.scot.nhs.uk/Services/Pages/PortreeCommunityHospital.aspx; Fancyhill IV51 9BZ) There's a minor injury unit and dental surgery here.

ⓘ Getting There & Away

BOAT

Despite the bridge, there are still a couple of ferry links between Skye and the mainland. Ferries also operate from Uig on Skye to the Outer Hebrides.

The **CalMac** (☎ 0800 066 5000; www. calmac.co.uk) ferry between Mallaig and Armadale (passenger/car £3/9.95, 30 minutes, eight daily Monday to Saturday, five to seven on Sunday) is very popular on weekends and in July and August. Book ahead if you're travelling by car.

The **Glenelg–Skye Ferry** (☎ 07881 634726; www.skyeferry.co.uk; car with up to 4 passengers £15; ☉ Easter–mid-Oct) runs a tiny vessel (six cars only) on the short Kylerhea to Glenelg crossing (five minutes, every 20 minutes). The ferry operates from 10am to 6pm daily (till 7pm June to August).

BUS

There are buses from Glasgow to Portree (£47, seven hours, three daily), and Uig (£47, 7½ hours, two daily) via Crianlarich, Fort William and Kyle of Lochalsh, plus a service from Inverness to Portree (£28, 3¼ hours, two daily).

CAR & MOTORCYCLE

The Isle of Skye became permanently tethered to the Scottish mainland when the Skye Bridge opened in 1995. The controversial bridge tolls were abolished in 2004 and the crossing is now free.

ⓘ Getting Around

BICYCLE

You can hire bikes from **South Skye Cycles** (☎ 01471-833484; www.southskyecycles.co.uk; Westmans Pottery, Teangue IV44 8RE; per day/week £20/100; ☉ 9am-5pm) in Sleat, and Skye Bike shack (p382) near Portree.

BUS

Getting around the island by public transport can be a pain, especially if you want to explore away from the main Kyleakin–Portree–Uig road. Here, as in much of the Highlands, there are fewer buses on Saturday and only a handful of Sunday services.

Stagecoach operates the main bus routes on the island, linking all the main villages and towns. Its Skye Dayrider/Megarider ticket gives unlimited bus travel for one/seven days for £9.50/35.50. For timetable info, call Traveline (p98).

CAR

Much of the driving on Skye is on single-track roads – remember to use passing places to allow any traffic behind you to overtake. There are petrol stations at Broadford (open 24 hours), Armadale, Portree, Dunvegan and Uig.

TAXI

You can order a taxi or hire a car (arrange for the car to be waiting at Kyle of Lochalsh train station) from **Kyle Taxi Company** (☎ 01599-534323; www.skyecarhire.co.uk; car hire per day/week from around £45/250).

Kyleakin (Caol Acain)

☑ 01599 / POP 100

Poor wee Kyleakin had the carpet pulled from under it when the Skye Bridge opened and it went from being the gateway to the island to a backwater bypassed by the main road. It's now a pleasant, peaceful little place, with a harbour used by yachts and fishing boats.

About 3 miles southwest of Kyleakin, a minor road leads southwards to **Kylerhea**, where there's a 1½-hour nature trail to a shore-front otter hide, where you stand a good chance of seeing these elusive creatures. A little further on is the jetty for the car ferry to Glenelg (p373) on the mainland.

Bright Water Visitor Centre   VISITOR CENTRE (☎ 01599-530040; www.eileanban.org; The Pier; tours adult/child £8/7; ☉ 10am-4pm Mon-Fri Easter-Sep) This community-run visitor centre serves as a base for tours of **Eilean Ban** – the island used as a stepping stone by the Skye Bridge – where Gavin Maxwell (author of *Ring of Bright Water*) spent the last 18 months of his life in 1968–69, living in the lighthouse-keeper's cottage. The island is now a nature reserve, and 1½-hour tours (departing 2pm weekdays) are available – book in advance, or be at the visitor centre for 1pm to buy a ticket on the day.

The visitor centre also houses a child-friendly exhibition on Maxwell, the lighthouse and the island's wildlife.

Broadford (An T-Ath Leathann)

☑ 01471 / POP 750

The long, straggling village of Broadford is a service centre for the scattered communities of southern Skye. It has a 24-hour petrol station, a bank and a large Co-op supermarket with an ATM.

There are lots of B&Bs in and around Broadford and the village is well placed for exploring southern Skye by car.

🛏 Sleeping & Eating

Skye Basecamp HOSTEL £
(🖪 01471-820044; www.skyebasecamp.co.uk; Lime Park; dm/q from £20/70; 🅿 🛜) Run by the mountaineers at Skye Guides (p374), this well-equipped hostel is set in a converted residential house with great views across the sea towards the Crowlin Islands and the Applecross hills. Maps, guidebooks, weather forecasts and walking advice are all to hand.

Oystercatchers COTTAGE ££
(🖪 07931 108378; www.oystercatchers-cottage-breakish-skye.co.uk; 22 Lower Breakish; 4 nights £365-555; 🅿 🛜) Nestled next to an inlet of the sea, this traditional whitewashed cottage has been modernised to a high standard with a bright and spacious kitchen-dining room, one double and two twin bedrooms, and a cute garden with Weber barbecue and a breathtaking view across the water to the Red Cuillin. Peak rates Easter and June to September, minimum four-night stay.

Skye Picture House B&B ££
(🖪 01471-822531; www.skyepicturehouse.com; Ard Dorch; s/d from £45/90; 🅿 🛜) Perched just a stone's throw above the sea, the setting of this welcoming B&B could hardly be better. Two of the three bedrooms have views across the water to the island of Scalpay, with the chance of spotting an otter. Breakfast is usually a help-yourself buffet, and evening meals may be available (check first, though).

★ Cafe Sia CAFE ££
(🖪 01471-822616; www.cafesia.co.uk; Rathad na h-Atha; mains £7-17; ⊗10am-9pm; 🛜 📶) 🖋 Serving everything from eggs Benedict and cappuccino to cocktails and seafood specials, this appealing cafe specialises in wood-fired pizzas (also available to take away) and superb artisanal coffee. There's also an outdoor deck with great views of the Red Cuillin. Takeaway coffee from 8am.

Armadale & Sleat

If you cross over the sea to Skye on the ferry from Mallaig you arrive in Armadale, at the southern end of the long, low-lying peninsula known as Sleat (pronounced 'slate'). The landscape of Sleat itself is not exceptional, but it provides a grandstand for ogling the magnificent scenery on either side – take the steep and twisting minor road that loops through Tarskavaig and Tokavaig for stunning views of the Isle of Rum, the Cuillin Hills and Bla Bheinn.

Armadale itself is little more than a grocery store, a post office, a cluster of craft shops and a scattering of houses.

Museum of the Isles MUSEUM
(🖪 01471-844305; www.armadalecastle.com; adult/child £9/5; ⊗9.30am-5.30pm Apr-Oct, 10am-3pm Mon-Fri Mar & Nov; 🅿 🐾) Just along the road from Armadale pier is the part-ruined Armadale Castle, former seat of Lord MacDonald of Sleat. The neighbouring museum will tell you all you ever wanted to know about Clan Donald, and also provides an easily digestible history of the Lordship of the Isles. Prize exhibits include rare portraits of clan chiefs, and a wine glass that was once used by Bonnie Prince Charlie. The ticket also gives admission to the lovely castle gardens.

Shed CAFE ££
(🖪 01471-844222; mains £9-15; ⊗9am-6pm May-Sep, call to check Oct-Apr; 🅿) A cute little wooden shed at Armadale pier has some outdoor tables and serves good seafood salads, pizzas, fish and chips, and coffee. You can sit in or take away.

❶ Getting There & Away

From late May to August there are three to five buses a day (three on Sunday) from Armadale to Broadford (£4.25, 30 minutes) and Portree (£7.95, 1¼ hours), timed to meet the arrival of ferries from Mallaig. Outside the summer season, services are less frequent and may not coincide with ferry times.

Isleornsay & Around

This pretty bay, 8 miles north of Armadale, lies opposite Sandaig Bay on the mainland, where Gavin Maxwell lived and wrote his much-loved memoir *Ring of Bright Water*. It's home to an atmospheric old hotel and bar, and an arts and crafts gallery.

Torabhaig Distillery DISTILLERY
(🖪 01471-833447; www.torabhaig.com; Teangue; tours per person £10; ⊗10am-5pm Mon-Fri) A converted farmstead overlooking the sea

houses Skye's second distillery, opened in 2017. There's a visitor centre and cafe; tours are best booked in advance.

★**Toravaig House Hotel**   HOTEL **£££**
(☑ 01471-820200; www.toravaig.com; Toravaig; r from £249; P 🛜) This hotel, 3 miles south of Isleornsay, is one of those places where the owners know a thing or two about hospitality – as soon as you arrive you'll feel right at home, whether relaxing on the sofas by the log fire in the lounge or admiring the view across the Sound of Sleat from the lawn chairs in the garden.

The spacious bedrooms – ask for room 1 (Colonsay), with a pair of armchairs in the bay window looking over the sea – are luxuriously equipped, from the crisp bed linen to the huge, high-pressure shower heads. The elegant restaurant serves the best of local fish, game and lamb. After dinner you can retire to the lounge with a single malt and flick through the yachting and angling magazines.

Hotel Eilean Iarmain   HOTEL **£££**
(☑ 01471-833332; www.eileaniarmain.co.uk; r from £240; P 🛜 🐾) A charming old Victorian hotel with log fires, chintzy traditional decor, a candlelit restaurant and 12 luxurious rooms (plus another six in the Garden House), many with sea views. The hotel's cosy, wood-panelled **Prában Bar** (mains £11-22; ⊙ noon-2.30pm & 5.30-9pm; 🐾) hosts live folk music and serves delicious, upmarket pub grub.

An Crùbh   CAFE **££**
(☑ 01471-833417; www.ancrubh.com; Duisdale Beag; mains £7-14; ⊙ 10am-4.30pm Wed-Sun Apr-Sep; P 🛜) This gorgeous modern community centre has a cafe with fantastic views over the sea to the mainland mountains of Ladhar Bheinn and Beinn Sgritheall, outdoor tables for summer and sofas in front of a wood-burning stove for winter. As well as coffee and cake, there are soups, salads and sandwiches that make the most of local produce.

Elgol (Ealaghol)

On a clear day, the journey along the road from Broadford to Elgol is one of the most scenic on Skye. It takes in two classic postcard panoramas – the view of Bla Bheinn across Loch Slapin (near Torrin), and the superb view of the entire Cuillin range

from Elgol pier. Elgol itself is a tiny settlement at the end of a long, single-track road.

The only places to eat are the cafe above the car park halfway down the hill towards the pier, and the restaurant at **Coruisk House** (☑ 01471-866330; www.coruiskhouse.com; r from £170; ⊙ Mar-Oct; P 🛜). You can buy groceries and get takeaway soup and sandwiches at the **Elgol Shop** (☑ 01471-866329; IV49 9BJ; mains £4-8; ⊙ 10am-5pm Mon-Sat; P) nearby.

Spar Cave   CAVE
Just east of Elgol is the Spar Cave, famously visited by Sir Walter Scott in 1814 and mentioned in his poem 'Lord of the Isles'. The 80m-deep cave is wild, remote and filled with beautiful flowstone formations. It is a short walk from the village of Glasnakille, but the approach is rough going over seaweed-covered boulders and is only accessible for one hour either side of low water. Check tide times before setting off; there's more info at www.walkhighlands.co.uk/skye/sparcave.shtml.

Aquaxplore   BOATING
(☑ 0800 731 3089; www.aquaxplore.co.uk; Elgol Pier; ⊙ Apr-Oct) Runs 1½-hour high-speed boat trips from Elgol to an abandoned shark-hunting station on the island of Soay (adult/child £34/24), once owned by *Ring of Bright Water* author Gavin Maxwell. There are longer trips (£60/48, four hours) to Rum, Canna and Sanday to visit breeding colonies of puffins, with the chance of seeing minke whales on the way.

★**Misty Isle**   BOATING
(☑ 01471-866288; www.mistyisleboattrips.co.uk; Elgol Pier; adult/child £30/15; ⊙ Apr-Oct) The pretty, traditional wooden launch *Misty Isle* offers a three-hour cruise (two daily) from Elgol harbour to the remote Loch na Cuilce, an impressive inlet surrounded by soaring peaks. On a calm day, you can clamber ashore to make the short walk to Loch Coruisk in the heart of the Cuillin Hills. You get 1½ hours ashore and visit a seal colony en route. No Sunday trips.

★**Mary's Thatched Cottages**   COTTAGE **£££**
(☑ 07856 783169; www.isleofskyecottages.com; 3/7 nights from £570/945; ⊙ Apr-Sep; P 🛜 🐾) These thatch-roofed dwellings (each sleeping two to four people) by the roadside as you arrive in Elgol from Broadford must be the island's cutest accommodation. Four

THE FAIRY POOLS EFFECT

From being the preserve of a few hardy hill walkers and wild swimmers 20 years ago, the Fairy Pools in Glen Brittle have become one of the most visited places in Skye.

A general rise in tourist numbers combined with the influence of TV, travel magazines and social media has seen visitor numbers to this photogenic spot rise to more than 1000 a day in 2020. All in a remote glen served by a solitary single track road.

A new 150-space car park (£5 per car) and toilets, and an upgraded footpath, has only seen numbers increase still further, heading for 200,000 a year. And it's not alone. The Old Man of Storr, the Quiraing, the Fairy Glen at Uig, and Neist Point are all suffering from overcrowding.

So what can you do to help? Our number one tip is to just slow down. Instead of a whirlwind tour of the Instagram honeypots, try to spend a couple of days in one of the quieter corners of the island – Sleat, Elgol or Waternish, for example – and explore it thoroughly. Visit the pubs and cafes, browse the artists' studios, talk to the locals.

You'll come away with a deeper understanding of the island and its history, rather than just a handful of Twitter-tastic snapshots.

beautifully reconstructed stone cottages have been designed with modern comforts in mind – the stone slab floors have underfloor heating. Minimum stay is three nights, Friday to Monday; book as far in advance as possible.

❶ Getting There & Away

Bus 55 runs from Broadford to Elgol (£3.80, 40 minutes, three daily Monday to Friday only).

Cuillin Hills

The Cuillin Hills are Britain's most spectacular mountain range (the name comes from the Old Norse *kjöllen*, meaning 'keel-shaped'). Though small in stature – Sgurr Alasdair, the highest summit, is only 993m – the peaks are near-alpine in character, with knife-edge ridges, jagged pinnacles, scree-filled gullies and hectares of naked rock.

While they are a paradise for experienced mountaineers, the higher reaches of the Cuillin are off limits to the majority of hikers. The good news is that there are also plenty of good low-level hikes within the ability of most walkers.

There are two main bases for exploring the Cuillin – Sligachan to the north (on the Kyle of Lochalsh–Portree bus route), and Glenbrittle to the south (no public transport).

One of the best hikes (on a fine day) is the steep climb from Glenbrittle campsite to Coire Lagan (6 miles round trip; allow at least three hours). The impressive upper corrie contains a lochan for bathing (for the hardy!), and the surrounding cliffs are a playground for rock climbers – bring your binoculars.

Even more spectacular, but much harder to reach on foot, is Loch Coruisk (from the Gaelic Coir'Uisg, the Water Corrie), a remote loch ringed by the highest peaks of the Cuillin. Accessible by boat trip from Elgol, or via an arduous 5.5-mile hike from Kilmarie, Coruisk was popularised by Sir Walter Scott in his 1815 poem 'Lord of the Isles'. Crowds of Victorian tourists and landscape artists followed in Scott's footsteps, including JMW Turner, whose watercolours were used to illustrate Scott's works.

Collie & Mackenzie Statue   STATUE

A bronze statue close to the old bridge at Sligachan, unveiled in 2020, commemorates Norman Collie and John Mackenzie, an English chemistry professor and a Skye crofter turned mountain guide, who made many first ascents together in the Cuillin mountains in the late 19th century.

Glenbrittle Campsite   CAMPSITE £

(☏01478-640404; www.dunvegancastle.com/glenbrittle/campsite; Glenbrittle; sites per adult/child incl car £11/7; ☺Apr-Sep) Excellent site, close to mountains and sea, with a shop selling coffee, food and outdoor kit. The midges can be diabolical, though.

Glenbrittle Youth Hostel   HOSTEL £

(HS; ☏01478-640278; www.hostellingscotland.org.uk; Glenbrittle; dm/tw £22/59; ☺Apr-Sep; ℗) Scandinavian-style timber hostel that quickly fills up with climbers on holiday weekends.

NORTHERN HIGHLANDS & ISLANDS CUILLIN HILLS

Sligachan Hotel

HOTEL ££

(☎ 01478-650204; www.sligachan.co.uk; Sligachan; s/d from £80/125; P 🛜) The Slig, as it has been known to generations of climbers, is a near village in itself, encompassing a comfortable hotel, a microbrewery, self-catering cottages, a small mountaineering museum, a big barn of a pub – **Seamus Bar** (Sligachan Hotel; mains £9-18; ⊗ food served noon-9pm Apr-Oct, to 3pm Nov-Mar; 🛜 🎨) – and an adventure playground.

There's a basic **campsite** (www.sligachan. co.uk/camping; Sligachan; sites per adult/child £8/4; ⊗ Apr-Oct) across the road from the hotel. Be warned – this spot is a midge magnet. Electric hook-up £5 extra; no bookings.

Raasay

☎ 01478 / POP 160

Raasay is the rugged, 10-mile-long island that lies off Skye's east coast. The island's fascinating history is recounted in the book *Calum's Road* by Roger Hutchinson.

There are several good walks here, including one to the flat-topped conical hill of **Dun Caan** (443m), and another to the extraordinary ruin of **Brochel Castle**, perched on a pinnacle at the northern end of Raasay. The Forestry Commission publishes a free leaflet (available in the ferry waiting room) with suggested walking trails.

Accommodation is very limited – don't turn up without a reservation unless you are planning to wild camp (there are plenty of places to do so in the east and north of the island).

Raasay Distillery

DISTILLERY

(☎ 01478-470178; www.raasaydistillery.com; Borodale House; tours £10-15; ⊗ 9.30am-5.30pm Mon-Sat; P) Raasay's first ever (legal!) distillery opened in 2017, and comes with a twist – you can stay the night here, in one of the six designer bedrooms (double from £320) in the Victorian hotel that has been incorporated into the modern building.

★ Raasay House

HOSTEL, B&B £££

(☎ 01478-660266; www.raasay-house.co.uk; d from £230 incl full board & activities; P 🛜) 🌊 Beautifully renovated Raasay House (originally the laird's residence), just a short walk from the ferry pier, provides outdoor activity courses and accommodation ranging from dorm bunks to luxury B&B. The bar and restaurant (mains £11 to

£22) serves good-quality seafood, beef and game, and locally brewed beers.

🛈 Getting There & Away

CalMac (www.calmac.co.uk; return passenger/car £4/13) ferries run from Sconser, on the road from Portree to Broadford, to Raasay (25 minutes, nine daily Monday to Saturday, twice daily Sunday). There are no petrol stations on the island, nor is there any public transport.

Minginish

Loch Harport, to the north of the Cuillin, divides the Minginish peninsula from the rest of Skye. On its southern shore lies the village of **Carbost**, home to Talisker malt whisky.

Magnificent **Talisker Bay**, 5 miles west of Carbost, is framed by a sea stack and a waterfall.

As well as the excellent **Skyewalker** (☎ 01478-640250; www.skyewalkerhostel.com; Fiskavaig Rd, Portnalong; dm £20-22; P) hostel and the **Old Inn** (☎ 01478-640205; www.theoldinnskye.co.uk; Carbost; bunkhouse per person from £30, B&B s/d/tr £100/120/150; P), there are several B&Bs and self-catering cottages. As ever, book ahead to avoid being caught without a bed.

Talisker Distillery

DISTILLERY

(☎ 01478-614308; www.malts.com/en-gb/brands/ talisker; Carbost; tours from £15; ⊗ 9am-5.30pm Mon-Sat, 10am-5.30pm Sun Apr-Oct, shorter hours Nov-Mar; P) Skye's oldest distillery (established in 1830) produces smooth, sweet and smoky Talisker single malt whisky. The guided tour includes a free dram (book in advance).

Oyster Shed

SEAFOOD £

(www.facebook.com/oystershedskye; Carbost; mains £5-20; ⊗ 11am-6pm Mon-Fri Apr-Oct, shorter hours Nov-Mar) 🌊 A farm shop selling fresh local seafood to take away, including oysters (£1.30 each), cooked mussels and scallops, lobster and chips, and seafood platters (£40).

🛈 Getting There & Away

Macdonald Skye Tours (www.skyetaxi. co.uk) runs two buses a day on weekdays, one on Saturday, from Portree to Carbost and Portnalong (£6, 50 minutes) via Sligachan.

Portree (Port Righ)

📞 01478 / POP 2320

Portree is Skye's largest and liveliest town. It has a pretty harbour lined with brightly painted houses, and there are great views of the surrounding hills. Its name (from the Gaelic for King's Harbour) commemorates James V, who came here in 1540 to pacify the local clans.

⊙ Sights & Activities

Aros Centre   CULTURAL CENTRE
(📞 01478-613750; www.aros.co.uk; Viewfield Rd; ⊙9am-5pm; 🅿 ♿) FREE On the southern edge of Portree, the Aros Centre is a combined visitor centre, book and gift shop, restaurant, theatre and cinema. The 45-minute movie *Skye Story* is screened hourly from 10am to 4pm (admission per adult/child £8.50/free) and allows you to take a virtual tour of the island and its history. The centre is a useful rainy-day retreat, with an indoor soft play area for children.

MV Stardust   BOATING
(📞 07795 385581; www.skyeboat-trips.co.uk; Portree Harbour; adult/child £20/10) MV *Stardust* offers 1½-hour boat trips around Portree Bay, with the chance to see seals, porpoises and – if you're lucky – white-tailed sea eagles. There are longer two-hour cruises to the Sound of Raasay (adult/child £25/15). You can also arrange fishing trips, or to be dropped off for a hike on the Isle of Raasay and picked up again later.

🛏 Sleeping

Portree is well supplied with B&Bs, but accommodation fills up fast from April to October, so be sure to book ahead.

Portree Youth Hostel   HOSTEL £
(HS; 📞 01478-612231; www.hostellingscotland.org.uk; Bayfield Rd; dm/d from £25/70; 🅿 🛜) This HS hostel offers brightly decorated dorms and private rooms, a stylish lounge with views over the bay, and outdoor seating areas. Its location in the town centre just 100m from the bus stop is ideal.

Torvaig Campsite   CAMPSITE £
(📞 01478-611849; www.portreecampsite.co.uk; Torvaig; sites with 2 adults from £23; ⊙Apr-Oct; 🛜 🐕) An attractive, family-run campsite located 1.5 miles north of Portree, on the road to Staffin.

Ben Tianavaig B&B   B&B ££
(📞 01478-612152; www.ben-tianavaig.co.uk; 5 Bosville Tce; r £110; 🅿 🛜) 🌱 A warm welcome awaits from the Irish-Welsh couple who run this appealing B&B bang in the centre of town. All three bedrooms have a view across the harbour to the hill that gives the house its name, and breakfasts include free-range eggs and vegetables grown in the garden. Two-night minimum stay; no credit/debit cards.

Woodlands   B&B ££
(📞 01478-612980; www.woodlands-portree.co.uk; Viewfield Rd; r £85; ⊙Mar-Oct; 🅿 🛜) A great location, with views across the bay, and unstinting hospitality make this modern B&B, a half-mile south of the town centre, an excellent choice.

Cuillin Hills Hotel   HOTEL £££
(📞 01478-612003; www.cuillinhills-hotel-skye.co.uk; Scorrybreac Rd; r from £245; 🅿 🛜) Located on the eastern fringes of Portree, this luxury hotel enjoys a superb outlook across the harbour towards the Cuillin mountains. The more expensive rooms cosset guests with four-poster beds and panoramic views, but everyone can enjoy the scenery from the glass-fronted restaurant and well-stocked whisky bar.

🍴 Eating

Isle of Skye Baking Co   CAFE £
(www.facebook.com/IsleofSkyeBaking; Old Woollen Mill, Dunvegan Rd; mains £4-9; ⊙9am-4pm Mon-Sat; 🅿 ♿) 🌱 Famous for its 'lunch bread' – a small loaf baked with a filling inside, like cheese and leek, or beef stew – and platters of Scottish cheese and charcuterie, this cafe is also an art gallery and craft shop.

Dulse & Brose   MODERN SCOTTISH ££
(📞 01478-612846; www.bosvillehotel.co.uk; Bosville Hotel, 7 Bosville Tce; mains £9-17; ⊙noon-3pm & 6-10pm May-Sep, 6-8.15pm Oct-Apr; 🛜) 🌱 This hotel restaurant sports a relaxed atmosphere, an award-winning chef and a menu that makes the most of Skye produce – including lamb, game, seafood, cheese, organic vegetables and berries – and adds a French or Asian twist to traditional dishes.

★ Scorrybreac   MODERN SCOTTISH £££
(📞 01478-612069; www.scorrybreac.com; 7 Bosville Tce; 4-course dinner £60; ⊙5-9pm Tue-Sat Mar-Oct, limited opening Nov & Dec) 🌱 Set in the front rooms of what was once a private

house, and with just eight tables, Scorrybreac is snug and intimate, offering fine dining without the faff. Chef Calum Munro (son of Donnie Munro, of Gaelic rock band Runrig fame) sources as much produce as possible from Skye, including foraged herbs and mushrooms, and creates the most exquisite concoctions.

ⓘ Information

Portree Tourist Office (☑ 01478-612992; www.visitscotland.com/destinations-maps/ isle-skye; Bayfield Rd; ◷ 10am-4pm Mon-Sat year-round, longer hours Jun-Aug; ☎) The only tourist office on the island.

ⓘ Getting There & Around

BUS

The main bus stop is at Somerled Sq. There are four Scottish Citylink buses every day from Kyle of Lochalsh to Portree (£8, one hour), continuing to Uig.

Local buses run from Portree to the following:
Armadale (£7.95, 1¼ hours) Connecting with the ferry to Mallaig late May to August.
Broadford (£6.30, 45 minutes) Two to five daily.
Dunvegan Castle (£5.50, 50 minutes) Three daily Monday to Saturday.

There are also three buses a day on a circular route around Trotternish (in both directions), taking in Flodigarry (£4.75, 40 minutes), Kilmuir (£5.10, 45 minutes) and Uig (£4.20, 30 minutes).

BICYCLE

You can hire bikes from **Skye Bike Shack** (☑ 07826 842160; www.skyebikeshack.com; 6 Carbost, Skeabost Bridge; bike hire per day from £30; ◷ 9am-1pm Tue-Sat) – it's 4 miles west of Portree, on the road towards Dunvegan.

Dunvegan (Dun Bheagain)

Dunvegan, an unremarkable village on the western side of Skye, is famous for its historic namesake castle that has links to Sir Walter Scott and Bonnie Prince Charlie.

Dunvegan Castle   CASTLE
(☑ 01470-521206; www.dunvegancastle.com; adult/child £14/9; ◷ 10am-5.30pm Easter–mid-Oct; ℗) Skye's most famous historic building, and one of its most popular tourist attractions, Dunvegan Castle is the seat of the chief of Clan MacLeod. In addition to the usual castle stuff – swords, silver and

family portraits – there are some interesting artefacts, including the Fairy Flag, a diaphanous silk banner that dates from some time between the 4th and 7th centuries, and Bonnie Prince Charlie's waistcoat and a lock of his hair, donated by Flora MacDonald's granddaughter.

The oldest parts are the 14th-century keep and dungeon, but most of it dates from the 17th to 19th centuries, when it played host to Samuel Johnson, Sir Walter Scott and, most famously, Flora MacDonald. Look out for Rory Mor's Drinking Horn, a beautiful 16th-century vessel of Celtic design that could hold half a gallon of claret. Upholding the family tradition in 1956, John MacLeod – the 29th chief, who died in 2007 – downed the contents in one minute and 57 seconds.

Duirinish & Waternish

The Duirinish peninsula to the west of Dunvegan, and Waternish to the north, boast some of Skye's most atmospheric hotels and restaurants, plus an eclectic range of artists' studios and crafts workshops.

The sparsely populated Duirinish peninsula is dominated by the distinctive flat-topped peaks of Helabhal Mhor (469m) and Helabhal Bheag (488m), known locally as **MacLeod's Tables**. There are some fine walks from Orbost, including the summit of **Helabhal Bheag** (allow 3½ hours return) and the 5-mile trail from Orbost to **MacLeod's Maidens**, a series of pointed sea stacks at the southern tip of the peninsula.

It's worth making the long drive beyond Dunvegan to the western side of the Duirinish peninsula to see the spectacular sea cliffs of **Waterstein Head** and to walk down to **Neist Point lighthouse** with its views to the Outer Hebrides.

Eco Bells Glamping   CAMPSITE **££**
(☑ 01470-521461; www.facebook.com/skye ecobells; Orbost, Duirinish; cabin/tent per night £92/75; ◷ Apr-Sep; ℗) ✎ Tucked away in a remote corner, on a minor road about 3 miles south of Dunvegan, this place offers accommodation in three cosy cabins and a large bell tent in a rural setting. Each cabin or tent sleeps up to three adults (or two adults and two children) and has beds, heating, a fire pit and barbecue. Two-night minimum stay.

★ **Hillstone Lodge** B&B £££
(☎ 01470-511434; www.hillstonelodge.com; 12
Colbost; s/d from £175/195; ⊙ Apr-Oct; P ⊠)
🖉 You can't help notice the many new
houses on Skye that bear the hallmarks
of award-winning local architects Rural Design – weathered timber walls and
modern materials used with traditional
shapes and forms. Hillstone is one of the
best, with tasteful modern styling and
stunning views across Loch Dunvegan. It's
about 1km north of the **Three Chimneys**
(☎ 01470-511258; www.threechimneys.co.uk;
Colbost; mains £30-35; ⊙ 12.15-1.45pm Mon-Sat
mid-Mar–Oct, plus Sun Easter-Sep, 6.30-9.15pm
daily year-round; P ⊠) 🖉, above the pier.

Cafe Lephin CAFE £
(☎ 01470-511465; www.cafelephin.co.uk; 2 Lephin, Glendale; mains £5-8; ⊙ 11am-6pm Mon-Sat;
⊠ 🔌 ⊠) A mixture of modern and rustic,
with touches of tweed and sheepskin, this
wee cafe captures the spirit of enterprise
that's bringing life back to areas of Skye
that were deserted during the Highland
Clearances. Great coffee, comfy sofa and a
menu that includes haggis panini!

Stein Inn PUB FOOD ££
(☎ 01470-592362; www.stein-inn.co.uk; Stein,
Waternish; mains £9-17; ⊙ kitchen noon-3pm &
6-9pm Easter-Oct, shorter hours Nov-Easter; P)
This old country inn dates from 1790 (but
was refurbished in 2020) and has a lively
little bar and a delightful beer garden beside the loch – a real suntrap on summer
afternoons. The bar serves real ales from
the Isle of Skye Brewery and excellent bar
meals. Food is served in winter too, but call
ahead to confirm hours.

There's also a handful of bedrooms here
(£100 to £160 per room), all with sea views.

★ **Loch Bay** SEAFOOD £££
(☎ 01470-592235; www.lochbay-restaurant.
co.uk; Stein, Waternish; 6-course dinner £95;
⊙ 12.15-1.45pm Wed-Sun, 6.15-9pm Tue-Sat
Apr-early Oct; P) 🖉 This cosy farmhouse
kitchen of a place, with terracotta tiles and
a wood-burning stove, is one of Skye's most
romantic restaurants and was awarded a
Michelin star in 2018. The menu includes
most things that swim in the sea or live in
a shell, but there are non-seafood choices,
too. Best to book ahead.

DINOSAUR FOOTPRINTS ON SKYE

The occasional dinosaur bone has
been turning up in the Jurassic rocks
of the Trotternish peninsula since 1982
– intriguing, but nothing very exciting.
Then, following a storm in 2002, a set
of fossilised dinosaur footprints was
exposed at An Corran in Staffin Bay.
Their interest piqued, geologists began
taking a closer interest in the Trotternish rocks and, in 2015, a major discovery was made near Duntulm Castle
– a 170-million-year-old trackway of
footprints left by a group of sauropods.
Skye is now a major focus for research
into dinosaur evolution.

A collection of Jurassic fossils and
further information on dinosaur sites
in Skye can be found at the **Staffin
Dinosaur Museum** (☎ 01470-562321;
www.staffindinosaurmuseum.com; 3
Ellishadder, Staffin; adult/child £2/1;
⊙ 9.30am-5pm; P).

Trotternish

The Trotternish peninsula to the north of
Portree has some of Skye's most beautiful
– and bizarre - scenery. A loop road allows
a circular driving tour of the peninsula
from Portree, passing through the village of
Uig, where the ferry to the Outer Hebrides
departs.

⊙ Sights

★ **Quiraing** NATURAL FEATURE
Staffin Bay is dominated by the dramatic
basalt escarpment of the Quiraing: its impressive land-slipped cliffs and pinnacles
constitute one of Skye's most remarkable
landscapes. From a parking area at the highest point of the minor road between Staffin
and Uig you can walk north to the Quiraing
in half an hour.

Old Man of Storr NATURAL FEATURE
(P) The 50m-high, pot-bellied pinnacle of
crumbling basalt known as the Old Man of
Storr is prominent above the road 6 miles
north of Portree. Walk up to its foot from
the car park at the northern end of Loch
Leathan (2-mile round trip). This seemingly unclimbable pinnacle was first scaled in
1955 by English mountaineer Don Whillans,

a feat that has been repeated only a handful of times since.

Fairy Glen
AREA

Just south of Uig, a minor road (signposted 'Sheader and Balnaknock') leads a mile or so to the Fairy Glen, a strange and enchanting natural landscape of miniature conical hills, rocky towers, ruined cottages and a tiny roadside lochan.

Skye Museum of Island Life
MUSEUM

(📞 01470-552206; www.skyemuseum.co.uk; Kilmuir; adult/child £4/50p; ⊙ 9.30am-5pm Mon-Sat Easter-late Sep; 🅿) The peat-reek of crofting life in the 18th and 19th centuries is preserved in the thatched cottages, croft houses, barns and farm implements of the Skye Museum of Island Life. Behind the museum is **Kilmuir Cemetery**, where a tall Celtic cross marks the grave of Flora MacDonald – the cross was erected in 1955 to replace the original monument, of which 'every fragment was removed by tourists'.

🛏 Sleeping

★ Cowshed
Boutique Bunkhouse
HOSTEL £

(📞 07917 536820; www.skyecowshed.co.uk; Uig; dm/pod/q £23.50/95/120; 🅿🛜🐕) This hostel enjoys a glorious setting overlooking Uig Bay, with superb views from its ultra-stylish lounge. The dorms have custom-built wooden bunks that offer comfort and privacy, while the camping pods (sleeping up to four, but more comfortable with two) have heating and en-suite shower rooms; there are even mini 'dog pods' for your canine companions.

Shulista Croft
CAMPSITE £

(📞 01470-552314; www.shulistacroft.co.uk; North Duntulm, Shulista; pod per night £95; ⊙ Mar-Nov) 🌿 Set on a working croft amid sheep, lambs and chickens, Shulista has luxury timber camping pods with great views (two-night minimum stay, three in July and August; up to two adults and two kids). Each one is heated and insulated, and has an en-suite shower room, basic kitchenette and even a TV.

Dun Flodigarry
Hostel & Camping
HOSTEL, CAMPSITE £

(📞 01470-552212; www.flodigarry-hostel.scot; Flodigarry; dm/tw £20/48, tent sites per person £12; 🅿@🛜) A bright and welcoming hostel that enjoys a stunning location over-looking the sea, with views across Raasay to the mainland mountains. A nearby hiking trail leads to the Quiraing (p383) rock formation (2.5 miles away), and there's a hotel bar barely 100m from the door. You can also camp nearby and use all the hostel facilities.

OUTER HEBRIDES

POP 27,670

The Western Isles, or Na h-Eileanan an Iar in Gaelic – also known as the Outer Hebrides – are a 130-mile-long string of islands lying off the northwest coast of Scotland. There are 119 islands in total, of which the five main inhabited islands are Lewis and Harris (two parts of a single island, though often described as if they are separate islands), North Uist, Benbecula, South Uist and Barra. The middle three (often referred to simply as 'the Uists') are connected by road-bearing causeways.

The ferry crossing from Ullapool or Uig to the Western Isles marks an important cultural divide – more than a third of Scotland's registered crofts are in the Outer Hebrides, and no less than 60% of the population are Gaelic speakers.

If your time is limited, head straight for the west coast of Lewis with its prehistoric sites, preserved blackhouses (traditional houses) and beautiful beaches.

❶ Information

The only tourist office is in Stornoway (p387). See www.visitouterhebrides.co.uk for tourist information.

❶ Getting There & Away

AIR

There are airports at Stornoway (Lewis), Benbecula and Barra.

Loganair (📞 0344 800 2855; www.loganair. co.uk) flights operate to Stornoway from Edinburgh, Inverness and Glasgow. There are also flights (weekdays only) between Stornoway and Benbecula.

There are daily Loganair flights from Glasgow to Barra, and from Monday to Saturday to Benbecula. At Barra, the planes land on the hard-sand beach at low tide, so the schedule depends on the tides.

BOAT

Standard one-way fares on **CalMac** (📞 0800 066 5000; www.calmac.co.uk) ferries:

Crossing	Duration (hours)	Car (£)	Driver/ Passenger (£)
Ullapool– Stornoway	2¾	52	9.75
Uig–Loch-maddy	1¾	32	6.50
Uig–Tar-bert	1½	32	6.50
Oban–Castlebay	4¾	70	15.15
Mallaig–Lochbois-dale	3½	59	10.75

There are two or three ferries a day to Storno-way, one or two a day to Tarbert and Lochmaddy, and one a day to Castlebay and Lochboisdale. See the website for ferry timetables.

Advance booking for cars is recommended (essential in July and August); foot and bicycle passengers should have no problems. Bicycles are carried free.

ℹ️ Getting Around

Despite their separate names, Lewis and Harris are actually one island. Berneray, North Uist, Benbecula, South Uist and Eriskay are all linked by road bridges and causeways. There are car ferries between Leverburgh (Harris) and Berneray, and between Eriskay and Castlebay (Barra).

The local council publishes timetables of all bus and ferry services within the Outer Hebrides, which are available at tourist offices. Timetables can also be found online at www.cne-siar.gov.uk.

BICYCLE

Bikes can be hired from **Bike Hebrides** (☎ 07775 943355; www.bikehebrides.com; 6 Sand St, Stornoway; per day/week £25/100; ⊙ 9am-5pm Mon-Sat) in Stornoway (Lewis), **Horgabost Bike Hire** (☎ 07469 196079; www. facebook.com/horgabostbikehire; Horgabost Campsite, South Harris HS3 3HR; per half-/full day £15/20; ⊙ 9am-5pm Mon-Sat) in South Harris and Barra Bike Hire (p394) in Castlebay (Barra).

BUS

The bus network covers almost every village on the islands, with around four to six buses a day on all the main routes; however, there are no buses at all on Sunday. You can pick up timetables from Stornoway tourist office (p387), or call Stornoway bus station (p387) for information.

CAR & MOTORCYCLE

Apart from the fast, two-lane road between Tarbert and Stornoway, most roads are single track. The main hazard is posed by sheep wandering about or sleeping on the road. Petrol stations are far apart (almost all of those on Lewis and Harris are closed on Sunday), and fuel is about 10% more expensive than on the mainland.

There are petrol stations at Stornoway, Barvas, Borve, Uig, Lochs, Ness, Tarbert and Leverburgh on Lewis and Harris; Lochmaddy and Bayhead on North Uist; Balivanich and Creagorry on Benbecula; Howmore, Lochbois-dale and Daliburgh on South Uist; and Castle-bay on Barra.

Cars can be hired from around £41/202 per day/week from **Car Hire Hebrides** (☎ 01851-706500; www.carhire-hebrides.co.uk; Ferry Terminal, Shell St, Stornoway), with offices at Stornoway ferry terminal, Stornoway airport and Benbecula airport.

Lewis (Leodhais)
☎ 01851 / POP 19,000

The northern part of Lewis is dominated by the desolate expanse of the Black Moor, a vast, undulating peat bog dimpled with glittering lochans, seen clearly from the Stornoway–Barvas road. But Lewis' finest scenery is on the west coast, from Barvas southwest to Mealista, where the rugged landscape of hill, loch and sandy strand is reminiscent of the northwestern Highlands. The Outer Hebrides' most evocative historic sites – Callanish Standing Stones (p387), **Dun Carloway** (Dun Charlabhaigh; P) and Arnol Blackhouse (p387) – are also to be found here.

Stornoway (Steornabhagh)
☎ 01851 / POP 5715

Stornoway is the bustling 'capital' of the Outer Hebrides and the only real town in the whole archipelago. It's a surprisingly busy little place, with cars and people swamping the centre on weekdays. Though set on a beautiful natural harbour, the town isn't going to win any prizes for beauty or atmosphere, but it's a pleasant enough introduction to this remote corner of the country.

◉ Sights & Activities

Museum nan Eilean   MUSEUM
(www.lews-castle.co.uk; Lews Castle; ⊙ 10am-5pm Mon-Wed, Fri & Sat Apr-Sep, 1-4pm same days Oct-Mar; P) FREE The 'Museum of the Isles'

occupies a modern extension built onto the side of Lews Castle. Artefacts, photos and videos celebrate the culture and history of the Outer Hebrides and explore traditional island life. The highlights of the collection are six of the famous Lewis chess pieces (p388), discovered at Uig in west Lewis in 1831. Carved from whale and walrus ivory, they are thought to have been made in Norway more than 800 years ago.

Lews Castle CASTLE
(☑ 01851-822750; www.lews-castle.co.uk; HS2 0XS; ⊙ 8am-5pm; P) FREE The Baronial mansion across the harbour from Stornoway town centre was built in the 1840s for the Matheson family, then owners of Lewis; it was gifted to the community by Lord Leverhulme in 1923. A major redevelopment completed in 2017 saw it converted to luxury self-catering accommodation, but the grand public rooms on the ground floor are free to visit when not in use. There's also an excellent cafe (mains £7-15; ⊙ 8am-4pm; 🛜🚻), one of the few local eateries to open on Sundays.

The beautiful wooded grounds, crisscrossed with walking trails, are open to the public and host the Hebridean Celtic Festival.

An Lanntair Arts Centre ARTS CENTRE
(☑ 01851-708480; www.lanntair.com; Kenneth St; ⊙ 10am-5pm Tue & Wed, to midnight Thu-Sat, 11am-4pm last Sun of month) FREE The modern, purpose-built An Lanntair (Gaelic for 'lighthouse'), complete with art gallery, theatre, cinema and restaurant, is the centre of the town's cultural life. It hosts changing exhibitions of contemporary art and is a good source of information on cultural events.

Hebridean Adventures WILDLIFE WATCHING
(☑ 07871 463755; www.hebrideanadventures. co.uk; 22 North Beach; adult/child £120/90; ⊙ Apr-Sep) Seven-hour whale-watching trips out of Stornoway harbour in a converted fishing boat with a cosy saloon to shelter from any wild weather (must be prebooked).

🎉 Festivals & Events

Hebridean Celtic Festival MUSIC
(www.hebceltfest.com; ⊙ Jul) A four-day extravaganza of folk, rock and Celtic music held in the second half of July.

🛏 Sleeping

★ Heb Hostel HOSTEL £
(☑ 01851-709889; www.hebhostel.com; 25 Kenneth St; dm/s/d £20/50/55; @🛜) The Heb is an easy-going hostel close to the ferry, with comfy wooden bunks, a convivial living room with peat fire, and a welcoming owner who can provide all kinds of advice on what to do and where to go. You can also stay in a shepherd's hut in the garden (per night £75, minimum three nights).

29 Kenneth Street B&B ££
(☑ 07917 035295; www.stornowaybedandbreak fast.co.uk; 29 Kenneth St, HS1 2DR; s/d from £65/95; 🛜) Nine smartly fitted out bedrooms spread between two houses (the other is across the street at No 32) offer great-value accommodation, just five minutes' walk from the ferry terminal.

Hal o' the Wynd B&B ££
(☑ 01851-706073; www.halothewynd.com; 2 Newton St; s/d from £55/85; 🛜) Touches of tartan and Harris tweed lend a traditional air to this welcoming B&B, conveniently located directly opposite the ferry pier. Most rooms have views over the harbour to Lews Castle.

Park Guest House B&B ££
(☑ 01851-702485; www.the-parkguesthouse.com; 30 James St; s/d from £78/98; P🛜) A charming Victorian villa with a conservatory and six luxurious rooms (mostly en suite), the Park Guest House is comfortable and central and has the advantage of an excellent restaurant specialising in Scottish seafood, beef and game plus one or two vegetarian dishes (mains £15 to £30). Rooms overlooking the main road can be noisy on weekday mornings.

🍴 Eating

Artizan Cafe CAFE £
(☑ 01851-706538; www.facebook.com/artizan stornoway; 12-14 Church St; mains £4-8; ⊙ 9.30am-5pm Mon-Sat; 🛜🚻) Recycled timber and cool colours mark out this cafe-gallery as one of Stornoway's hip hang-outs, serving great coffee and cake and light lunches (12.30pm to 2.30pm). Turns into a cocktail bar on Saturday nights from 6pm to 11pm.

An Lanntair Cafe Bar BISTRO ££
(https://lanntair.com/cafebar; Kenneth St; mains £9-18; ⊙ 10am-8pm Mon-Sat; 🛜🖊🚻) The stylish and family-friendly cafe-bar at the

arts centre serves a broad range of freshly prepared dishes, from tasty bacon rolls at breakfast to burgers, salads and fish and chips for lunch, and chargrilled steaks or local scallops for dinner.

❶ Information

Sandwick Rd Petrol Station (Engebret Ltd; ☑ 01851-702304; www.engebret.co.uk; Sandwick Rd; ⊘ 6am-11pm Mon-Sat, 10am-4pm Sun) The only shop in town that's open on a Sunday, selling groceries, alcohol, hardware, fishing tackle and outdoor kit. The Sunday papers arrive around 2pm.

Stornoway Tourist Office (☑ 01851-703088; www.visitouterhebrides.co.uk; 26 Cromwell St; ⊘ 10am-4pm Apr-Oct, closed Sun Nov-Mar)

❶ Getting There & Away

The **bus station** (☑ 01851-704327; South Beach) is on the waterfront next to the ferry terminal (left luggage 30p to £1.50 per piece). Bus W10 runs from Stornoway to Tarbert (£4.80, one hour, four or five daily Monday to Saturday) and Leverburgh (£6.80, two hours).

The Westside Circular bus W2 runs a circular route from Stornoway through Callanish, Carloway, Garenin and Arnol; the timetable allows you to visit one or two of the sites in a day.

Arnol

Arnol Blackhouse   HISTORIC BUILDING
(HES; ☑ 01851-710395; www.historicenvironment.scot; Arnol HS2 9DB; adult/child £6/3.60; ⊘ 9.30am-5.30pm Mon-Sat Apr-Sep, 10am-4pm Mon, Tue & Thu-Sat Oct-Mar; ℗) One of Scotland's most evocative historic buildings, the Arnol Blackhouse is not so much a museum as a perfectly preserved fragment of a lost world. Built in 1885, this traditional blackhouse – a combined byre, barn and home – was inhabited until 1964 and has not been changed since the last inhabitant moved out. The museum is about 3 miles west of Barvas.

The staff faithfully rekindle the central peat fire every morning so you can experience the distinctive peat-reek; there's no chimney, and the smoke finds its own way out through the turf roof, windows and door – spend too long inside and you might feel like you've been kippered!

At nearby Bragar, a pair of whalebones forms an arch by the road, with the rusting harpoon that killed the whale dangling from the centre.

Garenin (Na Gearrannan)

The picturesque and fascinating Gearrannan Blackhouse Village is a cluster of nine restored thatch-roofed blackhouses perched above the exposed Atlantic coast. One of the cottages is home to the **Blackhouse Museum** (☑ 01851-643416; www.gearrannan.com; adult/child £3.60/1.20; ⊘ 9.30am-5.30pm Mon-Sat Apr-Sep; ℗), a traditional 1955 blackhouse with displays on the village's history, while another houses a **cafe** (mains £3-6; ⊘ 9.30am-5.30pm Mon-Sat).

Some of the blackhouses in the village are let out as self-catering **holiday cottages** (☑ 01851-643416; www.gearrannan.com; HS2 9AL; 2-person cottage for 3 nights £350; ℗).

Callanish (Calanais)

Callanish, on the western side of Lewis, is famous for its prehistoric standing stones. One of the most atmospheric prehistoric sites in the whole of Scotland, its ageless mystery, impressive scale and undeniable beauty leave a lasting impression.

Callanish Standing Stones   HISTORIC SITE
(HES; www.historicenvironment.scot; ⊘ 24hr) FREE The Callanish Standing Stones, 15 miles west of Stornoway on the A858 road, form one of the most complete stone circles in Britain. It is one of the most atmospheric prehistoric sites anywhere. Sited on a wild and secluded promontory overlooking Loch Roag, 13 large stones of beautifully banded gneiss are arranged, as if in worship, around a 4.5m-tall central monolith.

Some 40 smaller stones radiate from the circle in the shape of a cross, with the remains of a chambered tomb at the centre. Dating from 3800 to 5000 years ago, the stones are roughly contemporary with the pyramids of Egypt.

Calanais Visitor Centre   MUSEUM
(☑ 01851-621422; www.callanishvisitorcentre.co.uk; admission free, exhibition £3; ⊘ 9.30am-8pm Mon-Sat Jun-Aug, 10am-6pm Mon-Sat Apr, May, Sep & Oct, 10am-4pm Tue-Sat Nov-Mar; ℗) This visitor centre near the Callanish Standing Stones is a tour de force of discreet design. Inside is a small exhibition that speculates on the origins and purpose of the stones, and an excellent **cafe** (mains £4-8; ⊘ 9.30am-8pm Mon-Sat Jun-Aug, 10am-6pm Mon-Sat Apr, May, Sep & Oct, 10am-4pm Tue-Sat Nov-Mar; ℗).

Western Lewis

The B8011 road (signposted Uig, on the A858 Stornoway–Callanish road) from Garrynahine to Timsgarry (Timsgearraidh) meanders through scenic wilderness to some of Scotland's most stunning beaches. At **Miavaig**, a loop road detours north through the Bhaltos Estate to the pretty, mile-long white strand of **Reef Beach**; there's a basic but spectacular **campsite** (Cnip; Traigh na Beirigh; tent sites £10; ⊙May-Sep) in the machair behind the beach.

From Miavaig, the road continues west through a rocky defile to Timsgarry and the vast, sandy expanse of **Traigh Uige** (Uig Sands). The famous 12th-century **Lewis chess pieces**, made of walrus ivory, were discovered in the sand dunes here in 1831.

The minor road that continues south from Timsgarry to **Mealista** passes a few smaller, but still spectacular, white-sand and boulder beaches on the way to a remote dead end. On a clear day you can see St Kilda on the horizon.

There are precious few places to eat out here, so check that your accommodation offers evening meals if you don't want to go hungry.

Uig Museum MUSEUM
(www.ceuig.co.uk; Timsgarry; adult/child £2/free; ⊙noon-5pm Mon-Sat Apr-Oct) This small community museum, housed in the local school, has lots of info on the Lewis chess pieces (discovered nearby in 1831) and on other historic sites in western Lewis.

SeaTrek BOATING
(☑01851-672469; www.seatrek.co.uk; Miavaig Pier) From April to September, SeaTrek runs two-hour boat trips (adult/child £38/28, Monday to Saturday) in a high-speed RIB to spot seals and nesting seabirds. There are also three-hour trips (£48/38) to deserted islands in Loch Roag, with time ashore to go exploring.

★**Carnish Cabins** CABIN £££
(☑07855 843375; www.carnishcabins.co.uk; Carnais, Uig; per week £795-895) These designer timber cabins set on an old croft with a stunning outlook across the sands of Uig Bay take 'glamping' to a new level, with beautifully thought-out accommodation that includes fully equipped kitchens, en-

suite shower rooms and a little deck with outdoor seating.

Baile-na-Cille B&B £££
(☑01851-672242; www.bailenacille.co.uk; Timsgarry; per person £75; ⊙Apr-Oct; P🅿️) This lovely old house hidden away at the northern end of Uig Bay is well worth seeking out for its friendly, old-fashioned hospitality, comfortable rooms and stunning location; there's even a tennis court and croquet lawn. Evening meals are available most nights (book in advance) for £35 per person.

Harris (Na Hearadh)

☑01859 / POP 2000

Harris, to the south of Lewis, is the scenic jewel in the necklace of islands that comprise the Outer Hebrides. It has a spectacular blend of rugged mountains, pristine beaches, flower-speckled machair and barren rocky landscapes. The isthmus at Tarbert splits Harris neatly in two: North Harris is dominated by mountains that rise forbiddingly above the peat moors to the south of Stornoway – Clisham (799m) is the highest point in the whole island chain. South Harris is lower-lying, fringed by beautiful white-sand beaches in the west and a convoluted rocky coastline to the east.

Harris is famous for Harris tweed, a high-quality woollen cloth still hand-woven in islanders' homes. The industry employs around 400 weavers; staff at Tarbert tourist office can tell you about weavers and workshops you can visit.

Tarbert (An Tairbeart)

☑01859 / POP 480

Tarbert is a harbour village with a spectacular location, tucked into the narrow neck of land that links North and South Harris. It is one of the main ferry ports for the Outer Hebrides, and home to the Isle of Harris Distillery.

Village facilities include two petrol stations, a bank, an ATM and two general stores.

Isle of Harris Distillery DISTILLERY
(☑01859-502212; www.harrisdistillery.com; Main St; tours £12; ⊙10am-5pm Mon-Sat; P) This distillery only filled its first batch of whisky barrels in 2017, and its first single malt, called The Hearach (Gaelic for a person

from Harris), will not be bottled until the management decides it has reached perfection; meanwhile, it's producing Isle of Harris gin, too. The modern building is very stylish – the lobby feels like a luxury hotel – and 75-minute tours depart two or three times daily (weekdays only) in summer; book in advance. There's a cafe here, too.

Isle of Harris Sea Tours   BOATING
(☑01859-502060; www.isleofharrisseatours.co.uk; East Loch Tarbert Marina; adult/child from £60/40) Three-hour boat trips in a 10m twin-hulled cruiser let you explore the deeply indented east coast of Harris, or go in search of otters and seals. Longer trips make a circumnavigation of Harris, or head to the remote Shiant Isles.

🛏 Sleeping & Eating

Harris Hotel   HOTEL £££
(☑01859-502154; www.harrishotel.com; s/d from £109/129; P🗢) Run since 1903 by four generations of the Cameron family, the Harris is a 19th-century sporting hotel built in 1865 for visiting anglers and deer stalkers, and retains a pleasantly old-fashioned atmosphere. It has spacious, comfy rooms and a decent restaurant; look out for JM Barrie's initials on the dining-room window (the author of *Peter Pan* visited in the 1920s).

Hotel Hebrides   HOTEL £££
(☑01859-502364; www.hotel-hebrides.com; Pier Rd; s/d from £85/170; 🗢) The location and setting don't look promising – a nondescript building squeezed between the ferry pier and car park – but this modern establishment brings a dash of urban glamour to Harris, with flashy fabrics and wall coverings, luxurious towels and toiletries, and a stylish restaurant and lounge bar. There are also luxury suites (from £225 per night) in a separate building.

Distillery Canteen   CAFE £
(Isle of Harris Distillery, Main St; mains £6-10; ⊙10am-4pm Mon-Sat) The cafe at the Isle of Harris Distillery, with its communal, scrubbed-timber tables and chunky benches, is bright and convivial. The menu is not extensive – a choice of soups, cafe, homebaked bread and platters of cheese or seafood – but the quality of the food, most of it sourced directly from Harris, shines brightly.

Hebscape   CAFE £
(www.hebscapegallery.co.uk; Ardhasaig; £3-7; ⊙10.30am-4.30pm Tue-Sat Apr-Oct; P🗢) 🖉 This stylish cafe and art gallery, a couple of miles outside Tarbert on the road north towards Stornoway, occupies a hilltop site with breathtaking views over Loch A Siar. Enjoy home-baked cakes or scones with Suki tea or freshly brewed espresso, or a hearty bowl of homemade soup, while admiring the gorgeous landscape photography of co-owner Darren Cole.

❶ Getting There & Away

There are four or five daily buses, Monday to Saturday, from Tarbert to Stornoway (£4.80, one hour) and Leverburgh (£3.20, 50 minutes) via the west-coast road.

Tarbert also has ferry connections to Uig (car/pedestrian £32/6.50, 1½ hours, one or two daily) on Skye.

North Harris

Magnificent North Harris is the most mountainous region of the Outer Hebrides. There are few roads here, but many opportunities for climbing, walking and birdwatching.

The B887 leads west, from a point 3 miles north of Tarbert, to **Hushinish**, where there's a lovely silver-sand beach. Along the way the road passes an old whaling station, one of Lord Leverhulme's failed development schemes, and the impressive shooting lodge of **Amhuinnsuidhe Castle** (www.amhuinnsuidhe.com), now exclusive holiday accommodation.

Golden Eagle Observatory   BIRDWATCHING
Between the old whaling station and Amhuinnsuidhe Castle, at Miavaig, a parking area and gated track gives hikers access to a golden eagle observatory, a 1.3-mile walk north from the road. On Wednesday from April to September, local rangers lead a 3½-hour guided walk (£5 per person) in search of eagles; details from www.north-harris.org.

South Harris

South Harris' west coast has some of the most beautiful beaches in Scotland. The blinding white sands and turquoise waters of Luskentyre and Scarasta would be major holiday resorts if they were transported to somewhere with a warm climate; as it is, they're usually deserted.

The east coast is a complete contrast to the west – a strange, rocky moonscape of naked gneiss pocked with tiny lochans, the bleakness lightened by the occasional splash of green around the few crofting communities. Film buffs will know that the psychedelic sequences depicting an alien landscape in *2001: A Space Odyssey* were shot from an aircraft flying over Harris' east coast.

The narrow, twisting road that winds along this coast is known locally as the **Golden Road** because of the vast amount of money it cost per mile. It was built in the 1930s to link all the tiny communities known as 'The Bays'.

◎ Sights & Activities

★ Luskentyre   BEACH

(Losgaintir) Luskentyre is one of the biggest and most beautiful beaches in Scotland, famed for its acres of low-tide white sands and turquoise waters. A minor road leads along the northern side of the bay to a parking area beside an ancient graveyard; from here you can walk west along the beach or through the grassy dunes with gorgeous views across the sea to the island of Taransay.

Clò Mòr   MUSEUM

(🖉 01859-502040; Old School, Drinishader; ⊙9am-5.30pm Mon-Sat Mar-Oct; 🅿) FREE The Campbell family has been making Harris tweed for 90 years, and this exhibition (behind the family shop) celebrates the history of the fabric known in Gaelic as *clò mòr* (the 'big cloth'); ask about live demonstrations of tweed weaving on the 70-year-old Hattersley loom. Drinishader is 5 miles south of Tarbert on the east-coast road.

St Clement's Church   HISTORIC BUILDING

(Rodel; ⊙9am-5pm Mon-Sat) FREE At the southernmost tip of the east coast of Harris stands the impressive 16th-century St Clement's Church, built by Alexander MacLeod of Dunvegan between the 1520s and 1550s, only to be abandoned after the Reformation. There are several fine tombs inside, including the cenotaph of Alexander MacLeod, finely carved with hunting scenes, a castle, a *birlinn* (the traditional longboat of the islands) and various saints, including St Clement clutching a skull.

Talla na Mara   ARTS CENTRE

(🖉 01859-503900; www.tallanamara.co.uk; Pairc Niseaboist; ⊙9am-5pm Mon-Sat; 🅿) FREE Opened in 2017 as a community enterprise, this beautiful modern building houses several artists' studios and an exhibition space that displays works celebrating the landscapes and culture of Scotland's Western Isles.

Sea Harris   BOATING

(🖉 01859-502007; www.seaharris.com; Leverburgh Pier; per person £220; ⊙Apr-Sep) Operates 10-hour day trips to St Kilda in a fast boat with four to five hours ashore.

Kilda Cruises   BOATING

(🖉 01859-502060; www.kildacruises.co.uk; Leverburgh Pier; per person £235) Operates 12-hour day trips to the remote and spectacular island group of St Kilda. Daily from mid-April to mid-September.

🛏 Sleeping

Lickisto

Blackhouse Camping   CAMPSITE £

(🖉 01859-530485; www.lickistoblackhousecamping.co.uk; Liceasto; tent sites per adult/child £14/7, yurt £80; 🐕) 🖉 Remote and rustic campsite on an old croft, with pitches set among heather and outcrops and chickens running wild. Campers can use a communal kitchen-lounge in a converted blackhouse, and there are two yurts with wood-burning stove and gas cooker (no electricity). Bus W13 from Tarbert to Leverburgh stops at the entrance.

Am Bothan   HOSTEL £

(🖉 01859-520251; www.ambothan.com; Ferry Rd, Leverburgh; dm £25; 🅿🛜) An attractive, chalet-style hostel, Am Bothan has small, neat dorms and a great porch where you can enjoy morning coffee with views over the bay. The hostel has bike hire and can arrange wildlife-watching boat trips.

Sorrel Cottage   B&B ££

(🖉 01859-520319; www.sorrelcottage.co.uk; 2 Glen, Leverburgh; s/d from £70/90; 🅿🛜🐕) Sorrel Cottage is a pretty crofter's house with beautifully modernised rooms, about 1.5 miles west of the ferry at Leverburgh. Vegetarians and vegans are happily catered for. Bike hire available.

★ Borve Lodge Estate   COTTAGE £££

(🖉 01859-550358; www.borvelodge.com; Rock House per 4/7 nights £1343/2350; 🅿🛜) This estate on the west side of South Harris has developed some of the most spectacular self-catering accommodation in the Outer Hebrides, including the Rock House, a turf-roofed nook built into the hillside with sweeping views over the sea, and the stunning Broch, a three-storey rock tower based on Iron Age designs (both sleep two people).

✕ Eating

★ Skoon Art Café   CAFE £
(☎ 01859-530268; www.skoon.com; Geocrab; mains £5-9; ⊙10am-4.30pm Tue-Sat Apr-Sep, reduced hours Oct-Mar; P) ✒ Set halfway along the Golden Rd, this neat little art gallery doubles as an excellent cafe serving delicious homemade soups, sandwiches, cakes and desserts (try the gin-and-tonic cake).

Temple Cafe   CAFE £
(☎ 07876 340416; www.facebook.com/thetemple cafe; Northton; mains £5-12; ⊙10.30am-5pm Tue-Sun Apr-Sep, reduced hours Oct-Mar; P 🐾) Set in a cute stone-and-timber 'hobbit house' that was originally a visitor centre, and strewn with cushions covered in Harris tweed, this rustic cafe serves homemade scones, soups, salads and hot lunch specials to a soundtrack of '70s tunes. Evening meals 6.30pm to 8pm Friday to Sunday in summer (must be booked in advance).

An Traigh   CAFE ££
(☎ 01859-550258; https://antraigh.com; Talla na Mara; mains £8-14; ⊙11am-5pm; P 🛜 🐾) The cafe-bar in this community centre and art gallery enjoys a stunning location, with views across the sea to the island of Taransay, and an outdoor deck that makes the most of any sunny weather. The menu includes local seafood, plus sandwiches, fish and chips, and burgers.

❶ Getting There & Away

A CalMac (p384) car ferry zigzags through the reefs of the Sound of Harris from Leverburgh to Berneray (car/pedestrian £13.90/3.70, one hour, three or four daily Monday to Saturday, two or three Sunday).

There are two to four buses a day (except Sunday) from Tarbert to Leverburgh; W10 takes the main road along the west coast (£3.20, 40 minutes), while W13 winds along the Golden Rd on the east coast (£3.20, one hour).

North Uist (Uibhist A Tuath)

☑ 01876 / POP 1255

North Uist, an island half-drowned by lochs, is famed for its **trout fishing** (www.nuac.co.uk) but also has some magnificent beaches on its north and west coasts. For birdwatchers this is an earthly paradise, with regular sightings of waders and wildfowl ranging from redshank to red-throated diver to red-necked phalarope. The landscape is less wild and mountainous than Harris, but it has a sleepy, subtle appeal.

Little **Lochmaddy** is the first village you hit after arriving on the ferry from Skye. It has a couple of stores, a bank with an ATM, a petrol pump, a post office and a pub.

◉ Sights

Balranald RSPB Reserve   WILDLIFE RESERVE
(www.rspb.org.uk; P) FREE Birdwatchers flock to this Royal Society for the Protection of Birds (RSPB) nature reserve, 18 miles west of Lochmaddy, in the hope of spotting the rare red-necked phalarope or hearing the distinctive call of the corncrake.

There's a visitor centre with a resident warden who offers 1½-hour guided walks (£6), departing at 10am Tuesday from May to September.

St Kilda Viewpoint   VIEWPOINT
(P) From the westernmost point of the road that runs around North Uist, a minor, drivable track leads for 1.5 miles to the summit of Clettraval hill, where a lookout point with telescope affords superb views west to the distant peaks of St Kilda and the Monach Isles.

Taigh Chearsabhagh   ARTS CENTRE, MUSEUM
(☎ 01870-603970; www.taigh-chearsabhagh. org; Lochmaddy; arts centre free, museum £3; ⊙10am-5pm Mon-Sat Apr-Oct, to 4pm Nov-Mar; P) Taigh Chearsabhagh is a museum and arts centre that preserves and displays the history and culture of the Uists, and is also a thriving community centre, post office and meeting place.

The centre's cafe (mains £4 to £6, closes at 3pm) dishes up homemade soups, sandwiches and cakes.

ST KILDA

St Kilda is a collection of spectacular sea stacks and cliff-bound islands about 45 miles west of North Uist. The largest island, **Hirta**, measures only 2 miles by 1 mile, with huge cliffs along most of its coastline. Owned by the National Trust for Scotland (NTS), the islands are a Unesco World Heritage Site and are the biggest seabird nesting site in the North Atlantic, home to more than a million birds.

Hirta is the only island on which visitors can land. In addition to watching the birdlife, you can explore the remains of the island's only settlement at **Village Bay**, where there's a ranger's office and small museum, and climb to the summit of Conachair (430m), the island's highest point.

There is no accommodation on St Kilda other than a tiny campsite at Village Bay on Hirta (£20 per person, no more than six people) with toilets, showers and a drinking-water supply; the maximum permitted stay is five nights. Must be arranged in advance through the NTS (details at www.kilda.org.uk).

Boat tours to St Kilda are a major undertaking – day trips are at least seven-hour affairs, involving a minimum 2½-hour crossing each way, often in rough seas; all must be booked in advance and are weather-dependent (April to September only).

Tour operators include the following:

Go To St Kilda (☏ 07789 914144; www.gotostkilda.co.uk; Stein Jetty; per person £260) Trips depart from Skye.

Kilda Cruises (p390)

Uist Sea Tours (p393)

Sea Harris (p390)

🛏 Sleeping & Eating

Balranald Campsite
CAMPSITE £

(☏ 01876-510304; www.balranaldhebrideanholidays.com; Balranald Nature Reserve, Hougharry; sites £8-10, plus per person £2; ☏) You can birdwatch from your tent at this lovely campsite set on the machair alongside the RSPB's Balranald Nature Reserve (p391), and listen to rare corncrakes calling as the sun goes down beyond the neighbouring white-sand beach.

There's also a two-bed timber camping pod looking out over the reserve (per night £50).

Rushlee House
B&B ££

(☏ 01876-500274; www.rushleehouse.co.uk; Lochmaddy; s/d £60/78; P ☏) A lovely modern bungalow with three luxuriously appointed bedrooms and great views of the hills to the south. No evening meals, but it's just a short walk to the restaurant at Hamersay House.

The B&B is 0.75 miles from the ferry pier; take the first road on the right, then first left.

★ Langass Lodge
HOTEL £££

(☏ 01876-580285; www.langasslodge.co.uk; Locheport; s/d from £105/130; P ☏) The delightful Langass Lodge hotel is a former shooting lodge set in splendid isolation overlooking Loch Langais. Refurbished and extended, it now offers a dozen appealing rooms, many with sea views.

It is also home to one of the Hebrides' best **restaurants** (www.langasslodge.co.uk; Locheport; mains £16-25, 3-course dinner £40; ☺6-8.30pm), noted for its fine seafood and game.

Hamersay House
HOTEL £££

(☏ 01876-500700; www.hamersayhouse.co.uk; Lochmaddy; s/d from £110/145; P ☏ ☏) Hamersay House is Lochmaddy's most luxurious accommodation, with nine designer bedrooms, a lounge with leather sofas set around an open fire.

There is also a good restaurant (mains £14 to £21, open 6pm to 8.30pm) with sea views from the terrace.

Hebridean Smokehouse
FOOD & DRINKS

(☏ 01876-580209; www.hebrideansmokehouse.com; Clachan; ☺8am-5.30pm Mon-Fri, plus 9am-5pm Sat Easter-Oct) Smokehouse shop selling locally sourced, peat-smoked salmon, sea trout, scallops, lobster and mackerel.

Benbecula (Beinn Na Faoghla)

☎ 01870 / POP 1305

Benbecula, which sits between North Uist and South Uist, and is connected to both by causeways, is a low-lying island with a flat, lochan-studded landscape that's best appreciated from the summit of **Rueval** (124m), the island's highest point. There's a path around the southern side of the hill (signposted from the main road; park beside the landfill site) that is said to have been the route taken to the coast by Bonnie Prince Charlie and Flora MacDonald during the prince's escape in 1746.

The main village is **Balivanich**, which has a bank with an ATM, a post office, a couple of supermarkets and a petrol station (open on Sunday). It is also the location of Benbecula airport.

South Uist (Uibhist A Deas)

☎ 01878 / POP 1755

South Uist is the second-largest island in the Outer Hebrides and saves its choicest corners for those who explore away from the main north–south road. The low-lying west coast is an almost unbroken stretch of white-sand beach and flower-flecked machair – a waymarked hiking trail, the **Hebridean Way**, follows the coast – while the multitude of inland lochs provide excellent trout fishing (www.southuistfishing.com). The east coast, riven by four large sea lochs, is hilly and remote, with spectacular **Beinn Mhor** (620m) the highest point.

Driving south from Benbecula you cross from the predominantly Protestant northern half of the Outer Hebrides into the mostly Roman Catholic south, a religious transition marked by the granite statue of **Our Lady of the Isles** on the slopes of Rueval and the presence of many roadside shrines.

The ferry port of **Lochboisdale** is the island's largest settlement, with a bank, ATM, grocery store and petrol station.

◎ Sights & Activities

Kildonan Museum   MUSEUM
(☎ 01878-710343; www.kildonanmuseum.co.uk; Kildonan; adult/child £3/free; ◎ 10am-5pm Apr-Oct; ℗) Six miles north of Lochboisdale, Kildonan Museum explores the lives of local crofters through its collection of artefacts, an absorbing exhibition of B&W photography and first-hand accounts of harsh Hebridean conditions. There's also an excellent tearoom (mains £4 to £8, open 11am to 4pm) and craft shop.

Half a mile south of the museum, amid Milton's ruined blackhouses, a cairn marks the site of **Flora MacDonald's birthplace**.

Eriskay   ISLAND
There's not much to see on Eriskay, but you'll pass through it on the way to the car ferry that crosses to Ardmhor at the northern end of Barra; Eriskay itself is connected to South Uist by a causeway that was constructed in 2001.

In 1745 Bonnie Prince Charlie first set foot in Scotland on the west coast of Eriskay, on the sandy beach (immediately north of the ferry terminal) still known as **Prince's Strand** (Coilleag a'Phrionnsa).

More recently the SS *Politician* sank just off the island in 1941. The islanders salvaged much of its cargo of around 250,000 bottles of whisky and, after a binge of dramatic proportions, the police intervened and a number of the islanders landed in jail. The story was immortalised by Sir Compton Mackenzie in his comic novel *Whisky Galore,* made into a famous film in 1949 and remade in 2016.

Uist Sea Tours   BOATING
(☎ 07833 690693; www.uistseatours.co.uk; The Pier, Lochboisdale; adult/child from £40/25; ◎ mid-Apr–mid-Sep) This outfit runs two-hour boat trips from Lochboisdale to spot bottlenose dolphins in the Sound of Barra (Monday, Wednesday and Friday evenings), and six-hour trips from Eriskay harbour (adult/child £70/50) to see nesting puffins on the island of Mingulay (Friday). There are also seven-hour day trips to St Kilda (£175/100).

🛏 Sleeping & Eating

Tobha Mor Crofters' Hostel   HOSTEL £
(www.gatliff.org.uk; Howmore; dm adult/child £16/8, camping per person £10) An atmospheric hostel housed in a restored thatched black-house, about 12 miles north of Lochboisdale.

Uist Storm Pods   CAMPSITE ££
(☎ 01878-700845; www.uiststormpods.co.uk; Lochboisdale; per pod £77; ◎ Mar-Oct; ℗ ✿) This place has two Scandinavian-style timber camping pods set on a hillside on

a working farm. Each has an outdoor deck and barbecue overlooking the sea, a mini-kitchen, fridge and chemical toilet, and can sleep up to four people. The pods are a short walk from the ferry; take the second road on the left, immediately before the RBS bank.

★ Polochar Inn   INN ££
(☑ 01878-700215; www.polocharinn.com; Polochar; s/d from £99/109; P ☎) This 18th-century inn has been transformed into a stylish, welcoming hotel with a stunning location looking out across the sea to Barra. The excellent restaurant and bar menu (mains £11 to £22; booking recommended) includes seafood chowder, venison casserole, local salmon and scallops, and Uist lamb.

Polochar is 7 miles southwest of Lochboisdale, on the way to Eriskay.

Lochside Cottage   B&B ££
(☑ 01878-700472; www.lochside-cottage.co.uk; Lochboisdale; s/d/f £45/70/90; P ☎) Lochside Cottage is a friendly B&B, 1.5 miles west of the ferry, and has rooms with views and a sun lounge barely a fishing-rod's length from its own trout loch. There are also two six-berth caravans in the garden (£180 a week). Alasdair, the owner, is a ghillie who can advise on the local fishing.

❶ Getting There & Away

Bus W17 runs about four times a day (except Sunday) between Berneray and Eriskay via Lochmaddy, Balivanich and Lochboisdale. The trip from Lochboisdale to Lochmaddy (£5.30) takes 1¾ hours.

CalMac (p384) ferries run between Lochboisdale and Mallaig.

Barra (Barraigh)

☑ 01871 / POP 1175

With its beautiful beaches, wildflower-clad dunes, rugged little hills and strong sense of community, diminutive Barra – just 14 miles in circumference – is the Outer Hebrides in miniature. For a great view of the island, walk up to the top of Heaval (383m), a mile northeast of Castlebay (Bagh a'Chaisteil), the largest village.

You can hire bikes from Barra Bike Hire (☑ 07876 402842; www.barrabikehire.co.uk; Buth Bharraigh Community Shop, Castlebay; per half-/full day £12/18; ☉ 9am-5pm Mon-Sat).

◎ Sights & Activities

The uninhabited islands of Pabbay, Mingulay and Berneray, gifted to the National Trust for Scotland (NTS) in 2000, are important breeding sites for seabird species such as fulmar, black guillemot, common and Arctic tern, great skua, puffin and storm petrel.

Uist Sea Tours (p393) runs boat trips to the islands from Lochboisdale in South Uist in settled weather. The puffin season lasts from June to early August.

Kisimul Castle   CASTLE
(HES; ☑ 01871-810313; www.historicenvironment. scot; Castlebay; adult/child incl ferry £6/3.60; ☉ 9.30am-5.30pm Apr-Sep) Castlebay takes its name from the island fortress of Kisimul Castle, first built by the MacNeil clan in the 11th century. A short boat trip (weather permitting) takes you out to the island, where you can explore the fortifications and soak up the view from the battlements.

The castle was restored in the 20th century by American architect Robert MacNeil, who became the 45th clan chief. He gifted the castle to Historic Scotland in 2000 for an annual rent of £1 and a bottle of whisky (Talisker single malt, if you're interested).

Traigh Mor   BEACH
This vast expanse of firm golden sand (the name means 'Big Strand') serves as Barra's airport (a mile across at low tide, and big enough for three 'runways'), the only beach airport in the world that handles scheduled flights. Watching the little Twin Otter aircraft come and go is a popular spectator sport. In between flights, locals gather cockles, a local seafood speciality, from the sands.

☐ Sleeping & Eating

Accommodation on Barra is limited, so make a reservation before committing to a night on the island. Wild camping (on foot or by bike) is allowed almost anywhere; campervans and car campers are restricted to official sites – check www.isleofbarra.com for details.

Dunard Hostel   HOSTEL £
(☑ 01871-810443; www.dunardhostel.co.uk; Castlebay; dm/tw/pod from £25/55/50; P ☎) Dunard is a friendly, family-run hostel just a five-minute walk from the ferry terminal. There are also two camping pods in the

garden, with shared use of hostel facilities. The owners can help to organise sea-kayaking trips.

Tigh na Mara
B&B ££

(☎01871-810304; www.tighnamara-barra.co.uk; Castlebay; s/d from £55/90; ☺Apr-Oct; P 🛜) A lovely cottage B&B with a brilliant location just above the ferry pier, looking out over the bay and Kisimul Castle. Ask for the ensuite double bedroom with bay view.

Castlebay Hotel
HOTEL £££

(☎01871-810223; www.castlebayhotel.com; Castlebay; s/d from £79/140; P 🛜) The Castlebay Hotel has spacious bedrooms decorated with a subtle tartan motif – it's worth paying a bit extra for a sea view – and there's a comfy lounge and conservatory with grand views across the harbour to the islands south of Barra. The hotel bar is the hub of island social life, with regular sessions of traditional music.

The restaurant specialises in local seafood and game (often rabbit).

Deck
CAFE £

(www.hebrideantoffeecompany.com; Castlebay; mains £4-10; ☺10am-5pm Mon-Wed, to 4pm Thu, 9am-7pm Fri & Sat Apr-Sep, Thu-Sat only Oct-Mar) There are only outdoor seats at this cafe (attached to the Hebridean Toffee factory), on a wooden deck overlooking the bay, but it's worth waiting for a fine day to sample the freshly baked scones, homemade cakes and local seafood.

🛈 Getting There & Around

There are daily flights from Glasgow to Barra airport.

CalMac (p384) ferries link Eriskay with Ardmhor (car/pedestrian £10.85/3.15, 40 minutes, three to five daily) at the northern end of Barra. Ferries also run from Castlebay to Oban.

A bus service links ferry arrivals and departures at Ardmhor with Castlebay (£1.80, 20 minutes). Bus W32 makes a circuit of the island up to five times daily (except Sunday), and also connects with flights at the airport.

NORTHERN HIGHLANDS & ISLANDS BARRA (BARRAIGH)

AT A GLANCE

POPULATION
45,000

**NUMBER OF
INHABITED
ISLANDS**
36

BEST SUNSET
St Ninian's Isle
(p424)

**BEST ISLAND
RETREAT**
West Manse (p414)

**BEST DESIGNER
ROOMS**
Storehouse (p404)

WHEN TO GO
Jan Shetland's Up
Helly Aa: horned
helmets and burning
Viking ships on the
beach.

Jun Orkney rocks to
the St Magnus Festi-
val: book accommo-
dation ahead.

Jul Summer sunlight
and Scotland's long-
est daylight hours.

Skara Brae (p407)
PAUL WILLIAMS - FUNKYSTOCK/GETTY IMAGES ©

Orkney & Shetland

U p at Britain's top end it can feel more Scandinavian than Scottish, and no wonder. For the Vikings, the jaunt across the North Sea was as easy as a stroll to the local mead hall and they soon controlled these windswept, treeless archipelagos, building longhouses alongside prehistoric remains.

An ancient magic hovers here, endowing Orkney and Shetland with an allure that lodges firmly in the soul. It's in the misty seas, where seals, whales and porpoises patrol lonely coastlines; it's in the air, where squadrons of seabirds wheel above huge nesting colonies; and it's on land, where standing stones catch late summer sunsets and strains of folk music disperse in the wind before it gusts shut the pub door.

Orkney & Shetland Highlights

1 Skara Brae
(p407) Shaking your head in astonishment at extraordinary prehistoric perfection that predates the pyramids.

2 Maeshowe
(p407) Sensing the gulf of years in this ancient tomb enlivened by later Viking graffiti.

3 Hoy (p411)
Soaking up the glorious scenery and making the hike to the spectacular Old Man of Hoy.

4 Northern Islands (p412)
Island-hopping through Orkney, where crystal azure waters lap against glittering white-sand beaches.

5 Scapa Flow
(p413) Submerging yourself among the sunken warships of Scapa Flow.

6 Lerwick (p421)
Discovering your inner Viking at the Up Helly Aa festival.

7 Hermaness National Nature Reserve (p427)
Capering with puffins and dodging dive-bombing skuas at Shetland's birdwatching centre.

8 Lighthouse Cottages (p422)
Staying in one of Shetland's romantic lighthouse cottages; one of the best is at spectacular Sumburgh.

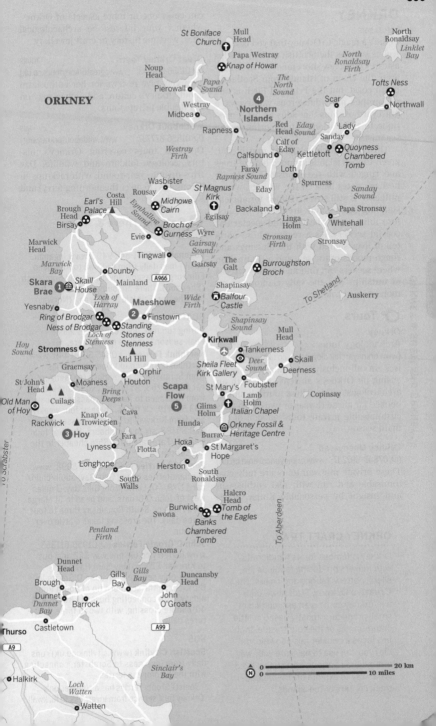

ORKNEY

St Boniface Church
Mull Head
Papa Westray
Knap of Howar
North Ronaldsay
Linklet Bay
Noup Head
North Ronaldsay Firth
Pierowall
Papa Sound
The North Sound
Tofts Ness
Scar
Northwall
Westray
Midbea
4 **Northern Islands**
Red Head
Eday Sound
Lady
Sanday
Rapness
Calfsound
Calf of Eday
Kettletoft
Quoyness Chambered Tomb
Westray Firth
Faray
Rapness Sound
Loth
Spurness
Sanday Sound
Wasbister
Eday
Rousay
St Magnus Kirk
Backaland
Linga Holm
Papa Stronsay
Whitehall
Costa Hill
Earl's Palace
Midhowe Cairn
Egilsay
Brough Head
Birsay
Broch of Gurness
Wyre
Stronsay Firth
Stronsay
Marwick Head
Evie
Gairsay Sound
The Galt
Burroughston Broch
Tingwall
Gairsay
Marwick Bay
Dounby
Skaill House
Mainland
A966
Shapinsay
Auskerry
Skara Brae
1
Yesnaby
Loch of Harray
Maeshowe
Balfour Castle
To Shetland
Ring of Brodgar
Ness of Brodgar
2 Finstown
Wide Firth
Mull Head
Standing Stones of Stenness
Loch of Stenness
Hoy Sound
Stromness
Mid Hill
Kirkwall
Tankerness
Skaill
Shapinsay Sound
Deerness
Graemsay
Orphir
Houton
Scapa Flow
5
Deer Sound
Sheila Fleet Kirk Gallery
Foubister
St John's Head
Moaness
Bring Deeps
St Mary's
Copinsay
Old Man of Hoy
Cuilags
Cava
Lamb Holm
Italian Chapel
Rackwick
Knap of Trowieglen
3 Hoy
Fara
Glims Holm
Hunda
Orkney Fossil & Heritage Centre
Lyness
Flotta
Hoxa
Burray
South Ronaldsay
Longhope
Herston
St Margaret's Hope
South Walls
Swona
Halcro Head
Tomb of the Eagles
Burwick
Banks Chambered Tomb
To Aberdeen
Stroma
Pentland Firth
Dunnet Head
Gills Bay
Duncansby Head
Brough
Gills Bay
John O'Groats
Dunnet
Barrock
Dunnet Bay
Castletown
Thurso
A99
A9
Halkirk
Sinclair's Bay
Loch Watten
Watten

N
0   20 km
0   10 miles

ORKNEY

POP 22,900

There's a magic to Orkney that you begin to feel as soon as the Scottish mainland slips astern. Only a few short miles of ocean separate the chain of islands from Scotland's north coast, but the Pentland Firth is one of Europe's most dangerous waterways, a graveyard of ships that adds an extra mystique to these islands shimmering in the sea mists.

This is an archipelago of mostly flat, green-topped islands stripped bare of trees and ringed with red sandstone cliffs. Its heritage dates back to the Vikings, whose influence is still strong. Famed for ancient standing stones and prehistoric villages, for sublime sandy beaches and spectacular coastal scenery, it's a region whose ports tell of lives shared with the blessings and rough moods of the sea, and a destination where seekers can find melancholy wrecks of warships and the salty clamour of remote seabird colonies.

Tours

Orkney Archaeology Tours

TOURS

(www.orkneyarchaeologytours.co.uk) Specialises in all-inclusive multiday tours focusing on Orkney's ancient sites, with an archaeologist guide. These tours should be booked far ahead (a year or two). Also runs customisable private tours outside of the main season.

Orkney Uncovered

TOURS

(☑07841 697237; www.orkneyuncovered.co.uk) These private minivan tours are fully customisable and run with real enthusiasm and insight by personable Kinlay. Tours

can cover one or more aspects of Orkney, whether your interest be archaeological sites, wartime history or craft jewellery.

Great Orkney Tours

TOURS

(☑01856-861443; www.greatorkneytours.co.uk) Jean gets rave reviews for her enthusiasm about Orkney's culture and archaeology on her flexible private tours.

Wildabout Orkney

BUS

(☑01856-877737; www.wildaboutorkney.org) Operates tours covering Orkney's history, ecology, folklore and wildlife. Day trips operate year-round, with pick-ups in Stromness (to meet the morning ferry) and Kirkwall.

Getting There & Away

AIR

Loganair (☑0141-642 9407; www.loganair.co.uk) flies daily from Kirkwall to Aberdeen, Edinburgh, Glasgow, Inverness and Sumburgh (Shetland). There are summer services to Manchester, Fair Isle and Bergen (Norway).

BOAT

During summer, book car spaces ahead. Peak-season fares are quoted here.

Northlink Ferries (☑0845 6000 449; www.northlinkferries.co.uk) Operates ferries from Scrabster to Stromness (passenger/car £20.45/63, 1½ hours, two to three daily), from Aberdeen to Kirkwall (passenger/car £33.50/119, six hours, three or four weekly) and from Kirkwall to Lerwick (passenger/car £20.85/88, six to eight hours, three or four weekly). Fares are up to 35% cheaper in the low season.

Pentland Ferries (☑0800 688 8998; www.pentlandferries.co.uk; Gills Bay; adult/child/car £17/9/40) Leave from Gills Bay, 3 miles west of John O'Groats, and head to St Margaret's Hope on South Ronaldsay three to four times daily. The crossing takes a little over an hour.

John O'Groats Ferries (☑01955-611353; www.jogferry.co.uk; one way £22, incl bus to Kirkwall £25; ☺May-Sep) Has a passenger-only service from John O'Groats to Burwick, on the southern tip of South Ronaldsay, with connecting buses to Kirkwall. A 40-minute crossing, with two to three departures daily.

BUS

Scottish Citylink (www.citylink.co.uk) runs daily from Inverness to Scrabster, connecting with the Stromness ferries.

John O'Groats Ferries has a summer-only 'Orkney bus' service from Inverness to Kirkwall.

ORKNEY CRAFT TRAIL

Orkney is famous for its handicrafts, with makers producing fabulous jewellery, pottery, fabrics and chairs. The **Creative Orkney Trail** (www.creative-orkney.com) is an association of small producers, mostly based in little communities or the countryside, that produces a booklet (also downloadable) you can use to navigate your way around their various workshops. It's a great way to explore off-the-beaten-track corners of the islands.

Tickets (one way £30, five hours) include bus-ferry-bus travel from Inverness to Kirkwall. There are two daily from June to August.

🛈 Getting Around

The *Orkney Transport Guide* details all island transport and is free from tourist offices. There are winter and summer versions – ferry sailings, flights and some bus services are reduced from October to April.

The largest Orkney island, Mainland, is linked by causeways to four southern islands; others are reached by air and ferry.

AIR

Loganair Inter-Isles Air Service (☏ 01856-872494; www.loganair.co.uk) Loganair operates inter-island flights from Kirkwall to the northern islands of Eday, Stronsay, Sanday, Westray, Papa Westray and North Ronaldsay. Fares are reasonable, with some special discounted tickets if you stay a night on the outer islands. You can book online but it's often easier by phone.

BICYCLE

Various locations on Mainland hire out bikes, including **Cycle Orkney** (☏ 01856-875777; www.cycleorkney.com; Tankerness Lane, Kirkwall; per day/3 days/week £25/50/100; ⊙ 9am-5.30pm Mon-Sat) and Orkney Cycle Hire (p411). Both offer out-of-hours pick-ups and options for kids. The Kirkwall tourist office has a list of providers on outer islands.

BOAT

Orkney Ferries (☏ 01856-872044; www.orkneyferries.co.uk) operates car ferries from Mainland to the islands. Bikes are carried free. An Island Explorer pass costs £44 for 10 days' passenger or cyclist travel from May to October.

BUS

Stagecoach (☏ 01856-870555; www.stagecoachbus.com) runs buses on Mainland and connecting islands. Most don't operate on Sunday. Dayrider (£9.30) and 7-Day Megarider (£20.55) tickets allow unlimited travel.

CAR

Small-car hire rates are around £90/240 per two days/week, though there are sometimes specials for as low as £30 per day. **Orkney Car Hire** (James D Peace & Co; ☏ 01856-872866; www.orkneycarhire.co.uk; Junction Rd, Kirkwall; car hire per day/2 days/week £62/90/240; ⊙ 8am-5pm Mon-Fri, 9am-1pm Sat) and **WR Tullock** (☏ 01856-875500; www.orkneycarrental.co.uk; Castle St; per day/2 days/week £65/95/260; ⊙ 8.30am-6pm

🛈 EXPLORING ORKNEY

There's an excellent range of tourist information on Orkney. The Kirkwall Information Centre (p405) has a good range of info and very helpful staff.

The **Orkney Explorer Pass** (www.historicenvironment.scot; adult/child/family £27/16/54; ⊙ Apr-Oct) covers all Historic Environment Scotland sites in Orkney, including Maeshowe, Skara Brae, the Broch of Gurness, the Brough of Birsay, the Bishop's Palace and Earl's Palace in Kirkwall and the Hackness Martello Tower on Hoy, as well as Jarlshof on Shetland. It lasts for 30 consecutive days and is only available from April to October.

Mon-Fri, to 5pm Sat) are both close to the bus station in Kirkwall. There are also operators in Stromness and on some of the outer islands.

Kirkwall

POP 7000

Orkney's main town is the islands' commercial centre and there's a comparatively busy feel to its main shopping street and ferry dock. It's set back from a wide bay, and its vigour, combined with the atmospheric paved streets and twisting wynds (lanes), give the Orcadian capital a distinctive character. Magnificent St Magnus Cathedral takes pride of place in the centre of town, and the nearby Earl's and Bishop's Palaces are also worth a ramble. Founded in the early 11th century, the original part of Kirkwall is one of the best examples of an ancient Norse town.

🔘 Sights

⭐ **St Magnus Cathedral**   CATHEDRAL
(☏ 01856-874894; www.stmagnus.org; Broad St; ⊙ 9am-6pm Mon-Sat, 1-6pm Sun Apr-Sep, 9am-1pm & 2-5pm Mon-Sat Oct-Mar) **FREE** Constructed from local red sandstone, Kirkwall's centrepiece, dating from the early 12th century, is among Scotland's most interesting cathedrals. The powerful atmosphere of an ancient faith pervades the impressive interior. Lyrical and melodramatic epitaphs of the dead line the walls and emphasise the serious business of 17th- and 18th-century bereavement. Tours

Kirkwall

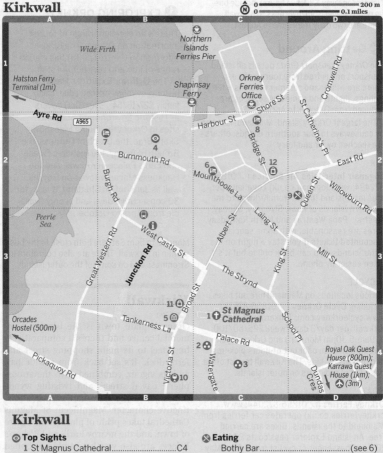

Kirkwall

◎ Top Sights
1 St Magnus Cathedral.............................C4

◎ Sights
2 Bishop's Palace C4
3 Earl's Palace C4
4 Orkney Distillery B2
5 Orkney Museum B4

⌂ Sleeping
6 Albert Hotel C2
7 Peedie Hostel..B2
8 Shore C2

⊗ Eating
Bothy Bar ....(see 6)
Judith Glue Real Food Cafe...........(see 11)
Shore ....(see 8)
9 Storehouse D2

♾ Drinking & Nightlife
10 Royal Cask B4

🛍 Shopping
11 Judith Glue...B3
12 Sheila Fleet C2

of the upper level (£8) run on Tuesday and Thursday; phone to book.

Earl Rognvald Brusason commissioned the cathedral in 1137 in the name of his martyred uncle, Magnus Erlendsson, who was killed by Earl Hakon Paulsson on Egilsay in 1117. Magnus' remains are entombed in an interior pillar. Another notable in-

terment is that of the Arctic explorer John Rae.

★ **Highland**
Park Distillery   DISTILLERY
(☏ 01856-874619; www.highlandparkwhisky.com; Holm Rd; tours adult/child £15/10; ⊙ tours 10am-4pm daily Apr-Oct, Mon-Fri Nov-Mar) Despite a dodgy Viking rebrand and an increasingly

corporate feel, this is still a good visit. It's a serious distillery that malts its own barley; see it and the peat kiln used to dry it on the excellent, well-informed, hour-long tour (book ahead). The standard 12-year-old is a soft, balanced malt, great for novices and aficionados alike; the 18-year-old is among the world's finest drams. This and older whiskies can be tasted on more specialised tours (£20 to £100), which you can prearrange.

There's also a shop in the centre of Kirkwall, good for merchandise but not doing tastings at time of research.

Earl's Palace
RUINS
(☑ 01856-871918; www.historicenvironment. scot; Watergate; adult/child £6/3.80; ⊙ 9.30am-5.30pm Apr-Sep) The intriguing Earl's Palace was once known as the finest example of French Renaissance architecture in Scotland. One room features an interesting history of its builder, Earl Patrick Stewart, a bastard in every sense of the word, who was beheaded in Edinburgh for treason. He started construction in about 1600, but ran out of money and never completed it. When it's closed you can still get a good look at it from the garden. Admission includes the adjacent **Bishop's Palace** (☑ 01856-871918; www.historicenvironment.scot; Watergate; entry incl in Earl's Palace; ⊙ 9.30am-5.30pm Apr-Sep).

Orkney Distillery
DISTILLERY
(☑ 01856-875338; www.orkneydistilling.com; Ayre Rd; tours adult/child £15/8; ⊙ tours 11am & 2pm Wed-Sat) Opened in 2018, this distillery and visitor centre on the waterfront is a showcase for the tasty Orkney spirit Kirkjuvagr. Tours run for an hour and include an audiovisual display and a tasting; it's wise to prebook online. There's also a cafe-bar here. For real enthusiasts, there's an in-depth day-long tour that lets you create your own gin.

Orkney Museum
MUSEUM
(☑ 01856-873191; www.orkney.gov.uk; Broad St; ⊙ 10.30am-5pm Mon-Sat year-round, closed 12.30-1.30pm Oct-Apr) **FREE** This labyrinthine display in a former merchant's house gives an overview of Orcadian history and prehistory, including Pictish carvings and a display on the ba', an anarchic cross between rugby and a street brawl that takes over the town at Christmastime. Most engaging are the last rooms, covering 19th- and 20th-century social history.

🎊 Festivals & Events

St Magnus Festival
PERFORMING ARTS, MUSIC
(☑ 01856-871445; www.stmagnusfestival. com; ⊙ late Jun) Running for a week over midsummer, this festival is a colourful celebration of music and the arts, with high-quality orchestral performances at the heart of it. It's held in various venues around Kirkwall.

🛏 Sleeping

Orcades Hostel
HOSTEL £
(☑ 01856-873745; www.orcadeshostel.com; Muddisdale Rd; dm/s/d £22/44/60; P@🛜) Book ahead to get a bed in this cracking hostel on the western edge of Kirkwall. It's a guesthouse conversion, so there's a very smart kitchen and lounge, and great-value doubles. Comfortable, spacious en suite dorms with just four bunks make for sound sleeping, and enthusiastic owners give the place spark. There are lockers for valuables at reception.

Peedie Hostel
HOSTEL £
(☑ 01856-877177; www.stayinkirkwall.co.uk; Ayre Rd; dm/s/tw £22/30/45; P🛜) Nestling into a corner at the end of the Kirkwall waterfront, this marvellously located, recently refurbished hostel set in former fisherfolk's cottages has a cute, tiny downstairs section and a more sizeable upper area. Most of the dorms have just two beds, and there are three separate kitchen areas. It's normally unstaffed but the owner is very helpful.

Laundry facilities are available.

Royal Oak Guest House
B&B ££
(☑ 01856-877177; www.royaloakhouse.co.uk; Holm Rd; s £60-66, d £85; P🛜) This likeable spot south of Kirkwall's centre has eight bright rooms, all with modern en suite bathrooms. Photos of Orkney decorate the guesthouse, which features a luminous dining room and guest access to fridge, microwave and lounge. Best is the great chat with owner Liz.

Karrawa Guest House
GUESTHOUSE ££
(☑ 01856-871100; www.karrawaguesthouseorkney. co.uk; Inganess Rd; s £70-76, d £90-95; P🛜) In a peaceful location on the southeastern edge of Kirkwall, this enthusiastically run guesthouse offers significant value for well-kept modern double rooms with comfortable

mattresses. Breakfast is generously proportioned and bikes are available for hire.

★ Albert Hotel
HOTEL £££

(☎ 01856-876000; www.alberthotel.co.uk; Mounthoolie Lane; s £118, d £148-163; ☎) Stylishly refurbished in plum and grey, this central but peaceful hotel is Kirkwall's finest address. Comfortable contemporary rooms in a variety of categories sport super-inviting beds and smart bathrooms. Staff are helpful, and will pack you a breakfast box if you've got an early ferry. A great Orkney base, with the more-than-decent **Bothy Bar** (☎ 01856-876000; www.alberthotel. co.uk; Mounthoolie Lane; mains £7-13; ☉ noon-2pm & 5-9pm; ☎) downstairs. Walk-in prices are often cheaper.

Shore
HOTEL £££

(☎ 01856-872200; www.theshore.co.uk; Shore St; s £90-100, d £130-155; ☎) Right on the harbour, the Shore has a can-do attitude and a friendly vibe. The rooms vary widely, from compact upstairs chambers to excellent, spacious premier doubles with water views (well worth the upgrade), but all are modern. Breakfast is also above average.

✕ Eating & Drinking

Judith Glue
Real Food Cafe
CAFE £

(☎ 01856-874225; www.judithglue.com; 25 Broad St; light meals £6-13; ☉ 9am-6pm Mon-Sat, 10am-6pm Sun mid-Sep–May, 9am-8pm Mon-Sat, 10am-6pm Sun Jun–mid-Sep; ☎) ✐ At the back of a lively craft shop opposite St Magnus Cathedral, this licensed cafe-bistro serves tasty sandwiches and salads, as well

THE BA'
....

Every Christmas Day and New Year's Day, Kirkwall holds a staggering spectacle: a crazy ball game known as the ba'. Two enormous teams, the Uppies and the Doonies, fight their way, no holds barred, through the streets, trying to get a leather ball to the other end of town. The ball is thrown from the Mercat Cross to the waiting teams; the Uppies have to get the ba' to the corner of Main St and Junction Rd, the Doonies must get it to the water. Violence, skulduggery and other stunts are common, and the event, fuelled by plenty of strong drink, can last hours.

as daily specials and succulent seafood platters. There's a strong emphasis on sustainable and organic ingredients, but put the feel-good factor aside for a moment when fighting for a table at lunchtime. Check Facebook for regular events.

★ Shore
SCOTTISH ££

(☎ 01856-872200; www.theshore.co.uk; 6 Shore St; bar meals £9-11, restaurant mains £17-22; ☉ food noon-2pm & 6-9pm Mon-Fri, 10am-9pm Sat & Sun, reduced hours winter; ☎) This popular harbourside place is a convivial spot with a helpful attitude. It offers high-standard bar meals and excellent evening meals in the restaurant section, which features local seafood and beautifully prepared meat dishes. Upstairs are some very decent rooms.

Storehouse
SCOTTISH ££

(☎ 01856-252250; www.thestorehouserestau rantwithrooms.co.uk; Bridge St Wynd; dinner £14-22; ☉ 5-9.30pm Tue-Sat; ☎) This transformation of a listed 19th-century herring warehouse into an Orcadian restaurant is a marvellous success of architecture and design. Much that is great about the Orkney Islands – quality produce, craft traditions, literary history – is artfully blended here in the restaurant and eight sumptuous, luxurious, individually designed rooms upstairs (doubles £150 to £190).

★ Foveran
SCOTTISH £££

(☎ 01856-872389; www.thefoveran.com; St Ola; mains £16-27; ☉ 6.30-8.30pm mid-May–mid-Sep, Fri & Sat or by appt mid-Sep–mid-May; ☎) ✐ Three miles down the Orphir road, one of Orkney's best dining options is surprisingly affordable for its quality. Tranquilly located, with a cosy eating area overlooking the sea, it shines with its classic Orcadian ingredients – the steak with haggis and whisky sauce is feted, while North Ronaldsay lamb comes in deliciously tender cuts.

A medley of toothsome vegetables accompanies the mains, and interesting wines complement the dishes. If you like the spot – and why wouldn't you? – there are compact, comfortable, Laura Ashley–decorated rooms available (single/double £85/125).

Royal Cask
PUB

(☎ 01856-873477; www.orkneyhotel.co.uk; 40 Victoria St; ☉ 11am-midnight Mon-Wed, 11am-1am Thu-Sat, noon-midnight Sun; ☎) Tucked away in the Orkney Hotel, this refurbished bar is best visited for its fabulous selection of single malt whisky, with more than 800 different bottlings and lots of knowledge about them. There are also bar meals available to soak it all up.

🛍 Shopping

Kirkwall has some gorgeous jewellery and crafts along Albert St, as well as shops selling quality Orcadian food and drink.

Sheila Fleet　　　　　　　　JEWELLERY
(✆01856-861203; www.sheilafleet.com; 30 Bridge St; ⊙10am-5pm or 6pm Mon-Sat) Orkney's best-known jewellery designer creates some exquisite pieces seemingly lit from within. She draws on local traditions and storytelling for her creations. If you like them, make sure you pay a visit to her striking gallery and cafe in Tankerness.

Judith Glue　　　　　　ARTS & CRAFTS
(✆01856-874225; www.judithglue.com; 25 Broad St; ⊙9am-6pm Mon-Sat, 10am-6pm Sun mid-Sep–May, 9am-8pm Mon-Sat, 10am-6pm Sun Jun–mid-Sep) This absorbing shop has some fine handmade knitwear as well as an eclectic range of Orkney crafts and souvenirs.

ℹ Information

Balfour Hospital (✆01856-888000; www. ohb.scot.nhs.uk; Foreland Rd)
Kirkwall Tourist Office (✆01856-872856; www.visitorkney.com; West Castle St; ⊙9am-5pm Mon-Sat Nov-Mar, to 6pm Sep-Oct & Sep-Oct, to 6pm daily May-Aug) Has a good range of Orkney info and helpful staff. Shares a building with the bus station.

ℹ Getting There & Away

AIR
Kirkwall Airport (✆01856-872421; www.hial. co.uk) is located 2.5 miles southeast of town and is served regularly by bus 4 (15 minutes).

BOAT
Ferries to Orkney's northern islands depart from the pier in the centre of town. Here, too, is the **Orkney Ferries office** (✆01856-872044; www.orkneyferries.co.uk; Shore St; ⊙7am-5pm Mon-Fri, 7am-noon & 1-3pm Sat) for bookings. Ferries to Shapinsay depart from the next pier to the west.

Ferries to Aberdeen and Shetland use the Hatston Ferry Terminal, 2 miles northwest. Bus X10 heads there to coincide with departures.

BUS
All services leave from the **bus station** (West Castle St):

Bus X1 Stromness (£3.35, 30 minutes, hourly Monday to Saturday, seven on Sunday); in the other direction to St Margaret's Hope (£3.15).
Bus 2 Orphir and Houton (£2.20, 20 minutes, four or five daily Monday to Saturday, five on Sunday from mid-June to mid-August).
Bus 6 Evie (£3.65, 40 minutes, three to five daily Monday to Saturday) and Tingwall (Rousay ferry). Runs Sunday in summer to Tingwall only.

East Mainland to South Ronaldsay

After a German U-boat sank battleship HMS *Royal Oak* in 1939, Winston Churchill had causeways of concrete blocks erected across the channels on the eastern side of Scapa Flow, linking Mainland to the islands of Lamb Holm, Glims Holm, Burray and South Ronaldsay. The Churchill Barriers, flanked by rusting wrecks of blockships, now support the main road from Kirkwall to Burwick.

East Mainland

Sheila Fleet Kirk Gallery & Café　　　　　JEWELLERY
(✆cafe 01856-861758, gallery 01856-861203; www.sheilafleet.com; Tankerness; ⊙10am-5pm Mon-Sat, 11am-5pm Sun) You've normally got the rings sorted out before you walk down the aisle, but not at this audacious conversion of a parish church into a design gallery for Sheila Fleet's shimmering jewellery. It's near the water in Tankerness, 6 miles southeast of Kirkwall beyond the airport, and is a striking sight inside. It's complemented by a lovely conservatory cafe.

The cafe does really tasty breakfasts and lunches (light meals £7 to £12) using local produce. You'd better book a table ahead in summer.

Lamb Holm

Italian Chapel　　　　　　CHURCH
(✆01856-781268; Lamb Holm; adult/child £3/ free; ⊙9am-6.30pm Jun-Aug, to 5pm May & Sep, 10am-4pm Mon-Sat, to 3pm Sun Apr & Oct, 10am-1pm Nov-Mar) The Italian Chapel is all that remains of a POW camp that housed the Italian soldiers who worked on the Churchill Barriers. They built the chapel in their spare time, using two Nissen huts, scrap metal and their considerable artistic skills. It's quite extraordinary inside and

the charming backstory makes it an Orkney highlight. One of the artists returned in 1960 to restore the paintwork.

Orkney Wine Company
DRINKS

(☑ 01856-781736; www.orkneywine.co.uk; Lamb Holm; ☉ 10am-4pm Mon-Thu & Sat, 10am-2pm Fri, plus noon-4pm Sun Jul & Aug, reduced hours winter) The Orkney Wine Company has handmade wines produced with berries, flowers and vegetables, all naturally fermented. Get stuck into some strawberry-rhubarb wine or blackcurrant port – unusual flavours but surprisingly delicious. You can also taste a rum distilled next door.

Burray

This small island, a link in the chain joined by the Churchill Barriers, has a fine beach at Northtown on the east coast, where you may see seals. The village has a shop and places to stay, and there's a worthwhile museum on the island.

★ Fossil & Heritage Centre
MUSEUM

(☑ 01856-731255; www.orkneyfossilcentre. co.uk; adult/child £5.10/3.40; ☉ 10am-5pm mid-Apr–Sep) This eclectic museum is a great visit, combining some excellent 360-million-year-old Devonian fish fossils found locally with a well-designed exhibition on the world wars and Churchill Barriers. Upstairs is a selection of household and farming implements. There's a good little gift shop and an enjoyable coffee shop. Coming from Kirkwall, it's on the left half a mile after crossing onto Burray.

Sands Hotel
HOTEL £££

(☑ 01856-731298; www.thesandshotel.co.uk; s/d/ste £105/140/250; 🅿 🐾) This commodious, refurbished 19th-century herring station is right on the pier in Burray village. Rooms have stylish furnishings, and all have great water views. Families and groups should consider a suite: a brilliant two-level self-contained flat that sleeps four and has a kitchen. There's a good restaurant (noon to 2pm and 5pm to 9pm, reduced winter hours) with a genteel nautical feel.

South Ronaldsay

South Ronaldsay's main village, pristine St Margaret's Hope, was named after the Maid of Norway, who died here in 1290 on her way to marry Edward II of England (strictly a political affair: Margaret was only seven years old). The island has some intriguing prehistoric tombs and fine places to stay and eat, and is also the docking point of two of the three mainland ferries.

⊙ Sights

★ Tomb of the Eagles
ARCHAEOLOGICAL SITE

(☑ 01856-831339; www.tomboftheeagles.co.uk; Cleat; adult/child £7.80/3.50; ☉ 9.30am-5.30pm Apr-Sep, 10am-noon Mar, 9.30am-12.30pm Oct) Two significant archaeological sites were found here by a farmer on his land. The first is a Bronze Age stone building with a firepit, indoor well and plenty of seating (a communal cooking site, or the original Orkney pub?). Beyond, in a spectacular clifftop position, the neolithic tomb (wheel yourself in prone on a trolley) is an elaborate stone construction that held the remains of up to 340 people who died some five millennia ago.

An excellent personal explanation is given at the visitor centre, where you meet a few spooky skulls and can handle some of the artefacts, plus absorb information on the Mesolithic period. It's about a mile's airy walk to the tomb from the centre, which is signposted near Burwick at South Ronaldsay's southern tip.

Banks Chambered Tomb
ARCHAEOLOGICAL SITE

(Tomb of the Otters; ☑ 01856-831605; www.bankschamberedtomb.co.uk; Cleat; adult/child £6/3; ☉ 11am-5pm Apr-Sep) Discovered while digging was under way for a car park, this 5000-year-old chambered tomb has yielded a vast quantity of human bones, well preserved thanks to the saturation of the earth. The tomb, dug into bedrock, is an atmospheric if claustrophobic visit. The guided tour mixes homespun archaeological theories with astute observations. Within the adjacent bistro, you can handle discoveries of stones and bones, including the remains of otters, who presumably used this as a den. Follow signs for Tomb of the Eagles.

🍴 Sleeping & Eating

★ Bankburn House
B&B ££

(☑ 01856-831310; www.bankburnhouse.co.uk; A961, St Margaret's Hope; s/d £65/100, without bathroom £50/80; 🅿 @ 🐾 🐕) 🍴 This large rustic house does everything right, with

SKARA BRAE

Idyllically situated by a sandy bay 8 miles north of Stromness, and predating Stonehenge and the pyramids of Giza, extraordinary **Skara Brae** (☑ 01856-841815; www. historicenvironment.scot; Sandwick; adult/child Nov-Mar £7/4.20, Apr-Oct incl Skaill House £8/5; ⊙ 9.30am-5.30pm Apr-Sep, 10am-4pm Oct-Mar), one of the world's most evocative prehistoric sites, is northern Europe's best-preserved neolithic village. Even the stone furniture – beds, boxes and dressers – has survived the 5000 years since a community lived and breathed here. It was hidden until 1850, when waves whipped up by a severe storm eroded the sand and grass above the beach, exposing the houses underneath.

There's an excellent interactive exhibit and short video, arming visitors with facts and theory, which will enhance the impact of the site. You then enter a reconstructed house, giving the excavation (which you head to next) more meaning. The official guidebook, available from the visitor centre, includes a good self-guided tour.

In the summer months, your ticket also gets you into adjacent Skaill House (p409).

Bus 8S runs here sporadically from Stromness and Kirkwall; otherwise a taxi, cycle or hitch from Stromness is the easiest option. Mobility scooters are available at the visitor centre to cut out the walk to the site.

smashing good-sized rooms and an engaging owner who puts on quality breakfasts and takes pride in constantly innovating to improve guests' comfort levels. The huge lawn overlooks St Margaret's Hope and the bay – perfect for sunbathing on shimmering Orkney summer days. Prices drop substantially for multinight stays.

Robertsons CAFE £
(☑ 01856-831889; www.facebook.com/coffeehoosebar; Church Rd, St Margaret's Hope; light meals £3-9; ⊙ food 10am-9pm Mon-Sat, 11am-9pm Sun, closed Mon-Wed off-season; 🛜) Tastefully renovated, this characterful high-ceilinged former general store with chessboard tiles makes an atmospheric venue for a morning coffee and filled roll, or light meals such as soups and cheeseboards with local varieties (available for purchase). It also does cocktails and opens as a bar until late.

Skerries Bistro SEAFOOD £
(☑ 01856-831605; www.skerriesbistro.co.uk; Cleat; lunch £6-10; ⊙ 11am-4pm Mon-Fri & Sun Apr-Sep) This cafe-bistro occupies a spectacular setting at the southern end of South Ronaldsay. It's a smart, modern glass-walled building with a deck and great clifftop views. Meals range from soups and sandwiches to daily fish and shellfish specials. Dinners may be available in summer. For sale at time of research.

West & North Mainland

This part of Mainland island is sprinkled with outstanding prehistoric monuments: the journey to Orkney is worth it for these alone and they stand proud as some of the world's most important neolithic sites. It would take a day to see all of them – if pushed for time, visit Skara Brae then Maeshowe, but book your visit to the latter in advance.

Bus 8S links Kirkwall and Stromness via a loop past the Ring of Brodgar, Skara Brae (£3.65, 55 minutes) and other prehistoric sights. It runs twice a day, usually every day in summer and two to three times a week in winter.

⦿ Sights

The Heart of Neolithic Orkney is Unesco-listed and consists of four standout archaeological sites (Skara Brae, Maeshowe, the Standing Stones of Stenness (p408) and the Ring of Brodgar (p408)). These and other associated sites are not to be missed. It's important to prebook your entry slot to Maeshowe ahead of time.

⭐**Maeshowe** ARCHAEOLOGICAL SITE
(☑ 01856-761606; www.historicenvironment. scot; adult/child £9/5.40; ⊙ 10am-5pm Apr-Sep, to 4pm Oct-Mar, last tour 1hr before close) Constructed about 5000 years ago, Maeshowe is an extraordinary place, a Stone Age tomb built from enormous sandstone blocks,

some of which weighed many tonnes and were brought from several miles away. Creeping down the long stone passageway to the central chamber, you feel the indescribable gulf of years that separate us from the architects of this mysterious tomb.

Entry is by 45-minute guided tours (prebooking online is strongly advised) that leave by bus from the visitor centre at nearby Stenness.

Though nothing is known about who and what was interred here, the scope of the project suggests it was a structure of great significance.

In the 12th century, the tomb was broken into by Vikings searching for treasure. A couple of years later, another group sought shelter in the chamber from a three-day blizzard. Waiting out the storm, they carved runic graffiti on the walls. As well as the some-things-never-change 'Olaf was 'ere' and 'Thorni bedded Helga', there are also more intricate carvings, including a particularly fine dragon and a knotted serpent.

Prebook tickets online, as recommended, or buy them at the visitor centre in Stenness, from where the tour buses depart. Guides tend to only show a couple of the Viking inscriptions, but they'll happily show more if asked. Check out the virtual-reality tour in the visitor centre while you wait.

For a few weeks around the winter solstice, the setting sun shafts up the entrance

A NEOLITHIC CAPITAL

The spectacular finds from ongoing excavations at **Ness of Brodgar** (www.nessofbrodgar.co.uk; ⊘tours early Jul-late Aug), an archaeological site between the Standing Stones of Stenness and the Ring of Brodgar, have revolutionised understanding of the neolithic in Britain. What was probably a major centre of power and religion has been revealed; in use for over a millennium, the settlement had a mighty wall, a large building (a temple or palace?) and as many as 100 other structures, some painted. During the summer dig season, there are free guided tours; check the website for times and dates.

passage and strikes the back wall of the tomb in spooky alignment.

Standing Stones of Stenness ARCHAEOLOGICAL SITE
(www.historicenvironment.scot; ⊘24hr) FREE
Part of this Mainland area's concentration of neolithic monuments, four mighty stones remain of what was once a circle of 12. Recent research suggests they were perhaps erected as long ago as 3300 BCE, and they impose by their sheer size – the tallest measures 5.7m in height. The narrow strip of land they're on, the Ness of Brodgar, separates the Harray and Stenness lochs and was the site of a large settlement inhabited throughout the neolithic period (3500–1800 BCE).

Barnhouse Neolithic Village ARCHAEOLOGICAL SITE
(www.historicenvironment.scot; ⊘24hr) FREE
Alongside the Standing Stones of Stenness are the excavated remains of a village thought to have been inhabited by the builders of Maeshowe. Don't skip this: it brings the area to life. The houses are well preserved and similar to Skara Brae with their stone furnishings. One of the buildings was entered by crossing a fireplace: possibly an act of ritual significance.

Ring of Brodgar ARCHAEOLOGICAL SITE
(www.historicenvironment.scot; ⊘24hr) FREE A mile northwest of Stenness is this wide circle of standing stones, some over 5m tall. The last of the three Stenness monuments to be built (2500–2000 BC), it remains a most atmospheric location. Twenty-one of the original 60 stones still stand among the heather. On a grey day, with dark clouds thudding low across the sky, the stones are a spine-tingling sight.

Unstan Chambered Cairn ARCHAEOLOGICAL SITE
(www.historicenvironment.scot; A965; ⊘24hr) FREE This atmospheric neolithic tomb, on a smaller scale than nearby Maeshowe, is a site that you may well get to yourself. It's a very tight squeeze down the entrance passage; once inside, you can appreciate several different burial compartments divided by vertical stone slabs. The modern roof protects the structure.

Orkney Brewery BREWERY
(☑01856-841777; www.orkneybrewery.co.uk; Quoyloo; tours adult/child £7.50/4.25; ⊘10am-

4.30pm Mon-Sat, 11am-4.30pm Sun mid-Mar–Dec) The folk here have been producing their brilliant Orcadian beers – Dark Island is a standout, while Skull Splitter lives up to its name – for years now, and this brewery's visitor centre is a great place to come and try them. Tours run regularly and explain the brewing process, while the cafe-bar, fashionably decked out in local stone, is atmospheric.

Skaill House HISTORIC BUILDING

(☎01856-841501; www.skaillhouse.co.uk; Sandwick; adult/child £5/4 or incl with Skara Brae; ⊙9.30am-5.30pm Apr-Sep, 10am-4pm Oct) Next to Skara Brae, and entered on a joint ticket, Skaill House is an imposing step-gabled Orcadian mansion built for the bishop in 1620. Catapulting straight from the neolithic to the 1950s decor is a time-travel experience, but it's an interesting sight in its own right. You can see a smart hidden compartment in the library as well as the bishop's original 17th-century four-poster bed. There are often falconry displays in the grounds, and they make a decent gin here.

In the 19th century, a storm revealed some stones in the dunes of the laird of Skaill House, who began excavating; and revealed Skara Brae to the world.

Birsay

The small village of Birsay is 6 miles north of Skara Brae, set amid peaceful countryside. It has some excellent attractions, including the Brough of Birsay, which makes a tempting picnic destination if you plan the tides right.

Brough of Birsay ARCHAEOLOGICAL SITE

(www.historicenvironment.scot; adult/child £6/3.60; ⊙9.30am-5.30pm mid-Jun–Sep) At low tide (check tide times at any Historic Environment Scotland site) you can walk out to this windswept island, which is the site of extensive Norse ruins, including a number of longhouses and the 12th-century **St Peter's Church**. There's also a replica of a Pictish stone found here. This is where St Magnus was buried after his murder on Egilsay in 1117, and the island became a pilgrimage place. The attractive lighthouse has fantastic views. Take a picnic, but don't get stranded...

The Brough features heavily in George Mackay Brown's excellent novel *Magnus*.

Earl's Palace RUINS

(⊙24hr) FREE The ruins of this palace, built in the 16th century by the despotic Robert Stewart, Earl of Orkney, dominate the village of Birsay. Today it's a mass of half walls and crumbling columns; the size of the palace is impressive, matching the reputed ego and tyranny of its former inhabitant.

Barony Mill HISTORIC BUILDING

(☎01856-721439; www.baronymill.com; A967; adult/child £3.50/free; ⊙11am-4.30pm May-Sep) This working watermill is a satisfying sight – it's still running, and producing flour from bere (a type of barley) that you'll find in baked morsels across the Orkney Islands. In summer you can visit on a guided tour, when its workings will be explained.

Birsay Bay Tearoom CAFE £

(☎01856-721399; www.birsaybaytearoom.co.uk; light meals £3-8; ⊙10.30am-5pm Thu-Mon Apr-Sep, 10.30am-4pm Thu-Mon Feb, Mar & early Oct, 10.30am-4pm Thu-Sun Nov & Dec; 🖅) A pleasant spot with sweeping views over green grass, black cows and blue-grey sea, this cafe (slowly) serves tea, coffee, home baking and light meals. It's a good place to wait for the tide to go out before crossing to the Brough of Birsay (in plain sight). Check the website for latest winter opening times as these vary substantially.

❶ Getting There & Away

Bus 7 runs twice daily Monday to Saturday between Kirkwall (£3.65, 35 minutes) and Stromness (£3.65, 40 minutes) via Birsay.

Evie

Broch of Gurness ARCHAEOLOGICAL SITE

(www.historicenvironment.scot; Evie; adult/child £6/3.60; ⊙9.30am-5.30pm Apr-Sep) Here's a fine example of the drystone fortified towers that were both a status symbol for powerful farmers and useful protection from raiders some 2200 years ago. The imposing entranceway and sturdy stone walls – originally 10m high – are impressive; inside you can see the hearth and where a mezzanine floor would have fitted. Around the broch are a number of well-preserved outbuildings, including a curious shamrock-shaped house. The visitor centre has some interesting displays on the culture that built these remarkable fortifications.

The broch is on an exposed headland at Aikerness, a 1.5-mile walk northeast from the strung-out village of Evie.

Stromness

POP 1800

This appealing grey-stone port has a narrow, elongated, flagstone-paved main street and tiny alleys leading down to the waterfront between tall houses. It lacks the size of Kirkwall, Orkney's main town, but makes up for that with bucketloads of character, having changed little since its heyday in the 18th century, when it was a busy staging post for ships avoiding the troublesome English Channel during European wars. Stromness is ideally located for trips to Orkney's major prehistoric sites.

◉ Sights

Stromness, formerly a slightly rough-edged maritime town, has gone all arty, with a string of quirky craft shops, galleries and boutiques along the picturesque main shopping street. It's great for browsing.

★ Stromness Museum   MUSEUM
(☑01856-850025; www.stromnessmuseum.co.uk; 52 Alfred St; adult/child £5/1; ☉10am-5pm daily Apr-Sep, 10am-5pm Mon-Sat Oct, 11am-3.30pm Mon-Sat Nov-Mar) This superb museum, run with great passion, is full of knick-knacks from maritime and natural-history exhibitions covering whaling, the Hudson's Bay Company and the German fleet sunk after WWI. Recent finds from the jaw-dropping excavations at the Ness of Brodgar are on display and there's always an excellent summer exhibition. You can happily nose around for a couple of hours. Across the street is the house where local poet and novelist George Mackay Brown lived.

Pier Arts Centre   GALLERY
(☑01856-850209; www.pierartscentre.com; 30 Victoria St; ☉10.30am-5pm Thu-Sat year-round, plus Mon Jun-Sep) FREE This gallery has really rejuvenated the Orkney modern-art scene with its sleek lines and upbeat attitude. It's worth a look as much for the architecture as for its high-quality collection of 20th-century British art and changing exhibitions.

★‍ Festivals & Events

Orkney Folk Festival   MUSIC
(www.orkneyfolkfestival.com; ☉late May) A four-day event in late May, with folk concerts, ceilidhs (evenings of traditional Scottish entertainment) and casual pub sessions. Stromness packs out, and late-night buses from Kirkwall are laid on. Book tickets and accommodation ahead.

⎸ Sleeping

Brown's Hostel   HOSTEL £
(☑01856-850661; www.brownsorkney.com; 45 Victoria St; s/d from £25/45, d/q with bathroom from £50/90; �@) On Stromness' main street, this handy, sociable place has cosy private rooms – no dorms, no bunks – at a very good price. There's an inviting common area where you can browse the free internet or swap pasta recipes in the open kitchen. There are good en suite rooms in a house up the street, and an apartment sleeping four.

Point of Ness
Caravan & Camping Park   CAMPSITE £
(☑office hours 01856-873535, site 01856-850532; https://orkney.campstead.com; Ness Rd; tent sites per small tent/adult £8.80/7.40; ☉Apr-Sep; P🐾🐾🐾) This breezy, fenced-in campsite has a super location overlooking the bay at the southern end of Stromness and is as neat as a pin.

★ Brinkies
Guest House   B&B ££
(☑01856-851881; yvonneski@btinternet.com; Brownstown Rd; s £65-70, d £80-90; P🐾) Just a short walk from the centre of Stromness, but with a lonely, king-of-the-castle position overlooking the town and bay, this exceptional place offers five-star islander hospitality. Compact, modern rooms are handsome, stylish and comfortable, and the public areas are done out attractively in wood, but it's the charming owner's flexibility and can-do attitude that makes this place so special.

Breakfast is 'continental Orcadian' – a stupendous array of quality local cheese, smoked fish and homemade bere bannocks (a wheat-barley bread). Want a lie-in? No problem; saunter down at 10am. Don't want breakfast? How about a packed lunch instead?

To get here, take Outertown Rd off Back Rd, turn right on to Brownstown Rd and keep going.

Burnside Farm
B&B ££

(☑ 01856-850723; www.burnside-farm.com; North End Rd/A965; s/d £80/100; 🅿 🛜) On a working dairy farm at Stromness' edge, this place has lovely views over green fields, town and harbour. Rooms are elegant and maintain the style from when the house was built in the late 1940s, with attractive period furnishings. The top-notch bathrooms, however, are sparklingly contemporary. Breakfast comes with views, and the kindly owner couldn't be more welcoming.

Lindisfarne B&B
B&B ££

(☑ 01856-850082; www.stayinstromness.co.uk; off A965; s/d £55/75) Set among green fields with views down over Stromness, Lindisfarne is run by a charming young Orcadian family and makes a great base. It's a modern, spacious home with four commodious bedrooms, common areas for guests and self-catering options. Breakfast is delicious, and a warm welcome from Deborah, Kevin and the kids is guaranteed.

It's not signposted from the main Kirkwall–Stromness road: turn left just after passing the right turn to Birsay and Sandwick a mile short of Stromness.

✖ Eating

★ Hamnavoe Restaurant
SEAFOOD ££

(☑ 01856-850606, 01856-851226; 35 Graham Pl; mains £15-24; ⊙ 7-9pm Tue-Sun Jun-Aug) Tucked away off the main street, this Stromness favourite specialises in excellent local seafood in an intimate, cordial atmosphere. There's always something good off the boats, and the chef prides himself on his lobster. Booking is a must. It opens some weekends in low season; it's worth calling ahead to check.

Ferry Inn
PUB FOOD ££

(☑ 01856-850280; www.ferryinn.com; 10 John St; mains £10-19; ⊙ food 7am-9pm Apr-Oct; 🛜) Every port has its pub, and in Stromness it's the Ferry. Convivial and central, it warms the cockles with folk music, local beers and characters, and eating in a refurbished dining area that offers good local seafood and cheery service.

ⓘ Getting There & Around

BICYCLE
Orkney Cycle Hire (☑ 01856-850255; www.orkneycyclehire.co.uk; 54 Dundas St; per day £10-15; ⊙ 8am-5pm) Family options include kids' bikes and child trailers.

BOAT
Northlink Ferries (p400) Runs services from Stromness to Scrabster on the mainland (passenger/car £20.45/63, 1½ hours, two to three daily).

BUS
Bus X1 runs regularly to Kirkwall (£3.35, 30 minutes, hourly Monday to Saturday, seven Sunday), with some going on to St Margaret's Hope (£6.05, 1¼ hours).

Hoy

Orkney's second-largest island, Hoy (meaning 'High Island'), got the lion's share of the archipelago's scenic beauty. Shallow turquoise bays lace the east coast and massive sea cliffs guard the west, while peat and moorland cover Orkney's highest hills. Much of the north is a reserve for breeding seabirds. The Scrabster–Stromness ferry gives you a decent perspective of the island's wild good looks.

◉ Sights

Old Man of Hoy
NATURAL FEATURE

Hoy's best-known sight is this 137m-high rock stack jutting from the ocean off the tip of an eroded headland. It's a tough ascent and for experienced climbers only, but the walk to see it is a Hoy highlight, revealing much of the island's most spectacular scenery. You can also spot the Old Man from the Scrabster–Stromness ferry.

The easiest approach to the Old Man is from Rackwick Bay, a 5-mile walk by road from Moaness Pier (in Hoy village on the east coast, where the ferries dock) through the beautiful Rackwick Glen. You'll pass the 5000-year-old **Dwarfie Stane** (Rackwick Glen; ⊙ 24hr) FREE, the only example of a rock-cut tomb in Scotland. On your return you can take the path via the Glens of Kinnaird and Berriedale Wood, Scotland's most northerly tuft of native forest.

From Rackwick Bay, where there's a hostel, the most popular path climbs steeply westwards then curves northwards, descending gradually to the edge of the cliffs opposite the Old Man of Hoy. Allow seven hours for the return trip from Moaness Pier, or three hours from Rackwick Bay.

Scapa Flow Visitor Centre & Museum
MUSEUM

(☎01856-791300; www.orkney.gov.uk; Lyness; ☉10am-4.30pm Mon-Sat Mar, Apr & Oct, 9am-4.30pm Mon-Sat, 1st to last ferry Sun May-Sep) FREE Lyness was an important naval base during both world wars, when the British Grand Fleet was based in Scapa Flow. This fascinating museum and photographic display, located in an old pump house that once fed fuel to the ships, is a must-see for anyone interested in Orkney's military history. Take your time to browse the exhibits and have a look at the folders of supplementary information – letters home from a seaman lost when the *Royal Oak* was torpedoed are particularly moving.

It's easily visited, just by the ferry slip at Lyness, and there's a decent cafe. The museum was being renovated at time of research, due to reopen in 2021. During renovations there is a temporary exhibition in the Hoy Hotel, half a mile from the Lyness ferry terminal.

Hackness Martello Tower & Battery
FORT

(www.historicenvironment.scot; Hackness; adult/child £6/3.60; ☉9.30am-5.30pm daily Apr-Sep, 10am-4pm Mon-Sat Oct) Built during the Napoleonic Wars, when French ships passed through the Pentland Firth to prey on North Sea merchant vessels, this battery, accompanied by two towers (one across the water), never saw action but is an impressive piece of military architecture. The custodian gives an excellent tour of the barracks and tower – there's a lovely view from the gun platform on top – that really evokes the period.

🛏 Sleeping & Eating

Hoy Centre
HOSTEL £

(☎office hours 01856-873535, warden 07918 367560; https://orkney.campstead.com; dm/tw £21.90/61.50; P🅿☎) This clean, bright, modern hostel has an enviable location, around 15 minutes' walk from Moaness Pier, at the base of the rugged Cuilags. Rooms are all en suite and include good-value family options; there is also a spacious kitchen and DVD lounge. It's open year-round: book via the website to avoid an admin fee (private rooms only).

Stromabank Hotel
INN ££

(☎01856-701494; www.stromabank.co.uk; Longhope; s/d £75/100; P☎) Perched on the hill above Longhope, this small atmospheric hotel has very acceptable, refurbished en suite rooms, as well as tasty home-cooked meals, including seafood and steaks (£8 to £14) using lots of local produce.

Meals are served 6pm to 8pm Friday to Wednesday, plus noon to 2pm Sunday. It does meals for residents only on Thursday and takeaways on Saturday evenings.

Beneth'ill Cafe
CAFE £

(☎01856-791119; www.benethillcafe.co.uk; Hoy Village; light meals £7-9; ☉10am-6pm Apr-Sep) Handy for the Moaness ferry, this cafe has a spectacular location by the water with great views of the brooding Hoy hills. It offers home baking and light meals such as salads and quiches. There's also a daily hot dish, often something hearty like stew, which is great after a walk. The food is pleasingly fresh, tasty and well presented.

ℹ Getting There & Around

Orkney Ferries (p401) runs a passenger/bike ferry (adult £4.55, 30 minutes, two to six daily) between Stromness and Moaness at Hoy's northern end, and a car ferry to Lyness (with one service to/from Longhope) from Houton on Mainland (passenger/car £4.55/14.40, 40 minutes, up to seven daily Monday to Friday, two or three Saturday and Sunday); book cars well in advance. Sunday service is from May to September only.

A bus meets ferries at Lyness and goes on to Houton; it also runs to the Moaness ferry on Sunday.

Northern Islands

The group of windswept islands north of Mainland is a haven for birds, rich in archaeological sites and blessed with wonderful white-sand beaches and azure seas. Though some are hillier than others, all offer a broadly similar landscape of flattish green farmland running down to scenic coastline. Some give a real sense of what Orkney was like before the modern world impinged upon island life.

Accessible by reasonably priced ferries or planes, the islands are well worth exploring. Though you can see 'the sights' in a matter of hours, the key is to stay a day or two and relax into the pace of island life.

Note that the 'ay' at the end of island names (from the Old Norse for 'island') is pronounced closer to 'ee'.

Orkney Ferries (p401) and Loganair Inter-Isles Air Service (p401) serve these islands. It's possible to make day trips to many of the islands from Kirkwall.

Most islands offer a bus service that meets ferries: you may have to call to book this. The same operator often offers island tours.

Westray

If you have the time to visit only one of Orkney's Northern Islands, make Westray (www.westraypapawestray.co.uk) the one. The largest of the group, it has rolling farmland, handsome sandy beaches, great coastal walks and several appealing places to stay.

◉ Sights & Activities

★ **Noltland Castle**   CASTLE
(www.historicenvironment.scot;   ⊙9.30am-5.30pm Apr-Sep, 10am-4pm Oct-Mar) FREE A half-mile west of Pierowall stands this sturdy ruined tower house, built in the 16th century by Gilbert Balfour, aide to Mary, Queen of Scots. The castle is atmospheric and bristles with shot holes, part of the defences of the deceitful Balfour, who plotted to murder Cardinal Beaton and, af-

ter being exiled, the king of Sweden. Like a pantomime villain, he met a sticky end.

At the nearby Links of Noltland, archaeological investigation is regularly unearthing interesting neolithic finds. Most intriguing has been a chamber built over a spring, which was possibly used as a sauna.

Noup Head   NATURE RESERVE
FREE This bird reserve at Westray's northwestern tip is a dramatic area of sea cliffs, with vast numbers of breeding seabirds from April to July. You can walk here along the clifftops from a car park, passing the impressive chasm of **Ramni Geo**, and return via the lighthouse access road (4 miles).

Westray
Heritage Centre   MUSEUM
(☑01857-677414;   www.westrayheritage.co.uk; Pierowall;   adult/child £3/50p;   ⊙11.30am-5pm Mon, 9am-noon & 2-5pm Tue-Sat, 1.30-5pm Sun May-Sep, 2-4pm Wed or by arrangement Oct-Apr) This heritage centre has displays on local history, nature dioramas and archaeological finds, with some famous neolithic carvings (including the 5000-year-old 'Westray Wife'). These small sandstone figurines are the oldest known depictions of the human form so far found in the British Isles.

DIVING SCAPA FLOW

One of the world's largest natural harbours, Scapa Flow has been in near constant use by fleets from the time of the Vikings onwards. After WWI, 74 German ships were interned here; when the armistice dictated a severely reduced German navy, Admiral von Reuter, in charge of the fleet, took matters into his own hands. A secret signal was passed around and the British watched incredulously as every German ship began to sink. Fifty-two of them went to the bottom, with the rest left aground in shallow water.

Most were salvaged, but seven vessels remain to attract divers. There are three battleships – the *König*, the *Kronprinz Wilhelm* and the *Markgraf*. The first two were partially blasted for scrap, but the *Markgraf* is undamaged and considered one of Scotland's best dives.

Numerous other ships rest on the sea bed. HMS *Royal Oak*, sunk by a German U-boat in October 1939 with the loss of 833 crew, is a war grave and diving is prohibited.

It's worth prebooking diving excursions far in advance. You'll need plenty of experience to dive the wrecks, some of which are 47m deep, plus have recent drysuit experience: this can be organised for you. Boats that you can charter for dives include **MV Karin** (www.scapaflow.com) and **MV Jean Elaine** (www.jeanelaine.co.uk). In Stromness, **Scapa Scuba's Red Shed** (☑01856-851218; www.scapascuba.co.uk; Lifeboat House, Dundas St; ⊙2-6pm Mon-Sat, 4-6pm Sun) is a dive shop with good equipment for purchase and hire.

Westraak TOURS
(📞01857-677777; www.westraak.co.uk; Pierowall; adult half-/full day £49/70) This husband-and-wife outfit runs informative and engaging trips around Westray, covering everything from Viking history to puffin mating habits. It also runs the island's taxi service.

🛏 Sleeping & Eating

★ **West Manse** B&B £
(📞01857-677482; www.westmanse.co.uk; Westside; r per person £25; P🛜🐾) 🦮 Be free from timetables at this imposing house with arcing coastal vistas; make your own breakfast when you feel like it. The welcoming hosts have introduced a raft of green solutions for heating, fuel and more. Kids will love this unconventional place, with its play nooks and hobbit house, while art exhibitions, eclectic workshops, venerably comfortable furniture and clean air are drawcards for parents.

There's also a self-catering apartment, Brotchie (£300 per week). And the owners let out a fabulous little waterside cottage in Pierowall that's totally designed for the needs of a visitor with a disability, accompanied by a carer.

Chalmersquoy & the Barn HOSTEL £
(📞01857-677214; www.chalmersquoywestray. co.uk; Pierowall; dm/s/q £25/33/75, B&B s/d £58/80, apt for 4/6 £60/100, tent sites £9-12 plus adult/child £2/1; P🛜) This excellent, intimate, modern hostel is an Orcadian gem. It's heated throughout and has pristine kitchen facilities and an inviting lounge; rooms sleep two or three in comfort. Out front, the lovely owners have top self-catering apartments with great views, and spacious en suite B&B rooms. There's also a campsite and a fabulous byre that hosts atmospheric concerts. A recommended all-round choice.

Bis Geos COTTAGE ££
(📞01857-677420; www.bisgeos.com; per week from £469; P) There are stunning views at this spectacular, quirky and cosy self-catering option between Pierowall and Noup Head. Of the three separate units, the largest sleeps eight and offers the finest vistas. Shorter stays are sometimes available.

Braehead Manse B&B ££
(Reid Hall; 📞01857-677861; www.braeheadmanse. co.uk; Braehead; s/tw/d £55/70/80; P🛜) 🦮 A top-notch conversion of a former village hall behind the church in the middle of Westray, this place has two luminous, high-ceilinged rooms with modern en suite bathrooms and a swish open-plan kitchen/living/dining area with excellent facilities.

Pierowall Hotel PUB FOOD £
(📞01857-677472; www.pierowallhotel.co.uk; Pierowall; mains £9-14; ⏰food noon-2pm & 5-8.30pm May-Sep, noon-1.30pm & 6-8pm Oct-Apr; 🛜) The heart of the Westray community, this refurbished local pub is famous throughout Orkney for its popular fish and chips – whatever has turned up in the day's catch from the hotel's boats is displayed on the blackboard. There are also some curries, but the sea is the way to go here. It also has rooms.

❶ Getting There & Around

There are daily flights with Loganair (p401) from Kirkwall to Westray (one way £37, 20 minutes).

Orkney Ferries (p401) links Kirkwall with Rapness (passenger/car £8.85/20.90, 1½ hours, daily). A bus to the main town, Pierowall, meets the ferry. You can hire bikes at the Rendall's grocery store in Pierowall (📞01856-677389 or 📞07796 538035); it also runs the island's taxi service.

Papa Westray

Known locally as Papay, this exquisitely peaceful, tiny island (4 miles by 1 mile) is home to possibly Europe's oldest domestic building, the 5500-year-old **Knap of Howar** (⏰24hr) FREE, and largest Arctic tern colony. Plus the two-minute hop from Westray is the world's shortest scheduled air service. It's a charming island with seals easily spotted while walking its coast.

Papay Ranger TOURS
(📞07931 235213; www.papawestray.co.uk) The Papay ranger runs excellent day-long tours of Papay in summer that include lunch and afternoon tea (£60/30 per adult/child). It also organises guided boat visits to Holm of Papay (£25/10), bike hire on the island and bespoke tours.

Beltane House GUESTHOUSE, HOSTEL £
(📞01857-644224; www.papawestray.co.uk; Beltane; dm/s/d £28/33/55; P🛜🐾) Owned by the local community, this is Papa Westray's hub. It has the only shop, and functions as a makeshift pub on Saturday nights. One

wing is a hostel with bunks, the other a guesthouse with immaculate rooms with en suites. There are two kitchens, zippy wi-fi (when it works), a big lounge/eating area and views over grassy fields to the sea beyond.

It's just over a mile north of the ferry.

There's a surcharge for one-night stays. You can also camp here (adult/tent £6/6) and there are camping pods that sleep two (£20 per person plus £5 for bedding).

🛈 Getting There & Away

AIR
There are two or three daily flights with Loganair (p401) to Papa Westray (£18, 20 minutes) from Kirkwall. The £21 return offer (you must stay overnight) is great value. Some of the Kirkwall flights go via Westray (£17, two minutes, the world's shortest scheduled flight) or North Ronaldsay (£17, 10 minutes).

BOAT
A passenger-only ferry with Orkney Ferries (p401) runs from Pierowall on Westray to Papa Westray (£4.40, 25 minutes, three to six daily in summer); the crossing is free if you've come straight from the Kirkwall–Westray ferry. From October to April the boat sails by arrangement (call ☎01857-677216). On Tuesday and Friday a car ferry from Kirkwall makes the journey to Papa Westray.

Rousay

Just off the north coast of Mainland, hilly Rousay merits exploration for its fine assembly of prehistoric sites, great views and relaxing away-from-it-all ambience. Connected by regular ferry from Tingwall, it makes a great little day trip, but you may well feel a pull to stay longer. A popular option is to hire a bike from Trumland Farm near the ferry and take on the 14-mile circuit of the island.

★ Midhowe Cairn
& Broch   ARCHAEOLOGICAL SITE
(www.historicenvironment.scot; ⊘24hr) FREE
Six miles from the ferry on Rousay, mighty Midhowe Cairn has been dubbed the 'Great Ship of Death'. Built around 3500 BCE, this enormous ship is divided into compartments, in which the remains of 25 people were found. Covered by a protective stone building, it's nevertheless memorable. Adjacent Midhowe Broch, the sturdy stone lines of which echo the rocky shoreline's striations, is a muscular Iron Age fortified

compound with a mezzanine floor. The sites are on the water, a 10-minute walk downhill from the main road.

Prehistoric Sites   ARCHAEOLOGICAL SITE
(www.historicenvironment.scot; ⊘24hr) FREE
Rousay's major archaeological sites are clearly labelled from the road ringing the island. Heading west from the ferry, you soon come to **Taversoe Tuick**, an intriguing burial cairn constructed on two levels, with separate entrances. Perhaps a joint tomb for different families, it's a semi-detached solution in posthumous housing. Not far beyond are two other significant cairns: **Blackhammer** and **Knowe of Yarso**, the latter a fair walk up the hill but with majestic views.

Trumland Farm   HOSTEL £
(☎01856-821252; trumland@btopenworld.com; dm £17-20, camping £8; P 🐾) 🚭 An easy stroll from the ferry (turn left at the main road), this organic farm has a wee hostel with two dorms and a pretty little kitchen and common area. You can pitch tents and use the facilities; there's also well-equipped self-catering in a cottage and various farm buildings. Linen is £2 extra. Bikes can be hired here.

Taversoe   INN ££
(☎01856-821325; www.taversoehotel.co.uk; s £55-70, d £90-105; ⊘Feb-Dec; P 🐾) Two miles west from the ferry pier, Rousay's only hotel is an attractively low-key place, with renovated rooms offering excellent bathrooms – one suitable for people with disabilities – and beautiful water vistas. The best views are from the dining room, which serves good-value meals. The friendly owners will collect you from the ferry.

🛈 Getting There & Around

A small ferry connects Tingwall on Mainland with Rousay (passenger/bicycle/car £4.55/free/14.40, 30 minutes, up to six daily) and the nearby islands of Egilsay and Wyre.

Rousay Tours (☎01856-821234; www.rousaytours.co.uk; adult/child £38/12) offers taxi service and recommended guided tours of the island, including wildlife-spotting (seals and otters), visits to the prehistoric sites and an optional tasty packed lunch.

Sanday

Aptly named, blissfully quiet and flat, Sanday is ringed by Orkney's best beaches –

with dazzling-white sand of the sort you'd expect in the Caribbean. It's a peaceful, green, pastoral landscape with the sea revealed at every turn.

Quoyness
Chambered Tomb
ARCHAEOLOGICAL SITE

(☉24hr) FREE There are several archaeological sites on Sanday, the most impressive being this chambered tomb, similar to Maeshowe and dating from the 3rd millennium BCE. It has triple walls, a main chamber and six smaller cells.

Sanday
Heritage Centre
MUSEUM

(☎01857-600724; www.sanday.co.uk; Lady; donations appreciated; ☉9.30am-5pm daily May-Oct, Sat-Sun Nov-Apr) FREE This museum in the former temperance hall has intriguing displays on various aspects of island history, including fishing, WWI, archaeology and shipwrecks. In an adjacent field a typical croft house is preserved.

Ayre's Rock Hostel & Campsite
HOSTEL, CAMPSITE £

(☎01857-600410; www.ayres-rock-hostel-orkney.com; tent sites £8-10, pods £35, dm/s/tw £19.50/23.50/39; P ⊛ ⛺) This super-friendly spot by a beach 6 miles north of the Sanday ferry offers a cosy three-room hostel sleeping two or four, and a sweet, grassy campsite by the water. As well as tent pitches, there are heated two-person pods and a static caravan. Evening meals are available. It has a craft shop and Saturday chip shop, and the hosts are extremely helpful.

Backaskaill
B&B ££

(☎01857-600305; www.bedandbreakfastsandayorkney.com; s/d £65/90; P ⊛) Set on a working cattle farm by the sea, this place offers comfortable accommodation in a noble stone farmhouse. The polished interior features an eclectic collection of art and curios. The hospitality is cordial and professional. Rooms feel light and modern, and there's a fabulous guest lounge. The island's best dinners (mains £10 to £16) are here and can be booked by non-guests.

🛈 Getting There & Away
There are flights with Loganair (p401) from Kirkwall to Sanday (one way £37, 20 minutes, once or twice daily).

Orkney Ferries (p401) runs from Kirkwall (passenger/car £8.85/20.90, 1½ hours), with a link to Eday. A bus meets the boat (book on ☎01857-600438).

North Ronaldsay

North Ronaldsay is a real outpost surrounded by rolling seas and big skies. Delicious peace and quiet and the island's excellent birdwatching lure visitors. There are enough semi-feral sheep to seize power, but a 13-mile drystone wall running around the island keeps them off the grass; they make do with seaweed, which gives their meat a distinctive flavour.

North Ronaldsay Lighthouse
LIGHTHOUSE

(www.northronaldsay.co.uk; ☉10am-5pm May-Aug or by arrangement) At the northern end of the island is this lighthouse, over 100ft high and one of many built across Scotland by the Stevenson family. A visitor centre and licensed cafe are here, as are bikes for hire and a gift shop selling the woollens made from yarn supplied by the local seaweed-eating sheep. You can climb the lighthouse itself and/or visit the woollen mill on a tour (☎07703-112224, 01857-633257; www.northronaldsay.co.uk; lighthouse or mill adult/child £6/3, combined £8/5).

On the shore to the south of the lighthouse is an earlier model, an 18th-century beacon tower some 70ft high.

Observatory Guest House
B&B, HOSTEL ££

(☎01857-633200; www.nrbo.co.uk; campsites £5, dm/s/d £19.50/44.50/89; P ⊛) 🐾 Powered by wind and solar energy, this place offers first-rate accommodation and ornithological activities next to the ferry pier. There's a cafe-bar with lovely coastal views and convivial communal dinners (£16) in a (sometimes) sun-kissed conservatory; if you're lucky, local lamb might be on the menu. You can also camp here.

🛈 Getting There & Away
There are two or three daily flights with Loganair (p401) to North Ronaldsay (£18, 20 minutes) from Kirkwall. The £21 return offer (you must stay overnight) is great value.

Orkney Ferries (p401) runs from Kirkwall on Friday (passenger/car £8.85/20.90, 2½ hours), plus Tuesday in summer.

SHETLAND

Close enough to Norway geographically and historically to make nationality an ambiguous concept, the Shetland Islands are Britain's most northerly outpost. There's a Scandinavian lilt to the local accent, and streets named King Haakon or St Olaf are reminders that Shetland was under Norse rule until 1469, when it was gifted to Scotland in lieu of the dowry of a Danish princess.

The stirringly bleak setting – it's a Unesco geopark – still feels uniquely Scottish though, with deep, naked glens flanked by steep hills, twinkling, sky-blue lochs and, of course, sheep on the roads.

Despite the famous ponies and woollens, it's no agricultural backwater. Offshore oil makes it quite a busy, comparatively well-heeled place, despite drops in barrel prices. Nevertheless, nature still rules the seas and islands, and the birdlife (p427) is spectacular: pack binoculars.

Tours

Discover Shetland TOURS
(☑ 07387-167205; www.discovershetland.net)
Customisable tours of Shetland with a knowledgable guide, who's strong on the natural world and the ecology of the archipelago.

Shetland Nature WILDLIFE
(☑ 01595-760333; www.shetlandnature.net) This operator specialises in otter-watching excursions but also runs birdwatching trips all around the archipelago as well as scenic tours.

Adventure Shetland TOURS
(☑ 07827 324671; www.adventureshetland.com)
Archaeologist Jon runs a range of tailored tours that can focus on the island's prehistoric heritage, coastal hikes and more.

ℹ Information

Lerwick Tourist Office (p422) In the centre of the Shetland's main town, with comprehensive information on the islands.

Brochures are also available at Sumburgh Airport. Visit www.shetland.org, an excellent website with good info on accommodation, activities and more.

The archipelago is replete with handicraft workshops, many working to produce artisanal jewellery and Shetland's famous woollens. The **Shetland Craft Trail** (☑ 07447-377856;

SHETLAND ROOTS

The seafaring Shetlanders have made their way to all corners of the globe and many visitors come here to investigate their islander forebears. There are some excellent resources to help you do so. The Shetland Family History Society (www.shetland-fhs.org.uk) is a good first port of call; another is the brilliant database at www.bayanne. info/Shetland, which has hundreds of thousands of names in accurate family trees.

Museums across the islands also have useful archives, such as the Shetland Museum (p418) and the Unst Heritage Centre (p427).

In all cases you will get much better information by contacting these organisations ahead of your visit.

Every couple of decades Shetland holds a Hamefarin, a year to ceremonially welcome back descendants of Shetlanders to the archipelago with a series of events and information. The last was in 2010.

www.shetlandartsandcrafts.co.uk) publishes a useful brochure of makers across the islands; the info is also available on its website.

ℹ Getting There & Away

AIR

Sumburgh Airport (☑ 01950-460905; www. hial.co.uk), 25 miles south of Lerwick, is Shetland's main airport. **Loganair** (☑ 0141-642907; www.loganair.co.uk) runs daily services to Aberdeen, Kirkwall, Inverness, Edinburgh and Glasgow, and summer services to Manchester and Bergen (Norway).

BOAT

Northlink Ferries (☑ 0845 600 0449; www.northlinkferries.co.uk; 🐾) runs daily overnight car ferries between Aberdeen and Lerwick (high-season passenger/car one way £36/124, 12 to 15 hours), some stopping at Kirkwall, Orkney. With a basic ticket you can sleep in recliner chairs or the bar area. It's £39.50 for a berth in a shared cabin and from £91 to £150 for a comparatively luxurious double cabin. Sleeping pods (£18) are comfortable, reclinable seats. Ferries have a cafe, bar, paid lounge and cinema on board, plus slow wi-fi.

ℹ Getting Around

Public transport within and between the islands of Shetland is managed by **ZetTrans** (www.zettrans.org.uk). Timetable information for all air, bus and ferry services can be obtained at http://travel.shetland.org, from the ZetTrans website and from Lerwick's Viking Bus Station (p422).

AIR

The **Shetland Inter-Island Air Service** (Airtask; ☑ 01595-840246; www.airtask.com) is operated by Airtask from Tingwall airport, 6.5 miles northwest of Lerwick. There are big discounts for under-25s. Flights run to Papa Stour, Foula and Fair Isle.

BICYCLE

If it's fine, cycling on the islands' excellent roads can be an exhilarating way to experience the stark beauty of Shetland. It can, however, be very windy and there are few spots to shelter. You can hire bikes from several places, including Grantfield Garage in Lerwick.

BOAT

Ferry services run by Shetland Islands Council (www.shetland.gov.uk/ferries) link Mainland to other islands from various points.

BUS

An extensive bus network radiates from Lerwick to all corners of Mainland, with connecting services to the islands of Yell, Fetlar and Unst. The schedules aren't generally great for day tripping from Lerwick as they're suited to people coming into the capital for the day.

CAR

Shetland has broad, well-made roads (due to oil money). Car hire is gloriously fuss-free, and vehicles can be delivered to transport terminals. Prices are usually around £40/200 for a day/week.

Bolts Car Hire (☑ 01595-693636; www.boltscarhire.co.uk; North Rd; ⊘ 9am-5.30pm Mon-Fri, to 4pm Sat Apr-Oct, 9am-5.30pm Mon-Fri, to 1pm Sat Nov-Mar) Has an office in Lerwick and by the airport; delivers to Lerwick's ferry terminal.

Grantfield Garage (☑ 01595-692709; www.grantfieldgarage.co.uk; Esplanade; ⊘ 9am-5.30pm Mon-Fri, to 5pm Sat) No longer a garage; this is generally the cheapest.

Star Rent-a-Car (☑ 01595-692075; www.starrentacar.co.uk; 22 Commercial Rd; ⊘ 8am-7pm Mon-Fri, to 6pm Sat, noon-5pm Sun) Opposite Lerwick's Viking Bus Station. Has an office at Sumburgh Airport as well.

Lerwick

POP 7000

Built on the herring trade and modernised by the oil trade, Lerwick is Shetland's only real town, home to a third of the islands' population. It has a solidly maritime feel, with aquiline oil boats competing for space in the superb natural harbour with the dwindling fishing fleet. Wandering along atmospheric Commercial St is a delight, and the excellent Shetland Museum provides cultural background. Fans of the TV series *Shetland* will easily recognise several buildings around town.

◉ Sights & Activities

★ **Shetland Museum**   MUSEUM
(☑ 01595-695057; www.shetlandmuseumandarchives.org.uk; Hay's Dock; ⊘ 10am-5pm Mon-Sat, noon-5pm Sun Apr-Sep, 10am-4pm Tue-Sat Oct-Mar) FREE This museum houses an impressive collection of 5000 years' worth of culture, people and their interaction with this ancient landscape. Comprehensive but never dull, it covers everything from the archipelago's geology to its fishing industry, via local mythology – find out about scary *nyuggles* (ghostly horses), or detect *trows* (fairies). Pictish carvings and replica jewellery are among the finest pieces. The museum also includes a working lighthouse mechanism, a small gallery, a boat-building workshop and an archive for tracing Shetland ancestry.

Shetland Textile Museum   MUSEUM
(Böd of Gremista; ☑ 01595-694386; www.shetlandtextilemuseum.com; Gremista Rd; adult/child £3/free; ⊘ noon-4pm Tue-Sat) A mile north of the centre of Lerwick, this four-square stone house, birthplace of P&O founder Arthur Anderson, was also once a fish-curing station. It now holds a good display on the knitted and woven textiles and patterns that Shetland is famous for. You can get here on Bus 1.

Clickimin Broch   RUINS
(Clickimin Rd; ⊘ 24hr) FREE This fortified site, just under a mile southwest of Lerwick's town centre, was occupied from the 7th century BCE to the 6th century CE. It's impressively large, and its setting on a tongue of land in a small loch gives it a feeling of being removed from the present day.

Lerwick

Knab VIEWPOINT

(Knab Rd) This headland gives a marvellous perspective of the entrance to Lerwick's harbour, as well as Breiwick (bay) and Bressay. There's a golf course, parkland, a cemetery and fortifications to ramble around.

Shetland Wildlife Boat Tours BOATING

(☎ 07876-522292; www.thule-charters.co.uk; adult/child £50/40; ⊗ Apr-Sep) This outfit runs two daily trips to Noss in summer in a small catamaran. An underwater camera

Lerwick

offers glimpses of the birds diving in the depths.

**Shetland
Seabird Tours** BIRDWATCHING
(☏ 07767 872260; www.shetlandseabirdtours. com; adult/child £45/25; ⊙ Apr-Oct) With two daily departures, these three-hour cruises head out to watch gannets feeding, observe the raucous seabird colonies of Bressay and Noss, and do a bit of seal-spotting. You can book online.

★⁂ Festivals & Events

**Shetland
Folk Festival** MUSIC
(www.shetlandfolkfestival.com; ⊙ late Apr or early May) This four-day festival sees local and international folk musicians playing in various venues across Lerwick and beyond.

🛏 Sleeping

Lerwick has very average hotels but excellent B&Bs. There are no campsites within 15 miles.

Woosung B&B £
(☏ 01595-693687; www.woosung-bb.com; 43 St Olaf St; d £65, s/d without bathroom £30/60; ☞🐾) A budget gem in the heart of Lerwick B&B-land, this place has a wise and welcoming host and comfortable, clean, good-value rooms with fridge and microwave. Two of them share a compact but spotless bathroom. The solid stone house dates from the 19th century, built by a clipper captain who traded tea out of the Chinese port for which it's named.

**Islesburgh
House Hostel** HOSTEL £
(☏ 01595-745100; www.shetland.gov.uk; King Harald St; dm/s/tw/q £23/42/48/66; 🅿@☞)

This typically grand Lerwick mansion houses an excellent hostel, with comfortable dorms, a shop, a laundry, a cafe and an industrial kitchen. Electronic keys offer reliable security and no curfew. It's wise to book ahead in summer. If nobody's about, you can check in at the nearby community centre.

★**Fort Charlotte
Guesthouse** B&B ££
(☏ 01595-692140; www.fortcharlotte.co.uk; 1 Charlotte St; s/d £50/85; ☞) Sheltering under Fort Charlotte's walls, this friendly place offers summery en suite rooms, including great singles. Views down the pedestrian street are on offer in some; sloping ceilings and artful touches add charm to others. It has local salmon for breakfast and a bike shed. Very popular; book ahead.

Aald Harbour B&B ££
(☏ 01595-840689; www.aaldharbourbedandbreakfast.com; 7 Church Rd; s/d £60/85; ☞) With a handy location just off the pedestrian street, this upbeat spot has four cute rooms decked out in IKEA furniture, with Shetland fabrics and toiletries creating a cosy Nordic fusion. Rooms have fridges, good showers and wi-fi, and there are attractive public areas downstairs. Breakfast includes fresh-fruit and smoked-fish options.

**Rockvilla
Guest House** B&B ££
(☏ 01595-695804; www.rockvillaguesthouse. com; 88 St Olaf St; s/d £65/92; ☞🐾) Some of Shetland's B&Bs are aimed more at oil workers than visitors, but this is quite the reverse: a relaxing, welcoming spot in a fine house behind a pretty garden. The three rooms are colour themed: Blue is

bright, with a front-and-back outlook; Red is sultry, with a sofa in the window; and smaller Green is shyer, under the eaves.

Your hosts are friendly, and Jeff runs airport transfers (£35) plus day tours to Sumburgh, Eshaness or Unst, among other places.

Breiview
Guest House
B&B ££

(☏01595-695956; www.breiviewguesthouse. co.uk; 43 Kantersted Rd; s/d £60/85; P🗗) On a hill a little removed from Lerwick's centre, this sizeable guesthouse is a fine option with some water views. Rooms – some in the house next door – are spacious, light, furnished with blonde wood and have good bathrooms. Coming from the centre, turn left after passing the big Tesco supermarket and follow the signs.

Kveldsro
House Hotel
HOTEL £££

(☏01595-692195; www.shetlandhotels.com; Greenfield Pl; s/d £118/145; P🗗) Lerwick's best hotel overlooks the harbour and has a quiet but central setting. It's a dignified small set-up that will appeal to older visitors or couples. All doubles cost the same, but some are markedly better than others, with four-poster beds or water views. All boast new stylish bathrooms. The bar area is elegant and has fine perspectives.

Eating

Peerie Shop Cafe
CAFE £

(☏01595-692816; www.peerieshop.co.uk; Esplanade; light meals £3-8; ⊙8am-5pm Mon-Sat; 🗗) If you've been craving proper espresso since leaving the mainland, head to this gem, with art exhibitions, wire-mounted halogens and industrial-gantry chic. Newspapers, scrumptious cakes and sandwiches, hot chocolate that you deserve after that blasting wind outside, and – less often – outdoor seating give everyone a reason to be here.

Dowry
CAFE £

(☏01595-692373; www.thedowry.co.uk; 98 Commercial St; light meals £6-13; ⊙10am-10pm Mon & Thu, 10am-6pm Tue-Wed, 10am-11pm Fri & Sat; 🗗) This welcome addition to Lerwick's eating scene pulls in a keen crowd of Shetlanders for its lunches based on solid local produce. Sandwiches with tasty homemade focaccia or brioche, soups, thoughtful vegan choices, craft beer and sharing

platters of deli produce mean it's easy to eat well. Booth seating and water views up the back are where it's at.

★ Fjarå
CAFE, BISTRO ££

(☏01595-697388; www.fjaracoffee.com; Sea Rd; mains £8-22; ⊙8am-10pm Tue-Sat (food until 8pm), 10am-6pm Sun; 🗗) A cute wooden building in a super location, Fjarå is perched above a rocky shore and takes full advantage, with big picture windows looking out over the water and occasionally some basking seals. It does a bit of everything, with breakfasts, sandwiches, salads and bagels, plus beer, cocktails and some excellent dinner offerings, including creative burgers, game and local seafood.

It's across the road from the Tesco supermarket at the southern entrance to town.

🍷 Drinking & Entertainment

The Lounge
PUB

(☏01595-692231; 4 Mounthooly St; ⊙11am-1am; 🗗) Tucked away behind Lerwick's tourist office, the Lounge features an earthy downstairs bar populated by friendly local characters. The attractive upstairs space features live music several times a week and informal jam sessions at other times. It's well worth checking out.

Mareel
ARTS CENTRE

(☏01595-745500; www.mareel.org; Hay's Dock) Modern Mareel is a thriving arts centre with a cinema, concert hall and cafe in a great waterside location.

ORKNEY & SHETLAND LERWICK

UP HELLY AA

Shetland's long Viking history has rubbed off in more ways than just street names and square-shouldered locals. Most villages have a **fire festival** (www.uphellyaa.org; ⊙Jan), a continuation of Viking midwinter celebrations of the rebirth of the sun, with the most spectacular happening in Lerwick on the last Tuesday in January.

Squads of *guizers* dress in Viking costume and march through the streets with blazing torches, dragging a replica longship, which they then surround and burn, bellowing Viking songs from behind bushy beards.

ℹ Information

Gilbert Bain Hospital (☑ 01595-743000; www.shb.scot.nhs.uk; South Rd)

Lerwick Tourist Office (☑ 01595-693434; www.shetland.org; cnr Commercial & Mounthooly Sts; ⊙ 9am-5pm Mon-Sat & 10am-4pm Sun Apr-Sep, 10am-4pm Mon-Sat Oct-Mar) Helpful, with a good range of books and maps.

ℹ Getting There & Away

Northlink Ferries (p417) from Aberdeen and Kirkwall dock at Holmsgarth Terminal, a 15-minute walk northwest from the town centre.

From **Viking Bus Station** (☑ 01595-744868; Commercial Rd), buses service various corners of the archipelago, including regular services to/from Sumburgh Airport.

Bressay & Noss

These islands lie across Bressay Sound just east of Lerwick. Bressay (*bress*-ah) has interesting walks, especially along the cliffs and up **Ward Hill** (226m), which has good views of the islands. Much smaller Noss is a nature reserve, notable for its seabird life. As well as the crossing to Noss from Bressay, there are boat trips around the island from Lerwick.

OFFBEAT ACCOMMODATION

Shetland offers intriguing options for getting off the beaten accommodation track. There's a great network of *böds* – simple rustic cottages or huts with peat fires. They cost £14 per person, or £12 for the ones without electricity, and are available March to October. Contact and book via **Shetland Amenity Trust** (☑ 01595-694688; www.camping-bods.com; ⊙ 9am-5pm Mon-Thu, to 4pm Fri).

The same organisation runs three **Shetland Lighthouse Cottages** (☑ 01595-694688; www.shetlandlighthouse.com; per 3 days high season £350-420, per week £700-950), all commanding dramatic views of rugged coastline: one, renovated and classy, at Sumburgh; one on the island of Bressay near Lerwick; and one at Eshaness. They sleep six to seven, and prices drop substantially in the low season.

★ Isle of Noss NATURE RESERVE
(☑ 0800 107 7818; www.nature.scot; boat adult/child £3/1.50; ⊙ 10am-5pm Tue, Wed & Fri-Sun May–Aug) Little Noss, 1.5 miles wide, lies just east of Bressay. High seacliffs harbour more than 100,000 pairs of breeding seabirds, while inland heath supports hundreds of pairs of great skua. Access is by dinghy from Bressay; phone in advance to check that it's running. Walking anticlockwise around Noss is easier, with better cliff-viewing. There's a small visitor centre by the dock.

Maryfield House Hotel INN ££
(☑ 01595-820203; www.maryfieldhousehotel.co.uk; Maryfield, Bressay; r £120; 🅿 🐾) By the Bressay ferry slip, this solid old hotel has reopened and makes a fine alternative to staying in Lerwick. Comfortable rooms with good, large beds and refurbished bathrooms are complemented by friendly hosts. Decent bar meals are on offer, as well as items such as seafood platters, by preordering.

ℹ Getting There & Away

Ferries (passenger/car and driver return £5.90/14.40, seven minutes, frequent) link Lerwick and Bressay. The Noss crossing is 2.5 miles across the island.

Scalloway

POP 1200

Surrounded by bare, rolling hills, Scalloway (*scall*-o-wah) – Shetland's former capital – is a busy fishing and yachting harbour with a thriving seafood-processing industry. It's 6 miles from Lerwick.

There are pretty beaches and pleasant walks on the nearby islands (linked by bridges) of Trondra and East and West Burra.

Scalloway Museum MUSEUM
(☑ 01595-880734; www.scallowaymuseum.org; Castle St; adult/child £3/1; ⊙ 10am-4pm Mon-Sat, 2-4pm Sun mid-Apr–Sep; ♿) This enthusiastic modern museum by Scalloway Castle has an excellent display on Scalloway life and history, with prehistoric finds, witch-burnings and local lore all featuring. It has a detailed section on the Shetland Bus and a fun area for kids, as well as a cafe.

Scalloway Castle   CASTLE
(www.historicenvironment.scot; Castle St; ⊘24hr) FREE Scalloway's most prominent landmark is its castle, built around 1600 by Earl Patrick Stewart. The turreted and corbelled tower house is fairly well preserved. If you happen to find it locked, get keys from the Scalloway Museum.

Shetland
Bus Memorial   MONUMENT
(Main St) During WWII, the Norwegian resistance movement operated the 'Shetland Bus' from here. The trips were very successful, carrying agents, wireless operators and military supplies to Norway for the resistance and returning with refugees, recruits for the Free Norwegian Forces and, in December, Christmas trees for the treeless Shetland Islands.

This is a moving tribute on the waterfront, built with stones from both countries. The Norwegian stones are from the home areas of 44 Norwegians who died running the gauntlet between Norway and Scalloway.

Da Haaf   SEAFOOD ££
(☎01595-772480; www.nafc.uhi.ac.uk; NAFC Marine Centre; lunches £6-14, dinner mains £14-21; ⊘9am-4pm Mon-Fri plus 5.30-8pm Fri-Sat; ☏) In a fisheries college, this place has a slightly canteeny feel but great water views out of big windows. It does simple but tasty snacks all day and lunches from noon to 2.30pm. The kitchen comes into its own at weekend dinnertime (must be booked), when haddock, monkfish and other seafood specials are served.

❶ Getting There & Away
Buses run from Lerwick (£1.80, 25 minutes, roughly hourly Monday to Saturday, four Sunday) to Scalloway.

South Mainland
From Lerwick, it's 25 miles down this narrow, hilly tail of land to Sumburgh Head. Important prehistoric sights, fabulous birdwatching and glorious white-sand beaches make it one of Shetland's most interesting areas. The lapping waters are an inviting turquoise – if it weren't for the raging Arctic gales, you'd be tempted to have a dip.

ORKNEYINGA SAGA
Written around CE 1200, this saga is a rich tale of sorcery, political intrigue, and cunning and unscrupulous acts among the Viking earls of Orkney. Part myth and part historical fact, it begins with the capture of the islands by the king of Norway and recounts the tumultuous centuries until they became part of Scotland. It's a wonderful piece of medieval literature and well worth a read.

Head to the **Orkneyinga Saga Centre** (Orphir; ⊘9am-6pm Apr-Oct) FREE in the south coast village of Orphir for more background.

Sandwick & Mousa
Opposite the scattered village of Sandwick, where you pass the 60-degree latitude line, is the small isle of Mousa, an RSPB reserve protecting some 7000 breeding pairs of nocturnal storm petrels. Mousa is also home to rock-basking seals as well as impressive Mousa Broch, the best preserved of these northern Iron Age fortifications.

Mousa Broch   HISTORIC BUILDING
(Mousa; ⊘24hr) FREE On the island of Mousa, off Sandwick, this prehistoric fortified house, dating from some 2000 years ago, is an impressive sight. Rising to 13m, it's an imposing double-walled structure with a spiral staircase to access a 2nd floor. It has featured in Viking sagas as a hideout for eloping couples. In its walls nest hundreds of storm petrels, whose return to the nest at dusk is a stirring sight.

Mousa Boat   BOATING
(☎07901-872339; www.mousa.co.uk; Sandwick; ⊘Apr-Sep) This operator runs boat trips to Mousa (adult/child return £16/7, cash only, 15 minutes, daily except Saturday) from Sandwick, allowing three hours ashore on the island. It also offers night petrel-viewing trips (£30/10, dates on website) and short cruises. There's a small interpretation centre at the dock.

Mackenzies Farm
Shop & Café   CAFE £
(☎01950-477790; www.mackenziesfarm shop.co.uk; A970, Cunningsburgh; mains £6-15; ⊘8.30am-5.30pm Mon-Fri, 9am-4pm Sat,

ORKNEY & SHETLAND SOUTH MAINLAND

11am-4pm Sun, extended hours in summer; 🔊)
🖉 Local farmers supply the produce for
this excellent shop and cafe, which stocks
cheeses, quality meats and more, and presents dishes that range from quiches and
sandwiches to fuller offerings with Shetland lamb.

Bigton & Boddam

On the western side of the narrow southern
end of Mainland, a couple of miles beyond
Bigton, is a spectacular sight: the largest
shell-and-sand tombolo (sand or gravel
isthmus) in Britain leading to beautiful,
emerald-capped **St Ninian's Isle** (Bigton).
Walk across to find the ruins of a 12th-cen-
tury church where a famous hoard of silver
Pictish treasure was found. Sunsets can be
absolutely spectacular.

South of here, Shetland's best beach is
gloriously white **Scousburgh Sands** (Spig-
gie Beach; Scousburgh). Back on the main
road, a side road from small Boddam leads
to the **Shetland Crofthouse Museum**
(🖉01950-460557; www.shetlandmuseumandar-
chives.org.uk/crofthouse-museum;   Boddam;
adult/child £3.50/1.50; ⊙10am-1pm & 2-4pm Apr-
Sep) FREE. The years drop away when you
enter, stepping back into a primitive existence. Built in 1870, this former dwelling has
been restored, thatched and furnished with
19th-century furniture and utensils.

The Lerwick–Sumburgh bus stops right
outside.

Sumburgh

With sea cliffs, and grassy headlands jutting into sparkling blue water, Sumburgh
is one of the most scenic places on Mainland, with a far greener landscape than the
peaty north. It has a handful of excellent
attractions clustered near Shetland's major
airport.

★**Sumburgh Head**   BIRDWATCHING
(www.rspb.org.uk) At Mainland's southern tip,
these spectacular cliffs offer a good chance
to get up close to puffins and huge nesting
colonies of fulmars, guillemots and razorbills. If you're lucky, you might spot dolphins, minke whales or orcas. Also here is
the excellent Sumburgh Head Visitor Centre, in the lighthouse buildings.

★**Sumburgh Head**
Visitor Centre   LIGHTHOUSE, MUSEUM
(🖉01595-694688;   www.sumburghhead.com;
adult/child £6/2; ⊙11am-5.30pm Apr-Sep) High
on the cliffs at Sumburgh Head, this excellent attraction is set across several buildings. Displays explain about the lighthouse,
foghorn and radar station that operated
here, and there's a good exhibition on the
local marine creatures and birds. You can
visit the lighthouse itself on a guided tour
for an extra charge.

Jarlshof   ARCHAEOLOGICAL SITE
(🖉01595-460112;   www.historicenvironment.
scot; adult/child £6/3.60; ⊙9.30am-5.30pm
Apr-Sep, 9.30am-4.30pm Oct-Mar) Old and
new collide, with Sumburgh Airport right
by this picturesque, instructive archaeological site. Various periods of occupation
from 2500 BCE to CE 1500 can be seen
– the complete change upon the Vikings'
arrival is obvious, with their rectangular
longhouses presenting a marked contrast
to the preceding brochs, roundhouses and
wheelhouses. Atop the site is 16th-century
Old House, named 'Jarlshof' in a novel by
Sir Walter Scott. There's an informative audio tour included with admission.

Old Scatness   ARCHAEOLOGICAL SITE
(🖉01595-694688; www.shetlandamenity.org/
old-scatness; adult/child £6/4; ⊙May-Aug; 👶)
This dig brings Shetland's prehistory vividly to life; it's a must-see for archaeology
buffs but fun for kids too. Clued-up guides
in Iron Age costumes show you the site,
which has provided important clues on
the Viking takeover and dating of Shetland
material. It has an impressive broch from
around 300 BCE, roundhouses and later
wheelhouses. Best of all is the reconstruction with peat fire and working loom. Lack
of funding has badly restricted the opening
hours: check the website.

ⓘ Getting There & Away

Bus 6 runs to Sumburgh and Sumburgh Airport
from Lerwick (£2.90, one hour, roughly hourly
Monday to Friday, nine Saturday, five Sunday).

North Mainland

The north of Mainland is very photogenic – jumbles of cracked, peaty, brown hills
blend with grassy pastureland and extend
like bony fingers into numerous lochs and

out into the wider, icy, grey waters of the North Sea. Different shades of light give it a variety of characters.

Around Hillswick, there's stunning scenery and several good places to stay; this makes it one of the best places to base yourself in the Shetland Islands.

Brae

The crossroads settlement of Brae has several accommodation options and is an important service centre for the whole of northern Shetland. It's no beauty, despite its bayside location. South of Brae, Voe (Lower) is a pretty collection of buildings beside a tranquil bay on Olna Firth. With a cheap sleep and pub meals opposite, it can make a good stop.

★ **Busta House Hotel** HOTEL ££
(☑ 01806-522506; www.bustahouse.com; Busta; s/d £90/115; 🅿🛜🐕) 🏊 This genteel, characterful hotel near Brae has a long, sad history and inevitable rumours of a (friendly) ghost. Built in the late 18th century (though the oldest part, the sumptuous guest lounge, dates from 1588), it has creaks and quirks and compact, likeable rooms that retain a cosy charm. Sea views and/or a four-poster bed cost a bit more (£125).

There's also a fine restaurant and very helpful staff.

Frankie's Fish & Chips FISH & CHIPS £
(☑ 01806-522700; www.frankiesfishandchips. com; Brae; mains £6-12; ⊙ 9.30am-8pm Mon-Sat, noon-8pm Sun; 🛜) 🏊 This famous Shetland chippie uses only locally sourced and sustainable seafood. As well as chip-shop standards, the menu runs to tasty Shetland mussels in garlicky sauces and, when available, plump juicy scallops. It also does breakfast rolls, baked potatoes and fry-ups. Eat in, out on the deck with views over the bay, or take away.

❶ Getting There & Away

Buses from Lerwick to Brae (£2.90, 45 minutes, eight daily Monday to Saturday) run via Tingwall and Voe. Some continue to Hillswick.

Eshaness & Hillswick

Eleven miles northwest of Brae the road ends at the red basalt cliffs of Eshaness, site of some of Shetland's most impressive

SEA KAYAKING

Paddling is a great way to explore Shetland's tortuous coastline, letting you get up close to seals and bird life. **Sea Kayak Shetland** (☑ 01595-840272; www.seakayakshetland.co.uk; beginner session £30, half/full day £50/85) is a reliable operator catering for beginners and experts alike; it offers various guided trips.

coastal scenery. When the wind subsides there's superb walking and views from the headland lighthouse. On the way, the village of Hillswick is set on a pretty bay.

Tangwick Haa Museum MUSEUM
(☑ 01806-503389; www.tangwickhaa.org.uk; ⊙ 11am-5pm mid-Apr–Sep) FREE A mile east of Eshaness, a side road leads south to this museum, housed in a restored 17th-century house. The wonderful collection of old B&W photos captures the sense of community in this area.

★ **Almara** B&B ££
(☑ 01806-503261; www.almara.shetland.co.uk; s/d £40/80; ⊙ Apr-Oct; 🅿🛜) 🏊 Follow the puffin signpost a mile short of Hillswick to find Shetland's finest welcome. With sweeping views over the bay, this house has a great lounge, unusual features in the excellent rooms and bathrooms (including thoughtful extras such as USB chargers), and a good eye on the environment. You'll feel completely at home and appreciated; this is B&B at its best.

St Magnus Bay Hotel HOTEL ££
(☑ 01806-503372; www.stmagnusbayhotel.co.uk; Hillswick; s/d £90/120; 🅿🛜) This wonderful wooden mansion was built in 1896 and sociable owners have done a cracking job returning it to former glories. Renovated rooms are winningly wood-clad, with modern bathrooms; half boast big windows taking full advantage of the fine water views. The bar serves pub meals complemented by seafood specials: quantities are huge. Breakfast is also a winner; try the delicious smoked haddock.

Braewick Cafe CAFE £
(☑ 01806-503345; www.eshaness.moonfruit. com; Braewick; light meals £4-12; ⊙ 10am-5pm daily Jun-Aug, 10am-4.30pm Thu-Mon early Mar-

MIGRATING BIRDS ON FAIR ISLE

It's worth making the stomach-churning ferry ride to one of Scotland's most remote inhabited islands for stunning cliff scenery, isolation and squadrons of winged creatures. About halfway to Orkney, Fair Isle is only 3 miles by 1.5 miles in size and is probably best known for its patterned knitwear, still produced in three workshops on the island.

It's also a paradise for birdwatchers, who form the bulk of the island's visitors. Fair Isle is in the flight path of migrating birds, and thousands breed here. They're monitored by the **bird observatory** (www.fairislebirdobs.co.uk; P @ 📞), which collects and analyses information year-round; visitors are more than welcome to participate. The observatory building and accommodation burned down in 2019 but a rebuild is in the works.

There are also a few B&B and self-catering options on the island, including **South Light** (📞 07752 566231; www.southlightfairisle.co.uk; s/d incl all meals £85/160; 📞), in the keepers' cottage by the Stevenson lighthouse at the southern tip of the island.

From Tingwall, Shetland Inter-Island Air Service (p418) operates flights to Fair Isle (£93 return, 25 minutes). There's also a weekly service from Sumburgh in summer.

The small ferry **Good Shepherd IV** (📞 01595-760363; neilthomson1951@gmail.com) sails from Grutness (near Sumburgh) and some from Lerwick (one way passenger/car and driver £17.60/7.60, three hours) two to three times weekly. Book by phone or email.

May & Sep–mid-Oct; 📞) 🍴 At the excellent caravan park and campsite at Braewick, this licensed cafe has tasty light meals served with stunning views over St Magnus Bay's eye-catching crags. Much food is sourced from the owners' croft next door.

❶ Getting There & Away

Three buses from Lerwick run to Hillswick (£3.50, 1¼ hours, Monday to Saturday), with a feeder bus on to Eshaness. Two buses run the return route. There are other connections at Brae.

The North Isles

Yell, Unst and Fetlar make up the North Isles of the Shetland Islands, which are connected to each other by ferry, as is Yell to Mainland. All are great for nature watching; Unst has the most to offer overall.

Yell

POP 1000

Yell if you like but nobody will hear; the desolate peat moors here are typical Shetland scenery. The bleak landscape has an appeal, though. Yell is all about colours: the browns and vivid, lush greens of the bogland, grey clouds thudding through the skies, and the steely blue waters of the North Atlantic, which are never far away.

The peat makes the ground look cracked and parched, though it's swimming most of the year. Though many folk fire on through to Unst, Yell offers several good hill walks, especially around the Herra peninsula, about halfway up the west coast.

Old Haa Museum   MUSEUM
(📞 01957-722339; www.oldhaa.com; Burravoe; ⊙10am-4pm Mon-Thu & Sat, 2-5pm Sun mid-Apr–Sep) FREE This museum has a medley of curious objects (pipes, piano, a doll in cradle, tiny Bibles, ships in bottles and a sperm-whale jaw), as well as an archive of local history and a tearoom. It's in Burravoe, 4 miles east of the southern ferry terminal in Ulsta.

Lumbister   BIRDWATCHING
Red-throated divers, merlins, skuas and other bird species breed at this birdwatching hot spot on the Shetland moorland. The area is home to a large otter population, too, best viewed around Whale Firth, where you may also spot common and grey seals.

Quam B&B   B&B ££
(📞 01957-766256; www.quambandbyellshetland.co.uk; Westsandwick; d £80; P 📞) Just off the main road through Yell island, this farm B&B has friendly owners and three good rooms. Breakfast features eggs from the farm, which also has cute ponies that you can meet. Dinners (£15 per person) can be arranged and bikes hired.

ⓘ Getting There & Away

Yell is connected with Mainland by **ferries** (☑ 01595-745804; www.shetland.gov.uk/ferries) between Toft and Ulsta (return per adult/car and driver £5.90/14.40, 20 minutes, frequent). It's wise to book car space in summer.

An integrated bus-and-ferry connection runs once daily Monday to Saturday from Lerwick to Yell (£3.80, 1¼ hours), connecting with ferries to Fetlar and Unst. Connecting services cover other parts of the island.

Unst

POP 600

You're fast running out of Scotland once you cross to rugged Unst (www.visit-unst. com). Scotland's most northerly inhabited island is prettier than nearby Yell, with bare, velvety-smooth hills and settlements clinging to waterside locations, fiercely resisting the buffeting winds.

⊙ Sights

★**Hermaness National
Nature Reserve**   NATURE RESERVE
(www.nnr.scot) At marvellous Hermaness headland, a 4.5-mile round walk takes you to cliffs where gannets, fulmars and guillemots nest, and numerous puffins frolic. You can also see Scotland's most northerly point, the rocks of **Out Stack**, and **Muckle Flugga**, with its lighthouse built by Robert Louis Stevenson's uncle. Duck into the **Hermaness Visitor Centre** (☑ 01595-711278; ⊙ 9am-5pm Apr-early Sep) FREE, with its poignant story about one-time resident Albert Ross.

The path to the cliffs is guarded by a squadron of great skuas who nest in the nearby heather, and dive-bomb at will if they feel threatened. They're damn solid birds too, but don't usually make contact.

Unst Bus Shelter   LANDMARK
(Bobby's Bus Shelter; www.unstbusshelter.shetland.co.uk; Baltasound) At the turn-off to Littlehamar, just past Baltasound, is Britain's most impressive bus stop. Enterprising locals, tired of waiting in discomfort, decided to do a job on it, bringing in comfortable seats and much more. It now gets decorated to a different theme every year.

Unst Boat Haven   MUSEUM
(☑ 01957-711809; Haroldswick; adult/child £3/free, combined ticket with Unst Heritage Centre £5; ⊙ 11am-4pm Mon-Sat, 2-4pm Sun May-Sep)

This large shed is a boatie's delight, packed with a beautifully cared for collection of Shetland rowing and sailing boats, all with a backstory. Old photos and maritime artefacts speak of the glory days of Unst fishing. There's a seasonal tearoom out front.

Unst Heritage Centre   MUSEUM
(☑ 01957-711528; www.unstheritage.com; Haroldswick; adult/child £3/free, combined ticket with Unst Boat Haven £5; ⊙ 11am-4pm Mon-Sat, 2-4pm Sun May-Sep) This heritage centre houses a modern museum with a history of the Shetland pony and a recreation of a croft house.

🛏 Sleeping & Eating

Self-caterers can stock up at Baltasound's Skibhoul Stores, which has a bakery and cafe, and the Final Checkout, between Baltasound and Haroldswick. Known locally as 'the garage', the Final Checkout has an ATM, and sells petrol and diesel.

★**Gardiesfauld Hostel**   HOSTEL £
(☑ 01957-755279; www.facebook.com/gardiesfauldhostel; 2 East Rd, Uyeasound; per adult/child sites £8/4, dm £16/9; ⊙ Apr-Sep; P 🐾) This

---

SHETLAND WILDLIFE

For birdwatchers, Shetland is paradise – a stopover for migrating Arctic species and host to vast seabird breeding colonies. June is the height of the season.

Every bird has its own name here: rain geese are red-throated divers, bonxies are great skuas, and alamooties are storm petrels. Clownish puffin antics are a highlight. The **Royal Society for the Protection of Birds** (RSPB; www.rspb.org.uk) maintains several reserves, plus there are national nature reserves at **Hermaness**, **Keen of Hamar** and **Noss**. **Foula** and **Fair Isle** also support large seabird populations.

Keep an eye on the sea: sea otters, orcas and other cetaceans are regularly sighted. Latest sightings are logged at useful www.nature-shetland.co.uk.

Shetland Nature Festival (www.shetlandnaturefestival.co.uk; ⊙ early Jul) has guided walks, talks, boat trips, open days and workshops.

spotless hostel has very spacious dorms with lockers, family rooms, a garden, an elegant lounge and a wee conservatory dining area with great bay views. You can camp here, too; there are separate areas for tents and vans. The bus stops right outside. Bring 20p coins for the showers. It will open in winter if you prebook.

Baltasound Hotel HOTEL **££**
(☑ 01957-711334; www.baltasoundhotel.co.uk; Baltasound; s £85, d £130-138; ☺ Apr–mid-Oct; P ☎) Brightly decorated rooms – some bigger than others – are complemented by wooden chalets arrayed around the lawn. Rooms feel a little overpriced so it's worth the small upgrade to the 'large doubles', which sport modern bathrooms. There's a lovely country outlook, and evening bar meals in a dining room dappled by the setting sun. Contact the hotel for winter opening details.

ℹ Getting There & Around

Unst is connected with Yell and Fetlar by ferries (p427) between Gutcher and Belmont (free if coming from Mainland that day; otherwise adult/car and driver £5.90/14.40 return, 10 minutes, frequent).

An integrated bus and ferry connection runs once a day Monday to Saturday from Lerwick to Baltasound and other Unst villages (£4.40, 2¼ hours). There are connecting services around Unst itself.

Fetlar

Fetlar, a notable birdwatching destination, is the smallest but most fertile of the North Isles. Its name is derived from the Viking term for 'fat land'.

Fetlar Interpretive Centre VISITOR CENTRE
(☑ 01957-733206; www.fetlar.org; Houbie; adult/child £3/free; ☺ 11am-4pm Mon-Sat, 12.30-4pm Sun May-Sep) This excellent centre has photos, audio recordings and videos on the island and its history. You'll find it 4.5 miles from the ferry, by the water in the hamlet of Houbie.

ℹ Getting There & Away

Four to nine daily ferries (p427) (free if coming from Mainland that day; otherwise adult/car and driver £5.90/14.40 return, 25 minutes) connect Fetlar with Gutcher on Yell and Belmont on Unst.

Understand Scotland

History

Scotland was forged from the melting pot of several cultures and grew to wield great cultural, scientific and manufacturing influence globally. From the Vikings' decline onwards, Scottish history has been intertwined, often violently, with that of its southern neighbour, England. Battles and border raids were commonplace until a shared monarch, then political union, drew the two together. Even then, Jacobite risings reflected divisions in Scottish and British society. More recently a trend towards self-determination led to a devolved parliament in 1999, and an independence referendum in 2014.

Early Days

Hunters and gatherers have left fragments of evidence of Scotland's earliest human habitation. These people came in waves from northern Europe and Ireland as glaciers retreated in the wake of the last ice age around 10,000 BC.

The Neolithic period was similarly launched by arrivals from mainland Europe. Scotland's Stone Age has left behind an astonishing diary of human development – unforgettable memories in stone of a distant past. Caithness, Orkney and Shetland have some of the world's best-preserved prehistoric villages, burial cairns and standing stones. Further south, crannogs (round structures built on stilts over a loch) were a favoured form of defensible dwelling through the Bronze Age.

The Iron Age saw the construction of a remarkable series of defence-minded structures of a different sort. Brochs (again a northeastern island development) were complex, muscular stone fortresses, some of which still stand well over 10m high.

Top Prehistoric Sites

Jarlshof (Shetland)

Skara Brae (Orkney)

Maeshowe (Orkney)

Kilmartin Glen (Argyll)

Callanish (Lewis)

Tomb of the Eagles (Orkney)

Scottish Crannog Centre (Kenmore)

Romans & Picts

The Roman occupation of Britain began in AD 43, almost a century after Julius Caesar first invaded. However, the Roman onslaught ground to a halt in the north, not far beyond the present-day Scottish border. Between 78 and 84, governor Agricola marched northwards and spent several years trying to subdue tribes the Romans called the Picts (from the Latin *pictus,* meaning 'painted'). By the 2nd century Emperor Had-

TIMELINE	4000 BC	2200 BC	AD 43
	Neolithic farmers move to Scotland from mainland Europe; sites from these ancient days dot Scotland, with the best concentrated in Orkney.	Beaker culture arrives in Scotland. The Bronze Age produces swords and shields. Construction of hill forts, crannogs and mystifying stone circles.	Claudius begins the Roman conquest of Britain, almost a century after Julius Caesar first invaded. By AD 80 a string of forts is built from the Clyde to the Forth.

rian, tired of fighting in the north, decided to cut his losses and built the wall (122–28) that bears his name across northern England. Two decades later Hadrian's successor, Antoninus Pius, invaded Scotland again and built a turf rampart, the Antonine Wall, between the Firth of Forth and the River Clyde. In northern Britain, the Romans had met their match.

Little is known about the Picts, who inhabited northern and eastern Scotland. The Roman presence probably helped forge disparate Celtic tribes into a unified group; we can assume they were fierce fighters given the trouble the hardy Roman army had with them. The main material evidence of their culture is their fabulous carved symbol stones, found across eastern Scotland.

Eventually the Romans left Britain, and at this time there were at least two indigenous peoples in the northern region of the British Isles: the Picts in the north and east, and the Britons in the southwest. A new

Pictish Stones

St Vigeans Museum (Arbroath)

Aberlemno Stones (Angus)

Groam House Museum (Rosemarkie)

Meigle Museum (Meigle)

Inverness Museum (Inverness)

HISTORY ROMANS & PICTS

PICTISH SYMBOL STONES

The mysterious carved stones that dot the landscape of eastern Scotland are the legacy of the warrior tribes who inhabited these lands 2000 years ago. The Romans occupied the southern half of Britain from AD 43 to 410, but the region to the north of the firths of Forth and Clyde – known as Caledonia – was abandoned as being too dangerous, and sealed off behind the ramparts of the Antonine Wall and Hadrian's Wall.

Caledonia was the homeland of the Picts, a collection of tribes named by the Romans for their habit of painting or tattooing their bodies. In the 9th century they were culturally absorbed by the Scots, leaving behind only a few archaeological remains, a scattering of Pictish place names beginning with 'Pit', and hundreds of mysterious carved stones decorated with intricate symbols, mainly in northeast Scotland. The capital of the ancient Southern Pictish kingdom is said to have been at Forteviot in Strathearn; Pictish symbol stones are found throughout this area and all the way up the eastern coast of Scotland into Sutherland and Caithness.

It is thought that the stones were set up to record Pictish lineages and alliances, but no one is sure exactly how the system worked. They are decorated with unusual symbols, including z-rods (a lightning bolt?), circles (the sun?), double discs (a hand mirror?) and fantastical creatures, as well as figures of warriors on horseback, hunting scenes and (on the later stones) Christian symbols.

A free leaflet, *The Angus Pictish Trail* (download at https://aberlemno.org/the-stones) will guide you to the main sites (there are similar leaflets for Aberdeenshire and Moray). The finest assemblage of stones in their natural outdoor setting is at **Aberlemno**, and there are excellent indoor collections at **St Vigeans Museum** (p219) and the **Meigle Museum** (p209).

142	397	5th century	Early 500s
Building of Antonine Wall marks the northern limit of the Roman Empire. It is patrolled for about 40 years, but after this the Romans decide northern Britain is too difficult to conquer.	The first Christian mission beyond Hadrian's Wall, in Whithorn, is initiated by St Ninian. The earliest recorded church in Scotland is built to house his remains.	Roman soldiers are recalled to Rome as the Empire faces attack from barbarian tribes. The last Romans depart and Emperor Honorius tells Britons to fend for themselves.	A Celtic tribe, the Scots, crosses the sea from northern Ireland and establishes a kingdom in Argyll called Dalriada.

group, the Celtic Scots, probably arrived around AD 500, crossing from Ireland and establishing a kingdom called Dalriada in Argyll. St Ninian was the earliest recorded bringer of Christianity to the region, establishing a mission in Whithorn in Scotland's southwest. In the 6th century, St Columba, Scotland's most famous missionary, resumed St Ninian's work. Columba was a scholar and monk who was exiled, tradition has it, after involvement in a bloody battle. After fleeing Ireland in 563, he established a monastery on Iona – an island that retains an ancient, mystical aura – and also travelled northeast to take his message to the Picts. By the late 8th century most of Scotland had converted.

The First Kings of Scotland

The Picts and Scots were drawn together by the threat of a Norse invasion and by political and spiritual power from their common Christianity. Kenneth MacAlpin, first king of a united Scotland, achieved power using a mixture of blood ties and diplomacy. He set his capital in Pictland at Scone and brought to it the sacred Stone of Destiny, used in the coronation of Scottish kings.

Robert the Bruce Trail
....
Melrose Abbey
(Melrose)
....
Scone Palace
(Perth)
....
Bannockburn
(Stirling)
....
Arbroath Abbey
(Arbroath)
....
Dunfermline Abbey
(Dunfermline)

Nearly two centuries later, MacAlpin's descendant Malcolm II (r 1005–18) defeated the Northumbrian Angles, a Germanic tribe who had settled in eastern England, at the Battle of Carham (1018), bringing Edinburgh and Lothian under Scottish control and extending Scottish territory as far south as the Tweed.

But the Highland clans, inaccessible in their glens, remained a law unto themselves for another 700 years. A cultural and linguistic divide grew up between the Gaelic-speaking Highlanders and the Lowlanders who spoke the Scots tongue.

Robert the Bruce & William Wallace

When Alexander III fell to his death in Fife in 1286, the succession was disputed by no fewer than 13 claimants, but in the end it came down to two: Robert Bruce, lord of Annandale, and John Balliol, lord of Galloway.

THE DECLARATION OF ARBROATH

During the Wars of Independence, a group of Scottish nobles sent a letter to Pope John XXII requesting support for the cause of Scottish independence. Having railed against Edward I's tyranny and sung the praises of Robert the Bruce, the declaration famously stated: 'For so long as a hundred of us remain alive, we will yield in no least way to English dominion. For we fight, not for glory nor for riches nor for honours, but only and alone for freedom, which no good man surrenders but with his life'. The Pope initially supported the Scottish cause, but English lobbying changed his mind.

685	780	848	1040
The Pictish king Bridei defeats the Northumbrians at Nechtansmere in Angus, an against-the-odds victory that sets the foundations for Scotland as a separate entity.	From the 780s onwards, Norsemen in longboats from Scandinavia begin to pillage the Scottish coast and islands, eventually taking control of Orkney, Shetland and the Western Isles.	Kenneth MacAlpin unites the Scottish and Pictish thrones, uniting Scotland north of the Firth of Forth into a single kingdom.	Macbeth takes the Scottish throne after defeating Duncan. This, and the fact that he was later killed by Duncan's son Malcolm, are the only parallels with Shakespeare's version of the story.

Edward I of England was asked to arbitrate. He chose Balliol, whom he thought he could manipulate more easily.

Seeking to tighten his feudal grip on Scotland, Edward – known as the 'Hammer of the Scots' – treated the Scots king as vassal rather than equal. The humiliated Balliol finally turned against him and allied Scotland with France in 1295, thus beginning the enduring 'Auld Alliance' and ushering in the Wars of Independence.

Edward's response was bloody. In 1296 he invaded Scotland, and Balliol was incarcerated in the Tower of London. In another blow to Scots pride, Edward removed the Stone of Destiny from Scone and took it back to London.

Enter William Wallace. Bands of rebels were attacking the English occupiers and Wallace led one such band to defeat the English at Stirling Bridge in 1297. After Wallace's betrayal and execution, Robert the Bruce, grandson of the former claimant, saw his chance, defied Edward (whom he had previously aligned himself with), murdered his rival John Comyn and had himself crowned King of Scotland at Scone in 1306. Bruce mounted a campaign to drive the English out of Scotland but suffered repeated defeats. Persistence paid off and he went on to secure an illustrious victory over the English at Bannockburn in 1314, enshrined in Scottish legend as one of the finest moments in the country's history.

Scottish independence was eventually won in 1328, though 'the Bruce' died the next year. Wars with England and civil strife continued, however. In 1371 Robert the Bruce's grandson, Robert II, acceded to the throne, founding the Stewart (later written as Stuart) dynasty, which was to rule Scotland and, in time, the rest of Britain until 1714.

The Renaissance

James IV (r 1488–1513) married the daughter of Henry VII of England, the first of the Tudor monarchs, thereby linking the two royal families through 'the Marriage of the Thistle and the Rose'. This didn't prevent the French from persuading James to go to war against his in-laws, and he was killed at the Battle of Flodden in 1513, along with some 10,000 of his subjects. Renaissance ideas, in particular Scottish poetry and architecture, flourished during this time; some of the finest Scottish Renaissance buildings can be seen within the fortress of Stirling Castle.

Mary, Queen of Scots, & the Reformation

In 1542 James V, childless, lay on his deathbed – broken-hearted, it is said, after his defeat by the English at Solway Moss. Then news came that his wife had given birth to a baby girl. Fearing the end of the Stewart dynasty, and recalling its origin through Robert the Bruce's daughter, James sighed, 'It cam' wi' a lass, and it will gang wi' a lass'. He died shortly

Columba was a man of fixed ideas. On Iona he promptly set about banishing women and cows, as he believed that 'where there is a cow there is a woman, and where there is a woman there is mischief'. He wasn't a memory-foam-bed kind of person – he slept on the bare floor with a stone for a pillow.

1263	1296	1298–1305	1314
Norse power is finally broken at the Battle of Largs, which marks the retreat of Viking influence and eventually the handing back of the Western Isles to Scotland.	Edward I marches on Scotland with an army of 30,000 men, razing ports, butchering citizens and capturing the castles of Berwick, Edinburgh, Roxburgh and Stirling.	William Wallace is proclaimed Guardian of Scotland in March 1298. After Edward's force defeats the Scots at the Battle of Falkirk, Wallace resigns and goes into hiding, but he is fatally betrayed after his return in 1305.	Robert the Bruce wins a famous victory over the English at the Battle of Bannockburn, despite being outnumbered by his opponents.

afterwards, leaving his week-old daughter, Mary, to inherit the throne as Queen of Scots.

She was sent to France young, and Scotland was ruled by regents, who rejected overtures from Henry VIII of England urging them to wed the infant queen to his son. Furious, Henry sent his armies to take vengeance on the Scots. The 'Rough Wooing', as it was called, failed to win hearts and minds and in 1558 Mary was married to the French dauphin. When he became king the next year, Mary was briefly queen of France as well as Scotland.

While Mary was in France, being raised Catholic, the Reformation tore through Scotland, to where, following the death of her sickly French husband, the 18-year-old returned in 1561. She was formally welcomed to her capital city and held a famous audience with John Knox. The great reformer harangued the young queen and she later agreed to protect the budding Protestant Church in Scotland while continuing to practise Catholicism in private.

She married Lord Darnley in the Chapel Royal at Holyrood and gave birth to a son (later James VI) in 1565. Any domestic bliss was short-lived and, in a scarcely believable train of events, Darnley was involved in the

THE LORDS OF THE ISLES

In medieval times, when overland Highland travel was slow, difficult and dangerous, the sea lochs, firths (estuaries), kyles (narrow sea channels) and sounds of the west coast were the motorways of their time. Cut off from the rest of Scotland, but united by these sea roads, the west coast and islands were a world unto themselves.

Descended from the legendary Somerled (a half-Gaelic, half-Norse warrior of the 12th century), the chiefs of Clan Donald claimed sovereignty over this watery kingdom. It was John MacDonald of Islay who first styled himself Dominus Insularum (Lord of the Isles) in 1353. He and his descendants ruled their vast territory from their headquarters at Finlaggan in Islay, backed up by fleets of swift *birlinns* and *nyvaigs* (Hebridean galleys), an intimate knowledge of the sea routes of the west and a network of coastal castles.

Clan Donald held sway over the isles, often in defiance of the Scottish kings, from 1350 to 1493. At its greatest extent, in the second half of the 15th century, the Lordship of the Isles included all the islands on the west coast of Scotland, the west-coast mainland from Kintyre to Ross-shire, and the Antrim coast of northern Ireland. But in a greedy grab for territory, Clan Donald finally pushed its luck too far. John MacDonald made a secret pact with the English king Edward IV to divide Scotland between them. When this treason was discovered 30 years later, the Lordship was forfeited to James IV of Scotland, and the title has remained in possession of the Scottish, and later British, royal family ever since. Lord of the Isles is one of the many titles held today by Prince Charles, heir to the British throne.

1328	1410	1468–69	1488–1513
Continuing raids on northern England force Edward III to sue for peace and the Treaty of Northampton confirms Scotland's independence, with Robert I, the Bruce, as king.	One of Europe's most venerable educational institutions, the University of St Andrews, is founded.	Orkney and then Shetland are mortgaged to Scotland as part of a dowry from Danish king Christian I, whose daughter is to marry the future James III of Scotland.	The Scottish Renaissance produces an intellectual climate that encourages Protestantism, a reaction against the perceived wealth and corruption of the medieval Roman Catholic Church.

murder of Mary's Italian secretary Rizzio (rumoured to be her lover), before he himself was murdered, probably by Mary's new lover and third-husband-to-be, the Earl of Bothwell.

The Scots had had enough. Mary's enemies – an alliance of powerful nobles – finally confronted her at Carberry Hill, east of Edinburgh, and she was forced to abdicate in 1567 and thrown into prison at Castle Leven. She escaped and met her enemies in battle at Langside, but she was defeated and fled to England, where she was imprisoned for 19 years by Elizabeth I and finally executed in 1587.

History, however, has a habit of providing a twist in the tale. Mary's son James VI (r 1567–1625) had meanwhile been crowned at Stirling, and a series of regents ruled in his place. In England, Elizabeth died childless, and the English, desperate for a male monarch, soon turned their attention north. James VI of Scotland became James I of England and moved his court to London. His plan to politically unite the two countries, however, failed. For the most part, the Stuarts ignored Scotland from then on.

Mary Queen of Scots (1969) by Antonia Fraser is the classic biography of Scotland's ill-starred queen, digging deep behind the myths to discover the real woman caught up in the labyrinthine politics of the period.

Union with England

Civil war and 17th-century religious conflict left the country and its economy ruined. Scotland couldn't compete in this new era of European colonialism and, to add to its woes, during the 1690s famine killed up to a third of the population in some areas. Anti-English feeling ran high: the Protestant king William, who had replaced the exiled Catholic James VII/II to the chagrin of many in Scotland, was at war with France and employing Scottish soldiers and taxes – many Scots, sympathetic to the French, disapproved. This feeling was exacerbated by the failure of the Darien Scheme, an investment plan designed to establish a Scottish colony in Panama, which resulted in widespread bankruptcy in Scotland.

The failure made it clear to wealthy Scottish merchants and stockholders that the only way they could gain access to the lucrative markets of developing colonies was through union with England. The English parliament favoured union through fear of Jacobite sympathies in Scotland being exploited by its enemies, the French.

On receiving the Act of Union in 1707 in Edinburgh, the Chancellor of Scotland, Lord Seafield – leader of the parliament that the Act of Union abolished – is said to have murmured under his breath, 'Now there's an end to an auld sang'. Robert Burns later castigated the wealthy politicians who engineered the union in characteristically stronger language: 'We're bought and sold for English gold – such a parcel of rogues in a nation!'

1513	1567	1587	1603
James IV invades northern England and is soundly defeated (and killed) in Northumberland at the Battle of Flodden. This marks a watershed in war history, with artillery on the upswing and archery on the way out.	Mary, Queen of Scots, is deposed and thrown into prison. Though her last stand is still to come, the days of wilful royal action in Scotland seem to be over.	After 19 years in prison, Mary, Queen of Scots is beheaded for treason on the orders of Queen Elizabeth I of England.	James VI of Scotland inherits the English throne in the so-called Union of the Crowns, becoming James I of Great Britain.

The Jacobites

The Jacobite rebellions of the 18th century sought to displace the Hanoverian monarchy (chosen by the English parliament in 1701 to ensure a Protestant succession after the Stuart queens Mary II and Anne died without heirs) and restore a Catholic Stuart king to the British throne.

Jacobite, a term derived from the Latin for 'James', is used to describe the political movement committed to the return of the Catholic Stuart kings to the thrones of England and Scotland.

James Edward Stuart, known as the Old Pretender, was the son of James VII/II. With French support he arrived in the Firth of Forth with a fleet of ships in 1708 but was seen off by government men-of-war.

The Earl of Mar led another Jacobite rebellion in 1715 but proved an ineffectual leader; his campaign fizzled out soon after the inconclusive Battle of Sheriffmuir.

The Old Pretender's son, Charles Edward Stuart, better known as Bonnie Prince Charlie or the Young Pretender, landed in Scotland for the final uprising. He had little military experience, didn't speak Gaelic and had a shaky grasp of English. Nevertheless, supported by an army of Highlanders, he marched southwards and captured Edinburgh, except for the castle, in September 1745. He got as far south as Derby in England, but success was short-lived; a government army led by the Duke of Cumberland harried him all the way back to the Highlands, where Jacobite dreams were finally extinguished at the Battle of Culloden in 1746.

Although a heavily romanticised figure, Bonnie Prince Charlie was partly responsible for the annihilation of Highland culture, given the crackdown following his doomed attempt to recapture the crown. After returning to France he gained a reputation for drunkenness and mistreatment of mistresses. France had plans to invade Britain during the mid-18th century, but it eventually ceased to regard the prince as a serious character. When French ambitions were thwarted by British naval victories in 1759, the Bonnie Prince's last chance had gone. He died in Rome in 1788.

Bonnie Prince Charlie's flight after the Battle of Culloden is legendary. He lived in hiding in the remote Highlands and islands for months before being rescued by a French frigate. His narrow escape from Uist to Skye, dressed as Flora MacDonald's maid, is the subject of the 'Skye Boat Song'.

The Highland Clearances

In the aftermath of the Jacobite rebellions, Highland dress, the bearing of arms and the bagpipes were outlawed. The Highlands were put under military control and private armies were banned.

The clansmen, no longer of any use as soldiers and uneconomical as tenants, were evicted from their homes and farms by the Highland chieftains to make way for flocks of sheep. A few stayed to work the sheep farms; many more were forced to seek work in the cities, or to eke a living from crofts (smallholdings) on poor coastal land. Men who had never seen the sea were forced to take to boats to try their luck at herring fishing, and many thousands emigrated – some willingly, some

1692	1707	1745–46	1740s–1830s
The Massacre of Glencoe causes further rifts between those clans loyal to the Crown and those loyal to the old ways.	Despite popular opposition, the Act of Union – which brings England and Scotland under one parliament, one sovereign and one flag – takes effect on 1 May.	The culmination of the Jacobite rebellions: Bonnie Prince Charlie lands in Scotland, gathers an army and marches south. Though he gains English territory, he is eventually defeated at the Battle of Culloden.	Cultural and intellectual life flourishes during the Scottish Enlightenment. Meanwhile, the Industrial Revolution brings preeminence in the production of textiles, iron, steel and coal – and above all in shipbuilding.

under duress – to the developing colonies of North America, Australia and New Zealand.

If you do much walking in the Highlands and islands, you are almost certain to come across a pile of stones among the bracken – all that remains of a house or cottage. Look around and you'll find another, and another, and soon you'll realise that this was once a crofting settlement.

The Scottish Enlightenment

During the period known as the Scottish Enlightenment (roughly 1740–1830) Edinburgh became known as 'a hotbed of genius'. Philosophers David Hume and Adam Smith and sociologist Adam Ferguson emerged as influential thinkers, nourished on generations of theological debate. Medic William Cullen produced the first modern pharmacopoeia, chemist Joseph Black advanced the science of thermodynamics, and geologist James Hutton challenged long-held beliefs about the age of the Earth.

After centuries of bloodshed and religious fanaticism, people applied themselves with the same energy and piety to the making of money and the enjoyment of leisure. There was a revival in Scottish history and literature. The writings of Sir Walter Scott and the poetry of Robert Burns achieved lasting popularity. The cliched images that spring to mind when you say 'Scotland' – bagpipes, haggis, tartans, misty glens – owe much to the romantic depictions of the country developed at this time.

The Industrial Revolution

The development of the steam engine ushered in the Industrial Revolution. Glasgow, deprived of its lucrative tobacco trade following the American War of Independence (1776–83), developed into an industrial powerhouse, the 'second city' of the British Empire. Cotton mills, iron and steelworks, chemical plants, shipbuilding yards and heavy-engineering works proliferated along the River Clyde in the 19th century, powered by southern Scotland's abundant coal mines.

The Clearances and the Industrial Revolution had shattered the traditional rural way of life, and though manufacturing cities and ports thrived in these decades of Empire, wealth was generated for a select few by an impoverished many. Deep poverty forced many into emigration and others to their graves. The depopulation was exacerbated by WWI, which took a heavy toll on Scottish youth. The ensuing years were bleak and marked by labour disputes.

War & Peace

Scotland largely escaped the trauma and devastation wrought by WWII on the industrial cities of England (though Clydebank was bombed). Indeed, the war brought a measure of renewed prosperity to Scotland as

Charlie, Meg & Me by Gregor Ewing (2013) is an entertaining account of one man and his dog retracing Bonnie Prince Charlie's epic 500-mile trek through the Scottish Highlands in 1746.

Between 1904 and 1931 around one million people emigrated from Scotland to begin new lives in North America and Australasia.

1890–1910	1914–32	1941–45	1970s
The 'Glasgow Boys' bring European influence and international recognition to Scottish art, breaking away from the Edinburgh mainstream.	Scottish industry slumps during WWI and collapses in its aftermath in the face of overseas competition and the Great Depression. About 400,000 Scots emigrate between 1921 and 1931.	Clydebank is blitzed by German bombers in 1941, with 1200 deaths; by 1945 one out of four males in the workforce is employed in heavy industries to support the war effort.	The discovery of oil and gas in the North Sea brings new prosperity to Aberdeen and the surrounding area, and also to Shetland.

the shipyards and engineering works geared up to supply material. But the postwar period saw the collapse of shipbuilding and heavy industry, on which Scotland had become over-reliant.

After the discovery of North Sea oil off the Scottish coast, excitement turned to bitterness for many Scots, who felt that revenues were being siphoned off to England, though some parts of the country, such as Aberdeen, prospered. This issue, along with takeovers of Scottish companies by English ones (which then closed the Scots operation, asset-stripped and transferred jobs to England), fuelled increasing nationalist sentiment. The Scottish National Party (SNP) developed into a third force (then a second as it eclipsed the Conservatives, and then first as it won power from the Labour Party) in Scottish politics.

John Prebble's wonderfully written book *The Highland Clearances* (1963) tells the terrible story of how the Highlanders were driven out of their homes and forced into emigration.

Devolution

In 1979 a referendum was held on whether to set up a directly elected Scottish Assembly. Fifty-two per cent of those who voted said yes to devolution, but Labour prime minister James Callaghan decided that everyone who didn't vote should be counted as a no, so the Scottish Assembly was rejected.

From 1979 to 1997 Scotland was ruled by a Conservative government in London, for which the majority of Scots hadn't voted. Separatist feelings, always present, grew stronger. Following the landslide victory of the Labour Party in 1997, another referendum was held on the creation of a Scottish parliament. This time the result was overwhelmingly and unambiguously in favour.

Elections were held and the Scottish parliament convened for the first time in 1999 in Edinburgh, with Labour's Donald Dewar, who died in office the very next year, becoming first minister. Labour held power until 2007, when the proindependence Scottish National Party formed government. It was overwhelmingly re-elected in 2011 and pushed for a referendum on independence. The campaign engaged the nation and resulted in a huge turnout, but in September 2014 the Scots voted against becoming an independent nation by 55% to 45%.

One of the major factors for many Scots who voted to remain part of the UK was the guarantee of continued EU membership, so when in June 2016 the UK population narrowly voted to leave the EU – a process that became known as Brexit – this again brought the issue of Scottish independence into the spotlight. As the UK headed towards its final break with the EU at the end of 2020, polls revealed that a majority of Scots (56%, excluding 'don't knows') now supported independence.

1999–2004	2014	2016	2020
Scottish parliament is convened in May 1999 after a three-century hiatus. The new Parliament Building is opened in Edinburgh by Elizabeth II in 2004.	Scotland votes on, and rejects, becoming a fully independent nation by 55% to 45%, and so remains part of the UK.	Scots vote 62% to remain in the EU, but the UK as a whole votes to leave, raising further questions about Scotland's future path.	The UK formally exits the EU at the end of the year, and support for Scottish independence rises to 56%.

The Scottish Larder

Traditional Scottish cookery is all about basic comfort food: solid, nourishing fare, often high in fat, that will keep you warm on a winter's day spent in the fields or at sea. But Scotland has been a front runner in the recent British culinary revolution, and an inspiring array of local and sustainable produce is on offer. Scotland's traditional drinks – whisky and beer – have also found a new lease of life, with single malts being marketed like fine wines, and numerous new microbreweries.

Breakfast, Lunch & Dinner

The Full Scottish

Though it's making a comeback, surprisingly few Scots eat porridge for breakfast – these days a cappuccino and a croissant is just as likely – and even fewer eat it in the traditional way; that is, with salt to taste, but no sugar.

The typical 'full Scottish' breakfast offered in a B&B or hotel usually consists of fruit juice and cereal, toast and jam, a pot of coffee or tea, and a fry-up combination of any or all of bacon, sausage, black pudding (a type of sausage made with oatmeal, onion and pig blood), grilled tomato, mushrooms, potato scones and a fried egg or two. Most B&Bs offer a vegetarian version these days. An increasing number are eliminating the fried plate in favour of a healthier option such as fruit salad.

Fish for breakfast may sound strange but was not unusual in crofting (smallholding) and fishing communities where seafood was a staple. Many hotels still offer grilled kippers (smoked herrings) or smoked haddock (poached in milk and served with a poached egg) for breakfast – delicious with lots of buttered toast.

Scottish food writer Sue Lawrence's book *A Taste of Scotland's Islands* contains more than 100 recipes based on the use of fresh, seasonal Scottish produce.

Traditional Soups

Scotch broth, made with mutton stock, barley, lentils and peas, is nutritious and tasty, while cock-a-leekie is a hearty soup made with chicken and leeks. Warming vegetable soups include leek and potato soup, and lentil soup (traditionally made using ham stock – vegetarians, beware!).

Seafood soups include the delicious Cullen skink, made with smoked haddock, potato, onion and milk, and *partan bree* (crab soup).

Seafood Specialities

Scottish seafood is among the world's best, and it's a major highlight of a visit to the country, particularly along the west coast. There's an increasing awareness of sustainability issues and most serious seafood places will give information on provenance. Tucking into some local hand-dived scallops and creel-caught langoustines as the sun sets over a west-coast or island bay is one of Europe's great gastronomic pleasures.

And it's not all about crisp linen, claw crackers and finger bowls. A number of simple seafood shacks serve up delicious fresh fare in a very

SMOKIN'!

Scotland is famous for its smoked salmon, but there are many other varieties of smoked fish – plus smoked meats and cheeses – to enjoy. Smoking food to preserve it is an ancient art that has recently undergone a revival, but this time it's more about flavour than preservation.

There are two parts to the process – first the cure, which involves covering the fish in a mixture of salt and molasses, or soaking it in brine; and then the smoke, which can be either cold smoking (at less than 34°C), which results in a raw product, or hot smoking (at more than 60°C), which cooks it. Cold-smoked products include traditional smoked salmon, kippers and Finnan haddies. Hot-smoked products include *bradan rost* ('flaky' smoked salmon) and Arbroath smokies.

Arbroath smokies are haddock that have been gutted, de-headed and cleaned, then salted and dried overnight, tied together at the tail in pairs, and hot-smoked over oak or beech chippings for 45 to 90 minutes. Finnan haddies (named after the fishing village of Findon in Aberdeenshire) are also haddock, but these are split down the middle like kippers, and cold smoked.

Kippers (smoked herring) were invented in Northumberland, in northern England, in the mid-19th century, but Scotland soon picked up the technique, and both Loch Fyne and Mallaig were famous for their kippers.

no-frills manner – a great way to eat straight from the boats without busting the budget.

Juicy langoustines (also known as Dublin Bay prawns, Norway lobsters or, in some places, simply 'prawns') are a highlight; crabs, squat lobsters, lobsters, oysters, mussels and scallops are also widely available.

Scottish salmon is famous worldwide, but there's a big difference between the now-ubiquitous farmed salmon and the leaner, more expensive wild fish (there is now only one wild salmon fishery in Scotland). Also, there are concerns over the environmental impact and animal-welfare conditions of salmon farms.

Smoked salmon is traditionally dressed with a squeeze of lemon juice and eaten with fresh brown bread and butter. Trout, salmon's smaller cousin – whether wild, rod-caught brown trout or farmed rainbow trout – is delicious fried in oatmeal.

As an alternative to kippers, you may be offered Arbroath smokies (hot-smoked haddock), traditionally eaten cold. Herring fillets fried in oatmeal are good, if you don't mind picking out a few bones. Mackerel pâté and smoked or peppered mackerel (both served cold) are also popular.

Scottish Beef, Pork & Game

Steak eaters will enjoy a thick fillet of world-famous Aberdeen Angus beef, and beef from Highland cattle is much sought after. Venison, from red deer, is leaner and appears on many menus, particularly in the Highlands. Scotland, particularly Ayrshire, has some quality pork that appears in various forms.

A variety of meat-based deli products is beginning to appear from smaller, often organic, producers, with pork, mutton and venison being used in a very tasty array of smoked and charcuterie products.

Puddings

Traditional Scottish puddings are irresistibly creamy, high-calorie concoctions. Cranachan is whipped cream flavoured with whisky, and mixed with toasted oatmeal and raspberries. Atholl brose is a mixture of cream, whisky and honey, flavoured with oatmeal. Clootie dumpling is a rich steamed pudding filled with currants and raisins; it's so named because it's wrapped in a 'cloot' (linen cloth) for steaming.

Vegetarian & Vegan

Scotland has the same proportion of vegetarians as the rest of the UK – around 14% of the population – and vegetarianism is now firmly in the mainstream. Even the most remote Highland pub usually has at least one vegetarian dish on the menu, and there are many dedicated vegetarian restaurants in the cities. If you get stuck, there's almost always an Italian or Indian restaurant where you can get meat-free pizza, pasta or curry.

Vegans are much better catered for than in past years, and Pitlochry is now home to the UK's first ever 100% vegan hotel, Saorsa 1875 (p326).

One thing to keep in mind is that lentil soup, a seemingly vegetarian staple of Scottish pub and restaurant menus, is traditionally made with ham stock.

Most B&Bs offer a vegetarian fry-up option these days, though vegans are advised to explain to their host beforehand exactly what the term 'vegan' means – just in case.

Eating with Kids

Following the introduction of the ban on smoking in public places in 2006, many Scottish pubs and restaurants have had to broaden their appeal by becoming more family friendly. As a result, especially in the cities and more popular tourist towns, many restaurants and pubs now have family rooms and/or play areas. Children's menus are common but not usually very imaginative.

You should be aware, though, that children under the age of 14 are not allowed into the majority of Scottish pubs, even those that serve bar meals; and in family-friendly pubs (those in possession of a Children's Certificate), under-14s are only allowed in between 11am and 8pm, and must be accompanied by an adult aged 18 or older.

Farmers Markets & Food Festivals

Many towns, city districts and villages, particularly in the south of Scotland, have a regular farmers market that showcases local produce. There's an inspiring variety of new, sustainably grown fare, with everything from chorizo to tea being brought from farm to table by small-scale producers. Local food festivals are another increasingly popular way to publicise regional delicacies.

TOP 10 SEAFOOD RESTAURANTS

Ondine (p86), Edinburgh

Café Fish (p282), Tobermory

Haar (p194), St Andrews

Kishorn Seafood Bar (p371), Lochcarron

Tolbooth Restaurant (p230), Stonehaven

Lochleven Seafood Cafe (p334), Kinlochleven

Starfish (p260), Tarbert

Silver Darling (p226), Aberdeen

Loch Bay (p383), Skye

Captain's Galley (p358), Scrabster

Cookery Courses

More than a dozen places in Scotland offer courses in Scottish cookery. Two of the most famous:

Nick Nairn Cookschool (☎01877-389900; https://nicknairncookschool.com; Port of Menteith) One-day courses in modern Scottish cooking at the school owned by Scotland's top TV chef, Nick Nairn, author of *Wild Harvest* and *Island Harvest*.

Edinburgh New Town Cookery School (☎0131-226 4314; https://entcs.co.uk; 7 Queen St) Offers a huge range of courses from half-day to two weeks, including a one-day shellfish workshop (£170).

Beer

Scottish breweries produce a wide range of beers, with generic multinational lagers alongside traditional-style real ales and a huge and growing selection of craft-brewed beers from small regional brewing operations.

Traditional Scottish ales use old-fashioned 'shilling' categories to indicate strength (the number of shillings was originally the price per barrel; the stronger the beer, the higher the price). The usual range is from 60 to 80 shillings (written 80/-). You'll also see IPA, which stands for India Pale Ale, a strong, hoppy beer first brewed in the early 19th century for export to India (the extra alcohol meant that it kept better on the long sea voyage).

Draught beer is served in pints (568mL, usually costing from £2.70 to £4.50) or half pints; alcoholic content generally ranges from 3% to 6%. What the English call bitter, Scots call heavy, or export.

The craft-beer revolution of recent years has hit Scotland with full force, and a large number of small breweries are producing beers ranging from organic lagers to traditional Scottish ales, American-influenced pale ales and various styles of dark beer. An increasing number of pubs have given over one or more taps to local craft beers or real ales, immeasurably improving the Scottish beer scene.

Visit http://glasgowcamra.org.uk/breweries.php for a comprehensive list of Scottish breweries, both large and small.

Many craft breweries have their own pubs, or even combine pub and brewery in one place, such as Pitlochry's Moulin Hotel (p326),

HAGGIS – SCOTLAND'S NATIONAL DISH

Scotland's national dish is often avoided by visitors because of its ingredients, which admittedly don't sound promising – the finely chopped lungs, heart and liver of a sheep, mixed with oatmeal and onion and stuffed into a sheep's stomach bag. However, it actually tastes surprisingly good.

Haggis should be served with *champit tatties* and *bashed neeps* (mashed potatoes and turnips), with a generous dollop of butter and a good sprinkling of black pepper.

Although it's eaten year-round, haggis is central to the Burns Night celebrations of 25 January, in honour of Scotland's national poet, Robert Burns, when Scots worldwide unite to revel in their Scottishness. A piper announces the arrival of the haggis, and Burns' poem *Address to a Haggis* is recited to this 'Great chieftan o' the puddin-race'. The bulging haggis is then lanced with a *dirk* (dagger) to reveal the steaming offal within, 'warm-reekin, rich'.

Vegetarians (and quite a few carnivores, no doubt) will be relieved to know that veggie haggis is available in some restaurants.

Takeaways serve deep-fried haggis with chips – tasty, but don't tell your cardiologist.

Top Seafood platter

Bottom
Cranachan (p440)

NOIRCHOCOLATE/SHUTTERSTOCK ©

TOP FIVE SINGLE MALTS – OUR CHOICE

After a great deal of diligent research (and not a few sore heads), Lonely Planet's *Scotland* authors have selected their five favourite single malts from across the country.

Ardbeg (p263) (Islay) The 10-year-old from this noble distillery is a byword for excellence. Peaty but well balanced. Hits the spot after a hill walk.

Highland Park (p402) (Orkney) Full and rounded, with heather, honey, malt and peat. Award-winning distillery tour.

Isle of Arran (p252) (Arran) One of Scotland's newer distilleries, offering a lightish, flavoursome malt with flowery, fruity notes.

Macallan (p234) (Speyside) The king of Speyside malts, with sherry and bourbon finishes. The distillery is set amid waving fields of Golden Promise barley.

Talisker (p380) (Skye) Brooding, heavily peated nose balanced by a satisfying sweetness from this lord of the isles. Great post-dinner dram.

St Andrews' Brewing Co (p194) and Edinburgh's **Royal Dick** (☑0131-560 1572; www.summerhall.co.uk/the-royal-dick; 1 Summerhall; ⊙2-10pm; ☎; ☑41, 42).

Traditional Pubs

The traditional Scottish pub ranges from the grandiose, purpose-built, Victorian pubs typical of Edinburgh and Glasgow through former coaching inns dotted along ancient highways to cottage drinking dens hidden away in Highland glens and island villages.

What they have in common today is that they have preserved much of their original 18th- or 19th-century decor – timber-beamed ceilings, glowing mahogany bar tops, polished brass rails and stained-glass windows – and generally serve cask-conditioned real ales and a range of malt whiskies.

Pubs like these are often the social hub of rural communities, a meeting place and venue for live music, quiz nights and ceilidhs (p448).

Scotland's most famous soft drink is Barr's Irn-Bru: a sweet, fizzy drink, radioactive orange in colour, that smells like bubble gum and almost strips the enamel from your teeth. Many Scots swear by its restorative effects as a cure for a hangover.

Whisky

Scotch whisky (always spelt without an 'e' – whiskey with an 'e' is Irish or American) is Scotland's best-known product and biggest export. The spirit has been distilled in Scotland at least since the 15th century and probably for much longer.

At a bar, older Scots may order a 'half' or 'nip' of whisky as a chaser to a pint or half pint of beer (a 'hauf and a hauf'). Only tourists ask for 'Scotch' – what else would you be served in Scotland? The standard measure in pubs is either 25mL or 35mL.

As well as whiskies, there are whisky-based liqueurs such as Drambuie. If you must mix your whisky with anything other than water, try a whisky mac (whisky with ginger wine). After a long walk in the rain there's nothing better for putting a warm glow in your belly.

Whisky Bars

Some pubs, especially in the whisky-distilling region of Speyside, have become known as whisky bars because of their staggering range of single-malt whiskies – the famous Quaich Bar in the Craigellachie Hotel (p235), established in 1894, offers more than 900 varieties.

The revival of interest in single malts since the late 1990s has seen a new wave of whisky bars open across the country, mainly in the cities. Places such as Glasgow's Òran Mór (p130) have more than 300 malts stacked behind the bar.

Scottish Culture

The notion of 'the Scottish arts' often conjures up cliched images of bagpipe music, incomprehensible poetry and romanticised paintings of Highland landscapes. But Scottish artists have given the world a wealth of unforgettable treasures, from the songs and poems of Robert Burns and the novels of Sir Walter Scott to the architecture of Charles Rennie Mackintosh.

Literature

Scotland has a long and distinguished literary history, from the era of the medieval makars ('makers' of verses; ie poets) to the present-day crime novels of Val McDermid, Christopher Brookmyre, Louise Welsh and Ian Rankin.

Burns & Scott

Scotland's most famous literary figure is, of course, Robert Burns (1759–96). His works have been translated into dozens of languages and are known the world over. Burns wrote in Lowland Scots (Lallans); in fact, his poetry was instrumental in keeping Lallans alive to the present day. He was also very much a man of the people, satirising the upper classes and the church for their hypocrisy. Although he is best known for the comical tale of *Tam O'Shanter* and for penning the words to 'Auld Lang Syne', his more political poems – including 'Such a Parcel of Rogues in a Nation' (about the 1707 Act of Union) and 'A Man's a Man for a' That' (about class and solidarity) – reveal his socialist leanings.

The son of an Edinburgh lawyer, Sir Walter Scott (1771–1832) was Scotland's greatest and most prolific novelist. Scott was born in Edinburgh and lived at various New Town addresses before moving to his country house at **Abbotsford** (📞01896-752043; www.scottsabbotsford.com; visitor centre free, house adult/child £11.50/5; ⏰10am-5pm Apr-Oct, to 4pm Nov-Mar, house closed Dec-Feb). His early works were rhyming ballads, such as *The Lady of the Lake*, and his first historical novels – Scott effectively invented the genre – were published anonymously. Plagued by debt in later life, he wrote obsessively in order to make money, but will always be best remembered for classic tales such as *Waverley*, *The Heart of Midlothian*, *Ivanhoe*, *Redgauntlet* and *Castle Dangerous*.

RLS & Sherlock Holmes

Along with Sir Walter Scott, Robert Louis Stevenson (RLS; 1850–94) ranks as Scotland's best-known novelist. Born at 8 Howard Pl in Edinburgh into a family of famous lighthouse engineers, Stevenson studied law at Edinburgh University but was always intent on pursuing the life of a writer. An inveterate traveller, but dogged by ill health, he finally settled in Samoa in 1889, where he was highly respected by the locals and given the nickname of 'Tusitala' – the teller of tales. Stevenson is known and loved around the world for those tales: *Kidnapped*, *Catriona*, *Treasure Island*, *The Master of Ballantrae* and *The Strange Case of Dr Jekyll and Mr Hyde*.

Sir Arthur Conan Doyle (1859–1930), the creator of Sherlock Holmes, was born in Edinburgh and studied medicine at Edinburgh University. He

Essential Scottish Novels

Sunset Song (Lewis Grassic Gibbon, 1932)

The Prime of Miss Jean Brodie (Muriel Spark, 1961)

Greenvoe (George Mackay Brown, 1972)

Trainspotting (Irvine Welsh, 1993)

based the character of Holmes on one of his lecturers, the surgeon Dr Joseph Bell, who had employed his forensic skills and powers of deduction on several murder cases in Edinburgh.

The 20th Century

Scotland's finest modern poet was Hugh MacDiarmid (born Christopher Murray Grieve; 1892–1978). Originally from Dumfriesshire, he moved to Edinburgh in 1908, where he trained as a teacher and a journalist, but he spent most of his life in Montrose, Shetland, Glasgow and Biggar. His masterpiece is 'A Drunk Man Looks at the Thistle', a 2685-line Joycean monologue.

The poet and storyteller George Mackay Brown (1921–96) was born in Stromness in Orkney, and lived there almost all his life. Although his poems and novels are rooted in Orkney, his work, like that of Burns, transcends local and national boundaries. His best-known novel, *Greenvoe* (1972), is a poetic evocation of an Orkney community threatened by the coming of modernity.

Dame Muriel Spark (1918–2006) was born in Edinburgh and educated at James Gillespie's High School for Girls, an experience that provided material for perhaps her best-known novel, *The Prime of Miss Jean Brodie,* a shrewd portrait of 1930s Edinburgh.

As the millennium approached, the most widely known Scots writers included Iain Banks (1954–2013; *The Crow Road, 1982*), Irvine Welsh (b 1961; *Trainspotting, 1993*), Janice Galloway (b 1955; *The Trick Is to Keep Breathing, 1989*) and Ali Smith (b 1962; *Free Love & Other Stories, 1995*). The grim realities of modern Glasgow were vividly conjured in the short-story collection *Not Not While the Giro* (1983) by James Kelman (b 1946), whose controversial novel *How Late It Was, How Late* won the 1994 Booker Prize.

The Contemporary Scene

Following the publication of *The Panopticon* (2012), Jenni Fagan (b 1977), one time performance poet and singer in a grunge band, was listed as one

The Living Tradition (www.living tradition.co.uk) is a bimonthly magazine covering the folk and traditional music of Scotland and the British Isles, as well as Celtic music, with features and reviews of albums and live gigs.

SCOTTISH LANGUAGES

From the 8th to the 19th centuries the common language of central and southern Scotland was Lowland Scots (sometimes called Lallans), which evolved from Old English and has Dutch, French, Gaelic, German and Scandinavian influences. As distinct from English as Norwegian is from Danish, it was the official language of state in Scotland until the Act of Union in 1707.

Following the Union, English rose to predominance as the language of government, church and polite society. The spread of education and literacy in the 19th century eventually led to Lowland Scots being perceived as backward and unsophisticated – children were often beaten for speaking Scots in school instead of English.

The Scots tongue persisted, however, and has undergone a revival – there are now Scots language dictionaries, university degree courses in Scots language and literature, and Scots is studied as part of the school curriculum.

Scottish Gaelic (*Gàidhlig* – pronounced 'gaa-lik') is spoken by about 60,000 people in Scotland, mainly in the Highlands and islands. It is a member of the Celtic family of languages, which includes Irish Gaelic, Manx, Welsh, Cornish and Breton.

Gaelic culture flourished in the Highlands until the Jacobite rebellions of the 18th century. After the Battle of Culloden in 1746 many Gaelic speakers were forced from their ancestral lands, and Gaelic was regarded as little more than a 'peasant' language of no modern significance.

It was only in the 1970s that Gaelic began to make a comeback. After two centuries of decline, the language has been encouraged through financial help from government agencies and the EU, and Gaelic education is flourishing at every level, from playgroups to tertiary institutions.

of Granta's Best of Young British Novelists. Her latest offering, *Luckenbooth* (2021), begins with Satan's daughter rowing ashore in a coffin at Leith in 1910, and develops into a powerful and compelling tale that spans the subsequent nine decades.

Scottish-American author Douglas Stuart (b 1976) saw his debut novel *Shuggie Bain* – an epic portrayal of a working-class family in 1980s Glasgow – win the 2020 Booker Prize, while Kirsten Innes' (b 1980) first book *Fishnet* – a thought-provoking exploration of the underworld of the sex worker (soon to become a TV drama) – won the Guardian's 2015 Not the Booker Prize. Her much anticipated second novel, *Scabby Queen* (2020), takes a brutally honest look at the state of contemporary Scotland.

The Scottish crime-writing charts are topped by Val McDermid (b 1955), Ian Rankin (b 1960) and Denise Mina (b 1966). McDermid's novels feature private investigator Kate Brannigan and psychologist Tony Hill – *Wire in the Blood* became a successful TV series – while Mina's novel *The Long Drop* won the McIlvanney Prize for Scottish Crime Novel of the Year in 2017. Rankin's Edinburgh-based crime novels, featuring the hard-drinking, introspective Detective Inspector John Rebus, are sinister, engrossing mysteries that explore the darker side of Scotland's capital city. There are now 24 Rebus novels, from *Knots and Crosses* (1987) to the latest, *A Song for the Dark Times* (2020). He has a growing international following (his books have been translated into 22 languages).

Music

Traditional Music

Scotland has always had a strong folk tradition. In the 1960s and 1970s Robin Hall and Jimmy MacGregor, the Corries and the hugely talented Ewan McColl worked the pubs and clubs up and down the country. The Boys of the Lough, headed by Shetland fiddler Aly Bain, was one of the first professional bands to promote the Celtic music of Scotland and Ireland. It was followed by the Battlefield Band, Alba, Capercaillie and others.

The Scots folk songs you'll often hear sung in pubs and at ceilidhs (p448) draw on Scotland's rich history. A huge number of them relate to the Jacobite rebellions in the 18th century and, in particular, to Bonnie Prince Charlie – 'Hey Johnnie Cope', the 'Skye Boat Song' and 'Will Ye No Come Back Again', for example – while others relate to the Covenanters and the Highland Clearances.

In recent years there has been a revival in traditional music, often adapted and updated for the modern age. Bands such as Runrig pioneered with their own brand of Gaelic rock, while Shooglenifty blend Scottish folk music with anything from indie rock to electronica, producing a hybrid that has been called 'acid croft'.

But perhaps the finest modern renderings of traditional Scottish songs come from singer-songwriter Eddi Reader, who rose to fame with the band Fairground Attraction and its 1988 hit 'Perfect'. Her album *Eddi Reader Sings the Songs of Robert Burns* (2009) is widely regarded as one of the best interpretations of Burns' works.

Bagpipes

The bagpipe is one of the oldest musical instruments still in use today. Although no piece of film footage on Scotland is complete without the drone of the pipes, their origin probably lies in the Middle East; when they first arrived in Scotland is unknown, but it was certainly premedieval.

The traditional Highland bagpipe consists of a leather bag held under the arm, kept inflated by blowing through the blowstick; the piper forces air through the pipes by squeezing the bag with the forearm. Three of the

The Traditional Music & Song Association (www.tmsa. scot) website has listings of folk music, dance and cultural festivals around Scotland.

pipes, known as drones, play a constant note (one bass, two tenor) in the background; the fourth pipe, the chanter, plays the melody.

Highland soldiers were traditionally accompanied into battle by the skirl of the pipes, and the Scottish Highland bagpipe is unique in being the only musical instrument ever to be classed as a weapon. The playing of the pipes was banned – under pain of death – by the British government in 1747 as part of a scheme to suppress Highland culture in the wake of the Jacobite uprising of 1745. The pipes were revived when the Highland regiments were drafted into the British Army towards the end of the 18th century.

Bagpipe music may not be to everyone's taste, but Scotland's most famous instrument has been reinvented by bands like the Red Hot Chilli Pipers (https://rhcp.scot), who use pipes, drums, guitars and keyboards to create rock versions of trad tunes. They feature regularly at festivals throughout the country.

Ceilidhs

The Gaelic word *ceilidh* (*kay*-lay) means 'visit'. A *ceilidh* was originally a social gathering in the house after the day's work was over, enlivened with storytelling, music and song. These days, a *ceilidh* means an evening of traditional Scottish entertainment, including music, song and dance. To find one, check the village noticeboard, or just ask at the local pub; visitors are always welcome to join in.

Rock & Pop

It would take an entire book to list all the Scottish artists and bands that have made it big in the world of rock and pop. From Glasgow-born King of Skiffle, Lonnie Donegan, in the 1950s, to the chart-topping Dumfries DJ Calvin Harris today, the roll call is long and impressive, and only a few can be mentioned here.

The '90s saw the emergence of three bands that took the top three places in a 2005 vote for the best Scottish band of all time – melodic indie-pop songsters Belle and Sebastian, Brit-rock band Travis, and indie rockers Idlewild, who opened for the Rolling Stones in 2003. Scottish artists who have made an international impression in more recent times include Ayrshire rockers Biffy Clyro, indie rock group Frightened Rabbit, Glasgow synth-pop band Chvrches, and Edinburgh hip-hop trio Young Fathers.

The airwaves are awash with female singer-songwriters, but few are as gutsy and versatile as Edinburgh-born, St Andrews–raised KT Tunstall. Although she's been writing and singing since the late 1990s, it was her 2005 debut album *Eye to the Telescope* that introduced her to a wider audience. Others include Glasgow-born Amy Macdonald, who was only 20 years old when her first album *This Is the Life* (2007) sold three million copies – her latest is *The Human Demands* (2020) – and Karine Polwart, whose songs combine folk influences with modern themes and subjects.

Few male singer-songwriters are more popular than bespectacled twin brothers Craig and Charlie Reid, better known as The Proclaimers. Nine studio albums from 1987 to 2012 provided ample material for the hugely successful movie based on their music, *Sunshine on Leith* (2013).

But it's West Lothian–born Lewis Capaldi who has taken the world by storm. His million-selling debut album *Divinely Uninspired to a Hellish Extent* (2019) topped charts around the globe, and his single 'Someone You Loved' reached number one on the Billboard Hot 100.

Painting

Perhaps the most famous Scottish painting is the portrait of *Reverend Robert Walker Skating on Duddingston Loch* by Sir Henry Raeburn (1756–1823), held in the National Gallery of Scotland. This image of a Presbyterian minister at play beneath Arthur's Seat, with all the poise of a ballerina and

Scottish Pop Playlist

'Suddenly I See', KT Tunstall

'Letter from America', The Proclaimers

'This Is the Life', Amy Macdonald

'Someone You Loved', Lewis Capaldi

the hint of a smile on his lips, is a symbol of Enlightenment Edinburgh, the triumph of reason over wild nature. However, recent research has suggested it may not be the work of Raeburn after all, but may have been painted by French artist Henri-Pierre Danloux.

Scottish portraiture reached its peak during the Scottish Enlightenment in the second half of the 18th century with the paintings of Raeburn and his contemporary Allan Ramsay (1713–84), while Sir David Wilkie (1785–1841), whose genre paintings depicted scenes of rural Highland life, was one of the greatest artists of the 19th century.

In the early 20th century the Scottish painters most widely acclaimed outside the country were the group known as the Scottish Colourists – SJ Peploe (1871–1935), Francis Cadell (1883–1937), Leslie Hunter (1877–1931) and JD Fergusson (1874–1961) – whose striking paintings drew on French post-Impressionist and Fauvist influences. Peploe and Cadell, active in the 1920s and 1930s, often spent the summer painting together on the Isle of Iona, and reproductions of their beautiful landscapes and seascapes appear on many a print and postcard.

For a guide to Scottish film locations, check out www.scotlandthemovie.com.

Cinema

Perthshire-born John Grierson (1898–1972) is acknowledged around the world as the father of the documentary film. His legacy includes the classic *Drifters* (1929; about the Scottish herring fishery) and the Oscar-winning *Seawards the Great Ships* (1961; about Clyde shipbuilding). Writer-director Bill Forsyth (b 1946) is best known for *Local Hero* (1983), a gentle comedy about an oil magnate seduced by the beauty of the Highlands, and *Gregory's Girl* (1980), about an awkward teenage schoolboy's romantic exploits.

In the 1990s the rise of the director-producer-writer team of Danny Boyle (English), Andrew Macdonald and John Hodge (both Scottish), who wrote the scripts for *Shallow Grave* (1994), *Trainspotting* (1996) and *A Life Less Ordinary* (1997), marked the beginnings of what might be described as a home-grown Scottish film industry. A *Trainspotting* sequel, *T2: Trainspotting,* was released in 2017.

Other Scottish directorial talent includes Kevin Macdonald, who made *Touching the Void* (2003), *State of Play* (2009) and the award-winning documentary *Whitney* (2018); and Lynne Ramsay, who directed *Morvern Callar* (2002), the BAFTA-nominated *We Need To Talk About Kevin* (2011) and *You Were Never Really Here* (2017), which won Best Screenplay at Cannes.

Rob Roy (1995) is a witty and moving cinematic version of Sir Walter Scott's tale of the outlaw MacGregor – despite dodgy Scottish accents from Liam Neeson and Jessica Lange.

Architecture

The leading Scottish architects of the 18th century were William Adam (1684–1748) and his son Robert Adam (1728–92), whose revival of classical Greek and Roman forms influenced architects throughout Europe. Among the many neoclassical buildings they designed are Hopetoun House, Culzean Castle and Edinburgh's Charlotte Sq, possibly the finest example of Georgian architecture anywhere.

Alexander 'Greek' Thomson (1817–75) changed the face of 19th-century Glasgow with his neoclassical designs, while in Edinburgh, William Henry Playfair (1790–1857) continued Adam's tradition in the Greek temples of the National Monument on Calton Hill, the Royal Scottish Academy and the National Gallery of Scotland.

The 19th-century resurgence of interest in Scottish history and identity, led by writers such as Sir Walter Scott, saw architects turn to the towers, pointed turrets and crow-stepped gables of ancient castles for inspiration. The Victorian revival of the Scottish Baronial style, which first made an appearance in 16th-century buildings such as Craigievar Castle, produced many fanciful abodes such as Balmoral Castle, Scone Palace and Abbotsford.

Scotland's best known 20th-century architect and designer was Charles Rennie Mackintosh (1868–1928), one of the most influential exponents of the art nouveau style. His finest building is the Glasgow School of Art (1896), which still looks modern more than a century after it was built.

Sport

Many Scots are sports-mad and follow football or rugby with fierce dedication, identifying closely with local teams and individuals. The most popular games are football, rugby union, shinty, curling and golf, the last two of which the Scots claim to have invented.

Football

Football (soccer) in Scotland is not so much a sport as a religion, with thousands turning out to worship their local teams on Wednesdays and weekends throughout the season (August to May). Sacred rites include standing in the freezing cold of a February day, drinking hot Bovril and eating a Scotch pie as you watch your team getting gubbed.

Scotland's top 12 clubs play in the Scottish Premiership (www.spfl.co.uk), but two teams – Glasgow Rangers and Glasgow Celtic – have dominated the competition. On only 18 occasions since 1890 has a team other than Rangers or Celtic won the league; the last time was when Aberdeen won in 1985.

> Outlander's Scotland (2018) by Phoebe Taplin is an excellent companion for anyone interested in visiting Scottish locations featured in popular TV series.

Rugby Union

Traditionally, football was the sport of Scotland's urban working classes, while rugby union (www.scottishrugby.org) was the preserve of middle-class university graduates and farmers from the Borders. Although this distinction is breaking down – rugby's popularity soared after the 1999 World Cup was staged in the UK, and the middle classes have invaded the football terraces – it persists to some extent.

Each year, from January to March, Scotland takes part in the Six Nations Rugby Championship. The most important fixture is the clash against England for the Calcutta Cup – it's always an emotive event; Scotland won in 2018 and in Twickenham, London, in 2021.

At club level, the season runs from September to May, and among the better teams are those from the Borders such as Hawick, Kelso and Melrose. At the end of the season, teams play a rugby sevens (seven-a-side) variation of the 15-player competition.

Golf

Scotland is the home of golf. The game was probably invented here in the 12th century, and the world's oldest documentary evidence of a game being played (dating from 1456) was on Bruntsfield Links in Edinburgh.

Today there are more than 550 golf courses in Scotland – that's more per capita than in any other country (see www.scottishgolfcourses.com). The sport is hugely popular and much more egalitarian than in other countries, with lots of affordable, publicly owned courses. There are many world-famous championship courses, too, including Muirfield in East Lothian, Turnberry and Troon in Ayrshire, Carnoustie in Angus and St Andrews' Old Course in Fife.

> Curling, a winter sport that involves propelling a 19kg granite stone along the ice towards a target, was probably invented in Scotland in medieval times. For more information, see www.scottishcurling.org.

Highland Games

Highland games are held in Scotland throughout the summer, and not just in the Highlands. You can find dates and details of Highland games held all over the country on the Scottish Highland Games Association website (www.shga.co.uk).

The traditional sporting events are accompanied by piping and dancing competitions. Some events are peculiarly Scottish, particularly those that involve trials of strength: tossing the caber (heaving a tree trunk into the air), throwing the hammer and putting the stone. The biggest Highland games are staged at Dunoon, Oban and Braemar.

Natural Scotland

Visitors revel in rural Scotland's solitude and dramatic scenery. Soaring peaks, steely lochs, deep inlets, forgotten beaches and surging peninsulas evince astonishing geographic diversity. Scotland's wild places harbour Britain's most majestic wildlife, from the emblematic osprey to the red deer, its bellow reverberating among stands of native forest. Seals, dolphins and whales patrol the seas, islands moored in the Atlantic are havens for species long hunted to extinction further south, while the northern archipelagos clamour with seabird colonies of extraordinary magnitude.

The Land

Scotland's mainland divides neatly into three parts. The Southern Uplands, ranges of grassy rounded hills bounded by fertile coastal plains, occupy the south and are divided from the Lowlands by the Southern Uplands Fault.

The Central Lowlands lie in a broad band stretching from Glasgow and Ayr in the west to Edinburgh and Dundee in the east. This area is underlain by sedimentary rocks, including beds of coal that fuelled Scotland's Industrial Revolution. It's only a fifth of the nation by land area, but it has most of the country's industry, its two largest cities and 80% of the population.

Another geological divide – the Highland Boundary Fault – marks the southern edge of the Scottish Highlands. These hills, with most of their summits around 900m to 1000m, were scoured by ice-age glaciers, creating a series of deep, U-shaped valleys, some now flooded by the long, narrow sea lochs that today are such a feature of west Highland scenery. The Highlands form 60% of the Scottish mainland, and are cut in two by the Great Glen, a long, glacier-gouged valley running southwest to northeast.

Despite their pristine beauty, the wild, empty landscapes of the western and northern Highlands are artificial wildernesses. Before the Highland Clearances (p436) many of these empty corners of Scotland supported sizeable rural populations.

Offshore, some 900 islands are concentrated in four main groups: the Shetland Islands, the Orkney Islands, the Outer Hebrides and the Inner Hebrides.

Scotland accounts for one-third of the British mainland's surface area, but it has a massive 80% of Britain's coastline and only 10% of its population.

The Water

It rains a lot in Scotland – some parts of the western Highlands get over 4m of rainfall a year, compared to 2.3m in the Amazon Basin – so it's not surprising that there's plenty of water about. Around 3% of Scotland's land surface is fresh water. The numerous lochs, rivers and burns (streams) form the majority of this, but about a third is in the form of wetlands: the peat bogs and marshes that form a characteristic Highland and island landscape.

But it's salt water that really shapes the country. Including the islands, there's more than 10,000 miles of tortuous, complex Scottish shoreline.

Some 90% of Britain's surface fresh water is found in Scotland, and Loch Lomond is Britain's largest body of fresh water (by area).

WILDLIFE SAFARIS

If you're pushed for time, you can improve your chances of spotting wildlife by joining a 'wildlife safari'. Many operators around the country run full- or half-day 4x4 safaris searching for eagles, deer and other species, or operate boat trips to spot seals, dolphins, whales and seabirds.

Ecoventures (☎01381-600323; www.ecoventures.co.uk; Cromarty Harbour; adult/child £32/25)

Hebridean Whale Cruises (☎01445-712458; www.hebridean-whale-cruises.com; Pier Rd; ⊙Apr-Oct)

Highland Safaris (☎01887-820071; www.highlandsafaris.net; ⊙9am-5pm; ♿)

Nature Scotland (☎07743 956380; www.naturescotland.com)

Hebridean Adventures (☎07871 463755; www.hebrideanadventures.co.uk; 22 North B; adult/child £120/90; ⊙Apr-Sep)

Mammals

While the Loch Ness monster still hogs headlines, Scotland's wild places harbour a wide variety of animals, including red deer, otters and 75% of Britain's red squirrels.

Other small mammals include the Orkney vole and various bats, as well as stoats and weasels. The mountain hare swaps a grey-brown summer coat for a pure-white winter one.

Rarer beasts slaughtered to the point of near-extinction in the 19th century include pine martens, polecats and Scottish wildcats. Populations of these are small and remote but, except for the wildcat, are slowly recovering.

Of course, most animals you'll see will be in fields or obstructing you on single-track roads. Several indigenous sheep varieties are still around, smaller and stragglier than the purpose-bred supermodels to which we're accustomed. Other emblematic domestic animals include the Shetland pony and the gentle Highland cow, with its broad horns and shaggy reddish-brown coat and fringe.

The waters are rich in marine mammals. Dolphins and porpoises are fairly common, and in summer minke whales are regular visitors. Orcas are regularly sighted around Shetland and Orkney. Seals are widespread. Both the Atlantic grey and common seal are easily seen on coasts and islands.

One of the best-loved pieces of Scottish wildlife writing is *Ring of Bright Water* (1960) by Gavin Maxwell, in which the author describes life on the remote Glenelg peninsula with his two pet otters in the 1950s.

Birds

Scotland has an immense variety of birds. For birdwatchers, Shetland is paradise – 21 of the British Isles' 24 seabird species are found here, breeding in huge colonies. Being entertained by the puffins' clownish antics is a highlight for visitors.

Large numbers of red grouse – a popular game bird – graze the heather on the moors. The ptarmigan plays the Arctic trick of changing its plumage from mottled brown in summer to dazzling white in winter. In heavily forested areas you may see the capercaillie, a black, turkey-like bird that is the largest member of the grouse family. Millions of greylag geese winter on Lowland stubble fields.

The Royal Society for the Protection of Birds (RSPB; www.rspb.org.uk) is very active in Scotland. Several species have been successfully reintroduced, and the populations of other precariously placed species have stabilised, including those of ospreys (absent for most of the 20th century), golden eagles, white-tailed eagles, peregrine falcons and hen harriers.

Scottish Natural Heritage (www.nature.scot) is the government agency responsible for the conservation of Scotland's wildlife, habitats and landscapes. A key initiative is to reverse biodiversity loss.

National Parks

Scotland has two national parks – Loch Lomond and the Trossachs, and the Cairngorms. There's a huge range of other protected areas: 43 national nature reserves (www.nnr.scot) span the country, and there are also marine areas under various levels of protection.

Environmental Issues

Scotland's abundance of wind and water means the government hasn't had to look far for sources of renewable energy. The ambitious grand plan is to reach net zero carbon emissions by 2045, and things are going to plan with 90% of electricity generation coming from renewable sources by early 2020, and a solid commitment to reject fracking and nuclear power.

FIVE ICONIC SCOTTISH SPECIES

Red Deer

The red deer, Britain's largest land animal, is present in large numbers in Scotland. You're bound to see them if you spend any time in the Highlands; in winter especially, harsh weather will force them down into the glens to crop the roadside verges. The most spectacular time to spot them is during the rutting season (late September and October), when stags roar and clash antlers in competition for females.

Best places to spot Jura, Rum, Torridon, Galloway

Golden Eagle

Perhaps the most majestic wildlife sight on moor and mountain is the golden eagle, which uses its 2m wingspan to soar on rising thermals as it hunts for its favourite prey, the mountain hare. Almost all of the 400-or-so pairs known to nest in the UK are to be found in the Scottish Highlands and islands, as they prefer remote glens and open moorland well away from human habitation.

Best places to spot Harris, Skye, Rum, Mull

Red Squirrel

Scotland's woods are home to 75% of Britain's red-squirrel population; in most of the rest of the UK they've been pushed out by the dominant grey squirrel, introduced from North America. The greys often carry a virus that's lethal to the reds, so measures are in place to try to prevent their further encroachment.

Best places to spot Galloway Forest Park, Glen Affric, Perthshire, Rothiemurchus

Otter

From a low point in the late 20th century, when the population was decimated by hunting, pollution and habitat loss, otters have made a comeback and are now widespread in Scotland. They frequent fresh and salt water but are easiest to spot along the coast, where they time their foraging to coincide with an ebbing tide (river otters tend to be nocturnal).

Best places to spot Orkney, Shetland, Skye, Outer Hebrides; the piers at Kyle of Lochalsh and Portree are otter hotspots, as they've learned to scavenge from fishing boats

Scottish Wildcat

Trapping, hunting, habitat loss and interbreeding with feral domestic cats have made the Scottish wildcat Britain's most endangered mammal; it's thought that fewer than 400 pure-bred individuals survive. It hunts around the edges of woodland at dawn and dusk and is very wary of humans; seeing one in the wild is extremely rare.

Best places to spot Angus Glens, Strathpeffer area, Highland Wildlife Park (in captivity)

Golden eagle (p453)

Though a major goal is to halt a worrying decline in biodiversity, climate change is a huge threat to existing species. Temperature rises would leave plenty of mountain plants and creatures with no place to go; a steady decline in Scotland's seabird population is also surmised to have been partly caused by the effects of a temperature-induced decrease in plankton on fish numbers.

The main cause, however, of the worrying level of fish stocks is clear: we've eaten them all. In 2010 the *Marine (Scotland) Act* was passed. It's a compromise solution that tries to both protect vulnerable marine stocks and sustain the flagging fishing industry, which is pinning its hopes on Brexit freeing it from the EU's Common Fisheries Policy.

Survival Guide

Directory A–Z

Accessible Travel

Travellers with disabilities will find a strange mix of accessibility and inaccessibility in Scotland. Most new buildings are accessible to wheelchair users, so modern hotels and tourist attractions are fine. However, most B&Bs and guesthouses are in hard-to-adapt older buildings, which means that travellers with mobility problems may pay more for accommodation. Things are constantly improving, though.

It's a similar story with public transport. Newer buses have steps that lower for easier access, as do trains, but it's wise to check before setting out. Tourist attractions usually reserve parking spaces near the entrance for drivers with disabilities.

Many places such as ticket offices and banks are fitted with hearing loops to assist the hearing-impaired; look for a posted symbol of a large ear.

An increasing number of tourist attractions have audio guides. Some have Braille guides or scented gardens for the visually impaired.

Download Lonely Planet's free Accessible Travel guides from https://shop.lonelyplanet.com/categories/accessible-travel.

VisitScotland (www.visitscotland.com/accommodation/accessible) Details accessible accommodation; many tourist offices have leaflets with accessibility details for their area. Also produces the guide *Accessible Scotland* for travellers using wheelchairs. Many regions have organisations that hire out wheelchairs; contact the local tourist office for details. Many nature trails have been adapted for wheelchair use.

Disability Rights UK (www.disabilityrightsuk.org) An umbrella organisation for voluntary groups for people with disabilities. Many wheelchair-accessible toilets can be opened only with a special Royal Association of Disability & Rehabilitation (Radar) key, which can be obtained via the website or from tourist offices for £5.70.

Disabled Persons Railcard (www.disabledpersons-railcard.co.uk) Discounted train travel. Costs £20.

Tourism for All (📞0845 124 9971; www.tourismforall.org.uk) Publishes regional information guides for travellers with disabilities and can offer general advice.

Children

Scotland offers a range of child-friendly accommodation and activities suitable for families.

It's worth asking in tourist offices for local family-focused publications. *The List* magazine (available at newsagents and bookshops) has a section on children's activities and events in and around Glasgow and Edinburgh.

The **National Trust for Scotland** (📞0131-458 0200; www.nts.org.uk; annual membership adult/family £61.20/114) and **Historic Environment Scotland** (HES; 📞0131-668 8999; www.historicenvironment.scot; annual membership adult/adult with children/family £58/63/106) organise family-friendly activities at their properties throughout summer.

Children are generally well received around Scotland, and every area has some child-friendly attractions and B&Bs. Even dryish local museums usually make an effort with an activity sheet or child-focused information panels.

More hotels and guesthouses these days provide child-friendly facilities, including cots. Many restaurants (especially the larger ones) have high chairs and decent children's menus.

See also Lonely Planet's *Travel with Children*.

Customs Regulations

Britain had a two-tier customs system: one for goods bought duty-free outside the EU; the other for goods bought in another EU country where tax and duty is paid. After leaving the EU in 2020, changes are expected to these arrangements.

For the latest go to www.gov.uk/duty-free-goods.

Duty-free The duty-free limit for goods includes 200 cigarettes or equivalent in cigars, 4L of wine, 1L of spirits and other goods worth up to £390.

Tax and duty on imports Customs officials use the following guidelines to distinguish personal use from commercial imports from the EU: 800 cigarettes, 200 cigars, 10L of spirits, 90L of wine and 110L of beer. Still enough to have one hell of a party.

Discount Cards

Historic Sites

Membership of Historic Environment Scotland (HES) and/or the National Trust for Scotland (NTS) is worth considering, especially if you're going to be in Scotland for a while. Both are organisations dedicated to the preservation of the environment, and both care for hundreds of spectacular sites. You can join at any of their properties.

Historic Environment Scotland (HES; ☎0131-668 8999; www.historicenvironment.scot; annual membership adult/adult with children/family £58/63/106) This organisation cares for hundreds of sites of historical importance. Membership gives free entry to HES sites (half-price entry to sites in England and Wales). Also offers a short-term Explorer Pass – valid for seven consecutive days for £40. It can be great value, particularly if you visit both Edinburgh and Stirling Castles.

National Trust for Scotland (☎0131-458 0200; www.nts.org.

uk; annual membership adult/family £61.20/114) NTS looks after hundreds of sites of historical, architectural or environmental importance. Membership offers free access to all NTS and National Trust properties (in the rest of the UK). If you're aged 16 to 24, it's a great deal at only £33.

Hostel Cards

If travelling on a budget, membership of **Hostelling Scotland** (HS; ☎01786-891400; www.hostellingscotland.org.uk; annual membership 26yr & over/25yr & under £15/6, life membership £150) is a must.

Senior Cards

Discount cards for those over 60 years of age are available for train travel (p466).

Student & Youth Cards

The most useful card is the International Student Identity Card (www.isic.org), which displays your photo. It gives you discounted entry to many attractions and on many forms of transport.

Electricity

Type G
230V/50Hz

Health

➔ If you're an EU citizen, your European Health Insurance Card (EHIC) may no longer cover you for medical treatment in the UK from 1 January 2021 onward; make sure you have travel insurance that covers the duration of your trip.

➔ Citizens from non-EU countries should find out if there is a reciprocal arrangement for free medical care between their country and the UK. Australian travellers are eligible for free essential health care, for example.

➔ If you do need health insurance, make sure you get a policy that covers you for the worst possible scenarios, including emergency flights home.

➔ No jabs (vaccinations) are required to travel to Scotland.

Ticks & Lyme Disease

Ticks are tiny invertebrates (barely 1mm or 2mm across) that feed on the blood of sheep, deer and, occasionally, humans. They lurk amid vegetation and clamber on as you brush past; then they find a spot of bare flesh and tuck in. Their bites are painless and, for the most part, harmless (they will drop off once full). But a small percentage of ticks are known to transmit Lyme disease, a potentially serious infection.

Ticks occur all over Scotland in woodlands, moorlands and long grass, but mainly in the wetter areas of the western Highlands. They are active mainly between March and October. Tips for avoiding ticks include sticking to paths, wearing long trousers tucked into socks, and using insect repellent. Check yourself (and your children and pets) for ticks after hiking, especially around the hairline, in the navel, groin and armpits, between the toes, and behind the ears and knees. Outdoor shops sell plastic tick-removal tools.

More information: www.mountaineering. scot/safety-and-skills/ health-and-hygiene/ticks.

Insurance

Insurance covers you not only for medical expenses, theft and loss but also for cancellation of, or delays in, any of your travel arrangements.

Lots of bank accounts give their holders automatic travel insurance – check if this is the case for you.

Always read the small print carefully. Some policies specifically exclude 'dangerous activities', such as scuba diving, motorcycling, skiing, mountaineering and even trekking.

There's a variety of policies, and your travel agent can give recommendations. Make sure the policy includes healthcare and medication in the countries you may visit on your way to/ from Scotland.

You may prefer a policy that pays doctors or hospitals directly rather than forcing you to pay on the spot and claim the money

back later. If you have to claim later, make sure you keep all documentation. Some policies ask you to call back (reverse charges) to a centre in your home country, where an immediate assessment of your problem will be made.

Not all policies cover ambulances, helicopter rescue or emergency flights home. Most policies exclude cover for pre-existing illnesses.

Worldwide travel insurance is available at www. lonelyplanet.com/travel-insurance. You can buy, extend and claim online anytime – even if you're already on the road.

Internet Access

➡ 3G and 4G mobile broadband coverage is good in urban areas, but limited or sometimes nonexistent in rural areas. 5G is on its way but is currently not widespread.

➡ EU citizens can currently use their own mobile/ cellphone data roaming allowance in the UK for no charge. This may change after Brexit, however, so check before you travel.

➡ Travellers from non-EU countries will usually incur

high roaming charges – so buy a local SIM card or stick to wi-fi networks.

➡ Most hotels, B&Bs, hostels, stations, libraries and coffee shops (even some trains and buses) offer wi-fi access.

➡ Internet cafes are now very few and far between. If you're stuck, public libraries often have computers with free internet access.

Language Courses

Scotland is a popular place to learn English, and there are numerous places to do it. Dedicated language academies offer intensive tuition at a price and can also arrange accommodation in residences or with local families. Much cheaper are colleges, some of which even offer free English classes for foreigners.

A good resource to start you off is the English UK Scotland (www.englishukscotland.com) website, which has details of many colleges and language schools, mostly in Edinburgh and Glasgow.

Legal Matters

➡ The 1707 Act of Union preserved the Scottish legal system as separate from the law in England and Wales.

➡ Police have the power to detain, for up to 24 hours, anyone suspected of having committed an offence punishable by imprisonment (including drug offences).

➡ If you need legal assistance, contact the **Scottish Legal Aid Board** (☑0131-226 7061; www.slab. org.uk; 91 Haymarket Tce).

➡ Possession of cannabis is illegal, with a spoken warning for first offenders with small amounts. Fines and prison sentences apply for repeat offences and larger quantities.

MIDGES

If you've never been to the Scottish Highlands and islands before, be prepared for an encounter with dreaded midges. These tiny, 2mm-long blood-sucking flies appear in huge swarms in summer, and can completely ruin a holiday if you're not prepared to deal with them.

They proliferate from late May to mid-September, but especially mid-June to mid-August – which unfortunately coincides with the main tourist season – and are most common in the western and northern Highlands. Midges are at their worst during the twilight hours, and on still, overcast days – strong winds and bright sunshine tend to discourage them.

The only way to combat them is to cover up, particularly in the evening. Wear long-sleeved, light-coloured clothing (midges are attracted to dark colours) and, most importantly, use a reliable insect repellent.

Possession of harder drugs is much more serious. Police have the right to search anyone they suspect of possessing drugs.

LGBTIQ+ Travellers

Although most Scots are tolerant of homosexuality, couples overtly displaying affection away from ac-knowledged 'gay' venues or districts may encounter disapproval.

Edinburgh and Glasgow have small but flourishing gay scenes. *Scene Alba* (www.scenealba.co.uk) is a monthly magazine covering queer culture in Scotland, with listings of gay-friendly pubs and clubs in Edinburgh and Glasgow.

Maps

If you're going to do some hill walking, you'll require maps with far greater detail than the free maps supplied by tourist offices. The Ord-nance Survey (OS) caters to walkers, with a wide variety of maps at scales of 1:50,000 and 1:25,000. Alternatively, look out for the excellent walkers maps published by Harvey; they're at scales of 1:40,000 and 1:25,000.

Money

ATMs

ATMs (called cashpoints in Scotland) are widespread and you'll usually find at least one in small towns and villages. You can use Visa, Mastercard, Amex, Cirrus, Plus and Maestro to withdraw cash from ATMs belonging to most banks and building societies in Scotland.

Cash withdrawals from some ATMs may be subject to a small charge, but most are free. If you're not from the UK, your home bank will

likely charge you for with-drawing money overseas – it pays to be aware of how much, as it may be much better to withdraw larger amounts less often.

If there's no ATM, it's often possible to get 'cash back' at a hotel or shop in remote areas – ie make a payment by debit card and get some cash back (the cash amount is added to the transaction).

Credit & Debit Cards

Credit and debit cards can be used almost everywhere except for some B&Bs that only accept cash. Make sure bars or restaurants will accept cards before you order, as some don't. The most popular cards are Visa and Mastercard; American Express is only accepted by the major chains, and virtually no one will accept Diners or JCB. Chip-and-PIN is the norm for card trans-actions; only a few places will accept a signature. Contactless card payments (up to £45) are now widely accepted.

Moneychangers

Be careful using bureaux de change; they may offer good exchange rates but frequently levy outrageous commissions and fees. The best-value places to change money in the UK tend to be travel agents. A handy tool for finding the best rates is the website http://travel-money.moneysavingexpert.com/buy-back.

You'll normally find bet-ter rates in London than in Scotland, so do your chang-ing there if you're visiting that city first.

Banks, post offices and some of the larger hotels will change cash and travel-lers cheques.

Opening Hours

Hours may vary throughout the year; in rural areas many places have shorter hours

EATING PRICE RANGES

The following price ranges refer to the average price of a main course from the dinner menu.

£ less than £12

££ £12–22

£££ more than £22

from around October to April. In the Highlands and islands, Sunday opening is restricted.

Banks 9.30am–4pm Monday to Friday, some to 1pm Saturday.

Nightclubs 9pm–1am Thursday to Saturday.

Post offices 9am–6pm Monday to Friday, to 12.30pm Saturday.

Pubs 11am–11pm Monday to Thursday, to 1am Friday and Saturday, 12.30–11pm Sunday; lunch noon–2.30pm, dinner 6–9pm daily.

Restaurants Lunch noon–2.30pm, dinner 6–9pm.

Shops 9am–5.30pm Monday to Saturday, often 11am–5pm Sunday.

Post

The **UK Post Office** (www.postoffice.co.uk) is a reliable service with a network of dedicated mail centres as well as shops with post-of-fice facilities. Mail sent within the UK can go either 1st or 2nd class. First-class mail is faster (there's nor-mally next-day delivery) and slightly more expensive.

Public Holidays

Although bank holidays are general public holidays in the rest of the UK, in Scotland they only apply to banks and some other com-mercial offices.

Scottish towns normally have four days of public

PRACTICALITIES

Radio Find out what's hitting the headlines on BBC Radio Scotland (www.bbc.co.uk/radioscotland) by listening to *Good Morning Scotland* from 6am to 9am weekdays.

Newspapers Leaf through Edinburgh's *Scotsman* (www.scotsman.com) or Glasgow's *Herald* (www.heraldscotland.com), or the independence-supporting *National* (www.thenational.scot). Have a giggle at rival tabloids the *Daily Record* and the *Scottish Sun*, or try the old-fashioned *Sunday Post* for a nostalgia trip.

TV Watch BBC1 Scotland, BBC2 Scotland and ITV stations STV or Border. Channels Four and Five are UK-wide channels with unchanged content for Scotland. BBC Scotland is dedicated to Scottish content, and BBC Alba broadcasts in Scottish Gaelic.

Smoking In Scotland you can't smoke in any public place that has a roof and is at least half enclosed. That means pubs, bus shelters, restaurants and hotels – basically, anywhere you might want to smoke.

Weights and Measures Scotland uses the metric system for weights and measures, with the exception of road distances (in miles) and beer (in pints). The pint is 568mL, more than the US version.

holiday, which they allocate themselves; dates vary from year to year and from town to town. Most places celebrate St Andrew's Day (30 November) as a public holiday.

General public holidays:

New Year 1 and 2 January

Good Friday March or April

Christmas Day 25 December

Boxing Day 26 December

Telephone

Phone booths are a rarity these days, but can be useful in remote areas with a poor or nonexistent mobile-phone signal. You'll mainly see two types: one takes money (and doesn't give change), while the other uses prepaid phonecards and credit cards. Some phones accept both coins and cards. Payphone cards are widely available.

The cheapest way of calling internationally is via the internet, or by buying a discount-call card. You'll see these in newsagents, along with tables of countries and the number of minutes you'll get for your money.

Mobile Phones

The UK uses the GSM 900/1800 network, which covers the rest of Europe, Australia and New Zealand but isn't compatible with the North American GSM 1900 network. Most modern mobiles can function on both networks, but check before you leave home just in case.

The UK's decision to leave the EU (aka 'Brexit') means that British networks will eventually be able to charge for roaming in Europe, and EU network subscribers will have to pay roaming fees once again when visiting the UK. However, the EU roaming agreement should remain in force until at least 2021.

Unless you have a global roaming deal, it will be cheaper to get a UK number. Make sure your phone is unlocked before you depart, then pick up a SIM on arrival. Alternatively, consider a cheap pay-as-you-go phone (aka a 'burner' phone) with a local SIM card (from £20 including calling credit) for local calls, using your own phone where you can access free wi-fi (ie cafes, museums and your accommodation). Operators offer a variety of packages that include UK calls, messages and data; a month's worth will typically cost around £20.

Though things are improving, coverage in Highland and island areas can be sketchy; don't rely 100% on mobile data.

Phone Codes & Useful Numbers

Dialling the UK Dial your country's international access code, then 44 (the UK country code), then the area code (dropping the first 0) followed by the telephone number.

Dialling out of the UK The international access code is 00; dial this, then add the code of the country you wish to dial.

Making a reverse-charges (collect) international call Dial 155 for the operator. It's an expensive option, but not for the caller.

Area codes in Scotland Begin with 01; eg Edinburgh 0131, Wick 01955.

Directory assistance There are several numbers; 118500 is one.

Mobile phones Codes usually begin with 07.

Free calls Numbers starting with 0800 or 0808 are free; calls to 0845 numbers are charged at local rates.

Time

Scotland is on UTC/GMT +1 hour during summer daylight-saving time (late March to late October) and UTC/GMT +0 the rest of the year.

Toilets

➡ Public toilets are increasingly uncommon but still found in larger cities.

➡ Usually free, but some charge a small fee.

Tourist Information

The Scottish Tourist Board is known as VisitScotland (www.visitscotland.com). You can request regional brochures to be posted out to you, or download them from the website.

Only a handful of larger towns have tourist offices ('information centres', or 'iCentres') that open from 9am or 10am to 4pm or 5pm Monday to Friday, and at weekends in summer. In smaller places, particularly in the Highlands, tourist offices only open from Easter to September.

If you want to email a tourist office, it's [insert-townname]@visitscotland.com.

Visas

➡ If you're a citizen of the EEA (European Economic Area) nations or Switzerland, you don't need a visa to enter or work in Britain – you can enter using your national identity card.

➡ Visa regulations are always subject to change, which is especially likely

after Britain's exit from the EU from 1 January 2021, so it's essential to check before leaving home.

➡ Currently, if you're a citizen of Australia, Canada, New Zealand, Japan, Israel, the US and several other countries, you can stay for up to six months (no visa required) but are not allowed to work.

➡ Nationals of many countries, including South Africa, will need to obtain a visa: for more info, see www.gov.uk/check-uk-visa.

➡ The Youth Mobility Scheme, for Australian, Canadian, Japanese, Hong Kong, Monégasque, New Zealand, South Korean and Taiwanese citizens aged 18 to 31, allows working visits of up to two years but must be applied for in advance.

➡ Commonwealth citizens with a UK-born parent may be eligible for a Certificate of Entitlement to the Right of Abode, which entitles them to live and work in the UK.

➡ Commonwealth citizens with a UK-born grandparent could qualify for a UK Ancestry Employment Certificate, allowing them to work full time for up to five years in the UK.

➡ British immigration authorities have always been tough; dress neatly and carry proof that you have sufficient funds with which to support yourself. A credit card and/or an onward ticket will help.

Volunteering

Various organisations offer volunteering opportunities in Scotland, with conservation, organic-farming and animal-welfare projects to the fore.

Women Travellers

Solo women travellers are likely to feel safe in Scotland.

The contraceptive pill is available only on prescription; however, the 'morning-after' pill (effective against conception for up to 72 hours after unprotected sexual intercourse) is available over the counter at chemists.

Work

Whatever your skills, it's worth registering with a number of temporary employment agencies; there are plenty in the cities.

Low-paid seasonal work is available in the tourist industry, usually in restaurants and pubs.

From 1 January 2021 a new immigration system applies to people arriving in the UK, and EU citizens moving to the UK to work will need to get a work visa in advance.

The Youth Mobility scheme allows working visits for some foreign nationals.

Transport

GETTING THERE & AWAY

Flights, cars and tours can be booked online at www.lonely-planet.com/bookings.

Entering the Country

Entering or leaving the UK was straightforward and hassle-free prior to 'Brexit' and the Covid-19 pandemic, save for the occasional inconvenience of long queues at passport control and security.

Since 2020, things have changed, with a range of testing and quarantining restrictions. Check www.gov.uk/uk-border-control for up-to-date information direct from the UK government.

EU, EEA and Swiss citizens will continue to be able to travel to the UK for holidays or short trips without needing a visa. You'll be able to cross the UK border using a valid passport, but not an identity card.

Air

There are direct flights to Scottish airports from other parts of the UK, lots of European countries, the Middle East, the US and Canada. From elsewhere, you'll probably have to fly into a European or Middle Eastern hub and get a connecting flight to a Scottish airport – London has the most connections. This will often be a cheaper option anyway if flying in from North America.

Airports

Scotland has four main international airports: Aberdeen, Edinburgh, Glasgow and Glasgow Prestwick, with a few short-haul international flights landing at Inverness. London is the main UK gateway for long-haul flights. Sumburgh on Shetland has summer service from Norway.

Aberdeen Airport (☎0344 481 6666; www.aberdeenairport.com) Located at Dyce, 6 miles northwest of the city centre. There are regular flights to numerous Scottish and UK destinations, including London and Belfast, and international flights to several European countries.

Edinburgh Airport (EDI; ☎0844 448 8833; www.edinburghairport.com) Eight miles west of the city, this airport has numerous flights to other parts of Scotland and the UK, Ireland and mainland Europe, as well as long-haul flights to the US, Canada, the UAE and Qatar.

Glasgow Airport (GLA; ☎0344-481 5555; www.glasgowairport.com; ☎) Glasgow's principal airport offers connections all over Scotland, Britain and Europe. Long-haul destinations include the US, Canada and Dubai.

Glasgow Prestwick Airport (PIK; ☎0871-223 0700; www.glasgowprestwick.com; ☎) Southwest of Glasgow near Ayr, this airport is a Ryanair hub serving mainly holiday destinations in southern Europe.

Inverness Airport (INV; ☎01667-464000; www.invernessairport.co.uk) At Dalcross, east of the city, this airport has direct flights to several British and Western European destinations.

London Gatwick (www.gatwickairport.com) London's second airport, with numerous flights to Scotland.

London Heathrow (www.heathrow.com) Britain's principal international airport.

Land

Bus

Buses are usually the cheapest way to get to Scotland from other parts of the UK.

Megabus (☎0141-352 4444; www.megabus.com) One-way fares from London to Glasgow from as little as £1 if you book well in advance. Has some fully reclinable sleeper services.

National Express (☎0871 781 8181; www.nationalexpress.com) Regular services from London and other cities in England and Wales to Glasgow and Edinburgh.

Scottish Citylink (☎0871 266 3333; www.citylink.co.uk) Daily service between Belfast and Glasgow and Edinburgh via Cairnryan ferry.

Car & Motorcycle

Drivers of EU-registered vehicles will find bringing a car or motorcycle into Scotland for up to six months straightforward, but check the latest situation before travelling.

The vehicle must have registration papers and a nationality plate, and you must have insurance. The International Insurance Certificate (Green Card) isn't compulsory, but it's excellent proof that you're covered.

If driving from mainland Europe via the Channel Tunnel or ferry ports, head for London and follow the M25 orbital road to the M1 motorway, then follow the M1 and M6 north.

Train

Travelling to Scotland by train is faster and usually more comfortable than the bus, but it's more expensive. Taking into account check-in and travel time between city centre and airport, the train is a competitive alternative to air travel from London.

The **National Rail Enquiry Service** (☎03457 48 49 50; www.nationalrail.co.uk) has timetable and fare info for all trains in Britain.

Avanti West Coast (www.avantiwestcoast.co.uk) Trains between London Euston and Glasgow (4½ hours, hourly).

Caledonian Sleeper (www.sleeper.scot) This is an overnight service connecting London Euston with Edinburgh, Glasgow, Stirling, Perth, Dundee, Aberdeen, Fort William and Inverness. There are two departures nightly from Sunday to Friday.

Crosscountry (☎03447 369 123; www.crosscountrytrains.co.uk) Trains from Wales, and central and southwest England to Glasgow, Edinburgh and Aberdeen.

Eurostar (www.eurostar.com) You can travel from Paris or Brussels to London in around two hours on the Eurostar service. From St Pancras, it's a quick and easy change to Kings Cross or Euston for trains to Edinburgh or Glasgow.

LNER (www.lner.co.uk) Trains between London Kings Cross and Edinburgh (4½ hours, every half-hour).

TransPennine Express (www.tpexpress.co.uk) Trains from Manchester to Glasgow and Edinburgh.

Sea

Car-ferry links between Northern Ireland and Scotland are operated by **Stena Line** (☎03447 70 70 70; www.stenaline.co.uk) and **P&O** (www.poferries.com). Stena Line travels the Belfast–Cairnryan route and P&O Irish Sea the Larne–Cairnryan route.

GETTING AROUND

Air

Most domestic air services are geared to business needs, or are lifelines for remote island communities. Flying is a pricey way to cover relatively short distances, but it's certainly worth considering if you're short of time and want to visit the Outer Hebrides, Orkney or Shetland.

Airlines in Scotland

Loganair (☎0344 800 2855; www.loganair.co.uk) The main domestic airline in Scotland, with flights from Glasgow to Inverness, Campbeltown, Islay, Tiree, Barra, Benbecula, Stornoway, Kirkwall and Sumburgh; from Edinburgh to Campbeltown, Islay, Tiree, Barra, Stornoway, Kirkwall and Sumburgh; from Aberdeen to Inverness, Kirkwall and Sumburgh; from Inverness to Benbecula, Stornoway, Kirkwall and Sumburgh; and from Stornoway to Benbecula. It also operates inter-island flights in Orkney.

Hebridean Air Services (☎0845 805 7465; www.hebrideanair.co.uk; Oban Airport, North Connel) Flies from Connel airfield near Oban to the islands of Coll, Tiree, Colonsay and Islay.

Bicycle

Scotland is a compact country, and travelling around by bicycle is a perfectly feasible proposition if you have the time. Indeed, for touring the islands a bicycle is both cheaper than driving (for ferry fares) and more suited to the islands' small sizes and leisurely pace of life. For more information, see www.visitscotland.com/cycling and the Sustrans (www.sustrans.org.uk/national-cycle-network) pages about the National Cycle Network.

Boat

Caledonian MacBrayne (CalMac; ☑0800 066 5000; www.calmac.co.uk) Serves the west coast and islands. A comprehensive timetable booklet is available from tourist offices and online. There's a summer timetable and one for winter, when services are reduced. CalMac offers 30 Island Hopscotch tickets, giving reduced fares for various combinations of crossings; these are listed online and in the timetable booklet. Bicycles travel free with foot-passenger tickets.

Northlink Ferries (☑0845 6000 449; www.northlink ferries.co.uk) Ferries from Aberdeen and Scrabster (near Thurso) to Orkney, from Orkney to Shetland and from Aberdeen to Shetland.

Bus

Scotland is served by an extensive bus network that covers most of the country. In remote rural areas, however, services are geared to the needs of locals (getting to school or the shops in the nearest large town) and may not be conveniently timed for visitors.

First (www.firstgroup.com) Operates local bus routes in several parts of Scotland.

Scottish Citylink (www.citylink.co.uk) National network of comfy, reliable buses serving main towns. Away from main roads, you'll need to switch to local services.

Stagecoach (www.stagecoach-bus.com) Operates local bus routes in many parts of Scotland.

Bus Passes

National Entitlement Card (www.entitlementcard.org.uk) Available to seniors and people with disabilities who are Scottish citizens; allows free bus travel throughout the country. The youth version, for those aged 11 to 26, gives discounted travel, and Hostelling Scotland (HS) members receive a 20% discount on Scottish Citylink services. Students do, too, by registering online.

Scottish Citylink Explorer Pass Offers unlimited travel on Scottish Citylink services (and selected other bus routes) within Scotland for any three days out of five (£49), any five days out of 10 (£74) or any eight days out of 16 (£99). Also gives discounts on various regional bus services, on Northlink and CalMac ferries, and in HS hostels. Can be bought in the UK by both UK and overseas citizens.

Car & Motorcycle

Scotland's roads are generally good and are far less busy than those in England, making driving more enjoyable.

Motorways (designated 'M') are toll-free dual carriageways, limited mainly to central Scotland. Main roads ('A') are dual or single carriageways and are sometimes clogged with slow-moving trucks and caravans; the A9 from Perth to Inverness is notoriously busy.

Life on the road is more relaxed and interesting on the secondary roads (designated 'B') and minor roads (undesignated), though in the Highlands and islands there's the added hazard of sheep wandering onto the road (be particularly wary of lambs in spring).

Petrol is more expensive than in countries such as the US or Australia, but roughly in line with the rest of Western Europe. Prices tend to rise as you get further from the main centres and can be more than 10% higher in remote areas, where petrol stations are widely spaced and sometimes closed on Sundays.

Car Hire

Car hire in the UK is competitively priced by European standards, and shopping around online can unearth some great deals, which can drop to as low as £15 per day for an extended hire period. Hit comparison sites such as Kayak to find some of the best prices.

The minimum legal age for driving is 17, but to rent a car, drivers must usually be aged 23 to 65 – outside these limits special conditions or insurance requirements may apply.

If planning to visit the Outer Hebrides or Shetland, it'll often prove cheaper to hire a car on the islands rather than pay to take a hire car across on the ferry.

Avis (www.avis.co.uk)

Budget (www.budget.co.uk)

Europcar (www.europcar.co.uk)

Hertz (www.hertz.co.uk)

Sixt (www.sixt.co.uk)

Driving Licences

A non-UK licence is valid in Britain for up to 12 months from time of entry into the country. If bringing a car from Europe, make sure you're adequately insured.

Road Rules

The *Highway Code*, widely available in bookshops, and also online and downloadable at www.gov.uk/highway-code, details all UK road regulations.

➡ Vehicles drive on the left. Seat belts are compulsory if fitted; this technically applies to buses, too.

➡ The speed limit is 30mph (48km/h) in built-up areas, 60mph (96km/h) on single carriageways and 70mph (112km/h) on dual carriageways.

➡ Give way to your right at roundabouts (traffic already on the roundabout has right of way).

➡ Motorcyclists must wear helmets. They are not compulsory for cyclists.

➡ It is illegal to use a hand-held mobile phone or similar device while driving.

➡ The maximum permitted blood-alcohol level when driving is 50mg/100mL (22mg per 100mL of breath); this is lower than in the rest of the UK but equivalent to the limit in many other countries.

➡ Traffic offences (illegal parking, speeding etc) usually incur a fine for which you're given 30 to 60 days to pay. In Glasgow and Edinburgh the parking inspectors are numerous and without mercy – never leave your car around the city centres without a valid parking ticket, as you risk a hefty fine.

Hitching

Hitching is fairly easy in Scotland, except around big cities and in built-up areas, where you'll need to use public transport. Although the northwest is more difficult because there's less traffic, long waits are unusual (except on Sunday in 'Sabbath' areas). On some islands, where public transport is infrequent, hitching is so much a part of getting around that local drivers may stop and offer you lifts without your even asking.

> **SINGLE-TRACK ROADS**
>
> In many rural areas, especially in the Highlands and islands, you will find single-track roads that are only wide enough for one vehicle. Passing places (usually marked with a white diamond sign, or a black-and-white striped pole) are used to allow oncoming traffic to get by. Remember that passing places are also for overtaking – you must pull over to let faster vehicles pass. It's illegal to park in passing places.

It's against the law to hitch on motorways or their immediate slip roads; make a sign and use approach roads, nearby roundabouts or service stations.

Hitching is never entirely safe, however, and Lonely Planet doesn't recommend it. Travellers who hitch should understand that they are taking a small but potentially serious risk.

Tours

There are numerous companies in Scotland offering all kinds of tours, including historical, activity-based and backpacker tours. It's a question of picking the tour that suits your requirements and budget.

Discreet Scotland
(☑ 07989 416990; www.discreetscotland.com) Luxurious private tours in an upmarket 4WD that range from day trips from Edinburgh to full weeks staying in some of Scotland's finest hotels.

Timberbush Tours
(☑ 0131-226 6066; www.timberbush-tours.co.uk) Comfortable small-group minibus tours around Scotland, with Glasgow and Edinburgh departures.

Train

Scotland's train network extends to all major cities and towns, but the railway map has a lot of large, blank areas in the Highlands and the Southern Uplands where you'll need to switch to road transport. The West

Highland line from Glasgow to Fort William and Mallaig, and the Inverness to Kyle of Lochalsh line, offer two of the world's most scenic rail journeys.

National Rail Enquiry Service (www.nationalrail.co.uk) Lists timetables and fares for all trains in Britain.

ScotRail (www.scotrail.co.uk) Operates most train services in Scotland; its website has downloadable timetables.

Costs & Reservations

Train travel is more expensive than the bus, but it's usually more comfortable.

Reservations are recommended for intercity trips, especially on Fridays and public holidays. For shorter journeys, just buy a ticket at the station before you go. On certain routes, including the Glasgow–Edinburgh express, and in places where there's no ticket office at the station, you can buy tickets on the train.

Children under five travel free; those five to 15 years usually pay half-fare.

Bikes are carried free on all ScotRail trains, but space is sometimes limited. In 2020 ScotRail introduced Active Travel Carriages, with room for up to 20 bikes and recharging point for e-bikes, on the Glasgow–Oban–Fort William–Mallaig line. Bike reservations are compulsory on certain routes, including the Glasgow–Oban–Fort William–Mallaig line and the Inverness–Kyle of Lochalsh line; they're recommended on many others. You can

TRAIN FARES

The complex British train-ticketing system rewards advance planning, particularly on long routes. A one-way fare from London to Edinburgh, for example, can cost over £170, but a fare purchased well in advance, at off-peak times, can be as low as £40. Regional fares in Scotland have a lot less variation.

make reservations for your bicycle from eight weeks to two hours in advance at main stations, or when booking tickets by phone or online.

There's a bewilderingly complex labyrinth of ticket types. In general, the further ahead you book, the cheaper your ticket will be.

Advance Purchase Book by 6pm on the day before travel; cheaper than Anytime tickets.

Anytime Buy any time and travel any time, with no restrictions.

Off Peak There are time restrictions (you're not usually allowed to travel on a train that leaves before 9.15am); relatively cheap.

It's always worth checking the ScotRail website for current family or senior offers.

Discount Cards

Discount railcards are available for people aged 60 and over, for people aged 16 to 25 (or mature full-time students), for two over-16s travelling together, and for those with a disability.

The **Senior Railcard** (www.senior-railcard.co.uk; per year £30), **16-25 Railcard** (Young Persons Railcard; www.16-25railcard.co.uk; per year £30), **Two Together Railcard** (www.twotogether-railcard.co.uk; per year £30), **Family & Friends Railcard** (www.familyandfriends-railcard.co.uk; per year £30) and **Disabled Persons Railcard** (www.disabledpersons-railcard.co.uk; per year £20) are each valid for a year and give one-third off most train fares in Scotland, England and Wales.

You'll find they pay for themselves pretty quickly if you plan to take a couple of long-distance journeys or a handful of short-distance ones. Fill in an application at any major station. You'll need proof of age (birth certificate, passport or driving licence) for the 16-25 and Senior Railcards (proof of enrolment for mature-age students) and proof of entitlement for the Disabled Persons Railcard. You'll need a passport photo for all of them. You can also buy railcards online, but you'll need a UK address to have them sent to.

Train Passes

ScotRail (☎0344 811 0141; www.scotrail.co.uk) has a range of good-value passes for train travel. You can buy them online, by phone or at stations throughout Britain. Note that Travelpass and Rover tickets are not valid for travel on certain (eg commuter) services before 9.15am weekdays.

Central Scotland Rover Covers unlimited train travel between Glasgow, Edinburgh, North Berwick, Stirling and Fife. Costs £55 for three consecutive days.

Spirit of Scotland Travelpass Gives unlimited travel on all Scottish train services (with some restrictions), all CalMac ferry services and on certain Scottish Citylink coach services (on routes not covered by rail). It's available for four days' travel out of eight (£149) or eight days' out of 15 (£189).

Highland Rover Allows unlimited train travel from Glasgow to Oban, Fort William and Mallaig, and from Inverness to Kyle of Lochalsh, Aviemore, Aberdeen and Thurso. It also gives free travel on the Oban/Fort William–Inverness bus, on the Oban–Mull and Mallaig–Skye ferries, and on buses on Mull and Skye. It's valid for four days' travel out of eight (£95).

Scottish Grand Tour Allows unlimited train travel from Glasgow to Kyle of Lochalsh, Inverness and Edinburgh, and all stops in between. It's valid for four days' travel out of eight (£89).

Glossary

bag – reach the top of (as in to 'bag a couple of peaks' or 'Munro bagging')

bailey – the space enclosed by castle walls

birlinn – Hebridean galley

blackhouse – low-walled stone cottage with thatch or turf roof and earth floors; shared by both humans and cattle and typical of the Outer Hebrides until the early 20th century

böd – once a simple trading booth used by fishing communities, today it refers to basic accommodation for walkers etc

bothy – hut or mountain shelter

brae – hill

broch – defensive tower

burgh – town

burn – stream

cairn – pile of stones to mark path or junction; also peak

camanachd – Gaelic for *shinty*

ceilidh (*kay*-li) – evening of traditional Scottish entertainment including music, song and dance

Celtic high cross – a large, elaborately carved stone cross decorated with biblical scenes and Celtic interlace designs dating from the 8th to 10th centuries

chippy – fish-and-chip shop

Clearances – eviction of Highland farmers from their land by *lairds* wanting to use it for grazing sheep

Clootie dumpling – rich steamed pudding filled with currants and raisins

close – entrance to an alley

corrie – circular hollow on a hillside

craic – lively conversation

craig – exposed rock

crannog – an artificial island in a *loch* built for defensive purposes

crofting – smallholding in marginal agricultural areas following the Clearances

Cullen skink – soup made with smoked haddock, potato, onion and milk

dene – valley

dirk – dagger

dram – a measure of whisky

firth – estuary

gloup – natural arch

Hogmanay – Scottish celebration of New Year's Eve

howff – pub or shelter

HS – Historic Scotland

laird – estate owner

linn – waterfall

loch – lake

lochan – small *loch*

machair – grass- and wildflower-covered dunes

makar – maker of verses

Mercat Cross – a symbol of the trading rights of a market town or village, usually found in the centre of town and usually a focal point for the community

motte – early Norman fortification consisting of a raised, flattened mound with a keep on top; when attached to a *bailey* it is known as a motte-and-bailey

Munro – mountain of 3000ft (914m) or higher

Munro bagger – a hill walker who tries to climb all the *Munros* in Scotland

NNR – National Nature Reserve, managed by the *SNH*

NTS – National Trust for Scotland

nyvaig – Hebridean galley

OS – Ordnance Survey

Picts – early inhabitants of north and east Scotland (from Latin *pictus*, or 'painted', after their body paint decorations)

provost – mayor

RIB – rigid inflatable boat

rood – an old Scots word for a cross

RSPB – Royal Society for the Protection of Birds

Sassenach – from Gaelic 'Sasannach': anyone who is not a Highlander (including Lowland Scots)

shinty – fast and physical ball-and-stick sport similar to Ireland's hurling

SMC – Scottish Mountaineering Club

SNH – Scottish Natural Heritage, a government organisation directly responsible for safeguarding and improving Scotland's natural heritage

sporran – purse worn around waist with the kilt

SYHA – Scottish Youth Hostel Association

wynd – lane

GAELIC & NORSE PLACE NAMES

The Gaelic language has left a rich legacy of place names, often intermixed with Old Norse names brought by the Vikings who occupied the western and northern islands. The spellings may be Anglicised, but the meaning is usually still clear.

Gaelic Place Names

ach, auch	from *achadh* (field)
ard	from *ard* or *aird* (height, hill)
avon	from *abhainn* (river or stream)
bal	from *baile* (village or homestead)
ban	from *ban* (white, fair)
beg	from *beag* (small)
ben	from *beinn* (mountain)
buie	from *buidhe* (yellow)
dal	from *dail* (field or dale)
dow, dhu	from *dubh* (black)
drum	from *druim* (ridge or back)
dun	from *dun* or *duin* (fort or castle)
glen	from *gleann* (narrow valley)
gorm	from *gorm* (blue)
gower, gour	from *gabhar* (goat), eg Ardgour (height of the goats)
inch, insh	from *inis* (island, water-meadow or resting place for cattle)
inver	from *inbhir* (rivermouth or meeting of two rivers)
kil	from *cille* (church), eg Kilmartin (Church of St Martin)
kin, ken	from *ceann* (head), eg Kinlochleven (head of Loch Leven)
kyle, kyles	from *caol* or *caolas* (narrow sea channel)
more, vore	from *mor* or *mhor* (big), eg Ardmore (big height), Skerryvore (big reef)
strath	from *srath* (broad valley)
tarbert, tarbet	from *tairbeart* (portage), meaning a narrow neck of land between two bodies of water, across which a boat can be dragged
tay, ty	from *tigh* (house), eg Tyndrum (house on the ridge)
tober	from *tobar* (well), eg Tobermory (Mary's well)
tom	small hill

Norse Place Names

a, ay, ey	from *ey* (island)
bister, buster, bster	from *bolstaor* (dwelling place, homestead)
geo	from *gja* (chasm)
holm	from *holmr* (small island)
kirk	from *kirkja* (church)
pol, poll, bol	from *bol* (farm)
quoy	from *kvi* (sheep fold, cattle enclosure)
sker, skier, skerry	from *sker* (rocky reef)
ster, sett	from *setr* (house)
vig, vaig, wick	from *vik* (bay, creek)
voe, way	from *vagr* (bay, creek)

Behind the Scenes

SEND US YOUR FEEDBACK

We love to hear from travellers – your comments keep us on our toes and help make our books better. Our well-travelled team reads every word on what you loved or loathed about this book. Although we cannot reply individually to your submissions, we always guarantee that your feedback goes straight to the appropriate authors, in time for the next edition. Each person who sends us information is thanked in the next edition – the most useful submissions are rewarded with a selection of digital PDF chapters.

Visit **lonelyplanet.com/contact** to submit your updates and suggestions or to ask for help. Our award-winning website also features inspirational travel stories, news and discussions.

Note: We may edit, reproduce and incorporate your comments in Lonely Planet products such as guidebooks, websites and digital products, so let us know if you don't want your comments reproduced or your name acknowledged. For a copy of our privacy policy visit lonelyplanet.com/privacy.

WRITER THANKS

Isabel Albiston

Many thanks to everyone who helped me on my travels. Thanks to Sandie and my fellow authors, and to my friends and family for your support, especially to Alison and her family.

Andy Symington

Many thanks to those who were generous with their time and advice, particularly in tourist offices. I am especially grateful, as ever, to Jenny Neil and Brendan Bolland, to Neil Wilson and my other co-authors on this project and to Sandie Kestell and the LP team.

Neil Wilson

Thanks to the helpful tourist office staff all over Scotland; to Morag and Alisdair at Lochside Cottage, Steven Fallon, Keith Jeffrey, Fiona Garven, Derek McCrindle, Brendan Bolland, Jenny Neil, Tom and Christine Duffin, Steve Hall, Elaine Simpson, Duncan and Maja Pepper, Dona Milne and Alastair Short; and, as ever, to Carol Downie. Thanks also to my co-authors, and the LP team.

Barbara Woolsey

A heartfelt thanks to all those who supported in this research, and particularly to my wonderful big Scottish family. Special shout-outs to: Clair Woolsey, Remy Woolsey, René Frank, Marlene Dow and Ardelle Kuchinka.

ACKNOWLEDGEMENTS

Climate map data adapted from Peel MC, Finlayson BL & McMahon TA (2007) 'Updated World Map of the Köppen-Geiger Climate Classification', *Hydrology and Earth System Sciences*, 11, 1633–44.

Illustrations pp62-63, 102-103, 196-197 by Javier Zarracina

Cover photograph: Ruin at Greenan castle, Ayr, Scotland, Jim McDowall/Getty Images©

THIS BOOK

This 11th edition of Lonely Planet's *Scotland* guidebook was researched and written by Isabel Albiston, Andy Symington, Neil Wilson and Barbara Woolsey. The previous two editions were also written by Andy and Neil.

This guidebook was produced by the following:
Senior Product Editor Sandie Kestell
Cartographer Mark Griffiths
Product Editors Fergus O'Shea, Bruce Evans
Book Designer Virginia Moreno

Assisting Editors Janet Austin, Andrew Bain, Andrea Dobbin, Carly Hall, Kirsten Rawlings, Gabrielle Stefanos, Maja Vatrić, Brana Vladisavljev
Cover Researcher Fergal Condon
Thanks to Amy Lynch, Matthew Southerland

Index

Map Legend

Sights

- Beach
- Bird Sanctuary
- Buddhist
- Castle/Palace
- Christian
- Confucian
- Hindu
- Islamic
- Jain
- Jewish
- Monument
- Museum/Gallery/Historic Building
- Ruin
- Shinto
- Sikh
- Taoist
- Winery/Vineyard
- Zoo/Wildlife Sanctuary
- Other Sight

Activities, Courses & Tours

- Bodysurfing
- Diving
- Canoeing/Kayaking
- Course/Tour
- Sento Hot Baths/Onsen
- Skiing
- Snorkelling
- Surfing
- Swimming/Pool
- Walking
- Windsurfing
- Other Activity

Sleeping

- Sleeping
- Camping
- Hut/Shelter

Eating

- Eating

Drinking & Nightlife

- Drinking & Nightlife
- Cafe

Entertainment

- Entertainment

Shopping

- Shopping

Information

- Bank
- Embassy/Consulate
- Hospital/Medical
- Internet
- Police
- Post Office
- Telephone
- Toilet
- Tourist Information
- Other Information

Geographic

- Beach
- Gate
- Hut/Shelter
- Lighthouse
- Lookout
- Mountain/Volcano
- Oasis
- Park
- Pass
- Picnic Area
- Waterfall

Population

- Capital (National)
- Capital (State/Province)
- City/Large Town
- Town/Village

Transport

- Airport
- Border crossing
- Bus
- Cable car/Funicular
- Cycling
- Ferry
- Metro station
- Monorail
- Parking
- Petrol station
- S-Bahn/Subway station
- Taxi
- T-bane/Tunnelbana station
- Train station/Railway
- Tram
- U-Bahn/Underground station
- Other Transport

Routes

- Tollway
- Freeway
- Primary
- Secondary
- Tertiary
- Lane
- Unsealed road
- Road under construction
- Plaza/Mall
- Steps
- Tunnel
- Pedestrian overpass
- Walking Tour
- Walking Tour detour
- Path/Walking Trail

Boundaries

- International
- State/Province
- Disputed
- Regional/Suburb
- Marine Park
- Cliff
- Wall

Hydrography

- River, Creek
- Intermittent River
- Canal
- Water
- Dry/Salt/Intermittent Lake
- Reef

Areas

- Airport/Runway
- Beach/Desert
- Cemetery (Christian)
- Cemetery (Other)
- Glacier
- Mudflat
- Park/Forest
- Sight (Building)
- Sportsground
- Swamp/Mangrove

Note: Not all symbols displayed above appear on the maps in this book

OUR STORY

A beat-up old car, a few dollars in the pocket and a sense of adventure. In 1972 that's all Tony and Maureen Wheeler needed for the trip of a lifetime – across Europe and Asia overland to Australia. It took several months, and at the end – broke but inspired – they sat at their kitchen table writing and stapling together their first travel guide, *Across Asia on the Cheap*. Within a week they'd sold 1500 copies. Lonely Planet was born.

Today, Lonely Planet has offices in Tennessee, Dublin and Beijing, with a network of over 2000 contributors in every corner of the globe. We share Tony's belief that 'a great guidebook should do three things: inform, educate and amuse'.

OUR WRITERS

Isabel Albiston

Inverness & the Central Highlands After six years working for the *Daily Telegraph* in London, Isabel left to spend more time on the road. A job as writer for a magazine in Sydney, Australia was followed by a four-month overland trip across Asia and five years living and working in Buenos Aires, Argentina. Isabel started writing for Lonely Planet in 2014 and has contributed to 15 guidebooks. She's currently based in Ireland.

Andy Symington

Southern Scotland, Southern Highlands & Islands, Orkney & Shetland Andy has written or worked on over a hundred books and other updates for Lonely Planet (especially in Europe and Latin America) and other publishing companies, and has published articles on numerous subjects for a variety of newspapers, magazines, and websites. He part-owns and operates a rock bar, has written a novel and is currently working on several fiction and non-fiction writing projects. Andy, from Australia, moved to Northern Spain many years ago. When he's not off with a backpack in some far-flung corner of the world, he can probably be found watching the tragically poor local football side or tasting local wines after a long walk in the nearby mountains.

Neil Wilson

Edinburgh, Central Scotland, Northeast Scotland, Northern Highlands & Islands Neil was born in Scotland and has lived there most of his life. Based in Perthshire, he has been a full-time writer since 1988, working on more than 80 guidebooks for various publishers, including the Lonely Planet guides to Scotland, England, Ireland and Prague. An outdoors enthusiast since childhood, Neil is an active hill-walker, mountain-biker, sailor, snowboarder and rock-climber, and a qualified fly-fishing guide and instructor. He has climbed and tramped in four continents, including ascents of Jebel Toubkal in Morocco, Mount Kinabalu in Borneo, the Old Man of Hoy in Scotland's Orkney Islands and the Northwest Face of Half Dome in California's Yosemite Valley.

Barbara Woolsey

Glasgow Barbara Woolsey was born and raised on the Canadian prairies to a Filipino mother and Irish-Scottish father – and that multicultural upbringing has fuelled a life's passion for storytelling across cultures and borders. Barbara's voyaged across five continents and almost 50 countries by plane, train and motorbike. In addition to writing for Lonely Planet, Barbara contributes as a journalist to newspapers, magazines, and websites with readerships around the world. She spends most of her time in her adopted home of Berlin, Germany.

Published by Lonely Planet Global Limited
CRN 554153
11th edition – August 2021
ISBN 978 1 78701 642 2
© Lonely Planet 2021   Photographs © as indicated 2021
10 9 8 7 6 5 4 3 2 1
Printed in Singapore